JOURNAL FOR THE STUDY OF THE OLD TESTAMENT
SUPPLEMENT SERIES
105

Editors
David J.A. Clines
Philip R. Davies

Executive Editor
John Jarick

Editorial Board
Richard J. Coggins, Alan Cooper, Tamara C. Eskenazi,
J. Cheryl Exum, Robert P. Gordon, Norman K. Gottwald,
Andrew D.H. Mayes, Carol Meyers, Patrick D. Miller

JSOT Press
Sheffield

Re-Establishing Justice

Legal Terms, Concepts and Procedures in the Hebrew Bible

Pietro Bovati

translated by
Michael J. Smith

Journal for the Study of the Old Testament
Supplement Series 105

Published by JSOT Press
JSOT Press is an imprint of
Sheffield Academic Press Ltd
343 Fulwood Road
Sheffield S10 3BP
England

Typeset by Sheffield Academic Press
and
Printed on acid-free paper in Great Britain
by Bookcraft
Midsomer Norton, Somerset

British Library Cataloguing in Publication Data

A catalogue record for this book is available
from the British Library

ISBN 1-85075-290-7

CONTENTS

PREFACE

This study was presented as a doctoral thesis in Biblical Science at the Pontifical Biblical Institute in Rome; some additions and some bibliographical reordering have been made between the dissertation's defence in May 1985 and its present publication.

The work was carried out under the direction of Fr Luis Alonso Schökel SJ, who played a decisive role in the choice of subject and the shape of the research; his extremely wide knowledge of literary learning and his knowledge of the humanities were of invaluable assistance to me. It is to him first that I must put on record my gratitude for accepting me as a student, for the faith he put in me and for his unfailing support at every stage of the investigation.

Fr Dennis McCarthy SJ was for several years the dissertation's second reader; his unexpected death in August 1983 deprived me of a most perceptive reader and a close friend: I would like to honour his memory here. His place was kindly taken by Fr Pierre Proulx SJ, to whom I owe a great deal for his suggestions, his information and his numerous accurate observations; his erudite collaboration has filled some of the gaps in my work.

My thanks go to those who in various ways have made possible the drafting and publication of this study: Fr Paul Beauchamp SJ, my lecturer in Sacred Scripture in the Theology Faculty at Fourvière, who passed on to me his rich, penetrating and lively approach to the biblical text; Fr Denis Vasse SJ and the Lyons Communauté du Pélerin, who gave me an unfailing welcome whose warmth stimulated my researches; Drs Domenico Comite and Claudio Simonini, who introduced me into the complex world of the law; Mrs Maria Grazia Franzese and Miss Bruna Costacurta for their care and attention in the typing and correction of the manuscript; and Fr James Swetnam SJ, who saw to its preparation for the series Analecta Biblica.

I would also like to thank Fr Carlo M. Martini, Fr Maurice Gilbert and Fr Albert Vanhoye SJ, Rectors of the Biblical Institute, for the kindness and understanding they have shown to my studies; I would also like to put on record my gratitude to the Professors of the Institute for their sound teaching. My thanks go too to my colleagues and friends for their help and encouragement during these years of prolonged work. Especial thanks are due to Miss Vittoria Casanova, whose generosity met a large proportion of the publication costs.

Rome, January 1986,
Pietro Bovati SJ

PREFACE TO THE ENGLISH EDITION

This English translation, published eight years after the Italian edition and without substantial changes, brings to a much wider audience the complex world of the juridical procedures of ancient Israel. In the meantime there have been no studies covering the whole of the area covered here, and this has rather served to confirm the validity and usefulness of my analysis and interpretation.

The biblical writers make extensive use of juridical language in speaking of God and of interpersonal relations. It is essential for a correct theological interpretation of the message of the Scriptures to distinguish the procedure of *controversy* from that of *the trial* and to understand their articulation. Pardon and reconciliation are the goals of authentic justice. My discussion follows these lines; so too does my desire.

I wish to thank most sincerely Professor David J.A. Clines for having accepted this work for publication in the *JSOT* Supplement Series. My thanks also go to Fr Michael Smith, my translator, and to the staff of Sheffield Academic Press, particularly my desk editor, Dr J. Webb Mealy, for making the project possible.

ABBREVIATIONS

AB	Anchor Bible
AION	*Annali dell'istituto universitario orientale di Napoli*
AJSL	*American Journal of Semitic Languages and Literatures*
ALUOS	*Annual of the Leeds Oriental Society*
AnBib	Analecta Biblica
AnGr	Analecta (Pont. Univ.) Gregoriana
AnStEbr	*Annuario di studi ebraici*
AOAT	Alter Orient und Altes Testament
ArOr	*Archiv orientálni*
ASTI	*Annual of the Swedish Theological Institute (in Jerusalem)*
ATA	Alttestamentliche Abhandlungen
ATANT	Abhandlungen zur Theologie des Alten und Neuen Testaments
ATR	*Anglican Theological Review*
AusBR	*Australian Biblical Review*
AUSS	*Andrews University Seminary Studies*
BA	*Biblical Archaeologist*
BASOR	*Bulletin of the American Schools of Oriental Research*
BBB	Bonner biblische Beiträge
BDB	F. Brown, S.R. Driver and C.A. Briggs, *A Hebrew and English Lexicon of the Old Testament* (Oxford, 1975)
BeiBibExT	Beiträge zur biblischen Exegese und Theologie
BeO	*Bibbia e oriente*
BETL	Bibliotheca ephemeridum theologicarum lovaniensium
BEvT	Beiträge zur evangelischen Theologie
BHT	Beiträge zur historischen Theologie
Bib	*Biblica*
BibB	Biblische Beiträge
BibFe	*Biblia y Fe*
BibLeb	*Bibel und Leben*
BiblSt	Biblische Studien
BJRL	*Bulletin of the John Rylands Library*
BK	Biblischer Kommentar
BO	*Bibliotheca Orientalis*
BotAT	Botschaft des Alten Testaments
BSac	*Bibliotheca Sacra*
BSHT	Breslauer Studien zur historischen Theologie
BTB	*Biblical Theology Bulletin*

BVSAW PH	Berichte über die Verhandlungen der sächsischen Akademie der Wissenschaften zu Leipzig—Philologisch-historische Klasse
BWANT	Beiträge zur Wissenschaft vom Alten und Neuen Testament
BWAT	Beiträge zur Wissenschaft vom Alten Testament
BZ	*Biblische Zeitschrift*
BZAW	Beihefte zur Zeitschrift für die Alttestamentliche Wissenschaft
BZfr	Biblische Zeitfragen
BZNW	Beihefte zur Zeitschrift für die Neutestamentliche Wissenschaft
CalvTJ	*Calvin Theological Journal*
CalwTMon	Calwer theologische Monographien
CBQ	*Catholic Biblical Quarterly*
ConBOT	Coniectanea Biblica, Old Testament Series
Cuadbíb	*Cuadernos Bíblicos*
CuBíb	*Cultura Bíblica*
DBSup	*Dictionnaire de la Bible, Supplément*
Dhorme	*La Bible*, L'Ancien Testament, I-II, ed. E. Dhorme (Paris, 1956, 1959)
DictSpir	*Dictionnaire de spiritualité*
DielhBlAT	*Dielheimer Blätter zum Alten Testament*
DissAbstr	*Dissertation Abstracts*
Einheitsübersetzung	*Einheitsübersetzung der Heiligen Schrift* (Das Alte Testament; Stuttgart, 1974)
ErfTSt	Erfurter theologische Studien
EstAT	Estudios de Antiguo Testamento
EstBíb	*Estudios bíblicos*
EstE	*Estudios eclesiásticos*
ETL	*Ephemerides theologicae lovanienses*
EuntDoc	*Euntes docete*
EurHS	Europäische Hochschulschriften
EvQ	*Evangelical Quarterly*
EvT	*Evangelische Theologie*
ExpTim	*The Expository Times*
ForBib	Forschung zur Bibel
ForTLing	Forum theologiae linguisticae
FreibTSt	Freiburger theologische Studien
FRLANT	Forschungen zur Religion und Literatur des Alten und Neuen Testaments
Gesenius	W. Gesenius, *Hebräisches und aramäisches Handwörterbuch über das Alte Testament* (Berlin–Göttingen–Heidelberg, 17th edn, 1915)
GK	W. Gesenius and E. Kautzsch, *Gesenius' Hebrew Grammar* (2nd English edn by A.E. Cowley; Oxford, 1910)
GUOST	*Glasgow University Oriental Society Transactions*
HALAT	L. Koehler and W. Baumgartner, *Hebräisches und aramäisches Lexicon zum Alten Testament* (Leiden, 3rd edn, 1967)

HAT	Handbuch zum Alten Testament
HSM	Harvard Semitic Monographs
HTR	*The Harvard Theological Review*
HUCA	*Hebrew Union College Annual*
ICC	International Critical Commentary
IEJ	*Israel Exploration Journal*
IndTSt	*Indian Theological Studies*
Int	*Interpretation*
IsrOrSt	*Israel Oriental Studies*
JANES	*Journal of the Ancient Near Eastern Society*
JAOS	*Journal of the American Oriental Society*
JBL	*Journal of Biblical Literature*
JBR	*Journal of Bible and Religion*
JJS	*Journal of Jewish Studies*
JLCR	Jordan Lectures in Comparative Religion
JNES	*Journal of Near Eastern Studies*
JNSL	*Journal of Northwest Semitic Languages*
Joüon	P. Joüon, *Grammaire de l'hébreu biblique* (Rome, 2nd edn., 1965)
JPTh	*Jahrbücher für protestantische Theologie*
JQR	*Jewish Quarterly Review*
JSOT	*Journal for the Study of the Old Testament*
JSS	*Journal of Semitic Studies*
JTS	*Journal of Theological Studies*
KAT	Kommentar zum Alten Testament
KD	*Kerygma und Dogma*
LD	Lectio divina
LSSt	Leipziger semitistische Studien
LuVitor	*Lumen*
Materiales	L. Alonso Schökel, *et al.*, *Materiales para un diccionario bíblico hebreo–español* (Rome, 1985)
NAWG	Nachrichten der Akademie der Wissenschaften in Göttingen
NBE	*Nueva Biblia Española* (translation directed by L. Alonso Schökel and J. Mateos; Madrid, 1975)
NEB	New English Bible (Oxford, 2nd edn, 1970)
NRT	*Nouvelle revue théologique*
NStB	Neukirchner Studienbücher
OBO	Orbis biblicus et orientalis
OLZ	*Orientalistische Literaturzeitung*
OnsGeestLev	*Ons Geestelijk Leven*
OrAnt	*Oriens antiquus*
OrBiLov	Orientalia et biblica lovaniensia
OrSyr	*L'orient syrien*
OTL	Old Testament Library
OTS	*Oudtestamentische Studiën*

OTWerkSuidA	Die Ou Testamentiese Werkgemeenskap in Suid-Afrika
PEQ	*Palestine Exploration Quarterly*
PTMS	Pittsburgh Theological Monograph Series
QDisp	Quaestiones Disputatae
RAC	*Reallexikon für Antike und Christentum*
RB	*Revue biblique*
REJ	*Revue des études juives*
RHPR	*Revue d'histoire et de philosophie religieuses*
RIDA	*Revue internationale des droits de l'antiquité*
RivB	*Rivista biblica*
RSR	*Recherches de science religieuse*
RSV	*Revised Standard Version*
RTL	*Revue théologique de Louvain*
RTP	*Revue de théologie et de philosophie*
Salm	*Salmanticensis*
SANT	Studien zum Alten und Neuen Testament
SBFLA	*Studii biblici franciscani liber annuus*
SBLDS	Society of Biblical Literature, Dissertation Series
SBLMS	Society of Biblical Literature, Monograph Series
SBM	Stuttgart biblische Monographien
SBS	Stuttgarter Bibelstudien
SBT	Studies in Biblical Theology
ScEccl	*Sciences Ecclésiastiques*
Scr	*Scripture*
Sem	*Semitica*
SemBEsp	Semana Biblica Española
SGKIO	Studien zur Geschichte und Kultur des islamischen Orients
SHAW PH	Sitzungsberichte der Heidelberger Akademie der Wissenschaften, Philosophisch-historische Klasse
SJLA	Studies in Judaism in Late Antiquity
SJT	*Scottish Journal of Theology*
SNVAO	Skrifter utgitt av det norske videnskaps-akademi i Oslo
SSN	Studia semitica neerlandica
STRT	Studia theologica rheno-traiectina
TArb	Theologische Arbeiten
TBü	Theologische Bücherei
THAT	*Theologisches Handwörterbuch zum Alten Testament*, I-II (ed. E. Jenni and C. Westermann; Munich, 1971, 1976)
ThSt	Theologische Studien
ThWAT	*Theologisches Wörterbuch zum Alten Testament* (ed. G.J. Botterweck, H. Ringgren; Stuttgart, 1970)
TLZ	*Theologische Literaturzeitung*
TOB	*Traduction oecuménique de la Bible*, Ancien Testament, Paris, 1976
TP	*Theologie und Philosophie*

TRE	*Theologische Realenzyklopädie*
TRu	*Theologische Rundschau*
TThSt	Trierer theologische Studien
TTZ	*Trierer theologische Zeitschrift*
TüTQ	*Tübinger theologische Quartalschrift*
TWANT	*Theologisches Wörterbuch zum Neuen Testament* (ed. G. Kittel; Stuttgart, 1933-)
TynBul	*Tyndale Bulletin*
TZ	*Theologische Zeitschrift*
UF	*Ugarit-Forschungen*
Vaccari	*La Sacra Bibbia* (tradotta dai testi originali con note a cura del Pontificio Istituto Biblico di Roma, 9 vols.; Florence 1957–1958)
VD	*Verbum Domini*
VF	*Verkündigung und Forschung*
VTSup	*Vetus Testamentum*, Supplements
WDienst	*Wort und Dienst*
WegFor	Wege der Forschung
WMANT	Wissenschaftliche Monographien zum Alten und Neuen Testament
ZAW	*Zeitschrift für die Alttestamentliche Wissenschaft*
ZDMG	*Zeitschrift der deutschen morgenländischen Gesellschaft*
ZDPV	*Zeitschrift des deutschen Palästina-Vereins*
Zorell	F. Zorell, *Lexicon hebraicum et aramaicum Veteris Testamenti* (Rome, 1968)
ZST	*Zeitschrift für systematische Theologie*
ZTK	*Zeitschrift für Theologie und Kirche*

INTRODUCTION:

ORIGIN OF THE WORK AND METHODOLOGICAL PREMISES

The birth and taking shape of a manuscript is often influenced if not brought about by two apparently contradictory phenomena which are in reality complementary. On the one hand, a series of meaningful accidents befalls a particular person, demonstrating the importance and topicality of the subject; on the other hand, the person perceives an ability to add something useful and original to the debate. I think the origin of the present study can be explained in this way.

Exegetes have always taken an interest in *the theme of justice*, but the last decade has seen more specific and systematic research into it. Three basic routes have been followed in this regard.

1. Contemporary history has taken increasing account of serious social problems within individual countries and in the wider context of international relations; there has been a clash of theories and ideologies designed to explain and resolve the conflicts of such situations, and not just at an academic level. Even the world of exegesis has been called upon to put forward a systematic presentation of the contents of Scripture as a tool for the correct interpretation of history and as a means to a conception of society attuned to the data of Revelation. Moreover, this has to be seen in the context of a renewed effort to inculturate the gospel message, which is based on Old Testament tradition and is not identical with legal dogma derived from Roman law.[1] It is natural that the main object of

1. I refer not only to the complex theological movement of Latin America and its different theologies of liberation, but more generally to the restatement, in other cultural areas as well, of the social question and its theoretical and pastoral implications; both the Second Vatican Council and the documents of the recent Popes witness to the importance of the subject. As regards Sacred Scripture directly, I note some recent works in which a further bibliography may be found: M. Schwantes, *Das*

the research should be the prophetic books, in which the denunciation of social injustice occurs insistently.[2]

2. Theology on the other hand has been constantly concerned with the theme of justice: urged on in particular by the Pauline message concerning justification, which relates to Old Testament tradition, scholars have attempted to formulate the characteristics of 'biblical justice' in general and to map out the

Recht der Armen (BeiBibExT, 4; Frankfurt am Main, 1977); L. Brummel *et al.*, (eds.), *Los pobres: Encuentro y compromiso* (Buenos Aires, 1978); C. Boerma, *Rich Man, Poor Man—and the Bible* (Leiden, 1979); W. Schottroff and W. Stegeman (eds.), *Traditionen der Beifreiung* (Sozialgeschichtliche Bibelauslegung, Bd. 1. Methodische Zugänge; Munich, 1980); J. Pons, *L'oppression dans l'Ancien Testament* (Paris, 1981); A. Penna, *I diritti umani: Dottrina e prassi* (Opera collettiva diretta da G. Concetti; Rome, 1982), pp. 61-95; L. Epsztein, *La justice sociale dans le Proche-Orient ancien et le peuple de la Bible* (Paris, 1983); D. McCarthy, 'Les droits de l'homme et l'Ancien Testament', in *Droits de l'Homme: Approche chrétienne* (Fédération Internationale des Universités Catholiques, Centre de Coordination de la Recherche; Rome, 1984), pp. 11-25.

2. Among the more recent contributions I may quote: H.-J. Kraus, 'Die prophetische Botschaft gegen das soziale Unrecht Israels', *EvT* 15 (1955), pp. 295-307; H. Donner, 'Die soziale Botschaft der Propheten im Lichte der Gesellschaftsordnung in Israel', *OrAnt* 2 (1963), pp. 239-45; G.J. Botterweck, 'Die soziale Kritik des Propheten Amos', in *Die Kirche im Wandel der Zeit* (FS J. Hoeffner; Cologne, 1971), pp. 39-58; *idem*, '"Sie verkaufen den Unschuldigen um Geld." Zur sozialen Kritik des Propheten Amos', *BibLeb* 12 (1971), pp. 215-31; K. Koch, 'Die Entstehung der sozialen Kritik bei den Propheten', in *Probleme biblischer Theologie* (FS G. von Rad; Munich, 1971), pp. 236-57; G. Wanke, 'Zu Grundlagen und Absicht prophetischer Sozialkritik', *KD* 18 (1972), pp. 2-17; M. Fendler, 'Zur Sozialkritik des Amos. Versuch einer wirtschafts- und sozialgeschichtlichen Interpretation alttestamentlicher Texte', *EvT* 33 (1973), pp. 32-53; S. Holm-Nielsen, 'Die Sozialkritik der Propheten', in *Denkender Glaube* (FS C.H. Ratschow; Berlin, 1976), pp. 7-23; E. Hernando, 'Los profetas y el derecho de gentes', *LuVitor* 28 (1979), pp. 129-52; J.L. Sicre, *Los dioses olvidados: Poder y riqueza en los profetas preexílicos* (Madrid, 1979); B. Lang, 'Sklaven und Unfreie im Buch Amos (II 6, VIII 6)', *VT* 31 (1981), pp. 482-88; *idem*, 'The Social Organisation of Poverty in Biblical Times', *JSOT* 24 (1982), pp. 47-63; C.H.J. de Geus, 'Die Gesellschaftskritik der Propheten und die Archäologie', *ZDPV* 98 (1982), pp. 50-57; H.B. Huffmon, 'The Social Role of Amos' Message', in *The Quest for the Kingdom of God* (FS G.E. Mendenhall; Winona Lake, IN, 1983), pp. 109-16; I.M. Zeitlin, 'Classical Prophecy and the Concern for Social Justice', in *Ancient Judaism: Biblical Criticism from Max Weber to the Present* (Cambridge, 1984), pp. 208-57; J.L. Sicre, *'Con los pobres de la tierra': La justicia social en los profetas de Israel* (Madrid, 1984).

relationship between God's justice and humanity's sin in particular.[3]

3. Since modern science demands rigour and precision in terminology and makes unvarying demands for categorization, exegesis

3. Here I can quote only some of the more important publications, referring the reader for further bibliography to: H. Gross, '"Rechtfertigung" nach dem Alten Testament', in *Kontinuität und Einheit* (FS F. Mussner; Freiburg, 1981), pp. 17-29; F. Noetscher, *Die Gerechtigkeit Gottes bei den vorexilischen Propheten: Ein Beitrag zur alttestamentlichen Theologie* (ATAbh, VI/I; Münster, 1915); N.H. Snaith, *The Distinctive Ideas of the Old Testament* (London, 1944), pp. 51-78; G. von Rad, '"Gerechtigkeit" und "Leben" in den Psalmen', in *Festschrift A. Bertholet* (Tübingen, 1950), pp. 418-37; O. Schilling, 'Die alttestamentliche Auffassung von Gerechtigkeit und Liebe', in *Vom Wort des Lebens* (FS M. Meinertz; Münster, 1951), pp. 9-27; H. Cazelles, 'A propos des quelques textes difficiles relatifs à la justice de Dieu dans l'Ancien Testament', *RB* 58 (1951), pp. 169-88; A.H. van der Weijden, *Die 'Gerechtigkeit' in den Psalmen* (Nimwegen, 1952); E. Beaucamp, 'La justice de Yahvé et l'économie de l'alliance', *SBF* 11 (1960–61), pp. 5-55; *idem*, 'Justice divine et pardon', in *A la rencontre de Dieu* (Mém A. Gelin; Le Puy, 1961), pp. 129-44; *idem*, 'La justice en Israël', in *Populus Dei*. I. *Israel* (Studi in onore del Card. A. Ottaviani; Rome, 1966), pp. 201-35; H.H. Schmid, *Gerechtigkeit als Weltordnung: Hintergrund und Geschichte des alttestamentlichen Gerechtigkeitsbegriffes* (BHT, 40; Tübingen, 1968); M. Barth, *Rechtfertigung: Versuch einer Auslegung paulinischer Texte im Rahmen des Alten und Neuen Testamentes* (TS, 90; Zürich, 1969); P. Dacquino, 'La formula "Giustizia di Dio" nei libri dell'Antico Testamento', *RivB* 17 (1969), pp. 103-19, 365-82; J.L. Crenshaw, 'Popular Questioning of the Justice of God in Ancient Israel', *ZAW* 82 (1970), pp. 380-95; H. Reventlow, *Rechtfertigung im Horizont des Alten Testaments* (BEvT, 58; Munich, 1971); U. Luck, 'Gerechtigkeit der Welt—Gerechtigkeit Gottes', *WDienst* 12 (1973), pp. 71-89; H.H. Schmid, 'Gerechtigkeit und Barmherzigkeit im Alten Testament', *WDienst* 12 (1973), pp. 31-41; V. Subilia, *La giustificazione per fede* (Brescia, 1976), esp. pp. 329-51; L.J. Kuyper, 'Righteousness and Salvation', *SJT* 30 (1972), pp. 233-52; W. Zimmerli, 'Alttestamentliche Prophetie und Apokalyptik auf dem Wege zur "Rechtfertigung des Gottlosen"', in *Rechtfertigung* (FS E. Käsemann; Tübingen–Göttingen, 1976), pp. 575-92; A. Dihle, 'Gerechtigkeit', *RAC*, X (Stuttgart, 1978), pp. 233-60; J.H. Stek, 'Salvation, Justice and Liberation in the Old Testament', *CalvTJ* 13 (1978), pp. 133-65; G. de Gennaro (ed.), *Amore–Giustizia*: *Analisi semantica dei due termini e delle loro correlazioni nei testi biblici veterotestamentari e neotestamentari* (L'Aquila, 1980); W.H. Schmidt, '"Rechtfertigung des Gottlosen" in der Botschaft der Propheten', in *Die Botschaft und die Boten* (FS H.W. Wolff; Neukirchen–Vluyn, 1981), pp. 157-68; B. Mogensen, '*ṣ^{e}dāqā* in the Scandinavian and German Research Traditions', in K. Jeppesen and B. Otzen (eds.), *The Productions of Time: Tradition History in Old Testament Scholarship* (Sheffield, 1984), pp. 67-80.

has backed up its researches with biblical vocabulary studies. As well as the recent dictionaries of Old Testament theology,[4] there has been a highly significant exegetical output concerned with one or more words belonging directly to the theme of justice.[5]

4. I obviously refer to *THAT*, I–II and to *ThWAT*, which is still being published. The *TWNT* also makes a significant contribution to Hebrew terminology. For certain words, the *DBSup* supplies useful lexicographical references.

5. The studies quoted in n. 3 are often based on a careful lexicographical investigation of the root *ṣdq* (and its synonyms and related words); among these, cf. in particular H.H. Schmid, *Gerechtigkeit als Weltordnung* (Tübingen, 1968).

The concept of justice and law has occasioned a series of contributions on the most important Hebrew terms: E. Kautzsch, *Ueber die Derivate des Stammes* sdq *im alttestamentlichen Sprachgebrauch* (Tübingen, 1881); H. Ferguson, 'The verb *špṭ*', *JBL* 8 (1888), pp. 130-36; G. Wildeboer, 'Die älteste Bedeutung des Stammes *tsdq* [= *ṣdq*]', *ZAW* 22 (1902), pp. 167-69; K. Cramer, 'Der Begriff *ṣdqh* bei Tritojesaja', *ZAW* 27 (1907), pp. 79-99; H.W. Hertzberg, 'Die Entwicklung des Begriffes *mšpṭ* im Alten Testament', *ZAW* 40 (1922), pp. 256-87 and *ZAW* 41 (1923), pp. 1-76; K.H.J. Fahlgren, *Ṣ^edāḳā, nahestehende und entgegengesetzte Begriffe im Alten Testament* (Uppsala, 1932); O. Booth, 'The Semantic Development of the Term *mšpṭ* in the Old Testament', *JBL* 61 (1942), pp. 105-10; J. van der Ploeg, 'Shāphaṭ et Mishpāṭ', *OTS* 2 (1943), pp. 144-55; F. Rosenthal, 'Ṣedaqa, charity', *HUCA* 23 (1950–1951), pp. 411-30; J.H. Eybers, 'The Stem š-p-ṭ in the Psalms', in *Studies on the Psalms* (OTWerkSuidA, 6; Potchefstroom, 1963), pp. 58-63; J.P. Justesen, 'On the Meaning of *ṣādaq*', *AUSS* 2 (1964), pp. 53-61; A. Jepsen, '*Ṣdq* and *ṣdqh* im Alten Testament', in *Gottes Wort und Gottes Land* (FS H.-W. Hertzberg; Göttingen, 1965), pp. 78-89; E. Toaff, 'Evoluzione del concetto ebraico *zedāqa*', *AnStEbr* (1968–1969), pp. 111-22; E. Berkovits, 'The Biblical Meaning of Justice', '*Ṣedeq* and *Ṣ'daqa*', in *Man and God: Studies in Biblical Theology* (Detroit, 1969), pp. 224-52 and 292-348; J.J. Scullion, 'Ṣedeq–ṣedaqah in Isaiah cc. 40–66 with Special Reference to the Continuity in Meaning between Second and Third Isaiah', *UF* 3 (1971), pp. 335-48; W.A.M. Beuken, 'Mišpat. The First Servant Song in its Context', *VT* 22 (1972), pp. 1-30; J. Jeremias, '*Mišpaṭ* im ersten Gottesknechtlied (Jes. XLII 1–4)', *VT* 22 (1972), pp. 31-42; C.F. Whitley, 'Deutero-Isaiah's Interpretation of *ṣedeq*', *VT* 22 (1972), pp. 469-75; F. Crüsemann, 'Jahwes Gerechtigkeit (*ṣ^edāqā/ṣädäq*) im Alten Testament', *EvT* 36 (1976), pp. 427-50; F.V. Reiterer, *Gerechtigkeit als Heil: Ṣdq bei Deuterojesaja. Aussage und Vergleich mit der alttestamentlichen Traditionen* (Graz, 1976); D. Cox, 'Ṣedaqa and mišpat. The Concept of Righteousness in Later Wisdom', *SBFLA* 27 (1977), pp. 33-50; B. Johnson, 'Der Bedeutungsunterschied zwischen *ṣädäq* und *ṣedaqa*', *ASTI* 11 (1977–1978), pp. 31-39; S.H. Scholnick, 'The Meaning of *mišpaṭ* in the Book of Job', *JBL* 101 (1982), pp. 521-29; J.M. Bernal Giménez, 'El siervo como promesa de "mišpāṭ". Estudio bíblico del término "mišpāṭ" en Is 42.1-4' in *Palabra y vida* (FS J. Alonso Diaz; Madrid, 1984), pp. 77-85.

My own study is greatly indebted to this cultural ferment and the problems, methodologies and contributions that have come out of it.

The context of social relations, although at first sight appearing to be a partial context, has the undoubted advantage of permitting a consideration of justice linked to events and institutions more directly under the control of the complex world of ideas. But above all it has the merit of bringing to light the very nucleus of the whole problem of justice. In his *Theology of the Old Testament*, G. von Rad emphasized the way in which the concept of *ṣ^{e}dāqâ* does not so much express an individual's reference to an ethical norm as much as the relationship between two beings, a relationship that is communication through a life of communion.[6] This definition had then to be worked out in the reality of history, in which there are not subjects in general but just and unjust subjects. From this it follows that the most difficult, but at the same time the most decisive relationship is the one that the just establishes with the unjust (or those considered so): the just is called upon in fact not only to deal correctly with the other, but to *re-establish justice*, so as to promote a right relationship between all the members of the society.

The area mapped out is substantially the same as the field of penal law. Since the study of law requires a certain wholeness, I have taken as my heuristic scheme modern penal law, following in this instance the researchers who have preceded me.[7] This allows me to single out and manifest the links between the individual manifestations of the legal process, granted that the *procedure* is precisely a series of acts whose specific function is comprehensible only if inserted into an organic whole. Two fundamental procedural structures arising from the biblical text have been described fairly autonomously: that of the bilateral controversy (examined in Part One of this essay) and that of the truly

6. G. von Rad, *Theologie des Alten Testaments*, I (Munich, 1957), pp. 368-69.

7. Given that we are dealing with an ancient culture of whose juridical activity we have only fragmentary elements, the only way forward is to situate these elements in the more systematic framework provided by another culture. The appropriateness and relevance of such a choice may then be debated (cf. H.J. Boecker, *Redeformen des Rechtslebens im Alten Testament* [Neukirchen, 1964], pp. 14-15); the fact remains that the fundamental concepts of Roman law (the basis of contemporary legislation) seem to be generally accepted as a useful tool for the description and organization of the Old Testament data. I am aware that a heuristic scheme runs the risk of turning into an interpretative thesis or hypothesis; but just as recourse to the terminology of our penal code is inevitable (Boecker, *Redeformen*, pp. 17-18), so it is impossible to avoid a more or less theoretical comparison between ancient legal practice and ours.

legal judgment (to which Part Two is given over).[8] At the beginning of Part One I describe the rise and development of the controversy and its link to the judicial process; I therefore put off until that point a description of the contents of our undertaking.

The burden of demonstration of our research is supplied by a study of the Hebrew *vocabulary* relating to procedures of a penal kind, both its technical terms[9] and those in common usage.[10] The vocabulary turns out to be semantically necessary for an exact understanding of the legal procedures and their meaning. The particular aim of my investigation has been not only to make a reasonably complete collection of words and phrases pertaining to legal procedure, but to go on to study the structural relations between them. Looking beyond a series of discrete 'judicial' words, the intention has been to examine the semantic field;[11] rather than studying isolated words it is necessary to study the surrounding phrase and speech, thus engaging in a paradigmatic and

8. Because of its specific nature, I have not discussed in the present essay the so-called 'sacred right'; I reserve the right to deal with this subject in a subsequent publication.

9. Following contemporary practice, by 'technical term', as opposed to 'ordinary term', I simply mean 'the special terminology used by a particular science, discipline or profession' (*Dizionario Enciclopedico Italiano*, XII [Rome, 1961], p. 19).

10. As regards terminology in common usage, I note with I.L. Seeligmann the difficulty of defining the language of judicial procedure with precision: 'Wörter, die in einem bestimmten Zusammenhang einen spezifisch forensischen Sinn haben, werden sonstwo in ganz allgemeiner Bedeutung ausgewandt' (I.L. Seeligmann, 'Zur Terminologie für das Gerichtsverfahren im Wortschatz des biblischen Hebräisch', *VTSup* 16 [1967], pp. 253-54).

11. Taking up and adapting to our subject the observations of J.F.A. Sawyer, *Semantics in Biblical Research* (London, 1972), pp. 32-33, it may be said, for example, that the question of the meaning of *ryb* is different from that of the meaning of the controversy in the Old Testament: to answer the first, the theory of semantic fields is useful; but for the second it is an essential tool. For the concept of 'semantic field', cf. S. Ullmann, *The Principles of Semantics* (Oxford–Glasgow, 2nd edn, 1957), pp. 152-70; *idem*, *Semantics: An Introduction to the Science of Meaning* (Oxford, 1970), pp. 236-58; G. Mounin, *Clefs pour la sémantique* (Paris, 1972); J. Lyons, *Semantics*, I (Cambridge, 1977), pp. 230-69; H. Geckeler, *Strukturelle Semantik und Wortfeldtheorie* (Munich, 1982). As regards research on the text of the Bible, I might mention the pages on methodology by I. Riesener, *Der Stamm* 'bd *im Alten Testament: Eine Wortuntersuchung unter Berücksichtigung neuerer sprachwissenschaftlicher Methode* (BZAW, 149; Berlin, 1979), especially pp. 54-75 (with bibliography).

syntagmatic treatment of the material available to us.

In essence, this essay is presented as a synchronic consideration[12] of the Hebrew linguistic data; and the procedural elements have been organized into a system that is not to be found—at least with the same precision and completeness—in any of the biblical texts. I think it necessary to forestall the natural objections in this regard.

A diachronic treatment of the Hebrew vocabulary would of course have been desirable and methodologically more rigourous; unfortunately, current knowledge of the subject is so scarce or disputed that a projected history of judicial terminology would risk being based on foundations that were too hypothetical. The various dictionaries and word lists, although occasionally providing useful distinctions,[13] do not comment except in passing on the possible chronological relationship between the various terms and phrases. Moreover, although it is possible to establish, with relative likelihood, the date of a text,[14] the decision

12. Cf. J. Barr, 'Semantic Philology and the Interpretation of the Old Testament', in *Tradition and Interpretation* (FS G.W. Anderson; Oxford, 1979), pp. 61-63.

13. Recent dictionaries of biblical theology in general, and *THAT* systematically, provide statististical data about the presence of words in the Old Testament and its individual books. But as E. Jenni writes in the introduction to *THAT*, I, p. XVIII; 'Der Wert der statistischen Angaben wäre für die Sprachgeschichte natürlich bedeutend grösser, wenn sie nicht mechanisch nach biblischen Büchern, sondern nach der Abfassungszeit der einzelnen literarischen Komplexe hätten geordnet werden können. Da aber die literarische Analyse und die Datierung vieler Texte umstritten oder unmöglich ist, konnte dieser Weg für die Wortstatistik nicht oder nur in Ausnahmfällen beschritten werden.' Cf. also L. Koehler, 'Problems in the Study of the Language of the Old Testament', *JSS* 1 (1956), p. 3.

14. Studies that tackle the problem of dating using purely linguistic criteria are of undoubted interest; I might quote, in particular, if only for the methodological problems implicit in them, the works of D.A. Robertson, *Linguistic Evidence in Dating Early Hebrew Poetry* (SBLDS, 3; Missoula, MT, 1972); R. Polzin, *Late Biblical Hebrew: Toward an Historical Typology of Biblical Hebrew Prose* (HSM, 12; Missoula, MT, 1976); the various contributions of A. Hurvitz: 'The Chronological Significance of "Aramaisms" in Biblical Hebrew', *IEJ* 18 (1968), pp. 234-40; *Bein Lashon Lelashon* (*Biblical Hebrew in Translation: A Study in Post-Exilic Hebrew and its Implications for the Dating of the Psalms*) (Hebrew; Jerusalem, 1972); 'The Evidence of Language in Dating the Priestly Code. A Linguistic Study in Technical Idioms and Terminology', *RB* 81 (1974), pp. 24-56; 'The Date of the Prose-Tale of Job Linguistically Reconsidered', *HTR* 67 (1974), pp. 17-34; *A Linguistic Study of the Relationship between the Priestly Source and the Book of Ezekiel: A New Approach to an Old Problem* (Cahiers de la Revue Biblique, 20; Paris, 1982). Cf. also G.M. Landes, 'Linguistic Criteria and the Date

regarding a single word or a particular syntagm remains difficult, given that for the most part the degree of harmonization exercised over the final redaction eludes us. As far as legal circles are concerned, they may be considered by nature to tend to conservatism,[15] and it is therefore not absurd to imagine the same terminology lasting for centuries, bearing in mind jurisprudence's constant effort to get legally significant words and formulae to agree between themselves.

The evolution of legal institutions and therefore of the procedures connected with them seems to be a generally recognized and attested fact, but even so, the passage from generalized statement to precise content reveals the difficulty of outlining with certainty the course of this evolution.[16] In this essay I have tried not to get involved in specific details, but to stay on the level of facts for which there is substantial documentation throughout Israel's history. It is certain, for example, that the advent of the monarchy modified, or, more accurately, defined certain features of the legal process; however, it does not appear to me to have changed structurally the idea of jurisdiction or the nature of the process. In this sense it seems to me to be mistaken, because not based on the texts, to suppose that it was only with the constitution of Israel as a state (at the time of the monarchy) that a rigorous judicial procedure became established.[17]

As is clear from the Table of Contents, this study follows the logical and temporal development of the various procedures. This may make the content of the essay clear, but where I stand in the history of research is less so.

It is therefore incumbent upon me to acknowledge the authors to whom my investigation is particularly indebted; given the nature of the

of the Book of Jonah', *Eretz-Israel* 16 (1982), pp. 147*-70*.

15. Cf. Seeligmann, 'Zur Terminologie', p. 255.

16. Cf. G. D'Ercole, 'The Juridical Structure of Israel from the Time of her Origin to the Period of Hadrian', in *Populus Dei*. I. *Israel* (Studi in onore del Card. A. Ottaviani; Rome, 1969), pp. 389-461. Boecker, while not attempting a systematic outline of the history of Israelite law, thinks it is possible to identify two important points in the historical development of the Hebrew people that had a juridical and institutional influence: the change to a sedentary way of life and the institution of the monarchy (*Redeformen*, pp. 10-12). I agree on the importance of these events, although it seems difficult to draw conclusions from them as to the possibility of specific laws (such as the 'amphictyonic law').

17. Cf. C. Macholz, 'Die Stellung des Königs in der israelitischen Gerichtsverfassung', *ZAW* 84 (1972), pp. 157-82.

work, which necessarily has had to contain a very wide subject in quite a restricted space, very rarely have I been able to make precise comparisons between the authors quoted. Leaving aside that which is concerned exclusively with linguistics and the theory of law, it is possible to group under three principal headings the studies that have preceded and fertilized my research.

1. I may mention, in the first place, those authors who have concerned themselves with juridical procedures within the framework of legislation or, more generally, of the institutions of the people of Israel. The results arrived at by these scholars allow us to reconstruct coherently, or at least plausibly, Old Testament procedure, on the basis of legal texts, stories, or other sources of information present in the biblical literature, often integrated with and compared to other literatures and other juridical systems.

Nowadays, the works of the past are no longer quoted in exegetical bibliographies, preference being given to more modern and condensed studies which serve as speedily consulted manuals; among these, those of J. Pedersen and (above all) R. de Vaux enjoy particular esteem.[18] The brief essay by L. Koehler, entitled 'Die hebräische Rechtsgemeinde'[19] continues to be a worthwhile introduction to matters juridical in the Old Testament. Greater influence has been exercised on my work, even though some of them deal with aspects which are only on the fringe of the subject discussed here, by the writings of D. Daube, B. Cohen, W. Falk, B.S. Jackson, H.J. Boecker and K.W. Whitelam.[20] In this list, despite some reservations about assigning it here, I believe the contribution of A. Gamper to be significant.[21]

In view of its specific content, this literature has been of particular

18. J. Pedersen, *Israel: Its Life and Culture*, II (Copenhagen, 1926), esp. pp. 378-410; R. de Vaux, *Les institutions de l'Ancien Testament*, I (Paris, 1958), pp. 231-50.

19. The essay, written in 1931, was added as an appendix to *Der hebräische Mensch* (Tübingen, 1953), pp. 143-71.

20. D. Daube, *Studies in Biblical Law* (Cambridge, 1947); B. Cohen, *Jewish and Roman Law: A Comparative Study*, I–II (New York, 1966); Z.W. Falk, *Hebrew Law in Biblical Times* (Jerusalem, 1964); *idem*, *Introduction to Jewish Law of the Second Commonwealth*, I–II (Leiden, 1972); H.J. Boecker, *Recht und Gesetz im Alten Testament und im Alten Orient* (NStB, 10; Neukirchen–Vluyn, 1976); K.W. Whitelam, *The Just King: Monarchical Judicial Authority in Ancient Israel* (JSOTSup, 12; Sheffield, 1979).

21. A. Gamper, *Gott als Richter in Mesopotamien und im Alten Testament: Zum Verständnis einer Gebetsbitte* (Innsbruck, 1966).

inspiration in Part Two of this study, the part concerned with judicial institutions; from these studies I have drawn the texts judged to be of the greatest importance for an understanding of the law-suit's structure.

For reasons of competence, as well as because of the adoption of a different methodology, I have not buttressed my analysis with a comparison between the biblical data and those from the literature of the Ancient Near East. For the same reason, I have not situated biblical procedures against the background of other important juridical traditions, such as the rabbinical and Roman. I recognize therefore that my work has a certain quality of incompleteness, which it may be possible to fill out elsewhere; however, I do not think that I have transgressed the principles of a serious scientific investigation. On the one hand, the positive results of comparative studies of the language and juridical institutions are to be found in the textbooks and specialized works on the subject, and it did not seem indispensable to go over point by point the relevant documentation. On the other hand, there is undoubtedly the possibility that on particular questions more light can be shed or that my line of argumentation can be called into question, starting from a knowledge of other juridical procedures or models; I believe that this is the normal position for a science, which remains structurally open to integration and correction.

2. In the second place, but not secondary in importance, mention must be made of those authors who have concerned themselves with the juridical literary genres of Scripture. Exegetical output in this area is particularly noteworthy for its abundance and quality;[22] I can therefore

22. For the history of the research, as well as the works that have been quoted in the following notes, mention should be made of the following: H. Gressmann, *Die älteste Geschichtsschreibung und Prophetie Israels* (Göttingen, 1910), pp. 323-28; *idem*, 'Die literarische Analyse Deuterojesajas', *ZAW* 34 (1914), pp. 254-97; H. Gunkel, 'Die Propheten als Schriftsteller und Dichter', in H. Schmidt, *Die grossen Propheten* (Göttingen, 1915), pp. xxxvi–lxxii; L. Koehler, *Deuterojesaja stilkritisch untersucht* (BZAW, 36; Giessen, 1923), pp. 110-20; J. Lindblom, *Die literarische Gattung der prophetischen Literatur* (Uppsala, 1924); J. Begrich, *Studien zu Deuterojesaja* (BWANT, 77; Stuttgart, 1938); E. Würthwein, 'Der Ursprung der prophetischen Gerichtsreden', *ZTK* 49 (1952), pp. 1-16; F. Hesse, 'Wurzelt die prophetische Gerichtsrede im israelitischen Kult?', *ZAW* 65 (1953), pp. 45-53; H.B. Hummon, 'The Covenant Lawsuit in the Prophets', *JBL* 78 (1959), pp. 285-95; C. Westermann, *Grundformen prophetischer Rede* (Munich, 1960); H.J. Boecker, 'Anklagereden und Verteidigungsreden im Alten Testament. Ein Beitrag zur Formgeschichte alttestamentlicher Prophetenworte', *EvT* 20 (1960),

only mention the works which have had the greatest influence on my investigation. H.J. Boecker's classic work, *Redeformen des Rechtslebens im Alten Testament*[23] is the one that most closely examines texts and phrases in search of formulae characteristic of the juridical process; even though it is not directly concerned with the problem of literary genres, it has had a noteworthy influence upon research that is so concerned. J. Harvey's study on the so-called prophetic *rîb*[24] on the other hand is concerned with the scheme or *pattern* of the juridical contest, and with the problems traditionally connected with its *Sitz im Leben*. The chief merit of G. Gemser's work[25] is to suggest how legal matters might have a concrete influence on the various biblical literary contexts, including the sapiential. I believe that exegesis that has been particularly concerned with the controversies between God and Israel has obscured the contribution of J. Vella,[26] who led the way towards a more exact understanding of the bilateral contest; I think that not keeping in mind the difference between this and judicial procedure is one of the greatest causes of unconvincing interpretations of many biblical texts.

From the studies just mentioned (and others to be found in the general bibliography), I have drawn the biblical texts starting from which Part One in particular has been constructed; methodologically, I could

pp. 398-412; J. Harvey, 'Le "Rîb-Pattern", réquisitoire prophétique sur la rupture de l'alliance', *Bib* 43 (1962), pp. 172-96; E. von Waldow, *Der traditionsgeschichtliche Hintergrund der prophetischen Gerichtsreden* (BZAW, 85; Berlin, 1963); J. Limburg, 'The Root *ryb* and the Prophetic Lawsuit Speeches', *JBL* 88 (1969), pp. 291-304; A. Schoors, *I Am God Your Saviour: A Form-Critical Study of the Main Genres in Is XL–LX* (VTSup, 24; Leiden, 1973), pp. 176-295; R.V. Bergren, *The Prophets and the Law* (*HUCA* Monograph Series, 4; Cincinnati, 1974); K. Nielsen, *Yahweh as Prosecutor and Judge: An Investigation of the Prophetic Lawsuit* (*Rib-Pattern*), (JSOTSup, 9; Sheffield, 1978); M. de Roche, 'Yahweh's *rîb* against Israel: A Reassessment of the so-called "Prophetic Lawsuit" in the Preexilic Prophets', *JBL* 102 (1983), pp. 563-74.

23. WMANT, 14; Neukirchen–Vluyn, 1964.

24. J. Harvey, *Le plaidoyer prophétique contre Israël après la rupture de l'alliance: Etude d'une formule littéraire de l'Ancien Testament* (Studia, 22; Bruges, 1967).

25. B. Gemser, 'The *rîb*- or Controversy-Pattern in Hebrew Mentality', in M. Noth and D. Winton Thomas (eds.), *Wisdom in Israel and the Ancient Near East* (VTSup, 3; Leiden, 1955), pp. 120-37.

26. J. Vella, *La giustizia forense di Dio* (Brescia, 1964); *idem*, 'Una trama letteraria di liti di Dio con il suo popolo: schema di teologia biblica', XXVI SemBEsp (Madrid, 1969), pp. 113-31.

count on a consensus that these passages were susceptible to a specifically juridical interpretation.

3. The final group of writings affecting my work consists of the various contributions to Hebrew lexicography concerned with juridical affairs. I refer not only to the essential tools, such as the Dictionaries of Theology (already mentioned), but to those books or articles that discuss the Hebrew vocabulary for legal proceedings in a more or less systematic way. Some of the authors quoted in the previous paragraphs tackle their subject by way of an examination of Hebrew juridical vocabulary. Among these, special mention may be given to Boecker, Gamper, Gemser and even Harvey. I.L. Seeligmann's article[27] is important, because even though it does not attempt a complete and organized treatment of trial vocabulary it does discuss some of the principal terms. Among the monographs dedicated to a more specific subject and more directly related to this study, I would like to mention those of R. Knierim[28] and J. Pons[29] for the quality of their analyses of the respective semantic fields undertaken, and the essay of J.F.A. Sawyer,[30] especially for its contribution of a methodological nature.

The material that I present is by way of a synthesis: the intention is not just to assemble the material and relevant observations that are the results of my predecessors' research, but to go further, and by my personal investigation to lay out as an organized whole the subjects, acts and procedures by which the Hebrew vocabulary of the Old Testament defines the juridical action taken against injustice.

The result is probably a framework, which because of its systematised nature may appear at least in part rigid and simplistic. Given my chosen aim, it has not been possible, among other things, to discuss even the principal texts that underpin my thesis according to traditional exegetical methods. Instead preference has been given to a continual comparison of the texts with each other, in search of identical, similar, equivalent or opposed words and phrases, in an easily discernible effort to establish

27. I.L. Seeligmann, 'Zur Terminologie für das Gerichtsverfahren im Wortschatz des biblischen Hebräisch', in *Hebräische Wortforschung* (VTSup, 16; FS W. Baumgartner; Leiden, 1967), pp. 251-78.

28. R. Knierim, *Die Hauptbegriffe für Sünde im Alten Testament* (Gütersloh, 1965).

29. J. Pons, *L'oppression dans l'Ancien Testament* (Paris, 1981).

30. J.F.A. Sawyer, *Semantics in Biblical Research: New Methods of Defining Hebrew Words for Salvation* (SBT 2nd Ser., 24; London, 1972).

their paradigms. Sometimes I have introduced a text (especially a narrative one) in a descriptive fashion, for the sole purpose of prefacing, by way of a significant example, the course of the line I am about to take. Since I have been more concerned to highlight linguistic and institutional phenomena and establish their role in juridical procedures than to make an exhaustive list of all occurrences, the quotations of biblical texts do not contain statistical data, nor do they intend to exhaust the possible occurrences; on the contrary, they open up the possibility of a deeper understanding of the subject by the addition of corrections, nuances and further distinctions. The coherence of the framework thus established is for me a significant criterion in support of the thesis.

At the beginning of this Introduction I noted the theological interest aroused by the subject of justice; I admit that the ultimate aim of my research has been a better understanding of the biblical message which—when speaking of the ways of God and humanity with each other—makes favoured use of juridical language. I have therefore frequently followed my lexicographical analyses with reflections on the subject in question, the scientific status of which are not comparable with the preceding matter. Considerations of this kind may be found in exegetical studies, particularly in essays in biblical theology, where the line of argument is less rigorously documented than in the strictly exegetical sector; it is not customary, however, to find lexicographical analysis side by side with speculative reflection. I therefore invite the reader to consider the reflective parts as an *attempt* to contribute to the general debate about the meaning of justice and some important themes in biblical theology.

Part I

THE JURIDICAL CONTROVERSY (*RÎB*)

INTRODUCTION TO PART I

The *rîb* is a controversy that takes place between two parties[1] on questions of law. For the contest to take place, the individuals in question must have had a previous juridical bond between them (even if not of an explicit nature), that is, it is necessary that they refer to a body of norms that regulates the rights and duties of each. This underlying relationship between the individuals affects not just the origin but also the progress of a dispute that is substantiated by juridical arguments and requires a solution in conformity with the law.[2]

The ownership of large and small property, economic contracts and political treaties, individual or collective rights sanctioned by tradition or a code, and so on—these, as universal experience testifies, are the perennial object of dispute;[3] the person who feels injured or defrauded instigates a lawsuit against whomever is the cause (real or presumed) in order to put matters to right; one takes on the role of 'prosecutor' and 'avenger' against the other party, and the juridical action is carried forward until a solution is reached that is seen by both sides to be just, that is, in conformity with the law or equity.[4]

In a further attempt to clarify the nature and meaning of the *rîb*, I

1. There are controversies between two persons (Gen. 21.25; 31.26; Jer. 12.1 etc.), between two groups (Gen. 13.7; 26.20-21 etc.) and even between an individual and a group (Judg. 8.1; 12.2; Neh. 5.7 etc.); however, these variations do not constitute special juridical forms, because what is really at issue is the difference between the two parties. The concept of 'symmetrical' and 'asymmetrical' used by Liedke (*THAT*, II, pp. 771-77) in his treatment of the *rîb*, does not seem to me to be based on the texts, nor to be relevant to a strictly juridical treatment of the controversy.

2. With reference to disputes during the patriarchal period, Gamper distinguishes between conflicts with 'strangers' and disputes 'within the tribe itself'; but he too admits that, on the one hand, even disputes with strangers are based on a precise law and that, on the other hand, both develop in a similar way (*Gott als Richter*, pp. 109-10).

3. Cf. Gemser, 'The *Rîb*- or Controversy-Pattern', pp. 120-22.

4. Cf. Begrich, *Deuterojesaja*, p. 20.

would like to offer the following description: to begin with there is a period of agreement between two parties, a situation of peaceable understanding; there then occurs an episode that upsets this relationship because it brings into question an element on which the understanding between the two was (explicitly or implicitly) based.[5] At this point we see the offended party intimate a breach of trust and justice to the other party and so recovers a relationship that respects the nature of both. If the *rîb* achieves its effect the two parties can, in truth and justice, renew their relationship, perhaps even more intensely, and lay the foundations for a peace agreement that will shape relations between those concerned in a new way.

From what I have said it seems clear that a *rîb* is a sort of juridical crisis poised between two situations with a tendency to stability. Since it is my intention at this point to sketch in the argument that I will develop in the following chapters, it seems useful to me to anticipate, in an overall way, the main stages of the controversy, putting particular emphasis on the ways in which it can be resolved.

The first stage, the one that decides the beginning of the *rîb* and gives it its internal dynamism, is the accusation, that is, that initiative by the party (that feels) injured that addresses the other party with a demand for justice.

Faced with this juridical action of accusation, we have the response by the accused, which can take one of two opposed forms: (1) the accused may confess guilt and admit being wrong, or (2) he may protest his innocence and provide sufficient reason for doing so.

The different reactions of the accused determine the different forms of reply by the accuser, which give rise to the different forms of conclusion of the *rîb*. (1) If the accused admits guilt and requests pardon, the conflict can be resolved by the injured party holding out reconciliation. But if the accuser does not grant pardon and compensation or a similar offer is refused, the controversy continues: the accused will be brought before a judge, who will hand down a sentence proportionate to the wrong committed, or the accused will be 'punished' directly by action

5. It is taken for granted that there is a system of law common to the disputants, at least the so-called natural law or law of the nations. A treaty (cf. Gen. 21.22-24 in relationship with 25), living in a covenant relationship (such as that between YHWH and Israel), or being bound by a law that makes all concerned compatriots, fellow-citizens and comrades, brings to the fore the possibility of a controversy, precisely because of the clarity of the rights explicitly attributed to each.

taken against him or her. (2) But if the accused maintains innocence, we get solutions parallel to those described above, although with different motives and nuances. It may happen (a) that the accuser accepts the accused's arguments, recognizing at the same time the baselessness of the original law suit; but it may also happen (b) that the accuser feels dissatisfied with the other's response and persists in the accusation. Whereas in case (a) the two parties can reach a compromise and an understanding and so bring about reconciliation, offered this time by the party unjustly accused, in case (b) the *rîb* cannot be concluded without recourse to an impartial tribunal that will declare who is in the right and who is in the wrong; if there is no such tribunal, then 'words give way to deeds', fisticuffs or war, which is seen as a kind of justice of last resort.[6]

The following table is a simplification and schematization of what has been said above:

BEGINNING	DEVELOPMENT		CONCLUSION
accuser	*accused*	*accuser*	*both*
the accuser begins the *rîb*	the accused confesses guilt	the accuser grants pardon	Reconciliation
		the accuser refuses the pardon (or some other arrangement)	Tribunal /War
	the accused protests innocence	the accuser persists in the accusation	Tribunal /War
		the accuser drops his accusation	Reconciliation

This schematic outline, which will be fleshed out and explained below, is the background on which I shall place those elements of the Hebrew vocabulary that I have studied.

6. As Boecker writes, 'Es ist eine im Alten Testament verbreitete Auffassung, den Krieg, in dem der Kriegsgott durch Sieg oder Niederlage die Rechtenscheidung trifft, als einen Rechtsstreit anzusehen' (*Redeformen*, p. 51). For typical examples see Pss. 76 and 7 (cf. R. Hubbard, 'Dynamistic and Legal Processes in Psalm 7', *ZAW* 94 [1982], pp. 267-79).

It seems important to me to have shown that there is a distinction and link between a 'two-party dispute' and a trial before a judge: the former has its own juridical character and can proceed to a resolution without outside mediation; on the other hand, the intervention of a judge can in certain circumstances bring about a reasonable conclusion to proceedings that originally involved only the two parties in dispute.

From a biblical point of view it is extremely deceptive to undervalue the pre-judicial nature of a two-party controversy,[7] believing it to have less juridical rigour than a trial before a judge, or trying to ascribe to it archaic procedures that disappeared when Israel achieved a sufficient level of cultural evolution.

According to the text of the Bible, the institution of a body of judges authorized 'to resolve in justice disputes between brothers' goes back to the desert period (Exod. 18.13-26; Deut. 1.9-18).[8] It is generally allowed that it was in this period that Israel was formed into a people subject to a precise juridical system by the promulgation of a common law; hence it may be thought that from that time forwards trial proceedings overseen by a judge became an integrated part of the history of Israel and infused, if not the totality, at least the better part of its juridical activities.

Actually things are more complicated. The two-party controversy retained its validity throughout the history of Israel; this depended both on the nature of the individuals who came into dispute and on the nature of the wrong alleged by one party against the other.

In patriarchal times, disputes between individuals and groups could be resolved only by agreement (or a fight) between the parties, given the lack of a superior authority endowed with suitable jurisdiction; but despite the Mosaic institution of the 'heads of the people' (Exod. 18.21; Deut. 1.15) certain conflicts—between the different tribes for example—could not subsequently find a tribunal competent to give judgment until

7. This is the terminology used by Boecker, *Redeformen*, pp. 25-34.

8. The texts quoted suggest that previously Moses alone exercised the office of judge, but there is no indication of when he began this activity. As will be shown in Chapter 5, authority and jurisdiction seem to coincide in the institutions of Israel.

H. Reviv examines the text of Exod. 18.13-27; Num. 11.16-25 and Deut. 1.9-17 and comes to the conclusion that they reflect respectively the time of David prior to Absalom's rebellion), of Jehoshaphat (2 Chron. 19.8-11) and of Hezekiah or Josiah ('The Traditions concerning the Inception of the Legal System in Israel: Significance and Dating', *ZAW* 94 [1982], pp. 566-75).

the appearance of the monarchy. But even after the king had been recognized as having supreme jurisdiction over the whole of Israel, there remained cases where the king was not competent to judge, for example those in which he himself was one of the parties involved,[9] or those that arose between the leaders of different nations. Turning to the overall covenant relationship laid down between the people of Israel and YHWH,[10] it can clearly be seen that there cannot be any real tribunal capable of judging between these two parties when they are in a situation of mutual controversy.[11]

It must also be noted that a certain number of juridical disputes arise for reasons that do not necessarily require—according to the law of Israel—the intervention of a judge, but can be resolved by agreement or reconciliation between the parties. Typical of these are injuries that concern honour, the conflict situation between debtor and creditor, involuntary wrongs and the like, where the controversy can be decided by compensation or pardon. If an individual, in these and similar cases, is faced with an accusation that he knows to be well-founded, it is in his interest to settle the quarrel directly and without recourse to a judge; in a

9. Typical in this respect is the affair between Saul and David, where it is possible to discern the characteristics of a contest for the kingship as laid claim to, legitimately or illegitimately, by various persons in the course of history. I might mention also the cases in which a dispute occurs between prophet and king (Samuel and Saul, Elijah and Ahab, etc.). After the disappearance of the monarchy, conflict situations continue as a result of the different forms of authority that are established in Israel (cf. e.g. Neh. 5.7; 13.11, 17)

10. Harvey, *Le plaidoyer prophétique*, pp. 139-41, followed by Limburg, 'The Root *ryb*', pp. 303-304, has shown the relationship between international law and the prophetic *rîb*, claiming that the Sitz im Leben of the latter should be sought in the covenant treaties between sovereign and vassal of the ancient Near East. I would maintain that in order for a controversy to take shape it is necessary that there should be some sort of relationship between the two disputants; therefore if the two have a covenant relationship the reason for the contention becomes plainer. I would add: *rîb*s between two kings and *rîb*s between God and Israel can have various elements in common as regards structure and vocabulary, precisely because both exhibit the same structure, that of a controversy, which cannot be resolved by the mediation of a third juridical individual (judge). Yet it is not necessarily the case that a *rîb* is 'une formule rattachée au droit divin, et concrètement au droit royal' (Harvey, *Le plaidoyer prophétique*, p. 138).

11. This problem is put into terms of the individual and raised by Job in his controversy with God: Job 9.32-33; 16.21; 31.35 (cf. M.B. Dick, 'The Legal Metaphor in Job 31', *CBQ* 41 [1979], pp. 45-49).

public judgment he would not only be shamed in front of everyone, but would moreover receive a harsher punishment, which he may (at least in part) be able to avoid if he puts his trust in dialogue and the fairness of his accuser.[12] Lastly, if the wrong is so widespread that everyone has a share in the blame, what sense does recourse to a judge make? The condemnation of everyone, to the benefit of no one, is not a reasonable goal.

These considerations, taken along with others that I shall make in the course of my work, show why the two-party controversy occurs frequently in the Bible and why it deserves separate treatment of its method and function.

12. Cf. Mt. 5.25-26.

Chapter 1

THE JURIDICAL DISPUTE IN GENERAL

Two conflicts that took place between the Ephraimites and the 'judges' Gideon and Jephtha are recounted in Judg. 8.1-3 and 12.1-6; in both cases the disagreement arises because the Ephraimites were not called upon to do battle against Israel's enemies (the Midianites in 8.1; the Ammonites in 12.1). Whereas 8.1 says explicitly that here is a *rîb (wayrîbûn 'ittô b*^{e}*ḥozqâ)*, 12.1 gives no precise juridical description of the episode.

In 1 Samuel 24 and 26, we can read two accounts that parallel this; David, even though hounded to death by Saul, spares the king's life after he falls helpless into his hands. Whereas in 1 Sam. 24.16 the controversy between the two is called a *rîb*, the same terminology is not used in ch. 26.

These and many other similar cases demonstrate that an analysis of juridical controversies cannot be limited to cases in which the 'technical terminology' appears. However, so as to be in a position to highlight the structurally critical elements of the controversy and show their relevance in a way that conforms to the principles of a reasonable methodology, I shall begin my first chapter with the word group that has the root *ryb* itself at its heart.[1]

1. I do not agree with Begrich (*Deuterojesaja*, p. 31), when he states that *ryb* 'ist die technische Bezeichnung der Verhandlung des Streites vor Gericht'; a controversy as such is not necessarily forensic, as is proved among other things by the very texts quoted by Begrich to support his opinion (Jer. 2.29; Job 9.3; 33.13; Mic. 6.1, 2; Isa. 3.13).

Liedke (*THAT*, II, pp. 771-77) maintains that *ryb* and its derivates are found in the Old Testament in three interlinked life and language fields (*Sitz im Leben*): those of (a) extra-judicial, (b) pre-judicial and (c) judicial conflicts. I admit that I do not understand the relevance of the distinction between extra-judicial and pre-judicial: if the first term is meant to cover litigation that does not have the characteristics of the judicial process, then it is unclear, for example, why the disputes over wells

1. *The Subjects of the rîb*

The subjects of a controversy do not, generally speaking, have a specific title as opponents; the proper names of categories and groups are normally used when recounting or alluding to a particular lawsuit.

We may consider the expression in Deut. 19.17 as typical and almost definitive when it refers to the opponents as: *š^e^nê hā'^a^nāšîm '^a^šer lāhem hārîb*. However, one of the litigants may be described by the phrase in 2 Sam. 15.2: *hā'îš '^a^šer yihyeh lô rîb* (cf. also v. 4).[2] Even more specifically, someone who is the object of contention, and therefore subject to threats and accusations, is called *'îš rîb* (Judg. 12.2; Jer. 15.10).[3]

On the other hand, the accuser, the one who brings a case against another, is called by Job 31.35 *'îš rîbî*; and speaking of the enemies of Israel, God calls them *'anšê rîbekā* (Isa. 41.11);[4] in these two cases, it seems that the pronominal suffix added to the noun *rîb* completely alters the meaning of the phrase.

(Gen. 13.7-8; 36.20-33) should fall into this category. What I have to say later in this chapter will seek to demonstrate that 'war' and 'anger' are by no means foreign to juridical discourse in the Old Testament.

At any rate, I think an analysis of the root *ryb* constitutes a convenient point of departure for a study of juridical conflict: it will be relatively easy to single out the few cases in which a controversy occurs in the degraded form of altercation and uproar. Limburg ('The Root *ryb*', pp. 298-99 n. 19) considers, for example, that Deut. 33.7 (if corrections are not made) is the only text in the Old Testament in which the root *ryb* means a physical struggle; in Exod. 21.18, and likewise Neh. 13.25, it may be imagined that a verbal dispute turned into a riot (cf. S. Paul, *Studies in the Book of the Covenant* [VTSup 18; Leiden, 1970], p. 67).

2. Note that someone who interferes in a controversy of which he is not a lawful subject is described as: *mit'abbēr 'al rîb lō' lô* (Prov. 26.17).

3. In Judg. 12.2 the complete phrase is *'îš rîb hāyîtî '^a^nî w^e^'ammî ûb^e^nê 'ammôn m^e^'ōd*; the context makes it clear that Gideon has been attacked by the Ammonites. In Jer. 15.10, we read: *'îš rîb w^e^'îš mādôn l^e^kol hā'āreṣ*; here too the rest of the verse shows that Jeremiah has been set upon by everybody without reason.

Different opinions about this are expressed by Limburg, 'The Root *ryb*', p. 298, who gives the phrase *'îš rîb* the general meaning of 'legal adversary'; and Gemser, 'The *Rîb*- or Controversy-Pattern', who translates 'a person with a case, a feud against...' (p. 121), or simply 'adversary' (p. 123).

4. It is clear that both Job 31.35 and Isa. 41.11 deal with adversaries; to my knowledge, no scholar concerned with the vocabulary of the *rîb* has pointed up the importance of the pronominal suffix. Zorell (under *rîb*) correctly distinguishes between *'îš rîb* 'cui obloquuntur' Jer. 15.10, 'adversarius' Job 31.35 and *'anšê rîbekā* 'qui tibi obloquuntur' Isa. 41.11.

Again along the lines of an adversary understood juridically as someone who attacks another person according to legal principles, we have the noun *yārîb* (Isa. 49.25; Jer. 18.19; Ps. 35.1) and the participle *mērîb* (1 Sam. 2.10);[5] but here too we have again pronominal suffixes which modify them. If instead of the root *ryb* we take a synonym, we see the same phenomenon recur (*'anšê maṣṣutekā* and *'anšê milḥamtekā*: Isa. 41.12).[6]

The subject who intervenes in a lawsuit can be described in Hebrew by a construct state, in which *rîb* acts as a *nomen regens* and the 'juridical subject' by a *nomen rectum*: however, only from the context can it be deduced whether the subject is the accuser or the accused. Although on the one hand we have *rîb b^e^nê yiśrā'ēl* (Exod. 17.7) or *rîb yhwh* (Mic. 6.2),[7] where the allusion is to accusers, we also find *rîb ṣiyyôn* (Isa. 34.8), where the reference is certainly to the one attacked; in yet other cases, it is known only that someone is involved in a *rîb*, but his juridical role cannot be clearly deduced (Exod. 23.3, 6; Isa. 1.23; Prov. 18.17, etc.).[8]

In conclusion, the juridical subjects of a controversy are referred to by the role that they play, and which can very often be deduced only from the context, rather than by a univocal technical vocabulary.

5. The text of Hos. 4.4 is the object of various interpretations. There seems to be a certain consensus in contemporary exegesis to correct the MT to *w^e^'imm^e^kā rîbî kōhēn* (H.W. Wolff, *Dodekapropheton*. I. *Hosea* [BK, 14/1; Neukirchen, 1961], p. 88).

6. It is likely that the phrase *'îš* + *šālôm* + pronominal suffix is the antonym of *'îš* + *rîb* + pronominal suffix: cf. Ps. 41.10 (*'îš š^e^lômî*); Jer. 20.10 (*'^e^nôš š^e^lômî*), Jer. 38.22 (*'anšê š^e^lōmekā*); Obad. 7 (*'anšê š^e^lōmekā*). It is a noteworthy paradox that, in the texts quoted, the friend (*'îš š^e^lômî*...) turns out to be an adversary (*'îš rîbî*...). Cf. also *šôl^e^mî* in Ps. 7.5 (H. Tigay, 'Psalm 7.5 and Ancient Near Eastern Treaties', *JBL* 89 [1970], pp. 182-86).

7. The designation of the accuser is clear when we have a reference to the accused in the same syntagm: *rîb l^e^yhwh 'im*...(Hos. 4.1; 12.3; Mic. 6.2); *rîb l^e^yhwh b^e^*...(Jer. 25.31); *rîbām* (of the servants) *'immādî* (against me) (Job 31.13).

8. When I analyse the vocabulary of the debate in Part II, Chapter 7, further elements will be given regarding the subjects of a juridical dispute. In the meantime, it may be observed that, despite the fact that accuser and accused are two logically opposed terms, it is not always easy to assign these functions with precision to the actual subjects of a lawsuit, given that they often exchange roles.

2. *The Controversy Situation: The Word ryb*

In this section I shall examine the word *ryb*, to see how it expresses the situation of the juridical dispute.[9] In the first place, bearing in mind the prepositions with which it is constructed, or more generally its grammatical complement, a clear distinction should be made between two meanings of the word: in the first case the *rîb* is directed *against* someone (an accusation *rîb*); in the second *on behalf* of someone (a defence *rîb*).[10]

2.1. *Ryb as a Juridical Action against Someone (ryb 'et/'im/b*^{e}*/'el)*

To begin with, the word *ryb* is compounded with a group of prepositions that have no noticeable distinction between themselves,[11] but all of them are used to define the action of accusation against a given person or group.

9. Limburg sums up the positions of those authors who have explicitly dealt with the meaning of *ryb* like this: 'The lexicons and literature understand the primary meaning for *ryb* as ranging from the broad "strive, contend" through a more restricted "conduct a legal process" to a most restricted "accuse, make an accusation"' ('The Root *ryb*', p. 292); as a result of his personal inquiries, first into non-theological contexts and then into the controversies between God and Israel (in the prophets), he believes he can show that *ryb* always has the meaning of to accuse (pp. 290, 301). I agree with the statement the the root *ryb* refers to a juridical upholding of the law; I would add, however, that grammatical construction and sometimes context may indicate whether this action is directed for or *against* someone.

10. The logical distinction between an accusation *rîb* and a defence *rîb* does not mean that one action can be separated from the other; although it is necessary to acknowledge the linguistic fact and hence the different kinds of juridical intervention, it has to be said that even when the *rîb* is on behalf of someone, it can never be dissociated from a certain position-taking against someone else: the defence *rîb* is, so to say, a second stage intervention which supposes a *rîb* already underway. Cf. for example:

Isa. 49.25	*w*^{e}*'et y*^{e}*rîbēk 'ānōkî 'ārîb*	(accusation)
	w^{e}*'et bānayik 'ānōkî 'ôšîa'*	(defence)
Prov. 22.23	*kî yhwh yārîb rîbām*	(defence)
	w^{e}*qāba' 'et qōb*^{e}*'êhem nāpeš*	(defence)

(Cf. A. Cody, 'Notes on Proverbs 22.21 and 22.23b', *Bib* 61 [1980], pp. 418-26).

11. Cf. Limburg, 'The Root *ryb*', p. 296. Boecker, on the other hand (*Redeformen*, p. 54 n. 2), brings out the following nuances: *ryb* in the absolute state, *ryb 'im* and *ryb 'et* generally refer to the whole controversy proceeding; *ryb b*^{e} refers to the plaintiff; *ryb 'el* means to level an accusation against someone. There are different classifications again in Gamper, *Gott als Richter*, p. 185, and Harvey, *Le plaidoyer prophétique*, pp. 116-17.

ryb 'et	Num. 20.13; Judg. 8.1; Isa. 45.9; 49.25; 50.8; Jer. 2.9; Ps. 35.1; Prov. 23.11; 25.9; Neh. 5.7; 13.11, 17[12]
ryb 'im	Gen. 26.20; Exod. 17.2; Num. 20.3; Judg. 11.25; Job 9.3; 13.19; 23.6; 40.2; Prov. 3.30 (Q); Neh. 13.25 The noun *rîb* is compounded with *'im* in Hos. 4.1; 12.3; Mic. 6.2; Job 31.13
*ryb b^e^*	Gen. 31.36; Judg. 6.32;[13] Hos. 2.4 The noun *rîb* is compouned with *b^e^* in Jer. 25.31
ryb 'el	Judg. 21.22; Jer. 2.29; 12.1; Job 33.13

The preposition *b^e^* is used to indicate the medium or form of the *rîb* in Judg. 8.1; Amos 7.4;[14] Job 23.6; and the preposition *'al* refers to the

12. In Mic. 6.1, the phrase *ryb 'et* is problematic by comparison with all the other occurrences.

The ancient versions (LXX, Syriac, Targums), give *ryb 'et* (6.1) a meaning not unlike that of *rîb 'im* (6.2).

Modern translations, on the other hand (TOB, RSV, Einheitsübersetzung, NBE, Vaccari), bring out more or less clearly the calling together of mountains and hills (*ryb 'et*: 6.1) and God's quarrel with the people of Israel (*rîb 'im*: 6.2). The commentators highlight this difference, attributing to the mountains the function of witnesses to the controversy; cf. M.P. Smith (ICC; Edinburgh, 1912), pp. 118-20; T.H. Robinson (HAT I/14; Tübingen, 1954), pp. 144, 146; R. Ungern-Sternberg (BotAT, 23/3; Stuttgart, 1958), p. 134; W. Rudolph (KAT, 13/3; Gütersloh, 1975), pp. 106-107, 109; J.L. Mays (OTL; London, 2nd edn, 1980), p. 127; L. Alonso Schökel, *Profetas*, II (Madrid, 1980), p. 1064. This line is also followed by Gamper, *Gott als Richter*, p. 185, and by Harvey, *Le plaidoyer prophétique*, p. 42.

H.W. Wolff, *Dodekapropheton* (BK, 14/4; Neukirchen, 1982), pp. 139-46, takes an original position. Precisely because *ryb 'et* is never attested in the sense of 'hold a controversy in the presence of', he maintains that 6.1 concerns a *rîb* against the mountains and hills ('symbol' of the idolatrous nations; cf. 5.14), and 6.2 begins YHWH's *rîb* against his people (in this latter controversy the mountains are given the role of witnesses).

13. I think the phrase *yāreb bô habba'al* in Judg. 6.32 should be translated: 'may Baal sue him', 'may Baal accuse him'; and not 'may Baal defend himself', as would be natural as a reprise of v. 31, where however we have *hû' yāreb lô*. This observation is moreover to be taken with the obvious pun on the name Jerub-baal.

14. The preposition *b^e^* in Amos 7.4 (*w^e^hinnēh qōrē' lārīb **bā'ēš** 'ădōnāy yhwh*) indicates the medium or form of the *rîb*, not the accused; something similar is to be found in Judg. 8.1 (*wayrîbûn 'ittô **b^e^**ḥozqâ*) and in Job 23.6 (*hab^e^rob kōaḥ yārîb 'immādî*). The quotation in Harvey's list in *Le plaidoyer*, p. 116 n. 7 therefore seems mistaken. D.R. Hillers, 'Amos 7.4 and in Ancient Parallels', *CBQ* 26 (1964), pp. 221-

reason for the controversy in Gen. 26.21, 22; Job 10.2.

2.2. *Ryb as a Juridical Action on Behalf of Someone* (*ryb lᵉ/rîb* + *pronominal suffix*)

The word *ryb* has a different meaning from the aforesaid when it is compounded with the preposition *lᵉ* or with an internal accusative: in this case, it has the sense of 'to intervene in a trial on behalf of (someone)', 'to take over a case for (someone)', 'to defend'.

ryb lᵉ	Deut. 33.7; Judg. 6.31 (3×); Job 13.8
ryb 'et rîb + pronominal suffix	1 Sam. 24.10; 25.39;[15] Jer. 50.34; 51.36; Prov. 23.11
ryb rîb + pronominal suffix	Mic. 7.9; Ps. 43.1; 74.22; 119.154; Prov. 22.23; 25.9;[16] Lam. 3.58[17]

Only in a few cases of self-defence (Deut. 33.7; Judg. 6.31b; Ps. 74.22; Prov. 25.9) does the word *ryb* take on the reflexive meaning of 'defend oneself'; in the other cases it signals (or calls for) the intervention of a third subject who will make common cause with the accused.

25, followed by Wolff, *Dodekapropheton*, p. 338, has proposed the correction of *lrb b'š* to *lrbb 'š* (rain of fire); if this proposal is accepted, there is no further reason to discuss the special meaning of the syntagm *ryb bᵉ* in Amos 7.4. The phrase *ryb bā'ēš* seems plausible however when compared with similar phrases (where the grammatical subject is God): *'nh bā'ēš* (1 Kgs 18.24); *bw' bā'ēš* (Isa. 66.15); *špṭ* (*Ni*) *bā'ēš* (Isa. 66.16).

15. The exact phrase in 1 Sam. 25.39 is (*bārûk yhwh 'ᵃšer*) *rāb 'et rîb ḥerpātî*; the latter term specifies both the subject involved in the *rîb* (by means of the pronominal suffix) and the cause of the controversy (by means of the noun *ḥerpâ*) (cf. Ps. 74.22).

16. We may mention the systems by which a defensive or accusatory intervention is expressed:

Prov. 23.11	*hû'*	*yārîb 'et rîbām*	*'ittāk*
Prov. 25.9	(thou)	*rîbᵉkā rîb*	*'et rē'ekā*
1 Sam. 25.39	*(yhwh)*	*rāb 'et rîb ḥerpātî*	*miyyad nābāl*
Ps. 43.1	(God)	*rîbâ rîbî*	*miggôy lō' ḥāsîd*

17. Instead of the pronominal suffix, Lam. 3.58 has the equivalent noun *nepeš*: *rabtā 'ᵃdōnāy rîbê napšî.*

2.3. *The Word ryb with other Constructions, but with the Same Meanings*

As well as the usages noted above, the word *ryb* can be used absolutely, or with a direct object; in such cases only the context allows a decision between the meaning of 'to accuse' and that of 'to defend'.

Ryb used absolutely (*a*) *to accuse*: Isa. 3.13; 57.16; Hos. 4.4; Amos 7.4; Ps. 103.9; Prov. 25.8;[18] (*b*) *to defend*: 19.20.

Ryb used with a direct object[19] (*a*) *to accuse*: Deut. 33.8;[20] Isa. 27.8; Job 10.2; (*b*) *to defend*: Isa. 1.17; 51.22.

3. *Verbs Parallel or Related to ryb*[21]

The fundamental distinction mapped out above for the verb *ryb* between a meaning of accusation and a meaning of defence is brought to the fore by the system of synonymous parallelism that is so frequent in biblical literature. Although the degree of synonymity is not always clear and it is often difficult to decide whether the verbs are parallel or related, it seems possible to establish the following two-way division:

a. with reference to an action of *accusation* (intervention against), we have these chief synonyms of *ryb*:

18. The 'aggressive' meaning of *ryb* used absolutely can also be detected in Exod. 21.18, where the debate turns into a brawl.

19. It may be noted that when *ryb* has a personal suffix as its object (3×) its meaning is 'to accuse'; but when its object is a noun (twice) the meaning is 'to defend'. However, I do not feel I can state that this constitutes a grammatical and semantic rule.

20. The text of Deut. 33.8 is not altogether clear: the verb *ryb* is in parallel with the verb *nsh* (*Pi*), which leads one to suppose that it is not an intervention on behalf of, though Gamper, *Gott als Richter*, p. 185, says it is. The fact that the episode at Massah and Meribah is the object of different interpretations in Scripture itself (Exod. 17.1-7; Num. 20.1-13; Pss. 81.8; 95.8-9; 106.32) is of no help to us in deciding on the exact meaning to attribute to the quotation from Deuteronomy.

21. In this section I will also point out some parallels of the noun *rîb*, because in some cases it refers not just to the event of the dispute, but has the same function as the verb, that of distinguishing the subject and object of the charge (Hos. 4.1; Mic. 6.2 etc.).

ykḥ	(*Hi*)		= *ryb*	Hos. 4.4
	(*Hi*)	+ acc.	= *ryb ʻim*	Job 40.2
	(*Hitp*)	*ʻim*	= *rîb ʻim*	Mic. 6.2[22]
nišpaṭ[23]		l^e	= *rîb* b^e	Jer. 25.31
lḥm	(*Qal*)	*'et*	= *ryb 'et*	Ps. 35.1
	(*Ni*)	b^e	= *ryb ʻim*	Judg. 11.25
qṣp			= *ryb*	Isa. 57.16
nṭr			= *ryb*	Ps. 103.9

b. indicating on the other hand an action of *defence* (intervention on behalf of), we have:

yšʻ (*Hi*)	+ acc.	= *ryb* l^e		Judg. 6.31
(*Hi*)		= *ryb*		Isa. 19.20
špṭ	+ acc.(*miyyad–*)	= *ryb 'et rîb*	+ pron. suff.	1 Sam. 24.16
	+ acc.	= *ryb*	+ acc.	Isa. 1.17 (cf. 1.23: *rîb*)
	+ acc. pron. suff.	= *ryb rîb*	+ pron. suff.	Ps. 43.1
ʻśh mišpāṭ	+ pron. suff.	= *ryb rîb*	+ pron. suff.	Mic. 7.9[24]
g'l	+ acc. pron. suff.	= *ryb 'et rîb*	+ pron. suff.	Jer. 50.34; Prov. 23.11
	+ acc. pron. suff.	= *ryb rîb*	+ pron. suff.	Ps. 119.154 (cf. also the equivalent in Lam. 3.58)
nqm (*Pi*)	+ int. obj.	= *ryb 'et rîb*	+ pron. suff.	Jer. 51.36

This list deserves some comments so as to fill out our examination of the Hebrew lexicon and likewise to demonstrate the relevance of the overall thrust of my argument in the Introduction to Part One. My observations will be spread over two sections, corresponding to the subdivision which I made above.

3.1. *The Synonyms of ryb as an Intervention against Someone*

With attention directed to the terms (verbs, phrases) that are used in parallel with *ryb* (or *rîb*) and have the meaning of intervention against

22. There is further confirmation of the synonymity between the root *ryb* and *ykḥ* in Job 13.6-7 and 33.19.

23. By *nišpaṭ* I mean the *Niphal* of the verb *špṭ*, which does not have a passive meaning (Cf. GK 51d; Joüon 51c).

24. For *ʻśh mišpaṭ* + pronominal suffix, see also Lam. 3.58-59. I would also like to point out other roots that show synonymity with *ryb* as a defence intervention: *nṣl* (*Hi*): Isa. 19.20; *plṭ* (*Pi*) *min*: Ps. 43.1; *ʻēzer min*: Deut. 33.7.

(someone), I will try to clarify their meaning more precisely and see what part they play in the juridical terminology of the controversy.

3.1.1. *The Root ykḥ.* Among the synonyms of *ryb* as an accusing intervention, I pointed first to the verb *ykḥ*, which is almost always found in the *Hiphil* (*Niphal*: Isa. 1.18; Job. 23.7; Gen. 20.16; this latter text is somewhat disputed; *Hophal:* Job 33.19; *Hitpael:* Mic. 6.2) and exhibits a range of meanings in which at first sight it is difficult to discern a unity.[25] The different prepositions with which the verb is compounded do not appear to allow a distinction between the various nuances of meaning, which can therefore only be arrived at by an analysis of their exact context; unfortunately, since the root is mostly used in poetic contexts, even this operation is far from straightforward.

However, it is certain that the subject to whom the action of the verb *ykḥ* is attributed is to some extent a *censor*: he criticises, warns, calls to account, intervenes in order to establish justice. It may well be, then, that the important thing is to see who is intervening, at whom the criticism is directed, what the environment is in which the activity of *ykḥ* occurs.

Although there are divergent opinions about the original environment of this Hebrew root,[26] I think it can at least be stated that there is an ethical and sapiential nuance to be kept always in mind. The way I see it is that the verb *ykḥ* is used to describe a father's educative correction of his son (2 Sam. 7.14; Prov. 3.12);[27] what is more, it is frequently parallel or correlative to the root *ysr* (Jer. 2.19; Pss. 6.2; 38.2; 94.10; Job 5.17; 40.2; Prov. 3.12; 9.7),[28] which is universally acknowledged as

25. As well as the Dictionary articles (*THAT*, I [ed. G. Liedke], p. 730-32, and *ThWAT*, III [ed. G. Mayer], pp. 620-28), cf. V. Maag, *Text, Wortschatz und Begriffswelt des Buches Amos* (Leiden, 1951), pp. 152-54; Gemser, 'The *Rîb* or Controversy-Pattern', pp. 124-25 n. 4; Boecker, *Redeformen*, pp. 45-47; Seeligmann, 'Zur Terminologie', pp. 266-68; R.R. Wilson, 'An Interpretation of Ezekiel's Dumbness', *VT* 22 (1972), pp. 98-100; E. Kutsch, '"Wir wollen miteinander rechten". Zu Form und Aussage von Jes 1.18-20', in *Künder des Wortes* (FS J. Schreiner; Würzburg, 1982), pp. 29-31.

26. Liedke (*THAT*, I, p. 730) distinguishes between those who hold that the root *ykḥ* found its original context in the field of judicial procedure (Boecker, Horst) and those on the other hand who believe in a sapiential origin (Maag). I incline rather to the second opinion, taking into consideration among other things the particularly frequent use of the root *ykḥ* in the book of Proverbs.

27. Cf. also Prov. 29.15.

28. Cf. the frequent parallel in Proverbs between *tôkaḥat* and *mûsār*: 3.11; 5.12; 10.17; 12.1; 13.18; 15.5, 32; in 6.23 we also have *tôkᵉḥôt mûsār*, while in

belonging to the sapiential lexicon ('to impart a lesson'); finally, it is often to be found in the same context as terms and expressions that are generally ascribed to the Wisdom genre (Isa. 11.1-5; Ps. 141.3-5; Job 6.24-26; 15.2-3; 32.11-14; Prov. 9.7-8; 15.12; 19.25; 25.12).[29]

However, this in no way excludes the root *ykḥ* from being relevant to matters juridical, both because certain texts demonstrate it incontrovertibly (Gen. 21.25;[30] 31.37; Isa. 1.18; 29.21; Amos 5.10; Ps. 50.8, 21; Job 9.33; 13.10, 15; 22.4; Prov. 22.23-25),[31] and because it is generally thought that the fields of Wisdom and jurisdiction are closely linked.

Thus, rather than maintaining that this verb has a different meaning according to context, it seems more logical to imagine that it expresses the sapiential phase of the justice procedure, using criticism, accusation and punishment. It is not altogether true, for example, to state that the father–son relationship is alien to the juridical world; on the contrary, paternal authority works within the family circle on a par with that of a civic leader in the community, and vice versa;[32] if a father allows natural feelings of affection to overrule rigorously upright conduct, he sanctions evil within the circle of responsibility which has been entrusted to him (family jurisdiction) and ends up guilty himself (1 Sam. 3.13); on the other hand, the parental right to punish is so widely recognized that when the parents cannot correct their children, they may be reduced to handing a son over to the public authorities even for capital punishment (Deut. 21.18-21).[33]

Ps. 39.12 we find the syntagm *ysr (Pi) b^e^tôkāḥôt.*

29. I might mention the parallelism between *tôkaḥat* and *'ēṣâ* in Prov. 1.25, 30; in the book of Proverbs the noun *tôkaḥat* clearly belongs within the field of sapiential terminology (cf. 5.12-13; 12.1; 15.5, 31, 32; 29.15).

30. The identity of function between *ykḥ* and *ryb* as verbs referring to a juridical contest comes out clearly in a comparison between two texts in Genesis:

21.25:	*w^e^hôkiaḥ 'abrāhām*	*'et '^a^bîmelek*	*'al 'ōdôt b^e^'ēr hammayim*
26.20:	*wayyārîbû rō'ê g^e^rār*	*'im rō'ê yiṣḥāq*	*lē'mōr: lānû hammāyim*
26.21:	*...wayyārîbû gam*		*'āleyā*

31. The noun *tôkaḥat* means taking up a position in the debate in Hab. 2.1; Ps. 38.16; Job 13.6; 23.4.

32. Cf. R.R. Wilson, 'Enforcing the Covenant: the Mechanisms of Judicial Authority in Early Israel', in *The Quest for the Kingdom of God* (FS E. Mendenhall; Winona Lake, IN, 1983), p. 64.

33. Cf. E. Bellefontaine, 'Deuteronomy 21.18-21: Reviewing the Case of the Rebellious Son', *JSOT* 13 (1979), pp. 13-31; P.R. Callaway, 'Deut. 21.18-21: Proverbial Wisdom and Law', *JBL* 103 (1984), pp. 341-52.

Juridical procedure should not be confused with forensic procedure: the former may remain within the sphere of a simple (private) interpersonal relation, without precise (public) formal structures; but it is a juridical procedure to the extent that there is perceived to be an intervention of accusation based upon the recognition of a misdeed and linked to an acknowledged agency of punishment. This holds good for the father–son relation and in normal relationships between citizens (Lev. 19.17; Prov. 24.23-25; 28.23). The fact that in certain cases this censuring function is carried out 'at the gates', that is, in the law-court, means that since the *rîb* could not be settled within a two-party context, it has been brought before a judge and submitted to his decision (Isa. 29.21; Amos 5.10).

It is important, however, to note the sapiential dimension evoked by the verb *ykḥ*; if, on the one hand, it underlines the relationship between juridical procedure and punishment (2 Kgs 19.4; Hab. 1.12; Pss. 94.10; 105.14), on the other hand it brings in a finality which is not limited to the pure application of 'retributive (punitive) justice': the corrective intentionality of the controversy shows that the aim of the juridical procedure is the *amendment* of one's adversary, not simply his punishment; sometimes punishment is the necessary means, but it is the human reality of the 'adversary as subject' which one tries to touch and have an influence upon.[34] From this it may be deduced that the action of *ykḥ* and even the action of punishment represent a process of justice to the extent that they are motivated by *love* for the other; it is in fact a mark of love to act in such a way that the other's life may be directed into the way of justice (Lev. 19.17-18; Prov. 3.11-12; 6.23; 10.17; 13.24; 15.10; 27.5-6), while an accusation dictated by hate is opposed to Wisdom and true justice.[35]

As regards the particular shades of meaning determined by the verb *ykḥ*'s governing prepositions, we may note a fundamental distinction:

1. *ykḥ* used absolutely (Isa. 1.18; 29.21; Hos. 4.4; Amos 5.10 etc.), with a direct object (2 Sam. 7.14; Jer. 2.19; Pss. 6.2; 38.2; 50.8 etc.), or followed by the prepositions *'im* (Mic. 6.2; Job 23.7), *'et* (Gen. 21.25; Lev. 19.17; Job 13.10; Prov. 3.12), *b^e^* (2 Kgs 19.4 = Isa. 37.4; Prov. 30.6), *'el* (Job 13.3; cf. 13.15), *l^e^* (Isa. 2.4 = Mic. 4.3; Job 32.12;

34. Cf. J. Scharbert, *Der Schmerz im Alten Testament* (BBB, 8; Bonn, 1955), pp. 190-94.

35. Cf. M. Ogushi, *Der Tadel im Alten Testament: Eine formgeschichtliche Untersuchung* (EurHS, 23; Frankfurt, 1978), especially pp. 148-52.

Prov. 9.7, 8; 15.12; 19.25), where it means to criticise, to correct, to accuse, and the like.

It should be noted that, unlike the verb *ryb* even with the preposition *l*ᵉ, the verb *ykḥ* is the equivalent of the action of accusing (the sole exception is Isa. 11.4[36]); just as with the verb *ryb*, the preposition *'al*

36. Job 16.21 has a special formula which deserves some comment. The MT has *wᵉyôkaḥ lᵉgeber 'im 'ᵉlôah—ûben 'ādām lᵉrē'ēhû*. Essentially, there are two philological problems in this verse: (1) the meaning of the verb *ykḥ*; (2) the meaning of the prepositions governed by the verb; the various responses to these two questions give rise to the plurality of interpretations of the whole verse.

The ancient versions (LXX, Syriac, Targums) give *ykḥ* the meaning of to accuse; only the Vulgate translates: *atque utinam sic iudicaretur vir cum Deo* (meaning 'to judge'; and *wywkḥ*, read as a *Hophal*). As for the meaning of the prepositions, I would point out that all translate *ben 'ādām* as 'son of man' (i.e. none has read the preposition *bên* with *scriptio defectiva*); moreover, in the second stich (with the exception of the LXX), they introduce an element of comparison ('like' a man...); in addition it may be noted that the Targums, again in the second stich, substitute *'im* for *l*ᵉ. It all goes to show that the ancient translators had a certain amount of difficulty with the Hebrew text.

Among the modern commentators (S.R. Driver and G.B. Gray, *The Book of Job* [ICC; Edinburgh, 1921]; G. Fohrer, *Das Buch Hiob* [KAT, 16; Gütersloh, 1963]; F. Horst, *Hiob* [BK 16/1; Neukirchen, 1968]; H. Pope, *Job* [AB, 15; Garden City, NY, 1974]; R. Gordis, *The Book of Job: Commentary, New Translation and Special Studies* (New York, 1978); L. Alonso Schökel and J.L. Sicre, *Job: Comentario Teologico y literario* (Madrid, 1983), the majority opinion has 'to judge' as the meaning of the verb *ykḥ* (Gordis, Alonso Schökel) or 'to decide' (Driver, Fohrer); they commonly correct *ben* to *bên*, and they give the various prepositions (*l*ᵉ... *'im; bên*... *l*ᵉ) a similar meaning; as an example, we may quote Alonso Schökel's version: 'que juzgue entre un varón y Dios, entre un hombre y su amigo'.

Driver and Gray, on the other hand, attribute a specific nuance to the prepositions *l*ᵉ and *'im* in the first stich ('decide for...in his contest with...'). Pope takes an original stand, in as much as he follows the MT at *ben 'ādām*, but introduces an element of comparison (*waw comparationis?*) in the second stich and gives the same nuance to the preposition *l*ᵉ in both stichs: 'he pleads for a man with God, as a fellow does for his friend'.

M. Dahood's highly innovative reading, 'For can a mere man argue with God / Or a human mind discern his intentions?') is based upon debatable philological arguments; in any case, it is not a great help in the analysis of the verb *ykḥ* and its prepositions ('The Phoenician Contribution to Biblical Wisdom Literature', in W.A. Ward [ed.], *The Role of the Phoenicians in the Interaction of Mediterranean Civilization* [Beirut, 1968], p. 124).

In conclusion, if the position of Driver, Gray and Pope is accepted, we have another case besides Isa. 11.4 in which the syntagm *ykḥ* (*Hi*) *l*ᵉ means a juridical

specifies the motive or reason for the accusation (Gen. 21.25; Pss. 50.8; 105.14 = 1 Chron. 16.21);[37] while b^e expresses the kind or means of intervention (2 Sam. 7.14; Isa. 11.4; Pss. 6.2; 38.2; Job. 15.3; 33.19).

As the synonymous equivalent of *mērîb* (and *'îš rîb* + pron. suff.) we have *môkîaḥ* (Job 32.12; 40.2; Prov. 9.7; 24.25; 25.12; 28.23; with the specification *baššaʻar*: Isa. 29.21; Amos 5.10) and *'îš môkîaḥ* (Ezek. 3.26;[38] cf. also Hos. 4.4). An equivalent of *'îš rîb* (the accused) is *'îš tôkāḥôt* (Prov. 29.1).

2. *ykḥ* followed by *bên* (Gen. 31.37; Job. 9.33) can be taken as meaning 'to take sides' with a meaning similar to 'to arbitrate', or even 'to decide'. In this meaning, although without the preposition *bên*, could perhaps be taken the cases of Gen. 24.14, 44;[39] 31.42. Job 16.21[40] represents an original formula which probably belongs to this sphere of meaning.

The semantic problem of how a juridical action against someone can be likened to an arbitration or sentence (cf. the parallelism between *ykḥ* and *špṭ* in Isa. 2.4 = Mic. 4.3; Isa. 11.3-4) will be developed below when I deal with the judgment (Chapter 5).

intervention on behalf (of someone).

37. The commentators give a generally adversative meaning to the *ykḥ* (*Hi*) *'al* syntagm of Job 19.5b (*w*ᵉ*tôkîḥû 'ālay ḥerpātî*), since the preposition *'al* governs a pronominal suffix which refers to the accused: Driver and Gray: 'and argue against me my reproach'; Fohrer: 'und mit meine Schmach vorhalten?'; Horst: 'und mir zu Lasten schändlich Tun beweisen'; Pope: 'and argue my disgrace against me'; Alonso Schökel: 'echandome en cara mi afrenta?' Gordis on the other hand has a different position, given that he attributes a declarative meaning to the verb *ykḥ* ('declare right, justify'): 'and justify the humiliation I have suffered'.

38. R.R. Wilson maintains that the phrase *'iš môkîaḥ* means mediator or arbiter; the command to be silent given by God to Ezekiel, governed by the phrase *w*ᵉ*lō' tihyeh lāhem l*ᵉ*'îš môkîaḥ* means, according to this author, the end of Ezekiel's activity as a prophetic mediator and the beginning of his role as one proclaiming divine punishment ('An Interpretation of Ezekiel's Dumbness', *VT* 22 [1972], especially pp. 98-104). I would say rather that Ezek. 3.26 marks the passage from a *rîb* in words (accusation) to a *rîb* in deeds (punishment), motivated by a refusal to listen on the part of the people.

39. Isaac's choice of a bride is undoubtedly a juridical act of great importance, since it decided the ancestry of the people of Israel; it is therefore attributed to the intervention of God himself.

40. Cf. n. 36.

3.1.2. *The Form špṭ (Ni)*. Only in a few cases (Pss. 9.20; 37.33; 109.7) is the form *nišpaṭ* used as the passive of the verb *špṭ*; elsewhere it means 'to enter into a controversy with someone', 'to be at odds legally'.[41] As with the verbs *ryb* and *ykḥ*, different prepositions, similar in meaning, denote the juridical subject against whom the action is directed: *'et* (1 Sam. 12.7; Isa. 66.16; Ezek. 17.20; 20.35, 36; 38.22; Prov. 29.9),[42] *'im* (Joel 4.2; 2 Chron. 22.8; cf. also Sir. 8.14), *l*^{e} (Jer. 25.31). In this case too the preposition *'al* indicates the motive for the legal action (Jer. 2.35; Joel 4.2), and the preposition *b*^{e} the kind or means (Isa. 59.4; 66.16; Ezek. 38.22).

The fact that underlying the *nišpaṭ* form there is the semantic force of the root *špṭ* leads us to see the juridical controversy as a 'submitting to judgment' of the case which has arisen between the two parties;[43] whether this takes place before a third party (cf. 1 Sam. 12.7) or not (cf. Exod. 20.35) does not modify the sense of the confrontation substantially, the aim of which is to establish justice and the truth.

3.1.3. *The Controversy and War (= Armed Clash)*. I will have occasion in the second part of my work (especially Chapter 7) to illustrate the relationship that exists between the juridical controversy and war. Here I note just two particularly significant points: (1) the *rîb* is 'like' a war: because the accusation carries the burden of re-establishing justice, it brings with it elements of aggression and force (Judg. 8.1; Jer. 50.34; Ps. 35.1; Job 9.3; 23.6; Prov. 23.11) which tend to be imposed despite the accused's opposition; (2) the *rîb* necessarily breaks out into war when the two parties are unable to reach a fair understanding by words; it might be said that the dynamism of the *rîb* brings the whole body into play, until one of the two admits that the other is right.

41. GK 51d notes the reciprocal aspect of the *Niphal* (= to be at odds with), clearly seen in Isa. 43.26: *niššāp*^{e}*ṭâ yāḥad*, with which Isa. 1.18 may be associated by analogy of meaning: *l*^{e}*kû nā' w*^{e}*niwwāk*^{e}*ḥâ*, and also 2 Sam. 19.10: *wayhî kol hā'ām nādôn b*^{e}*kol šibṭê yiśrā'ēl*. The reciprocity disappears however when *nišpaṭ* takes an object—the meaning then is 'to be at odds *with someone*'.

42. I believe that only in Jer. 2.35 (*nišpāṭ 'ôtāk*) could *'et* be considered a particle indicating the accusative (cf. however Joüon 103k); in Isa. 66.16; Ezek. 20.36; Prov. 29.9, it is preferable to see the preposition meaning 'with/against'.

43. This is confirmed by the parallelism between the phrase *bw' b*^{e}*mišpāṭ* (or *bammišpāṭ*) *'im* with the verbs *ryb* (Isa. 3.13) and *ykḥ* (Job 22.4).

3.1.4. *Wrath*

a. *The Terminology.* Among the synonyms of *ryb*, I have quoted above some verbs that belong to the semantic field of wrath; alongside the terminology that refers to the controversy as a juridical action of accusation, therefore, we have to consider the word group that expresses, so to speak, the emotional side of the contest.

The Hebrew vocabulary of wrath is quite rich; the following are the most important terms: *'np–'ap, ḥēmâ, ḥrh–ḥārôn, 'ebrâ, qṣp–qeṣep, z'm–za'am, z'p, qn'–qin'â.*[44]

b. *The Relationship between the Vocabulary of the Juridical Contest and that of Wrath.* It seems useful to point out, from a literary point of view, the complex system of relationships that exist between juridical language (*ryb, ykḥ, nišpaṭ*) and that of wrath.

In the first place, we have a *parallelism* which may be considered synonymous: as well as Isa. 57.16 and Ps. 103.9, Isa. 41.11; 66.15; Jer. 2.35 may be quoted.[45] To these texts, where the relationship of identity lies in the immediate juxtaposition of the terms, should be added those in which the same intervention is described with the vocabulary of the dispute and with the vocabulary of wrath, in the same literary unit but some verses apart. For example, in Jeremiah 25, the manifestation of God's wrath against all the nations (*ḥēmâ–ḥ^{a}rôn 'appô* and sword: vv. 15-16 [27-29]) counterbalances his controversy against every individual (*ryb–nišpaṭ* and sword: v. 31); in Ezek. 38, YHWH's great wrath (*ḥēmâ–'ap–qin'â–'ebrâ*) against Gog (vv. 18-19) is interpreted as a juridical action (*nišpaṭ*: v. 22).[46]

In the second place, the manifestation of anger is sometimes literarily linked to the action of the *rîb*; even though the nature of the relationship

44. J. Fichtner, '*orgē*', *TWNT*, V, pp. 392-94: the author also includes in the terminology of wrath the words *k's, rgz, rûaḥ*; cf. also E. Johnson, '*'ānap*', *ThWAT* I, pp. 379-83; G. Sauer, '*'ap* Zorn', *THAT*, I, p. 224; M.I. Gruber, *Aspects of Nonverbal Communication in the Ancient Near East* (Studia Pohl, 12, II; Rome, 1980), pp. 480-553.

45. The parallelism between 'wrath' and dispute vocabulary in Jer. 2.35 lies in the chiastic construction of the verse:

wattō'm^{e}rî kî niqqêtî — *'ak šāb 'appô mimmennî*
hin^{e}nî nišpāṭ 'ôtāk — *'al 'omrēk lō' ḥāṭā'tî.*

46. There is also a synonymous relationship between the cessation of wrath and a juridical intervention on behalf of (cf. Isa. 51.21-22; Mic. 7.9).

is difficult to determine, I think one may speak of reciprocal implication (or at least of co-presence within the span of one event) of wrath and accusation. In Gen. 31.36 and Neh. 5.6-7, we find the sequence: wrath (*ḥrh*)—juridical action of a dispute (*ryb b^{e}/'et*)—word that explains the accusation; in Neh. 13.25 the sequence is somewhat modified: dispute action (*ryb 'im*)—manifestation of wrath—word that specifies the accusation. One confirmation of the phenomenon can be seen in the fact that the kind of juridical intervention is expressed by the preposition *b^{e}*;[47] for example, when we read that a controversy occurs *bā'ēš* (Isa. 66.16; Amos 7.4; cf. also Ezek. 38.22), we may imagine that we are dealing with an intervention characterized by the 'heat' of wrath; on the other hand, it is explicitly said that a juridical intervention is possible, even if not desirable, in the form of wrath (Ps. 6.2: *b^{e}'app^{e}kā*; 38.2: *b^{e}qeṣp^{e}kā*).[48]

Furthermore, and this is the weightiest literary phenomenon to take into consideration, the lexicon of anger takes the place to be assigned in the juridical structure to the lexicon of the *rîb*; we therefore have a phenomenon of (synonymous) *substitution*, which is the chief indication that a particular terminology belongs to the same paradigm. As I shall demonstrate fully in the next chapter, a *rîb* is made up of three elements: (1) acknowledgement of a misdeed, (2) accusation, (3) appropriate punishment. For the time being it is noteworthy that the terminology of wrath often takes the place of the second element.[49] As particularly relevant texts I would quote Gen. 34.7-31; 39.19-20; Exod. 22.22-23; 32.9-10; Num. 11.1; Deut. 32.19. More broadly speaking, the scheme sin—God's wrath—punishment is even more frequent than that of sin—*rîb* action—punishment (cf. Num. 11.33; 12.9; Deut. 6.16; 7.4; 11.7; Judg. 2.11-15, 19-22 etc.).

c. *The Meaning of the Terminology of Wrath.*[50] I shall try in this section to provide some interpretative tools that will clarify at least partially the

47. Cf. pp. 40, 48, 49.

48. The book of Proverbs, which repeatedly condemns disputes (6.19; 10.12; 16.28; 17.14; 26.21; 29.22), points out the relationship between wrath and controversies (6.34-35; 15.18; 20.33).

49. Cf. H.J. Fahlgren, *Ṣ^{e}dāḳā, nahestehende und entgegengesetzte Begriffe im Alten Testament* (Uppsala, 1932), pp. 56-64.

50. The considerations dealt with in this section are in large measure based upon the treatise of M. Viller, 'Colère', *DictSpir*, II (Paris, 1953), pp. 1053-77. This article, and above all *TWNT*, V, pp. 383-92 (H. Kleinknecht) sums up the problem of the theme of anger as seen by classical antiquity.

meaning and function of the lexicon of wrath in a juridical context.

I shall start with the difficulty experienced by every reader of Scripture, and tackled systematically by exegetes:[51] the current understanding of the word is that wrath (and its possible synonyms) is defined as 'a disordered movement of the mind as a result of which it is violently excited against someone';[52] its connotation is therefore clearly negative, inasmuch as it implies a loss of self-control (irrationality) and a manifestation of violence towards others. This gives rise to a problem when a concept like this is applied to a juridical context (characterized by rationality and the absence of emotional violence), and when wrathful behaviour is attributed to God,[53] behaviour condemned elsewhere as a capital offence.

To try to answer this difficulty it seems necessary to reflect on the ambiguity of wrath, illustrating the two complementary aspects in which it is externally manifested.

51. Exegesis has been much concerned to discuss the theological meaning of the 'jealousy' and 'wrath' of God, linking these notions to the themes of sin and punishment; I have not, however, come across any studies that situate these emotions against the background of a suitable anthropological analysis, nor an overall treatment of the vocabulary which describes them. Cf. F. Küchler, 'Der Gedanke des Eifers Jahwes im Alten Testament', *ZAW* 28 (1908), pp. 42-52; R.V. Tasker, *The Biblical Doctrine of the Wrath of God* (London, 1951); K.-H. Bernhardt, *Gott und Bild: Ein Beitrag zur Begründung und Deutung des Bildverbotes im Alten Testament* (TArb, 2; Berlin, 1956), pp. 86-92; S. Lyonnet, *De peccato et redemptione*, I (Rome, 1957), pp. 40-41; *idem*, *De Peccato*, II (Rome, 2nd edn, 1972), pp. 69-71; B. Renaud, *Je suis un Dieu jaloux: Evolution sémantique et signification théologique de qin^{e}'ah* (LD, 36; Paris, 1963); H. Ringgren, 'Einige Schilderungen des göttlichen Zorns', in *Tradition und Situation: Studien zur alttestamentliche Prophetie* (FS A. Weiser; Göttingen, 1963), pp. 107-13; H.A. Brongers, 'Der Eifer des Herrn Zebaoth', *VT* 13 (1963), pp. 269-84; *idem*, 'Der Zornesbecher', *OTS* 15 (1969), pp. 177-92; S. Erlandsson, 'The Wrath of Yhwh', *TynBul* 23 (1972), pp. 111-16; D.J. McCarthy, 'The Wrath of Yahweh and the Structural Unity of the Deuteronomistic History', in *Essays in Old Testament Ethics* (FS J.P. Hyatt; New York, 1974), pp. 97-110; W. Harrelson, 'A Meditation on the Wrath of God: Psalm 90', in *Scripture in History and Theology* (FS J.C. Rylaarsdam; Pittsburgh, 1977), pp. 181-91; C. Westermann, 'Boten des Zorns. Der Begriff des Zornes Gottes in der Prophetie', in *Die Botschaft und die Boten* (FS H.W. Wolff; Neukirchen–Vluyn, 1981), pp. 147-56.

52. This is the definition given by F. Palazzi, *Novissimo dizionario della lingua italiana* (Milan, 1974), p. 723. Other dictionaries give essentially similar definitions.

53. I might note that in the Old Testament words expressing anger are used very frequently to mean the divine wrath (about 375 times) and not human wrath (about 80 times): *TWNT*, V, p. 395.

(1) *Falling into Wrath*. It seems as though wrath can be described as the reaction that a subject undergoes when faced with something intolerable;[54] it is because there is an excess of evil, it is because bounds have been overstepped, that a spontaneous reaction is produced in a person which, by its 'excesses', is a precise indication of the intolerability of the situation.[55]

From this point of view, anger has to be considered a blameworthy act, if it shows that a (wrathful) individual has been disturbed and 'set on fire'[56] by something that does not justify such behaviour;[57] but there is also the possibility of *just anger*, which is indignation in the face of an objectively intolerable fact. The 'wrath of God' obviously falls into this second category: like the wrath of a king or a just man, God's indignation expresses his non-connivance with evil and is the right reaction in the face of a grave situation of injustice.[58]

(2) *The 'Breaking Out' of Wrath*. Anger is an emotion that drives the body to want to get rid of whatever is experienced as intolerable. Here too there are two opposing forms: that of wrath rooted in pride and jealousy, which discharges its hate by turning into bitterness and a ruthless vendetta against someone else, and that of wrath inspired by justice, which works to rid the world of evil.[59] In this second case, wrath

54. 'La colère a donc pour cause un mécontentement éprouvé en face de ce qui paraît inadmissible et qui réagit en volonté de défense, de réprobation et, s'il y a lieu, de châtiment' (*DictSpir*, p. 1056).

55. J.L. Palache maintains that the meaning of the root *'pp* is 'to submerge' ('overwhelm') (*Semantic Notes on the Hebrew Lexicon* [Leiden, 1959], pp. 8-9); this would account for the connotations of excess and destruction characteristic of wrathful outbursts.

56. Cf. P. Dhorme, *L'emploi métaphorique des noms de parties du corps en hébreu et en akkadien* (Paris, 1923), p. 81.

57. Cf. *TWNT*, V, pp. 394-95, which gives a list of the biblical texts (particularly in the Wisdom literature) that criticise anger dictated by egoistic motives.

58. S. Lyonnet speaks of God's anger as a metaphor used to describe, by way of the effect it has on the sinner, 'repugnantiam absolutam inter Deum et peccatum' (*Exegesis Epistulae ad Romanos* [Cap. I ad IV; Rome 1963], pp. 125-26).

59. This is the context in which so-called 'retributive justice' is to be viewed; cf. St Augustine: 'Meminerimus sane iram Dei sine ulla affectione turbulenta intelligere: ira quippe eius dicitur, ratio iusta vindictae; tamquam si lex dicatur irasci, cum ministri eius secundum eam commoti vindicant' (*Enarrationes in Psalmos*, Ps LXXXII, 12). I do not therefore agree with the interpretation of F. Horst when he gives lopsided emphasis to the unjust aspect of anger: 'Der Grimm weist aber die Verhandlung ab

is equivalent to a punitive intervention;[60] if it occurs within a judicial structure, the manifestation of wrath is equivalent to the sentence of guilt that inflicts the penalty.[61] In a two-party controversy structure, on the other hand, punitive anger—to the extent that it proceeds from a desire for justice—is directed towards a party that refuses to listen to words and can only be reached and touched by bodily suffering; it is a means to the end of correcting the guilty and, at the end of the day, being reconciled with them.[62]

In conclusion: seen in the perspective of the juridical procedures that we are studying, the force of wrath *accompanies* and sometimes *takes the place of* the action of words in a *rîb*.

Wrath can in fact describe the indignation of the 'just person' in the face of evil, and the perception of the danger which it conceals; it therefore drives one to utter an urgent and threatening warning. This would explain the literary phenomenon of the parallel link between the lexicon of the *rîb* and the lexicon of wrath.

On another level, however, wrath is just the passage from words to deeds, from threat to punishment; it therefore comes after the *rîb* (made

und suspendiert das Recht. Wo Zorn waltet, tritt das Recht zurück. Die Suspendierung von Recht wird aber notwendig zum Unrechthandeln abgestempelt, wenn die eigene Rechtheit und Lauterkeit zum Mass genommen wird, um daran Gottes Zornhandeln zu messen' (*Hiob* [BK 16/I; Neukirchen, 1968], p. 150).

60. Even the root *ryb* sometimes refers to a punitive intervention; Isa. 27.8; Jer. 25.31; Hos. 12.3; Amos 7.4.

61. Cf. ch. 8, section 2.1.1.

62. A characteristic of wrath in a two-party controversy is that it can be calmed by the guilty party's sign of repentance (cf. ch. 4); moreover, it is interesting to note that God says of himself that his anger lasts 'for a moment', that he does not bear grudges (Isa. 54.7-8; Jer. 3.5, 12; Pss. 30.6; 103.9; Lam. 3.31-33). This means that we are not dealing with a judicial sentence, one of the specific hallmarks of which is irrevocability.

The sapiential understanding of punishment has already been outlined above; I would like to refer to it again here, recalling that if a father does not 'strike' he does not show love for his son (Prov. 13.24; cf. also 3.11-12; 19.18; 22.15; 23.13-14; 29.15, 17; Deut. 8.5; Wis. 11.9-10). At first glance, 'anger' and 'compassion' are felt by us to be simultaneously incompatible emotions in the same individual. However, they are attested as jointly present when they express the relation between two different people (cf. for example Exod. 22.23: God's wrath towards the wicked; 22.26: kindness towards the oppressed); what is more, the same manifestation of anger may not be at odds with tenderness (Jer. 31.20; and also Isa. 49.14-15; Hos. 11.8-9; Hab. 3.2).

up of words) and forms a necessary complement. It might be said that the manifestation of wrath is the *rîb* 'in deeds' as opposed to the *rîb* 'in words'; this explains why the terminology of anger sometimes takes the place of more narrowly juridical language in the structure of the controversy.

3.2. *The Synonyms of ryb as an Intervention on Behalf of Someone*
We can make a clear semantic division between the synonyms of *ryb* (as defence): on the one hand those that mean a 'salvific' intervention, and on the other hand those that mean a 'retributive' intervention.

3.2.1. *Judgment and Salvation.* We have seen that the verbs *špṭ, yš' (Hi)* and *g'l*, plus the phrase *'śh mišpāṭ*, are used in synonymous parallelism with the verb *ryb*, when the latter has the meaning of a defence intervention.

As can easily be seen, it is a matter of an action that intervenes when a *rîb* is already under way; now since my intention in this chapter is to give just a general introduction to the vocabulary and structure of the controversy, we may consider this aspect ancillary to it, and leave it to one side for the moment. In Part II, when confrontations before a judge are dealt with (Chapters 5 and 7), the relevance and precise meaning of the above-mentioned lexicon will become obvious.

3.2.2 *Vengeance.*[63] Among the synonyms of the defence *rîb* appears *nqm*, which forms part of the semantic field of vengeance.[64] This is not

63. Cf. E. Merz, *Die Blutrache bei den Israeliten* (BWAT, 20; Leipzig, 1916); M. Buttenweiser, 'Blood Revenge and Burial Rites in Ancient Israel', *JAOS* 39 (1919), pp. 303-21; P. Ducrot, 'De la vendetta à la loi du talion', *RHPR* 6 (1926), pp. 350-65; Fahlgren, *Ṣ^e^dāḳā*, pp. 64-66; R.H. Swartzback, 'A Biblical Study of the Word "Vengeance"', *Int* (1952), pp. 451-57; E. Neufeld, 'Self-Help in Ancient Hebrew Law', *RIDA* (3rd Ser.) 5 (1958), pp. 291-98; E. Pax, 'Studien zum Vergeltungsproblem der Psalmen', *SBFLA* 11 (1960–61), pp. 56-112; H. McKeating, 'Vengeance is Mine. A Study of the Pursuit of Vengeance in the Old Testament', *ExpTim* 74 (1962–63), pp. 239-45; H.A. Brongers, 'Die Rache- und Fluchpsalmen im Alten Testament', *OTS* 13 (1963), pp. 21-42; P. Rémy, 'Peine de mort et vengeance dans la Bible', *ScEccl* 19 (1967), pp. 323-50; L. Alonso Schökel, 'La Rédemption oeuvre de solidarité', *NRT* 93 (1971), pp. 449-72; G.E. Mendenhall, 'The Vengeance of Yahweh', in *The Tenth Generation: The Origins of the Biblical Tradition* (Baltimore–London, 1973), pp. 69-104; W. Dietrich, 'Rache: Erwägungen zu einem alttestamentlichen Thema', *EvT* 36 (1976), pp. 450-72.

64. Among the words with a similar meaning, G. Sauer notes *gml, šlm* (*Pi*), *pqd*

without its perplexities; the fact is that whereas an intervention calculated to save looks like an ethically noble and warranted act, retaliation seems to have more the character of a wicked and objectionable act. Furthermore, in contemporary language, the concept of vengeance is at odds with a juridical outlook on interpersonal relationships, inasmuch as it represents the overstepping of legal bounds in the pursuit of private and arbitrary satisfaction or redress.[65] Hence can be seen the difficulty, theologically speaking, of attributing vengeful activity to God.[66] It may be useful at this point to make it clear that the verb *nqm* (and synonyms) has a generalized meaning that could be summed up as 'to inflict harm on someone in exchange for harm received'.[67] In accordance with its particular nature and circumstances, law and ethics evaluate it differently. The decisive factors in this context are, primarily, the proportion between harm sustained and harm inflicted, and secondarily, the normative control of society.

Although disproportionate retaliation is to be condemned in every case (cf. Gen. 4.23-24), a proportional response to evil is in conformity with the axiom of justice that each should be done by as he or she does.[68]

The nature of the control over this kind of response to evil remains to be made clear, a control that varies according to juridical structures, legislation and custom. When the parties involved are not subject to a higher authority, for example in a conflict between states, a sort of law of nations seems to operate, though since in the main it is not codified it leaves scope for controversial behaviour.[69] In a conflict between

and *šwb* (*Hi*) (*THAT*, II, p. 108). The verb *g'l*, especially in the phrase *gō'ēl haddām*, should also be included in this number.

65. *Dizionario Enciclopedico Italiano*, XII (Rome, 1961), p. 673.

66. Cf. especially Deut. 32.35; Nah. 1.2; Ps. 94.1. The difficulties laid upon the interpretation of the biblical texts by the concept of vengeance are well summed up by Dietrich, 'Rache', pp. 450-53.

67. This is the definition of 'vengeance' in the *Enciclopedia Filosofica*, VIII (Rome, 2nd edn, 1979), p. 631.

68. On this subject, see the important collection of articles in K. Koch (ed.), *Um das Prinzip der Vergeltung in Religion und Recht des Alten Testaments* (WegFor, 125; Darmstadt, 1972).

69. Even when the parties have signed treaties or conventions, 'legitimate' retaliation is rarely made clear; at any rate, this is always the object of critical discussion. In Scripture, we often meet with the expectation of a just retaliation (Jer. 11.20; 15.15; 20.12; Ps. 58.11 etc.); but it may be noted that it is preferred to leave the intervention

'citizens' it is up to state law to regulate retributive action, or the usage sanctioned by tradition; in both cases, society recognizes and disciplines the practice.

Modern juridical provisions entrust the task of carrying out a retaliation to precise bodies in conformity with rigorously defined norms; for practical purposes, this abolishes the institution of self-defence, and condemns the 'private' vendetta, which consists of administering justice on one's own, without submitting one's rights as an individual to public authority.

Something analogous occurs in the world of the Bible, despite appearances to the contrary. As with many ancient peoples, 'vengeance' is an institution publicly recognized by society[70] and regulated by precise juridical arrangements.[71] Let us take, for example, premeditated murder.[72] Everybody in Israel knew that the guilty person deserved death as the punishment proportionate to the crime (the eye for an eye rule); the *gō'ēl haddām* saw justice done by seeking out and striking down the assassin; he was no more than an executioner, the means necessary to re-establish justice. It may be noted in fact that vengeance is neither arbitrary nor left to the offended party's judgment; in the case of an involuntary murder, the act of retribution is linked to a possible flight by the killer to a city of refuge[73] (Exod. 21.13-14; Num. 35.9-34; Josh.

to God, precisely because of the ambiguity inherent in the retributive reaction itself (cf. Lev. 19.18; 1 Sam. 24.13; 25.31; 33.39; 26.10; Prov. 20.22; 25.21-22; Sir. 28.1-7).

70. According to M. David, 'vengeance' is explained by a privatized concept of crime: 'Even the requital for murder or corporal harm done to a member of the community rested on the families concerned. In other words also the most serious crimes had without exception the character of private delicts' ('The Codex Hammurabi and its Relation to the Provisions of Law in Exodus', *OTS* 7 [1950], pp. 169-70). The fact that the State does not intervene directly in the penal procedure (unless there is a dispute and request for 'judgment') does not mean that crimes and retaliations are private affairs; on the contrary, they are public inasmuch as Israel is well aware that a crime does not concern just one family, but the whole community; the procedural system which relies on the *gō'ēl haddām* is in every case a juridical institution subject to collective control.

71. Cf. B. Cohen, 'Self-Help in Jewish and Roman Law', *RIDA* 3 (2nd ser.) (1955), pp. 107-33; de Vaux, *Institutions*, I, pp. 26-28, 247-50; A. Phillips, 'Another Look at Murder', *JJS* 28 (1977), pp. 111-14.

72. M.-J. Lagrange, 'L'homicide d'après le Code de Hammourabi et d'après la Bible', *RB* 13 (1916), pp. 440-71.

73. N.M. Nicolsky, 'Das Asylrecht in Israel', *ZAW* 48 (1930), pp. 146-75;

20.1-9). For someone who had spilt blood not entirely wittingly, this represented a way out that pulled him out of the injured party's line of fire; but this procedure also represented a recognition of retaliation's inherent justice, because it permitted the *gō'ēl haddām* to pursue the murderer right up to the gates of the city of refuge; there a 'trial' took place, and the verdict of the elders decided whether the punishment should be carried out or not (Num. 35.12, 24-26; Deut. 19.12; Exod. 21.14; Josh. 20.4-6).

In Israel, therefore, 'vengeance' was recognized as a right and a duty; but it was subject to the overall control of the community,[74] and, in some cases, to the specific control of the local or central tribunal. Moreover, if the unjust act was committed by a strongman and the injured party did not have the power necessary to carry out the retaliation, the lawcourt itself was charged with avenging the innocent by passing a verdict of capital punishment and striking down the malefactor with the sword. The king and God himself are very much the agents who use righteous force to re-establish justice, because the blood of the poor is dear to them and they know how to stand up firmly to the arrogance of the

M. David, 'Die Bestimmungen über die Asylstadte in Joshua XX: Ein Beitrag zur Geschichte des biblischen Asylrechts', *OTS* 9 (1951), pp. 30-48; M. Greenberg, 'The Biblical Concept of Asylum', *JBL* 78 (1959), pp. 125-32; L. Delekat, *Asylie und Schutzorakel am Zionheiligtum: Eine Untersuchung zu den privaten Feindpsalmen* (Leiden, 1967), esp. pp. 290-320; A.G. Auld, 'Cities of Refuge in Israelite Tradition', *JSOT* 10 (1978), pp. 26-40; M. Fishbane, 'Biblical Colophons, Textual Criticism and Legal Analogies', *CBQ* 42 (1980), pp. 443-46; J. Milgrom, 'Sancta Contagion and Altar/City Asylum', in J.A. Emerton (ed.), *Congress Volume, Vienna, 1980* (VTSup, 32; Leiden, 1981), pp. 278-310; cf. also G. Pidoux, 'Quelques allusions au droit d'asile dans les Psaumes', in *Maqqél shâqédh* (FS W. Vischer; Montpellier, 1960), pp. 191-97.

74. As P. Rémy writes: 'Le régime "vie pour vie" n'est pas la conséquence d'une autorégulation du sentiment. Il apparaît au contraire comme le fruit d'une instance supérieure tendant à en limiter les manifestations. Tout se passe comme si, entre les groupes hostiles, un accord tacite survenait autour d'un principe ralliant tous les suffrages, celui de l'égalité. Il pourra être enfreint par excès: venger un mort par plusieurs; mais on aura alors des réactions en chaîne, qui tendront désespérément et rageusement à réaffirmer le principe égalitaire que ces excès veulent nier. On évoquera l'image d'un pendule qui ne cesse de viser une position d'inertie par le jeu même de ses oscillations divergentes, sans pouvoir y atteindre. Dans la vengeance, le point d'inertie, l'équilibre, c'est l'égalité. Il n'est pas atteint par le sentiment de puissance, mais par l'obéissance à une motivation supérieure, caractère nettement éthique' ('Peine de mort et vengeance dans la Bible', *ScEccl* 19 [1967], p. 327).

wicked (Ps. 72.14). Thus it may be seen how a defence *rîb* can be the same as an act of vengeance.[75] If we took away this concept from the structure of jurisdiction, we would be letting it be seen that, on the one hand, the guilty can go unpunished, and on the other hand, that the death of (or injury to) the victim does not matter.[76]

4. *The Development of a Controversy*[77]

The verb *ryb* and its synonyms should not be seen only paradigmatically and syntagmatically; they need to be placed in their literary (especially

75. This fact is brought out by the phrase *gō'ēl haddām*: the verb *g'l* means to ransom or redeem (innocent blood which has been spilt), but the syntagm as a whole is equivalent to 'revenger'; cf. P. Joüon, 'Notes de lexicographie hébraique', *Bib* 6 (1925), pp. 317-18; B. Santos Olivera, '"Vindex" seu "Redemptor" apud hebreos', *VD* 11 (1931), pp. 89-94; N.H. Snaith, 'The Hebrew Root *g'l* (I)', *AnLeeds* 3 (1961–62), pp. 60-67; *ThWAT*, I, p. 886.

Alonso Schökel in particular has demonstrated the relationship between *g'l* and *nqm*, viewing it in the general context of justice as an intervention of solidarity: 'La vengeance (*neqama*) peut être considerée comme l'accomplissement du devoir du *go'el haddam*; ainsi le rapport *g'l/nqm* est semblable au rapport *g'l/qny*; l'un et l'autre présentent une racine commune et une application différente, d'un côté aux délits de sang, del'autre aux propriétés aliénées' ('La rédemption oeuvre de solidarité', p. 454).

76. Paradoxically, the death penalty and blood vendetta have the aim of showing the absolute importance of life: 'Le principe "vie pour vie" a une grandeur éthique tragique. Une vie humaine est à ce point précieuse qua sa perte ne peut être sanctionnée que par une perte semblable, du côté des coupables. Rien n'égale une existence humaine sinon une autre. L'irréparable de l'offence ne peut être compensé que par l'irréparable de la sanction... Le tragique est ici: pour affirmer cette valeur incomparable de la vie humaine, on est amené paradoxalement à la détruire' (Rémy, 'Peine de mort et vengeance dans la Bible', p. 329).

Although linked to the death penalty, the concept of vengeance is not identical to it; in my opinion, it is 'proportionate retribution' which has to be given symbolic expression. The sense of proportion and the way it is expressed may vary in accordance with peoples' cultural evolution, so that the 'right' punishment corresponds to a better and better sense of the absolute dignity of human beings.

77. My brief description of the development of a controversy beginning with the narrative text may be filled out and compared with other studies of particular *rîbs*. I would give special mention to the examples supplied by Gamper, *Gott als Richter*, pp. 105-10. On the controversy between Laban and Jacob (Gen. 31), cf. Boecker, *Redeformen*, pp. 41-45; C. Mabee, 'Jacob and Laban: The Structure of Judicial Proceedings (Genesis XXXI 25–42)', *VT* 30 (1980), pp. 192-207; see further my Chapter 2 n. 18. On the *rîb* between Saul and David (1 Sam. 24 and 26),

narrative) context too, so as to widen the controversy's semantic field and establish the elements that are structurally significant for this juridical procedure.

To gain our bearings, I would suggest Judg. 8.1-3, which because of its brevity and relative literary autonomy provides us with a useful framework of reference.

In v. 1, the contending parties are presented: on the one hand the Ephraimites, on the other Gideon; the former launch the action of the *rîb*, which is represented as particularly serious (*wayrîbûn 'ittô b^ehozqâ*).

The same verse also puts forward the *reason* for the conflict: it has to do with the fact that Gideon did not call upon the Ephraimites in an attack upon the Midianites, probably breaking an implicit military co-operation agreement and depriving them of possible booty. It may be noted how, in our text, the reason for the controversy is expressed in a phrase directed at Gideon by the Ephraimites (*wayyō'm^erû 'ēlâw*), and in particular how it takes the form of a question (*mâ haddābār hazzeh 'āśîtā lānû*...). The motive for the controversy is an element of great

L. Alonso Schökel, *Treinta Salmos: Poesia y Oración* (Madrid, 1981), pp. 199-201; and the contributions by G. von Rad, 'Zwei Ueberlieferungen von König Saul' (1968), in *Gesammelte Studien zum Alten Testament*, II (TBü, 48; Munich, 1973), pp. 199-211; D.M. Gunn, *The Fate of King Saul: An Interpretation of a Biblical Story* (JSOTSup, 14; Sheffield, 1980), pp. 91-96, 102-106; R.P. Gordon, 'David's Rise and Saul's Demise: Narrative Analogy in I Samuel 24–26', *TynBul* 31 (1980), pp. 37-64. The story of Joseph (Gen. 37–50) can be seen as a dynamic complex about the reconciliation between brothers; the biblical text has been studied from various points of view, including questions specific to literary criticism; I give here only some of the more recent bibliographical references: G. von Rad, *Die Josephgeschichte* (BiblSt, 5; Neukirchen, 4th edn, 1964); L. Ruppert, *Die Josepherzählung der Genesis: Ein Beitrag zur Theologie der Pentateuchquellen* (SANT, 11; Munich, 1965); D.B. Redford, *A Study of the Biblical Story of Joseph (Genesis 37–50)* (VTSup, 20; Leiden, 1970); H. Donner, *Die literarische Gestalt der alttestamentlichen Josephsgeschichte* (SHAW PH; Heidelberg, 1976); G.W. Coats, *From Canaan into Egypt: Structural and Theological Context for the Joseph Story* (CBQMS, 4; Washington, 1976); H. Seebass, *Geschichtliche Zeit und theonome Tradition in der Joseph-Erzählung* (Gütersloh, 1978); H.-C. Schmitt, *Die nichtpriesterliche Josephgeschichte. Ein Beitrag zur neuesten Pentateuchkritik* (BZAW, 154; Berlin, 1980); M. Savage, 'Literary Criticism and Biblical Studies: A Rhetorical Analysis of the Joseph Narrative', in C.D. Evans (ed.), *Scripture in Context: Essays on the Comparative Method* (Pittsburgh, 1980), pp. 79-100; A. Schenker, *Versöhnung und Sühne: Wege gewaltfreier Konfliktlösung im Alten Testament mit einem Ausblick auf das Neue Testament* (BibB, 15; Freiburg), pp. 15-40.

noted how, in our text, the reason for the controversy is expressed in a phrase directed at Gideon by the Ephraimites (*wayyō'meʾrû 'ēlâw*), and in particular how it takes the form of a question (*mâ haddābār hazzeh 'āśîtā lānû*...). The motive for the controversy is an element of great importance: it may be introduced, as I have already pointed out, by the preposition *'al* (Gen. 26.21, 22; Job 10.2, etc.) or by the conjunction *kî* (Judg. 6.32; Jer. 2.9-10; Hos. 2.4), but more frequently it is expressed by an accusatory 'saying', which can take on the verificatory (Gen. 26.20; Exod. 17.2; Neh. 5.7) or interrogative (Gen. 31.36; Num. 20.3-5; Isa. 45.9; Neh. 13.11, 17; cf. also Jer. 12.1; Mic. 6.1-3).[78]

Verses 2-3a contain Gideon's response to the question posed by the Ephraimites; here too we find the interrogative form (response to a question with a question), by which the accused defend themselves and to some extent twist the accusation back on itself; in fact they remind their accusers that although they had arrived late (to pick over the spoils), they had gleaned more than the harvesters themselves (Gideon and his men). *The accused's response* and the reasons therein therefore seems to be an element necessarily bound up with the *rîb*.

In v. 3b we have the conclusion of the quarrel: the Ephraimites' animosity cools down in the face of Gideon's reply. The account contains no further information about the relationship between the contending parties once the controversy ceased. Other biblical texts, however (Gen. 31.43-54, for example), deal very fully with the element that ratifies *the end* of the *rîb*.

The elements that mark the development and conclusion of the controversy, which I have touched on very briefly here, will form the subject matter of the following chapters, which will deal precisely with the accusation (the motive for the *rîb*), with the accused's reply, and finally with the conclusion of the *rîb*.

78. A motiveless controversy is probably expressed in Hebrew by the syntagm *ryd 'im...ḥinnām* (Prov. 3.30).

Chapter 2

THE ACCUSATION

The *rîb* takes shape when the accusation is made, and lasts as long as this remains in operation between two subjects. This is the reason why a controversy, despite the fact that it can involve a multiplicity of relationships and a certain complexity of procedures, tends in many cases to be identified with the juridical action of the accuser.

The accusation may be crystallized when a juridical subject lays the responsibility for an illegal or forbidden act upon a particular person (or group); it comes to an end when such measures are taken by the accused regarding the accusation and the accused himself that the accuser can feel that justice has been done. In an effort to make these concepts clear and relate them to the linguistic structures and vocabulary of the Bible, I would say that there are three elements in the structure of the accusation:

1. In the first place, it is necessary that someone should become aware of an injustice or a crime committed by a given subject.
2. Next it is necessary that whoever is aware of the crime should speak out, denouncing the guilty party.
3. Finally, given the intrinsic relationship between crime and punishment, it is necessary that the denunciation should carry a certain negative charge, indicating, whether implicitly or explicitly, the punishment in mind.

The present chapter will attempt to link these three aspects of the accusation.

1. *The 'Notitia Criminis'*

The first condition required for there to be an accusation (and therefore a *rîb*) is that a 'misdeed' should have been committed, and that this can be ascribed to a particular person responsible. I speak of a 'misdeed' and use a very general word in order to include a whole range of acts that are contrary to justice and law.[1] Our juridical provisions, like those of the Bible, our language, like Hebrew, contain a long list of terms that express synonymously the same concept of a misdeed. This variety in terminology is traceable to different factors; often there is a scale of value between the terms in step with the seriousness of the act committed (a seriousness that is made obvious by the kind of punishment foreseen by the law or tradition); sometimes the variety is brought about by the need to make it clear against which measure or group of laws the act has been perpetrated. But above all, different terminology corresponds to different subjects and their cultural environments, who interpret the same phenomenon using their own way of expressing themselves and with a preference for one term over another. They do so in accordance with their own verbal and conceptual system. Let us take some examples from English: what the judge might define as a 'crime of homicide' may

1. It is true that the word 'misdeed' does not have the technical precision that modern juridical science attempts to achieve in its terminology. Contemporary penal law constantly refers to *penal norms*, which are provisions of law arising from prohibition by the State of what is contrary to the State's own ends. From the penal code comes the definition of a '*crime*', which is the infraction of a command or prohibition imposed by that same law, or, more exactly, 'that human behaviour which, in the judgment of the legislator, is at variance with the state's aims and demands as punishment a (criminal) sentence' (F. Antolisei, *Manuale di Diritto Penale* [Milan, 7th edn, 1975], p. 132). The term crime (which is to be distinguished from misdemeanour or contravention) is therefore to be preferred in a rigorously juridical treatment of the biblical texts (cf. H. Cazelles, 'La transgression de la loi en tant que crime et délit', in *Populus Dei*. I. *Israel* [FS Card. A. Ottaviani; Rome, 1969], pp. 521-28; P. Maon, 'Responsabilité', *DBSup*, X, pp. 359-64).

My argument, however, takes place at a level that does not necessarily presuppose the existence of a normative, definitive penalty; and therefore where the interpretation of human behaviour is sometimes referred just to personal awareness of good and evil, of justice and injustice, to sometimes no more than a particular tradition or custom. As a result I have preferred to use the term misdeed, which, despite its generality, has the ability to indicate a deed at variance with the nature of good, however that may be defined. In the same way, I can term the author of a 'misdeed' an 'evildoer'.

Attempting to find an analogy with biblical vocabulary, it could be said that the concept of a misdeed is expressed by the Hebrew syntagm *'śh rā'â*, while that of the evildoer is expressed by *pō'ᵃlê 'āwen* (cf. P. Humbert, 'L'emploi du verbe *pā'al* et de ses dérivés substantifs en hébreu biblique', *ZAW* 65 [1953], p. 39).

perhaps be called 'a shocking horror', 'a barbarity' by public opinion; the prosecution will use the term 'crime', 'wrongdoing', 'injury', while the defence peroration will try to impose the concept of 'involuntary offence', or even 'error'. The mother of the defendant will have it that her child has committed 'something slight', 'has been led astray', 'has followed the wrong path'; the criminal's friends might say he had been 'stupid', 'was trying to be clever'; a priest would perhaps talk of 'sin' or 'evil', while a tolerant philosopher might speak of 'transgression' or 'rebellion', and so on. The event referred to is the same in every case, but the vocabulary used to define it is very varied.

If it is difficult in our own language to carry out a paradigmatic study of the concept of 'misdeed', it is even more so in Hebrew, where the shades of interpretation are intermixed and superimposed. In my work I can do no more than establish the important function that the concept of misdeed performs in the syntagmatic relation I am studying; it is up to the researcher studying a particular term or series of terms,[2] or to the interpreter of the various biblical texts, to assign a degree, a value and a point of reference to a given set of terms. For example, I do not have a specific interest in the exact distinction between *tô'ēbâ* and *n^ebālâ*, or which terms might be used to describe idolatry, or why crimes of such

2. I would mention in particular the lexicographical studies of Š. Porúbčan, *Sin in the Old Testament* (Rome, 1965), and of R. Knierim, *Die Hauptbegriffe für Sünde im Alten Testament* (Gütersloh, 1965).

In biblical studies, problems of an ethical or theological nature have generally obscured a more painstakingly juridical consideration of human deeds; in fact, the few works on the categories and procedures of penal law in Israel are in contrast with an abundant supply concerned with sin and its moral and religious repercussions. It probably needs to be asked whether the relationship between juridical and theological categories should not be rethought more accurately, recognizing that in Scripture juridical categories constitute a valid synthesis for the understanding of human experience and one of the most important ways in which divine revelation itself is communicated.

Among the studies which have tackled the theme of sin in a way more relevant in my subject, I would point to L. Diestel, 'Die religiösen Delicte im israelitischen Strafrecht', *JPTh* 5 (1879), pp. 246-313; G. Quell, '*hamartanō*. Die Sünde im Alten Testament', *TWNT*, I, pp. 267-88; V. Monty, 'La nature du péché d'après le vocabulaire hébreu', *ScEccl* 1 (1948), pp. 95-109; *idem*, 'Péchés graves et légers d'après le vocabulaire hébreu', *ScEccl* 2 (1949), pp. 129-68; C.R. Smith, *The Bible Doctrine of Sin* (London, 1953), pp. 15-56; S. Lyonnet, *De peccato et redemptione*. I. *De notione peccati* (Rome, 1957), esp. pp. 27-51; E. Beaucamp, 'Péché. I. Dans l'Ancien Testament. Le vocabulaire hébraïque', *DBSup*, VII, pp. 407-71.

different nature and seriousness are described simply as *hārā'*; what holds my attention is the juridical form of the criminal action.[3]

1.1. *The Misdeed according to the Hebrew Lexicon*

Here I give a summary list of terms referring to the misdeed[4] which by their frequency achieve especial importance in the sphere of biblical

3. Since I have mentioned above questions concerning the method of research into and interpretation of biblical terminology, it seems useful to note that in lexicographical studies a distinction is sometimes adopted between a 'theological' and a 'profane' use in the various hebraic terms present in Scripture. This split is made systematically in *TWNT*, and obviously in the works which depend upon it. This is undoubtedly useful when the intention is to demonstrate the extension of a given set of terms, but risks becoming misleading when it tends to underline a structural diversity of meaning within the same vocabulary. Unless a term has an exclusively religious use, or it can be shown that the term has a technical application in cultic matters, it seems necessary for a correct methodology to highlight the 'profane' meaning, retaining it (analogously) even when used in a religious context.

There is nothing new about this principle. As N.W. Porteous wrote: 'To arrive at the distinctive Biblical meaning of the religious terms it is necessary that we should recognise that they are being drawn into relationship with each other by the compelling power of the reality which is seeking to make itself known but which can only be grasped indirectly by the use of words which have their own ordinary association' ('Semantics and Old Testament Theology', *OTS* 8 [1950], pp. 6-7). Along the same lines cf. also Koehler, *Deuterojesaja*, 37; and H.W. Wolff, '"Wissen um Gott" bei Hosea als Urform von Theologie', in *Gesammelte Studien zum Alten Testament* (Munich, 2nd edn, 1973), p. 184.

As regards my study, there is first of all a problem of translation (R. Knierim, *Die Hauptbegriffe für Sünde*, pp. 66-67). For example, translating *ḥṭ'* as 'to sin' may create difficulties when we are dealing with a code of penal procedure (Boecker, *Redeformen*, p. 112). There then comes a conceptual problem: in Israel, 'to make a mistake', 'to commit a crime', 'to be criminals', and so on, are juridical concepts of such relevance to justice so as necessarily to involve reference to God, who is the giver of the Law and the guarantor of its application. The juridical sphere must therefore be studied as structurally autonomous and its terminology respected precisely because it retains its metaphorical or symbolic value when it referred to the sphere of the divine (cf. G. D'Ercole, 'The Organic Structure of Israel in Terms of her Moral Order and Dogmatic Order of Cult', in *Populus Dei*. I. *Israel* [FS Card. A. Ottaviani; Rome, 1969], p. 605, with bibliography).

4. My list may be extended by comparing it with those of Fahlgren, *Ṣᵉdāḳā*, pp. 1-50; Porúbčan, *Sin in the Old Testament*, pp. 4-107; and Beaucamp, 'Péché', pp. 407-71.

Even these monograph studies encounter two difficulties acknowledged by their own authors: in the first place, it appears impossible to make a complete

jurisdiction. This list is by no means exhaustive; even a whole monograph devoted to the subject would have to make a choice.

I am also giving references to some biblical texts in order to show how the vocabulary spans the different books of Scripture, in quite different historical and cultural contexts. I have given preference to passages in which the juridical meaning is more obvious, and in which the reference is to crimes committed against people.

The following can be seen as the building-blocks for a paradigm to be filled out and linked together elsewhere.

ḥṭ’		Gen. 20.9; Deut. 19.15; 1 Sam. 2.25; 1 Kgs 8.31; Jer. 37.18; Ps. 51.6; Job 8.4
	ḥēṭ’	Gen. 41.9; Deut. 21.22; 22.26; 24.16; Isa. 1.18; Ps. 103.10
	ḥ^{a}ṭā’â	Gen. 20.9; Exod. 32.21; Ps. 32.1
	ḥaṭṭā’â	*only in* Exod. 34.7 and Isa. 5.18
	ḥaṭṭā’t	Gen. 31.36; Deut. 19.15; Num. 5.6; 1 Sam. 20.1; Ezek. 3.20; Ps. 59.4; Job 10.6; 13.23
‘wh		2 Sam. 24.17; 1 Kgs 8.47; Est. 1.16
	‘āwōn	Deut. 19.15; 1 Sam. 20.1; Isa. 59.3; Ps. 36.3; Job 10.6
pš‘[5]		Isa. 59.13; Jer. 2.8
	peša‘	Gen. 31.36; Exod. 22.8; Amos 1.3; Ps. 59.4; Job 13.23; Prov. 10.12
‘wl		*only in* Isa. 26.10 and Ps. 71.4
	‘āwel	Deut. 25.16; Lev. 19.15, 35; Jer. 2.5; Ps. 7.4; Job 34.10
	‘awlâ	Ezek. 28.15; Mic. 3.10; Zeph. 3.5; Mal. 2.6; Ps. 37.1; Job 6.30
r‘‘ (*Hi*)		Gen. 19.7; Judg. 19.23; 1 Sam. 26.21; Isa. 1.16; Prov. 24.8
	ra‘	Deut. 17.2; 2 Sam. 12.9; 1 Kgs 3.9; Isa. 5.20; Jer. 7.30; Pss. 36.5; 51.6; Job 1.1; Prov. 21.20
	rā‘â	Gen. 39.9; Judg. 20.12; 1 Sam. 12.17; 24.12; Jer. 2.13; Hos. 7.2; Ps. 15.3; Job 22.5; Prov. 3.29

catalogue of all the terms and phrases which, directly or indirectly, enter into such a wide semantic field; and, in second place, it seems that in the current state of research it is difficult to offer a systematic organization of such concepts in their own sphere of meaning and in the relationship between them (cf. G. te Stroete, ‘Sünde im Alten Testament. Die Wiedergabe einiger hebräischer Ausdrücke für Sünde, in fünf gangbaren west-europäischen Bibelübersetzungen’, in *Übersetzung und Deutung* [FS A.R. Hulst; Nijkerk, 1977], pp. 164-75).

5. Cf. H.W. Hertzberg, ‘Die “Abtrünningen” und die “Vielen”. Ein Beitrag zu Jesaja 53’, in *Verbannung und Heimkehr* (FS W. Rudolph; Tübingen, 1961), pp. 97-102.

rš‘ (*Qal*)		1 Kgs 8.47; Ps. 18.22
(*Hi*)		Ps. 106.6; Dan. 9.5; Neh. 9.33
	reša‘	1 Sam. 24.14; Jer. 14.20; Ps. 10.15; Job 34.10; Qoh. 3.16
m‘l[6]		Num. 5.27; Ezek. 14.13; Prov. 16.10
	ma‘al	Josh. 7.1; Ezra 9.4
mrd		Num. 14.9; Ezek. 2.3
	mered	*hapax*: Josh. 22.22
mrh (*Qal*)		Deut. 21.18, 20; Isa. 1.20; Ps. 78.8
(*Hi*)		Deut. 9.7; Ezek. 20.8
	m^{e}*rî*	1 Sam. 15.23; Isa. 30.9; Ezek. 2.5
srr		Deut. 21.20; Isa. 1.23; Ps. 78.8
	sārâ	Deut. 19.16; Isa. 1.5
t‘b (*Hi*)[7]		1 Kgs 21.26; Ezek. 16.52
	tô‘ēbâ	Deut. 13.15; 17.4; Jer. 6.15; Ezek. 5.9; Prov. 12.22
‘šq		Deut. 24.14; 1 Sam. 12.3; Jer. 7.6; Ezek. 22.29; Job 10.3; Prov. 14.31
	‘ōšeq	Isa. 59.13; Jer. 6.6; Ps. 62.11; Qoh. 5.7
	n^{e}*bālâ*[8]	Deut. 22.21; Judg. 20.6; 2 Sam. 13.12; Jer. 29.23
	zimmâ	Lev. 19.29; Judg. 20.6; Isa. 32.7; Job 31.11; Prov. 10.23
	’āwen	Isa. 10.1; Jer. 4.14; Hos. 6.8; Mic. 2.1; Hab. 1.3; Pss. 5.6; 36.5; Job 34.22
	‘āmāl[9]	Num. 23.21; Hab. 1.3, 13; Pss. 7.17; 10.7; 55.11; Job 15.35

As I said, my list could be extended with terms belonging more specifically to religion, that is, with language taken from the sphere of

6. Cf. J. Milgrom, 'The Concept of *ma‘al* in the Bible and the Ancient Near East', *JAOS* 96 (1976), pp. 236-47; *idem, Cult and Conscience: The Asham and the Priestly Doctrine of Repentance* (Leiden, 1976), pp. 16-35.

7. P. Humbert, starting from a root *y‘b*/*’yb*, maintains that the noun *tô‘ēbâ* refers to 'ce qui présente une tare, un défaut, un vice, ce qui passe donc pour impur...et inspire, à ce titre, dégout, horreur, aversion, blâme et interdiction' ('L'étymologie du substantif *to‘ēbā*', in *Verbannung und Heimkehr* [FS W. Rudolph; Tübingen, 1961], p. 159). This description makes quite clear the difficulty of defining a Hebrew term with such precision that the meaning fits all the different biblical occurrences (cf. also the same author's 'Le substantif *to‘ēbā* et le verbe *t‘b* dans l'Ancien Testament', *ZAW* 72 [1960], pp. 217-237).

8. Cf. Boecker, *Redeformen*, pp. 18-19; A. Phillips, 'Nebalah—A Term for Serious Disorderly and Unruly Conduct', *VT* 25 (1975), pp. 237-41.

9. Cf. J.L. Palache, *Semantic Notes on the Hebrew Lexicon* (Leiden, 1959), pp. 54-56, which traces the semantic development: work, labour—suffering, pain—evil, wickedness.

the sacral, or with terms that are the 'proper names of crimes', and then used metaphorically to describe wicked or perverse behaviour in general: for example, *bgd*, *znh*, *ḥll*, *ḥnp*, *ṭm'*, *kzb*, *'qš*, etc.; and the nouns: *mirmâ*, *šāw'*, *šeqer*, *ḥāmās*, etc.

The verb *'šm*,[10] which is often included in lists similar to mine, does not properly refer to the commission of a crime, but rather to becoming liable for it (Gen. 26.10; Lev. 5.23; Judg. 21.22; Jer. 2.3 etc.). The nouns *'āšām* (guilt), *'ašmâ*, (culpability) and *'āšēm* (guilty) are to be seen as linked by the same nuances as the verb.[11]

1.2. *Awareness of a Misdeed*

It is obvious that a misdeed can become the occasion of or reason for a juridical process in the strict sense only to the extent to which it is recognized to be a misdeed. Now for this to happen an individual needs a double framework of awareness.[12]

10. Cf. Milgrom, *Cult and Conscience*. This monograph is only concerned with the root *'šm* in its cultic use. The author considers that the verb *'šm* has two fundamental meanings, linked by a different grammatical regime: (1) followed by the preposition *l*[e] and a personal object, it means 'to be held liable for reparation by someone'; (2) without an object, it refers to the internal experience of being held liable, and means 'to feel guilty' (p. 3); cf. also the same author's 'The Cultic *'šm*: A Philological Analysis', in *Proceedings of the Sixth World Congress of Jewish Studies*, I (Jerusalem, 1977), pp. 299-308. This material can be harmonized with the studies of P. Joüon, 'Notes de lexicographie hébraique. XV. Racine *'šm*', *Bib* 19 (1938), pp. 454-59; H.C. Thomson, 'The Significance of the Term 'Asham in the Old Testament', *GUOST* 14 (1953), pp. 20-26; L. Morris, ''Asham', *EvQ* 30 (1958), pp. 196-210; P. Maon, 'Responsabilité', *DBSup*, X, pp. 359-61.

11. Consideration should also be given to the particular study of the Hebrew terminology for crimes that fall into the categories of negligence, imprudence, inexperience, equivalent perhaps to the ethical concept of inadvertence (cf. Antolisei, *Manuale di diritto penale*, pp. 289-303). I would point out in particular the Hebrew root *šgg*: R. Knierim, '*šgg*, sich versehen', *THAT*, II, pp. 869-72; J. Milgrom, 'The Cultic *š*[e]*gāgā* and its Influence on Psalms and Job', *JQR* 58 (1967), pp. 115-25; Alonso Schökel, *Treinta Salmos*, p. 100.

12. In this short paragraph I am referring, on the one hand, to what jurists call 'legislative sources', and on the other to 'interpretation of the penal code' (Antolisei, *Manuale di diritto penale*, pp. 43-75). The former aspect is obvious: written, and in some cases customary, laws are the 'knowledge bank' of the penal code, following the traditional principle *nullum crimen, nulla poena sine lege*. The latter aspect is more debatable, but at any rate the necessity can be maintained of 'that mental exercise by which the meaning of a law is sought and explained. Without this clarificatory process, it would obviously be impossible to apply a norm to a particular

On the one hand, there has to be an objective system of norms that lay down what is good and what is bad. Knowledge of the *Law* (be it written or handed down orally) is necessary for civilized social life,[13] and it is indispensable in those who undertake for society the task of prosecuting the evildoer: their activity will be the more fitting the more it is in tune with the letter and spirit which they are putting across in the norm.[14]

case... In any case, an interpreter must not rest content with what is to be gleaned immediately from the words, that is to say, the surface meaning, but must seek the profounder, more inward meaning of the disposition and its practical significance' (*Manuale di diritto penale*, pp. 59-60, with bibliography).

13. Cf. Antolisei, *Manuale di diritto penale*, pp. 325-46, where among other things he deals with the problem of the distinction between *ignorance* and *error* in the field of penal legislation. We may recall in this context the well-known axiom: *ignorantia legis non excusat.* Cf. also D. Daube, 'Error and Accident in the Bible', *RIDA* 2 (1949), pp. 189-213; *idem*, 'Error and Ignorance as Excuses in Crime', in *Ancient Jewish Law: Three Inaugural Lectures* (Leiden, 1981), pp. 49-69.

14. In Israel, an accuser may do so 'in the name of the Law' or in the name of the One who gave the Law; he draws all (his) authority by reference to the Legislator, from whom in practice he draws wisdom and purpose. I would like to note here the prophet's role as a public prosecutor (cf. especially H.J. Kraus, *Die prophetische Verkündigung des Rechts in Israel* [ThSt, 51; Zollikon, 1957]; C. Westermann, *Grundformen prophetischer Rede* [Munich, 1960]; R. North, 'Angel–Prophet or Satan–Prophet?', *ZAW* 82 [1970], pp. 31-67; S. Amsler, 'Le thème du procès chez les prophètes d'Israël', *RTP* 24 [1974], pp. 116-31; R.V. Bergren, *The Prophets and the Law* [*HUCA* Monograph Series, 4; Cincinnati, 1974]; A. Phillips, 'Prophecy and Law', in *Israel's Prophetic Tradition* [FS P.R. Ackroyd; Cambridge, 1982], pp. 217-32).

One's understanding of the prophetic role obviously has an immediate effect upon one's idea of God himself: 'Je nach der Beschreibung der Stellung und des Auftrags der Propheten wird sich das Verständnis von Gott ändern: Gott als Ankläger und Richter, Gott als Pädagoge und Vater, der fordernde und strafende Gott, der mahnende und scheltende Gott' (L. Markert, *Struktur und Bezeichnung des Scheltworts* [Berlin, 1977], p. 41). As a result, it seems important to me not only to recognize the prophet's accusatory role, but also to deepen the meaning of the accusation itself.

The prophetic claim to be the voice of the Legislator must in its turn be submitted to scrutiny: a typical case can be found in the trial of Jeremiah, in which the whole question is knowing in whose name the prophet is speaking (Jer. 26). On the subject of true or false prophets, cf. H.-J. Kraus, *Prophetie in der Krisis: Studien zu Texten aus dem Buch Jeremia* (BiblSt, 43; Neukirchen-Vluyn, 1964); T.W. Overholt, *The Threat of Falsehood: A Study in the Theology of the Book of Jeremiah* (StBibT 2nd ser., 16; London, 1970); J.L. Crenshaw, *Prophetic Conflict: Its Effect upon*

On the other hand, it is also indispensable that there should be a clear mental link with the actual *life-stories* of people, since they are the actual locus of good and evil. People understand what a misdeed is if they can detect behaviour that conforms or does not conform to the Law. The latter aspect becomes obvious only when the violation of the norm takes unmistakable forms; but when it is borne in mind that the evil-doer has a natural tendency to cloak activities with a veil of legitimacy, it is understandable why a sure touch in recognizing misdeeds is difficult to achieve but on the other hand is of decisive importance for the individual and the community.[15]

It now remains to be shown by examples from the biblical texts how the action of the *rîb* makes explicit reference to that logically prior moment which is the *notitia criminis*, demonstrating also the kind of terminology generally used. As regards this latter aspect, the analysis I shall make of the 'witness' in a courtroom context (Chapter 7) is a necessary complement.

The different Hebrew verbs that refer to the *notitia criminis*[16] have a similar meaning and function; they are structurally linked to the procedure of the *rîb* seen from an accusatory or punitive point of view. Naturally I shall give only a few examples, with the aim of demonstrating the relevance of my comments.

Israelite Religion (BZAW, 124; Berlin, 1971); F.L. Hossfeld and I. Meyer, *Prophet gegen Prophet: Eine Analyse der alttestamentlichen Texte zum Thema: wahre und falsche Propheten* (BiBei, 9; Fribourg, 1973).

15. Anyone who becomes aware of a misdeed becomes, by that very fact, a potential accuser of the guilty party. This general principle holds good especially for Israel, which does not distinguish between citizens appointed '*ex officio*' to carry out the task of denouncing crimes (public 'officials') and anyone else, who may but is not obliged to do so. As the heirs of an elaborate juridical tradition, we are accustomed to go on to distinguish between the complainant, the prosecutor and the witness, even though we know that in some modern processes these different functions tend to overlap. Under the biblical system, the interchangeability of these figures is almost constant; in this first part of my work I will regularly use the word 'accuser', which seems to me more general and more directly linked to the function of speaking, the subject to be developed in the next section.

16. The verbs that refer to the notice of the crime can be used separately or together: cf. Deut. 17.4: *ngd* (*Ho*)—*šm'*; Gen. 21.26: *yd'*—*ngd* (*Hi*)—*šm'* (all in the negative); Exod. 3.7: *r'h*—*šm'*—*yd'*; Exod. 2.24: *šm'*—*r'h*—*yd'* etc. As a complement, cf. Chapter 6, section 3 (the Preliminary Phase).

1.2.1. *The Verb šm'*. Neh. 5.6: The ordinary people, especially the women, tell Nehemiah that they have been subjected to slavery by their own fellow-Jews (vv. 1-5). Nehemiah *listens* (*ka'ašer šāma'tî 'et za'aqātām*); he is moved to *anger* (*wayyiḥar lî me'ōd*) and *accusation* (*wā'ārîbâ 'et haḥōrîm we'et hassegānîm*).

1 Sam. 2.22: Eli *becomes aware* of the misdeeds committed by his sons (*wešāma' 'et kol 'ašer ya'aśûn bānâw*) and therefore he *accuses* them (*lāmmâ ta'aśûn kaddebārîm hā'ēlleh*).

Consideration may also be given to Gen. 34.7; Num. 11.1; Deut. 13.13-14.

1.2.2. *The Verb* **ngd** *(Ho).* Gen. 31.22: Laban is informed of Jacob's flight (*wayyuggad lelābān*); he therefore sets off in pursuit to accuse him of theft (v. 26).

1 Kgs 2.41: Solomon is told of the trespass committed by Shimei (*wayyuggad lišlōmōh kî...*); the king holds a court case, in this instance a sort of trial *in absentia*.

Gen. 38.24: Judah is informed (*wayyuggad lîhûdâ*) of his daughter-in-law Tamar's prostitution; as 'pater familias' he immediately passes a punitive sentence.

Other texts: Deut. 17.4; 1 Sam. 14.33; Est. 2.2.

1.2.3. *The Verb* **r'h**. Neh. 13.15-17: Nehemiah is made aware (*rā'îtî*) of the breaking of the sabbath; the juridical action that follows is one of a *rîb* against the authorities (*wā'ārîbâ 'et ḥōrê yehûdâ*).

Gen. 6.5-6: God sees evil spread throughout humankind (*wayyar' yhwh kî...*) and passes sentence on it.

Cf. also: 2 Kgs 9.26; Jer. 23.13-15; Prov. 25.7b-8; Neh. 13.23-25.

1.2.4. *The Verb* **yd'**. Neh. 13.10-11: Nehemiah realizes that the Temple has been neglected (*wā'ēde'â kî...*); here too he breaks out into an accusation against those responsible (*wā'ārîbâ 'et hassegānîm*).

Prov. 24.12: God's knowledge of evil (*hû' yēdā'*) settles the sentence.

For the verb *yd'* (*Ho*), see also Lev. 4.23, 28. For the *Niphal*, cf. 1 Sam. 22.6.

2. *The Verbal Form of the Accusation*

In this section I would like to deal with the verbal expression of the controversy, and in particular the verbal form of the accusation. It is important to realize that in the biblical texts the verb (or noun) *ryb* is often immediately followed by the verb *'mr*, which explains and qualifies the nature of the dispute (Gen. 26.20; 31.36; Exod. 17.2; Num. 20.3; Judg. 8.1; Isa. 45.9; Neh. 5.7; 13.11, 17). It is not, however, necessary that the coupling *ryb–'mr* should be present in order for the dispute to take on a juridical nature; the juridical side of it is to be found more in the structure of the verbal form that is directed at the other person, as I shall be demonstrating below.

2.1. *The Verbal Clash*

I have already said several times that a *rîb* tends to be identified with the opening speech of one individual accusing another. Properly speaking, this is only the start of the dispute, but since it comes at the beginning it takes on such importance as to push what follows into the background or cause it to be forgotten altogether.

If, however, I want to get an exact grip on the *rîb* in general, and if I want to understand the very nature of the accusation, I have to see that a controversy implies a speech that appeals to the other party's response. The individual making the accusation is indeed convinced that his speech brings to bear all the reasons that lie behind his accusation, and the consequences that flow from them; but when this internal awareness takes the form of words it demands to be listened to, accepted or criticized in words by whoever is the object of the accusation. When one individual speaks he stimulates another individual to speak (paradoxically, at the precise moment when it seems to want to crush him), so that a mutual recognition of the truth can be reached, the indispensable basis of a just relationship.

A *rîb* is, in fact, a dialogue. It is a dialogue which calls one of the disputants to account, but does so precisely so that he can assert himself as an authentic 'individual'.

It is no wonder, therefore, that the controversy situation finds expression in narratives that recount the verbal clash between the two parties involved. The verbs used by the biblical narrator are *generic* (*'mr, 'nh,*[17] *šwb* [*Hi*], etc.), verbs which can be used in other contexts for other purposes, but which in the particular case of a controversy or dispute take on the force of accusation, reply, prosecution, defence.

This holds good whether the dialogue is strictly limited to the two

17. The importance of the verb *'nh* has been pointed out by Begrich, *Deuterojesaja*, pp. 31-32.

disputants (cf., for example, Gen. 31.26-44)[18] or whether it is brought before a judge (cf. 1 Kgs 3.16-28); and it holds good not just for narratives but also for that 'literary genre' which occurs regularly, particularly in the prophetic tradition and is known as the *rîb*; here the dialogue is sometimes set on foot by the speaker himself, who sums up in his speech his adversary's position[19] (cf., for example, Mal. 1.6-8;[20] Jer. 2.4-37, especially vv. 20, 23, 25, 27, 31, 35). The book of Job is the archetype of this dialogic structure, both because of its overall framework, which represents it as a great debate between Job and his 'friends'

18. For the *rîb* between Laban and Jacob in Gen. 31, cf. C. Mabee, 'Jacob and Laban. The Structure of Judicial Proceedings (Genesis XXXI 25-42)', *VT* 30 (1980), pp. 192-207. The author makes a careful analysis of the motivation and development of the controversy, which he sees as beginning at v. 25. I believe that such frequently used terms as 'judicial proceedings', 'judicial encounter' and 'judicial authority' (applied to the accuser, Laban) and the like are not the happiest—they suggest in fact that in order to be *juridical* every proceeding must show signs of being *judicial* (one of the two parties becomes the judge); not only does this not correspond to the structure of the controversy, but it is likewise ruled out by the author himself with reference to the text he is examining: 'The judicial encounter is narrated as one event, skillfully raising the spectre of a third-party mediation, but remaining throughout fundamentally a two-party dispute' (p. 203).

On this same text (Gen. 31.25-42), cf. also the *Excursus* of Boecker, who looks on it as a typical example of 'pre-forensic confrontation' (*Redeformen*, pp. 41-45), and further, C.H. Gordon, 'The Story of Laban and Jacob in the light of the Nuzi Tablets', *BASOR* 6 (1937), pp. 25-27; D. Daube and R. Yaron, 'Jacob's Reception by Laban', *JSS* 1 (1956), pp. 60-62; M. Greenberg, 'Another Look at Rachel's Theft of the Teraphim', *JBL* 81 (1962), pp. 239-48; D. Daube, *The Exodus Pattern in the Bible* (London, 1963), pp. 62-72; R. Frankena, 'Some Remarks on the Semitic Backround of Chapters XXIX-XXXI of the Book of Genesis', *OTS* 17 (1972), pp. 53-64; J.P. Fokkelman, *Narrative Art in Genesis: Specimens of Stylistic and Structural Analysis* (SSN, 17; Assen, 1975), pp. 164-96; M.A. Morrison, 'The Jacob and Laban Narrative in the Light of Near Eastern Sources', *BA* 46 (1983), pp. 155-64; E. Blum, *Die Komposition der Vätergeschichte* (WMANT, 57; Neukirchen–Vluyn, 1984), pp. 117-32.

19. In Gunkel's vocabulary, this is to be linked up with the literary genre of the dispute: *Streitgespräch, Disputation* ('Die Propheten als Schriftsteller und Dichter', in H. Schmidt, *Die grossen Propheten*, II. 2 [Göttingen, 1915], pp. LXIX-LXXI). For the history of research into this subject, see the recent monograph by A. Graffy, *A Prophet Confronts his People: The Disputation Speech in the Prophets* (AnBib, 104; Rome, 1984), pp. 2-23.

20. Cf. E. Pfeiffer, 'Die Disputationsworte im Buche Maleachi (Ein Beitrag zur formgeschichtlichen Struktur)', *EvT* 12 (1959), pp. 546-68.

and between Job and God, and because of the continual references to 'saying' and 'answering' by the disputants within the individual speeches (cf., for example, Job 9.14-16; 13.22).

2.2. *The Word of Accusation*

There is no one word in Hebrew that refers univocally to the act of accusation; however, we can find *verba dicendi* which, in their syntagm, have exactly this semantic force.

I have noted above the coupling *ryb–'mr* as one of the possible ways in which to describe the accusatory side of a controversy. Another possibility is provided by the verb *'nh*, which, in a context of proceedings, refers to a juridically relevant declaration or testimony (Exod. 23.2; Deut. 21.7; 25.9), and which in the syntagm *'nh bᵉ* takes on the more specific nuance of 'to accuse' (1 Sam. 12.3; 2 Sam. 1.16; Isa. 3.9; 59.12; Jer. 14.7; Mic. 6.3; Hos. 5.5; 7.10; Job 15.6);[21] the grammatical subject of the verb may be an individual, who takes on the role of prosecutor, or, by metonomy, the misdeed itself.

The verb *dbr* (*Pi*) *bᵉ* (= against someone) probably also belongs to this paradigmatic series; its meaning fluctuates between to criticise and to accuse (Num. 12.1, 8; 21.5, 7; Jer. 31.20; Pss. 50.20; 78.19; Job 19.18; cf. also *dbr* (*Pi*) *'im* in Gen. 31.24, 29).[22]

The verb *ngd* (*Hi*) may also belong to the series of verbs which express the act of accusation. As we will see,[23] in an actual courtroom context this verb has the meaning of to act as a witness, often with the nuance of for the prosecution. In the case of a *rîb à deux*, the aspect emphasized is that of the 'notification' or disavowal of the crime, the juridical act that justifies the subsequent punitive action. The object of the verb is one of the terms that define the misdeed; use of the preposition *lᵉ* refers it to one's adversary in the dispute (Isa. 58.1; Ezek. 23.36; Mic. 3.8; Job 36.9; cf. also Isa. 57.12, where the object *ṣidqātēk* is obviously ironic, and Job 21.31, where instead of *lᵉ* we find the equivalent *'al pānâw*).

According to H.J. Boecker,[24] the verb *spr* (*Pi*) is also characteristic of an accusation; in addition to Isa. 43.26, which he puts forward as proof,

21. The syntagm *'nh bᵉ* denotes the action of a prosecution witness in a trial before a judge; this will be dealt with in detail in Chapter 7.

22. Cf. also the phrase *dbr (Pi) 'et 'ôyᵉbîm baššā'ar* (Ps. 127.5).

23. Cf. Chapter 7, section 1.6.2.

24. *Redeformen*, pp. 55-56.

the following might be considered pertinent: Ezek. 12.16; Pss. 59.13; 64.6; 73.15 and, with particular nuance of a suit, 2 Kgs 8.6.[25]

Finally, I would point out the verb *yd'* (*Hi*): Ezek. 16.2; 20.4; 22.2; Job 10.2; 13.23.

2.3. *Forms in Which an Accusation Occurs*

The variety of ways in which an accuser can launch an accusation prevents any strict talk of 'formulae' or 'characteristic vocabulary'; this does not remove the possibility of fixing upon and examining the rhetorical forms in which notification of a charge is generally given in Hebrew, about which I shall make some observations as to content and method.

The notification of the charge can be expressed in a *declarative* or in an *interrogative* form. These two forms are sometimes juxtaposed in one and the same accusation (cf., for example, Gen. 44.5-6; Exod. 5.15-16; Judg. 2.2; 2 Sam. 12.9); but mostly one or the other is to be found apart. They appear to be equivalent as regards the meaning they have and role they exercise in the controversy, as may be seen from a comparison of more or less stereotypical phrases meaning, 'who can accuse?'

2 Sam. 16.10	*ûmî*	*yō'mar*	*maddûa'*	*'āśîtâ kēn*	interrogative
Job 9.12	*mî*	*yō'mar 'ēlâw*	*mah*	*ta'ᵃśeh*	interrogative
Qoh. 8.4	*ûmî*	*yō'mar lô*	*mah*	*ta'ᵃśeh*	interrogative
Job 36.23	*ûmî*	*'āmar*	*pā'altā*	*'awlâ*	declarative

The declarative form occurs in a great variety of expressions and terms, but it can easily be recognized just on the basis of its semantic content, given that it refers to something that belongs to the category of 'misdeed' (cf. Gen. 16.5; 26.20; Exod. 32.30; Judg. 11.13; 1 Sam. 22.8; 1 Kgs 14.8-9; Isa. 1.2-3; 43.22-27; Jer. 2.13; Job 36.23; Ezra 10.10; Neh. 5.9).

More alien to our mentality (but not to that of the Ancient Near East)

25. Begrich, *Deuterojesaja*, p. 26 n. 2, with regard to Isa. 43.26, maintains that the verb *zkr (Hi)* is also important: 'Die Bedeutung "anzeigen" erhält das Wort im gerichtlichen Zusammenhange dadurch, dass der Anklagende den Richtern den Namen dessen nennt, gegen den er eine Verhandlung beantragt. Für diese Auffassung spricht ferner die Wendung *hzkyr 'wn*, welche die Gerichtspraxis zu entstammen und die Anzeige eines Vergehens zu bezeichnen scheint. Hes 21.28 und namentlich Nu 5.15 ist das m.E. noch deutlich zu erkennen.' As may be seen, however, the verb *hzkyr* belongs ultimately to the series of verbs of accusation used in a courtroom rather than to those of accusation of a crime made directly to the opposing party.

is the *interrogative form* of the accusation; it is for this reason that I think it will be useful to provide a more detailed description and explanation of the motive behind this phenomenon.

The question is introduced by interrogative pronouns or adverbs, with the meaning peculiar to each of them, but without this variety introducing different juridical forms.[26] One of the characteristic forms[27] is that introduced by *mah*, of which I shall give some examples in order to demonstrate the variations on one and the same syntagm:

Isa. 45.9	*mah*					*ta‘aśeh*	
Gen. 4.10	*meh*					*‘āśîtā*	
Judg. 18.18	*mâ*				*’attem*	*‘ōśîm*	
Gen. 20.9	*meh*					*‘āśîtā*	*lānû*
Gen. 3.13	*mah*	*zō’t*				*‘āśît*	
Judg. 2.2	*mah*	*zō’t*				*‘aśîtem*	
Jonah 1.10	*mah*	*zō’t*				*‘āśîtā*	
Gen. 12.18	*mah*	*zō’t*				*‘āśîtā*	*lî*
Gen. 26.10	*mah*	*zō’t*				*‘āśîtā*	*lānû*
Judg. 8.1	*mâ*	*haddābār*	*hazzeh*			*‘āśîtā*	*lānû*
Neh. 2.19	*mâ*	*haddābār*	*hazzeh*	*’ašer*	*’attem*	*‘ōśîm*	
Gen. 44.15	*mâ*	*hamma‘aśeh*	*hazzeh*	*’ašer*		*‘aśîtem*	
Neh. 13.17	*mâ*	*haddābār hārā‘*	*hazzeh*	*’ašer*	*’attem*	*‘ōśîm*	
Judg. 20.12	*mâ*	*hārā‘â*	*hazzō’t*	*’ašer*		*nihyetâ*	*bākem*
Josh. 22.16	*mâ*	*hamma‘al*	*hazzeh*	*’ašer*		*me‘altem*	*bē’lōhê*
						yiśrā’ēl	

In addition to using *mah*[28] to introduce questions, Hebrew frequently begins them with ‘why...?’: *lāmmâ* (Exod. 2.13; Num. 21.5; 1 Sam. 2.29; 15.19; 22.13; 26.18 etc.) and *maddûa‘* (Exod. 1.18; Lev. 10.27; Judg. 12.1; 2 Sam. 12.9; 1 Kgs 1.6; Jer. 2.31; Neh. 13.11 etc.).[29] Other interrogatives too have a similar function: *mî*[30] (‘who’...?) (Judg. 6.29;

26. In Judg. 12.1 there is a distinction made between two accusations introduced respectively by *maddûa‘* and *lāmmâ*; various interrogatives can be found in one and the same accusation (cf. Gen. 29.25; 31.26-30; Jer. 2.31 etc.).

27. According to the terminology of Boecker, it relates to the ‘Beschuldigungsformel’ (*Redeformen*, pp. 26-31).

28. As well as ‘what’?, *mah* can also mean ‘why?’ (cf. Zorell, p. 413); in the latter sense it can introduce an accusation (cf. Exod. 17.2; Isa. 45.10; Jer. 49.4).

29. Cf. A. Jepsen, ‘Warum? Eine lexikalische und theologische Studie’, in *Das ferne und nahe Wort* (FS L. Rost; BZAW, 105; Berlin, 1967), pp. 106-13.

30. The interrogative pronoun *mî* seems to express the denunciation of unknowns (cf. also Gen. 21.26).

15.6; Isa. 50.1; Job 9.24); *'êk* ('how...?') (Gen. 26.9; 2 Sam. 1.14; Jer. 2.21, 23); *'ê* ('where...?') (Gen. 4.9; Isa. 50.1; Mal. 1.6).[31]

2.4. *The Meaning of an Accusation in the Interrogative Form*

J. Harvey[32] distinguishes three fundamental elements in the structure of a *rîb*, which, preceded by the 'prologue' (the preliminaries of the trial) and followed by the 'threats and sentence' (or 'decree or ultimatum') make up the skeleton of this literary genre. These three elements are: (1) *the questioning* directed by the judge, who is at the same time the prosecutor ('plaignant') of the accused; this questioning never expects an answer from the accused and never gets one; (2) *the recital*, generally in historical terms, which narrates the kindnesses of the plaintiff and the infidelities of the accused party...(3) the accused party's *official declaration of guilt*, a declaration that is closely tied to the recital.[33]

From a strictly logical point of view, the distinctions made by Harvey seem in order: the questioning (however linked to the accused's ultimate reply) is different from the recital (directed towards a 'jury'?), and above all from the declaration of guilt, linked to the sentence. But I have not a few difficulties with sharing this formulation of the *rîb*.[34] The element that we need to subject to revision at this point is the *questioning*, which is seen as separate and distinct from the other two.[35]

31. Sometimes the simple interrogative particle h^a or $h^a l\bar{o}'$ can introduce a notification of crime, often in the form of a rhetorical question: cf. Deut. 32.6; 2 Sam. 19.22; 1 Kgs 21.19; Isa. 57.4b; Neh. 2.19. (Cf. H.A. Brongers, 'Some Remarks on the Biblical Particle $h^a l\bar{o}'$', *OTS* 21 [1981], pp. 177-89).

32. Harvey, *Le plaidoyer prophétique*, esp. pp. 90-100.

33. Harvey, *Le plaidoyer prophétique*, p. 55.

34. A rigorous examination of Harvey's text is not possible at this point; I must mention, however, that the logical scheme put forward by the author does not always correspond to the substance of the biblical texts (as the author himself admits: *Le plaidoyer prophétique*, pp. 81, 91); moreover, the attribution of one expression (or another) or one (or another) of the elements does not seem to be carried out in accordance with methodologically exacting principles; finally, the choice of biblical texts in which the *rîb*'s form is sought seems arbitrary, and as a consequence there is the continual risk of extrapolating unjustified conclusions.

35. In his literary scheme of the 'réquisitoires complets' (Isa. 1.2-20; Mic. 6.1-8; Jer. 2.4-13, 29; Ps. 50), Harvey further distinguishes between the 'preliminaries' (element 1): (a) the assembling of heaven and earth and the calling to order; (b) declaration of YHWH's uprightness and accusation of the people (*Le plaidoyer prophétique*, pp. 54-55). What I call 'the accusation' is spread, according to Harvey, across a full four separate elements in the structure of the *rîb*.

To start with, it is not enough for there to be an interrogative phrase for something to be called a 'questioning'; rather, this term is characteristic of the questioning phase of a trial, which has the role of verifying the facts and responsibility for them so that the judge can hand down a verdict in accordance with truth and justice; in a *rîb*, on the other hand, an accusatory questioning occurs even when the accused has been caught *in flagrante delictu* (cf. Exod. 2.13; Gen. 44.15; Judg. 8.1 etc.) and has the precise aim of signalling to one party (which becomes the adversary) the reason for the dispute. In a controversy, on the other hand, the questions can have a quite different force and meaning, and should not therefore be lumped together under the same heading:[36] sometimes a question is equivalent to an accusation, but at other times—as we shall see—to a declaration of innocence on the part of the speaker (cf. Jer. 2.5; Mic. 6.3); other times again it is the rejection in interrogative form of sacrificial compensation to be presented (Isa. 1.11-12; cf. also Mic. 6.6-7; Ps. 50.13; Isa. 57.6; 58.5-7; Jer. 6.20a).[37]

In the second place, the accusation may be a simple formula or may take the form of a complex argument;[38] if we bear in mind that the end purpose of the accusation is to be acknowledged as the truth by the opposing party, it is only to be expected that it should proceed by employing all the tactics of rhetoric and should exploit all the resources of the reasoned and reasonable discourse; this is frequently the case when the accused is slow to admit guilt in the misdeed that is the cause of the dispute. However, this does not set up structurally distinct elements within the controversy, since an element is only structural to the extent to which it can be defined by precise opposition to the others and a precise function within the whole.

36. Cf. Boecker, 'Anklagereden', p. 407. The importance must also be borne in mind of the *rhetorical question*, in its different forms and functions (H. Lausberg, *Handbuch der literarischen Rhetorik* [Munich, 1960], pp. 379-84); cf. R. Gordis, 'A Rhetorical Use of Interrogative Sentences in Biblical Hebrew', *AJSL* 49 (1932–33), pp. 212-17; G.W. Coats, 'Self-Abasement and Insult Formulas', *JBL* 89 (1970), especially pp. 22-23; W. Brueggemann, 'Jeremiah's Use of Rhetorical Questions', *JBL* 92 (1973), pp. 358-74.

37. Even the pronouncement of the penalty can be expressed in the form of a question: Deut. 32.30; Isa. 42.24; Jer. 2.14; 5.9, 29 etc.

38. Begrich comments: 'Die Appellationsrede des Anklagende hat mit der des Angeschuldigten die freie Anordnung der Aufbauglieder gemein, eine Wiederspiegelung der Erregung, in welcher beide Parteien miteinander reden' (*Deuterojesaja*, p. 27).

Lastly, the structure (of a literary genre, of a text or very generally of the *rîb* itself) should not be confused with a particular literary schema;[39] even if sometimes there is a material coincidence, there is an essential difference between the two things. A structure is a logical organization, abstract and conceptual by nature, which in the way of things allows for an indefinite series of variations and transformations; what matters is not the order of appearance of the elements or their material formulation, but the interplay of rigorous logic between them; and although the structure is arrived at by the analysis of a certain *corpus* of texts, none of the texts reproduces it as such, since it is an interpretative phenomenon of the understanding.[40]

A literary schema, on the other hand, is a technique resembling a formula, discernible through stereotypes, order and repetition; it governs the compositions of a number of authors desirous to manifest fidelity to a particular literary tradition, the meaning of which they take to themselves by putting it into practice. Leaving aside, therefore, the question of deciding whether there actually exists a literary schema for the *rîb*, the thrust of my study is to define the *structural* elements of the controversy as a juridical procedure. It is this that gives rise to the literature used to interpret the relationship existing between YHWH and the people of Israel. From this point of view I would assert that the accusation is an essential factor in the *rîb*,[41] whether it occurs in a declarative or interrogative form.

What remains is to find, or at least suggest, the reason for this difference in form of the accusation, and in particular the reason for the interrogative form. I have already pointed out (2.1) that a *rîb* may be seen as a dialogue encounter between two parties, or, more precisely, as a verbal interchange initiated and backed up by the accusation. The fact that this may occur in an interrogative form does not take away at all from its juridical nature or its threatening force (cf., for example, Judg.

39. The terminology 'litigation schema' is used, for example, by P. Buis ('Les conflits entre Moïse et Israël dans l'Exode et Nombres', *VT* 28 [1978], pp. 257-70), who finds three different narrative dispute schemes in the accounts of Exodus and Numbers (each of them with variations), which sometimes overlap one another.

40. P. Beauchamp, 'Propositions sur l'alliance de l'Ancien Testament comme structure centrale', *RSR* 58 (1970), pp. 192-93.

41. Harvey himself seems to prefer the term 'formula' (*Le plaidoyer prophétique*, pp. 28-30). M. Mannati seems to concede the existence of the *rîb*'s 'literary formula', though denying its applicability to Ps. 50 ('Le Psaume 50 est-il un *rîb*?', *Sem* 23 [1973], pp. 27-50).

12.1), but emphasizes the fact that its purpose is achieved only to the extent the opposed party has had the opportunity to bring forward arguments in self-justification or to accept the accuser's reasoning. A dispute begun without the accused being able to reply makes nonsense of a juridical controversy, inasmuch as it does not allow for the common recognition of what is right; on the other hand, a dispute whose very literary form allows for the other party's reply and encourages it, stands as 'right' precisely because—despite any move by arrogance or violence—it agrees to undergo critical examination by the accused and to receive the other party's (evildoer's, criminal's, sinner's) own guarantee of the justice of which it is the interpreter.

2.5. *Integrating Elements in the Accusation and their Purpose*

When the accuser begins to speak, he or she is not restricted just to notifying the other of the misdeed; since, as I have said, the crime has often not been immediately recognized as such by its author, the accusing party sometimes brings into the accusation speech elements which on the one hand serve to guarantee the statements and on the other reveal their purpose.

The accuser,[42] especially in controversies with a more complex literary form, makes explicit reference (when possible) to a third party (an individual, group or something similar) which is called upon or named as guarantor of the objectivity of the procedure. We may call such a person a *witness* or perhaps an *arbiter*; but both terms are only partial expressions of what this role brings to mind.[43] In fact, the calling into

42. I use the word 'accuser' even though sometimes it is the accused who is appealing to an arbiter: in fact, if the format of this recourse is examined carefully, it will be seen that the accused can do so only to the extent to which they believe themselves to be in the right and therefore to be able to accuse the accuser of wicked intentions (cf. Gen. 31.37, 41-42; 1 Sam. 24.13). Cf. on the subject Boecker, *Redeformen*, pp. 48-57. The situation is analogous to that which gives rise to a judgment when those believing themselves to be in the right have recourse to a judging authority.

43. The term 'witness' is more apt when the intervention is by someone able to back up and *confirm* the accuser's charge; the term 'arbiter' on the other hand is more apt when the third party is able to *make a decision* with objectivity about a controversy in progress. It is not always easy to assess the exact nuance to be attributed to the various parties called upon to take part in a juridical dispute; at any rate, it ought to be emphasized that a *rîb* remains a bilateral procedure, carried out by the two parties involved, unless there is some recognizable jurisdictional agency to whom the parties at odds refer the final decision.

play of a third party by the prosecution represents an impartial judicial agency that is either impossible or impractical without precise forensic structures.[44]

In controversies between human parties, the role of witness-arbiter may be assigned to others (Gen. 31.37; 1 Kgs. 20.7; 2 Kgs 5.7), or to God (Gen. 16.5; Exod. 5.21; Judg. 11.27; 1 Sam. 12.5-6; 25.13, 16; 26.23). In the *rîbs* conducted against his people, God calls upon his witnesses the cosmos (heaven and earth:[45] Deut. 32.1; Isa. 1.2; Ps. 50.4-6; heaven: Jer. 2.12; earth: Jer. 6.19; the mountains: Mic. 6.1-2) or even the pagan nations (Jer. 2.10; 6.18).[46] So Job, in his long controversy with God, demands the support of an arbiter, whose state is not clearly defined precisely because it is impossible to imagine anyone in a position to stand over the two litigants (Job 9.33; 16.19-21; 19.25).

In the majority of cases, the appeal to a witness-arbiter is presented literarily in the form of an imperative (or a jussive), by which someone is invited to listen or, more explicitly, to express an opinion (to declare that someone is 'in the right') about the dispute in progress. In fact, neither in the prose stories nor in the poetical controversy texts does an actual third party appear; this might be considered mere chance, but it seems reasonable to suppose that it is not really up to the witness-arbiter to regulate the progress and outcome of the controversy.

Reference to a third party is an *artifice* which means in the first place that the opposed party is not listening, in the second place that it refuses

44. The problem is fully discussed by E. von Waldow, *Der traditionsgeschichtliche Hintergrund der prophetischen Gerichtsreden* (BZAW, 85; Berlin, 1963), esp. pp. 12-19.

With reference to Mic. 6.1, Alonso Schökel prefers to use the expression 'notarial witnesses' (*Profetas*, p. 1064); this terminology offers the undoubted advantage of drawing on the examples of a recognised institution which has an authoritative role in our own day. I use the expression 'witness-arbiter' only because its generic nature also alludes to the task of 'arbitration' in a dispute.

According to G.E. Wright, 'The Lawsuit of God: A Form-Critical Study of Deuteronomy 32', in *Israel's Prophetic Heritage* (FS J. Muilenburg; New York, 1962), p. 47, 'the witnesses were perhaps a special type of "jury"', inasmuch as they had to listen to the accusations but not act as judges.

45. Cf. M. Delcor, 'Les attaches littéraires, l'origine et la signification de l'expression biblique "Prendre à témoin le ciel et la terre"', *VT* 16 (1966), pp. 8-25.

46. Cf. H. von Reventlow, 'Die Völker als Jahves Zeugen bei Ezechiel', *ZAW* 71 (1959), pp. 33-43. In Deut. 32.7, God calls upon the witness of the 'fathers' (of Israel).

to speak the truth, and, finally, that what the accusing party says is true, not 'self-interested'. The witness-arbiter does not pass a law court judgment, but the invocation of one has the same practical effect of declaring the innocent right and shaming whoever is in the wrong.

There is an interesting custom in this regard: the custom in a two-party controversy of presenting a *fictitious case*,[47] upon which the accused is called to deliver judgment (cf. 2 Sam. 12.1-7; 14.1-17; 1 Kgs 20.35-43; Isa. 5.1-7; Ezek. 23);[48] the accuser uses this device to avoid recourse to a juridical third party, but instead gives the accused a double role, and so manages to demonstrate the truth of the assertions.[49]

It is clear from this that the accuser's desire is not to vanquish but to *convince* the other. This is reinforced by the fact that the accuser's speech often takes the form of a pressing argument that culminates in an *invitation*, directed at the adversary, to *recognize* that he or she is in the wrong, and thereby admit that the accuser is in the right. Characteristic of this is the use of the verbs *yd'* and *r'h* (in the imperative), which as we have seen refer to the 'notitia criminis': here consciousness of the

47. Westermann, *Grundformen prophetischer Rede*, p. 145; *idem*, *Vergleiche und Gleichnisse im Alten Testament und Neuen Testament* (CalwTMon, 14; Stuttgart, 1984), p. 77.

48. As well as the Commentaries, see, for 2 Sam. 12: R.A. Carlson, *David, the Chosen King: A Traditio-Historical Approach to the Second Book of Samuel* (Stockholm, 1964), pp. 152-62; A. Phillips, 'The Interpretation of 2 Sam. 12.5-6', *VT* 16 (1966), pp. 242-44; V. Simon, 'The Poor Man's Ewe-Lamb. An Example of a Juridical Parable', *Bib* 48 (1967), pp. 207-42; H. Seebass, 'Nathan und David in 2 Sam 12', *ZAW* 86 (1974), pp. 203-11; J.P. Fokkelman, *Narrative Art and Poetry in the Books of Samuel*, I (SSN, 20; Assen, 1981), esp. pp. 71-82; A. Schenker, *Versöhnung und Sühne* (BibB, 15; Freiburg, 1981), pp. 41-53. For 2 Samuel 14: H.J. Hoftijzer, 'David and the Tekoite Woman', *VT* 20 (1970), pp. 419-44; L. Alonso Schökel, 'David y la mujer de Tecua: 2 Sam. 14 como modelo hermenéutico', *Bib* 57 (1976), pp. 192-205; D.M. Gunn, *The Story of King David: Genre and Interpretation* (JSOTSup, 6; Sheffield, 1978), pp. 40-43; Fokkelman, *Narrative Art and Poetry*, I, pp. 126-62. For Isaiah 5: W. Schottroff, 'Das Weinberglied Jesajas (Jes. 5.1-7). Ein Beitrag zur Geschichte der Parabel', *ZAW* 82 (1970), pp. 68-91; H.W. Hoffmann, *Die Intention der Verkündigung Jesajas* (BZAW, 136; Berlin, 1974), pp. 86-90; J.T. Willis, 'The Genre of Isaiah 5.1-7', *JBL* 96 (1977), pp. 337-62; A. Graffy, 'The Literary Genre of Isaiah 5.1-7', *Bib* 60 (1979), pp. 400-409; G.A. Yee, 'A Form-Critical Study of Isaiah 5.1-7 as a Song and a Juridical Parable', *CBQ* 43 (1981), pp. 30-40.

49. It may be noted that a typical case is to persuade the king to 'pass judgment' on a case that involves him as one of the parties concerned.

crime becomes recognition of one's own injustice, and in a certain way approval of the accusation.[50] Among the most important passages we may mention Exod. 10.10; 1 Sam. 12.17; Jer. 2.23; 3.2, 13; Job 5.27; 11.6.[51]

In literarily large-scale *rîb*s the debating aspect is particularly obvious; it is difficult to demonstrate the form and detail of this here. In fact, since it is up to the accuser not only to bring home to the other party his crime, but also to break down resistance which is the fruit of passion or distorted ideology, all the resources of irony, dialectic and impassioned rhetoric are brought to bear in order to induce the adversary to accept the truth which comes to light in the words of the accuser.[52]

3. *The Relationship with Sanction*

The accuser, declaring the other party responsible for a particular misdeed, equally serves notice at the same time that this carries with it some sort of punitive sanction.

Another element comes into play here, one that is indispensable for defining an accuser in rigorous terms: I am referring to the fact that accusers must dispose of a certain amount of *force* in order to impose themselves.

The term *force* is not the happiest form from a juridical point of view; the term '*power*' would perhaps be more suitable, since it is more in line with tradition in the context of a recognized structure of social relationships, where it can take on the nuance of authority, faculty and competence.[53]

50. We shall see (Chapter 7) how the coupling *r'h–yd'* constitutes the element which defines a witness in a law suit.

51. An analogy may be seen in the invitation to confess one's misdeed using the imperative of *ngd (Hi)* (cf. Josh. 7.19; 1 Sam. 14.43; Jon. 1.18). This will be dealt with especially in the next chapter.

52. Cf. S.H. Blank, 'Irony by Way of Attribution', *Semitics* 1 (1970), pp 1-6; G. Warmuth, *Das Mahnwort: Seine Bedeutung für die Verkündigung der vorexilischen propheten Amos, Hosea, Micha, Jesaja und Jeremia* (BeiBibExT, 1; Frankfurt, 1976); Y. Gitay, *Prophecy and Persuasion: A Study of Isaiah 40–48* (ForTLing, 14; Bonn, 1981).

53. According to Chiovenda (*Principi di diritto processuale civile* [Napoli, 1965], pp. 45-46), a juridical action is a potestative right, that is, 'the juridical power to bring about the conditions for realizing the aim of the law. The action is a power that involves the adversary, with reference to whom it produces the effect of realizing the

If I have used the word '*force*', it is in order to point out explicitly that a juridical procedure must dispose of a certain element of *coercion* against whoever does not observe the norms of justice, given that in general such people do not willingly submit themselves to the punitive consequences of their infractions. A law without force cannot be applied and is therefore meaningless (*telum imbelle*).

This holds good for the system whose potestative peak is the 'judge'; it obviously also holds good in two-party controversies for whoever undertakes the juridical activity of accuser. Two examples will allow me to illustrate the scope of this problem.

The first is drawn from the *rîb* between Laban and Jacob. The accusation of the former against the latter (Gen. 31.26-28) is linked to the claim, 'It would be in my power to do you harm' (*yeš l*[e]*'ēl yādî la'*[a]*śôt 'immākem rā'*),[54] where I think we may detect not just an abstract juridical faculty but the definite possibility of applying a punitive sanction.

The second example concerns the incident that took place between Abner and Ishbaal (2 Sam. 3.6-11): Abner, who 'had become powerful in the house of Saul' (v. 6), was accused by Ishbaal of having taken Saul's concubine to himself (v. 7). It seems clear that the accusation was legitimate and that Abner had abused his power; however, the continuation of the story tells us that the ferocious reaction of the accused—who had military power to hand—prevented Ishbaal from carrying forward his grievance and taking possible sanctions: 'He could not answer a word to Abner, because he was afraid of him (*w*[e]*lō' yākōl 'ôd l*[e]*hāšîb 'et 'abnēr dābār miyyir'ātô 'ōtô*)' (v. 11).[55]

So we may say that an accusation is really true to its nature if it does not just limit itself to charging the accused with an offence, but carries with it the specific means to apply a suitable punishment to the guilty. It

law. The adversary is in no way bound by this power: he is simply subject to it. The action ends with its exercise, that is, without the adversary being able to do anything either to prevent it or satisfy it' (quoted by G. Leone, *Manuale di Diritto Processuale Penale* [Napoli, 9th edn, 1975], pp. 62-63).

54. W.G.E. Watson ('Reclustering Hebrew *l'lyd*', *Bib* 58 [1977], pp. 213-15) has proposed a different division of the Hebrew text (*yeš l' l*[e]*yādî...*); however, the meaning of the verse remains as suggested in my translation (*l'* = 'power'). For the expression *l*[e]*'ēl yad-*, cf. Deut. 28.32; Mic. 2.1; Prov. 3.27; Neh. 5.5; Sir. 5.1.

55. Cf. also Judg. 18.20-26; Zeph. 1.12. The theme of being afraid of power, which prompts flight from accusation, can be found in Jer. 1.8, 17 and perhaps Amos 5.13.

is obvious that, from a logical point of view, accusation and sanction are distinct: punishment does not occur when the accused make good their arguments, or (in certain cases) when the accused achieve a sort of friendly compromise, or offer spontaneously and generously to repay the wrong. Despite this, it may be said that to be under accusation is *de facto* to be under the *threat* of some sort of sanction, just as 'accusing' or 'starting a *rîb* against' someone tends to become synonymous with 'undertaking a punitive action' against that party (cf. Jer. 25.31; Hos. 4.1-3; 12.3; Judg. 20.12). This deserves to be kept clearly in mind, even when the accuser does not make explicit reference to the consequences that follow from the charge.

But it is the Law itself, in whose name the accuser speaks, which defines the crime as an act that deserves to be punished;[56] without sanctions, there would be no way of indicating the essential difference between a good and an evil life in society, between justice and injustice. The way 'crime pays' is what brings most into question a juridical system and, in the Bible, represents one of the most radical criticisms of God's own justice (that is, in the literal sense of 'justice') in the world (cf. Jer. 12.1-2; Hab. 1.2-4; Mic. 3.14-15; Ps. 73.2; Job 21.7; Qoh. 7.15).

The logical link between accusation and punishment may not be emphasized by particular syntactical structures; for example, in Judg. 12.1, the Ephraimites say to Jephtha: 'Why did you go out to fight against the Ammonites and you did not call on us? We will burn you and your house'. The simple parataxis (with change of tense) does not prevent an understanding of the connection between the question (accusatory) and the statement (which threatens punishment) (cf. also Gen. 31.28-29; Judg. 2.2-3;[57] Jon. 1.10-12). For the most part, however,

56. 'Penal norms are generally made up of two elements: the precept (*praeceptum legis*) and the sanction (*sanctio legis*). The precept is the command to maintain a certain conduct, that is, not to do a particular thing or carry out a given action; the sanction is the juridical sanction which must follow an infraction of the precept' (Antolisei, *Manuale di Diritto Penale*, p. 32).

57. In Judg. 2.2-3 we have the following juxtaposition: *wā'ōmar*: the Law, the misdeed and the accusation (*w*^{e}*lō' š*^{e}*ma'tem b*^{e}*qōlî—mah zō't '*^{a}*śîtem*)—*w*^{e}*gam 'āmartî*: punishment (for the emphasising force of the particle *gam*, cf. B. Jacob, 'Erklärung einiger Hiob-Stellen', *ZAW* 32 [1912], pp. 279-82; C.L. Labuschagne, 'The Emphasizing Particle *gam* and its Connotations', in *Studia Biblica et Semitica* [FS T.C. Vriezen; Wageningen, 1966], pp. 193-203).

In Isa. 66.3-4 we find: *gam hēmmâ* (misdeed)—*gam '*^{a}*nî* (punishment); in Deut. 32.21: *hēm* (misdeed)—*wa'*^{a}*nî* (punishment); in Mal. 2.8-9: *w*^{e}*'attem*

a particle (or conjunction, or adverb) points up the logical link with the sanction, which in this way is explicitly *motivated*:[58]

a. The misdeed is introduced by a causal conjunction; this gives the reason for the punishment which follows immediately: very frequent are *kî* (Deut. 32.20; Judg. 6.30; 2 Sam. 12.12; Jer. 6.19 etc.) and *ya'an* (sometimes followed by *kî* or *'*^{a}*šer*: Num. 11.20; 1 Sam. 15.23; 1 Kgs 11.11; Jer. 19.4; 25.8 etc.).

b. The sanction is announced by an adverb which indicates the (punitive) consequence of the charged crime. Frequent are *lākēn* (Judg. 10.13; 1 Sam. 2.30; 1 Kgs 14.10; Jer. 7.20 etc.) and *w*^{e}*'attâ* (Judg. 20.13; Jer. 7.13; 2 Sam. 12.10 etc.).[59]

Also worthy of consideration is the use of *hinnēh*,[60] which, linked or

(misdeed)—*w*^{e}*gam '*^{a}*nî* (punishment): in all these cases a similarity of vocabulary may be noted between the criminal act and the juridical act which punishes it, along the lines of what is said in Jer. 5.19: 'Since (*ka'*^{a}*šer*) you have abandoned the Lord and have served foreign gods in your land, therefore (*kēn*) you will serve foreigners in a land that is not yours'.

58. Cf. H.W. Wolff, 'Die Begründungen der prophetischen Heils- und Unheilssprüche', *ZAW* 52 (1934), pp. 1-22; H.W. Hoffmann, *Die Intention der Verkündigung Jesajas* (BZAW, 136; Berlin, 1974), esp. pp. 31-34.

59. As regards the characteristic particles that signal the links in a discourse, A. Laurentin points out the importance of *w*^{e}*'attâ* in texts of a juridical bent ('*w*^{e}*'attah—Kai nun*. Formule caractéristique des textes juridiques [à propos de Jean 17.5]', *Bib* 45 [1964], pp. 168-97). He states that in a legal context the particle is used both to summon the accused and to hand down the sentence (pp. 178-82). It must be noted, however, that the particle has the function of pointing to a logical connection rather than indicating a specific function or point in the juridical procedure; essentially it depends on the context, that is, on the relationship between the elements, to clarify the precise nature of this link.

For a philological discussion of some of these particles of correlation (adverbs, conjunctions...), cf. J. Muilenberg, 'The Linguistic and Rhetorical Usages of the Particle *ky* in the Old Testament', *HUCA* 32 (1961), pp. 135-60; H.A. Brongers, 'Bemerkungen zum Gebrauch des adverbialen *w*^{e}*'attāh* im Alten Testament', *VT* 15 (1965), pp. 289-99; R. Frankena, 'Einige Bemerkungen zum Gebrauch des Adverbs *'al kēn* im Hebräischen', in *Studia Biblica et Semitica*, pp. 94-99; D.E. Gowan, 'The Use of *ya'an* in Biblical Hebrew', *VT* 21 (1971), pp. 168-85; E. Jenni, 'Zur Verwendung von *'attā* "jetzt" im Alten Testament', *TZ* 28 (1972), pp. 5-12; M.J. Mulder, 'Die Partikel *ya'an*', *OTS* 18 (1973), pp. 49-83; B. Jongeling, '*Lākēn* dans l'Ancien Testament', *OTS* 21 (1981), pp. 190-200; A. Schoors, 'The Particle *ky*', *OTS* 21 (1981), pp. 240-76.

60. Cf. P. Humbert, 'Die Herausforderungsformel "*hinnenî êlékâ*"', *ZAW* 51

not to other expressions referring to the misdeed, signals in the text the appearance of the punitive sanction: 1 Sam. 2.31; 2 Sam. 12.11; 1 Kgs 14.10; 21.21; 2 Kgs 21.12; Jer. 5.14; 6.19, 21; 7.20; 25.9; 29.21 etc.).

As noted at the beginning of this section, as shown by the syntactical examples listed above, the act of accusation is often presented *as though it were a sentence* (a judicial verdict) upon the defendant (cf., in a legal context, the relationship between Jer. 26.11 and Jer. 26.16); the risk of confusion between these two juridical forms is increased by the fact that, in the biblical texts, the accusation very often does not receive an answer, and sometimes is linked immediately to the actual act of punishment, as though we had a judge handing over the accused, considered guilty, into the hands of the executor of justice.[61]

The similarity in tone between these two forms of juridical procedure should not, however, make us forget the radical difference between them, a difference that I may put like this: *the accusation is always the conditional anticipation of the sentence.* The word 'conditional' expresses the limit and function of the accusation; the fact is that an

(1933), p. 101-108; *idem*, 'La formule hébraïque en *hineni* suivi d'un participe', *REJ* 97 (1934), pp. 58-64; D. Vetter, 'Satzformen prophetischer Rede', in *Werden und Wirken des Alten Testaments* (FS C. Westermann; Neukirchen, 1980), pp. 185-92. See also my own Chapter 6, n. 62.

61. Boecker (*Redeformen*, pp. 21-24), has emphasized the *formula of handing over* the defendant for execution, directed by the local juridical assembly to the *pater familias*, who possesses authority over the members of his household and so is the only person who can grant authorization for punishment (Judg. 6.30; cf. also 2 Sam. 14.5-7, and, by extension to a tribe, Judg. 20.13). On the subject of the *patria potestas*, cf. also A. Phillips, 'Some Aspects of Family Law in Pre-Exilic Israel', *VT* 23 (1973) pp. 349-61; A.M. Rabello, 'Les effets personnels de la puissance paternelle en droit hébraïque, à travers la Bible et le Talmud', in *Mélanges à la mémoire de M.-H. Prevost* (Paris, 1982), pp. 84-101.

The texts on which the deductions of Boecker are based do not seem sufficient to guarantee with certainty the nature and extension of this juridical procedure (which would indicate a conflict between amphictyonic and family jurisdiction, the latter being typical of the nomadic period). In my opinion, it is very important to stress that we are always in a situation of *controversy between two parties* (in Judg. 6.31 this is made explicit by the terminology of the *rîb*): the consent requested from the *pater familias* (of the clan or tribe) is a clear manifestation that we are dealing with an accusation (not a verdict). The linking of the accusation to the sanction, as I have shown above, is a constant of juridical procedures, but it cannot be confused with the verdict, which lays down the punishment, because this is handed down by an impartial authority (to whom the two parties are subject) after listening to accusation and defence.

accusation continues to be such only to the extent to which—implicitly or explicitly—it is subject to a second speech (in a two-party controversy, this speech is that of the accused), and it is by this that it is confirmed or rebutted; the sentence, on the other hand, brings all other interventions to a close and by its nature cannot be appealed against.

Therefore, for an individual to enter into a controversy with another individual is to pronounce the sentence as a *threat*, as a possibility conditional upon what the adversary does and says.

J. Harvey, in his study of prophetic *rîbs*,[62] distinguishes between 'absolute' *rîbs* (in which the penalty is expressed in the form of a threat and not a sentence) and 'mitigated' *rîbs* (in which a positive decree is issued, which lays down the new behaviour demanded of the accused in order to avoid incurring an 'absolute' *rîb*). I believe that this distinction is only between rhetorical variations: by its nature a threat is an offer—in negative form—of the same possibility offered—in positive form—by the decree which imposes a chance of conversion.[63] The word 'ultimatum' used by Harvey[64] for the decree can certainly also be used for the 'threat', given that it stresses the definitive and dramatic aspect of the accusation; it should be enough, in this respect, to recall the preaching of Jonah in Nineveh to see how a threat with all the appearances of an ultimatum ('Forty more days and Nineveh will be destroyed', Jon. 3.4)[65] is implicitly the offer of a saving conversion (cf. also 2 Kgs 20.1-6; Jer. 26.18-19).[66]

It is true that in the controversies between God and his people the alternative put before the accused is expressly laid out (cf. Isa. 1.18-20;

62. Harvey, *Le plaidoyer prophétique*, pp. 100-105. The controversies examined by the author are limited to those undertaken by God against Israel after the breaking of the Covenant.

63. Cf. T.M. Raitt, 'The Prophetic Summons to Repentance', *ZAW* 83 (1971), pp. 30-49; H.W. Hoffmann, *Die Intention der Verkündigung Jesajas* (BZAW, 136; Berlin, 1974).

64. Harvey, *Le plaidoyer prophétique*, p. 103.

65. Regarding the complex problem of Jonah's prophecy, cf. in particular L. Schmidt, '*De Deo*' (BZAW, 143; Berlin, 1976), pp. 4-130. On the subject of the prophetic threat that is not fulfilled, cf. L. Alonso Schökel, 'L'infaillibilité de l'oracle prophétique', in E. Castelli (ed.), *L'infaillibilité: Son aspect philosophique et théologique* (Paris, 1970), pp. 495-503.

66. Cf. J. Fichtner, 'Die "Umkehrung" in der prophetischen Botschaft. Eine Studie zu dem Verhältnis von Schuld und Gericht in der Verkündigung Jesajas', *TLZ* 78 (1953), pp. 459-66.

Mic. 6.8; Ps. 50.14-15, 23), but the 'if'[67] (*'im/'im lō'*)[68] and the 'otherwise' (*pen*)[69] belong structurally to the nature of the accusation itself even when they are not clearly expressed, indeed even when the

67. The text of Isa. 1.19-20 is extremely clear in its formulation of the alternative offered by God (the accuser) to the leaders of the people (the accused): 'If (*'im*) you are willing to obey, you shall eat the good things of the earth. But if (*wᵉ'im*) you persist in rebellion, the sword shall eat you instead'. Cf. G. Fohrer, 'Jesaja 1 als Zusammenfassung der Verkündigung Jesajas', in *Studien zur alttestamentlichen Prophetie (1949–1965)* (BZAW, 99; Berlin, 1967), p. 161: 'Dieses Entweder-Oder der gegenwärtigen Entscheidung ist ein wesentlicher Grundzug der vorexilischen Prophetie'. This opinion is shared by H.W. Hoffmann, *Die Intention der Verkündigung Jesaja* (Berlin, 1974), pp. 46-47, whose criticism I share of G. Sauer's thesis in 'Die Umkehrforderung in der Verkündigung Jesajas', in *Wort—Gebot—Glaube: Beiträge zur Theologie des Alten Testaments* (ATANT, 59; Zürich, 1970), pp. 277-97.

A parallel to Isa. 1.19-20 may be seen in Solomon's statement regarding Adonijah, who had attempted to seize the royal power and had been disavowed by David's decision: 'Should (*'im*) he behave honourably, not one hair of his shall fall to the ground; but if (*wᵉ'im*) he is found malicious, he shall die' (1 Kgs 1.52).

The proposal of conditions is part, as we shall see in Chapter 4, of the attempt to restore the relationship between the two contestants; as regards the *rîbs* between YHWH and Israel, it may be noted that an offer in the form of an alternative (*'im/'im lō'*) is often present in the words of the accuser (cf. 1 Sam. 12.14-15; Isa. 58.9, 13; Jer. 4.1; 26.4; Mal. 2.2 etc.); even in the dispute begun by YHWH against Pharaoh, the punishment (the plagues) is sometimes expressly introduced by the phrase 'if (*'im*) he refuses to...' (Exod. 7.27; 8.17; 9.2; 10.4).

In Ezek. 33.1-20 we find expressed a general thesis about God's behaviour towards sinful man: here, denouncing evil and foretelling disaster, the prophet constantly places an alternative before the man who listens; God's threat works towards the conversion of the wicked, if he heeds it; in this lies the 'right dealing of God' (Ezek. 33.20).

Finally, it may be noted that an alternative is contained structurally in the very stipulations of a pact (Exod. 15.26; Deut. 11.26-28; 28.1, 15; 2 Sam. 7.14; cf. Gen. 31.50); proposing an alternative during a controversy is equivalent to proposing a renewed covenant.

68. For a purely philological discussion, in addition to the Grammars, cf. C. van Leeuwen, 'Die Partikel *'im*', *OTS* 18 (1973), pp. 15-48. It should be remembered, however, that the concept of 'condition' or 'alternative' is not limited in Hebrew to a single form of expression.

69. The particle *pen* can in certain contexts signal the negative event which will inevitably follow if suitable steps are not taken; in this sense it expresses the threatening aspect of an accusation (Judg. 14.15; Ps. 50.22; Jer. 4.4; 6.8; 21.12; Hos. 2.5; Amos 5.6). Regarding the semantic nuances of the particle *pen*, cf. P. Joüon, 'Etudes de sémantique hébraïque', *Bib* 2 (1921), pp. 340-42.

accuser pronounces a woe (*hôy*)[70] or intones a funeral dirge.[71]

These observations of mine allow us to define better the fundamental intention of the accusation in a *rîb* (between two parties): what is sought after is not punishment but a right relationship with the other;[72] the

70. In the Isa. 1.10-20 *rîb* we have the alternative noted above (vv. 19-20); in that of 1.2-9 on the other hand we find a 'woe' (v. 4); it is impossible to imagine that there is an essential difference between the two; it can only be maintained that a 'woe' represents an underscoring of the threat contained implicitly in the alternative (H.W. Hoffmann, *Die Intention der Verkündigung Jesajas* [Berlin, 1974], p. 103).

For the expression *hôy* as a threat accompanied by the denunciation of injustice, cf. Isa. 5.8, 11, 18, 20, 21; 10.1, 5; 28.1; 29.15; 30.1; 31.1; 33.1; 45.9-10; Jer. 22.13; 23.1; Ezek. 13.3, 18; 34.2; Amos 6.1; Mic. 2.1; Nah. 3.1; Hab. 2.6, 9, 12, 15, 19; Zeph. 2.5; 3.1; Zech. 11.17.

With the form *'ôy*, cf. Isa. 3.9, 11; Jer. 13.27; Ezek. 16.23; 24.6, 9; Hos. 7.13; Lam. 5.16 (cf. also Job 10.15, with *'alᵉlāy*).

For a discussion of the origin and meaning of invective, especially in the prophets, cf. Westermann, *Grundformen prophetischer Rede*, pp. 137-42; E. Gerstenberger, 'The Woe-Oracles of the Prophets', *JBL* 81 (1962), pp. 249-63; R.J. Clifford, 'The Use of *hôy* in the Prophets', *CBQ* 28 (1966), pp. 458-64; G. Wanke, '*'ôy* und *hôy*', *ZAW* 78 (1966), pp. 215-18; J.G. Williams, 'The Alas-Oracles of the Eighth Century Prophets', *HUCA* 38 (1967), pp. 75-91; H. Wildberger, *Jesaja* (BK, 10/1; 1968), pp. 175-202; H.W. Wolff, *Dodekapropheton*. II. *Joel und Amos* (BK, 14/2; 1969), pp. 284-87; W. Janzen, '*'Ašrê* and *hôy* in the Old Testament', *HTR* 62 (1970), pp. 432-33; H.J. Zobel, 'hôj', *ThWAT*, II, pp. 382-88; E. Otto, 'Die Stellung der Wehe-Worte in der Verkündigung des Propheten Habakuk', *ZAW* 89 (1977), pp. 73-107; D.R. Hillers, '*Hôy* and *Hôy*-Oracles. A Neglected Syntactic Aspect', in *The Word of the Lord Shall Go Forth* (FS D.N. Freedman; Winona Lake, IN, 1983), pp. 185-88. For the problems connected with the literary genre of invective, see in particular L. Markert, *Struktur und Bezeichnung des Scheltworts* (BZAW, 140; Berlin, 1977).

71. There is undoubted relationship between the cry *hôy* and the funeral dirge (cf. Jer. 22.18; 34.5). The literary genre of the *qînâ* is widely used in the prophetic tradition to affirm the inevitability of the disaster foretold; cf. H. Jahnow, *Das hebräische Leichenlied im Rahmen der Völkerdichtung* (BZAW, 36; Giessen, 1923); P. Heinisch, *Die Totenklage im Alten Testament* (BZfr, 13 F., 9/10; Münster, 1931), esp. pp. 42-51, 64-82; O. Eissfeldt, *Einleitung in das Alte Testament* (Tübingen, 2nd edn, 1956), pp. 109-14; W. Janzen, *Mourning Cry and Woe Oracle* (BZAW, 125; Berlin, 1972), H.-J. Krause, '*hôj* als prophetische Leichenklage über das eigene Volk im 8. Jahrhundert', *ZAW* 85 (1973), pp. 15-46. The study by C. Hardmeier, *Texttheorie und biblische Exegese: Zur rhetorischen Funktion der Trauermetaphorik in der Prophetie* (BEvt, 79; Munich, 1978), seemed to me excessively complicated.

72. In his commentary on the episode in Josh. 22.9-34, Boecker notes that the purpose of the accusation is to bring about an understanding in line with the law;

desire is that the accused should reform and live in a just relationship, not that the accused should be taken away in the name of some abstract principle of retributive justice. To accuse means, then, to want the other to escape from the unjust situation[73] by an act of truth and justice; but it certainly does not mean 'to condemn', if this word is taken as sanctioning the end of the relationship between the two parties by the elimination (real or symbolic) of one of them.

To be sure, even in a *rîb* properly so-called, the accusation is often unheeded, the threat derided, and its fundamentally positive purpose—manifested in a lengthy attempt to win over—perversely interpreted as powerlessness to do harm (cf. Isa. 28.15-16; Jer. 5.12; Amos 9.10; Zeph. 1.12; Ps. 10.4). This is why the accuser has to proceed to deeds,[74] which put the words into practice and demonstrate the truth of what has been said. The accuser 'makes himself felt' by a punitive act which demonstrates in concrete terms the truth of the words of the accusation and the seriousness of the task taken on. Even in this case, however, the sanction is gradual, the sanction has to be applied as 'paternal correction', as medicine which is intended to cure and not to kill (Ps. 118.18; Prov. 19.18; 23.13-14), as an instrument for life, not one designed for death (cf. Lam. 3.31-33).

Along the same lines, it is useful to remember how Scripture sees in punishment a necessary means for the learning of wisdom: the word

hence he can state: 'Aber auch für die andere Fälle gilt es zu bedenken, dass das hebräische Verfahren nie auf die Strafe, sondern immer auf die Wiederherstellung gerechter und geordneter Verhältnisse abzielt. Wenn man dies ohne Verfahren erreichen kann, dann ist mit anderen Mitteln derselbe Zweck erfüllt' (*Redeformen*, p. 35).

73. In this context one may recall the image of the 'watchman' used by the prophets to describe their role in dealing with Israel: Isa. 21.6-12; Jer. 6.17; Ezek. 3.16-21; 33.1.20. Cf. H. von Reventlow, *Wächter über Israel: Ezechiel und seine Tradition* (BZAW, 82; Berlin, 1962), esp. pp. 126-30; G. Del Olmo Lete, 'Estructura literaria de Ez 33.1-20', *EstBíb* 22 (1963), pp. 5-31; P. Auvray, 'Le prophète comme guetteur', *RB* 71 (1964), pp. 191-205.

74. This is the sense in which I interpret the sign of silence imposed by God on the prophet Ezekiel (3.22-27); rather than an affirmation of the inevitability of punitive judgment (as maintained by E. Vogt, 'Die Lähmung und Stummheit des Propheten Ezechiel', in *Wort—Gebot—Glaube: Beiträge zur Theologie des Alten Testaments* [ATANT, 59; Zürich, 1970], p. 100; and also R. Wilson, quoted in Chapter 1 n. 38), I think that we are dealing with a sort of final 'threat', inasmuch as it foretells the dumb language of God's punitive action.

which recognizes the truth and not *še'ôl* (Isa. 38.18-19; Pss. 6.6; 88.11-13 etc.) is, in the *rîb*, the end ultimately aimed at by the words and actions of the accuser who wants to be known as genuinely just.

Chapter 3

THE RESPONSE OF THE ACCUSED

In the previous chapter we saw the nature of the accusation's internal links, and its function in the context of a controversy; in this chapter we will deal with the accused's response, upon which the outcome of the dispute in question essentially depends.

When biblical texts relate a *rîb*, they often reduce its internal structure to a simple clash of two affirmations:[1] that of the accuser and that of the accused—generally indicating only implicitly which of the two prevailed and brought about the end of the controversy (cf. Gen. 20.9-16; 21.25-27; Judg. 8.1-3; 12.1-4 etc.). We are undoubtedly being given a précis, which provides the essentials of the debate without dwelling on the shifts of speech, which—as experience attests and even the Bible[2] sometimes acknowledges—occur between one speaker and the other before settling down into an agreement or a definitive breakdown of the relationship.

In essence there are two ways in which the accused can respond to the accusation: either admit wrongdoing or protest innocence. Within this logical division may be found all the nuances expressing the complexities of psychology and particular situations; but the truth that

1. With reference to Disputationworte, Begrich writes: 'Die gegebenen Formen eines Streitgespräches zwischen zwei Parteien sind Frage und Antwort, Behauptung und Gegenbehaptung' (*Deuterojesaja*, p. 43).

2. As an example, we may quote those biblical texts in which the controversy is carried on as a dialogue (cf. Gen. 31.22-54; Mal. 1.6-14; and even Jer. 2.1-37); we may look especially to those disputes that are developed in different sections, each with its own outline, but all bound together in the context of a single controversy. I am referring to the conflict between God (represented by Moses and Aaron) and Pharaoh in chs. 5–11 of Exodus; or the one between Saul and David, which begins in ch. 17 of 1 Samuel (vv. 8-11), and which has symbolic episodes in chs. 24 and 26, and concludes in 2 Samuel 1 with the death of Saul when David shows he is not guilty of it, and we may recall above all the great controversy between the just person and God which forms the literary drama of the whole of the book of Job.

comes out in justice tends to organize the facts into a simple opposition between yes and no, good and evil, guilty and innocent, and so on. As a result, faced with an accusation, either the response is yes (and a declaration of guilt), or the response is no (and a proclamation of innocence); equivocations must sooner or later settle into one or other of these two straightforward responses.[3]

These two essential kinds of response provide the subject matter for the current chapter; by way of conclusion, starting from the juridical importance of the verb *'śh*, I shall make some observations on the importance of 'deeds' in a question of law. These observations will mark the transition from the subject matter of the dispute to that of its conclusion.

1. *The Admission of Guilt*

The various ways in which the accused in biblical texts confesses his guilt can be organized into three distinct kinds, each of which shows its own originality of expression. Reduced to their essentials, they may be formalized like this:

1. to confess (to make a confession);
2. (to say): I have sinned;
3. (to say): You are (in the) right.

These three forms are equivalent as regards overall meaning and as regards function: each of them is capable autonomously of representing the response of an accused who admits guilt: from this point of view they belong to a single paradigm, and are (at least to a certain extent) interchangeable.

For the most part, however, these three forms are linked to one another in such a way as to make up syntagms with two or three elements. Formalizing this logically, we have the following possibilities:

3. The logical distinction between innocent and guilty underlies the dynamic of all procedures, and naturally has its counterpart in a judicial context. In a trial, it is the judge who draws the distinction between the *ṣaddîq* and the *rāšā'* (cf. Chapters 5 and 8); in a controversy properly so-called, on the other hand (one which remains two-sided), it is the defendant who is asked for a juridically decisive declaration.

1.	2.	3.
to confess:	(to say) I have sinned	
to confess:		(to say) You are (in the) right
	(to say) I have sinned	You are (in the) right
to confess:	(to say) I have sinned	You are (in the) right

My treatment will deal in sequence with each of these three forms of admission of guilt, pointing out as occasion rises the relationship to the others.

1.1. *To Confess*

With the aim of understanding better the different expressions and terms in the Hebrew lexicon, I shall try to decide what are the significant features that define the juridical concept of a 'confession'.

It seems that a start can be made by saying that it is a *speech* act; even though certain gestures are equivalent to a confession, this really consists of a declaration, corresponding to the verbal nature of the controversy.

In the second place, the substance of confessing is admitting *one's guilt*; the specific content of a confession is a statement concerning the speaker, the recognition that one's behaviour (or a single act) should be defined as guilty (or a crime). Finally, this declaration has a *juridical* value, because its status is that of a response to an accusation (whether formulated explicitly or not), of which it recognizes the soundness and to which it gives assent. From this point of view, the content of a confession also makes reference to the other disputant, declaring the accuser (at least implicitly) to be the upholder of the law in speech and in juridical action. This, as we shall see, has decisive consequences upon the outcome of the controversy.

These formal distinctions will act as heuristic parameters in my treatment of the Hebrew lexicon; as a first step I shall seek out the terminology which can be allocated to the syntagm: *to confess—one's guilt*; only at the end of section 1 (1.3 and 1.5) will I provide some pointers to the syntagm that is to some degree equivalent: *to confess—the other right*.

1.1.1. *The Root ydh.* The root is the first to come to the mind of biblical scholars when 'confession' is discussed, on account of the specific interest directed towards the subject of 'sin'.[4] In the juridical argument

4. To be more exact, biblical exegesis is concerned with the problem of the expiation of sins; confession is one of the prerequisites or accompanying acts along

that I am developing, it does not have a privileged value with respect to other terminologies, but only enjoys technical precision in an avowedly religious context.[5]

with the rite of sacrifice to which expiatory efficacy is normally attributed.

Milgrom (*Cult and Conscience*, pp. 106-10; 118-20) shows how, in particular in Lev. 5.1-5; 16.21; 26.40 and Num. 5.7 (all attributed to the source P), it is explicitly *deliberate* sins that are being dealt with (public confession is not required for involuntary sins, and he states: 'Confession (*htwdh*), then, is a prerequisite for the ultimate expiation of deliberate sin: it means to "acknowledge" the sin by identifying it and accepting blame' (p. 10). His fundamental thesis is therefore that, according to the source P, confession transforms intentional sin into an 'oversight' (which can be expiated by sacrifice) because repentance and confession have a 'juridical function' (pp. 118-21). I cannot, however, see an explanation of why the confession of sins (and the repentance which is presupposed) should have such value and juridical efficacy.

5. Exegetical research in this field has followed two main lines complementary to one another. The first looks to the study of the root *ydh*, which because of its technical nature is accorded a privileged role in the context of the confession of sins. We may recall P. Joüon, 'Reconnaissance et remercîment en hébreu biblique', *Bib* 4 (1923), pp. 381-85; H. Grimme, 'Der Begriff von hebräischen *hwdh* und *twdh*', *ZAW* 58 (1940–41), pp. 234-40; R. Pautrel, '"Immola Deo sacrificium laudis". Ps. 50.15', in *Mélanges bibliques...en l'honneur de A. Robert* (Paris, 1957), pp. 234-40; F. Mand, 'Die Eigenständigkeit der Danklieder des Psalters als Bekenntnislieder', *ZAW* 70 (1958), pp. 185-99; G. Bornkamm, 'Lobpreis, Bekenntnis und Opfer', in *Apophoreta* (FS E. Haenchen; BZNW, 30; Berlin, 1964), pp. 46-63; H.J. Hermisson, *Sprache und Ritus im altisraelitischen Kult: Zur 'Spiritualisierung' der Kultbegriffe im Alten Testament* (WMANT, 19; Neukirchen, 1965), esp. pp. 31-43; W. Beyerlin, 'Die *tôdā* der Heilsvergegenwärtigung in den Klageliedern des Einzelnen', *ZAW* 79 (1967), pp. 208-24; A.E. Goodman, '*ḥsd* and *twdh* in the Linguistic Tradition of the Psalter', in *Words and Meanings* (FS D.W. Thomas; Cambridge, 1968), pp. 105-15; D. Bach, 'Rite et parole dans l'Ancien Testament. Nouveaux eléments apportés par l'étude de *tôdâh*', *VT* 28 (1978), pp. 10-19.

The second line of contributions touches upon the great post-exilic penitential prayers, in which ample expression is given to the confession of sins. The following are generally quoted as penitential prayers: (a) The collective confessions of Ezra 9.6-15; Neh. 1.5-11; 9.5-37; Dan. 9.4-19; Ps. 106. Some authors add Isa. 59.9-15; 63.7-64.11; Jer. 32.17-25; Lamentations 5 (cf. C. Giraudo, *Le struttura letteraria della preghiera eucaristica* [AnBib, 92; Rome, 1981], p. 110). In Greek, mention may also be made of Dan. 3.26-45 and Bar. 1.15–3.8; since my study is based on an analysis of Hebrew terminology, these latter texts will be left for specific treatment. (b) The individual confessions of Pss. 38; (39); 51; 130.

Among the bibliographical contributions of a general nature we may note R. Pettazzoni, *La confessione dei peccati*, II/2 (Bologna, 1935), pp. 140-311; J. Vella,

The general meaning of the root is to recognize, to admit, to declare;[6] the different forms in which the root occurs, the verbal object and the context dictate important nuances in the primary meaning.

a. In the *Hitpael* the verb is used absolutely, or with an object (governed by various prepositions); it occurs in the context of penitential liturgies[7] to indicate the response—usually public—of sinners to the *rîb* undertaken by God against them. Except for 2 Chron. 30.22,[8] the meaning is always that of 'to confess one's sin'; this is made clear by the verbal object:

htwdh	(absolute)		Ezra 10.1 Neh. 9.3 Dan. 9.4
htwdh	*ḥaṭṭā'tî* *w*^{e}*ḥaṭṭa't 'ammî* *yiśrā'ēl*		Dan. 9.20
htwdh	*'et ḥaṭṭā'tām*	*'*^{a}*šer 'āśû*	Num. 5.7

La giustizia forense di Dio (Brescia, 1964), pp. 109-26; P. Buis, 'Notification de jugement et confession nationale', *BZ* NS 11 (1967), pp. 193-205; E. Lipiński, *La liturgie pénitentielle dans la Bible* (LD, 52; Paris, 1969); Giraudo, *La struttura letteraria*, pp. 81-177.

As regards individual prayer passages, cf. A.C. Welch, 'The Source of Nehemia IX', *ZAW* 47 (1929), pp. 130-37; M. Rehm, 'Nehemias 9', *BZ* NS 1 (1957), pp. 59-63; M. Gilbert, 'La prière de Daniel Dn 9. 4-19', *RTL* 3 (1972), pp. 284-310; W.T. In Der Smitten, *Esra: Quellen, Ueberlieferung und Geschichte* (SSN, 15; Assen, 1973), pp. 25-34, 47-51; W. Beyerlin, 'Der nervus rerum in Psalm 106', *ZAW* 86 (1974), pp. 50-64; M. Gibert, 'La prière d'Azarias (Dn 3.26-45. Théodotion)', *NRT* 96 (1974), pp. 561-82; A. Lacocque, 'The Liturgical Prayer in Daniel 9', *HUCA* 47 (1976), pp. 119-42; M. Gilbert, 'La place de la Loi dans la prière de Néhémie 9', in *De la Tôrah au Messie* (FS H. Cazelles; Paris, 1981), pp. 307-16; Alonso Schökel, *Treinta Salmos*, pp. 189-230.

6. Cf. C. Westermann, '*jdh* hi. preisen', *THAT*, I, p. 675; G. Mayer, '*jdh*', *ThWAT*, III, p. 456.

7. When I say penitential liturgies I mean those collections of rites (words and gestures) that express the condition of the repentant sinner and ask God for mercy and succour. In this chapter I shall sometimes use the word 'penitential' to refer explicitly to the prayer that confesses sin.

8. The context of 2 Chron. 30.22 contains the syntagm *ydh* (*Hitp*) *l*^{e}*yhwh*: the immediate context (particularly v. 21) suggests the translation, 'to celebrate the Lord'; however it should be noted that the wider context concerns a ritual confession of sin and penitential action (vv. 15-20).

htwdh	*’et ‘^{a}wōnām* *w^{e}’et ‘^{a}wōn ’^{a}bōtām*	*b^{e}ma‘^{a}lām*	*’^{a}šer mā‘^{a}lû bî*	Lev. 26.40
htwdh (*‘ālâw*)	*’et kol ‘^{a}wōnōt b^{e}nê yiśrā’ēl* *w^{e}’et kol piš‘êhem*	*l^{e}kol haṭṭō’tām*		Lev. 16.21
htwdh	*‘al ḥaṭṭō’t b^{e}nê yiśrā’ēl*		*’^{a}šer ḥāṭā’nû lāk*	Neh. 1.6
htwdh	*‘al ḥaṭṭō’têhem* *wa‘^{a}wōnôt ’^{a}bōtêhem*			Neh. 9.2
htwdh	*’^{a}šer ḥāṭā’ ‘āleyhā*			Lev. 5.5

b. The use of the verb *ydh* in the *Hiphil* is different. In general it takes for its object a person different from the speaker (or the speaker's qualities and actions); the generic meaning of 'to recognize' takes on the specific connotation of *to praise*, to celebrate, and the like.[9]

In two cases, however, we clearly have the meaning of 'to confess guilt':

Ps. 32.5	Prov. 28.13
wa‘^{a}wōnî lō’ kissîtî	*m^{e}kasseh p^{e}šā‘âw lō’ yaṣlîaḥ*
’āmartî ’ôdeh ‘^{a}lê p^{e}šā‘ay l^{e}yhwh	*ûmôdeh w^{e}‘ōzēb*
w^{e}’attâ nāśā’tā ‘^{a}wōn ḥaṭṭā’tî	*y^{e}ruḥām*

In both cases we find the sequence: do not conceal—confess—forgiveness; in the text from Proverbs, the principle *môdeh* implies the noun *p^{e}šā‘âw* from the first part of the verse; in Psalm 32 we have the syntagm *hwdh ’^{a}lê p^{e}šā‘ay*, which recalls Neh. 1.6; 9.2.

It should also be observed that in Ps. 32.5 the complete phrase contains a second object, *l^{e}yhwh*, with the result that the whole thing is to be translated, 'I will confess my guilt to the Lord': we see here for the first

9. Westermann thinks it possible to establish a difference between *ydh* (*Hi*) and *hll* (*Pi*). In secular usage, the former is a response to an action or behaviour; the latter is a response to a way of life. This would correspond to theological usage, in which *ydh* would belong to narrative divine praise, whereas *hll* would belong to the descriptive form (*THAT*, I, pp. 674-75).

time the fact that a confession is made to the one against whom the sin has been committed.

It may be asked then if the syntagm *ydh* (*Hi*) *l*ᵉ always means 'to praise'. However, in other contexts the 'praise' expresses a recognition of one's guilt or, if preferred, a recognition of the other's right in a juridical controversy situation. This becomes clear if some passages from Solomon's great prayer at the inauguration of the Temple in Jerusalem are compared with one another:

1 Kgs 8.33-34[10]	1 Kgs 8.46-50
1. sin (*ḥṭ'*) and military defeat	1. sin (*ḥṭ'*) God's wrath and exile
2. conversion (*šwb*) plea (*htpll –hthnn*) formula: *hôdû 'et šᵉmekā*	2. conversion (*šwb*) plea (*htpll –hthnn*) formula: *ḥāṭā'nû wᵉhe'ᵉwînû rāšā'nû*
3. forgiveness (*slḥ*)	3. forgiveness (*slḥ*)

c. The noun *tôdâ* has shades of meaning that echo the verbal forms quoted above.[11] The most frequent meaning is that of *praise* (the prevalent meaning of the verb *ydh* in the *Hiphil*), but cases should be noticed where the 'recognition' of God is equivalent to a confession of one's guilt (analogously to my observation about 1 Kgs 8.33-35).

To begin with we have the expression *ntn tôdâ l*ᵉ *(yhwh)*. In Josh. 7.19 it seems that the invitation issued by Joshua to the guilty Achan should be interpreted as the other making a confession of guilt: the criminal, by publicly proclaiming his sin, gives 'glory' and 'recognition' to God, in other words he admits the rightness of him who has marked him out as guilty by lot.

śîm nā' kābôd lᵉyhwh 'ᵉlōhê yiśrā'ēl
wᵉten lô tôdâ

wᵉhagged nā' lî meh 'āśîtā
'al tᵉkaḥēd mimmennî[12]

In Ezra 10.10-11 we have the same expression, again in the imperative, in the broad context of a great penitential prayer (9.5-15), which is followed by the people's pledge to act according to the law of

10. The identical sequence as in vv. 33-34 occurs in 1 Kgs 8.35. For the theme of 'praise' linked to conversion after the Exile, cf. also Bar. 2.32 and 3.6-7.

11. Alonso Schökel, *Treinta Salmos*, p. 206.

12. The theme of '*do not hide*', parallel to 'to confess', recalls Ps. 32.5 and Prov. 28.13 quoted above.

God (10.1-9); here we have a declaration of guilt linked to an invitation to recognize God:

'attem m^{e}'altem...
l^{e}hôsîp 'al 'ašmat yiśrā'ēl
w^{e}'attâ t^{e}nû tôdâ l^{e}yhwh '^{e}lōhê '^{a}bōtêkem

Another expression deserving consideration is *zbḥ tôdâ* (*l^{e}*), which we find in Psalm 50 as a request from God to the people of the covenant; if the overall context is a *rîb*, it is natural to expect that the accuser (God) should ask the guilty party to recognize its guilt and, by the same token, to recognize that God is in the right[13] (among other things, the pun may be noted on the verb *kbd*, recalling Josh. 7.19).

Ps. 50.14-15	*z^{e}baḥ*	*lē'lōhîm*	*tôdâ...*	*ût^{e}kabb^{e}dēnî*
23	*zōbēaḥ*		*tôdâ*	*y^{e}kabb^{e}dān^{e}nî*
Josh. 7.19				*śîm nā' kābôd l^{e}yhwh...*
	w^{e}ten	*lô*	*tôdâ*	

1.1.2. *Other Verbs that Mean 'to Confess'*. We have seen that the verb *ydh* takes on the undoubted nuance of 'to confess' when it is closely linked to the terminology of the 'crime'. A similar syntagm can be detected with other verbs.

The most important of these is *yd'*; it is not used in the great post-exilic penitential prayers, and does not seem to presuppose the technical situation of a liturgical celebration. The meaning of the verb, in the examples I give, is clearly that of 'to recognize one's guilt':[14]

2 Sam. 19.21	*kî yāda' 'abd^{e}kā*	*kî '^{a}nî ḥāṭā'tî*
Jer. 14.20	*yāda'nû (yhwh)*	*riš'ēnû '^{a}wōn '^{a}bôtênû*
		kî ḥāṭā'nû lāk
Ps. 51.5		*(kî) p^{e}šā'ay*
	'^{a}nî 'ēdā'	
Isa. 59.12		*wa'^{a}wōnōtênû*
	y^{e}da'^{a}nûm	
Job 9.2	*'omnām yāda'tî*	*kî kēn*
		ûmah yiṣdaq '^{e}nôš 'im 'ēl
Job 9.28-29	*yāda'tî*	*kî lō' t^{e}naqqēnî*
		'ānōkî 'eršā'

13. Alonso Schökel, *Treinta Salmos*, pp. 210-11.

14. The act of *confessing* one's guilt as expressed by *yd'* should be seen in conjunction with all the means used by the accuser to *convince*; cf. ch. 2, section 2.5.

Another significant verb is *ngd* (*Hi*): in this case it is not the aspect of 'recognizing' which is highlighted, but that of 'manifesting': the speaker makes a self-denunciation, confesses to being a criminal. We may recall Ps. 38.19 (*kî ʿᵃwōnî 'aggîd*), Isa. 3.9 (*wᵉḥaṭṭā'tām...higgîdû*, in an ironic sense), and also Josh. 7.19 and 1 Sam. 14.43, in which an invitation to confess directed at the guilty party is expressed.

Along the same lines as the verb *ngd* (*Hi*), the verb *ydʿ* (*Hi*) should be considered as semantically equivalent in Ps. 32.5 (*ḥaṭṭā'tî 'ôdîʿᵃkā*).[15]

Lastly, verbs that are the antonyms of confession deserve attention, (to hide, conceal, etc.); when these are found *in the negative* they amount to the equivalent of a declaration of guilt. For the verb *ksh* (*Pi*) see Ps. 32.5; Prov. 28.13 and Job 31.33; for the verb *kḥd* (*Pi*), Josh. 7.19 and Isa. 3.9.

1.2. *The Formula of the Self-Confessed Criminal*

The second way in which the admission of one's guilt is expressed in Hebrew is quite similar to the first: here too we have in essence a syntagm made up of two elements, which may be likened to those described above; but the peculiarity of this second form consists in the fact that the first element is a generic verb meaning 'to say' (*'mr*), while the second contains, so to speak, *the formula*[16] with which a declaration of one's guilt is traditionally made. Hence the title of this section, which aims to suggest the stereotyped and technical way in which the speaker expresses guilt. The following scheme shows how the formula *ḥāṭā'tî* / *ḥāṭā'nû* reveals its paradigmatic development:

'mr ḥāṭā'tî	Exod. 9.27; Num. 22.34; 1 Sam. 15.30; 2 Kgs 18.14
'mr ḥāṭā'tî lᵉ...	Exod. 10.16; 2 Sam. 12.13; Ps. 41.5; (Mic. 7.9)
'mr ḥāṭā'tî kî...	1 Sam. 15.24
'mr ḥāṭā'tî... heʿᵉwêtî	2 Sam. 24.17
'mr ḥāṭā'tî wᵉyāšār heʿᵉwêtî	Job 33.27
'mr ḥāṭā'tî wᵉhārēaʿ hᵃrēʿōtî	1 Chron. 21.17

15. Perhaps mention should be made of the expression in Gen. 41.9: *'et ḥᵃṭā'ay 'ᵃnî mazkîr hayyôm:* here, however, the admission of guilt is not made to the accusing injured party but to the authorities.

16. Cf. Boecker, *Redeformen*, pp. 111-17 (he, however, considers this formula as belonging to judicial debates); R. Knierim, *Die Hauptbegriffe für Sünde im Alten Testament* (Gütersloh, 1965), pp. 20-37.

— *ḥāṭā'tî l^{e}... w^{e}hāra' b^{e}'êneykā 'āśîtî*	Ps. 51.6
'mr ḥāṭā'tî l^{e}... w^{e}kāzō't w^{e}kāzō't 'āśîtî	Josh. 7.20
'mr ḥāṭā'tî... hiskaltî wā'ešgeh harbēh m^{e}'ōd	1 Sam. 26.21
'mr ḥāṭā'tî m^{e}'ōd '^{a}šer 'āśîtî... niskaltî m^{e}'ōd	2 Sam. 24.10
'mr ḥāṭā'tî m^{e}'ōd '^{a}šer 'āśîtî 'et haddābār hazzeh... niskaltî m^{e}'ōd	1 Chron. 21.8

The individual declaration (*ḥāṭā'tî*) is matched by the collective (*ḥāṭā'nû*); but unlike the former, this always occurs as the people's response when they confess their guilt to God in a religious and liturgical context:

'mr ḥāṭā'nû	Judg. 10.15; Neh. 1.6; cf. Num. 14.40; Lam. 5.16
'mr ḥāṭā'nû l^{e}...	Deut. 1.41; 1 Sam. 7.6; cf. Isa. 42.24; Jer. 3.25; 8.14; 14.7, 20
'mr ḥāṭā'nû kî...	Num. 21.7; 1 Sam. 12.10
'mr ḥāṭā'nû l^{e}...w^{e}kî	Judg. 10.10
'mr ḥāṭā'nû rāšā'nû	Dan. 9.15
'mr ḥāṭā'nû w^{e}he'^{e}wînû rāšā'nû	1 Kgs 8.47
'mr ḥāṭā'nû he'^{e}wînû w^{e}rāšā'nû	2 Chron. 6.37
— *ḥāṭā'nû... he'^{e}wînû hiršā'nû*	Ps. 106.6
'mr ḥāṭā'nû w^{e}'āwînû w^{e}hirša'nû ûmārādnû w^{e}sôr mimmiṣwōtekā ûmimmišpāṭeykā	Dan. 9.5

In the texts quoted above, one cannot fail to recognize the characteristic *formula* by which the criminal (individual or group) confesses its guilt.[17]

It should be remembered however that other expressions, in part modeled on the above-mentioned formula, have an identical value and function in the structure of a juridical controversy. In this connection we may examine two main groups.

1. In place of *ḥāṭā'tî* / *ḥāṭā'nû*, we may find *other* verbs belonging to the paradigm of the 'misdeed', and which instead of being juxtaposed to the former (as in the schemata listed above) replace them. Here I give some examples:

Lam. 1.20	*mārô mārîtî*
Ezra 10.2	*'^{a}naḥnû mā'alnû bē'lōhênû*
Dan. 9.9	*māradnû bô*
Lam. 3.42	*naḥnû pāša'nû ûmārînû*

Cf. also Isa. 59.12; 66.5; Jer. 14.7; Pss. 25.11; 65.4; Ezra 9.6; Neh. 1.7; 2 Chron. 28.13 etc.

17. Cf. Giraudo, *La struttura letteraria*, p. 89; B.O. Long, 'Two Question-and-Answer Schemata in the Prophets', *JBL* 90 (1971), pp. 132-33.

2. In place of *ḥāṭā'tî* / *ḥāṭā'nû* we may find *nouns*, again belonging to the misdeed paradigm, in nominal phrases; particular note should be given to the different prepositions:

Ps. 51.5	*kî p^{e}šā'ay '^{a}nî 'ēdā'*
	w^{e}ḥaṭṭā'tî negdî *tāmîd*
Isa. 59.12	***kî p^{e}šā'ênû 'ittānû***
	wa'^{a}wōnōtênû y^{e}da'^{a}nûm
1 Sam. 25.24	***bî '^{a}nî*** *'^{a}dōnî* ***he'āwōn***
2 Sam. 14.9	***'ālay*** *'^{a}dōnî hammelek* ***he'āwōn w^{e}'al bêt 'ābî***

Cf. also Gen. 4.13; Ezek. 33.10; (Job 19.4); Ezra. 9.15

1.3. *The Declaration that the Accuser is (in the) Right*

The specific nature of this kind of confession of guilt resides in the fact that the accused introduces into the speech not only a clear statement of self-consciousness (of having done wrong), but also one about the other party (and about the righteousness of the accuser's claim). The syntagm in this case appears to be tripartite: 1. an element of 'saying'; 2. a statement that the other party 'is right'; 3. a declaration of one's guilt. Elements 2. and 3. may be unattached, as, for example, in the great penitential prayers, but their mutual relationship is to be considered very relevant.[18]

To show that the other party (the accuser) is in the right, there is a characteristic use of *ṣaddîq* in a nominal phrase:

'mr	*yhwh haṣṣaddîq*	*wa'^{a}nî w^{e}'ammî har^{e}šā'îm*	Exod. 9.27
'mr	*ṣaddîqîm 'attem*	*hinnēh '^{a}nî qāšartî 'al '^{a}dōnî*	2 Kgs 10.9
'mr	*ṣaddîq 'attâ...*	*hin^{e}nû l^{e}pāneykā b^{e}'ašmātênû*	Ezra 9.15
'mr	*w^{e}'attâ ṣaddîq...*	*wa'^{a}naḥnû hiršā'nû*	Neh. 9.33
'mr	*ṣaddîq yhwh...*	*w^{e}lō' šāma'nû b^{e}qōlô*	Dan. 9.14
—	*ṣaddîq w^{e}yāšār hû'*	*šiḥēt lô... dôr 'iqqēš ûp^{e}taltōl*	Deut. 32.4-5
—	*ṣaddîq hû' yhwh*	*kî pîhû mārîtî*	Lam. 1.18

The text of Deut. 34.4-5, even though it occurs in a *rîb* as the statement of an accuser, forms part of this series. This is because the great canticle can be read on two levels, not just as an accusation (spoken by

18. The opposition between *ṣaddîq* and *rāšā'* in a *rîb* points to the relationship which necessarily exists between two disputants; the former refers to the disputant who is in the right 'either because his accusations are true or because the accusations of his adversary are false' (J. Vella, *La giustizia forense di Dio* [Brescia, 1964], p. 38). This also holds good in a two-party controversy, and even in a law court before a judge. I would like to point out (with reference to section 1.5 of this chapter) how the concept of true and false enters into the definition of 'innocent' and 'guilty'.

Moses against the people), but also as a confession of guilt (repeated by the people, who know it by heart: Deut. 31.19, 21).[19]

To the passages quoted in the schema should be added those in which the accused (though without using the word *ṣaddîq* in a nominal phrase) grants innocence (*ṣdq*) to the accuser, at the same time confessing his guilt: cf. Ps. 51.6; Neh. 9.8; Dan. 9.7, 18; 2 Chron. 12.6.

The syntagm *ṣdq min* forms a separate issue: the preposition *min* does not express a comparison ('to be juster than...') but a relative object ('to be just in relationship to', 'to be innocent regarding...'). When it occurs in the context of a two-sided controversy, the syntagm makes it clear that one party is right with respect to the other, and therefore that one is innocent and the other is guilty.[20]

Sometimes the one who speaks is the *accuser*, who recognizes that the accused is innocent (and therefore the speaker is the guilty one):

Gen. 38.26	(*'mr*) *ṣādᵉqâ mimmennî kî...*
1 Sam. 24.18	(*'mr*) *ṣaddîq 'attâ mimmennî kî...*

To these two passages (even though we do not have a *min*) may be likened:

Jer. 12.1	*ṣaddîq 'attâ yhwh kî 'ārîb 'ēleykā.*

Sometimes the speaker is the accused, but uses the syntagm *ṣdq min* to protest innocence (Job 35.2; cf. also 32.2; and the following section 2.2).

Finally, *ṣdq min* is used by a speaker not in self-reference but describing the relationship between one person and another in a more or less explicit controversy situation: cf. 1 Kgs 2.32; Jer. 3.11; Ezek. 16.52; Hab. 1.13; Job 4.17; in Job 9.2 and 25.4 the syntagm *ṣdq 'im* has an identical meaning; and Job 32.2 contains the expression *ṣdq* (*Pi*) *napšô min*.

The importance of the root *ṣdq* to declare innocence in a juridical confrontation has been widely noted; it has therefore been followed by a debate on its interpretation.[21]

19. Cf. G.E. Wright, 'The Lawsuit of God: A Form-Critical Study of Deuteronomy 32', in *Israel's Prophetic Heritage* (FS J. Muilenburg; New York, 1962), p. 56.

20. Cf. GK 33b n. 2; Boecker, *Redeformen*, pp. 126-29; F. Horst, *Hiob* (BK, 16; Neukirchen, 1968), pp. 74-76; Alonso Schökel, *Treinta Salmos*, p. 201.

21. On the meaning of the 'justice' of God, cf. M. Gilbert, 'La prère de Daniel. Dn 9.4-19', *RTL* 3 (1972), pp. 304-309, who discusses among others the opinion of S. Lyonnet (esp. in 'La notion de Justice de Dieu en Rom. 3.5 et l'exégèse paulinienne du "Miserere"', in *Sacra Pagina*, II [BETL, XIII; Paris, 1959], pp. 354-

At this point I think that it is useful to observe that, as well as this root, other synonymous words or expressions can take over the function of defining who in the controversy is in the right.

As well as *tām(îm)* and *yāšār*, synonyms for *ṣaddîq* in Deut. 32.4, and *ṭhr*, parallel to *ṣdq* in Job 4.17, I consider these important:

1. the root *nqh*: Num. 5.31; 32.22; Judg. 15.3; Ps. 19.13, 14; Job 10.14; etc.
2. the terms *'emet* (Neh. 9.33; Ps. 51.8; cf. also Ps. 25.10-11) and *'emûnâ* (Deut. 32.4; Ps. 40.10-13). The corresponding Greek in Dan. 3.27 may also be consulted.
3. the root *qdš*, pointed out by L. Alonso Schökel[22] as the transposition into a priestly key of the recognition of justice and innocence (Ezek. 20.39; 43.7-8; cf. also Ps. 106.47).
4. finally, the root *kbd* is of particular importance on account of its oppositional value to the terminology of *shame* (which refers—as we shall have the opportunity to see later—to the experience of juridical defeat).[23] I have noted the appearance of the rot *kbd* in Josh. 7.19 (to which may be likened 1 Sam. 6.5) and in Ps. 15.23; I would like further to quote, for *kbd* (*Pi*): 1 Sam. 2.29; 15.30; Isa. 24.14-15; 43.23; and for *kābôd*: Neh. 9.5; Isa. 42.8; 62.2; Jer. 13.16; Ezek. 39.21.

1.4. *Redundancy*

The response in which the accused admits guilt can be short, almost epigrammatic. For example, after Nathan has brought home to him his guilt and passed sentence (2 Sam. 12.1-12), David says only, 'I have sinned against the Lord (*ḥāṭā'tî leyhwh*)' (v. 13); the Jews respond to Ezra's denunciation (Ezra 10.10-11), 'Yes, we must act according to your word (*kēn kidbārekā* (Q) *'ālênû la'aśôt*)' (v. 12).

Many times, however, we have quite long replies, featuring accumulation and repetition; in the first place, within every kind of declaration, formulae are as it were stretched by the addition of synonymous expressions (cf. the examples in the schemas quoted above); in the

55) and Vella, *La giustizia forense di Dio*, pp. 48-50, 56-57.

22. *Treinta Salmos*, p. 224.

23. Cf. ch. 8, section 1.3.2. 'Shame' as an antonym for 'justice' in the two-sided relationship of a controversy appears clearly in Dan. 9.7:

lekā 'adōnāy	*haṣṣedāqâ*
welānû	*bōšet happānîm.*

second place, we may find several forms of confession of guilt joined together in a single reply (Exod. 9.27; Ezra 9.15; Ps. 51.5-6 etc.); finally, in the great post-exilic penitential prayers, the confession of sin is repeated several times almost like a refrain (Ezra 9.6-7, 10, 13, 15; Dan. 9.5-8, 9, 10, 13, 14, 15, 16, 18 etc.).

This redundancy certainly occurs on a more massive scale in the collective confession texts assigned to a late stage in the history of Israel;[24] but it would be an insufficient explanation to see it as a mere literary fact traceable to stylistic decadence. The declaration of guilt—both in ordinary anthropological experience and in its subsequent literary expression—is proportionate to the *awareness* of the seriousness of the situation, the crime committed, the accusation and the punishment.[25]

According to biblical history, individual and collective history appears as humanity's repeated falling into sin, which is followed by a repeated denunciation by God (by means of his 'messengers'); but little by little this repetition shows itself to be the practical manifestation of a total rejection which demands a total destruction.

As a result, the message of the prophetic tradition changes gradually from an accusation dealing with particular points in the behaviour of individuals and the people to a global denunciation[26] which embraces everyone in all times, a denunciation which becomes the threat of an irrevocable punishment.[27] Just as prophecy becomes almost monotonous as it reveals the refusal to heed the voice of God, in the same way post-exilic tradition expresses Israel's conscious response to prophecy,[28] filling out and constantly repeating the people's admission of guilt, this

24. With reference to Dan. 9.4-19, Gilbert writes of 'phrases amples, bourrées d'accumulations, dont le but semble être de faire sentir la totalité, la plénitude de la faute ou de la confusion de tout Israël' ('La prière de Daniel', p. 299).

25. The Exile period must undoubtedly be given great importance in the history of the religious consciousness of Israel; the end of the state (and sacral) institutions, along with the danger of disappearing into the melting-pot of the nations, prompted an in-depth search into the meaning of such a catastrophe.

26. Cf. J.F. Zink, '"Uncleanness and Sin": A Study of Job XIV 4 and Psalm LI 7', *VT* 17 (1967), pp. 354-61.

27. Cf. H. Gross, '"Anfang und Ende". Beobachtungen zum prophetischen Reden von Schöpfung, Gericht und Heil', in *Künder des Wortes* (FS J. Schreiner; Würzburg, 1982), pp. 295-98.

28. Cf. H. Gunkel, *Einleitung in die Psalmen* (Göttingen, 2nd edn, 1966), pp. 131-32.

being a recognition of the seriousness of the sin that brought about the disaster of the Exile. Faced with the prospect of a death of which there has to some degree already been a foretaste, the urgency of salvation necessarily finds expression in obsessive and insistent declarations that keep coming back to a single point, that of their own responsibility, linking it—as we shall see later—with a request for forgiveness and mercy.

1.5. *Confession and Praise*

In the course of my work we have seen how, starting with a study of the root *ydh* right through to the final form of confession of guilt (which is parallel to or coincident with a recognition of the accuser's 'justice'), there are two intertwined semantic lines, the penitential and the celebratory. Recognizing the irreprehensible nature of God, giving him 'glory', calling upon his 'holy' Name, and so forth incline writers towards literary forms that appear alien to penitential pleadings. In the great post-exilic public confessions the phenomenon is even more obvious: in them the proclamation of the divine titles (Neh. 1.5; 9.32; Dan. 9.4) and the invitations to blessing (*brk*: Neh. 9.5; Ps. 106.48; cf. also Dan. 3.26) and praise (*tᵉhillâ*: Neh. 9.5; Ps. 106.2, 47; Isa. 63.7; cf. Dan. 3.26 and Baruch 3.6-7; *hwdh*: Ps. 106.1, 47) create certain problems of classification for the experts in literary genres.[29]

My intention in this section is to provide a few illustrations of the semantic link that exists between confession and praise;[30] I believe that the concept of *truth* is the common basis of these two expressions of the

29. Cf. the discussion on the position of Gunkel in Gilbert, 'La prière de Daniel', pp. 285-86. As regards Psalm 106, cf. Kraus, *Psalmen*, II, p. 727; G. Castellino, *Libro dei Salmi* (Torino, 1955), pp. 706-708. For Psalm 51, see in particular H. Ridderbos, 'Psalm 51.5-6', in *Studia biblica et semitica* (FS T.C. Vriezen; Wageningen, 1966), pp. 310-11.

30. There have been various attempts to explain how praise finds its way into the juridical context (in the accusation and confession): cf. F. Horst, 'Die Doxologien im Amosbuch', *ZAW* 47 (1929), pp. 45-54; S.B. Frost, 'Asseveration by Thanksgiving', *VT* 8 (1968), pp. 380-90; G. Bornkamm, 'Lobpreis, Bekenntnis und Opfer', in *Apophoreta* (FS E. Haenchen; BZNW, 30; Berlin, 1964), pp. 46-63; G. von Rad, 'Gerichtsdoxologie', in *Schalom* (FS A. Jepsen; Stuttgart, 1971), pp. 28-37; G.C. Macholz, 'Gerichtsdoxologie und israelitisches Rechtsverfahren', *DielhBLAT* 9 (1975), pp. 52-69; J.L. Crenshaw, *Hymnic Affirmation of Divine Justice: The Doxologies of Amos and Related Texts in the Old Testament* (SBLDS, 24; Missoula, MT, 1975). Cf. also the latter author's '*YHWH ṣᵉbaʾôt šᵉmô:* A Form-Critical Analysis', ZAW 81 (1969), pp. 156-75.

human spirit, which sometimes seem to draw apart,[31] if not to exclude one another.

A controversy, which begins with the lodging of an accusation, has as its final aim the recognition of the truth, without which no act or ordinance whatever—even though objectively right—can receive the human distinction of being just. In fact, a person faced with unjust behaviour or an unjust structure does not simply have the problem of re-establishing a state of legality by means of more or less violent external operations; since it is a question of free-willed individuals, the real problem is to arrive at an internal acceptance of the external acts of justice. Now, since only the truth makes us free, and without freedom there is no intersubjective justice, the whole dynamic of the controversy, and indeed all jurisdictional procedures, tend to favour, promote and bring about the recognition of the truth.

Since we are dealing with a two-sided structure, every statement of truth comes as it were from two angles: the first is in relationship to the speaker, the second to the partner in the relationship. In order to illustrate this fact, we may take as an example a theme, namely, how *history* is viewed in the controversies between God and Israel.

In prophetic *rîb*s, in the actual accusation, what is said has the function of laying some blame upon the other party, and at the same time of asserting the innocence of the speaker. If mention is made of past history, this becomes at the same time an aggravation of the sin and a recognition of God's righteousness (cf. Deut. 32.7; Jer. 2.5; Mic. 6.4 etc.).

Within the accused's reply in the penitential prayers, we have a similar situation: the declaration of guilt makes reference to the history of sin, in which God's most upright behaviour is to the same degree a cause of celebration Ps. 106.7; Neh. 9.7 etc.). This gives rise to the alternation of confession and praise which is so characteristic of penitential pleas; it is not a simple matter of the mixing of two literary genres, but of the

31. Cf. Giraudo, *La struttura letteraria*, p. 162: the author points to 'an early recurrence of the root *ydh* in a confessional key consistent with admitting a two-sided situation at the heart of the covenant; in other words, on the one hand the inferiority and guilt of the human partner and on the other hand the natural superiority and sinlessness of the divine partner. It is onto this second aspect of the confessional act that occurrences of the root in a purely celebratory key are grafted at a second stage. In such a case, the intensive forms of *ydh* are to be found practically detached from any reference to the vassal's infidelity, from the moment when the prayer's attention is totally given over to the magnificence of God's works.' Cf. also E. Valgiglio, *Confessio nella Bibbia e nella letteratura cristiana antica* (Torino, 1980), pp. 56-60.

union of two expressions of the truth which need linking to one another.

However, this does not seem to me to be the last word on the question. Actually, history shows that sin does not block the 'path' of God's justice; repeated rebellion does not move the Other to betrayal. Paradoxically, human sin leads to a more genuine recognition of God, who is not simply just whereas human beings are unjust (Mic. 6.5), but is just towards those who are unjust. It is in this latter recognition of truth, which is simultaneously confession and praise, that the newness of the Christian message comes through.

2. *The Protestation of Innocence*[32]

We shall now have a look at what the other possible response to an accusation is and how it is expressed.

It would seem more difficult than in the previous section to provide a systematic framework within which to locate the forms of expression used for a declaration of innocence in a controversy;[33] the reason may lie in the fact that the protestation of innocence finds less of a place in liturgical contexts,[34] and so retains a freedom and variety of expression more in keeping with everyday experience.

At any rate, we may note that a protestation of innocence directly opposes the claims of the accuser (cf. Judg. 11.14 in comparison with 11.13); just as the latter has two forms, the declarative and the interrogative, so the response of innocence is a mirror image of the accusation itself, clothing itself in the same forms. On the other hand, a protestation of innocence is directly opposed to the confession of one's wrong; in this way we shall be able to recognize, in the terminology and

32. I shall not bring into my argument those assertions which maintain that the accused are guiltless if they claim that they are ignorant of the crime committed (cf. Gen. 21.26; 1 Sam. 22.15; 25.25). In this connection it should be noted that if 'ignorance' does not represent guiltlessness, it is a mitigating factor of great importance (cf. Gen. 38.16; Num. 22.34; Deut. 4.42; 19.4; Josh. 20.3, 5; 1 Sam. 2.32; 2 Sam. 3.26).

33. In the passages quoted in the course of this section, the protestation of innocence is sometimes not a response given to the other party, but a declaration made before a judge. These cases likewise presuppose the situation characteristic of a dispute (transferred to a judicial setting).

34. Cf. however, Pss. 7; 35; 57; 69, which, according to O. Eissfeldt, may to some extent refer to legal procedures linked to the cult (1 Kgs 8.31-32) (*Einleitung in das Alte Testament* [Tübingen, 4th edn, 1976], p. 160).

the formulae which I am about to list, the (oppositional) symmetry with what has been elaborated in the previous section.

To make things clearer, I would like to give here a simplified schema to use as a guide in what follows. In it appear the relationships to which I have just now alluded:

Accusation		*Response*		
	1. *ydh*	2. *ḥāṭā'tî*	*bî...he'āwōn*	3. *ṣaddîq 'attâ*
declarative	—	*lō' ḥāṭā'tî*	*b^e lî 'āwōn*	*ṣādaqtî*
interrogative	—	*meh ḥāṭā'tî*	*meh '^a wōnî*	—

2.1. *The Accused Justifies Himself*

We may note from the outset that there are no words in Hebrew opposed to those which express a confession as 'recognition' (*ydh*, *yd'*, etc.); it may be for the same reason that the language of self-justification is less formalized by comparison with that of a confession—that is, because it does not hold a significant position in the context of religious and cultic tradition.

I shall deal firstly with the declaration of guiltlessness which is symmetrical to the second kind of confession of guilt (*ḥāṭā'tî*).

Here too we have a syntagm made up of two basic elements: 1. a statement (the verb *'mr*, expressed or implied); 2. the terminology of a crime *which is denied*: within the latter element we may distinguish verbal and nominal phrases. I would like to give some examples that will make clear the direct opposition to a confession.

a. in declarative mode

'mr	*'ên b^e yādî*[35] *rā'â wāpeša'*	
	w^e lō' ḥāṭā'tî lāk (*w^e 'attâ*...)	1 Sam. 24.12
'mr	*w^e 'ānōkî lō' ḥāṭā'tî lāk* (*w^e 'attâ*...)	Judg. 11.27
'mr	*lō' ḥāṭā'tî*	Jer. 2.35
'mr	*lō' pā'altî 'āwen*	Prov. 30.20
'mr	*lō' 'āśîtî m^e 'ûmâ* (*kî*...)	Gen. 40.15
'mr	*lō' 'āśîtî kēn*	Neh. 5.15
—	*bal timṣā' zammōtî*	
	bal ya'^a bor pî	Ps. 17.3

35. I should underline the importance of the *hand* in these declarations of innocence: clean hands are presented as a metaphor for sinlessness (Alonso Schökel, *Treinta Salmos*, p. 200); cf. Gen. 20.5; 1 Sam. 12.5; 26.18; Pss. 7.4; 18.21, 25; 26.6 (L.A. Snijders, 'Psaume XXVI et l'innocence', *OTS* 13 [1963], pp. 112-30); Job 16.7; 1 Chron. 12.18.

'mr	*lō' ḥ^{a}môr 'eḥād mēhem nāśā'tî* *w^{e}lō' h^{a}rē'ōtî 'et 'aḥad mēhem*		Num. 16.15
—		*lō' piš'î w^{e}lō' ḥaṭṭā'tî* *b^{e}lî 'āwōn*	Ps. 59.4-5
'mr		*'ên pāša'*	Prov. 28.24
'mr		*b^{e}lō' ḥāmās b^{e}kappāy*	1 Chron. 12.18
—		*lō' ḥāmās b^{e}kappāy*	Job. 16.17

b. in interrogative mode[36]

'mr	*meh ḥāṭā'tî (kî...)*		1 Kgs 18.9
'mr	*meh ḥāṭā'tî l^{e}kā...(kî...)*		Jer. 37.18
'mr	*ûmeh ḥāṭā'tî lāk (kî...)*		Gen. 20.9
—	*mâ 'ep'al lāk*		Job 7.20
—	*ûmah šāgîtî*		Job 6.24
'mr	*meh 'āśîtî ('attâ kākem)*[37]		Judg. 8.2
—	*meh 'āśîtî l^{e}kā*	*ûmâ hel'ētîkā*	Mic. 6.3
'mr	*meh 'āśîtî*	*ûmah b^{e}yādî rā'â*	1 Sam. 26.18
'mr	*meh 'āśîtî*	*ûmah māṣā'tā b^{e}'abd^{e}kā*	1 Sam. 29.8
'mr	*mah māṣ^{e}'û '^{a}bôtêkem*	*bî 'āwel (kî...)*	Jer. 2.5
'mr	*meh 'āśîtî*	*meh '^{a}wōnî ûmeh* *ḥaṭṭā'tî...(kî...)*	1 Sam. 20.1
'mr		*mah piš'î mah* *ḥaṭṭā'tî (kî...)*	Gen. 31.36
'mr		*ûmeh '^{a}wōnēnû ûmeh* *ḥaṭṭā'tēnû* *'^{a}šer ḥāṭā'nû l^{e}...*	Jer. 16.10
—		*kammâ lî '^{a}wōnôt* *w^{e}ḥaṭṭā'ôt*	Job 13.23
—		*h^{a}yēš bilšônî 'awlâ*	Job 6.30
'mr	*'et šôr mî lāqaḥtî* *w^{e}'et mî 'āšaqtî* *'et mî raṣṣôtî*	*waḥ^{a}môr mî lāqaḥtî* *ûmiyyad mî lāqaḥtî kōper...*	1 Sam. 12.3

Still in the interrogative form, cf. Gen. 20.4; Num. 22.28; 1 Sam. 17.29; Isa. 5.4; Jer. 2.30. For interrogative phrases that have the force of exoneration to a third party, cf. 1 Sam. 20.32 and 2 Sam. 24.17.[38]

36. Boecker demonstrates the correspondence between the *Beschuldigungsformel* (*meh 'āśîtā*) and the *Beschwichtigungsformel* (*meh 'āśîtî*): *Redeformen*, pp. 31-34.

37. Only in Jer. 8.6 is the question *meh 'āśîtî* addressed to the speaker *himself*, and amounts to a certain extent to a self-accusation (cf. Boecker, *Redeformen*, p. 33).

38. Concerning the episode in 2 Samuel 24, cf. the monograph by A. Schenker, *Die Mächtige im Schmelzofen des Mitleids: Eine Interpretation von 2 Sam 24* (OBO, 42; Freiburg, 1982).

2.2. *The Accused Declares Himself Innocent*

We have seen that the third way of confessing one's guilt is to admit that the accuser is right (using the root *ṣdq* and its synonyms; used antagonistically, exoneration is the affirmation that one is innocent, that right is on one's own side). Whereas confession looks like this: 'You are (in the) right, I am guilty', a declaration of innocence takes more or less the form: 'I am innocent, but you/he...'

Hebrew does not use the formula *ṣaddîq '^{a}nî*, but as can be seen from the following outline we have equivalent expressions, such as *ṣādaqtî*, *'eṣdāq*, *zak '^{a}nî*, *nāqî 'ānōkî*. The passages listed below bring together both verbal and nominal phrases. Particular attention should be given to the recurrence of the roots *ṣdq—rš'*, *zkh/zkk*,[39] *nqh* and *tmm*;[40] note also the way in which the encounter with the opposing party is depicted: as well as making clear his opponent's behaviour, the accuser is called to task by the use of the preposition *min* or the phrase *b^e'êneykā*:[41]

'mr ṣādaqtî	*w^e'ēl hēsîr mišpāṭî...*	
...b^{e}lî pāšaʿ		Job 34.5-6
— *'^{a}nî 'eṣdāq*		Job 13.18
'mr ṣidqî mē'ēl		Job 35.2
— *lō' 'āsîr tummātî mimmennî*		
b^{e}ṣidqātî heḥ^{e}zaqtî...		
	y^{e}hî k^{e}rāšā' 'ōy^{e}bî	
	ûmitqôm^{e}mî k^e'awwāl	Job 27.5-7
— *lō' rāšaʿtî mē'^{e}lōhāy*		Ps. 18.22
		= 2 Sam. 22.22
— *lō' 'eršāʿ*[42]		Job 10.7
'mr zak '^{a}nî b^{e}lî pāšaʿ		
ḥap 'ānōkî w^{e}lō' 'āwōn lî		
	hēn t^{e}nû'ôt 'ālay yimṣā'	
	yaḥš^{e}bēnî l^e'ôyēb lô	Job 33.9-10

39. For the terminology regarding the 'pure' and 'impure', cf. W. Paschen, *Rein und Unrein: Untersuchung zur biblischen Wortgeschichte* (SANT, 24; Munich, 1970).

40. Cf. L. Ruppert, *Der leidende Gerechte* (ForBib, 5; Würzburg, 1972), pp. 29-30; W. Brueggemann, 'A Neglected Sapiential Word Pair', *ZAW* 89 (1977), pp. 234-58.

41. For the preposition *min*, cf. Judg. 15.3; Ps. 18.22; Job 25.5; the syntagm *swr* (*Hi*) *tummātî mimmennî* (Job 27.5) also deserves consideration in parallel with the simpler *swr* (*Hi*) *mišpāṭî* in Job 34.5; all of this should be taken in connection with what has been said above (p. 104) about *ṣdq min*. For the phrase *b^e'êneykā*, cf. 2 Kgs 20.3; Job 11.4.

42. The syntagm *lō' rš'* is used to declare a third person innocent in Job 34.10, 12.

'mr zak liqḥî		
ûbar hāyîtî bᵉ'êneykā[43]		Job 11.4
'mr zikkîtî libbî		
ṭāhartî mēḥaṭṭā'tî		Prov. 20.9
'mr nāqî 'ānōkî... min (crime)		2 Sam. 3.28
'mr	*dāmô bᵉrō'šô*	
wa'ᵃnaḥnû nᵉqiyyim		Josh. 2.19
'mr kî niqqêtî		Jer. 2.35
'mr niqqêtî... min (person)		Judg. 15.3
'mr bᵉtom lᵉbābî		
ûbᵉniqyōn kappay 'āśîtî zō't		Gen. 20.5
'mr wᵉhaṭṭôb bᵉ'êneykā 'āśîtî		2 Kgs 20.3

I think that these are the clearer forms of a declaration of innocence; to them may be added the more indirect ones (cf. for example Gen. 20.4); a fairly typical form is that used by someone praying for assistance *kᵉṣidqî* (Pss. 7.9; 18.21, 25), *kᵉṣidqātî* (2 Sam. 22.21, 25), *kᵉtummî* (Ps. 7.9).[44] We also find metaphorical expressions taken from dressing (Job 29.14) and washing (Pss. 26.6; 73.13; Job 9.30), from walking (2 Kgs 20.3; Pss. 17.4-5; 26.1, 11; 101.2; Job 23.11) and from weighing (Job 31.6).[45] I may note finally that the act of protesting innocence is introduced or governed by verbs with a juridical reference, whose meaning and relevance I have already pointed out. I would like to give some examples:

43. Cf. Ps. 24.4.

44. Cf. A. Barucq, 'Péché et innocence dans les Psaumes bibliques et les textes religieux de l'Egypte du Nouvel-Empire', in *Etudes de critique et d'histoire religieuses* (FS L. Vaganay; Lyon, 1948), pp. 111-37; Ruppert, *Der leidende Gerechte*, pp. 22-27.

45. It might also be mentioned that an oath, with an imprecation called down upon oneself, is also an important form of a declaration of innocence: Ps. 7.4-6; Job 31.7-23. Cf. on the subject H. Blank, 'The Curse, Blasphemy, the Spell and the Oath', *HUCA* 23 (1950–51), pp. 91-92; J. Lévêque, 'Anamnèse et disculpation: la conscience du juste en Job 29–31', in *La Sagesse de l'Ancien Testament* (BETL, 51; Gembloux, 1979), pp. 240-42. For innocence proclaimed in a cultic context, cf. K. Galling, 'Der Beichtspiegel. Eine gattungsgeschichtliche Studie', *ZAW* 47 (1929), pp. 125-30.

1 Sam. 24.12	*da‘ ûr^{e}’ēh*[46] *kî*	*’ên b^{e}yādî rā‘â wāpeša‘*
Job 10.7	*‘al da‘t^{e}kā kî*	*lō’ ’eršā‘*
Job 13.18	*yāda‘tî kî*	*’^{a}nî ’eṣdāq*
Job 13.23	*hōdī‘ēnî*	*piš‘î w^{e}ḥaṭṭā’tî*
Job 6.24	*hābînû lî*	*ûmah šāgîtî*
Mic. 6.3	*‘^{a}nēh bî*[47]	*meh ‘āśîtî l^{e}kā...*
1 Sam. 12.3	*‘^{a}nû bî...*	*’et šôr mî lāqaḥtî...*

2.3. *The Protestation of Innocence Becomes an Accusation*[48]

The declaration of blamelessness of which I have supplied some striking examples from biblical texts should not be considered apart from the overall situation of the juridical controversy; actually it is not a statement of absolute innocence but the appropriate response to a particular accusation, which often takes the form of a mortal threat.[49]

The fact that a protestation of innocence can be transformed into an accusation against the accuser forms part of the very structure of a bilateral encounter. I would like to give just a few examples to illustrate the phenomenon. In the *rîb* between Saul and David, the latter sets out to vindicate himself, and his statements lead the former ‘to confess his guilt’ (1 Sam. 24.18, *ṣaddîq ’attâ mimmennî*; 1 Sam. 26.21, *ḥāṭā’tî*). In the dispute between Laban and Jacob, Laban begins the accusing, but Jacob’s defence becomes a *rîb* against him (Gen. 31.36).[50] Yet again, the Ammonite king’s claim against Jephtha (and Israel) is turned into a declaration of guilt during a defence speech (Judg. 11.27: *w^{e}’ānōkî lō’ ḥāṭā’tî lāk—w^{e}’attâ ‘ōśeh ’ittî rā‘â l^{e}hillāḥem bî*).[51]

46. We may recall that the pairing *yd‘–r’h* is used to indicate the *notitia criminis* (cf. p. 71); and in the imperative it is used as invitation to admission of guilt (p. 82).

47. Cf. Boecker: ‘Da hier eine Gerichtssituation vorliegt, wird man *‘nh b* besser von seiner konkreten juristischen Bedeutung her mit “lege Zeugnis ab gegen mich” übersetzen’ (*Redeformen*, p. 103). This interpretation of the text of Mic. 6.3, accepted in the recent commentary by H. Wolff (*Dodekapropheton*. IV. *Micha* [BK, 14/4; Neukirchen, 1982], p. 147), finds a confirmation in the *Targum* (*’aśhēd bî = testimonium perhibe in me*) and in the Syriac (*’śhdyny = produc mihi testes*).

48. The fact that a protestation of innocence may be transformed into an accusation had already been noted by Begrich, *Deuterojesaja*, p. 24.

49. P. Beauchamp, *Psaumes nuit et jour* (Paris, 1980), pp. 27-30.

50. Cf. C. Mabee, ‘Jacob and Laban. The Structure of Judicial Proceedings (Genesis XXXI 25-42)’, *VT* 30 (1980), pp. 202-205.

51. The reversal of perspective, from defence to counter-accusation (cf. Gen. 20.9; Job 7.20; Jer. 16.10) is signalled by certain syntactical indications which I have noted in the above outlines. Attention should first be directed to a *kî* which carries forward

This leads on to a consideration of those Scripture texts which form, so to speak, the equivalent of the prophetic *rîb*s (YHWH against Israel): I am referring to the 'lamentations', in which the people declare themselves innocent and level a sort of accusation against God himself.

A typical example of this may be found in Psalm 44. The purpose of the recognition of God's saving acts in the past (vv. 2-9) is to bring out the inconsistency of what God is doing in the present (cf., with a reverse meaning, Jer. 2.3–5.11); the frequent mention of the people's innocence (esp. vv. 18-19, 21-22) is turned into an accusation against God (vv. 13, 23), an accusation that takes the form of the question 'why'? (vv. 24, 25). Psalms 74, 80 and 90 must be viewed on the same level, and some 'individual' lamentations may also belong to this set (cf. Pss. 22; 42; 77; 81 etc.), in which a form of rebuke to God linked to a declaration of innocence appears more or less clearly.

The book of Job puts forward a dispute in which a 'just' man feels himself to be unreasonably accused and punished by God. I think the juridical metaphor should be taken seriously and it should be stated that if we are faced with a controversy, one of the two disputants is in the wrong: either 'the just man', who is not just but claims to be so (a solution that makes his declaration of innocence pharisaical), or God, who punishes arbitrarily[52] (this solution being inadmissible for Job's friends and for every reader faithful to the theology of God's absolute justice).[53]

With the book of Job as my starting point, I would like to offer a brief reflection on the meaning of a protestation of innocence against God himself.[54]

the declaration of innocence, especially in the interrogative form (cf. e.g. Gen. 20.9; 31.36; 40.15; 1 Sam. 20.1; 1 Kgs 18.9; Jer. 2.5; 37.18); this particle introduces a criticism of whoever is doing the accusing, and lays the accuser under accusation. Moreover, a declaration of innocence often brings about an explicit comparison between the different behaviour of the two disputants, a comparison that is expressed like this: *I* am innocent, *but you/he* (*w*^{e}*'attâ/hû'*) (cf. Judg. 11.27; 1 Sam. 24.12; Job 33.9-11; 34.5-6 etc.).

52. Cf. B. Halpern, 'Yahweh's Summary Justice in Job XIV 20', *VT* 28 (1978), pp. 472-74.

53. Cf. M.B. Dick, 'The Legal Metaphor in Job 31', *CBQ* 41 (1979), p. 40.

54. I may be allowed to point out that the Exile event did not just produce the tradition of public (and private) confessions in Israel, which I touched upon in the previous section. Although less noticeable, a tradition gained ground that could be referred to the theme of *passio iusti*, the suffering of the righteous (for discussion and

The 'why'? of the complaint and objection against suffering and death (always to the extent that it is considered 'unjust') is legitimate, indeed it is a very clearly juridical appeal addressed to God asking him to reveal his justice. This question demands a 'justification', and in this light it has a clearly accusatory force. But we must now ask ourselves, 'When is an accusation just? When does its juridical value hold good?' The answer may be that an accusation is authentic to the extent that it remains a *question* that appeals to an interpersonal relationship and engages it. In other words, the 'why?' of the accusation is *unjust* to the extent to which it makes itself absolute, becomes a self-justification that *judges* the other, without waiting for him to finish speaking; on the other hand, the 'why?' of an accusation is *just* to the extent that it is based on a desire that God should be God, the principle of life, and that this should be made manifest in the day-to-day history of humankind.

So if a declaration of innocence is to take on the hint of an accusation, it must structure itself like an accusation, putting itself forward as a question, as an invitation and stimulus to speech by the other; this holds good for a controversy with God and it holds good for controversies with one's fellow human beings. Only if a protestation of innocence does not condemn can it be called authentically just in the history of humankind.[55]

I would like to add to the above another line of reflection which concerns the problem of the book of Job. It is obvious that we are dealing with a controversy from the vocabulary and content of the different speeches. Now I have stated several times that it is the accusation that fixes the beginning of the controversy, and that this lasts as long as the speech for the prosecution. To understand the nature of the debate, it is necessary to know who began, and what was the nature of the speech addressed to the other party.

All this may seem irrelevant, but in my opinion it is of prime

bibliography on this point, see Ruppert, *Der leidende Gerechte*). The symbolic figure of the Suffering Servant was evoked at a somewhat later date in a sapiential fashion by Wis. 1.1–6.21. It seems to me that the reflection distilled into the book of Job should also be assigned to this sphere.

55. I would like to point out again that my argument is pitched at the juridical level of the bilateral controversy, and that it holds good to the extent that one can speak of interpersonal history. As we shall see, the structure of a judgment, in which the condemnation of the guilty is an essential device for pointing up of innocence, is something different.

importance. Is it really true that God accuses Job, that he has struck and punished Job, as he himself and his friends repeatedly state?[56] To be sure, if God does accuse Job, then the latter, who is innocent, is bound to counterattack, tottering on the brink of blasphemy. But God does not accuse Job, either in the prologue to the book, where on the contrary he praises his irreproachable behaviour (Job 1.8; 2.3), nor in the speech which he is called upon to give (38.1–41.26; cf. also 42.7-8) after Job's ultimate appeal (31.35-37). Rather, God says that it is up to Job to do the accusing (40.2); God 'defends' himself by calling to mind not his historical kindness (as in the prophetic *rîb*s) but the secret marvels of the origin of the world.

It is Job who accuses God; the reason for his quarrel is the suffering and death that press upon him. He interprets these signs as a punishment, as a juridical act which God ought to impose *only on someone who is unjust*. But is the sign of death subject to this interpretation alone?[57]

3. *'Doing' as the Locus of a Juridical Intervention*

Before tackling the subject of the conclusion of the *rîb*, I think it is opportune to note the juridical importance of the verb *'śh* (and its equivalent synonyms);[58] this allows a certain review of what has been covered so far, as well as a juridical placement of acts that ask for forgiveness or reconciliation.

To start with, the verb *'śh* is used to describe an unjust act, a crime, a misdeed; I have pointed out[59] the relevant verbs and nouns most frequently used in the Bible; here I would like to note that the syntagm *'śh*+ x (misdeed) is one of the most recurrent. With no claim to be exhaustive, I would like to put forward the following list to illustrate

56. Cf. E.M. Good, *Irony in the Old Testament* (Bible and Literature Series, 3; Sheffield, 2nd edn, 1982), p. 238.

57. Cf. *Filosofia e religione di fronte alla morte* (Archivio di filosofia; Padova, 1981); in this collection of articles I would like to point particularly to that of J. Ellul, 'Réflexions sur les contradictions de la Bible au sujet de la mort', pp. 315-30.

58. What interests me is to sketch in the complex series of Hebrew terms used to describe a human *act*: in this sense it is necessary to consider not just the noun *ma'^{a}śeh* and the verb *p'l*, but the human body (especially the hand) and the terminology that expresses the complex sphere of 'what is done', which is the juridical locus *par excellence*.

59. Chapter 2, section 1.1.

the abundance and variety of these expressions:

'śh n^{e}*bālâ* (Gen. 34.7; Deut. 22.21; Job. 7.15; 2 Sam. 13.12; Jer. 29.23 etc.);—*d*^{e}*bar hann*^{e}*bālâ* (Judg. 19.24); *zimmâ ûn*^{e}*bālâ* (Judg. 20.6);—*zimmâ* (Ezek. 16.43; 22.9; Hos. 6.9; Prov. 10.23; cf. Ezek. 23.48)—*m*^{e}*zimmâ* (Jer. 11.15; Ps. 37.7);—*tô'ēbâ* (Lev. 18.27; Deut. 12.31; 2 Kgs 21.11; Mal. 2.11 etc.);—*d*^{e}*bar hattō'ēbâ* (Jer. 44.4);—*ra'* (Num. 32.13; Deut. 4.25; Judg. 2.11; 1 Sam. 15.19; 2 Sam. 12.9; Isa. 56.2; Jer. 7.30; Ps. 51.6; Prov. 2.14; Qoh. 8.11 etc.);—*rā'â* (Gen. 26.29; Judg. 11.27; 1 Sam. 12.17; Jer. 2.13; Ezek. 20.43; Ps. 15.3; Neh. 13.27 etc.); —*reša'* (Prov. 16.12); *riš'â* (Mal. 3.15, 19);—*'âwel* (Lev. 19.15, 35; Deut. 25.16; Ezek. 18.26; 33.13, 15, 18);—*'āwen* (Isa. 32.6)—*r*^{e}*miyyâ* (Pss. 52.4; 101.7);—*šeqer* (2 Sam. 18.13; Jer. 6.13; 8.10);—*ša*^{a}*rurit* (Jer. 18.13);—*ne'āṣâ* (Neh. 9.18, 26);—*'iwwelet* (Prov. 14.17);—*ḥōnep* (Isa. 32.6); *ḥaṭṭā't* (Num. 5.7), and so on.

The use of the verb *'śh* (with or without a noun specifying the misdeed) is also widely attested in the course of the controversy procedure;[60] in the declaration of *accusation* (Gen. 20.9; Judg. 6.29; 1 Sam. 26.16; 27.11; Ps. 50.21; Neh. 5.9; 13.18 etc.), in an accusation in interrogative form (Gen. 12.18; 26.10; 31.26; 44.15; Exod. 1.18; Judg. 2.2; 8.1; 1 Sam. 2.23; 2 Sam. 16.10; Isa. 45.9; Job 9.12; Qoh. 8.4; Neh. 13.17 etc.), in an invitation to *admit one's guilt* (1 Sam. 12.17; Jer. 2.23 etc.), in the confession of one's wrongdoing (Josh. 7.20; 2 Sam. 24.10; Ps. 51.6; 1 Chron. 21.8 etc.) and in the *proclamation of one's innocence*, both in interrogative form (Num. 22.28; Judg. 8.2; 1 Sam. 20.1; 26.18; 29.8; Mic. 6.3 etc.) and in declarative form (Gen. 20.5; 40.15; Judg. 15.11; Ps. 7.4; Neh. 5.15).

These brief indications have the primary function of emphasizing a lexicographical fact: in Hebrew we have a verb (*'śh*), of itself very generic in meaning, which is specified both by the object to which it is immediately bound (something which is quite common even in modern languages) and by the position it holds in the context of a juridical procedure (something for which our arrangement supplies no easy analogy, where little by little the vocabulary has become technical jargon). Bearing this in mind allows us not only to be aware of the phenomenon when translating or commenting upon Bible texts, but allows us on reflection to give importance to the verb 'to do' even when its

60. The parable in Isa. 5.1-7 comes to mind, for example, entirely constructed as it is upon the repeated mention of the verb *'śh* (7 times) (cf. Alonso Schökel, *Profetas*, I, p. 133).

direct object is a term opposed to those listed above, one's referring to 'good', 'justice', 'mercy' and so on; and this is both as regards humanity and as concerns God himself.

This allows us to pass on to some overall reflections about matters juridical and their structural procedures. Law is primarily concerned with the events which are consequent upon the actions of free and responsible subjects; in other words, juridical activity has as its specific concern the visible, the external and the objective; it looks to *facts* and not to internal experiences.[61]

Law is well aware of how decisive will and consciousness are in human activity.[62] And nevertheless it pays great attention to 'doing', to the tangible and objective, in which the intentions of the essentially invisible and unknowable mind are revealed. Activity, behaviour, acts, and externally tangible events are the theatre in which justice and injustice are revealed.

Injustice is a fact, a visible datum, an act that belongs to tangible history. Overcoming it starts with a verbal confrontation (a controversy), a confrontation that culminates in a confession of guilt on the part of the criminal. But that is not enough for the sphere of law; it is indeed necessary for internal change, a confession of one's misdeed is indeed required; but justice demands that something 'be done', an act of goodness as opposed to the act of evil that has been performed. Justice requires that it should be seen to be re-established in order to be a meaningful dimension of historical truth.

An act of good is required of the criminal and also of the injured party (who is bringing the accusation): on the one hand a journey of conversion taking the form of penance and reparation; on the other hand a journey of reconciliation that takes the 'sacramental' form of acts of peace and communion.

It is along these lines that we go on to examine the actions that signify the end of controversy.

61. Cf. Antolisei, *Manuale di diritto penale*, pp. 170-73.

62. Cf. Antolisei, *Manuale di diritto penale*, pp. 253-342, where the 'subjective' element necessary for the definition of a crime is dealt with at length. Cf. also what I have written in this chapter, section 1.5.

Chapter 4

THE RECONCILIATION

By way of introduction to the subject matter of this chapter, I would like to make some general observations about the meaning and concluding forms of the juridical dispute.

A controversy may be compared to a crisis in interpersonal relations, on account of the essentially fleeting nature of the confrontation. If in fact a *rîb* is a speech that lets fly a threat and so shows up a disagreement, its aim is to permit justice, i.e. agreement between the parties within a framework that expresses the enduring value of law.

The desire for an end to the *rîb* comes out clearly in the speeches made by Job during the debate in which he is both protagonist and victim. He finds himself struggling on two fronts: the first and most fundamental is the one on which God appears as an aggressor who intervenes silently with punishing force and thereby seems implicitly to accuse a 'man of uprightness and integrity'; the second is that of the verbal controversy which sets him against the friends who have come to console him and whose concern is to make clear the accusatory meaning of God's punishment, inviting Job in different ways to accept a degree of responsibility for sinfulness. All the players in this drama search one after another for a conclusion; for his part, Job feels crushed by the absurd situation in which he finds himself; he earnestly desires that the *rîb* against him should come to an end, but he equally earnestly desires that it should not end in the manner suggested to him by his friends; and, faced with a lack of other options, he is prepared to accept his own death (Job 6.8-11; 7.21; 10.18-22; 13.14-16; 17.11-16; 30.19), not as the real end of the dispute but as a disclosure of the radical problem of his experience and as a final appeal for the utterance of a truth that he cannot otherwise obtain (Job 16.18-22; 19.25-27).

This brief illustration shows that although a dispute strives for a conclusion it reaches it only when there is agreement in a statement that defines justice in accordance with truth; if there is a lack of enough wisdom to make or accept that statement, if a deliberate lie glosses over interior refusal, if above all some kind of prevarication occurs and puts an end to the *rîb*, then the dispute drags on; even though apparently finished, it will rise again, even from the ashes, to make felt its unstoppable desire for real justice, the only possibility of life for an individual with a soul.

When we get down to the particular ways in which the disputants reach agreement, we meet first *a recourse to tribunal*. This way, which will supply the subject matter for Part II of my study, can be considered a genuine conclusion to the controversy only to the extent to which both parties—given that reasons for disagreement persist—unanimously decide[1] to submit their case to a single verdict, and, moreover, only to the extent that the verdict looks to both parties like incontrovertible justice.[2] Nevertheless, as we shall see, this juridical method, which *imposes* justice in a coercive way by condemning one of the two disputants, remains structurally imperfect. Paradoxically, judgment is the institution that most deeply reveals the refusal (often unconscious) of one party to acknowledge the truth; as such, the real 'just person'[3] has recourse to it only as a 'last-ditch' solution.

The second way in which a controversy can end is war, or, in more general terms, *a physical clash*, in which weapons 'have their say'. This might look like a barbaric and prejuridical procedure, but the constant recourse to it in the biblical and extra-biblical world, from ancient times to the present day, compels more careful consideration. If, as we may recall, the dispute *has* to end, but on the other hand the mediation of an arbitrator turns out to be impossible, how else is agreement to be reached? We may observe that at least one of the parties cannot live if things are left as they are; the situation is materially or morally intolerable; on the other hand, one often cannot call upon a judge, either because there is nobody with binding power over that case, or because both disputants do not recognize the jurisdiction of an official authority, or

1. The decision to submit one's case to judgment by a tribunal may be laid down—by a sort of general consensus—by customary practice or the laws of the State.

2. If one party considers itself defrauded of its rights, the controversy will have a legal conclusion, but in substance will remain unresolved.

3. The phrase 'the real just person' is intended to describe those in society who pursue exclusively just ends. It is obvious that I mean to apply this title pre-eminently to God, who in any case possesses all the means to carry through his intentions.

because recourse to judgment has in the past turned out to be unsatisfactory and therefore has not set minds at rest, or because the urgency of doing justice cannot abide the rules of procedure foreseen by the penal code, and so on.

I have already referred to the various motives that do lead, almost inevitably, to a recourse to force; they demonstrate, on the one hand, that even yet the problem has not been overcome, and on the other hand that we are getting into an ambiguous area that is intrinsically bound to the use of force.

As a particular example let us take war, in an attempt to see how it expresses and resolves a legal controversy. It is to be supposed that whoever declares the war considers it to be just and indispensable; but a clash of arms is (more or less directly) *imposed* on the opposing side, which is necessarily drawn into that arena, and whose room for manoeuvre is limited to 'the choice of weapons'. This creates a puzzle as to the perspective from which some sort of agreement can be reached by such means. The continuance of hostilities even runs the risk that one of the disputants will be destroyed; the enemy's rout is indeed the sign of a perfectly successful war. Thus one's adversary has to fight to the death in order to affirm mutual respect for the absolute value of life. And when in the end one party is compelled to admit the other's supremacy, an armistice is reached, and this is the other side of surrender: the victor agrees not to 'hit a man when he's down', provided that the conquered admits defeat and submits to the conditions which are *imposed* on him. Certainly the dispute is over, but the agreement is so 'un-wanted' by the conquered that it is fair to ask whether the controversy has really finished.

This type of conclusion to the *rîb* likewise turns out to be the refusal by one (or both) parties to recognize truth and justice, and is the violent and dramatic version of judgment in a law court. It is tolerable to the just person as an extreme case of a distorted human encounter, which shows up (one's own) guilt in the search for justice.

The third form of conclusion for a *rîb* is *reconciliation.* Its peculiarity lies in the fact that it does not have recourse to a court of appeal (such as a tribunal) other than the disputants, nor does it put its trust exclusively in force in order to uphold the law (as in war); it is a complex act in which both disputants are involved—each uniquely—with the intention of re-establishing justice without constraints.[4]

4. After stating that the system of self-defence (*self-help*) gradually becomes

The essential element, the one that makes it completely different from the others, the 'chief' element, the one that makes it possible, is provided by the confession of guilt by the party that is in the wrong. The verbal agreement arrived at, in which both accuser and accused can recognize themselves, is the basis of truth which allows for a mechanism of perfect justice.

Beginning with the confession of guilt, we shall investigate the structure of the juridical act of reconciliation. My chapter falls into three parts, which follow the successive acts of the peaceful conclusion of a *rîb*: the plea for pardon (by the guilty); the pardon granted (by the innocent accuser); and the peace treaty (signed by both).

1. *The Plea for Pardon*

The confession of guilt (demanded by the accuser and conceded by the guilty), does not just have the function of bearing witness to the truth championed by the accuser, thus declaring that the juridical procedure under way is motivated 'in accordance with justice'. What guilty parties seek is the suspension of the threat that hangs over them, which means basically the possibility of an agreement that guarantees them safety and respect. In other words, the confession of guilt is closely linked to a plea for life.

At this point in the controversy, it is *the guilty as accused who takes the initiative*, struggling for the needed clemency. We can gather under two main headings the set of actions of which the accused may be the

dangerous to the security and existence of the State (cf. also E. Neufeld, 'Self-Help in Ancient Hebrew Law', *RIDA* [3rd Ser.] 5 [1958], pp. 291-98), B. Cohen shows how disputes can reasonably be concluded by conciliation and arbitration. With reference to conciliation he writes, 'By conciliation we mean a mode of pacific settlement of litigation without recourse to a third party, in contrast to arbitration, which denotes the settlement of dispute by referring the matter at issue to a selected person or persons for judgement. Conciliation therefore is similar to compromise, i.e. a coming to terms, or an arrangement of a dispute by concessions on both sides. Such settlement has the force equal to the authority of a thing adjudged in the civil law, and is also sustained in the common law in accordance with the maxim *Interest reipublicae ut sit finis litium*' (*Jewish and Roman Law: A Comparative Study*, II [New York, 1966], pp. 615-16). I would like to add that besides conciliation (compromise, deal, accommodation), there also exists *reconciliation* in which the litigants, though faced with a particular wrong attributed to one party, arrive at a peaceful conclusion to their controversy.

protagonist: the verbal request for pardon, and the gestures that accompany or follow them.

1.1. *The Verbal Plea*

In order to illustrate, by way of a concrete example, the vocabulary and function of the request for pardon, let us call to mind the story told in 1 Sam. 25.5.[5]

David, who has withdrawn to the wilderness, sends some of his men with peaceable intentions to the rich landowner Nabal in hopes of a gift at the propitious time of sheep-shearing. Not only does Nabal refuse to hand over any of his goods, but he insults David's messengers (vv. 10-11); this excites a reaction from David, who commits himself (even with an oath: vv. 22, 34) to doing justice (cf. vv. 31, 33) with the sword.

The situation created in this way is typical of the controversy: David has done nothing wrong[6] (vv. 7-8, 15-16, 21), and he has been returned evil for good (v. 21) in the form of welcome refused and insult (vv. 10, 14, 39). With the exception of the foolish Nabal, who has no idea what is going on, everybody is agreed as to who is innocent and who is guilty: not just David and his men, who are on the same side (vv. 21-22), but even Nabal's servants (vv. 15-17), Abigail (v. 25) and God himself (v. 39). The threat that hangs over the house of the guilty is no bluff, even before it is carried out, therefore there is an urgent need to take steps (v. 17).

It is at this point that Abigail takes the initiative in a move that turns out well. The important thing to emphasize is that the centrepiece of Abigail's action is a *word* (v. 24: *'mr; dibrê 'ᵃmātekā*), which on the one hand admits the wrong and on the other hand leads into an insistent and reasoned request for pardon (particularly vv. 25, 28, 31). It is significant moreover that this move is not made by the guilty Nabal but by someone else who shoulders another's guilt (v. 24) and begs pardon for it (v. 28).

5. Regarding 1 Samuel 25, cf. J.D. Levenson, '1 Samuel 25 as Literature and as History', *CBQ* 40 (1978), pp. 11-28; D.M. Gunn, *The Fate of King Saul* (Sheffield, 1980), pp. 96-102; R.P. Gordon, 'David's Rise and Saul's Demise, Narrative Analogy in 1 Sam. 24–26', *TynBul* 31 (1980), pp. 37-64.

6. The story (which is written from David's point of view) affords no criticism of the demand made upon Nabal; from an objective point of view, it might be asked whether it was not a question of a kind of extortion and the arbitrary imposition of protection money.

1.1.1. *The Hebrew Lexicon of Supplication and Intercession.* A *word* which is a confession and a plea halts the continuation of the controversy. In the example recalled above, as in other similar accounts, this very decisive act is introduced by a generalized terminology.[7] In the *rîbs* begun by God against his people (or in general against any guilty party), the importance of this 'word' is underlined by a specific lexicon, which, although belonging to the wider semantic field of the prayer, has a place and a specific function in the juridical dynamic we are examining: I am alluding to the concepts of 'supplication' and 'intercession', for which I would like to point out the most recurrent Hebrew terminology.[8]

The verb *pll* (*Hitp*)[9] is the most frequently used; it takes *l^e^* or *'el*, (which indicate the person or thing to whom/which the supplication is addressed), and with *ba'ad*[10] or *'al*[11] (which indicate for whom/what the plea is made); the latter prepositions are generally the grammatical indication of the 'intercession'.

The verb *'tr* (*'el/l^e^*; and *ba'ad*) expresses a prayer made in times of

7. When I speak of 'generalized' terminology I mean that it is not specialized into meaning something in opposition to other terms: the verb *'mr*, for example, is a generalized term for the introduction of prayers asking for pardon (cf. also 2 Sam. 19.20; 19.27); but once the relationship between 'saying' and 'requesting' has been grasped, it can be seen how it has a precise and specific function.

8. The terminology of the prayer extends to other terms besides the root *pll*; and this (in common with its synonyms) does not just refer to prayers that ask pardon. It is the context that decides the function of a particular supplication and its internal structure. This also holds good for the lexicon of which we shall speak below. In this context cf. D.R. Ap-Thomas, 'Notes on some Terms Relating to Prayers', *VT* 6 (1956), pp. 226-41; Giraudo, *La struttura letteraria*, pp. 98, 101.

9. Cf. J.F.A. Sawyer, 'Types of Prayer in the Old Testament. Some Semantic Observations on *Hitpallel, Hithannen*, etc.', *Semitics* 7 (1980), pp. 131-43.

10. The preposition *ba'ad* is used with various verbs and phrases to indicate an intercessory prayer, not necessarily a 'penitential' one (that is, not necessarily linked to a confession of guilt); with the verb *pll* (*Hitp*): Gen. 20.7; Num. 21.7; Deut. 9.20; 1 Sam. 7.5; 12.19, 23; 1 Kgs 13.6; Jer. 7.16; 11.4; 14.11; 29.7; 37.3; 42.2, 20; Ps. 72.15; Job 42.10; *nś' t^e^pillâ*: 2 Kgs 19.4 = Isa. 37.4; *'tr* (*Hi*): Exod. 8.24; *z'q*: 1 Sam. 7.9; *bqš* (*Pi*) (with object: God): 2 Sam. 12.16; *drš* (with object: God): 2 Kgs 22.13; Jer. 21.2; 2 Chron. 34.21; *kpr* (*Pi*): Exod. 32.30 (on this latter text, cf. S. Lyonnet, 'Expiation et intercession. A propos d'une traduction de Saint Jérôme', *Bib* 40 [1959], pp. 885-901); and with yet more phrases: Ezek. 22.30; Job 6.22; 42.8.

11. The preposition *'al*, in combination with *pll* (*Hitp*) is a substitute for *'el* in 1 Sam. 1.10; in general it indicates the reason for the prayer in Ps. 32.6 and 2 Chron. 32.20; it means 'on behalf of' (intercession) in Job 42.8; Neh. 1.6; 2 Chron. 30.18.

calamity, sometimes by those who explicitly recognize themselves guilty: in the *Qal* (Exod. 8.26; 10.18; Job 33.26) and in the *Hiphil* (Exod. 8.4, 5, 24, 25; 9.28; 10.17; Job 22.27) it means 'to pray'; in the *Niphal* (Isa. 19.22; 2 Chron. 33.13, 19) the verb is used to express the 'granting'.

A more specific case appears to be the verb *ḥnn* (*Hitp*), used for the plea for clemency by someone who has been or feels condemned (cf. Est. 4.8; 8.3); sometimes there is an explicit relationship with the prayer of the sinner experiencing the consequences of guilt (cf. 1 Kgs 8.33, 47; Job 8.5; 9.15).

The nouns *tᵉpillâ* (1 Kgs 8.49; 2 Kgs 20.5; Isa. 1.15; Dan. 19.3, 17, 21; Neh. 1.6, 11 etc.), *rinnâ* (Jer. 7.16; 11.14; 14.12; Ps. 106.44), *tᵉḥinnâ* (1 Kgs 8.38, 49; Jer. 36.7; 37.20; Dan. 9.20) and *taḥᵃnûnîm* (Dan. 9.3, 17, 18; 2 Chron. 6.21) form part of the same paradigmatic series.

1.1.2. *The Link between Confession and Supplication.*[12] We have seen above[13] how *ydh* (*Hitp*) is the technical term for expressing a confession of sin in the context of a penitential liturgy; well, in some of these great prayers this verb is preceded by *pll* (*Hitp*) (Ezra 10.1; Neh. 1.6; Dan. 9.4, 20). This is one way of demonstrating the link between confession and request.

This link is further confirmed by the fact that verbs of supplication are frequently juxtaposed to an explicit confession of guilt. I would like to give just a few examples, emphasizing again how the punishment imposed or threatened stimulates and grounds the supplication:

Num. 21.7: 'The people came to Moses and said, "We have sinned because we have spoken against the Lord and against you; beg (*pll*) the Lord to take away these serpents from us."'

1 Kgs 8.47-48: 'If in the land of their exile they come to themselves and repent, and entreat (*ḥnn*) you saying, "We have sinned, we have acted perversely and wickedly", and if they turn again to you...and pray (*pll*) to you...'

12. With reference both to the great post-exilic penitential prayers and to numerous other passages in which there is a confession of sin, M. Gilbert says that the 'structure' *aveu-prière*, often emphasized by the particle *wᵉ'attâ*, is typical ('La place de la Loi dans la prière de Néhemie 9', in *De la Tôrah au Messie* [FS H. Cazelles; Paris, 1981], pp. 307-16). The close link between confession and request for pardon is particularly clear in Ps. 51; cf. R. Dalglish, *Psalm Fifty-One in the Light of Ancient Near Eastern Patternism* (Leiden, 1962), pp. 103-72.

13. Cf. ch. 2, section 1.1.1.

1 Sam. 12.19: ‘The whole people said to Samuel: “Plead (*pll*) for your servants with the Lord that we may not die, for we have added to all our sins this evil of asking to have a king”’.

Some examples of the same structure can be seen in Exod. 9.28; 19.17; 1 Sam. 7.3-6; 32.5-6; Lam. 3.41-42.

The link between confession of guilt and supplication for forgiveness becomes very obvious upon examination of the supplications themselves. The plea made by/on behalf of whoever is guilty is in essence made up of two elements: (1) the declaration of one’s guilt, expressed in ‘indicative’ form; (2) an explicit request to be forgiven, which takes the imperative form. The relationship between the two elements is often underscored by a particle (the adverb *w^{e}‘attâ* or the conjunction *kî*)[14] which points up the logical connection between confession and request.

I would like to give some examples to show the regularity of the phenomenon over the variety of expressions used:

1 Sam. 25.24	(1) *bî ’^{a}nî ’^{a}dōnî he‘āwōn…*
25	(2) *’al nā’ yāśîm ’^{a}dōnî ’et libbô ’el ’îš habb^{e}liyya‘al hazzeh*
Exod. 10.16	(1) *ḥāṭā’tî l^{e}yhwh ’^{e}lōhêkem w^{e}lākem*
17	(2) ***w^{e}‘attâ*** *śā’ nā’ ḥaṭṭā’tî*
1 Sam. 15.24	(1) *ḥāṭā’tî …*
25	(2) ***w^{e}‘attâ*** *śā’ nā’ ’et ḥaṭṭā’tî*
2 Sam. 24.10	(1) *ḥāṭā’tî m^{e}’ōd ’^{a}šer ‘āśîtî*
	(2) ***w^{e}‘attâ*** *yhwh ha‘^{a}ber nā’ ’et ‘^{a}wōn ‘abd^{e}kā*
2 Sam. 19.20	(2) *’al yaḥ^{a}šob lî ’^{a}dōnî ‘āwōn…*
21	(1) ***kî*** *yāda‘ ‘abd^{e}kā kî ’^{a}nî ḥāṭā’tî*
Ps. 41.5	(2) *yhwh ḥonnēnî r^{e}pā’â napšî*
	(1) ***kî*** *ḥāṭā’tî lāk*
Ps. 51.3-4	(2) *ḥonnēnî ’^{e}lōhîm k^{e}ḥasdekā…*
5-6	(1) ***kî*** *p^{e}šā‘ay ’^{a}nî ’ēdā‘…*[15]

14. The texts quoted show the different ways in which *w^{e}‘attâ* and *kî* link the confession and request:

(a) confession	+	*w^{e}‘attâ*: request for pardon
(b) request for pardon	+	*kî*: confession.

15. Other texts link the indicative of the confession of guilt to the imperative of the request where this asks in more general terms for liberation from a threat or punishment (2 Kgs 18.14; Jer. 14.20-21; 1 Sam. 12.10; Judg. 10.15 etc.). On the other

1.1.3. *The Function and Effectiveness of the Request for Pardon.* By writing about the confession of guilt I have tried to show how this juridically important event, in the context of a controversy, is the expression of a declaration of truth jointly recognized as such by the disputants. It is the dynamic of this truth that is now played out, progressively bringing to light the hidden intentions revealed by a juridical dispute.

We have just seen how the confession of guilt is linked to the request for pardon; the first, in the indicative, makes known the truth; the second, in the imperative, looks forward to what is to be done in the future in such a way that the recognition of an 'evil' is a sensible one and reveals its positive side. Between a confession and the supplication asking forgiveness is a logical connection whose juridical significance I would like to clarify.

a. *The Imperative of the Request.* Whoever makes the request puts it as an imperative. It is certainly not a question of an 'order', which is based on the legitimate authority of someone who embodies the law; those who confess to being in the wrong explicitly renounce that they as persons should be the principle of the other's action (otherwise a just punishment should be the only outcome). The basis for the imperative contained in the supplication lies in the accuser, who has been recognized as 'just'; as it is, the request brings out the truth and justice that were implicit in the juridical action undertaken by the accuser.

This may seem paradoxical, but again it is a question of truth and justice (cf. Dan. 9.16; Ezra 9.15; Bar. 2.19), even though—usually—one is led to believe that other 'virtues' and other principles come into forgiveness. I on the other hand believe that the request for pardon has the function of making explicit the intention of the just action undertaken by the accuser.

Nobody questions the justness of the accusation but the supplication for pardon reveals whether the accuser was motivated by hate in the righting of wrong, whether the 'justice' done was purely external with no desire for a living relationship with the other party.[16] In that case the

hand, there is a striking relationship between the two indicatives in Lam. 3.42:

naḥnû pāšaʿnû ûmārînû
ʾattâ lōʾ sālāḥtā.

16. As is well known, Scripture understands the act of *pardon* extended by the

certainty of being in the right will lead the one who is objectively innocent to be pitiless towards the guilty party; it will lead one to 'justify oneself' to the hilt through an exemplary sentence on the criminal, to the point of wanting to do away with the guilty so as to appear the only just person fit to live. Hate cloaks itself in justice in order to be irreproachable, and makes use of the other's guilt to unleash the power of death, but the confession of guilt and request for pardon unmask it, because they denounce it as a justice that does not share the aims of justice.

Let us now consider the opposite attitude: if the accuser's action was motivated by love, that is, by desire for the other's good and communion in mutual truth, then when one is faced with a declaration that affirms this truth and with a request to re-establish communion, one can reveal a forgiving side without ambiguity. To pardon without bringing an accusation is to behave like an accomplice in evil; to pardon without a confession of guilt is to promote a relationship that does not take cognisance of the truth; and if one pardons without a request being made, the communion would be imperfect, because not sought by both parties.

b. *Motives for the Request for Pardon*. In my study I have presented the supplication for pardon in a schematic way, abstracting it not only from its context but also from the network of other words that accompany and underpin it. This was done not because the latter are less important, but because it is less easy to organize them into a paradigm, one that

offended party as a manifestation of love (Pss. 51.3; 103.8-14; Dan. 9.9; Neh. 9.32 etc.). It is therefore a reasonable deduction that the *refusal of pardon*—when all the necessary conditions are present—constitutes the sign of a mind possessed by *hate*, that is, by a desire for the other's death.

It should be borne in mind moreover that the root *śn'* (to hate), which is frequently used to describe the wicked persecutor *of the just* (= unjust hate: Gen. 37.4-8; Pss. 25.19; 34.22; 35.19; 38.20-21; 69.5; 109.3 etc.), is also used in a positive sense when referring to an action directed against *an evildoer* (= just hate: said of God: Jer. 12.8; Pss. 5.6-7; 11.5; Prov. 6.16-19; said of man: Pss. 119.113; 139.21-22; Prov. 13.5): in the latter case, hate expresses non-connivance with evil and a desire to do justice.

It seems to me that the *love* which pardons the *evildoer* is precisely formulated in the Old Testament only with reference to God; in the Christian message, the fulfilment of Old Testament logic, it is also put before humankind as the achievement of perfect justice (Mt. 5.20-26, 43-48).

might be entitled 'motives for the request'. Whereas the request for pardon has a substantially identical literary form in varied situations, its motives on the contrary display a variety of subject-matter and expression which are consistent with the many-sided characteristics of the disputants and their histories.

By the application of ruthless logic, however, we may try to organize the motives into two main groups, bearing particularly in mind those texts in which the disputants are God and the people of Israel, a reason being that they are the ones in which the request for pardon is most frequent and copiously motivated. The phrase *w*^{e}*'attâ*, which often introduces a request for pardon, allows us, because of its temporal nuance, to turn our attention to motives that are located in the past and in the future.

The supplicant interposes an account of the history that lies between the two parties who now find themselves in dispute; this calling to mind of the past has the effect of laying bare the nature of each as revealed in the acts each has committed. With regard to the innocent partner, this shows that it is characteristic of that person to want a relationship and to remain committed, without yielding, to upholding it. By narrating the history of the 'covenant', the guilty party tells the other, who is 'just', that being faithful to what the other has initiated belongs to the latter's own structure; there would, for example, be a contradiction in God's justice if by his decisions he failed to do what he has desired and promoted as an expression of his nature as a spiritual being.

Turning now to the future, the guilty party looks forward to a situation in which, on account of the pardon granted, a perfect recognition will be possible of the nature of the 'just party', a recognition expressed in praise (Pss. 51.16-17; 106.47). This praise is not just a compliment that offers superficial gratification to the party that has 'done well'; it expresses on the one hand the joyful condition of life in the one who is the offender, pointing up the offender's removal from a condition of death; for the one who is innocent, on the other hand, it is the bringing about of that communion in which lies perfect happiness. But if pardon is not granted, what will the future be like? Dust, Sheol and Death may be the signs of the terrible destructive power of evil (cf. 2 Sam. 14.14), but life, which is expressed in a hymn of praise, will not be manifested or encouraged for anybody (cf. Isa. 38.18; Pss. 6.6; 30.10; 88.11-13).[17]

17. Cf. C. Westermann, *Das Loben Gottes in den Psalmen* (Göttingen, 1954), pp. 116-20.

An important point in this regard is the reference that the guilty accused makes to 'witnesses' of the juridical dispute under way; I am referring in particular to the mention of what others will say, the nations, those who have seen the blossoming of the relationship between the two partners, who have been there during their controversy and will be spectators at its conclusion. We have seen how during the *rîb* the accuser makes reference to referee-witnesses who are called upon to back up and guarantee the objectivity of the accuser's words and juridical action (and among these witnesses—in the controversies between YHWH and his people—are sometimes mentioned the pagan nations).[18] Now, at the moment of the request for pardon, these same witnesses become an argument on behalf of the supplicant, since they will recognize the justice of God and the meaning of the history of his relationship with the people of Israel only to the extent that they perceive life signs superior to the logic of death foreseen by an exclusive consideration of guilt (Exod. 32.12; Num. 14.13-16; Deut. 19.28; cf. also Deut. 32.27; Ezek. 20.9).

To speak of motives means that the speaker brings in suitable arguments to demonstrate the truth of his or her assumption, in such a way as to convince the other of the truth of what is being stated. It is not, therefore, so much a question of rhetorical ability of base and self-serving craftiness, but of a speech full of wisdom and a sense of humaneness; at the end of the day a judgment has to be made as to where truth and an authentic sense of justice lies.

The accuser's *rîb* brought into play a series of reasons to convince the other that the inevitable prospect was a just punishment; the supplication for pardon seeks reason for the opposite solution, which is that of just clemency. Whereas the accusation concerns the criminal, the request for pardon concerns the innocent (Num. 14.9; Ps. 51.3; Neh. 9.32; 2 Chron. 30.18 etc.) and tends to summarize all the arguments into a simple: forgive because you are just, forgive for the sake of your name, forgive because you are you (cf. Isa. 43.25), so that the justice which belongs to your being may be fully carried out (Jer. 14.7,21; Pss. 25.11; 79.9; Dan. 9.19).

Granted, supplicants do sometimes draw attention to themselves, alleging attenuating circumstances: the criminal is a fool, who has acted without knowing what he or she was doing (Num. 12.11; 1 Sam. 25.25; 26.21; Ps. 32.6 etc.). These attenuating circumstances require delicate

18. Cf. ch. 2, section 2.5.

handling, and represent a double-edged weapon: they can in fact make the criminal seem even more dramatically bound up with the crime, making the guilty look like an animal (Ps. 32.9; cf. Isa. 1.3; Jer. 2.23; Pss. 49.21; 73.22), whose only behaviour principle is spontaneous instinct which—if wicked—has no hope of correction. Although stupidity does become a motive for pardon to the extent that—recognized as such—it appeals to the just one (Jon. 4.11) who ought to demonstrate wisdom in such a situation, yet the risk of folly is that it will drag the innocent into its spiral of senseless destruction (1 Sam. 25.31).

1.1.4. *The Intercession.*[19] Among the means used to convince the innocent to grant pardon, *intercession* plays a special part. The peculiarity of this form of supplication lies in its being made on behalf of the guilty by someone who is not guilty. Intercession is the more effective the more it takes the criminal's part, shouldering the guilt and asserting total solidarity with the person and fate of the guilty. From this point of view, an intercession means that pardon has already been granted by one human being; in fact there could not be a prayer of solidarity without a willingness to overcome the barrier of guilt. The intercessor is well aware that a crime has been committed, and is in no way conniving at it; it is worth remembering in this context that the great intercessors of biblical tradition were indeed representatives for the prosecution: from Moses—both in his confrontations with Pharaoh (Exod. 8.4; 9.28-29; 10.17-18) and with the people of Israel (Exod. 32.11-14; 30-32; Num. 14.13-19; 21.7; Deut. 9.25-29)—to Samuel (1 Sam. 12.23; Jer. 15.1) and the prophets (Jer. 7.16; 11.14; 14.11; Amos 7.2, 5),[20] who were sent to denounce sin and threaten appropriate retribution. But if the guilty manages by his request, sometimes only implicit, to bring about a change of function by the accuser in the dynamic of the *rîb* so that the accuser no longer speaks *against* but *on behalf of* the guilty, putting across the defence, then it is a reasonable assumption that nobody will speak up to accuse

19. On the subject of the intercession, cf. N. Johansson, *Parakletoi* (Lund, 1940), pp. 3-62; H. Reventlow, *Liturgie und prophetisches Ich bei Jeremia* (Gütersloh, 1963), pp. 140-205; A.B. Rhodes, 'Israel's Prophets as Intercessors', in *Scripture in History and Theology* (FS J.C. Rylaarsdam; Pittsburgh, 1977), pp. 107-28; E. Jacob, 'Prophètes et Intercesseurs', in *De la Tôrah*, pp. 205-17; S.E. Balentine, 'The Prophet as Intercessor: A Reassessment', *JBL* 103 (1984), pp. 161-73.

20. Cf. W. Brueggemann, 'Amos' Intercessory Formula', *VT* 19 (1969), pp. 385-99.

the guilty, who will thus be able to experience the joy of pardon.

The twofold function of the same character (the intercessor) should not be a cause for surprise, since the change is in accordance with that of the accused as well, and carries the logic exhibited in the course of the juridical procedure of the controversy. The fact that this twofold juridical form (accusation = speech against; and intercession = speech on behalf of) is embodied in the same person makes this person the *mediator* of the reconciliation and of the covenant that succeeds it.[21] More precisely still, it may be stated that this single person is already the sign of a communion between guilty and innocent, a sign of that impossible unity which we call reconciliation. The intercessor is in fact a concrete demonstration of the fact that the just can truly make out of justice a principle of salvation and justification for every human being, bringing about a life-giving relationship that has overcome the logic of death.[22]

1.2. *The Gestural Plea*

We saw in the previous section the place and structure of the system of words that ask for pardon; now we shall look at the parallel and complementary system that uses the *body* of the admittedly guilty person.

Going back to the story in 1 Samuel 25, it is easy for us to note that Abigail's prayer is made in an external posture of great humility: 'As soon as Abigail saw David she quickly dismounted from the donkey and, falling on her face before David, bowed down to the ground. *She fell at his feet and said...*' (vv. 23-24). This obviously corresponds to her internal disposition and words, which admit guilt and appeal for clemency.

What is more, Abigail took the trouble to take with her 'two hundred loaves, two skins of wine, five dressed sheep, five measures of parched grain, a hundred bunches of raisins and two hundred cakes of figs' (v. 18), which she now in her plea offered to David and his men as a gift (v. 27). The abundance and variety of the offerings show that they are

21. A full treatment of the concept of 'mediator' in the Old Testament is to be found in J. Scharbert, *Heilsmittler im Alten Testament und im Alten Orient* (QDisp, 23/24; Freiburg, 1964).

22. When I talk about the logic of death I am referring to the fact that a crime, being an act of violence, does not just put a sign of death on reality but also makes a juridical appeal for a 'proportionate' act of punishment. The accuser who stands outside the perspective of reconciliation is prosecuting a kind of justice that paradoxically tries to deny this sign of death by means of another corresponding to the first one, as though nothing could come out of evil (and death) except more evil (and death).

not just a courtesy gesture: in them can be read her concern to make up for the foolish and miserly action of Nabal, and her willingness to demonstrate a real readiness for friendship. David in fact *accepted* what she had brought and said, 'Go home in peace' (v. 35). David's hand lets go of his sword in order to receive from Abigail her offering of reconciliation, and the controversy ends peacefully.[23]

In the *rîbs* that take place between people and in those that involve God and Israel, we may observe at the moment of the request for pardon a complex series of gestures that take in the supplicant's whole body. I would now like briefly to list and describe these externals accompanying the plea, deferring until the end of the section a consideration of their overall meaning and juridical function.

1.2.1. *Prostration.*[24] One of the commonest acts signifying a request for pardon is that of throwing oneself to the ground at the feet of the one from whom pardon is being asked. As an action declaring personal unworthiness (guilt) it is the *act of supplication* par excellence, to the extent that it expresses submission to the decision made by the other party.

Different Hebrew terms are used to describe substantially the same action:

npl	1 Sam. 25.23	*'al pāneyhā*
	24	*'al raglāyw*
	2 Sam. 19.19	*lipnê hammelek*
	Gen. 44.14	*l^epānāyw 'ārṣâ*
	50.18	*l^epānāyw*
	cf. also in the *Hitp*	
	Deut. 9.25	*lipnê yhwh*

23. The first hint of a peaceful conclusion to the controversy may be detected in David's words, 'Go home in peace; see, I have listened to you and granted your request' (1 Sam. 25.35). The definitive reconciliation is to be seen later in the marriage of David to Abigail, after the death of Nabal (vv. 39-42).

24. I would like to bring up once more a question of method. When I say that prostration (and its associated vocabulary) functions as an act of request for pardon, I do not at all mean that it *always* has this meaning. What concerns me is to show how this act (which has the general meaning of submission, respect, reverence) takes on—by its placement in the structure we are examining—a specific function and meaning. This also holds good for the other 'penitential' gestures and the lexicon by which they are expressed.

qdd	Exod. 34.8	*'ārṣâ*
	Num. 22.31	
kr'	Ezra 9.5	*'al birkay*
ḥwh (Eštaf)[25]	1 Sam. 25.23	
	Exod. 34.8	
	Neh. 9.3	
	Num. 22.31	*lᵉ'appāyw*
kpp (Ni)	Mic. 6.6	
	Qal:	
	Isa. 58.5	
	cf. also Pss. 145.14; 146.8	

1.2.2. *Weeping, Fasting, Penitential Attire, Dust and Ashes.*[26] I would like to bring together in this one section various manifestations of the penitential attitude: generally they are linked to one another, but even singly they can express a confession of sin and request for pardon. These gestures have had a 'liturgical' consecration which has formalized and ritualized them.

My presentation will be an outline one because we are dealing with

25. On this point I am following HALAT (cf. also R. Meyer, *Hebräische Grammatik* [1966–1972], §§72.1d and 82.5c). On the other hand, Gesenius, Zorell and BDB (cf. also GK 75 kk and Joüon 79 t) attribute it to *šḥh (Hitpa'lel)*. Further discussions of this philological problem may be found in J.A. Emerton, 'The Etymology of *hištaḥᵃwāh*', *OTS* 20 (1977), pp. 41-55; and S. Kreuzer, 'Zur Bedeutung und Etymologie von *hištaḥᵃwāh/yštḥwy*', *VT* 35 (1985), pp. 39-60.

26. I have mentioned the penitential rites that occur most frequently. These acts are sometimes accompanied by other gestures with a similar or complementary meaning: cf., for example, lustration (1 Sam. 7.6; Ps. 51.9), tearing or shaving the hair and beard (Isa. 15.2; 22.12; Jer. 7.29; 41.5; Ezek. 7.18; Mic. 1.16; Ezra 9.3), making cuts on one's body (Jer. 41.5; 48.37; Hos. 7.14) and beating one's breast or thigh (Isa. 32.12; Jer. 31.19; Ezek. 21.17).

It should be noted that this ritual is substantially that of *mourning* (cf. 2 Sam. 1.11-12; 3.31-35; Jer. 6.26; Ezek. 24.16-17; 26.16-17; 27.30-32; Amos 8.10).

Among the studies on the subject, I would like to single out P. Heinisch, *Die Trauergebräuche bei den Israeliten* (BZfr, 13 F., 7/8; Münster, 1931); H.W. Wolf, 'Der Aufruf zur Volksklage', *ZAW* 76 (1964), pp. 48-56; E. Kutsch, '"Trauerbräuche" und "Selbstminderungsriten" im Alten Testament', in K. Lüthi, E. Kutsch, W. Dantine, *Drei Wiener Antrittsreden*, (ThSt, 78; Zürich, 1965), pp. 23-42; J. Giblet, 'Pénitence', *DBSup*, VII, pp. 631-32; E. Lipiński, *La liturgie pénitentielle dans la Bible* (LD, 52; Paris, 1969), pp. 27-41; E. de Ward, 'Mourning Customs in 1,2 Samuel', *JJS* 23 (1972), pp. 1-27, 145-66; M.I. Gruber, *Aspects of Nonverbal Communication in the Ancient Near East* (Studia Pohl, 12, II; Rome, 1980), pp. 401-79.

fairly well-known phenomena; the texts quoted are ones in which a gesture is not linked to the others listed in the title of this section (for a wider perspective, cf. the summary at the end of the section).

a. *Weeping* (*bkh*),[27] in our context, is the bodily expression of repentance: it speaks of an internal experience of guilt and the pain of remorse.[28] It is frequently linked to the terminology of grief (*'bl*)[29] and lamentation (*spd*, *nwd*, etc.)[30] and seems to point to the misfortune which has already occurred[31] (see Deut. 1.45; 1 Sam. 24.17; Isa. 30.19; Jer. 14.17).

b. *Fasting* (*ṣwm*),[32] one of the practices connected with funeral mourning (1 Sam. 31.13; 2 Sam. 1.12 etc.) occurs—in the context that concerns us—only in a *rîb* in which God is actively involved in the accusation and punishment. As a symbol of a life in danger, fasting declares that there can be no future without the intervention of a word of salvific consolation (cf. 1 Sam. 7.6, with a rite of lustration; 1 Kgs 21.9; Jer. 36.9; Joel 1.14; 2.15; Zech. 8.19.

c. *Attire*, even more than the above-mentioned actions, forms part of manifestations of penitence in order to emphasize their public aspect.[33]

27. Cf. J.L. Palache, 'Über das Weinen in der jüdischen Religion', *ZDMG* 70 (1916), pp. 251-56; E. De Martino, *Morte e pianto rituale nel mondo antico* (Turin, 1958); F.F. Hvidberg, *Weeping and Laughter in the Old Testament: A Study of Canaanite-Israelite Religion* (Leiden, 1962), especially pp. 98-146; T. Collins, 'The Physiology of Tears in the Old Testament', *CBQ* 33 (1971), pp. 18-38, 185-97.

28. F. Stolz, '*bkh* weinen', *THAT*, I, p. 314.

29. Cf. in particular Kutsch, 'Trauerbräuche', pp. 35-37.

30. Cf. de Ward, 'Mourning Customs in 1,2 Samuel', pp. 1-5, 155-59.

31. V. Hamp, '*bākâ*', *ThWAT*, I, pp. 640-42.

32. Lipiński mentions other practices generally linked with fasting, such as sexual abstinence and a ban on perfume and money-making activities (*La liturgie pénitentielle*, p. 29). On the subject of the ritual and meaning of fasting, cf. J. Behm, *TWNT*, IV, pp. 925-35; K. Hruby, 'Le Yom ha-kippurim ou Jour de l'Expiation', *OrSyr* 10 (1965), pp. 43-74, 161-92, 413-42; R. Arbesmann, 'Fasten', *RAC*, VII (Stuttgart, 1969), especially pp. 451-56; *idem*, 'Fasttage', *RAC*, VII, pp. 501-503; P. Gerlitz, 'Religionsgeschichtliche und ethische Aspekte des Fastens', in *Ex Orbe Religionum*, II (FS G. Widengren; Leiden, 1972), pp. 255-65; F. Stolz, '*ṣūm* fasten', *THAT*, II, pp. 536-38; H.A. Brongers, 'Fasting in Israel in Biblical and Post-Biblical Times', *OTS* 20 (1977), pp. 1-21 (in particular, pp. 10-13); S. P. de Vries, *Jüdische Riten und Symbole* (Wiesbaden, 1981), pp. 135-45.

33. The ultimate meaning of the penitential ritual as regards clothing is variously interpreted (cf. A. Lods, *La croyance à la vie future et le culte des morts dans l'antiquité israélite* [Paris, 1906], pp. 88-99; E. Haulotte, *Symbolique du vêtement selon la*

Clothing is torn (*qr'*) and sackcloth (*śaq)* is worn. It is the state of a defeated person (2 Sam. 13.19; cf. Mic. 1.8); ragged or shabby clothes are like liturgical vestments expressing the kind of prayer that asks for pardon and clemency (cf. 2 Kgs 19.1-2; Jer. 4.8; 36.24).

d. *Dust and ashes* (*'āpār, 'ēper*), sprinkled on the head, manifest an especial state of unhappiness, perhaps because the penitent is identifying, so to speak, with elements that are the sign of death[34] (Gen. 3.19; Isa. 26.19; Pss. 17.6; 22.16; 103.14; Job 7.21 etc.; cf. Job 2.8; 42.6;[35] Lam. 3.28-29; as well as Gen. 18.27; 30.19).

1.2.3. *'Compensation' and Gift*. The supplicant tries to get pardoned by backing the plea up with gifts which, on the one hand, represent a kind of compensation for the wrong caused, and, on the other hand, are a sort of request for a peaceful solution.

To start with, if something is presented to the angry accuser, it is something pleasing, something which—at least symbolically—is to be put in the balance against the misdeed that occasioned the *rîb*. Amends are made for the evil done by means of (proportionate) restitution, before it is exacted forcibly; something is restored, and the prior state is re-established. Not only that: the offering is made abundantly, generously, in awareness of the seriousness of the situation caused by the seriousness of the action previously performed. In this way the offended party is 'ingratiated'.

Secondly, the act of making an offering means that a peaceful solution

Bible [Paris, 1966], pp. 114ff.); it seems to me, however, that it is not possible to exclude the intention to manifest publicly one's pitiful condition and invite others' pity. In this connection I would like to quote 1 Kgs 20.31-32: 'The servants (of Ben-Hadad) said to him, "Look, we have heard that the kings of Israel are *merciful* kings (*malkê ḥesed hēm*). Let us put *sackcloth* (*nāśîmâ nā' śaqqîm*) round our waists and ropes on our heads and go out to the king of Israel; *perhaps he will spare our life!*" So they wrapped sackcloth round their waists and put ropes on their heads and went to the king of Israel and said, "Your servant Ben-hadad says, 'Spare my life'". "So he is alive?", he answered. "He is my brother!"'.

34. Cf. M. Jastrow (Jr), 'Dust, Earth and Ashes as Symbols of Mourning among the Ancient Hebrews', *JAOS* 20 (1900), pp. 133-50; N.H. Ridderbos, '*'āpār* als Staub des Totenortes', *OTS* 5 (1948), pp. 174-78. As H. Lesêtre writes, 'En signe de deuil, on se jetait de la poussière sur la tête...La poussière implique l'idée de la fragilité et surtout celle de la mort. Elle convenait donc bien à l'expression d'un chagrin qui entamait la vie' (*DB*, V, pp. 588-89).

35. For Job 42.6, cf. D. Patrick, 'The Translation of Job XLII 6', *VT* 26 (1976), pp. 369-71.

is being asked: accepting the gift is a *de facto* agreement to the supplication, whereas rejecting it is to maintain an attitude of aggressive anger.

This is what happens in controversies between people,[36] but we have an analogy in the *rîb*s between God and his people; here recourse is had to sacrificial victims (whose scent is 'pleasing' to God), and in more general terms to cultic acts that may be supposed to be a liturgical manifestation of conversion, reparation and the offer of reconciliation.[37]

As regards the Hebrew vocabulary, I would like to point out the most recurrent terminology:

minḥâ [38]	Gen. 32.14, 19, 21-22; 33.10;[39] 43.11, 15, 25-26; 1 Sam. 3.14; Isa. 1.13; 43.23; Jer. 14.12; 41.5; Amos 5.22; Mal. 1.10; 2.13; Ps. 40.7

36. I would like to mention a few episodes: Abimelech makes a gift (*ntn*) to Abraham of herds and flocks, male and female slaves, as well as a thousand pieces of silver, as compensation for having taken Sarah from him (Gen. 20.14-16); Abraham, who has accused Abimelech without foundation over a question of wells, makes him a gift (*ntn*) of herds and flocks (Gen. 21.27); Jacob, who is aware that he has offended Esau, attempts a reconciliation with his brother through a rich gift (*minḥâ*) (Gen. 32.21); as well as money, Joseph's brothers bring a gift (*minḥâ*) to obtain Simeon's release from prison and put an end to the controversy (Gen. 43.11). Cf. also the episode of Abigail and David (1 Sam. 25.27).

37. Cf. D. Schoetz, *Schuld- und Sündopfer im Alten Testament* (BSHT, 18; Breslau, 1930); R.J. Thompson, *Penitence and Sacrifice in Early Israel outside the Levitical Law* (Leiden, 1963); R. de Vaux, *Les sacrifices de l'Ancien Testament* (Cahiers de la Revue Biblique, 1; Paris, 1964), pp. 28-48; R. Schmid, *Das Bundesopfer in Israel: Wesen, Ursprung und Bedeutung der alttestamentlichen Schelamim* (SANT, 9; Munich, 1964); N.H. Snaith, 'The Sin-Offering and the Guilt-Offering', *VT* 15 (1965), pp. 73-80; A. Charbel, *Zebaḥ šelamîm: Il sacrificio pacifico; nei suoi riti e nel suo significato religioso e figurativo* (Jerusalem, 1967); A. Schenker, *Versöhnung und Sühne* (Freiburg, 1981), pp. 102-16; D. Kidner, 'Sacrifice—Metaphors and Meaning', *TynBul* 33 (1982), pp. 119-36.

38. As D.J. McCarthy states, 'Tribute, commonly expressed by *minḥâ* in Hebrew, is a tax levied on a vassal as a *consequence* of the relationship established by a vassal alliance'. Different from tribute is another kind of gift which 'aims at disposing a power to join the petitioner: it *precedes* the alliance. We might call it a bribe, and in fact in Hebrew it is called *šōḥad* in 1 Kgs 15.9; 2 Kgs 16.8' ('Hosea XII 2: Covenant by Oil', *VT* 14 [1964], pp. 216-17). I think there is an important distinction between the (free) gift that precedes a covenant and the (imposed) tribute that is the consequence of a particular vassal relationship; it does not, however, seem to me that the predominant meaning of the term *minḥâ* is tribute. As regards *šōḥad*, it will be dealt with more fully in Chapter 5, when there will also be a discussion of the 'criticism' of compensation sacrifices in controversies between God and Israel.

mattān	Gen. 34.12; Prov. 21.14 (18.16; 19.6)
*b*ᵉ*rākâ*	Gen. 33.11; 1 Sam. 25.27
kōper[40]	Job 33.24

As regards verbs, particular attention is due to:

a. the terminology of the offering:

ntn	Gen. 20.14, 16; 21.27; 34.11-12; 1 Sam. 25.27; 1 Kgs 18.14-16
bw' (*Hi*) *minḥâ*	Gen. 43.26; Isa. 1.13; Jer. 41.5
bw' (*Hi*) *b*ᵉ*rākâ*	1 Sam. 25.27

b. to which corresponds the terminology of acceptance:

lqḥ		1 Sam. 25.35; Ps. 50.9; Josh. 9.14
lqḥ	*minḥâ*	Gen. 33.10; Mal. 2.13
lqḥ	*b*ᵉ*rākâ*	Gen. 33.11
rṣh[41]		Gen. 33.10; Jer. 14.10; Mic. 6.7; Mal. 1.8
rṣh	*minḥâ*	Jer. 14.12; Amos 5.22; Mal. 1.10 (For the noun *rāṣôn*, cf. Jer. 6.20; Isa. 58.5)
ḥpṣ		Isa. 1.11
ḥpṣ	*minḥâ*	Ps. 40.7; (For the noun *ḥēpeṣ*, cf. Mal. 1.10)

1.2.4. *Summary of the Request for Pardon.* It is quite impossible to list all the texts which display elements that could be included in this paradigm which I have called the 'request for pardon'; and it is difficult and arbitrary to choose which passages should be considered the 'most important'. My aim is twofold, and on that basis I have made a selection which has no other value than to supply a certain amount of textual backing (1) to show the abundance of texts, and the variety of the situations and their historical and literary contexts, and (2) to show the

39. On the relationship between Jacob and Esau, cf. P. Fokkelman, *Narrative Art in Genesis* (Assen, 1975), pp. 223-30.

40. B.S. Jackson maintains that *kōper* (monetary compensation) was in widespread use in Israel, even in cases of murder (*Essays in Jewish and Comparative Legal History* [Leiden, 1975], pp. 43-46, 91-93).

41. E. Würthwein makes mention of the specifically cultic use of *rṣh* and *ḥpṣ* ('Kultpolemik oder Kultbescheid? Beobachtungen zu dem Thema "Prophetie und Kult"', in *Tradition und Situation: Studien zur alttestamentlichen Prophetie* [FS A. Weiser; Göttingen, 1963], pp. 115-31). Cf. also R. Rendtorff, *Studien zur Geschichte des Opfers im Alten Israel* (WMANT, 24; Neukirchen, 1967), pp. 253-60.

connection that exists between the various expressions of the penitential attitude despite the variety of those links.

	Suppli-cation[42]	Prostra-tion	Weeping	Fasting	Attire	Dust	Offering
Gen. 44	(18-34)*	14			13		(33)
Gen. 50	17	18					18
Exod. 34	9*	9					
Num. 14	13-19*	5			5		
Deut. 9	26-29*	18, 25		18			
Josh. 7	7-9*	6, 10			6	6	
Judg. 2			4				5
Judg. 20			26	26			26
1 Sam. 7	5, 8-9			6			9-10
1 Sam. 25	24-31*	23-24					27
2 Sam. 12	16		21, 22	16, 21-23	16		
2 Sam. 19	20-21*	19					(21)
1 Kgs 20	32*				31-32		34
1 Kgs 21				27	27		
2 Kgs 22			19		11, 19		
Isa. 22			12	(13)	12		
Isa. 58	(9)	(5)		3-6	5	5	
Jer. 6					26	26	
Jer. 14	11			12			12
Jer. 41			6		5		5
Ezek. 7				19	18		
Joel 1			5		8		
Joel 1	(14)			14	13		
Joel 2	17*		12, 17	12, 15	13		
Jon. 3	8			5, 7	5, 6, 8	6	
Mic. 1			10		8	10	
Mic. 6		6					6-7
Zech. 7	2		3	(3), 5			
Mal. 2			13				13
Ps. 35	13	14		13	13		
Ps. 50	14-15						8-13
Ps. 69	14		(11)	11	12		
Ps. 102	2		10	5		10	
Job 2			12		12	12	
Lam. 2	18-22		11, 18		10	10	
Est. 4			3	3	1, 3	1, 3	
Est. 8		3	3				

42. In the 'supplication' column, an asterisk means that the Hebrew text contains the explicit content of the plea.

	Supplication	Prostration	Weeping	Fasting	Attire	Dust	Offering
Ezra 9	5-15*	5			3, 5		(5)
Ezra 10	1	1	1	6			
Neh. 1	4-11*		4	4			
Neh. 9	5-37*	3		1	1	1	
Dan. 9	3-19*			3	3	3	(21)

1.2.5. *The Meaning of Body Gestures*. The gestures performed by the penitent are external ones, and as such they are referrable to a juridical context; their primary meaning is to give unreserved expression to a confession of guilt. By involving the whole of one's body, gestures of penitence confirm publicly that one is not 'hiding one's sin'; the public exhibition as a criminal corresponds to the nature of the crime, which has more or less obviously threatened the body politic with hurt. It may be noted on the other hand that a public act of penance creates witnesses who will be led to 'judge' the gesture which the offended accuser makes towards the guilty penitent.

Bodily gestures are not just an expression of guilt, they are also a request for pardon; the 'self-confessed criminal' demonstrates—in a symbolic way—the presence of a mortal threat that is poised to crush. In this way one invites one's accuser to show pity; one pleads to be saved from one's own deserved death. By showing the accuser the consequences of unbridled anger and by demonstrating, so to speak, the result of the threat, the accused asks that a sense of justice should not have death as its outcome; this could not bring about a 'spiritual result' (that is, a meaningful effect) greater than that which has already been made manifest.

In short, the external attitude points—again symbolically—to the change brought about in the guilty party and to his or her willingness for reconciliation; the gift, in particular, is intended to represent an act opposite to the misdeed previously committed. If a crime is, in essence, the manifestation of a rejection of a just relationship, then the gift expresses a desire for a relationship made up of interchange, generosity and mutual well-being.

Penitential gestures are *symbolic*: in them the external body speaks of the invisible state of the heart. They express *humiliation*[43] and

43. In expressing *humiliation*, I think the roots *kn‘* and *‘nh* are especially important.

(a) *kn‘* (*Ni*). In 2 Chron. 7.14 and 33.12-13 (19-23), humiliation is linked to supplication (*pll*); in 2 Chron. 12.6 (7, 12) it is identified with a declaration that 'YHWH is just'.

conversion,[44] these being acts that belong to the internal conscience, the source from which a just relationship springs. In such cases it is said that the heart has been touched, softened or broken,[45] not because it is possible to tell the invisible from the visible reality, but because it is necessary that the gestures should be revealing the truth, without which works are either wicked or perverse.

In 2 Kgs 22.19, on the other hand, humiliation refers to tearing one's clothes and weeping; and in 1 Kgs 21.27, 29 to an almost complete series of penitential acts (cf. A. Jepsen, 'Ahabs Busse. Ein kleiner Beitrag zur Methode literarhistorischer Einordnung', in *Archäologie und Altes Testament* [FS K. Galling; Tübingen, 1970], pp. 145-55).

(b) *'nh*. The root *'nh* (II) expresses the act of humiliation through various verbal forms: in the *Niphal* (Exod. 10.3: *mipp^e nê*...; Isa. 53.7; Ps. 119.107), in the *Pual* (Isa. 53.4; cf. also Lev. 23.29, where it seems that allusion is being made to 'fasting', which is often described by the formula *'nh* [*Pi*] [*'et*] *nepeš*: Lev. 23.27, 32; Num. 29.7; Lev. 16.29, 31; Isa. 58.3, 5; Ps. 35.13) and in the *Hitpael* (Dan. 10.12: *lipnê*...; cf. also Ezra 8.21). The noun *ta'^a nît* in Ezra 9.5 is a reference to a penitential rite.

The root *'nh* may also be thought of as expressing the intention of the one doing the punishing to 'humiliate' the guilty; in this regard see *'nh* (*Pi*): Deut. 8.2-3, 16; 1 Kgs 11.39; 2 Kgs 17.20; Isa. 64.11; Nah. 1.12; Ps. 119.75; Lam. 3.33; in the *Hiphil*: 1 Kgs 8.35; Ps. 55.20; and in the *Hitpael*: Ps. 107.17.

44. On the subject of conversion, cf. especially W.L. Holladay, *The Root šûbh in the Old Testament with Particular Reference to its Usages in Covenantal Contexts* (Leiden, 1958), pp. 116-57. Supplementary bibliography in *THAT*, II, pp. 888-90.

It seems useful to me to note how 'conversion' is linked to the verbal and gestural 'request' described in my text: in 2 Chron. 7.14 conversion (*šwb*) is linked to humiliation (*kn'*) and supplication (*pll*); in Joel 2.12-13 it is related to weeping, lamentation and rending the heart (as opposed to clothing); in Jon. 3.9-10 it is expressed by the penitential rites of fasting and putting on sackcloth, as well as prayer; in Isa. 55.6-7 it is especially linked with the prayer that obtains forgiveness.

45. I would like here to point to other expressions that can be the equivalents of the aforementioned:

Ps. 51.19	*rûaḥ nišbārâ–lēb nišbār w^e nidkeh*
Isa. 61.1	*nišb^e rê lēb*
Isa. 57.15	*dakkā' ûš^e pal rûaḥ–rûaḥ š^e pālîm–lēb nidkā'îm*
Joel 2.13	*w^e qir'û l^e babkem w^e 'al bigdêkem*
Lev. 26.41	*yikkāna' l^e bābām he'ārēl*
Ps. 34.19	*nišb^e rê lēb–dakk^e 'ê rûaḥ*

Reference may also be made to 1 Kgs 8.38; Dan. 3.39; Bar. 2.18; 3.1.

As regards the concept of 'contrition', cf. O. Garcia de la Fuente, 'Sobre la idea de contrición en el antiguo Testamento', in *Sacra Pagina* (BETL, XII-XIII, vol. 1; Gembloux, 1959), pp. 559-79.

At this point there arises the problem of sincerity of heart, on which the innocent accuser is called to make a decision. This constitutes the most important act of the 'just party', for a choice to exercise clemency risks derision in the very moment at which one brings to fulfilment the exercise of mercy.

2. *The Pardon*

The person bringing the accusation and threatening sanction responds to the initiative taken by the confessed criminal in the complex of acts called a request by suspending all current manifestations of punishment.

First I will give a synthetic presentation of the relevant Hebrew lexicon, divided into three sections according to their particular semantic aspect; then I will pause briefly to put this point in the juridical procedure in context.

2.1. *Forgiveness of Sins: The Hebrew Terminology*

Ignoring the distinction between forgiveness requested and forgiveness granted, I would like to give a simple list of the terminology most frequently used to describe the act of pardon,[46] which, more or less evidently, always has a juridical connotation. The object of a pardon is in fact a 'misdeed' (crime, sin); now if the controversy procedure was set in motion by a misdeed, the action that annuls it has to have an analogous juridical force opposed to that of the accusation. It is true that the grammatical object of the 'pardoning' is sometimes a malefactor (person), but I think that this phenomenon—common to various languages—must be derived by metonomy from the former.

a. *The Verb slḥ.*[47] The peculiarity of this verb of pardon, with respect to the others, is that it always has God as the subject of the action.[48] Taking

46. For a monograph treatment of the pardon from a lexicographical point of view, see J. Stamm, *Erlösen und Vergeben im Alten Testament* (Bern, 1940); Š. Porúbčan, *Sin in the Old Testament: A Soteriological Study* (Rome, 1963), pp. 287-325.

47. As well as the verb *slḥ*, we might bear in mind the meaning of the term *sallāḥ* (disposed/inclined to pardon) in Ps. 86.5, and *s*ᵉ*lîḥâ* (pardon): in the singular in Ps. 130.4 and Sir. 5.5; in the plural in Dan. 9.9; Neh. 9.17 (with the meaning of a superlative).

48. In the *Niphal*, the grammatical object of the verb is the 'sinner' (Lev. 4.20, 26, 31, 35; 5.10, 13, 16, 18, 26; 19.22; Num. 15.25, 26, 28), but here too we have a

our cue from the ‘objects’ at which the action is directed, we may distinguish:

GOD	*slḥ*	(absolute)		Num. 14.20; 1. Kgs 8.30, 39; 2 Kgs 24.4; Isa. 55.7; Amos 7.2; Lam. 3.42; Dan. 9.18; 2 Chron. 6.21, 30
		l^e (malefactor)		Num. 30. 6, 9, 13; Deut. 29.19; 1 Kgs 8.50; 2 Kgs 5.18; Jer. 5.1, 7; 50.20; 2 Chron. 6.39
GOD	*slḥ*	*l*^{e} (misdeed)	*ʿāwōn*	Num. 14.19; Jer. 31.34; 33.8; Pss. 25.11; 103.3
			ḥaṭṭā’t	1 Kgs 8.34, 36; 2 Chron. 6.25, 27; 7. 14
			ʿāwōn + *ḥaṭṭā’t*	Exod. 34.9; Jer. 36.3

b. *The Verb nś’*. Here we have a more complete picture: the subject of the verb can be either God or a human being; the object is the misdeed (rarely the malefactor):[49]

GOD	*nś’*	*l*^{e} (malefactor)	Gen. 18.24, 26; Num. 14, 19;[50] Isa. 2.9;[51] Hos. 1.6[52]

liturgical type formula; it is unequivocably YHWH who does the pardoning and not the priest who carries out the rite (cf. *THAT*, II, p. 151).

49. In the *Qal* passive the verb *nś’* has the meaning of ‘to be pardoned’ in Isa. 33.24 (*hāʿām…n*^{e}*śu’ ʿāwōn*) and Ps. 32.1 (*’ašrê n*^{e}*śûy pešaʿ*).

50. The ancient versions (LXX, Vulgate, Syriac, Targum) are unanimous in translating Num. 14.19 as ‘pardon’. Some modern translators prefer instead the meaning of ‘bear’ (NBE) or ‘support’ (Vaccari, Dhorme, TOB, NEB; cf. also J. de Vaux, *Les Nombres* [Sources Bibliques; Paris, 1972], p. 172), perhaps making reference to Exod. 19.4 (‘I have carried you on eagle’s wings’) or to Deut. 1.31 (‘the Lord your God has carried you as a man carries his own son’), where, however, we have *nś’ ’et* (cf. also Deut. 1.9).

I think that Num. 14.19 is to be read along the same semantic lines as 14.18 (*yhwh ’erek ’appayim w*^{e}*rab ḥesed* ***nōśē’ ʿāwōn wāpāšaʿ***) in accordance with the following parallelism:

s*^{e}*laḥ *nā’ la*^{ʿa}*wōn hāʿām hazzeh* | *k*^{e}*gōdel hasdekā*
w^e*ka’*^{a}*šer* ***nāśā’tâ*** *lāʿām hazzeh* | *mimmiṣrayim w*^{e}*ʿad hēnnâ.*

51. Even though many hold that the expression in Isa. 2.9 is a gloss, the commonly accepted meaning is that of ‘to pardon’ (denied) (cf. H. Wildberger, *Jesaja* [BK, 10/1; Neukirchen, 1972], pp. 93-94).

		l^e *pešaʿ*	Exod. 23.21[53]
		pešaʿ + ḥaṭṭā't	Josh. 24.19
		ḥaṭṭā't	Ps. 25.18
		ḥaṭṭā't	Exod. 32.32
		pešaʿ	Job 7.21
		ʿāwōn	Mic. 7.18; Ps. 85.3; Hos. 14.3
		ʿāwōn + pešaʿ	Num. 14.18
		ʿāwōn ḥaṭṭā't	Ps. 32.5
		ʿāwōn + pešaʿ + ḥaṭṭā't	Exod. 34.7
A HUMAN BEING	*nś'*	l^e *pešaʿ*	1 Sam. 25.28
		'et ḥaṭṭā't	1 Sam. 15.25
		ḥaṭṭā't	Exod. 10.17
		pešaʿ + ḥaṭṭā't	Gen. 50.17

Naturally, the aforementioned use of the verb *nś'* must be carefully distinguished from the expression *nś' ʿāwōn/ḥēṭ'*, which means to be 'chargeable with a crime', 'to run the risk of a crime', 'to bear the consequences of a crime' and the like[54] (Exod. 28.43; Lev. 5.1, 17; 7.18; Num. 5.31; 9.31; Ezek. 14.10; 44.10, 12 etc.). The resemblance between the two syntagms leads to hesitation over the meaning to be attributed to some texts (e.g. Lev. 10.17; Num. 18.1, 23; Isa. 53.12).

c. *The Verb kpr (Pi).* Scholars[55] hold various opinions as to the etymology and therefore the meaning of this verb; as far as my work is

52. Although the general meaning of Hos. 1.6 is clear, the syntactical justification for *kî nāśō' 'eśśā' lāhem* seems problematic (cf. H.W. Wolff, *Dodekapropheton*. I. *Hosea* [BK, 14/1; Neukirchen, 1961], p. 7). I think that the parallelism should be maintained between *'^{a}raḥēm 'et bêt yiśrā'ēl* and *'eśśā' lāhem*, both negated by *lō' 'ôsîp ʿôd* (L. Alonso Schökel and J.L. Sicre, *Profetas*, II [Madrid 1980], p. 871).

53. In Exod. 23.21 the subject of the action of pardoning is really a *mal'āk* sent by God.

54. For this important distinction, I refer the reader to *THAT*, II, pp. 113-14. Cf. also W. Zimmerli, 'Die Eigenart der prophetischen Rede bei Ezechiel. Ein Beitrag zum Problem an Hand von Ez 14.1-11', *ZAW* 66 (1954), pp. 9ff.

55. Cf. J. Herrmann, *Die Idee der Sühne im Alten Testament. Eine Untersuchung über Gebrauch und Bedeutung des Wortes* kipper (Leipzig, 1905); L. Moraldi, *Espiazione sacrificale e riti espiatori nell'ambiente biblico e nell'Antico Testamento* (AnBib, 5; Rome, 1956), pp. 192-209; S. Lyonnet, 'De notione expiationis', *VD* 37 (1959), pp. 336-52; F. Maas, '*kpr*, pi. sühnen,' *THAT*, I, pp. 842-44; B. Janowski, *Sühne als Heilsgeschehen: Studien zur Sühnetheologie der Priesterschrift und zur Wurzel KPR im Alten Orient und im Alten Testament* (WMANT, 55; Neukirchen, 1982); B. Lang, '*kippaer*', *ThWAT*, IV, pp. 303-18 (with abundant bibliography).

concerned, it is sufficient to consider it a paradigmatic variant, leaving it to further studies to decide on its precise meaning and its placement among the other verbs and expressions that describe the pardon. This verb too has God as its subject when it expresses the act of pardon.

GOD	*kpr* (*Pi*)	*l^e* (malefactor)		Deut. 21.8
		l^e (malefactor)	*l^ekol 'ašer 'āśît*	Ezek. 16.63
		'al (malefactor)	*min ḥaṭṭā't*	Lev. 16.34
		'āwōn		Ps. 78.38; Dan. 9.24
		peša'		Ps. 65.4
		'al ḥaṭṭā't		Ps. 79.9
		'al 'āwōn		Jer. 18.23

(In the *Pual*, with *'āwōn* as subject, cf. Isa. 22.14; 27.9[56]; Prov. 16.6; with *ḥaṭṭā't* as subject, Isa. 6.7)

d. *The Verb 'br.* In certain cases this root expresses the act of pardon; I do not think there is good reason to say that it suggests anything less perfect than the other terms:[57]

GOD	*'br*	(*Qal*)	*l^e* (malefactor)	Amos 7.8; 8.2
			'al peša'	Mic. 7.18
	'br	(*Hi*)	*'et 'āwōn*	2 Sam. 24.10 (= 1 Chron. 21.8); Job 7.21
			ḥaṭṭā't	2 Sam. 12.13
			'āwōn mē'al...	Zech. 3.4
A HUMAN	*'br*	(*Qal*)	*'al peša'*	Prov. 19.11

e. *The Verb ksh.* When linked to the terminology of the misdeed, the verb *ksh* (*Pi*) has a twofold meaning:[58]

1. If the subject is the *guilty* party, it is equivalent to a refusal to make confession of guilt;[59] it seems that the subject of 'covering blood' should be interpreted along these lines (Gen. 37.26; Isa. 26.21; Ezek. 24.7; Job 16.18; cf. also Ezek. 24.8).

56. On Isa. 27.9, cf. A.C.M. Blommerde, 'The Broken Construct Chain, Further Examples', *Bib* 55 (1974), pp. 551-52.

57. This is the opinion of Stamm (*Erlösen und Vergeben*, p. 72), followed by H.-P. Staehli ('*'br* vorüber-, hinübergehen', *THAT*, II, p. 204), according to whom *'br 'al* is 'only an imperfect and therefore not widespread image of forgiveness; in fact, it only expresses a disregarding and not minding, not the elimination of guilt'.

58. Cf. H. Ringgren, 'kāsāh', *ThWAT*, IV, p. 276.

59. Cf. ch. 2, section 1.1.1.

2. If the subject is the *offended* party, the verb *ksh* (*Pi*) is equivalent to granting pardon:

A HUMAN	*ksh*	(*Pi*)	*'al* (malefactor)	Deut. 13.9	(denied)
LOVE	*ksh*	(*Pi*)	*'al peša'*	Prov. 10.12	
ANYONE	*ksh*	(*Pi*)	*peša'*	Prov. 17.9	
GOD	*ksh*	(*Pi*)	*ḥaṭṭā't*	Ps. 85.3	
GOD	*ksh*	(*Pi*)	*'al 'āwōn*	Neh. 3.37	(denied)

In the *Qal* passive we have Ps. 32.1 (the grammatical subject is *ḥaṭṭā't*; the pardoner is God).

f. *The Purification Series of Verbs*. 1. We may consider the verb *mḥh*[60] as belonging to this metaphorical series.

GOD	*mḥh*	(*Qal*)	*peša'*	Ps. 51.3; Isa. 43.25
			peša' + ḥaṭṭā't	Isa. 44.22
			'āwōn	Ps. 51.11
	mḥh	(*Hi*)	*ḥaṭṭā't*	Jer. 18.23 (corr.)

In the *Niphal*, we have as the grammatical subject *ḥaṭṭā't* (Ps. 109.14; Neh. 3.27) and *ḥerpâ* (Prov. 6.33); God seems to be the subject of the action of pardoning. The text of Prov. 30.20 also seems relevant: 'This is the behaviour of the adulterous woman: she eats and *cleans* her mouth and says: I have done nothing wrong!'

2. The verbs *kbs*, *rḥṣ*, *ṭhr* appear together in the lustration ritual (e.g. *kbs* + *ṭhr* in Lev. 13.6, 34, 58; 14.8; Num. 8.7 etc.; *rḥṣ* + *ṭhr* in Lev. 14.8; Num. 19.19; Josh. 22.17; 2 Kgs 5.12, 13; Prov. 30.12 etc.). Reference to this, sometimes even critically, seems to be made in texts such as Isa. 1.16; Jer. 2.22; 4.14; Pss. 26.6; 73.13; Job 9.30.

These verbs can be the equivalent of 'to pardon'.

GOD	*kbs*	(*Pi*)	(malefactor)		Ps. 51.9
	kbs		(malefactor)	*min 'āwōn*	Ps. 51.4
			'āwōn		Mic. 7.19 (corr.)
GOD	*rḥṣ*		*ṣō'â + d^e^mê...*		Isa. 4.4
			(Cf. also in the *Pual*: Prov. 30.12)		
GOD	*ṭhr*		(malefactor)		Ezek. 24.13; 37.23; Mal. 3.3; Ps. 51.9
			(malefactor)	*min 'āwōn*	Jer. 33.8; Ezek. 36.33
			(malefactor)	*min ḥaṭṭā't*	Ps. 51.4
			(malefactor)	*min ṭum'â*	Ezek. 36.25

60. Cf. L. Alonso Schökel, 'māḥāh', *ThWAT*, IV, p. 805.

g. *The Series of Verbs Denoting Attention, Memory, etc.* I am including under this title expressions that are parallel to the traditional verbs of pardon and should be included in this paradigm: their peculiarity is that of being *in the negative.*[61]

Of them all, *lō' zkr*[62] is of especial importance, since it has analogies with our concept of *to grant amnesty* (at least as regards the etymology of the word):

GOD	*lō' zkr*	*ḥaṭṭā't*	Isa. 43.25
		ḥaṭṭā't + *peša'*	Ps. 25.7
		l^eḥaṭṭā't	Jer. 31.34
		'āwōn	Isa. 64.8; Ps. 79.8
A HUMAN	*lō' zkr*	*'et 'ašer he'ewâ* (the guilty)	2 Sam. 19.20

In the *Niphal*, cf. Ezek. 18.22; 33.16.
2 Sam. 19.20 provides the following expressions with *lō' zkr*:

lō' ḥšb l^e (malefactor) *'āwōn*	(cf. Ps. 32.2; subject: God)
lō' śym lēb 'el/'al (malefactor)	(cf. 1 Sam. 25.25)

Finally I would like to note:

lō' šyt 'al (malefactor) *ḥaṭṭā't*	(Num. 12.11)

The terms and phrases I have listed on the previous pages all belong, from a generic point of view, to one and the same paradigm, even though some of them are more frequently used or, from their use in specific cultural spheres, appear more 'technical'. It should be no surprise that metaphorical expressions[63] occur in this lexicon: the whole of

61. The verb *zkr*, in the positive, when its object is a misdeed, is equivalent to not pardoning (Ps. 109.14: *zkr // lō' mḥh*) and to punishing (Jer. 14.10; Hos. 8.13; 9.9: *zkr // pqd*).

62. On the importance of *zkr* with juridical force, cf. B.S. Childs, *Memory and Tradition in Israel* (SBT, 37; London, 1962), pp. 32-33; Boecker, *Redeformen*, pp. 106-11; and also W. Schotroff, *'Gedenken' im Alten Orient und im Alten Testament: Die Wurzel zākar im semitischen Sprachkreis* (WMANT, 15; Neukirchen–Vluyn, 1964), pp. 233-38, 279-83. The juridical meaning of the root *zkr* is only occasionally and indirectly referred to in H. de Boer, *Gedenken und Gedächtnis in der Welt des Alten Testaments* (Fr. Delitzsch–Vorlesungen, 1960; Stuttgart, 1962).

63. From among the metaphorical expressions I would like to single out in particular the verb *rp'* (to heal); in 2 Chron. 7.14 and Ps. 103.3 it is in parallel with *slḥ*; it seems clear therefore that it can belong to the pardon paradigm, referring especially to the aspect of restitution of the state of well-being to the one who has been 'struck' by

language, even the most rigorously conceptual, scientific and technical, is based upon the use of metaphor and symbol to describe referents which do not fall within immediate tangible experience. Even the juridical sphere cannot express its ideas without borrowing terms from common experience, which may seem less rigorous to us only because they do not have immediate equivalents in our juridical terminology.[64] If, on the other hand, the whole world of pardoning is bound together by a few great expressive symbols,[65] it is only natural that the world of pardoning should present semantic analogies: the various expressions do not correspond to different acts of varying value, but are rather the result of the richness of meaning contained in the event of pardoning itself.[66]

All this moreover is confirmed by the synonymous *parallelism* which occurs in the pardoning lexicon; I would like to adduce just a few texts to back up this statement: Deut. 13.9 (*'bh, ḥws, ḥml, ksh*); Isa. 43.25 (*mḥh, lō' zkr*); Jer. 31.34 (*slḥ, lō' zkr*); 33.8 (*ṭhr, slḥ*); Mic. 7.18 (*nś', 'br*); Pss. 32.1-2 (*nś', ksh, lō' ḥšb*); 85.3 (*nś', ksh*); 103.3 (*slḥ, rp'*); 109.14 ([*lō'*] *zkr, mḥh*); Job 7.21 (*nś', 'br*); Dan. 9.24 (*kl', kpr*); Neh. 3.37 (*ksh, mḥh*); 2 Chron. 7.14 (*slḥ, rp'*).

punishment. From among the particularly obvious texts, I would like to single out Jer. 3.22; Hos. 14.5 (the object of the verb is *m^e^šûbôt*); Isa. 6.10; 57.18; Ps. 41.5 (the object of the verb is the guilty). Cf. J. Hempel, *Heilung als Symbol und Wirklichkeit im biblischen Schrifttum* (NAWG, PH; Göttingen, 1958, no. 3), pp. 237-314.

64. Even modern juridical language, despite trying to be technical and univocal, makes use of such terms as: absolve, release, cancel, annul, amnesty, etc., which are definitely metaphorical; moreover, in current jurisprudence such terms often have a specific meaning, not superimposable upon each other, whereas popular speech considers them synonymous. The fact that the linguistic systems of two different idioms are not univocally correspondent makes it necessary to look in the target language for a metaphor closer to the meaning in the source language.

65. I refer in particular to the classic study by P. Ricoeur, *Finitude et culpabilité* (Paris, 1960). The diversity of *Sitz im Leben* should naturally be borne in mind as a determining factor in the lexicon's variety.

66. To describe pardon and its greatness, the biblical authors resort to some particularly expressive images; cf. e.g. Job 14.16-17: 'You would cease to spy on my sins; you would seal up my crime in a bag...'; Ps. 103.12: 'He takes our sins farther away than the east is from the west'; Isa. 1.18: 'Even if your sins were like scarlet, they would become like snow; even if they were red as purple, they would become like wool'; Mic. 7.19: 'He will turn and have pity on us, he will tread down our faults. You will cast our sins into the depths of the sea.'

2.2. *The Cessation of Anger*

In Chapter 1, section 3.1.4, I tried to show how anger belongs to the lexicon of the *rîb*, referring in particular to the kind of punishment in action against the accused. Now just as we found the structure: (1) crime, (2) *rîb*-accusation, (3) confession-supplication, (4) pardon, so we can find an equivalent structure with variations taken from the lexicon of wrath. These two structures are the 'logical' reproduction of two distinct lines of expression; but given their substantial identity of meaning, it is not rare that there should be cross-overs from one series to the other, and therefore interchangeable elements.

Two elements in the structure concern me at this point: on the one hand the action of the guilty (or whoever is interceding for the guilty party) who strives to rein in or calm the accuser's indignation; and on the other hand the action of the latter, who desists from 'the heat of his anger' and suspends or annuls the punitive action.

2.2.1. *Calming Anger*. Logically, this subject would have been dealt with previously under the title 'request for pardon' (cf. section 1 of this chapter), but I have preferred to put it here because of its specific link to the cessation of anger. The characteristic expression that I would like to examine is *ḥlh (Pi) ('et) pᵉnê-*.[67]

Except in Ps. 43.13, Job 11.19 and Prov. 19.6, where the meaning seems to be the generic one of 'to thank someone' (respectively: the queen, Job and a 'noble'), all the other occurrences of the expression bear the meaning of trying to calm the *anger of God*; the context therefore is one of a religiously-based controversy, and the act of calming has a sacral or liturgical connotation.

The act of calming the offended party's anger has the same aim as the supplication to obtain a pardon, as is shown by the juxtaposition of the two following texts which speak of the same event:

	Exod. 32.7-14	Exod. 32.30-35
denunciation of the sin	*šiḥēt 'ammᵉkā…*	*'attem* ***ḥᵃṭā'tem*** *ḥᵃṭā'â gᵉdōlâ*
	wᵉyiḥar 'appî *bāhem*	

67. Cf. J. Reindl, *Das Angesicht Gottes im Sprachgebrauch des Alten Testaments* (ErfTSt, 25; Leipzig, 1970), pp. 175-85.

kpr (*Pi*) *pᵉnê-* in Gen. 32.21, where Esau is placated with a gift (*minḥâ*), may be linked to the expression *ḥlh* (*Pi*) *'et pᵉnê-*. There may also be a reference in 2 Sam. 21.3 (*kpr bᵉ*) and Prov. 16.15 (where *kpr* is linked to anger).

	Exod. 32.7-14	Exod. 32.30-35
prayer of intercession	***wayḥal*** *mōšeh* ***'et p^{e}nê*** *yhwh '^{e}lōhāyw*	*w^{e}'attâ 'e'^{e}leh 'el yhwh* *'ûlay* ***'^{a}kapp^{e}râ*** *b^{e}'ad ḥaṭṭa't^{e}kem…*
	wayyō'mer	*wayyō'mar*
	lāmâ yhwh ***yeḥ^{e}reh*** ***'app^{e}kā*** *b^{e}'ammekā…*	*'ānnā'* ***ḥāṭā'*** *hā'ām hazzeh* *ḥ^{a}ṭā'â g^{e}dōlâ*
	šûb mēḥ^{a}rôn ***'appekā*** ***w^{e}hinnāḥēm*** *'al hārā'â* *l^{e}'ammekā*	*w^{e}'attâ 'im* ***tiśśā'*** ***ḥaṭṭā'tām***
result	*wayyinnāḥem yhwh* *'al hārā'â '^{a}šer* *dibber la'^{a}śôt* *l^{e}'ammô*	*mî '^{a}šer ḥāṭā' lî* *'emḥennû missiprî*

The text of 2 Kgs 13.2-5 is likewise a very clear illustration of the place of this action designed to calm anger (an action which is a 'supplication' in so far as it is 'heeded'); in this case God has already set the punishment in motion:

Crime	(v. 2):	'(Jehoahaz) did what is evil in the sight of the Lord; he persisted in the sin into which Jeroboam son of Nabal had led Israel; he did not give it up'.
Anger	(v. 30):	'The *anger* of the Lord blazed out against Israel and he delivered them without respite into the power of Hazael king of Aram and Ben-Hadad son of Hazael'.
Supplication	(v. 4):	'Jehoahaz, however, tried to placate the Lord'.
Result	(v. 5):	'The Lord heard him, for he had seen the oppression the king of Aram was inflicting on Israel'. 'They escaped the grip of Aram.'

It may be said therefore that the expression *ḥlh* (*Pi*) (*'et*) *p^{e}nê yhwh*, which is sometimes found with *pll* (*Hitp*) (1 Kgs 13.6; 2 Chron. 33.12), takes the place of the supplication element in the syntagm under consideration, emphasizing the link with anger, that is, the threatening and punitive aspect of the *rîb* (cf. Exod. 32.11; 2 Kgs 13.4; Jer. 26.19; Ps. 119.58; Dan. 9.13). Like every supplication that seeks to obtain pardon, the action of placating is also accompanied by gestures of humiliation (Zech. 7.2; 8.21-22; 2 Chron. 33.12) and is backed up by sacrificial offerings (1 Sam. 13.12; Mal. 1.9).

2.2.2. *The Cessation of Wrath.* The imperative (of the supplication) 'let your anger give way' is equivalent to 'pardon', just as the affirmation of calmed anger corresponds synonymously to pardon granted. Here too a few examples are sufficient to demonstrate this:

Mic. 7.18	***nōśē'*** *'āwōn* ***wᵉ'ōbēr*** *'al peša'...*	= pardon
	lō' heḥᵉzîq lā'ad ***'appô***	= end of wrath
Ps. 85.3-4	***nāśā'tā*** *'ᵃwōn 'ammekā*	
	kissîtā *kol ḥaṭṭā'tām*	= pardon
	'āsaptā kol ***'ebrātekā***	
	hᵉšîbôtā ***mēḥᵃrôn 'appekā***	= end of wrath
Hos. 14.5	***'erpā'*** *mᵉšûbātām*	= pardon
	kî šāb ***'appî*** *mimmennû*	= end of wrath
Ps. 78.38	***yᵉkappēr*** *'āwōn...*	= pardon
	wᵉhirbâ lᵉhāšîb ***'appô***	
	wᵉlō' yā'îr kol ***ḥᵃmātô***	= end of wrath
Isa. 64.8	*'al* ***tiqṣōp*** *yhwh 'ad mᵉ'ōd*	= end of wrath
	wᵉ'al lā'ad ***tizkōr*** *'āwōn*	= pardon
Deut. 29.19	*lō' yō'beh yhwh* ***sᵉlōaḥ*** *lô*	= no pardon
	kî 'āz ye'šan ***'ap*** *yhwh*	
	wᵉqin'ātô *bā'îš hahû*	= anger

The cessation of wrath, in the dynamic of the juridical action, expresses a change that takes place in the accuser and which leads the accuser into a different relationship with the guilty party. The terminology used to express the calming and extinguishing of wrath is varied and colourful, as usually happens when feelings are being described; two phrases, however, deserve to be singled out in particular:

1. the expression formed by the verb *šwb* (*Qal* or *Hiphil*) joined to a noun meaning 'anger', in accordance with the following syntagms:
   —*šwb* + *'ap* + *min* (malefactor): Isa. 5.25; 9.11; Jer. 2.35; 4.8; 30.24; Hos. 14.5; Job 14.13; Dan. 9.16 etc.
   —*šwb* + *min* + *ḥᵃrôn 'ap*: Exod. 32.12; Deut. 13.18; Josh. 7.26; 2 Kgs 23.26; Jon. 3.9; 2 Chron. 29.10 etc.
   —*šwb* (*Hi*) + *min* + *ḥᵃrôn 'ap*: Pss. 66.15; 78.38; 85.4; Job 9.13; Prov. 24.18; Ezra 10.14 etc.

2. the verb *nḥm* (*Ni*),[68] which is usually translated as 'to repent', well expresses the change which takes place in the accuser who is threatening or punishing; in practical terms it has the force of *revocation* of the proceedings under way (cf. *nḥm 'al hārā'â*: Exod. 32.14; Jer. 18.18; Jon. 3.10 etc.; and *nḥm 'el hārā'â*: 2 Sam. 24.16; Jer. 26.3, 13, 19; 42.10 etc.). The expression *lō' nḥm* indicates on the contrary an *irrevocable* decree or procedure (cf. 1 Sam. 15.29; Jer. 20.16), especially when linked to *lō'...šwb min* (Jer. 4.28; Exod. 24.14).[69]

2.3. *Having Mercy*[70]

The third and final way in which Hebrew expresses pardon is the one that brings out the element of 'mercy'. It might be said that the vocabulary that belongs to this paradigm has the aim of revealing the state of *heart* of the one who instigated the *rîb*, the intention of the accusation and of the whole juridical procedure. Clemency, pity, mercy and so forth are the revelation of love by someone dealing with a guilty person.

2.3.1. *The Relationship between Wrath and Mercy, and between Mercy and Pardon*. The admittedly guilty is aware that the accuser is full of anger against him or her, and that this anger is just; the hope, which is modulated into supplication and expectation (Lam. 3.25-33; Pss. 39.8-10; 130.5) rests on the conviction that compassion (i.e. justice heedful of the threatened or suffering person) can overcome anger (justice heedful of the crime). As a result, we frequently find in the biblical texts the opposition *anger–mercy*; the practical manifestations of these two emotions are quite distinct, but—in a perfectly just procedure—the former is subordinate to the latter, because it is the better manifestation

68. Cf. J. Jeremias, *Die Reue Gottes: Aspekte alttestamenlicher Gottesvorstellung* (BiblSt, 65; Neukirchen, 1975); H. van Dyke Parunak, 'A Semantic Survey of *nḥm*', *Bib* 56 (1975), pp. 512-32; H.J. Stoebe, '*nḥm pi.* trösten', *THAT*, II, esp. pp. 64-65; B. Maarsingh, 'Das Verbum *nāḥam, ni.*', in *Übersetzung und Deutung* (FS A.R. Hulst; Nijkerk, 1977), pp. 113-25; H. Simian-Yofre, '*nḥm*', *ThWAT*, V, esp. pp. 372-78.

69. The irrevocable decree is expressed by *lō' šwb* (*Hi*) in Amos 1.3, 6, 9 etc. It may be of interest to note that the act of pardoning, after a threat, is formulated like this: *yāšûb w^{e}niḥam* (Joel 2.14; Jon. 3.9).

70. The link between the confession of guilt and the mercy of God is amply demonstrated by Vella, *La giustizia forense*, pp. 65-107.

of the prospects for a loving relationship. Just as the one who is patient (*'erek 'appayim*) is already merciful (Num. 14.18; Jon. 4.2; Ps. 86.15; Neh. 9.17 etc.), so the person who is merciful lays aside the manifestations of his wrath (Mic. 7.18; Pss. 6.2-3; 78.10 etc.).

The *synonymousness* between *pardon* and the *act of mercy* is so well-known and obvious that it is sufficient to quote a few texts as examples: Exod. 34.7; Hos. 1.6; Ps. 51.3;[71] Dan. 9.9; Neh. 9.17.

2.3.2. *The Vocabulary of Mercy*. The peculiarity of this lexicon—and one that comes out especially in the verbs—is to take as its object of reference not the *wicked action or behaviour* (misdeed, crime, sin), but the person (evildoer, guilty person, sinner). The semantic importance of this linguistic phenomenon is worthy of note: confusing clemency with tolerance of guilt is as common as identifying the evildoer with the misdeed that has been committed.

The vocabulary of mercy finds expression on three levels:

1. As a noun or verb describing the supplication for pardon. As we saw in ch. 4, section 1.1.1, *t^{e}ḥinnâ*, *taḥ^{a}nûnîm* and *ḥnn* (*Hitp*)[72] are found in parallel with *t^{e}pillâ* and *pll* (*Hitp*).

2. As an adjective describing the *person* who has mercy. Especially important are the terms *ḥannûn* and *raḥûm*, which are attributed exclusively to God.[73] The nouns *hesed*, *'^{e}met* and *raḥ^{a}mîm* have the force of an adverb or adjective describing the person who pardons or the action of pardoning (cf. Num. 14.19; Pss. 25.10; 30.10; 51.3; Prov. 16.6; Neh. 9.31 etc.).[74]

71. Cf. P.E. Bonnard, 'Le vocabulaire du Miserere', in *A la rencontre de Dieu* (Mém A. Gelin; Le Puy, 1961), pp. 145-56.

72. As regards the root *ḥnn*, cf. D.R. Ap-Thomas, 'Some Aspects of the Root ḤNN in the Old Testament', *JSS* 2 (1957), pp. 128-48; and the lexicographical study by K.W. Neubauer, *Der Stamm CH N N im Sprachgebrauch des Alten Testaments* (Berlin, 1964).

73. Cf. J. Scharbert, 'Formgeschichte und Exegese von Exod. 34.6f., und seiner Parallelen', *Bib* 38 (1957), pp. 130-50; C. Dentan, 'The Literary Affinities of Exodus XXXIV 6f.', *VT* 13 (1963), pp. 34-51.

74. Cf. N. Glueck, *Das Wort ḥesed im alttestamentlichen Sprachgebrauche als menschliche und göttliche gemeinschaftsgemässe Verhaltungsweise* (BZAW, 47; Berlin, 1927); W.F. Lofthouse, 'Ḥen and Ḥesed in the Old Testament', *ZAW* 51 (1933), pp. 29-35; H.J. Stoebe, 'Die Bedeutung des Wortes *ḥäsäd* im Alten Testament', *VT* 2 (1952), pp. 244-54; N.H. Snaith, *The Distinctive Ideas of the Old Testament* (London, 1944), pp. 110-22, 127-30; F. Asensio, *Misericordia et Veritas: El* ḥesed y emet *divinos. Su influjo religioso-social en la historia de Israel* (AnGr, 48;

3. As a verb (or noun acting as a verb) that expresses the *action* of having mercy, granting grace or pardon. I would like to single out some of the most used verbs:

ḥnn	Exod. 13.19; Judg. 21.22; 2 Sam. 12.22; Isa. 30.18-19; Ps. 6.3; Job 33.24 etc. For *t^eḥinnâ*, cf. Josh. 11.20; Ezra 9.8; cf. also *ḥ^anînâ* in Jer. 16.13
rḥm (*Pi*)	Exod. 33.19; Hos. 1.16; Mic. 7.19; Isa. 27.11; Ps. 102.14 etc.
ḥml	Deut. 13.19; 1 Sam. 15.3, 9; Isa. 9.18; Jer. 13.14; 21.7
ḥws	This verb is used almost exclusively in the negative, to indicate the refusal of pardon: Deut. 13.9; 19.3, 21; Jer. 13.15; Ezek. 5.11; 7.4; Joel 2.17 etc.
'bh	Sometimes in a construction with *lislōaḥ* (Deut. 29.19; 2 Kgs 24.4), but also on its own referring to the granting of pardon (Deut. 13.9; Prov. 6.35).

2.4. *The Meaning of the Pardon*

I am not claiming at this point to offer a systematic reflection on the act of pardon, which would demand an approach from many angles and a somewhat vast analysis of an anthropological and theological kind; I am limiting myself to sketching in just a few of its important aspects in the context of the juridical procedures we are examining, starting from the data that I have marshalled in previous pages, and integrating them with others supplied by the biblical texts. The general assumption on which I would like to comment is this: pardon as an act has of itself dialectical aspects in which its authentic nature is revealed.

Pardon is firstly a *response* which meets a desire and a request. Since it is called for by the guilty in a series of actions (the verbal and gestural

Rome, 1949); W.L. Reed, 'Some Implications of Ḥēn for Old Testament Religion', *JBL* 73 (1954), pp. 36-41; U. Masing, 'Der Begriff *ḥesed* im alttestamentlichen Sprachgebrauch', in *Charisteria* (I. Köpp...oblata; Holmiae, 1954), pp. 26-63; A.R. Johnson, 'Ḥesed and Ḥāsîd', in *Interpretationes ad Vetus Testamentum pertinentes* (FS S. Mowinckel; Oslo, 1955), pp. 100-12; A. Jepsen, 'Gnade und Barmherzigkeit im Alten Testament', *KD* 7 (1961), pp. 261-71; G. Schmuttermayr, 'RḤM—Eine lexikalische Studie', *Bib* 51 (1970), pp. 499-532; G. Gerleman, 'Das übervolle Mass. Ein Versuch mit ḥæsed', *VT* 28 (1978), pp. 151-64; K.D. Sakenfeld, *The Meaning of Ḥesed in the Hebrew Bible: A New Inquiry* (HSM, 17; Missoula, MT, 1978); H.D. Preuss, E. Kamlah, M.A. Signer and G. Wingren, 'Barmherzigkeit', *TRE*, V, pp. 215-38; C.F. Whitley, 'The Semantic Range of *Ḥesed*', *Bib* 62 (1981), pp. 519-26; E. Kellenberger, *Ḥäsäd wä'^ämät als Ausdruck einer Glaubenserfahrung: Gottes Offen-Werden und Bleiben als Voraussetzung des Lebens* (Zürich, 1982).

request), the aim of which is to arouse an attitude of fairness in the innocent party, it might be said that pardon is proportional to and conditional upon the actions of the repentant evildoer.

Yet although pardon is a response, it remains a *free gift*: the supplicant cannot demand; the one granting is not carrying out a juridically necessary gesture, but gives expression to an act of freedom (Isa. 43.25). This fact is so important that it deserves to be backed up by precise references to data or expressions drawn from the biblical texts:

1. The guilty has no *rights* to press home;[75] a request for pardon is equivalent to handing oneself over to the decision and conditions laid down by the offended party, in the hope that his or her will might be inspired by benevolence.[76] The act of pardon is therefore a juridical act, but it is not so much the expression of a right (of the guilty party) as an act of renunciation—carried out by the accuser—of the right to punish.
2. Someone desiring pardon knows that the plea may *not* obtain what is being asked for; the uncertainty in this case does not mean a lack of trust but a consciousness of the disproportion between the offending act and that of the one from whom one is expecting pardon. The one making the request says, 'Perhaps you will hear me',[77] in this way expressing a hope that cannot be inferred except from the generosity of the offended party.
3. The accuser grants pardon only *on certain conditions*;[78] not only is it up to the accuser to fix them, but it is the accuser's

75. Cf. Begrich, *Deuterojesaja*, pp. 23-24; and C.F.D. Moule, '"As We Forgive..." A Note on the Distinction between Deserts and Capacity in the Understanding of Forgiveness', in *Donum Gentilicium* (FS D. Daube; Oxford, 1978), pp. 68-77 (especially pp. 71-72, 76).

76. That the guilty party cannot demand anything is implicitly contained in the plea which has as its object the declaration of the wrongdoing. The awareness of 'having no rights' is expressed like this in a formula, 'Do as you think right' (cf. Gen. 34.11-12; Judg. 10.15; 2 Sam. 19.28-29; 2 Kgs 18.14; Jer. 14.7).

77. It is interesting to note how the act of asking for pardon is linked to the uncertainty of the expectation by *'ûlay* (perhaps...he will pardon) (Gen. 32.21; Exod. 32.30; 1 Sam. 6.5; 1 Kgs 20.31; 2 Kgs 19.4; Amos 5.15; Zeph. 2.3; Lam. 3.29) or by *mî yôdēa'* (who knows...if he will not pardon) 2 Sam. 12.22; Joel 2.13-14; Jon. 3.8-9).

78. I have already mentioned how an alternative is often put before the accused in *rîbs* (ch. 2, section 3); in this are made explicit the conditions required to obtain a pardon; I may recall, at this point, such texts as Gen. 18.26; 1 Sam. 25.34; 1 Kgs 1.52; Jer. 5.1; 2 Chron. 33.23.

unquestionable judgment that decides whether they have been met or not.

4. Finally, *pardon may not be granted*; even God, of whom it is said that he is supremely merciful, in certain cases refuses to forgive.[79] This refusal, therefore, is not always the sign of a hard and wicked heart; it may rather be a sign that an expression of freely given love cannot be made without being

79. That a person might not forgive another person an offence is no cause for surprise; the vendetta, which takes the place of forgiveness (Gen. 4.23-24; 34.1-31; 2 Sam. 3.26-27; 13.1-29; Prov. 6.34-35 etc.) is recognized as an expression of the wickedness of the human mind and unreservedly condemned.

Perhaps we do not reflect enough upon the fact that in our society it is widely accepted that for certain crimes only punishment is laid down and not the possibility of a pardon; indeed in certain cases, even when the offended party would be inclined to 'pass it over', once the mechanism of justice has been set in motion, it works inexorably to the fulfilment of its punitive ends. From this point of view, the biblical texts that 'command' non-forgiveness for certain crimes (Deut. 7.2; 13.9; Josh. 11.20; 1 Kgs 2.28-34 etc.) are to be interpreted as a kind of justice that expresses the seriousness of the act perpetrated; nevertheless we may ask ourselves whether it is in harmony with the perfection of justice not to take account of the possibility of reconciliation which is offered in the act of pardon.

The fact that God himself, in certain cases, refuses pardon to a person or to an entire people seems even more problematic; and sometimes this happens even when they make gestures of repentance and the intercessory plea of a 'just person' occurs (Exod. 23.21; 32.33-34; Deut. 1.45; 29.19; Josh. 24.19; 1 Sam. 15.25-29; 2 Kgs 24.4; Jer. 5.7; Amos 7.8; Lam. 3.42 etc.). It may be mentioned straight away that the innocent pray for God not to pardon (Isa. 2.9; Pss. 59.6; 109.1, 14; Jer. 18.23; Neh. 3.6-7). This is abundant demonstration that pardon—for God—is not at all automatic, and that even in him, who is the very source of mercy, clemency is necessarily bound up with the disposition of the person receiving it.

So then, the statement made by YHWH in Exod. 33.19 seems very eloquent and complex: *w^e^ḥannōtî 'et 'ᵃšer 'āḥōn w^e^riḥamtî 'et 'ᵃšer 'ᵃraḥēm*. The Vulgate (like some modern translations: NBE, Einheitsübersetzung) brings out the modal meaning of the *yiqtol* with the nuance of 'to will' (Joüon, 113 n): 'et miserebor cui voluero et clemens ero in quem mihi placuerit'. The same line is taken by Vaccari, according to whom the expressions in the Hebrew text 'refer to a goodness inclined to do favours and pardon, but with full independence and freedom'. The TOB, on the other hand, in place of an evasive formula (cf. again Joüon, 158 o) prefers to read a reinforced expression, with the meaning of 'quand j'accorde ma bienveillance, c'est efficace'. I think that the nuance of 'to be able' may be seen in the *yiqtol* (I am gracious to whom I can be gracious); more generally, I hold that the phrase is put forward as a kind of enigma regarding the two attributes of YHWH (*ḥannûn* and *rāḥûm*) on the model of what is said about the divine name itself (Exod. 3.14).

> perverted; a facile pardon, indeed an automatic pardon, is to make guilt trivial, to give incentive to evil and to favour perversion of the guilty one's heart.

Following this line of reflection, I would like to note that pardon comes *at the end* of a juridical procedure: after the crime, the accusation has taken place, sometimes in a punitive way; this has been followed by the confession of guilt and supplication, the latter linked to an attitude of conversion on the part of the guilty which is expressed in gestures and promises. This whole course prepares for and makes sense of the act of remission of guilt.

And yet there is something about pardon that is previous even to the request, the possibility of being merciful—as opposed to that of prosecuting punishment—which cuts across the actual dynamic of the accusation in a two-sided controversy. This is brought out by the fact that sometimes it is exactly the accuser who offers pardon even before the accused is in a position to recognise the offence and ask clemency for it.[80] The prospect of reconciliation only opens up at the moment of pardon because it was already written into the accusation itself as its main aim.[81] Seen from this angle, pardon is a prior act, already in some ways unilaterally granted by the offended party, and only waiting for the opportunity to make itself seen when the guilty receives it.[82]

80. Taking Isa. 1.18-19 as typical, I hold that the prophetic preaching that finds expression in the genre of the *rîb* has as its basis the offer of God's pardon (cf. Jer. 5.1; 7.1-15; 26.1-6, 18-19 etc.).

81. K. Koch's article, 'Sühne und Sündenvergebung um die Wende von der exilischen zur nachexilischen Zeit', *EvT* 26 (1966), pp. 217-39, in which he supports the thesis that 'die göttliche Vergebung der Sünde spielt im vorexilischen Israel keine Rolle' (p. 219), seems to me one-sided and out of tune with the overall dynamic of prophetic revelation. The author's arguments (pp. 219ff.) seem to me no more than an illustration of how the post-exilic period was a particularly important period in Israel's meditation on God's forgiveness (right after the disaster foretold by the preaching of the prophets), a reflection that was linked to a liturgical/cultic organization suitable for celebrating and re-actualizing this forgiveness. In my opinion, the precise aim of pre-exilic prophecy is to bring about an understanding of what divine forgiveness is, pointing out the conditions required of a person and a people for them to receive it: the prediction of non-forgiveness is a manner of denouncing not only sin, but at the same time the obstinate wish to remain in it.

82. H.H. Schmid, 'Rechtfertigung als Schöpfungsgeschehen. Notizen zur

When a crime has been committed, it becomes part of history; inscribed forever on reality, it leaves visible traces for a long time, until it is wiped out like a dirty mark on a piece of cloth. The future is fatally conditioned by the evildoer's act.

Pardon, on the one hand, comes *after the crime*, and in this sense recognizes its terrible status; but it is important to realize that its claim is to annul what has been done, to consider the misdeed 'as though it had not happened' (cf. the metaphors of oblivion, of washing away, of wiping out and so on). This annulment of history is problematic,[83] and may look like no more than a fiction which touches neither the guilty nor the period of history spanned by wickedness. The 'as though' means that unfortunately things are otherwise from the interpretation laid upon them.

So the value of a pardon is in proportion to its timing: if the pardon is given *before the crime*, the future is not conditioned just by wickedness, but by the act that takes it over from a prior perspective of mercy and reconciliation. Perhaps it is not so surprising to see that the overwhelming majority of biblical texts say that God forgives; this means that forgiveness finds its true nature when it is referred to him who, as its origin, perfectly understands the rebelliousness, weakness and wretchedness of humankind and who, when entering into a covenant relationship, already foresees the possibility of betrayal and offence. It is as though God were to lend a huge sum to a poor man, well knowing that he will never be in a position to pay it back, and therefore deciding a priori to renounce his right to demand it at all costs. This built-in structure of remission becomes history at the point when the debtor asks for amnesty, but actually amnesty was in the creditor's mind even before the debtor noticed the impossibility of settling his account.

Pardon is therefore identical with a prior clemency towards the other

alttestamentlichen Vorgeschichte eines neutestamentlichen Themas', in *Rechtfertigung* (FS E. Käsemann; Tübingen, 1976), pp. 403-14.

83. E. Kutsch ('"Wir wollen miteinander rechten". Zu Form und Aussage von Jes. 1.18-20', in *Künder des Wortes: Beiträge zur Theologie der Propheten* [FS J. Schreiner; Würzburg, 1982], pp. 23-33) maintains that the alternatives in Isa. 1.18 should be translated by a question (expecting a negative answer) because otherwise one would end up saying that sin becomes non-sin, which according to the author is impossible: 'Eine Untat kann nicht in eine Guttat verwandelt werden; Mord bleibt Mord' (p. 206). He judges that Isaiah does not have the possibility of conversion in mind; with reference to 1.18b and 1.19-20, he says, 'beide rechnen nicht mit der Möglichkeit, dass Gott Sünde vergibt oder tilgt oder dass der Mensch von dem falschen Weg, von dem Sündigen sich abwendet, umkehrt' (p. 29).

party, with whom a relationship has been established (a contract, a pact or a covenant). This seems at odds with the biblical presentation of forgiveness, where the emphasis falls on the abrupt and apparently arbitrary passage from *anger* to *mercy*. Just as the sinner repents and is converted (*šwb*), so the offended party (particularly God) repents of the harm that he intended to do and 'turns away' (same root, *šwb*) from the heat of his anger. It is not known how and why sinners change their attitude; the transformation of God's attitude seems mysterious too. An all-embracing interpretation of Scripture, common not only in people of low scholarship, is one that assigns the manifestation of wrath to a particular period in history (for example, the Old Testament) or to particular categories of people (the Jews or the pagans); by contrast, the manifestations of mercy would be in a different period or to different categories of people.

I think that a correct interpretation of forgiveness cannot be arrived at without trying to bring together the two sides of it, which for us is almost impossible. God is *from the outset* always the same towards everybody: he is clemency, patience and mercy; *history* shows him really to be someone who gives up his just anger in order to treat everybody with mercy. It is in the movement, not historical but conceptual, from one dimension to the other that the nature of the divine is revealed.[84]

There remains one last point, of great importance, which leads on to what I will say in the next section. Forgiveness is meaningful to the extent to which it makes possible a relationship between people, that is, to the extent to which it is linked to the larger structure of a 'covenant relationship'. Indeed it might be said that forgiveness is the proposal and definite offer to live together within the bounds of justice. Now this presupposes a constant reference to law, which is the mediation of the relationship's meaning. Without law there is no covenant. If forgiveness is granted, it presupposes the possibility that *now* it is possible to respect the word that obliges both parties.

The proportion between the kind of forgiveness, the kind of covenant and the kind of law must be kept constantly in mind in order to grasp

84. I have no intention at all of reducing forgiveness to a pure theological concept attributable to God; on the contrary, forgiveness is a fact of history, which for Christians is revealed and given through Jesus Christ. What matters is just to note that if God's nature is revealed in Christ, what is made manifest in this historical event (not deduced by *a priori* logic) is God's turning away from anger to have mercy on the sinner.

the nature of the reconciliation which puts an end to the controversy between individuals.

3. *The End of the Controversy*

In this final section I would like to single out the ways in which the biblical texts describe the end of the controversy. Given the structure I have laid out previously, it is impossible for a dispute to end without reaching—more or less clearly—a sign of agreement that takes in *both disputants*; it is true that the controversy was started by the accuser alone, but to end it requires that some common understanding is reached, such that neither party has any more to say or with which to find fault.

Logic demands that the agreement should be a fully truthful one; since the dispute arouse out of a real or imagined injustice, one would expect that the one in the wrong would make an explicit declaration to that effect, and that the offended party would accept that and forgive. The facts, however (to which the biblical texts bear witness), are in practice more ambiguous; right and wrong are not clear-cut, and as a result, especially in controversies between people, forms of compromise often win out over a dynamic that responds to rigorous truth (Gen. 13.1-12;[85] 20.1-18; 21.25-34; 26.18-22; Exod. 17.1-7 etc.). I have also pointed out[86] that the accusation presupposes the exercise of a certain amount of power over the other party; it can happen that someone is in the right, but does not have sufficient power to bring a *rîb* and exact compensation (Gen. 29.20-28; 1 Sam. 24; 26). I would therefore like to say immediately that a lot of the time controversies end but without the reason for the dispute being sufficiently clarified and without the conditions for a mutual relationship of truth and justice being laid down.

My treatment will make reference to the most obvious kinds of end to the controversy, under three headings that correspond to the expressions—different but sometimes complementary—which we find at the conclusion of *rîb*s: (1) the agreement, (2) the peace, (3) the covenant.

3.1. *The Simple Agreement*

Many of the controversies recounted in the Bible are resolved because the accuser lays aside the complaint; faced with an accused who protests innocence or proffers valid excuses, the accuser is satisfied; thus the

85. In Gen. 13.1-12, P. Pajardi refers to 'commodus discessus' (*Un giurista legge la Bibbia* [Milan, 1983], p. 59).

86. Cf. ch. 2, section 3.

controversy no longer has a reason to drag on and expires for lack of content.

H.J. Boecker[87] points out that in these cases the formula *wayyîṭab bᵉʿênê-* is used, and quotes as examples Josh. 22.30, 33 (the dispute between the Transjordanian tribes and the rest of Israel) and 2 Sam. 3.36 (where David's fast at the death of Abner provides a sort of proof—accepted by the people—of his non-involvement in the assassination). To these passages might be added Lev. 10.20 (the end of the dispute between Moses and the sons of Aaron)[88] and perhaps also Gen. 34.18 (where a compromise is mentioned which apparently concluded the dispute between Shechem and the brothers of Dinah).

This formula shows that the *accuser* has been satisfied by the accused's reply. It may be recalled on the other hand that equivalent expressions exist on the lips of the *accused* (guilty) which declare one's assent to whatever the accuser decides, and as a result one will have no objection to lodge later: Josh. 9.25 (in the dispute between Israel and the Gibeonites, the latter say, *kaṭṭôb wᵉkayyāšār bᵉʿêneykā laʿᵃśôt lānû ʿᵃśēh*); Judg. 10.15 (a *rîb* of God against Israel: *ʿᵃśēh ʾattâ lānû kᵉkol haṭṭôb bᵉʿêneykā*); and 2 Sam. 19.28 (the controversy between David and Meribaal: *waʿᵃśēh haṭṭôb bᵉʿêneykā*).

The expression *yṭb/ṭôb bᵉʿênê-* seems therefore to be the pointer to an agreement proposed by one party to the other in order to resolve a particular question (cf. also Gen. 20.15; 1 Kgs 21.2; 2 Kgs 10.5).[89]

But there can be *rîb*s that end with a withdrawal of the accusation without the use of the aforementioned formula (Gen. 26.11; Judg. 6.32; 8.3; 1 Sam. 19.6; 2 Sam. 19.30-31 etc.); on the other hand, of itself the expression says nothing about the conditions and circumstances of the agreement, which can therefore be of quite different kinds and values.

87. *Redeformen*, pp. 38-40.

88. A discussion of this episode, which revolves around expiatory sacrifice, can be found in J. Milgrom, 'Two kinds of *ḥaṭṭāʾt*', *VT* 26 (1976), pp. 333-37.

89. An element of integration may come from a consideration of the term *ṭôb* as a technical term for the covenant relationship: cf. in this context D.R. Hillers, 'A Note on some Treaty Terminology in the Old Testament', *BASOR* 176 (1964), pp. 46-47; J.S. Croatto, 'Ṭôbā como "amistad (de Alianza)" en el Antiguo Testamento', *AION* 18 (1968), pp. 385-89; A.G. Lamadrid, 'Pax et bonum. "Shalôm" y "ṭôb" en relación con "berit"', *EstBíb* 28 (1969), pp. 61-77; M. Fox, 'Ṭôḇ as Covenant Terminology', *BASOR* 209 (1973), pp. 41-42; I. Johag, '*Ṭôb*—Terminus technicus in Vertrags- und Bündnisformularen des Alten Orients und des Alten testaments', in *Bausteine biblischer Theologie* (FS G.J. Botterweck; Bonn, 1977), pp. 3-23.

To end a controversy with a simple agreement, therefore, carries with itself a certain ambiguity: although on the one hand there is something very positive that consists in avoiding or bringing to an end a violent conflict, on the other hand we have to realize that an agreement is the expression of convergent *opinion*, a 'seeming', which has no precise objective verification, and it does not always offer guarantees of truth and justice.[90]

3.2. *Peace*

A situation of conflict takes the form of one party 'moving against another' (Judg. 21.22; 1 Sam. 24.15; 25.20-22 etc.) and develops into strife which resembles or turns into war. The cessation of a dispute, then, is marked by expressions to the contrary; it is said that everyone 'returns' to their own dwelling (Gen. 21.32b; 1 Sam. 24.23; 26.25; 1 Kgs 1.51) and often it is made clear that this return takes place *b*^{e}*šālôm* (Gen. 26.29, 31; 28.21; 1 Sam. 29.7; 2 Sam. 3.21-23) or *l*^{e}*šālôm* (Gen. 44.17; 1 Sam. 20.13, 42; 25.35; 2 Kgs 5.19).

Returning 'peacefully' is the sign of an end to hostilities in the case of war (Josh. 10.21; Judg. 8.9; 11.31; 2 Sam. 19.25-31; 1 Kgs 2.17, 27-28; Jer. 43.12; Ps. 55.19); in the case of a juridical controversy, it means that there are no more reasons for strife, because the relationship between the parties has moved from disagreement to agreement, from a punitive threat to a kind of friendly relationship.[91]

We may conclude from these observations that the concept of 'peace' is used to describe the end of a controversy (cf. Job 22.21). Its semantic force is many-sided, as has been highlighted by a number of monographs;[92] I would like to note here only that they really do deal with the juridical sphere.

90. Cf. Pajardi, *Un giurista legge la Bibbia*, pp. 467-68.

91. Cf. D.J. Wiseman, '"Is it Peace?"—Covenant and Diplomacy', *VT* 32 (1982), pp. 311-26.

92. Cf. H. Gross, *Die Idee des ewigen und allgemeinen Weltfriedens im Alten Orient und im Alten Testament* (TThSt, 7; Trier, 1956); J.J. Stamm, 'Der Weltfriede im Alten Testament', in J.J. Stamm and H. Bietenhard, *Der Weltfriede im Alten und Neuen Testament* (Zürich, 1959), pp. 7-63; W. Eisenbeis, *Die Wurzel* šlm *im Alten Testament* (BZAW, 113; Berlin, 1969), pp. 52-222; H. van Oyen, 'Schalom. Gesetz und Evangelium unter dem Aspekt des Friedens', in *Wort—Gebot—Glaube. Beiträge zur Theologie des Alten Testaments* (ATANT, 59; Zürich, 1970), pp. 157-70; J.I. Durham, '*šālôm* and the Presence of God', in *Proclamation and Presence* (FS G.H. Davies; London, 1970), pp. 272-93; L. Rost, 'Erwägungen zum Begriff *šālôm*',

I have already mentioned the opposition *war–peace*: this could form the basis for an understanding of why the prophetic preaching, especially in Jeremiah, insists upon a denial of the foretelling of peace (Jer. 4.10; 6.14; 8.11, 15; 12.12; 14.19; 23.17; Ezek. 13.10, 16; Mic. 3.5); this is the equivalent of declaring the *rîb* of YHWH against Israel still open; vice versa, the good news of peace after the destruction of Jerusalem has great force as the offer and promise of reconciliation (Isa. 52.7; 57.19).

The *relationship*, on the other hand, which exists between *justice* and *peace* is well known:[93] it is precisely injustice that sets in motion the accuser's juridical action, and only the re-establishment of just relations can bring peace between the people involved (cf. Exod. 18.23; Isa. 9.5-6; 26.2-3, 12; 32.17-18; 48.18; 59.7-8; 60.17; Pss. 72.7; 85.11; 122.7-8 etc.). As regards a two-sided controversy, it is significant that the act of justice that brings about peace is essentially the forgiveness granted by the offended party (cf. Isa. 57.14-21; Jer. 33.6-9); indeed we might well ask whether it is possible to reach real concord without an act of mercy that returns one's dignity and gives one back a place in civil life.

When all is said, however, the concept of 'peace' is rather vague; it can in fact mean no more than the cessation of hostilities without any request for a precise kind of relationship or friendship. Once again I would like to point out that it is necessary to bear in mind the dynamic of the whole controversy in order to evaluate the meaning of its conclusion.

3.3. *Covenant*

The concept of 'peace' noted in the previous section can be fleshed out by observing that, after the hostilities, the disputants normally feel the need to stipulate a pact between them for the future.[94]

At the outset I said that in order to engage in a controversy the subjects of it had to have a relationship with each other by way of some

in *Schalom: Studien zu Glaube und Geschichte Israels* (FS A. Jepsen; Stuttgart, 1971), pp. 41-44; H. Schmid, *Šalôm: "Frieden" im Alten Orient und im Alten Testament* (SBS, 51; Stuttgart, 1971); J.P. Brown, 'Peace Symbolism in Ancient Military Vocabulary', *VT* 21 (1971), pp. 1-23; E. Dinkler, 'Friede', *RAC*, VIII, esp. pp. 448-53; G. Gerlemann, '*šlm* genug haben', *THAT*, II, pp. 919-35.

93. Cf. F. Vattioni, 'I precedenti letterari di Isa. 32.17. Et erit opus iustitiae pax', *RivB* 6 (1958), pp. 23-32.

94. Perhaps the concept of *b*ᵉ*rît šālôm* (Num. 25.12; Isa. 54.10; Ezek. 34.25; 37.26) may be understood in this way. Cf. also Gen. 26.28-29, 31; 1 Kgs 5.26; Ps. 55.21 (J. Pedersen, *Israel*, p. 285).

sort of (often only implicit) structure which regulates their mutual rights and duties; now, when the controversy ends, it is this bond of relationship that is clarified, reinforced or renewed.[95]

From a literary point of view, it appears that a *rîb* in the Bible is often concluded by the stipulation of a *covenant*; a very obvious case is the one of the controversy between Laban and Jacob (Gen. 31.44-54),[96] but see also Gen. 21.27; Exod. 34.10; Josh. 9.14; 2 Sam. 3.12-21; 1 Kgs 20.34; Neh. 10.1. It is also well known that covenants are based on *mutual oaths* of fidelity,[97] and we may observe that, after the dispute, this sworn promise is clarified (Gen. 21.31; 26.31; 31.53; 1 Sam. 19.6; 24.23; 2 Sam. 19.24; 1 Kgs 1.51; 2.8; Neh. 5.6-13). Finally, the ritual of a covenant after a *rîb* may involve the parties to the contract eating a meal together[98] (Gen. 26.31; 2 Sam. 3.20) or making a sacrifice (Judg. 2.5; 2 Sam. 24.25) or giving other *signs* of their communal decision (cf. Gen. 21.27-28; 31.25; cf. also 1 Sam. 15.31; 2 Sam. 12.20).

It would be out of all proportion to the rest of my work to bury myself in an analysis of covenant structure;[99] all that matters is that it represents a way of concluding a controversy that is considerably richer semantically than those listed previously. Its value is firstly that precise norms are laid down to regulate the behaviour of each party in the future (the law); this will avoid (it is hoped) that series of fatal misunderstandings which arise out of an imperfect awareness of each other's rights and duties. Secondly, a covenant is a solemn promise of mutual fidelity, which is not only a declaration of present friendship but also is put forward as a guarantee for the future, inasmuch as oath-takers

95. A typical text in this regard is Gen. 21.22-23.

96. I do not concur with the opinion of G.W. Coats, 'Strife without Reconciliation—A Narrative Theme in the Jacob Tradition', in *Werden und Wirken des Alten Testaments* (FS C. Westermann; Neukirchen, 1980), pp. 82-106, who thinks that what is narrated in Gen. 31.44-54 does not represent an act of reconciliation (esp. p. 91). To be sure, it may be admitted that the reconciliation between Laban and Jacob is not perfect (among other things, there is no recognition of wrongdoing by either side), but I do not believe that a 'physical community' (p. 103) is necessary for a warm covenant relationship.

97. Cf. M.G. Kline, *By Oath Consigned* (Grand Rapids, 1968), pp. 14-22; D.J. McCarthy, *Treaty and Covenant: A Study in Form in the Ancient Oriental Documents and in the Old Testament* (AnBib, 21A; Rome, 2nd edn, 1978), *passim.*

98. Cf. W.T. McCree, 'The Covenant Meal in the Old Testament', *JBL* 45 (1926), pp. 120-28; McCarthy, *Treaty and Covenant*, pp. 254-56.

99. Cf. McCarthy, *Treaty and Covenant*, with a very wide bibliography.

call down upon themselves that just and infallible judgment which is the judgment of God. Lastly, especially in covenant rites that involve a banquet or sacrifice, a communion between the contracting parties is signified that goes far beyond a casual agreement or a truce in hostilities; taking part in the same source of life is the sign of a communion between people,[100] in which may be discerned the outlines of true justice.

But also in a covenant, as in all the other possible forms of conclusion of the *rîb*, the important thing is not to insist on the external form that signifies the end of the discord and the beginning of a new relationship. It is absolutely necessary to see how the whole controversy developed, and what level of truth the mutual relationship has reached.

Agreements fall apart, peaces are violated, covenants are infringed; this is not to deny their value and their respective functions, but it does leave doubts about the possibility of getting away from an interpersonal situation which is perpetually subject to crisis and uncertain as to its future. The history of Israel, as seen through the eyes of the Deuteronomist, looks like a monotonously repeated series of broken and reformulated agreements between God and Israel. This chain of betrayal makes re-proposals of the pact more and more insignificant as they go along, and makes a new attempt by the offended party unjustified.

There comes a moment in history when permission is no longer given to put the same old proposal on the table under the pretense of starting afresh; the moment comes when the old structure is judged to be decayed and finished for ever (Jer. 31.31-32). Then something new appears, which is not the updating of what has already been gone through, but something unheard of and unexpected (Isa. 48.6-8). The price of this new start—to which we attach the content of the new 'covenant'[101]—is the confession of human inability to be faithful to him who is 'just in all his actions', and the trust that his justice can be communicated as a personal gift of communion (the law) (Jer. 31.33). Authentic reconciliation, whose character is as fixed as the heavens (Jer. 31.35-37; 33.19-26), can only take place in the humble recognition that the wretchedness of the sinner is not so strong as to stand in the way of the mercy shown by the Just One (Isa. 45.21; Jer. 31.20; Hos. 11.8-9).

100. McCarthy, *Treaty and Covenant*, pp. 255-56.

101. Cf. esp. P. Beauchamp, *L'un et l'autre Testament: Essai de lecture* (Paris, 1976), pp. 249-74.

Part II

JUDGMENT (*MIŠPĀṬ*)

Introduction to Part II

In the first part of my work I dealt with the vocabulary and procedures governing a controversy between two parties in which, due to a lack of structures or by the spontaneous decision of the disputants, the re-establishment of peace occurred without the mediation of a judging authority.

I now want to talk about judgment, that is, the juridical structure in a strictly legal sense, and about its constituent elements, in such a way as to bring out the specific nature and vocabulary of this procedure by contrast with the ones previously analysed.

The general organization of a trial is familiar to everybody, even if non-specialists are unaware of the complex of studied techniques involved in modern criminal proceedings. Since my argument will proceed by following clearly distinguishable juridical steps, it does not seem necessary to give an overview of this second Part. It might be more useful to clarify the relationship with Part I from a vocabulary point of view and also the overall meaning to be attributed to the various juridical proceedings.

The continuation of the *rîb* is the trial, which seeks its conclusion in a judgment. This means that there are elements proper to the controversy that are carried over into a trial, and others that either undergo important modification or are characteristic of this kind of proceeding. The consequence of this observation is that it is easier to recognize vocabulary as 'juridical' than to assign it exactly to the proceedings to which it belongs. Since the 'notitia criminis', the charge, the debate between the parties, the punishment and so on are juridical factors common to both a controversy and a trial, we will find in a trial situation part of the lexicon we have already come across in the dispute situation; my task, however, will be to locate it as a step in the structure with a specific meaning and function. The operation we are preparing to carry out is not at all simple, if for no other reason than that, as is well-known, the Old Testament does not provide us with a textbook of proceedings to which reference can be made. The reconstruction I am attempting should, however, permit a reasonable and coherent systematization of the individual elements, except for the uncertainties that fatally undermine the treatment of linguistic phenomena and institutions known to us only through brief and fragmentary witnesses.

The *rîb* is carried over into a trial when the confrontation between the parties does not result in an agreement on the truth that can guarantee the re-establishment of justice. As we shall see, recourse to a judge shows that at least one of the parties refuses to confess that he is in the wrong. The judge—it is hoped—will manage to shed light on the situation, but will necessarily have to condemn the guilty and will not therefore be able to re-establish justice as the reconciliation of the parties. From this point of view, proceedings that involve forgiveness are more in line with true justice; so much is this true that it is in forgiveness that Israel recognizes 'divine' activity *par excellence* and the ideal human activity in society and history.

It does have to be remembered, however, that forgiveness is not always possible: if the felon persists in claiming to be in the right and carries on with arrogant and overbearing behaviour, the only recourse is to apply the court's superior authority for an intervention on behalf of the unjustly oppressed. Furthermore, forgiveness is not always appropriate; especially when it takes the form of a universal remission, an amnesty, or a generalized absolution, it is an act that seems to make light of the crime committed. The remission of guilt is a judicious, reasonable and just act to the extent that it still recognizes evil as evil—not because it declares good what is wicked, but because while condemning what is to be condemned it rescues people from the destructive power of their own wickedness. This means that forgiveness is aimed at humanity, but its intention can be misinterpreted, perverted and brought into the service of iniquity.

This leads to the affirmation that none of the juridical procedures concerned with the re-establishment of the conditions of justice is altogether free of ambiguity. It is a right and duty to be angry at injustice and to track down the guilty; however, the sapiential tradition counsels against being easily moved to fury (Prov. 4.17; 22.24; 29.22; 30.33) and useless litigation (Prov. 6.19; 10.12; 15.18; 17.14, 19; 18.6, 17 etc.). There is a well-known true saying, '*Summum jus, summa iniuria*', which means how easy it is to lose sight of equity in ruthless zeal against injustice.[1] On the other hand, it is laudable to be able to forgive another's faults; but sometimes it is wiser to punish than to tolerate, because forgiveness may encourage the habit of evil. As Isa. 26.10 reminds us, punishment teaches justice (*yuḥan rāšā' bal lāmad ṣedeq*), and as Prov. 29.15 advises, the rod is an instrument of wisdom (*šēbet wᵉtôkaḥat yittēn ḥokmâ*).

It seems, therefore, that the two proceedings have a complementary nature—the controversy ends, by way of forgiveness, with reconciliation, while the trial, by way of a sentence, ends with the punishment of the guilty—and this happens in such a way as to maintain the nature of the law in its integrity. In the development of human society, the relationship between these two proceedings has to be maintained as an interaction that has to be monitored constantly.

1. Cf. D. Daube, 'Summum Ius—Summa Iniuria', in *Studies in Biblical Law* (Cambridge, 1947), pp. 190-313; M. Fuhrmann, 'Philologische Bemerkungen zur Sentenz "Summum ius summa iniuria"', in *Studi in onore di E. Volterra*, II (Milan, 1971), pp. 53-81; E. Carcaterra, 'Ius summum saepe summast malitia', *ibid.*, IV, pp. 627-66.

Chapter 5

JUDGMENT IN COURT: GENERAL ELEMENTS AND VOCABULARY

In Part I of my work, I began my investigation beginning with the use and meaning of the root *ryb*; in Part II, the root *špṭ* will be my introduction to the subject of the courtroom judgment.

The distinction and link between the two aforementioned roots—and therefore between the two parts of my work—were suggested to me by the biblical texts, in which it is clearly said that the initial dispute situation (*rîb*) is resolved by the court's verdict (*špṭ*):

Deut. 25.1	***kî yihyeh rîb bên ʾanāšîm***
	weniggešû ʾel hammišpāṭ ûšepāṭûm
Deut. 19.17-18	***weʿāmedû šenê hāʾanāšîm ʾašer lāhem hārîb***
	lipnê yhwh lipnê hakkōhanîm wehaššōpeṭîm...
	wedārešû haššōpeṭîm hêṭēb
2 Sam. 15.2	***wayhî kol hāʾîš ʾašer yihyeh lô rîb***
	lābôʾ ʾel hammelek lammišpāṭ...[1]

It can also be seen from the texts I have quoted that the root *špṭ* has three distinct forms: (1) *šōpēṭ* (Deut. 19.7-8); (2) *špṭ* (Deut. 25.1); (3) *mišpāṭ* (Deut. 25.1; 2 Sam. 15.2). This triad occurs in one and the same text and shows in a succinct way the scope of the courtroom juridical action:

Deut. 16.18	***šōpeṭîm*** *wešōṭerîm titten lekā bekol šeʿāreykā...*
	wešāpeṭû *ʾet hāʿām*
	mišpaṭ *ṣedeq*
2 Chron. 19.6	*wayyōʾmer ʾel* ***haššōpeṭîm***
	reʾû mâ ʾattem ʿōśîm kî lōʾ leʾādām ***tišpeṭû*** *kî leyhwh*
	weʿimmākem bidebar ***mišpāṭ***

1. The transferability of the *rîb* to a courtroom situation is also attested by Exod. 23.3, 6; Deut. 1.12; 17.8; Isa. 1.23; 50.8; Ezek. 44.24; Job 31.13; Prov. 18.17; 22.22-23; Lam. 3.35-36; 2 Chron. 19.8-10.

Deut. 1.16-17 *wāʾaṣawweh ʾet* ***šōpᵉṭêkem*** *bāʿēt hahîʾ lēʾmōr*
šāmōaʿ bên ʾaḥêkem ***ûšᵉpaṭṭem*** *ṣedeq bên ʾîš ûbên ʾāḥîw ûbên gērô*
lōʾ takkîrû pānîm ***bammišpāṭ***

The internal arrangement of this chapter will therefore mirror the modes of the root *špṭ*: first I deal with the vocabulary used to describe the figure of the judge to whom the case is submitted for an authoritative decision (*šōpēṭ*, with its synonyms and paradigmatic equivalents); secondly, I will look at the general meaning of the verb *špṭ*, illustrating it in relationship to its synonyms; lastly, I will deal with the noun *mišpāṭ* and other terms which, according to the context or syntagm to which they belong, describe the nature, the procedure, the juridical situation or act of making a decisive judgment.

The aim of my treatment is to show how the semantic field of courtroom justice is not restricted to a technical lexicon of an explicitly 'legal' kind; what makes a term or expression juridically relevant is in fact the structure of relations to which they make reference in a particular context. The bird's eye view I will take of the general terminology of judging will also allow me to provide a framework of reference for the following analysis of courtroom procedure and its vocabulary at the specific stages out of which it is made.

1. *The Judge*

An essential element for the legal institution of the judgment is the jurisdiction[2] that belongs to the judge: he is the juridical individual to whom the right and power to do justice where it has been threatened or violated is submitted.

1.1. *The Hebrew Terms Used for the Role of the Judge*

1.1.1. *šōpēṭ*. Various terms are used to describe the function of judging; of these the most frequent is *šōpēṭ*.

2. 'Innumerable definitions of "jurisdiction" have been proposed, but the simplest and most expressive is still the one that cleaves to the actual etymology of the term (*jus dicere*) and has it consisting of the power to declare, with binding force, what is the will of the law in a definite particular case, in which the law has been, or is thought to have been, violated. In particular, *penal jurisdiction* consists in making known, with telling force, the penal law as it applies to a definite particular case and in applying sanctions' (Pisapia, *Compendio di procedura penale*, pp. 3-4).

Except in a few cases where it is used with finite value in a nominal clause (Judg. 4.4; 1 Sam. 3.13; 8.2; 2 Kgs 15.5; Ezek. 34.17), the participle of the verb *špṭ* is used to describe a post of public interest: it normally refers to the function of a magistrate,[3] but there is no lack of texts in which the participial noun refers in general terms to authority, a chief, a notable, and the like, and therefore where the juridical connotation is no longer clearly observable (cf., for example, Hos. 7.7; 13.10; Dan. 9.12; and the book of Judges). The term is used in the singular and in the plural, and it is a title attributed to God.[4]

1.1.2. *dayyān*. We find the term *dayyān* twice, both with reference to God; it is therefore important not so much for its frequency, but because it acts as the *nomen agentis* for *dyn*, as *šōpēṭ* does for *špṭ*.

In 1 Sam. 14.16, a whole string of verbs (*špṭ bên...ûbên, r'h, ryb 'et rîb, špṭ miyyād*), all of them belonging to the sphere of the courtroom, explain the meaning of the single noun *dayyān*: David appeals to the judgment of YHWH in his dispute with Saul, a judgment which, although unable to take the form of a normal courtroom trial, has the structural and linguistic characteristics of one.

In Ps. 68.6 (*'ᵃbî yᵉtômîm wᵉdayyan 'almānôt*), the reference to orphans and widows, who—as we shall see—are a typical object of judging activity, confirms the relevance of the term *dayyān* in the lexical series that designates the function of a judge.

1.1.3. *'āb*. The text just quoted reveals a parallelism between *dayyān* and *'āb* which leads me to ask about the latter term's use in describing the task of a judge.

3. In modern usage, judge and magistrate are two synonymous terms. In general terms, 'a *judge* is someone who has the capability or opportunity to hand down his opinion about a question, an opinion that is binding on the parties in dispute; in a narrower sense, it is the person invested by the State with the ability to hand down sentence in civil or criminal cases, that is, a *magistrate*' (G. Cesana, *Dizionario ragionato dei sinonimi e dei contrari* [Milan, 1981], p. 272).

4. In Ps. 58.12 we have the sole case in which the plural *šōpᵉṭîm* is applied to God: *'ak yēš 'ᵉlōhîm šōpᵉṭîm bā'āreṣ*. On Psalm 58, cf. in particular Alonso Schökel, *Treinta Salmos*, pp. 231-47.

On the relationship between 'the gods' and 'judgment' (with special reference to Psalm 82), cf. H.-W. Jüngling, *Der Tod der Götter: Eine Untersuchung zu Psalm 82* (SBS, 38; Stuttgart, 1969); M. Tsevat, 'God and the Gods in Assembly. An interpretation of Psalm 82', *HUCA* 40-41 (1969–70), pp. 123-37; Alonso Schökel, *Treinta Salmos*, pp. 287-304.

The metaphorical use of *'āb* to designate a protector seems to be widely recognized both by scholars of the Ancient Near East and of the world of the Bible.[5] The object of this responsibility and the sphere in which it is exercised give different nuances of meaning: we can have the 'master' (head teacher, master craftsman, principal) of a company of craftsmen (1 Chron. 4.14); the spiritual father (founder) of a prophetic brotherhood (2 Kgs 2.12; 13.14);[6] the priest in charge (chaplain, head priest) of a family or clan (Judg. 17.10; 18.19); the guardian of a socially or juridically disadvantaged class such as orphans, widows and the poor (Job 29.16; 31.18; cf. Sir. 4.10); and lastly a superintendent with a political role (Gen. 45.8; Isa. 22.21; cf. 1 Macc. 2.65). The two latter categories are of particular concern to me, because they are the most closely linked with matters juridical and responsibility for judgment in particular.[7]

'Father' of the orphans, (widows) and poor is a title generally received by those who look after such people; it must be observed, however, that the context is sometimes extremely juridical, to the extent that it could be said that a 'father' is someone who defends the rights of those who cannot do so for themselves (Lam. 5.3). In Job 29.16, for example, the phrase 'I will be a father for the poor' forms part of the description of the judging activity carried out by Job 'at the gates of the city' (29.7), where the wretched, the orphaned, the widowed and strangers (29.12-16) are saved from the violence of the wicked (*'awwāl*). The text of Sir. 4.10 (*hyh k'b lytwmym*) likewise makes a close link with the exercise of justice (cf. 4.9: *hwš' mwṣq mmṣyqyw w'l tqwṣ rwḥk bmšpṭ ywšr*).

The term 'father' applied to a political functionary, particularly a king,

5. E. Jenni, *''āb* Vater', *THAT*, I, p. 6; H. Ringgren, *''āb*', *ThWAT*, I, pp. 2-3, 6; P. Nel, 'The Concept "Father" in the Wisdom Literature of the Ancient Near East', *JNSL* 5 (1977), pp. 53-66. In a covenant context, cf. D.J. McCarthy, 'Notes on the Love of God in Deuteronomy and the Father–Son Relationship between Yahweh and Israel', *CBQ* 72 (1965), pp. 144-47; F.C. Fensham, 'Father and Son as Terminology for Treaty and Covenant', in *Near Eastern Studies* (FS W.F. Albright; Baltimore, 1971), pp. 121-35.

6. E. Jenni, *THAT*, I, pp. 5-6 (with bibliography). In particular see A. Phillips, 'The Ecstatics' Father', in *Words and Meanings* (FS D.W. Thomas; Cambridge, 1968), pp. 183-94; J. Coppens, 'Le roi idéal d'Is IX 5-6 et XI 1-5 est-il une figure messianique?', in *A la rencontre de Dieu* (Mém. A. Gelin; Le Puy, 1961), pp. 96-99.

7. P.A.H. de Boer notes that in Judg. 5.7 we find, attributed to Deborah, the title *'ēm b^eyiśrā'ēl* ('The Counsellor', in M. Noth and D. Winton Thomas [eds.], *Wisdom in Israel and in the Ancient Near East* [VTSup, 3; Leiden, 1955], p. 59).

seems more widespread in surrounding cultures than in the strictly Israelite[8] (cf. 1 Sam. 24.12; 2 Kgs 5.13; 16.7); however, the list of titles found in Isa. 9.5 includes among the attributes of the king *'ᵃbî'ad* too, which may be a way of indicating the king's constant care for this people, especially the poor, a care which is typical of good government[9] (Deut. 10.18; Pss. 10.14, 18; 72.12-13; 82.3-4 etc.). The title *'ābînû* (parallel to *gō'ᵃlēnû*) in Isa. 63.16 may be considered a title of sovereignty (cf. v. 19: *hāyînû mē'ôlām lō' māšaltā bām*).

1.1.4. *pālîl.*[10] The term *pālîl* is used three times in the plural. It seems to describe a category of *mediators* who enable a transaction or arrangement involving monetary compensation in Exod. 21.22,[11] whereas in Deut. 32.31 it seems rather to involve the figure of the *witness-judge* in a controversy; neither case is really concerned with a judging function so much as that of an intermediary, who does not pronounce a free or guilty verdict, but facilitates an agreement in case of dispute.[12]

8. *ThWAT*, I, pp. 2-3.

9. For a discussion of the kingly title list of Isa. 9.5 and in particular for the precise meaning to be attributed to *'ᵃbî'ad*, I refer to H. Wildberger, 'Die Thronnamen des Messias, Jes 9.5b', *TZ* 16 (1960), pp. 314-32; *idem*, *Jesaja* (BK, 10/1; Neukirchen, 1972), pp. 362-63, 376-86 (with full bibliographical documentation).

10. Cf. the bibliography in n. 42 of this chapter.

11. B.S. Jackson, *Essays in Jewish and Comparative Legal History* (Leiden, 1975), pp. 79-81, gives a critical discussion of all the difficulties in Exod. 21.22-25, and comes to the conclusion that *wᵉnātan biplīlîm* 'is an interpolation, representing the growth of state authority at the expense of self-help' (p. 81; in a footnote, the author adds, 'This does not necessarily imply a judicial function, since the role of the *pelilim* was probably that of assessing damages, not assigning liability'). Cf. also G. Liedke, *Gestalt und Bezeichnungen alttestamentlicher Rechtssätze* (WMANT, 39; Neukirchen, 1971), pp. 44-45.

12. Speaking of the juridical status of the tribes before their formation into a people under Moses, H. Cazelles says, 'Les conflits étaient des conflits de famille à famille, de tribus à tribus; pour les empêcher de dégénérer en interminables vendettas, des intercesseurs et arbitres (en hébreu *pelilim*) intervenaient pour régler à l'aimiable par des compositions et des concessions. C'étaient généralement des anciens qui, par leur autorité morale et leur expérience, finissaient par créer une sorte de jurisprudence coutumière, enregistrée dans des sentences ou *mishpâtim*' ('Le sens religieux de la Loi', in *Populus Dei.* I. *Israel*, p. 184).

I cannot tell from the biblical texts whether the rarely mentioned figure of the *pᵉlîlîm* is to be identified with that of the *zᵉqēnîm*, who have quite an important and well-defined juridical function. The latter probably intervened in order to secure a peaceful settlement of squabbles between families and perhaps between clans

The text of Job 31.11 (*w^ehû' 'āwōn p^elîlîm*), which refers to 31.28 (*gam hû' 'āwōn p^elîlî*), talks of a crime which, rather than demanding a court case, requires an intercessory intervention.

In conclusion, perhaps the likeliest thing is to hold that the meaning of the root *pll* (intercede) is also present in the noun *pālîl*, giving it the force of an intermediary, mediator or conciliator.[13]

1.2. *Those who Exercise a Judge's Function*[14]

It is generally accepted that there were three main jurisdictions to which those who submitted themselves for judgment had recourse: (1) that of the elders, 'at the gates of the city', (2) that of the priests, (3) that of the king.[15] We therefore have three nouns (*z^eqēnîm—kōh^anîm—melek*) which are often paradigmatic substitutes for the word 'judge', to the extent that they refer to the particular form of judicial competence required by the case in question.

It would be a mistake to believe, however, that the situation was clearly defined in Israel, either as regards the effective competence of the individual tribunals or as regards the persons who presided over them.[16]

(something which is plausible but not documented in the Bible), but they certainly presided over the trials which took place in the various 'cities' of Israel, even handing down capital sentences (cf. Deut. 21.18-21; 22.13-21; 1 Kgs 21.8-16).

As regards arbitration procedure, cf. B. Cohen, *Jewish and Roman Law: A Comparative Study*, II (New York, 1966), pp. 651-709; regarding the world of the Bible in particular, see pp. 658-63. See further n. 43 to this chapter.

13. J.L. Palache considers that it is inexact to distinguish between different *pll* roots; according to him, the basic idea of *pll* is that of 'splitting in two, separating', whence come *pillēl*, 'to judge, decide' (Latin *dirimere*) and *htpll*, 'to ask for a (favourable) judgment'. The author does not recognize *plyl* (*ym*) in the sense of an arbiter or judge, in any of the texts usually quoted (*Semantic Notes on the Hebrew Lexicon* [Leiden, 1959], pp. 59-60).

14. Cf. J.P.M. van der Ploeg, 'Les juges en Israël', in *Populus Dei*. I. *Israel*, pp. 463-507.

15. Regarding jurisdiction in its various forms, cf. R. de Vaux, *Les Institutions de l'Ancien Testament*, I (Paris, 1958), pp. 235-39; Z.W. Falk, *Hebrew Law in Biblical Times* (Jerusalem, 1964), pp. 56-57; Boecker, *Redeformen*, pp. 11-12; L. Rost, 'Die Gerichtshoheit am Heiligtum', in *Archäologie und Altes Testament* (FS K. Galling; Tübingen, 1970), pp. 225-31; K.W. Whitelam, *The Just King: Monarchical Judicial Authority in Ancient Israel* (JSOTSup, 12; Sheffield, 1979) (pp. 39-46 concern jurisdiction before the institution of the monarchy); R.R. Wilson, 'Enforcing the Covenant: The Mechanisms of Judicial Authority in Early Israel', in *The Quest for the Kingdom of God* (FS E. Mendenhall; Winona Lake, IN, 1983), pp. 59-75.

16. From Koehler's essay onwards ('Die hebräische Rechtsgemeinde', p. 152),

Prescinding from the problem posed by the change in institutions over the course of history,[17] we may ask who really were the 'elders', what was the jurisdiction of the priests and where was it exercised, what officials served in the royal law-court, whether this effectively represented a court of appeal, and so forth.[18]

We are so accustomed to the principles of our modern political institutions that we take it for granted that at least some such 'division of powers' existed in ancient Israel.[19] Now it turns out from the Bible on

the opinion has become widespread that judges (particularly those who presided over local court rooms) were not a specialized corps of functionaries in Israel; on the contrary—it is said—any citizen could, on occasion, be called upon to exercise the office of a judging magistrate, and likewise with the other functions of a defender or accuser required by a public trial (cf. Boecker, *Redeformen*, p. 13). My interpretation of the biblical texts is different: the role of judge was not exercised indiscriminately by everybody, but rather by those recognized as having some authority (of government): in accordance with spheres of competence and in accordance with the historical evolution of (civil or military) political authority, jurisdiction belonged to different people. This explains why the title of 'judge' is associated with *z^{e}qēnîm*, *śārîm*, *melek*, and so forth.

17. Cf. G. D'Ercole, 'The Juridical Structure of Israel from the Time of her Origin to the Period of Hadrian', in *Populus Dei*, I, pp. 389-461.

18. Regarding the difficulties in deciding jurisdictional competences with certainty, cf. A. Malamat, 'Organs of Statecraft in the Israelite Monarchy', *BA* 28 (1965), pp. 34-65; M. Weinfeld, *Deuteronomy and Deuteronomic School* (Oxford, 1972), pp. 233-36; G.C. Macholz, 'Die Stellung des Königs in der israelitischen Gerichtsverfassung', *ZAW* 84 (1972), pp. 157-82: this author denies that the king's law-court in Jerusalem acted as a court of appeal (p. 177), against de Vaux, *Institutions*, I, p. 234 (2 Sam. 14.4-11); Gamper, *Gott als Richter*, p. 181; H.J. Boecker, *Recht und Gesetz im Alten Testament und im Alten Orient* (Neukirchen, 1976), pp. 32-40.

19. By 'division of powers' it is meant that the three fundamental powers of the State—the legislative, the executive, both administrative and political, and the jurisdictional—should be exercised by groups of organs separate from and independent of one another. All other forms of authority (military, economic, domestic, educational, etc.) are regulated by the aforementioned organs in accordance with their different competences.

My interpretation of jurisdiction in Israel—in practice entrusted to those who wielded executive power—is not at odds with what N. Lohfink wrote (commenting on Deut. 16.18-18.22): 'Im ganzem gilt also dass eine früher vorhanden stärkere Machtkonzentration bei König und Priestern abgebaut und ein gewisses gleichgewicht der Kräfte zwischen vier verschiedenen Gewalten, nämlich Rechtsprechung, königlicher Regierung, Tempelpriestertum und freiem Charisma angestrebt wird. Wir können die Gewaltenteilung als Leitprinzip dieser Ämterverfassung bezeichnen, obwohl keine historische Kontinuität zur modernen Form der Gewaltenteilung vorliegt

the other hand that power tended to concentrate itself in the same hands, and that the important role of the judge was actually assigned to those who wielded other forms of authority (either civil or military, either political or religious).[20]

This explains on the one hand, why *šōpēṭ* sometimes refers just to an authoritative role in Israel, without any specific legal connotation; on the other hand, there is an inference that a jurisdictional meaning is to be detected in Hebrew words used to express 'authority', 'chief', and so on.

In this connection, it seems fitting to refer to the texts that deal explicitly with the instituting of 'judges'[21] by Moses: Exod. 18.13-27;[22]

und im einzelnen viele Unterschiede zu modernen Systemen vorhanden sind' ('Gewaltenteilung. Die Ämtergesetze des Deuteronomiums als gewaltenteiliger Verfassungsentwurf und das katholische Kirchenrecht', in *Unsere grossen Wörter* [Freiburg–Basel–Vienna, 1977], pp. 72-73).

Lohfink notes therefore that (as far as the law of Deuteronomy goes) the power of the State is not concentrated in a single person; this does not mean, however, that there are organs separate from and independent of each other for the three fundamental powers (legislative, executive, jurisdictional). Furthermore, certain problems arise in placing the prophet in the same line as the judges (= elders?), the king and the priests; the prophet, as well as being 'charismatic', does not seem to wield that element of coercion necessary for jurisdictional power. When he is recognized as a prophet, he seems rather to enjoy a moral authority, which allows him to give orders to all the (other) authorities in Israel.

20. Cf. J.P.M. van der Ploeg, 'Le pouvoir exécutif en Israel', in *Populus Dei*. I. pp. 509-19.

21. Cf. p. 33, n. 8. The terminology used to describe the *institution* of the 'judges' is the same as that employed for the other authoritative roles within Israel:

śym	someone	[JUDGE]	*šōpēṭ*	*bā'āreṣ*	2 Sam. 15.4
śym	someone		*l^{e}'îš śar w^{e}šōpēṭ*	*'ālênû*	Exod. 2.14
śym	someone		*šōp^{e}ṭîm*	*l^{e}yiśrā'ēl*	1 Sam. 8.1
śym			*śārê '^{a}lāpîm . . .*	*'^{a}lēhem*	Exod. 18.21
śym	someone		*b^{e}rā'šêkem*		Deut. 1.13
śym		[AUTHORITY]	*śārê '^{a}lāpîm*		1 Sam. 22.7
śym			*śārê '^{a}lāpîm*	*lô*	1 Sam. 8.12
śym			*melek l^{e}šopṭēnû*	*lānû*	1 Sam. 8.5
śym			*melek*	*'ālay*	Deut. 17.14
śym			*melek*	*'āleykā*	Deut. 17.15
ntn		[JUDGE]	*šōp^{e}ṭîm*	*l^{e}kā b^{e}kol*	
				š^{e}'āreykā	Deut. 16.18
ntn	someone		*rā'šîm*	*'^{a}lêkem*	
			śārê '^{a}lāpîm . . .	*l^{e}šibṭêkem*	Deut. 1.15

Deut. 1.9-18;[23] there are variations between the two redactions, but it is clear that they are dealing with the same event and the same problem.

The central question posed by these passages is the impossibility, for a *single man*, of governing a *numerous people* (Exod. 18.18: *kî kābēd mimmᵉkā haddābār lō' tûkal ʿᵃśōhû lᵉbaddekā*; Deut. 1.12: *'êkâ 'eśśā' lᵉbaddî ṭorḥᵃkem ûmaśśa'ᵃkem wᵉrîbᵉkem*; cf. also Exod. 8.24 and Deut. 1.9); the number of cases that require an authoritative decision makes it senseless to depend on a single person. However, this is not just a problem concerning the administration of justice, but, more generally, one of authority in a State; a single chief cannot in fact be present in all situations if the population is large or spread over a vast territory. Mention might be made, in this respect, of Num. 11.10-30, where Moses is faced with the people's hunger and has to admit the difficulty of dealing on his own with the people's needs (Num. 11.14: *lō' 'ûkal 'anōkî lᵉbaddî lāśē't 'et kol hāʿām hazzeh kî kābēd mimmennî*).[24]

The problem was solved by the creation of a *corps of judges* (Exod. 18.22-26; Deut. 1.16-17), which was not, however, a 'separate organ'

ntn		[AUTHORITY]	*melek lᵉšopṭēnû*	*lānû*	1 Sam. 8.6
ntn	someone		(*melek*)	*ʿāleykā*	Deut. 17.15
ntn			*melek wᵉśārîm*	*lî*	Hos. 13.10
ntn			*melek*	*lᵉkā*	Hos. 13.11
ntn			*nᵉgîdîm*	*bāhem*	2 Chron. 11.11
ʿmd (*Hi*)		[JUDGE]	*šōpᵉṭîm*	*bā'āreṣ*	2 Chron. 19.5
ʿmd (*Hi*)	someone	[AUTHORITY]	*lārō'š*		
			lᵉnāgîd	*bᵉ'eḥāyw*	2 Chron. 11.22

22. Cf. R. Knierim, 'Exodus 18 und die Neuordnung der mosaischen Gerichtsbarkeit', *BZAW* 73 (1961), pp. 146-71.

23. Cf. H. Cazelles, 'Institutions et terminologie en Deut. 1.16-17', in J.A. Emerton *et al.* (eds.), *Congress Volume, Geneva 1965* (VTSup, 15; Leiden, 1966), pp. 97-112.

24. Cf. S.R. Driver, *Deuteronomy* (ICC; Edinburgh, 3rd edn, 1902), pp. 14-19. Even Solomon presents the difficulty in governing as the imbalance between his youth (*naʿar qāṭōn*) and the multitude of people for whom provision has to be made (*ʿam rāb 'ᵃšer lō' yimmāneh wᵉlō' yissāpēr mērōb*) (1 Kgs 3.7-8); the terminology used in this passage (particularly vv. 8-9 in comparison with Exod. 18.18; Deut. 1.8-9; Num. 11.14) and the request for the gift of *wisdom* (which will be revealed in the famous trial in 1 Kgs 3.16-28) show how government and jurisdiction tend to be overlaid. Cf. F.C. Fensham, 'Legal Aspects of the Dream of Solomon', in *Fourth World Congress of Jewish Studies* (Jerusalem, 1967), pp. 67-70; Whitelam, *The Just King*, pp. 156-66; H.A. Kenik, *Design for Kingship: The Deuteronomic Narrative Technique in 1 Kgs 3.4-15* (SBLDS, 69; Chico, CA, 1983), pp. 143-46.

endowed with autonomy within its sphere of competence, but rather an organic group of people to whom a measure of power was delegated for minor cases.[25] The 'judges' were or became 'chiefs' in Israel; they were recognized as having received an authority that was also jurisdictional, in accordance with a well-defined hierarchical ladder[26] (Exod. 18.25: *wayyitēn 'ōtām rā'šîm 'al hā'ām śārê 'alāpîm śārê mē'ôt śārê ḥamiššîm weśārê 'aśārōt*; cf. also v. 21; Deut. 1.15: *wā'eqqaḥ 'et rā'šê šibṭêkem... wā'ettēn 'ōtām rā'šîm 'alêkem śārê 'alāpîm* etc.).

Finally, those who were chosen had to have particular qualities; in Exod. 18.21 they are described as *'anšê ḥayil*[27] *yir'ê 'elōhîm 'anšê 'emet śōne'ê bāṣa'* (cf. also v. 25), and in Deut. 1.13: *'anāšîm ḥakāmîm ûnebōnîm wîdū'îm* (cf. also v. 15).[28] However, if these qualities are

25. The system of government and judgment created in Israel foresaw in essence two levels of court: the first was that handed over to the local authorities, who dealt with simple or less serious cases, which did not require difficult interpretation of the law; the other was that reserved to Moses (or a central body), to which fell the task of deciding questions of especial importance for the life of the people or controversial questions (Exod. 18.22, 26; Deut. 1.17). This difference of levels may be noted also in Deut. 17.8-13 and 2 Chron. 19.5-11; this latter text, which refers to the measures taken by Jehoshaphat in his institutional reform, provides not only for a distinction between local authority (vv. 5-7) and central authority in Jerusalem (vv. 8-11) but also for a distinction between religious cases within priestly competence and 'civil' ones under royal competence (v. 11). Cf. W. Albright, 'The Judicial Reform of Jehoshaphat', in *A. Marx Jubilee Volume* (New York, 1950), pp. 61-82; Gamper, *Gott als Richter*, pp. 181-83; G.C. Macholz, 'Zur Geschichte der Justizorganisation in Juda', *ZAW* 84 (1972), pp. 314-40; Weinfeld, *Deuteronomy and Deuteronomic School*, pp. 235-36.

26. The hierarchical ladder has to be understood in the sense proposed by S.R. Driver: 'The passage does not state that the *whole* people was divided systematically into thousands, hundreds, fifties and tens, but only that chiefs commanding these numbers were appointed, who exercised judicial authority, not necessarily over those only who were under their immediate command, but over the people at large. Men were appointed with military rank and entrusted for the time with a share in the administration of justice' (*Deuteronomy* [ICC; Edinburgh, 3rd edn, 1902], p. 18).

27. Cf. J. van der Ploeg, 'Le sens de *gibbôr ḥail*', *RB* 50 (1941) = *Vivre et penser*, I, pp. 120-25; W. McKane, 'The *Gibbôr Ḥayil* in the Israelite Community', *GUOST* 17 (1957–1958), pp. 28-37.

28. The terminology of Exod. 18.12 and Deut. 1.13 is echoed, in an ironic tone, in the criticism of judges made by Isa. 5.21-23:

indispensable in judging, they are equally presumed in governing; if in fact on the one hand *force* (another word for power) (Isa. 9.5; 11.2, 4; 28.6; Ps. 2.9 etc.) is necessary for the good government of Israel, 'moral' qualities are also required, such as the love of truth, impartiality, the fear of God and above all wisdom (cf. Deut. 17.20; 2 Sam. 14.20; 1 Kgs 3.9-12, 28; Isa. 9.5-6; 11.1-5; Ps. 2.10-11; Prov. 8.15-16 etc.).[29]

I would like to draw from these observations some consequences that touch directly upon the subject with which I am dealing.

According to the period, local traditions and the author, we come across different titles in the biblical texts to describe authority; quite apart from the king (who, besides *melek*, is also called *rō'eh*, *mōšēl*, *rōzēn*, etc.), the various chiefs of the people are given the titles *rā'šîm*, *śārîm*, *q^{e}ṣînîm*, *n^{e}dîbîm*, *ḥōrîm*, *n^{e}gîdîm*,[30] *n^{e}śî'îm*, and others.[31] Specialists in Israel's institutions will perhaps be able to decide what was the origin,

Isa. 5.21	*hôy ḥ^{a}kāmîm b^{e}'ênêhem* *w^{e}neged p^{e}nêhem n^{e}bōnîm*	Deut. 1.13	*'^{a}nāšîm ḥ^{a}kāmîm* *ûn^{e}bōnîm*
Isa. 5.22	*hôy gibbôrîm lištôt yāyin* *w^{e}'anšê ḥayil limsōk šēkār*	Exod. 18.21	*'anšê ḥayil*
Isa. 5.23	*maṣdîqê rāšā' 'ēqeb šōḥad* *w^{e}ṣidqat ṣaddîqîm yāsîrû mimmennû*		*śōn^{e}'ê bāṣa'*

29. On *wisdom* as a 'judicial' gift, cf. M. Noth, 'Die Bewährung von Salomos "Göttlicher Weisheit"', in M. Noth and D. Winton Thomas (eds.), *Wisdom in Israel and in the Ancient Near East* (VTSup, 3; Leiden, 1955), pp. 225-37; N.W. Porteous, 'Royal Wisdom', *ibid*., pp. 247-61; P. Reymond, 'Le rêve de Salomon (1 Rois 3.4-15)', in *Maqqél Shâqédh* (FS W. Vischer; Montpellier, 1960), pp. 210-15; M. Clark, 'A Legal Background in the Yahwist's Use of "Good and Evil" in Genesis 2–3', *JBL* 88 (1969), pp. 266-78; Weinfeld, *Deuteronomy and Deuteronomic School*, pp. 244-47, 256; L. Kalugila, *The Wise King: Studies in Royal Wisdom as Divine Revelation in the Old Testament and its Environment* (ConBOT, 15; Lund, 1980).

The necessity for the *spirit* in good government is attested especially in Num. 11.10-30; cf. also Isa. 11.1-4 and Neh. 9.20.

30. The term *nāgîd* has been particularly studied: cf. P. Joüon, 'Notes de lexicographie hébraïque. X: *nāgîd* "préposé", d'où "chef"', *Bib* 17 (1936), pp. 229-33; W. Richter, 'Die *nāgīd*-Formel. Ein Beitrag zur Erhellung des *nāgīd*-Problems', *BZ* NS 9 (1965), pp. 71-84; T.N.D. Mettinger, *King and Messiah: The Civil and Sacral Legitimation of the Israelite Kings* (ConBOT, 8; Lund, 1976), pp. 152-74; B. Halpern, *The Constitution of the Monarchy in Israel* (HSM, 25; Chico, CA, 1981), pp. 1-11; S. Shaviv, '*Nābî'* and *nāgîd* in 1 Sam. IX.1–X.16', *VT* 34 (1984), pp. 111-12.

31. J. van der Ploeg discusses the meaning of 15 titles attributed to the chiefs of the people of Israel: *śar*, *nāgîd*, *nāśî'*, *nāsîk*, *rōzēn*, *'allûp*, *sāgān*, *qāṣîn*, *pera'*, *pinnâ*, *'ayil*, *šôa'*, *nādîb*, *ḥōrîm*, *rō'š*, in 'Les chefs du peuple d'Israël et leur titres', *RB* 57

specific competence and history of these officials;[32] the important fact for me is that they represented the face of *government* and *judgment* in the various cities of Israel. Although it is not always clear what the distinction was between the different classes of authorities and magistrates,[33] it seems obvious that in essence the application of the Law

(1950), pp. 40-61; cf. also by the same author, 'Les "nobles" israélites', *OTS* 9 (1951), pp. 49-64; E.A. Speiser, 'Background and Function of the Biblical *nāśī*', *CBQ* 25 (1963), pp. 111-17; J.R. Bartlett, 'The Use of the Word *r'š* as a Title in the Old Testament', *VT* 19 (1969), pp. 1-10; C. Schäfer-Lichtenberger, *Stadt und Eidgenossenschaft im Alten Testament: Eine Auseinandersetzung mit Max Webers Studie 'Das antike Judentum'* (BZAW, 156; Berlin, 1983), pp. 243-55 (on *śar/śārîm*), pp. 255-367 (on *nāśî'*); U. Rüterswörden, *Die Beamten der israelitischen Königszeit: Eine Studie zu śr und vergleichbaren Begriffen* (BWANT, 117; Stuttgart, 1985).

32. Cf. A. Phillips, *Ancient Israel's Criminal Law: A New Approach to the Decalogue* (Oxford, 1970), pp. 17-32.

33. I would like to make a distinction, on this subject, between different questions:

1. *The Problem of the 'Judges'* (before the institution of the monarchy). It is difficult to doubt that, at least in certain cases, they exercised actual legal jurisdiction (Gamper, *Gott als Richter*, pp. 118-20, gives as sure witnesses: Judg. 4.4-5; 1 Sam. 7.6, 15-17; 12; cf. also 1 Sam. 8.1-3), but it is equally clear that they had above all a military role in the conquest of the land of Canaan.

It seems reasonable to imagine that 'judge' in this case means a common point of authoritative reference in a period when the political institutions were not clearly defined; as 'chief', the Judge took decisions concerning war and all the other controversies that required mediation by authority. There was a natural passage from the 'Judge' to the 'King' (already anticipated by Abimelech, and later confirmed by the handing over of power from Samuel to Saul), to the extent that the people demanded stability in power (the king and his dynasty 'for ever') which was not sufficiently guaranteed by the charismatic and exclusively personal figure of the 'Judge'.

The subject has been quite thoroughly discussed; among the studies, I would like to single out O. Grether, 'Die Bezeichnung "Richter" für die charismatischen Helden der vorstaatlichen Zeit', *ZAW* 57 (1939), pp. 110-21; M. Noth, 'Das Amt des "Richters Israels"', in *Festschrift A. Bertholet* (Tübingen, 1950), pp. 404-17; F.C. Fensham, 'The Judges and Ancient Israelite Jurisprudence', *OTWerkSuidA* 2 (Potchefstroom, 1959), pp. 15-22; H.C. Thomson, '*Shopeṭ* and *Mishpaṭ* in the Book of Judges', *GUOST* 19 (1961–1962), pp. 74-85; J. Dus, 'Die "Sufeten" Israels', *ArOr* 31 (1963), pp. 444-69; W. Richter, 'Zu den "Richtern Israels"', *ZAW* 77 (1965), p. 40-72; K.-D. Schunck, 'Die Richter Israels und ihr Amt', in J.A. Emerton et al. (eds.), *Congress Volume, Geneva 1965* (VTSup, 15; Leiden, 1966), pp. 252-62; D.A. McKenzie, 'The Judge of Israel', *VT* 17 (1967), pp. 118-21; M.S. Rozenberg, 'The *šōpᵉṭîm* in the Bible', *Eretz-Israel* 12 (1972), pp. 77*-86*; T. Ishida, 'The Leaders of the Tribal Leagues "Israel" in the Pre-Monarchic Period', *RB* 80 (1973), pp. 514-30; A.D.H. Mayes, *Israel in the Period of the Judges* (SBT, 2nd Ser., 29;

depended on the king and the 'chiefs' of the people: they were in fact the institutional means by whose decrees and sentences 'the law was carried out' in Israel. Particular consideration is to be given then to the

London, 1974), pp. 56-67; J. Hauser, 'The "Minor Judges"—A Re-Evaluation', *JBL* 94 (1975), pp. 190-200; S.M. Warner, 'The Period of the Judges within the Structure of Early Israel', *HUCA* 47 (1976), pp. 57-79; C.H.J. de Geus, *The Tribes of Israel* (Assen, 1976), pp. 204-209; A. Malamat, 'Charismatic Leadership in the Book of Judges', in *Magnalia Dei: The Mighty Acts of God. Essays on the Bible and Archaeology in Memory of G.E. Wright* (Garden City, 1976), pp. 152-68; Z. Weisman, 'Charismatic Leadership in the Era of the Judges', *ZAW* 89 (1977), pp. 399-412; J.A. Soggin, 'Das Amt der "kleinen Richter" in Israel', *VT* 30 (1980), pp. 245-48; H.N. Rösel, 'Jephtah und das Problem der Richter', *Bib* 61 (1980), pp. 251-55; Schäfer-Lichtenberger, *Stadt und Eidgenossenschaft*, pp. 344-54.

2. *The Problem of the 'Elders' (zᵉqēnîm).* Discussion turns on the origin of this authoritative body and on the extent of their power in the course of Israel's history; cf. J.L. McKenzie, 'The Elders in the Old Testament', *Bib* 40 (1959), pp. 522-40; J. van der Ploeg, 'Les anciens dans l'Ancien Testament', in *Lex tua Veritas* (FS H. Junker; Trier, 1961), pp. 175-91; D.G. Evans, 'Rehoboam's Advisors at Shechem and Political Institutions in Israel and Sumer', *JNES* 25 (1966), pp. 273-79; Gamper, *Gott als Richter*, pp. 177-80; H. Cazelles, 'Rédactions et Traditions dans l'Exode', in *Studien zum Pentateuch* (FS W. Kornfeld; Vienna, 1977), pp. 41-42; H. Reviv, 'Elders and "Saviors"', *OrAnt* 16 (1977), pp. 201-204; S. Frick, *The City in Ancient Israel* (Missoula, MT, 1977), pp. 119-27; G. Bettenzoli, 'Gli "Anziani di Israele"', *Bib* 64 (1983), pp. 47-73; *idem*, 'Gli "Anziani" in Giuda', *Bib* 64 (1983), pp. 211-24. Finally I would like to single out the monograph, in Hebrew, by H. Reviv, *The Elders in Ancient Israel: A Study of a Biblical Institution* (Jerusalem, 1983).

3. *The Problem of the Lists of Officials.* These are so various as to require a specific examination of the individual texts so as to derive a precise picture of the institutional figure depicted on it. A further difficulty arises from the fact that it does not always seem clear whether the title *šōpᵉṭîm* always refers to a special *category* different from the others, or whether it is a specification of the *role* performed by particular officials. For example, Deut. 19.17-18 lists: *wᵉʿāmᵉdû...lipnê hakkōhᵃnîm wᵉhaššōpᵉṭîm...wᵉdārᵉšû haššōpᵉṭîm hêṭēb*: it may be asked whether we are dealing with a *waw explicativum* (cf. H.A. Brongers, 'Alternative Interpretation des sogenannten waw copulativum', *ZAW* 90 [1978], pp. 273-77; D.W. Baker, 'Further Examples of the *waw explicativum*', *VT* 30 [1980], pp. 129-36; B.A. Mastin, '*Wāw explicativum* in 2 Kgs VIII 9', *VT* 34 [1984], pp. 353-55), as a result of which the translation would be: ' the priests who have the role of judges', or whether it is a case of *waw* with separative force, as a result of which the translation would be: 'the priests or the judges' (a distinction between religious and civil authority: cf. Deut. 17.12). For this kind of problem see Exod. 2.14 (in comparison with 18.21-22); Deut. 17.9; 21.2 etc.

prophetic message which is not so much directed in general terms at the people, but specifically at its chiefs, those in charge, the authorities of Israel (cf., for example, Isa. 1.10-17; 3.1-15; Jer. 21–22; Ezek. 34; Hos. 4.4-6; 5.1; Amos 4.1; 6.1; Mic. 3.1; Zeph. 1.8-9; 3.1-5 etc.); if we bear in mind their 'judging' role, Israel's wicked authorities exalt evil by giving it the force of law, and pervert justice by using it as a tool of iniquity.[34]

In this context, particular importance is assumed by the theme of *YHWH the King* and the *Davidic Messiah* (which through Isaiah form part of exilic and post-exilic prophecy), for these themes contain the hope of a perfect re-establishment of justice after the disastrous experience of the corruption of Israel's leaders.[35]

4. *The Problem of Certain Officials.* It seems that certain officials were charged with accompanying or serving the main authority (that of the 'chief' or judge) (cf. M. Weinfeld, 'Judge and Officer in Ancient Israel and in the Ancient Near East', *IsrOrSt* 7 [1977], pp. 65-88). I would like to single out in particular:

a. The *šōṭᵉrîm*: these seem to have been officials who carried out orders by authority in the different circles in which it was exercised (J. van der Ploeg, 'Les *šoṭᵉrim* d'Israël', *OTS* 10 [1954], pp. 185-96; H. Cazelles, 'Institutions et terminologie en Deut. I 6-17', in J.A. Emerton *et al.* [eds.], *Congress Volume, Geneva 1965*, pp. 104-108).

b. The *sōpᵉrîm*: their task must have been that of taking down and recording in writing the authority's verdict (cf. T.N.D. Mettinger, *Solomonic State Officials: A Study of the Civil Government Officials of the Israelite Monarchy* [ConBOT, 5; Lund, 1971], pp. 25-51; K. Galling, 'Tafel, Buch und Blatt', in *Near Eastern Studies* [FS W.F. Albright; Baltimore, 1971], pp. 207-23).

c. The *mazkîr*: there is certainly no unanimity about the specific role of this official; cf. R. de Vaux, 'Titres et fonctionnaires égyptiens à la cour de David et Salomon', *RB* 48 (1939), pp. 395-97; J. Begrich, 'Sofer und Mazkir. Ein Beitrag zur inneren Geschichte des davidisch-salomonischen Grossreiches und des Königreiches Juda', *ZAW* 17 (1940–41), pp. 1-29; H. von Reventlow, 'Das Amt des Mazkir. Zur Rechtsstruktur des öffentlichen Lebens in Israel', *TZ* 15 (1959), pp. 161-75; H.J. Boecker, 'Erwägungen zum Amt des Mazkir', *TZ* 17 (1961), pp. 212-16; *idem*, *Redeformen*, pp. 106-108; W. Schottroff, *'Gedenken' im Alten Orient und im Alten Testament* (Neukirchen, 1964), pp. 253-71; Seeligmann, 'Zur Terminologie', pp. 260-61; Mettinger, *Solomonic State Officials*, pp. 7-24; de Geus, *The Tribes of Israel*, pp. 207-209.

34. Cf. also Pss. 58; 82; 94; Qoh. 3.16.

35. Cf. J. Lust, 'The Immanuel Figure: A Charismatic Judge-Leader', *ETL* 47 (1971), pp. 464-70 (with bibliography).

2. *The Act of Judging*

'Judging' is the act whereby a judge re-establishes violated justice. All a magistrate's actions are the mediation or paradigmatic substitution of this.[36]

2.1. *The Hebrew Verbs for 'to Judge'*

I would like to give a list of verbs that show a certain amount of synonymousness to each other and which in a general way express the act of 'judging'. The comments allow an evaluation of their relevance to the series.

2.1.1. *špṭ*.[37] The verb *špṭ* is usually translated as 'to judge'; only in certain cases is the more general 'to govern' preferred (Gen. 19.9; Ruth 1.1 etc.; cf. above the similar problem with *šōpēṭ*).

Judging normally presupposes a controverted situation in which good and evil,[38] right and wrong are not clearly defined. In the first instance, judging appears as the authoritative act of discerning, separating, deciding between what/whom is just and what/whom is unjust, between the innocent and the guilty.

This can be inferred from the syntactical construction in which the verb *špṭ* often appears: as well as the form with the accusative (with or without *'et*), we have *špṭ bên...ûbên* (Gen 16.5; Exod. 18.16; Num. 35.24; Deut. 1.16; Judg. 11.27; 1 Sam. 24.13, 16; Isa. 5.3; Ezek. 34.20). Identical with this is the expression *špṭ bên...l^e* in Ezek. 34.17, 22; and the simpler *špṭ bên* in Gen. 31.53 and Isa. 2.4 (= Mic. 4.3).[39]

36. As G. Leone writes, 'Il processo (penale) in senso stretto è il complesso degli atti diretti alla decisione giurisdizionale su una notizia di reato' (*Manuale di Diritto Processuale Penale* [Napoli, 1975], p. 12).

37. Cf. H. Ferguson, 'The verb *špṭ*', *JBL* 8 (1888), pp. 130-36; J. van der Ploeg, '*Shāpaṭ* et *mishpāṭ*' *OTS* 2 (1943), pp. 144-55; I.H. Eybers, 'The stem *š-p-ṭ* in the Psalms', in *Studies on the Psalms* (OTWerkSuidA, 6; Potchefstroom, 1963), pp. 58-63; Seeligmann, 'Zur Terminologie', pp. 272-78; Liedke, *Gestalt und Bezeichnungen*, pp. 62-73; *idem*, '*špṭ* richten', *THAT*, II, pp. 999-1009; Whitelam, *The Just King*, pp. 51-59.

38. A judge's task is *lišmōa' haṭṭôb w^{e}hārā'* (2 Sam. 14.17), or in similar terminology, *l^{e}hābîn bên ṭôb l^{e}rā'* (1 Kgs 3.9); the criticism of judges in Isa. 5.20 lists: *hôy hā'ōm^{e}rîm lāra' ṭôb w^{e}laṭṭôb rā'* (cf. M. Clark, 'A Legal Background to the Yahwist's Use of "Good and Evil" in Genesis 2–3', *JBL* 88 [1969], pp. 266-78).

39. The variations with which the preposition *bên* occurs have been analysed by

There are also very important texts in which the verb *špṭ* is clearly specified by the role of distinguishing between the *ṣaddîq* and the *rāšā'*. This is seen for example in Deut. 25.1: *...ûšᵉpāṭûm wᵉhiṣdîqû 'et haṣṣaddîq wᵉhiršî'û 'et hārāšā'*; likewise 1 Kgs 8.32: *...wᵉšāpaṭtā 'et ʿᵃbādeykā lᵉharšîa' rāšā' lātēt darkô bᵉrō'šô ûlᵉhaṣdîq ṣaddîq lātet lô kᵉṣidqātô*. In this context, Qoh. 3.17 may also be quoted: *'et haṣṣaddîq wᵉ'et hārāšā' yišpōṭ hā'ᵉlōhîm*; and Gen. 18.25, where we have the equivalent *'śh mišpāṭ* in place of *špṭ*: *ḥālīlâ lᵉkā mē'ᵃśōt kaddābār hazzeh lᵉhāmît ṣaddîq 'im rāšā' wᵉhāyâ kaṣṣaddîq kārāšā' ḥālīlâ lāk hᵃšōpēṭ kol hā'āreṣ lō' ya'ᵃśeh mišpāṭ*.[40]

2.1.2. *dyn*.[41] The parallelism with *špṭ* shows that the verb *dyn* may be considered one of its most important synonyms (Jer. 5.28; Ps. 9.9; Prov. 31.9; cf. also 1 Sam. 24.16); I will also show below how the semantic field of both verbs tend to be overlaid. It should be observed, however, that the verb never takes the construction *bên...ûbên*; this leads to the idea that this verb does not refer so much to the act of 'discernment' between guilty and innocent but to the judicial procedure (for or against). It would then be a case of a verb placed semantically between *špṭ* and *ryb* (cf. Qoh. 6.10), shading towards one or the other according to context.

2.1.3. *pll (Pi)*. There are those who maintain that the verb *pll* (*Pi*) has juridical force and means 'to be an arbiter, mediator, guarantor'; 1 Sam. 2.25; Ezek. 16.52; Ps. 106.30 are quoted in support.[42] As I have already

J. Barr, 'Some Notes on *bēn* "between" in Classical Hebrew', *JSS* 23 (1978), pp. 1-22.

40. From this point of view, it may be imagined that the kind of judgment Absalom claimed to hand down in opposition to the court of his father David did not have the characteristics of right judgment, to the extent that he seemed to rule in favour of all those who put forward a claim: *mî yᵉśīmēnî šōpēṭ bā'āreṣ wᵉ 'ālay yābô' kol 'îš 'ᵃšer yihyeh lô rîb ûmišpāṭ* ***wᵉhiṣdaqtîw*** (2 Sam. 15.4. Cf. J.P. Fokkelman, *Narrative Art and Poetry in the Books of Samuel* [Assen, 1981], pp. 167-68).

41. G. Liedke, '*dīn* richten', *THAT*, I, pp. 445-48: the root originally referred to the actual authoritative judging that occurred in a trial (p. 446); V. Hamp and G.J. Botterweck, '*dîn*', *ThWAT*, II, pp. 200-207: the original meaning of 'judgment' includes all acts of justice in favour of or against someone (p. 200). Cf. also M. Dahood, 'Is the Emendation of *yādîn* to *yāzîn* Necessary in Job 36.31?', *Bib* 53 (1972), pp. 539-41.

42. Cf. M.D. Goldman, 'The Root *pll* and its Connotation with Prayer (Attempted

said with reference to *pālîl*, I believe that the root *pll* expresses more a role of mediation than a strictly legal function of settling; for this reason *pll* (*Pi*) cannot be considered a real paradigmatic substitute for *špṭ*, even if it brings a 'third party' into the controversy.[43]

2.1.4. *šm' and dbr (Pi).* The verbs *šm'*[44] and *dbr* (*Pi*) can in certain contexts appear as synonyms of *špṭ* to the extent that they refer to two fundamental dimensions of a judge's activity, the '*audience*' (the debate phase) and the pronunciation of *sentence* (the concluding phase of a trial). It should be observed that in every case they are found in parallel with the verb *špṭ* or clearly take its place: for *šm'* cf. Deut. 1.16 (*bên...ûbên*),[45] 17; Judg. 11.10 (*bên*); 2 Sam. 15.3; 1 Kgs 3.9[46] (in 3.11: *šm' mišpāṭ*); Job. 31.5; for *dbr* (*Pi*) cf. 2 Kgs 25.6 (*mišpāṭ*); Isa. 63.1; Pss. 51.6; 58.2 (*ṣedeq*); Zech. 8.16 (*'ᵉmet*) etc.

Explanation of Deuteronomy XXXII.31)', *AusBR* 3 (1953), pp. 1-6; D.R. Ap-Thomas, 'Notes on some Terms relating to Prayer', *VT* 6 (1956), pp. 230-39; E.A. Speiser, 'The Stem PLL in Hebrew', *JBL* 82 (1963), pp. 301-306; H.P. Stähli, '*pll* hitp. beten', *THAT*, II, p. 427.

43. The existence in Israel of the practice of *arbitration* is attested in a few biblical passages and has great plausibility (cf. n. 12); it may also be hypothesized that this function of mediation in disputes, especially in matters of civil law, was exercised by the same people (endowed with at least moral authority) to whom the task of judgment was entrusted. But this does not mean that judging was a sort of conciliation of the parties, as Gemser seems to maintain ('The *rîb-* or Controversy-Pattern', p. 124): 'The decision given by the judges is more of the nature of a settlement through mediation, arbitration, than a verdict based on law-clauses'. This opinion seems to be derived from Koehler ('Die hebräische Rechtsgemeinde', p. 150), who, speaking of Israel's judging assembly, says, 'Sie ist das Institut der Friedlichlegung'. This is in blatant contrast with the task that biblical legislation assigns to judges in a penal context.

44. Weinfeld, following a suggestion by H. Cazelles ('Institutions et terminologie en Deut. I.6-17', in J.A. Emerton *et al.* (eds.), *Congress Volume, Geneva 1965*, pp. 109-10) maintains that the verb *šm'*, in connection with a judgment, has a special relationship to the sapiential tradition (*Deuteronomy and Deuteronomic School*, pp. 245-47).

45. The actual text of Deut. 1.16 represents an overloaded construction; for a stricter parallelism, *ûbên gērô* should be inserted immediately after *bên 'ᵃḥêkem*.

46. R. Brunner, 'Das hörendes Herz', *TLZ* 79 (1954), pp. 697-700; T.N.D. Mettinger, *King and Messiah* (Lund, 1976), pp. 238-46; H.A. Kenik, *Design for Kingship* (Chico, CA, 1983), pp. 132-41.

2.1.5. *'śh mišpāṭ*. The phrase *'śh mišpāṭ*[47] means to have an ethical attitude of conformity to the law (Jer. 5.1; Mic. 6.8; Prov. 21.7, 15); in certain contexts, however, it refers to a judicial action, as may be seen from: (a) the link with *špṭ* in clearly legal texts: Gen. 18.25; 1 Kgs 3.28 (= 2 Chron. 9.18); see also Pss. 9.17; 119.84; 146.7; (b) the fact that, like *špṭ*, it can be construed with *bên...ûbên* (Jer. 7.5) or *bên...lᵉ* (Ezek. 18.8).

Of particular importance are the texts in which *mišpāṭ* is found in the construct state and the *nomen rectum* refers to a category of 'those in the right' (cf. Deut. 10.18; 1 Kgs 8.59; Pss. 9.5; 140.13).

The most complete syntagm is *'śh mišpāṭ ûṣᵉdāqâ*, which generally refers to uprightness in behaviour (Gen. 18.19; Ezek. 18.5, 19, 21, 27 etc.) but has procedural force in 1 Kgs 10.9; Jer. 22.3, 15; Ps. 99.4; to these latter texts may be added 2 Sam. 8.15 (= 1 Chron. 18.14); Jer. 9.23; 23.5; 33.15; Ezek. 45.9.[48]

2.2. *The Impartiality Necessary for Right Judging*

From a general consideration of *špṭ* and its synonyms, we now proceed to deal with the sort of judging that corresponds to its real nature. In fact, it is not enough that there should be a judgment, it is necessary that it should be *just*.

Now if the judge's fundamental task is to tell the guilty from the innocent, the first and main characteristic of right judging is that of maintaining a certain equidistance between the two parties in dispute; in other words, one is required to be *impartial*, not to allow oneself to be corrupted by any element that could change the course of justice. It is possible, then, following a logical scheme, to establish two antithetical paradigms: on the one hand, the paradigm of 'just judgment', and on the other that of 'dishonest judgment'; the quality of impartiality belongs to the former, partiality to the other.

47. The particular meaning of *'śh mišpāṭ* with a suffix or in the construct state is dealt with below.

48. The root *ḥqq* also seems to have connections with the sphere of jurisdiction and the courtroom; relevant texts seem to be Isa. 10.1 (*Qal*); Prov. 31.5 (*Pu*); 8.15 (*Po*). Cf., in this context, J. van der Ploeg, 'Studies in Hebrew Law', *CBQ* 12 (1950), 250-52; Z.W. Falk, 'Hebrew Legal Terms', *JSS* 5 (1960), pp. 350-52; R. Hentschke, *Satzung und Setzender: Ein Beitrag zur israelitischen Rechtsterminologie* (BWANT, 5/3; Stuttgart, 1963); P. Victor, 'A Note on *ḥōq* in the Old Testament', *VT* 16 (1966), pp. 358-61; G.H. Jones, 'The Decree of Yahweh (Ps. II 7)', *VT* 15 (1965), pp. 336-44; Liedke, *Gestalt und Bezeichnungen*, pp. 154-86.

2.2.1. *The Opposition between 'Correct' and 'Corrupt' Judging*. The opposition between the two kinds of judging is made extremely clear in the legislative texts where directives are given to judges for the correct administration of justice:

Deut. 1.16	*...ûš*^{e}*paṭṭem ṣedeq* *bên 'îš ûbên 'āḥîw...*	
Deut. 1.17		*lō' takkîrû pānîm bammišpāṭ*
	kaqqāṭōn kaggādōl tišmā'ûn	
Lev. 19.15		*lō' ta*^{a}*śû 'āwel bammišpāṭ* *lō' tiśśā' p*^{e}*nê dāl* *w*^{e}*lō' tehdar p*^{e}*nê gādôl*
	b^{e}*ṣedeq tišpōṭ '*^{a}*mîtekā*	
Deut. 16.18	*...w*^{e}*šāp*^{e}*ṭû 'et hā'ām* *mišpaṭ ṣedeq*	
Deut. 16.19		*lō' taṭṭeh mišpāṭ* *lō' takkîr pānîm* *w*^{e}*lō' tiqqaḥ šōḥad*

Grouping the essential elements of the aforementioned texts schematically, we have:

1. *just judgment*:	*špṭ ṣedeq*	(Deut. 1.16)
	špṭ b^{e}*ṣedeq*	(Lev. 19.15)
	špṭ mišpaṭ ṣedeq	(Deut. 16.18)

to which corresponds *impartiality*: *kaqqāṭōn kaggādōl tišmā'ûn* (Deut. 1.17).

2. *dishonest judgment*:	*'śh 'āwel bammišpāṭ*	(Lev. 19.15)
	nṭh (Hi) mišpāṭ	(Deut. 16.19)

to which corresponds the attitude of *partiality* and *corruption*:

nkr (Hi) pānîm	(Deut. 1.17; 16.19)
nś' pānîm	(Lev. 19.15)
lqḥ šōḥad	(Deut. 16.19)

2.2.2. *The Vocabulary of Right Judging (Just Judgment)*. The experience that justice is often administered in a dishonest way explains why the trait of uprightness is frequently emphasized in the biblical texts along with the verb which expresses the legal action of judgment. As well as the phrase *'śh mišpāṭ ûṣ*^{e}*dāqâ* mentioned above, I would like to quote some examples of syntagms that express judging in conformity with justice:

špṭ	*mišpaṭ ṣedeq*	Deut. 16.18
špṭ	*mišpaṭ ʾemet*	Zech. 7.9
špṭ	*ʾemet ûmišpaṭ šālôm (bešaʿarêkem)*	Zech. 8.16
špṭ	*ṣedeq*	Deut. 1.16; (Jer. 11.20; Ps. 9.5; Prov. 8.16); 31.9
špṭ	*mêšārîm*	Ps. 58.2 (75.3)
špṭ	*mîšôr*[49]	Ps. 67.5
špṭ	*beṣedeq*	Lev. 19.15; Isa. 11.4; Ps. 9.9
špṭ	*beṣedeq...beʾemûnâ*	Ps. 96.13
špṭ	*beṣedeq...bemêšārîm*	Ps. 98.9
špṭ	*beʾemet*	Prov. 29.14
dyn	*beṣedeq...bemišpāṭ*	Ps. 72.2
dyn	*bemêšārîm*	Pss. 9.9; 96.10
dbr (Pi)	*ṣedeq*	Ps. 58.2
dbr (Pi)	*biṣedāqâ*	Isa. 63.1[50]

2.2.3. *Injustice in the Courtroom (Wicked Judgment).* In this section I would like to point out the generic phrases that are used in Hebrew to express unjust judging. It should be noted that it is always a question of an act carried out 'legally' in a law court (*bammišpāṭ*), by means of which, however, the law (*mišpāṭ*) is trampled on and overturned: the phrase 'perversion of justice' is therefore very exact when used in this context; use is being made of the law and its institutions to promote and compound injustice.

Alongside the phrases of a generic nature that describe unjust judgment, I would like to single out, each time they occur, other related elements; in particular, I would like to emphasize the appearance of two categories (the subject of examination in later sections) that bring out how/why injustice is practised in the courtroom: (1) *partiality*: having favourites, keeping a favourable eye on certain categories of people, leaning towards one of the two disputants in a trial is intrinsically to

49. In Isa. 11.4 we have *ykḥ (Hi) bemîšôr* in parallel with *špṭ beṣedek*. The verb *ykḥ* (Hi) is used as a synonym to *špṭ* also in Isa. 2.4 and 11.3; as I have pointed out above, it sometimes takes on the meaning of 'to arbitrate' between the parties in dispute, or 'to punish', which brings it close to the semantic field of judging.

Just as a defence intervention (for example *ryb rîb* + pronomial suffix) on behalf of someone in the right can be the equivalent of a genuine act of justice (cf. below), so an accusatory action (for example *ykḥ* in the *Hi*) against the guilty can be synonymous with doing justice.

50. I would also like to note the phrases *rdp ṣedeq* (Deut. 16.20), *rdp ṣedāqâ wāḥāsed* (Prov. 21.21), and *rdp (Pi) ṣedāqâ* (Prov. 15.9), which describe the intentions of anyone wanting to preside over right judgment.

negate the very act of judging: if the decision is to be inspired by truth and law, it is necessary that the judge should be equidistant from the parties, without personal involvement. (2) *corruption*: taking money or other forms of recompense in exchange for a 'favour' to be granted to someone on trial is to turn the law court into a market, in which the cost is borne fatally by the poor.

2.2.3.1. *The Importance of the Verb nṭh (Hi) (to Pervert Justice).* Because of its frequency and its relevance to the law court, the verb *nṭh* (*Hi*) deserves special consideration. It occurs in various syntagms:

a. Construed with the noun *mišpāṭ* (to pervert, to twist justice), sometimes with an indication of who is doing the wrong:

Deut. 16.19	*lō' taṭṭeh*	*mišpāṭ*		*lō' takkîr pānîm*		(1)
				w^{e}lō' tiqqaḥ šōḥad		(2)
1 Sam. 8.3				*wayyiṭṭû 'aḥ^{a}rê habbāṣa'*		(2)
				wayyiqḥû šōḥad		(2)
	wayyaṭṭû	*mišpāṭ*				
Deut. 24.17	*lō' taṭṭeh*	*mišpaṭ*	*gēr yātôm*			
Deut. 27.19	*'arûr maṭṭeh*	*mišpaṭ*	*gēr yātôm*	*w^{e}'almānâ*		
Exod. 23.6	*lō' taṭṭeh*	*mišpaṭ*	*'ebyōn^{e}kā*		*b^{e}rîbô*	
Lam. 3.35	*l^{e}haṭṭôt*	*mišpaṭ*	*gāber...*		*b^{e}rîbô*	
Lam. 3.36	*l^{e}'awwēt*		*'ādām*			

b. Construed with a complementary object indicating *the person to whom the wrong is being done*—sometimes a legal specification is added (by way of the preposition *b*^{e} or *min*):

Amos 5.12	*ṣōr^{e}rê ṣaddîq*	*lōq^{e}ḥê kōper*	(2)
	w^{e}'ebyônîm ***baššaʻar*** *hiṭṭû*		
Prov. 18.5		*ś^{e}'ēt p^{e}nê rāšā' lō' ṭôb*	(1)
	l^{e}haṭṭôt ṣaddîq ***bammišpāṭ***		
Isa. 10.2	*l^{e}haṭṭôt* ***middîn*** *dallîm*		
	w^{e}ligzōl mišpaṭ '^{a}niyyê 'ammî		
Isa. 29.21[51]	*maḥ^{a}ṭî'ê 'ādām b^{e}dābār*		

51. In Isa. 29.21, the verb *nṭh* (*Hi*) is followed by *b*^{e}, to which causal value may be given ('for nought'); this may be compared as regards meaning with Amos 2.6: *'al mikrām bakkesep ṣaddîq—w^{e}'ebyôn ba'^{a}bûr na'^{a}lāyim*; the modal *b*^{e} of Ps. 27.9 may also be mentioned: *'al taṭ b^{e}'ap 'abdekā*.

Another interpretation could be that of giving *b*^{e} the value of a preposition of place, along the lines of the syntagm in Prov. 18.5 (and Amos 5.12): *nṭh (Hi)—ṣaddîq/'ebyôn—baššaʻar/bammišpāṭ*. The tribunal (*šaʻar*, mentioned in the previous stich), would then be identified—in a savagely ironic way—with primordial chaos

w^e^lammôkîaḥ ***baššaʻar*** *y^e^qōšûn*
wayyaṭṭû battōhû ṣaddîq
Mal. 3.5 *ûb^e^ʻōš^e^qê ś^e^kar śākîr ʼalmānâ w^e^yātôm*
ûmaṭṭê gēr

c. In conjunction with *terms that mean ʻway, road, path'*, the verb *nṭh* (*Hi*) seems to mean that the *iter* of justice has been turned, that legal ways have been perverted:[52]

Prov. 17.23 *šōḥad mēḥêq rāšāʻ yiqqāḥ* (2)
l^e^haṭṭôt ʼōrḥôt mišpāṭ
Job 24.4 *yaṭṭû ʼebyônîm middārek*
Amos 2.7 *w^e^derek ʻ^a^nāwîm yaṭṭû*

d. Finally, we have the special case of *nṭh* (*Qal*) *ʼaḥ^a^rê*...Whereas, in the previous cases, *nṭh* (*Hi*) took the law or the person who embodies it (*ṣaddîq*) as its object, in the current syntagm the verb (in the *Qal*) refers rather to the one towards whom the judge ʻdeviatesʼ, this being the cause of the perversion of justice.

I have already quoted 1 Sam. 8.3, where the two meanings of the verb are clearly linked: *wayyiṭṭû ʼaḥ^a^rê habbāṣaʻ*...*wayyaṭṭû mišpāṭ*. The same phenomenon may be noticed in Exod. 23.2: (*lōʼ tihyeh ʼaḥ^a^rê rabbîm l^e^rāʻōt w^e^lōʼ taʻ^a^neh ʻal rīb*) *linṭōt ʼaḥ^a^rê rabbîm l^e^haṭṭōt*. It may be noted that in 1 Sam. 8.3 the perversion of law is caused by an inclination towards profit, while in Exod. 23.2 it is the fruit of the favouritism towards the people gathered in judgment; in this way we see appear again the two categories that give actual expression to legal

(*tōhû*), where there is no distinction between good and evil. For the opposition *tōhû*—*ṣedeq*/*mêšārîm*, cf. Isa. 45.19; in Isa. 59.4 *ṣedeq* and *ʼ^e^mûnâ* are in opposition to *tōhû*/*šāwʼ*/*ʻāmāl*/*ʼāwen*.

52. The concept of way (*derek* and synonyms) is often used metaphorically to mean behaviour, especially in the sapiential literature and in a religious context (cf. *THAT*, I, pp. 458-60). When the term *way* is construed with terms meaning *law*, justice, etc. (of the kind *ʼōraḥ mišpāṭ*), I think that it means ʻto proceedʼ in conformity with the law (cf. Isa. 26.8; 40.14; 59.8; Prov. 2.8; 8.20); when it is construed with nouns meaning the *innocent*, the *just*, the *poor* (of the kind: *derek ṣaddîqîm*) the syntagm may be included, as far as meaning goes, with the previous case (cf. Prov. 2.8; where *ʼōrḥôt mišpāṭ* and *derek ḥ^a^sîdāyw* are placed in parallel. Just ʻproceedingʼ, in certain contexts such as Prov. 17.23, may refer to law court procedure in conformity with the law (cf. V. Maag, *Text, Wortschatz und Begriffswelt des Buches Amos* [Leiden, 1951], p. 142). Seeligmann likewise states that *derek* sometimes means ʻjudgment, trialʼ, quoting (as well as Amos 2.7) Isa. 40.27 and Jer. 5.4 (where *derek* is in parallel with *mišpāṭ*), and Ps. 1.6 (ʻZur Terminologieʼ, p. 269).

injustice (or better, are the cause of it), as mentioned at the beginning of this section.[53]

2.2.3.2. *Generic Expressions Meaning Injustice in the Law Court.* I would like to give some examples that seem particularly important to me; the variety of expressions is quite large, but—I think—it can easily be seen how they can be formed into paradigms; it should be kept in mind, in particular, how the act or 'perversion' takes as its object both the law and whoever labours under it (the innocent person):

špṭ	*'āwel*	Ps. 82.2
'śh	*'āwel bammišpāṭ*	Lev. 19.15; 19.35
'śh	*'awlâ*	Zeph. 3.5
'wt (Pi)	*mišpāṭ*	Job 8.3; 34.12
'wt (Pi)	*ṣedeq*	Job 8.3
'wt (Pi)	*'ādām b^erîbô*	Lam. 3.36
'wt (Pi)	(pron. suff.)	Job 19.6; Ps. 119.78 (+ *šeqer*)
t'b (Pi)	*mišpāṭ*	Mic. 3.9
t'b (Pi)	*dōbēr tāmîm*	Amos 5.10
gzl	*mišpaṭ ^{'a}niyyê 'ammî*	Isa. 10.2
gzl	*dal...baššā'ar*	Prov. 22.22
gēzel	*mišpāṭ wāṣedeq*	Qoh. 5.7
swr (Hi)	*mišpāṭ* (+ pron. suff.)[54]	Job 27.2; 34.5
swr (Hi)	*ṣidqat ṣaddîqîm mimmennû*	Isa. 5.23
m's	*mišpaṭ 'abdî wa'^amātî b^erîbām 'immādî*	Job 31.13
m's	*tām*	Job 8.20
prr (Hi)	*mišpāṭ* (+ pron. suff.)	Job 40.8
'qš (Pi)	*'et kol hay^ešārâ*	Mic. 3.9[55]

2.2.4. *Impartiality and Partiality in Judgment.*[56] The legislative texts that speak of trials have it as a constant concern that judgment should be

53. To the two cases quoted above we may perhaps link Job 36.18: *w^erob kōper 'al yaṭṭekkā* (*nṭh* in the *Hiphil*). The text of Job 36.17-21 is particularly thick with problems (cf. Alonso Schökel and Sicre, *Job*, pp. 508-10); despite this it may be observed how the theme of corruption and that of the perversion of the law are closely connected.

54. In Zeph. 3.14, a similar expression (with the plural and a pronominal suffix) means 'to lift the condemnation', i.e. to grant amnesty.

55. I would also like to single out the special expression in Hab. 1.4: *'al kēn yēṣē' mišpāṭ m^e'uqqāl.*

56. On this subject, cf. J.M. Bassler, *Divine Impartiality: Paul and a Theological Axiom* (SBLDS, 59; Chico, CA, 1982), pp. 7-17.

impartial (cf. the texts already quoted from Exod. 23.2-3; Lev. 19.15; Deut. 1.17). Except for Deut. 1.17 (where impartiality is commanded: *kaqqāṭōn kaggādōl tišmā'ûn*), all the other texts prohibit or condemn partiality.

Two expressions with equivalent meaning are used for this (unjust) favouring of someone during a trial:

a. *nkr* (*Hi*) *pānîm*:

Deut. 1.17	*lō' takkîrû pānîm*	*bammišpāṭ*	
Deut. 16.19	*lō' takkîr pānîm*		
Prov. 24.23	*hakkēr pānîm*	*b^{e}mišpāṭ*	*bal ṭôb*
Prov. 28.21	*hakkēr pānîm*		*lō' ṭôb*

b. *nś' pānîm*:[57]

Deut. 10.17	*lō' yiśśā' pānîm*		
Mal. 2.9	*w^{e}nōś^{e}'îm pānîm*	*battôrâ*	
Job 13.10	*bassēter pānîm tiśśā'ûn*		
Lev. 19.15[58]	*lō' tiśśā' p^{e}nê* ***dāl***		
Job 34.19[59]	*lō' nāśā' p^{e}nê* ***śārîm***		
Job 32.21	*'al nā' 'eśśā' p^{e}nê* ***'îš***		
Prov. 18.5	*ś^{e}'ēt p^{e}nê* ***rāšā'***		*lō' ṭôb*
Ps. 82.2	*ûp^{e}nê* ***r^{e}šā'îm*** *tiś'û*		

2.2.5. *The Integrity and Corruption of Judges.* It is through an examination of the vocabulary referring to corruption in the law court that we will gain an indirect idea of the ideal of integrity fitting for right judgment.

Corruption is one of the most frequent elements pointing to injustice in the law court; the terminology used highlights certain *nouns* which tell

57. Cf. also the expression *maśśō' pānîm* in 2 Chron. 19.7. On the expression *nkr* (*Hi*) *pānîm* and *nś' pānîm*, cf. Seeligmann, 'Zur Terminologie', pp. 270-72; J. Reindl, *Das Angesicht Gottes im Sprachgebrauch des Alten Testaments* (ErfTSt, 25; Leipzig, 1970), pp. 189-90; A.S. van der Woude, '*pānīm* Angesicht', *THAT*, II, pp. 441-42, 457.

58. Cf. also Sir. 35.12-13: *ky 'lhy mšpṭ hw' w'yn 'mw* ***mśw' pnym—l' yś' pnym*** *'l dl wtḥnwny mṣwq yšm'*.

59. The text of Job 34.19, speaking of God's impartiality, uses at the same time the two verbs *nś'* and *nkr* (*Pi*):

'^{a}šer lō' ***nāśā'*** *p^{e}nê śārîm*
w^{e}lō' ***nikkar*** *šôa' lipnê dāl*

Cf. P. Joüon, 'Notes de lexicographie hébraïque. XIII. *šôa'* "grand" (socialement)', *Bib* 18 (1937), pp. 205-206.

of economic force overcoming truth and justice; the whole thing, naturally, is done 'by stealth' (Deut. 17.25; Prov. 17.23; 21.14; cf. also Job 13.10),[60] in such a way that the verdict pronounced always appears to be in the strictest conformity with legality.

a. *šōḥad*.[61] The general meaning of this term is of a gift offered in order to get some sort of advantage (1 Kgs 15.19; 2 Kgs 16.8); in practical terms, it concerns a form of payment for a service requested or received (cf. the parallel between *šōḥad* and *m^{e}ḥîr* in Isa. 45.13 and Mic. 3.11).

In the sphere of the court room, *šōḥad* is typically the indicator of a judge's corruption;[62] one of the frequent syntagms is *lqḥ šōḥad*, often linked to other expressions that suggest the perversion of the law:

Exod. 23.6				*nṭh (Hi) mišpāṭ*
	lqḥ šōḥad			
Deut. 10.17	*lqḥ šōḥad*	*nś'*	*pānîm*	
Deut. 16.19	*lqḥ šōḥad*	*nkr (Hi)*	*pānîm*	*nṭh (Hi) mišpāṭ*
1 Sam. 8.3	*lqḥ šōḥad*			*nṭh (Hi) mišpāṭ*
Prov. 17.23	*lqḥ šōḥad*			*nṭh (Hi) 'orḥôt mišpāṭ*
2 Chron. 19.7	*miqqaḥ šōḥad*	*maśśō'*	*pānîm*	

(Cf. also Deut. 27.25; Ezek. 22.12; Ps. 15.5)

Two texts seem particularly important to me with regard to jurisdiction and the law courts:

rā'šeyhā b^{e}šōḥad yišpōṭû (Mic. 3.11)

We should not overlook the syntagms *špṭ b^{e}ṣedeq* (Lev. 19.15; Isa. 11.4 etc.), *špṭ be'^{e}met* (Prov. 29.14) and the like, which give by contrast extraordinary emphasis to the words of the prophets.[63]

60. For the concept of 'stealth' in Deut. 27.25, cf. S.R. Driver, *Deuteronomy* (ICC; Edinburgh, 3rd edn, 1902), pp. 299-300; the aspect of 'stealth' suggested by the noun *ḥêq* (in Proverbs) is noted by G. André, '*ḥêq*', *ThWAT*, II, pp. 912-13.

61. The verb *šḥd* is used in Ezek. 16.33 and Job 6.22: in the first case, it is a matter of the reward given to lovers; in the second, of a gift made to free oneself from an adversary. A legal connotation may be seen in the text of Job, as in Sir. 35.12 (Hebrew): *'l tšḥd ky l' yqḥ* (note the relationship between *šḥd* and *lqḥ*).

62. A judge's corruption may be directed at the acquittal of the guilty (cf. Isa. 5.23; Prov. 6.35; 21.14), or at the condemnation of the innocent (cf. Deut. 27.25; Isa. 33.15; Exod. 22.12; Pss. 15.5; 26.9-10).

63. Cf. Liedke, *Gestalt und Bezeichnungen*, p. 69.

śārayik sôr^e^rîm w^e^ḥabrê[64] *gannābîm*
kullô 'ōhēb šōḥad w^e^rōdēp šalmōnîm
yātôm lō' yišpōṭû w^e^rîb 'almānâ lō' yābô' '^a^lêhem (Isa. 1.23)

This oracle is directed against the 'chief men' of Jerusalem, seen precisely as *judges*: they ignore the pleas of poor people because, greedy for profit, they join forces with those who rob orphans and widows.[65] The central part of the verse is particularly interesting as regards the vocabulary used:

1. The expression *'ōhēb šōḥad* is directly opposed to one of the titles attributed to God as just judge: *'ōhēb mišpāṭ*[66] (Isa. 61.8; Ps. 37.28), *'ōhēb ṣ^e^dāqâ ûmišpāṭ* (Ps. 33.5), *'ōhēb ṣaddîqîm* (Ps. 146.8);[67] or again, in verbal phrases: *ṣaddîq yhwh ṣ^e^dāqôt 'āhēb* (Ps. 11.7); *w^e^'ōz melek mišpāṭ 'āhēb* (Ps. 99.4).[68]

If the perfect king is characterized by a love for justice (cf. Ps. 45.8: *'āhabtā ṣedeq wattiśnā' reša'*), the prophets' criticisms present a contrary picture of the chief men of Israel; besides Isa. 1.23, see Mic. 3.2 (*śōn^e^'ê ṭôb w^e^'ōh^a^bê rā'â*), and the warning in Amos 5.15 (*śin'û rā' w^e^'eh^e^bû ṭôb—w^e^haṣṣîgû bašša'ar mišpāṭ*).

2. In its turn, the expression *rōdēp šalmōnîm* seems opposed to the expressions which mean 'the pursuit of justice'; cf. Isa. 51.1: *rōd^e^pê ṣedeq*; Prov. 15.9: *m^e^raddēp ṣ^e^dāqâ*: 21.21: *rōdēp ṣ^e^dāqâ*; and above all, in a context of warnings directed at judges: *ṣedeq ṣedeq tirdōp* (Deut. 16.20).[69]

64. The root *ḥbr* also suggests complicity in Ps. 94.20; Prov. 28.24; Job. 34.8.

65. On Isa. 1.21-28, as well as the commentaries, cf. E.W. Davies, *Prophecy and Ethics: Isaiah and the Ethical Traditions of Israel* (JSOTSup, 16; Sheffield, 1981), pp. 90-112.

66. Cf. the opposition: *śônē' mišpāṭ* in Job. 34.17.

67. Ps. 146 describes the actions of YHWH the king (cf. v. 10) in opposition to those of the princes (*n^e^dîbîm*). He does justice for the oppressed (v. 7), protects the stranger, the orphan and the widow (v. 9); his love for the innocent (*ṣaddîqîm*) (v. 8) makes sure the activities of the wicked (*derek r^e^šā'îm*) are ineffective (v. 9; cf. 1.6). This presentation of God's justice is in violent contrast with the denunciation of the activities of the chief men of Israel made in Isa. 1.23.

68. The commentaries are not unanimous about the text and syntax of Ps. 99.4, but there is a consensus on connecting the figure of the king with love of the law.

69. It may also be asked whether the expression *rōdēp šalmōnîm* in Isa. 1.23 (cf. J.J. Finkelstein, 'The Middle Assyrian *Šulmānu*-Texts', *JAOS* 72 [1952], p. 79) is not a play on the word *šālôm* (one of the fundamental objectives of the administration

b. *beṣa'*.[70] The term *beṣa'* is parallel to *šōḥad* in 1 Sam. 8.3 and Isa. 33.15, and certainly has to do with the administration of justice if the men chosen as judges by Moses had to be *śōn*ᵉ*'ê bāṣa'* (Exod. 18.21).[71] It is important in this context to see the term with reference to the authorities; they are deemed just or unjust according to their relationship with 'profit' (cf. Isa. 56.11; Jer. 22.17; Ezek. 22.27; Prov. 28.16).

c. *mattān*, *mattānâ*. These are generic terms that usually have a positive meaning; in the sapiential literature, however, they seem sometimes to refer to something close to corruption yet without the context ever being clearly legal (cf. Prov. 15.27; 18.16; 19.6; 21.14; Qoh. 7.7).

d. *kōper*. The term *kōper* refers technically to the monetary compensation offered as amends in the case of an offence caused to others (cf. Exod. 21.30; Num. 35.31-32; Job 33.24 etc.).[72] In some cases, however, *kōper* is used as a parallel (Prov. 6.35)[73] or a substitute for *šōḥad*—Amos 5.12: *lqḥ kōper* + *nṭh* (*Hi*) *'ebyônîm baššaʻar*; and perhaps Job 36.18, where there is a relationship between *kōper* and the verb *nṭh* (*Hi*).[74]

Wealth can in fact put one beyond punishment (Prov. 13.8; Ps. 49.7-9;

of justice: cf. Exod. 18.23; Isa. 9.5-6; 26.12; Zech. 8.16; Ps. 122.5 etc.); the relationship between *šālôm* and *rdp* can be seen in Ps. 34.15: *baqqēš šālôm w*ᵉ*rodpēhû*, which is however a general invitation, not one directed specifically at officers of justice. In this context, supposing a similar play on words, mention may be made of Mic. 7.3: *haśśar šō'ēl w*ᵉ*haššōpēṭ baššillûm*.

70. Cf. D. Kellermann, *ThWAT*, I, pp. 734-36; R. Bergmeier, 'Das Streben nach Gewinn—des Volkes *'āwōn*', *ZAW* 81 (1969), pp. 93-97.

71. The expression *śōnē' beṣa'* (Exod. 18.21; Prov. 28.16; cf. also Prov. 15.27: *śônē' mattānōt*) is opposed to *'ōhēb šōḥad*, as mentioned above.

72. Cf. F. Maas, '*kpr* pi. sühnen', *THAT*, I, p. 844. A discussion of the difference between the legislation in Exod. 21.29-30 and Num. 35.31-32 with reference to the monetary compensation in the case of homicide, and more generally about *kōper*, is to be found in B.S. Jackson, 'Reflections on Biblical Criminal Law', in *Essays in Jewish and Comparative Legal History* (Leiden, 1975), pp. 41-50.

73. The first stich of Prov. 6.35 (*lō'yiśśā' p*ᵉ*nê kol kōper*) presents some difficulties in translation which suggest a correction of the MT (cf. BHS: *pāneykā l*ᵉ*kōper*). At any rate, it seems that the synonymous parallelism between *kōper* and *šōḥad* is universally accepted.

74. Cf. n. 53. On (unjust) *kōper*, cf. A. Phillips, 'Another Look at Murder', *JJS* 28 (1977), pp. 105-26; B. Janowski, *Sühne als Heilsgeschehen* (Neukirchen, 1982), pp. 167-68.

cf. also Prov. 6.35), even in the case of a crime which does not permit forms of damages (cf. Num. 35.31-32); the *kōper* 'accepted' by an authority charged with upholding the law is in fact the same as a kind of corruption of justice. The text of 1 Sam. 12.3 is especially illuminating in this regard: Samuel, faced with the people's demand for a king, defends his activities as a judge; not only—he states—has he not oppressed anyone by exploiting his position of power, but he has not even entered into deals 'to turn a blind eye' to certain guilty people (*ûmiyyad mî lāqaḥtî kōper w^e'a'lîm 'ênay bô*).

The last-quoted text allows me to enter upon two kinds of reflection, both having the aim of reaching a better understanding of the activity of an honest judge, that is right judging.

We have already seen how *kōper* achieves its end when it gets a judge to wink at a particular crime, and therefore not intervene with an appropriate punishment; now this is to transgress one of a magistrate's essential duties; see Exod. 23.8: *w^ešōḥad lō' tiqqāḥ kî haššōḥad y^e'awwēr piqḥîm wîsallēp dibrê ṣaddîqîm*; Deut. 16.19 (same text as before, with the sole variation of *'ênê ḥ^akāmîm* in place of *piqḥîm*); Lev. 20.4; Job 9.24.[75] As I shall show in Chapter 6, in the section given over to the judicial inquiry, one of the chief tasks of judges is to cast light on the cases put to them, so as to see exactly who is guilty and apply the sanctions laid down by the law; it is obvious that anything which 'blinds' the magistrate is to be considered contrary to justice.

This is the point at which the essential difference between the structure of the (two-sided) controversy and that of the judgment is to be grasped: whereas in the former a *gift* expresses the guilty party's willingness to make amends, and its acceptance (*lqḥ*) by the *offended* party signifies the end of the controversy in a reconciliation of the parties, in a legal context the gift becomes *corruption* (a bribe) and its acceptance (*lqḥ*) by the judge becomes an act diametrically opposed to the judging role.[76]

75. Isa. 56.10-11 might also be quoted, where the chief men are called blind (*'iwrîm*), ignorant (*lō' yādā'û—lō' yād^e'û hābîn*) and only in search of profit (*beṣa'*).

Prov. 22.12 may be considered a text in opposition to the previous one, especially bearing in mind Exod. 23.8 and Deut. 16.19: *'ênê yhwh nāṣ^erû dā'at waysallēp dibrê bōgēd*.

76. I would like to recall Gen. 20.16, where Abimelech, offering a thousand 'pieces' of silver, says to Sarah: *hinnēh hû' lāk k^esût 'ênayim*; it is obvious that it is not a question of corrupting the woman, but a kind of amends for the offence caused her. This is another example of how, depending on the juridical structure in which they occur, similar phrases and gestures take on a quite different meaning.

Likewise the phrase *nś' pānîm*, usually suggesting partiality, has a different force depending on the juridical structure. In a controversy it refers to the act of *being kind*; perhaps it calls to mind the physical gesture of lifting up someone who prostrated on the ground in an act of humiliation and supplication (cf. Gen. 32.21 and 1 Sam. 25.35; in both texts, the phrase is with reference to the offering of a gift).[77] In a law court, having a favourable attitude towards one of the parties in dispute is an unfitting act for a judge; as a result *being kind* turns into playing favourites and so altering the impartiality of right judgment.

From this point of view, God's behaviour over sacrifices and other cultic offerings—of which there is frequent mention in the prophetic *rîb*s—becomes clear; if in the controversies with his people YHWH does not accept the gift put before him,[78] it is not necessarily because he

77. In a still more generic way, the expression *nś' pānîm* has the meaning of 'to look after', 'to grant the request of' someone in a pitiful condition (cf. Gen. 19.21; Deut. 28.50; 2 Kgs 3.14; Job 42.8-9; Lam. 4.16); *nś' rō'š* has a similar meaning in Gen. 40.13, 19-20; 2 Kgs 25.27 (= Jer. 52.31).

78. Of the more important biblical texts I would like to quote: Isa. 1.11-15; 43.22-24 (cf. T. Booij, 'Negation in Isaiah 43.22-24', *ZAW* 94 [1982], pp. 390-400); 58.3-5; Jer. 6.20; 7.21-22; 11-15; Hos. 5.6-7; 6.6; Amos 5.21-23; Mic. 6.6-7; Zech. 7.4-6; Pss. 50.8-13; 51.18-19; (40.7-9); cf. also Prov. 21.3; Sir. 34.18–35.24.

The list of texts supplied by Harvey (*Le plaidoyer prophétique*, pp. 24-25) does not seem exact to me, above all because he includes under the same heading the denunciation of cultic activities directed towards idols (sin) and the refusal of sacrificial amends. The author's thesis on the latter subject (pp. 97-99, with bibliography) may be summed up as follows:

1. The theme of the refusal of sacrifices arises from the fact that 'la situation vitale dans laquelle venait s'insérer le *rîb* était liturgique et comprenait un sacrifice... si bien qu'une référence à ce contexte cultuel et à ses limites d'efficacité s'est imposée de soi'.

2. The *rîb* should be understood in a precise historical context: the texts state only that 'les compensations rituelles *ne valent plus rien dans le moment présent*', given that the covenant has been broken. This means that respect for the covenant takes priority over every other religious manifestation.

I too believe that prophetic criticism of the cult is not equivalent to a generalized polemic against expressions of religious life (laid down by the Law apart from anything else); I diverge from Harvey, however, on the precise meaning to be attributed to this criticism.

Since the literature on this subject is particularly abundant, I would like to note just a few important contributions: P. Volz, 'Die radikale Ablehnung der Kultreligion durch die alttestamentlichen Propheten', *ZST* 14 (1937), pp. 63-85; H.W. Hertzberg, 'Die prophetische Kritik am Kult', *TLZ* 75 (1950), pp. 219-26; R. Rendtorff,

desires a 'spiritual' cult or because his demands as the 'offended' party would require proportionate amends.[79]

There are two closely-linked fundamental reasons why God refuses the 'sacrifices'. The first is this: cultic offerings are perverse when they intend to establish or perpetuate a situation of injustice, uncoupling the meaning (repentance, conversion, change of life) from the thing (cultic act, external sacrifice). Now, God does not love a thing as such, but rather the meaning in it; it is not the external rituals of offerings that please him, but a contrite and humble heart (Ps. 51.19), obedience to the law (1 Sam. 15.22) and recognition (*yd'*) of his truth and justice (Hos. 6.6), things that sacrifice can express if it is a lived sign and not just a thing, that is, if in worship the heart cleaves and there is a real offering of self that demands a life joined to God.

'Priesterliche Kulttheologie und prophetische Kultpolemik', *TLZ* 81 (1956), pp. 341-44; K. Roubos, *Profetie en Cultus in Israël* (Wageningen, 1956); R. Hentschke, *Die Stellung der vorexilischen Schriftpropheten zum Kultus* (BZAW, 75; Berlin, 1957); R. Press, 'Der Gerichtspredigt der vorexilischen Propheten und der Versuch einer Steigerung der kultischen Leistung', *ZAW* 70 (1958), pp. 181-84; N.W. Porteous, 'Actualization and the Prophetic Criticism of the Cult', in *Tradition und Situation* (FS A. Weiser; Göttingen, 1963), pp. 93-105; E. Würthwein, 'Kultpolemik oder Kultbescheid? Beobachtungen zu dem Thema "Prophetie und Kult"', in *idem*, pp. 115-31; M.J. Buss, 'The Meaning of Cult in the Interpretation of the Old Testament', *JBR* 32 (1964), pp. 317-25; P. Reymond, 'Sacrifice et "spiritualité", ou sacrifice et alliance? Jer. 7.22-24', *TZ* 21 (1965), pp. 314-17; H.J. Hermisson, *Sprache und Ritus im altisraelitischen Kult: Zur 'Spiritualisierung' der Kultbegriffe im Alten Testament* (WMANT, 19; Neukirchen, 1965), esp. pp. 131-45; M. Sekine, 'Das Problem der Kultpolemik bei den Propheten', *EvT* 28 (1968), pp. 605-609; G. Fohrer, 'Kritik an Tempel, Kultus und Kultusausübung in nachexilischer Zeit', in *Archäologie und Altes Testament* (FS K. Galling; Tübingen, 1970), pp. 101-16; H. Schüngel-Straumann, *Gottesbild und Kultkritik vorexilischer Propheten* (SBS, 60; Stuttgart, 1972); G. Braulik, *Psalm 40 und der Gottesknecht* (ForBib, 18; Würzburg, 1975), pp. 132-41; H. Gese, 'Psalm 50 und das alttestamentliche Gesetzesverständnis', in *Rechtfertigung* (FS E. Käsemann; Tübingen, 1976), esp. pp. 69-77; J. Milgrom, 'Concerning Jeremiah's Repudiation of Sacrifice', *ZAW* 89 (1977), pp. 273-75; H.J. Boecker, 'Überlegungen zur Kultpolemik der vorexilischen Propheten', in *Die Botschaft und die Boten* (FS H.W. Wolff; Neukirchen, 1981), pp. 169-80.

79. With reference to Psalm 50, M. Mannati is critical of those authors who hold that the Psalmist is foretelling a spiritual cult, or is opposed to formalism and the overvaluation of the cult, or insists on the moral disposition necessary for cult ('Le Psaume 50 est-il un *rîb*?', *Sem* 23 [1973], p. 32 n. 1); I cannot, however, find in the article an explanation of vv. 8-15 of Psalm 50. In this passage, cf. instead Alonso Schökel, *Treinta Salmos*, pp. 209-10.

There is another aspect to bear in mind as well: if we were in a completely bilateral structure (on the one hand the people which has sinned, on the other God who has been offended), then the act of repentance signified by supplication, penitential rites and offerings would be perfectly legitimate and fitting; and the Bible records that God is pleased by them. But the juridical structure that underlies the texts to which I am referring is more complex; the people is divided into two camps: there are the wicked (overbearing, violent) who commit injustice, and there are the victims (innocent, weak, defenceless). God intervenes on behalf of those who are unjustly oppressed, and his defence *rîb* amounts to a kind of judgment that aims to re-establish perverted justice. Thus, if he were to accept sacrificial offerings, he would be making use—like a wicked judge who allows himself to be corrupted for personal gain—of a situation of injustice against which his whole juridical action was directed.[80]

2.3. *The Apparent Partiality of Right Judging*

A judge must not lean towards either of the two parties who submit to judgment; no consideration of social status, honour or past history must influence a calm evaluation of the case. But this holds good only to the extent to which the judge does not know who is right and who is wrong: a magistrate cannot—consciously or unconsciously—avoid establishing *a priori* the classes or 'sorts' of guilty and/or innocent. But if it were or becomes known who is in the right, it is in accordance with justice and a duty of the judging authority to take up a position in favour of whoever is upholding the law, and, by extension, forcibly to oppose whoever, having violated the law (the guilty), deserves punishment.[81]

Therefore it is not at variance with right judging, nor contrary to a judge's absolute impartiality towards the disputants, that a magistrate should personally take on a cause, for this is not an individual case but the cause of truth and justice, which the judge is called upon to protect and promote; judging indeed means precisely abandoning neutrality in order to save the innocent (who is right) by smiting the guilty (who is wrong).[82]

80. This is the explicit interpretation given by Sir. 35.11-15.

81. Cf. J.J.M. Roberts, 'The Divine King and the Human Community in Isaiah's Vision of the Future', in *The Quest for the Kingdom of God* (FS G.E. Mendenhall; Winona Lake, IN, 1983), pp. 132-33.

82. It should be remembered that one of the characteristics of penal jurisdiction is its *inability to refuse*, which 'is obvious in the sense that a judge can never refuse to make a decision' (G.D. Pisapia, *Compendio di procedura penale* [Padova, 2nd edn, 1979], p. 7).

This fact is spelt in literary terms by numerous biblical texts, in which it may be observed that the generic expression for judging (*špṭ* or its synonyms) is developed, on the one hand, by positive terms suggesting benevolence, attention, a saving intervention for someone in the right, and on the other hand, by terms with a negative value, suggesting punishment, towards the evildoer and violator of justice. For example:

Isa. 11.3-4

1. *w^{e}lō' l^{e}mar'ēh ʿênayw* ***yišpōṭ***
   w^{e}lō' l^{e}mišmaʿ 'oznayw yôkîaḥ
2. *w^{e}šāpaṭ b^{e}ṣedeq* ***dallîm***
   w^{e}hôkîaḥ b^{e}mîšôr l^{e}ʿanwê 'āreṣ
3. *w^{e}hikkâ 'ereṣ b^{e}šēbeṭ pîw*
   ûb^{e}rûaḥ ś^{e}pātāyw yāmît ***rāšāʿ***

The same tripartite scheme may also be found in Jer. 11.20; 21.12; Pss. 7.9-10; 11-12; 9.5-6; 17-19; 75.8 etc. The two forms judgment can take (acquit–sentence), specified by the individual under the law towards whom the magistrate's action is directed, are sufficient by themselves to express the activity of judging (cf. Ps. 72.4; Job 22.29-30; 36.6-7 etc.).

2.3.1. *Judging someone in the Right.* Judging is in fact to intervene in defence of someone who is *ṣaddîq*, whose rights have been threatened or injured by a *rāšāʿ*. It should not be thought that this action *on behalf of* an innocent victim represents something alien to the juridical structure *à trois* which is characteristic of judicial procedure, since the action of judging 'between the parties in dispute' is the same as 'giving each his or her rights' and is therefore the same as defending and saving the innocent from his or her oppressor. A few supporting texts:

1 Sam. 24.13	*yišpōṭ yhwh bênî ûbênekā*	*ûn^{e}qāmanî yhwh mimmekkā*
1 Sam. 24.16	*w^{e}hāyâ yhwh l^{e}dayyān* *w^{e}šāpaṭ bênî ûbênekā*	*w^{e}yēre' w^{e}yārēb 'et rîbî* *w^{e}yišp^{e}ṭēnî miyyādekā*
1 Sam. 26.23	*w^{e}yhwh yāšîb lā'îš 'et* *ṣidqātô w^e'et '^{e}munātô…*	
24		*…w^{e}yaṣṣīlēnî mikkol ṣārâ*
Num. 35.24	*w^{e}šāp^{e}ṭû hāʿēdâ bên* *hammakkeh ûbên gō'ēl* *haddām…*	*…w^{e}hiṣṣîlû hāʿēdâ 'et*
25		*hārōṣēaḥ miyyad gō'ēl haddām*

Despite this close link between 'judging' and the 'innocent', we do not, however, find in the Bible the syntagm *špṭ* [or its synonyms] *ṣaddîq*, except in Qoh. 3.17;[83] but we do however have an equivalent syntagm in which the *ṣaddîq*'s place is taken by (a) someone who claims innocence, or (b) someone who is (or claims to be) poor, humble and oppressed. The latter case typically represents those who, on account of their own lack of power, are continually victims of the oppression.[84] A few examples will help show how the aforementioned syntagm works:

Ps. 7.9	*šopṭēnî yhwh*	*k^e ṣidqî ûk^e tummî 'ālāy*	(a)
Ps. 26.1	*šopṭēnî yhwh*	*kî '^a nî b^e tummî hālaktî*	(a)
Ps. 72.4	*yišpōṭ '^a niyyê 'ām*		
	yôšîa'	*libnê 'ebyôn*	(b)
Jer. 22.16	*dān dîn*	*'ānî w^e 'ebyôn*	(b)
Prov. 31.9	*š^e poṭ ṣedeq*		
	w^e dîn	*'ānî w^e 'ebyôn*	(b)
Isa. 1.17	*šiptû*	*yātôm*	
	rîbû	*'almānâ*	(b)

Cf. also Isa. 1.23; 11.4; Jer. 5.28; Pss. 10.18; 82.3; Prov. 29.14 etc.

From the texts quoted so far it can be seen how the verb *špṭ* is linked—as a synonym or by association—to verbs that mean to defend, to save and the like;[85] indeed, precisely because the *defence*[86] action often has as its object the category of the downtrodden, it is often turned into the equivalent of a gesture of *compassion*. In order to demonstrate this relationship I would like to take two Psalms that refer explicitly to a (human) judge and which give a paradigm of the elements that currently concern me:

83. In Qoh. 3.17 we have *'et hassaddîq w^e 'et hārāšā' yišpōṭ hā'^e lōhîm*; the phrase means that the judgment of God will bring to light who is innocent and who is guilty, unlike a (wicked) human law court (v. 16).

84. I will discuss this more fully in Chapter 7.

85. Cf. W.I. Wolverton, 'The King's "Justice" in Pre-Exilic Israel', *ATR* 41 (1959), pp. 276-86; J.F.A. Sawyer, 'What Was a Mošia'?', *VT* 15 (1965), pp. 475-86; *idem*, *Semantics in Biblical Research: New Methods of Defining Hebrew Words for Salvation* (SBT, 2nd Ser., 24; London, 1972); in this work Sawyer studies in particular *yš'* (*Hi*), *nṣl* (*Hi*), *'zr*, *plṭ* (*Pi*), *mlṭ* (*Pi*).

86. Like the verb *ryb* (in a defence sense) and its synonyms (cf. ch. 1, section 3), *špṭ* is also sometimes construed with the preposition *min* (1 Sam. 24.16; 2 Sam. 18.19, 31; cf. Ps. 43.1).

Psalm 72[87]

v. 2	*yādîn b^{e}ṣedeq*	*‘amm^{e}kā*	
		wa‘^{a}niyyeykā	
	b^{e}mišpāṭ		
v. 4	*yišpōṭ*	*^{a}niyyê ‘ām*	
	yôšîy‘	*libnê ’ebyôn*	*wîdakkē’ ‘ôšēq*
v. 12	*yaṣṣîl*	*’ebyôn m^{e}šawwēa‘*	
		w^{e}‘ānî w^{e}’ên ‘ōzēr lô	
v. 13	*yāḥōs*	*‘al dal w^{e}’ebyôn*	
		w^{e}napšôt ’ebyônîm	
	yôšîa‘		
v. 14			*mittôk ûmēḥāmās*
	yig’al	*napšām*	
	w^{e}yêqar…b^{e}‘ênāyw	*dāmām*	

Psalm 82

v. 3	*šipṭû*	*dal*	
		w^{e}yātôm	
		‘ānî	
		wārāš	
	haṣdîqû		
v. 4	*pall^{e}ṭû*	*dal*	
		w^{e}’ebyôn	
			miyyad r^{e}šā‘îm
	haṣṣîlû		

For the purpose of grouping under headings the main verbs that exhibit synonymous parallelism with *špṭ* (and its synonyms), I would like to propose the following categories:

a. ‘*judge*’ and ‘*save*’

špṭ	*yš‘* (*Hi*)	Ps. 72.4, 13; Ezek. 34.22
dyn	*yš‘* (*Hi*)	Ps. 54.3
špṭ	*nṣl* (*Hi*)	Pss. 72.12; 82.4 (*miyyad*)
		Num. 35.24-25
dyn mišpāṭ	*nṣl* (*Hi*)	Jer. 21.12 (*miyyad*)
‘śh mišpāṭ ûṣ^{e}dāqâ	*nṣl* (*Hi*)	Jer. 22.3
špṭ	*plṭ* (*Pi*)	Pss. 43.1 (*min*); 82.4
špṭ	*pdh*	Ps. 26.11[88]

87. Psalm 101, like Psalm 72, pictures the perfect governor and puts the emphasis more on the attitude of the king towards those in his service; it insists on opposition to the arrogant and lying rather than favour for the honest (v. 6).

b. '*judge*' and '*vindicate*'

špṭ	*nqm*	1 Sam. 24.13 (*min*)
špṭ	*g'l*	Ps. 72.14 (*min*); Lam. 3.58

c. '*judge*' and '*defend*'

špṭ	*ryb rîb* + pron. suff.	Ps. 43.1 (*min*)
'śh mišpāṭ + pron. suff.	*ryb rîb* + pron. suff.	Mic. 7.9
špṭ mišpāṭ + pron. suff.	*ryb rîb* + pron. suff.	Lam. 3.58-59
špṭ	*ryb*	Isa. 1.17

d. '*judge*' and '*have compassion*'

špṭ	*ḥws 'al*	Ps. 72.13
špṭ	*ḥnn*	Ps. 26.11[89]
dyn	*nḥm* (*Hitp*) *'al*	Ps. 135.14 (= Deut. 32.36)[90]
'śh mišpāṭ	*'hb*	Deut. 10.18
špṭ mišpaṭ '^{e}*met*	*'śh ḥesed w*^{e}*raḥ*^{a}*mîm*	Zech. 7.9

2.3.2. *Judging the Guilty*. If in a court of law where justice holds sway the innocent are acquitted and saved, then the guilty are condemned; the action by which a judge decrees a punitive sanction is also expressed by the verb *špṭ* and its synonyms.

The syntagm under consideration is therefore *špṭ* + *crime/the guilty*. As I have already observed in the previous section with reference to *špṭ ṣaddîq*, we do not find the syntagm *špṭ rāšā'* other than in Qoh. 3.17; its place in the paradigm is taken either by synonyms or by the subjects who, it turns out from the context, ought to be condemned.

On the other hand, it is important to observe that the Hebrew verbs

88. The association between *špṭ* and *pdh* (and *ḥnn*) is demonstrated by the inclusion in Psalm 26:

v. 1 *šopṭēnî yhwh*

kî '^{a}*nî b*^{e}*tummî hālaktî*

v. 11 *wa'*^{a}*nî b*^{e}*tummî 'ēlēk*

p^{e}*dēnî*

w^{e}*ḥonnēnî*

89. Cf. previous note.

90. Zorell, Gesenius, BDB and Halat give the same force as the *Niphal* to the *Hitpael* of *nḥm* in the texts quoted above, respectively: 'ad misericordiam se moveri sivit', 'um jem. Mitleid empfinden', 'be sorry, have compassion', 'es sich leid sein lassen'. The same dictionaries show that the same verbal form has the meaning of *to avenge oneself* in other texts (cf. Ezek. 5.13; Gen. 27.42).

that in general mean 'to judge' quite rarely have the explicit meaning of '*to condemn*':[91] for *špṭ*—if we exclude the book of Ezekiel[92]—we have only 1 Sam. 3.13 and 2 Chron. 20.12 (*b*^{e}); for *dyn*, Gen. 15.14; 1 Sam. 2.10; Isa. 3.13; Ps. 110.6;[93] for *'śh mišpāṭ*, Ps. 119.84 (*b*^{e}) and 149.9 (*b*^{e}).

The 'sentence' is manifested in a paradigmatic series of verbs directly opposed to those which we saw in the previous section, following a scheme which—at least as a first approximation—looks like this:

a. instead of *saving* we find *punishing*, striking, handing over to the executioner, and the like.
b. the terminology of *defending* has its counterpart in that of *wrath* (a synonym for a juridical action against...).
c. the lexicon of *having compassion* is used in the negative.

91. Perhaps it is of this special use of the verb *špṭ* that Koehler states, 'Richten heisst nicht deliktische Tatbestände feststellen und auf Grund dieser Feststellung urteilen und verurteilen, sondern im Hebräischen sind "Richten" und "Helfen" Parallelbegriffe' ('Die hebräische Rechtsgemeinde', p. 151); and again, 'Billige Vermittlung...nicht die Feststellung der Strafe, heisst genau *šāphaṭ*; der *šôphēṭ* ist in erster Linie der Helfer zum Recht, nicht der (strafende) Richter' (*Deuterojesaja*, p. 110).

It may be accepted that the primary purpose of judgment is the affirmation (or re-establishment) of law, but it cannot be denied that punitive sanctions are closely linked to judgment.

It might be important to remember, in this respect, that salvation is sometimes seen as 'getting away from' the judge: this means therefore that judgment—at least implicitly—has the threatening force of a sanction; e.g. Ps. 109.31: *l*^{e}*hôšîa' miššōp*^{e}*ṭê napšî*; Job 23.7: *wa'*^{a}*pall*^{e}*ṭâ lāneṣaḥ miššōp*^{e}*ṭî* (cf. also Job 9.15: *limšōp*^{e}*ṭî 'etḥannān*).

92. In dealing with the verb *špṭ*, the book of Ezekiel constitutes a linguistic exception. Only in Ezek. 34.17, 20, 22 (where we have *špṭ bên...l*^{e}, *špṭ bên...ûbên*, and, in v. 22, an explicit link with *yš'* [*Hi*]) and 44.24 (where the reference is to the priest's judging activity in the New Temple) does the verb *špṭ* have a meaning that is in line with that of the other biblical texts; elsewhere (17 occurrences) the meaning is always that of *handing down sentence*.

93. The text of Ps. 50.4: 'God calls together the heavens...and the earth *lādîn 'ammô*', is generally interpreted in a negative sense: 'to judge (that is, to bring in judgment against) his people'. M. Mannati is of the opposite opinion ('Le Psaume 50 est-il un *rîb*?', *Sem* 23 [1973], pp. 34-36) and translates: 'pour le jugement qu'il rendra en faveur de son peuple', citing as his reason that the verb *dyn* is generally used in the sense of 'to administer justice for...', and, in the few cases where it means 'to administer justice against...', it is a matter of a judgment *against* the nations *in favour of* Israel (cf. previously E. Beaucamp, 'La théophanie du Psaume 50 [49]. Sa signification pour l'interprétation du Psaume', *NRT* 81 [1959], pp. 903-906).

Since my observations seem semantically quite obvious, I will give only a couple of examples, taken from the book of Ezekiel:

7.3	*‘attâ haqqēṣ ‘ālayik*	
	w^{e}šillaḥtî ’appî bāk	anger
	ûš^{e}paṭṭîk kidrākāyik	
	w^{e}nātattî ‘ālayik ’ēt kol tô‘^{a}bōtāyik	JUDGMENT
4	*w^{e}lō’ tāḥôs ‘ênî ‘ālayik*	
	w^{e}lō’ ’eḥmôl	no compassion
16.38	*ûš^{e}paṭṭîk mišp^{e}ṭê nō’^{a}pôt*	
	w^{e}šōp^{e}kōt dām	JUDGMENT
	ûn^{e}tattîk dam ḥēmâ w^{e}qin’â	anger
39	*w^{e}nātattî ’ôtāk b^{e}yādām…*	hand over to the executioner of justice
40	*w^{e}he‘^{e}lû ‘ālayik qāhāl*	execution
	w^{e}rāg^{e}mû ’ôtāk bā’āben	
	ûbitt^{e}qûk b^{e}ḥarbôtām	
41	*w^{e}śār^{e}pû bāttayik bā’ēš*	
	w^{e}‘āśû bāk š^{e}pāṭîm l^{e}‘ênê nāšîm rabbôt[94]	

3. *Judgment*

After dealing with the *judge* and *the act of judging*, little remains to be said about the *judgment* as regards the understanding of the structure of a trial.

This section will therefore put forward some elements of a lexicographical nature.

My examination focuses upon nouns that have the same root as verbs expressing ‘judging’ in general:

špṭ	(*šōpēṭ*)	*mišpāṭ*
dyn	(*dayyān*)	*dîn, mādôn*
pll	(*pālîl*)	*p^{e}lîlâ, p^{e}lîliyyâ*
dbr (*Pi*)[95]	*dābār*	

94. The term *š^{e}pāṭîm* deserves mention, especially in the syntagm *‘śh š^{e}pāṭîm b^{e}*, being a typical way of describing an adverse verdict: cf. J.-L. Ska, ‘La sortie d’Egypte (Exod. 7.14) dans le récit sacerdotal (P^{g}) et la tradition prophétique’, *Bib* 60 (1979), pp. 206-208; P. Joüon, ‘Notes de lexicographie hébraïque’, *Bib* 8 (1927), p. 61.

95. The link between the verb *dbr* and the noun *dābār* with a specifically juridical meaning does not seem as close as in the other aforementioned pairs.

3.1. *mišpāṭ*[96]

This is by far the most important noun in the series I am presenting. It has something of a variety of interlinked meanings: it can mean the action of judging (a verbal noun: *mišpāṭ* equals *'śh mišpāṭ*), what is judged (as an internal object, of the kind *špṭ mišpaṭ-*), and the final act that concludes a judgment (*mišpāṭ* = sentence, verdict, as in *dbr* [*Pi*] *mišpāṭ*), as well as the result of jurisprudence (*mišpāṭ* as law, decree).[97]

3.1.1. *mišpāṭ as a Procedural Action*. a. Some texts in which this meaning can clearly be seen:

Lev. 19.15, 35	*lō' ta'ᵃśû 'āwel bammišpāṭ* (in 19.15 the expression to which it is directly opposed is: *bᵉṣedeq tišpōṭ 'ᵃmîtekā*)
Num. 35.12	*'ad 'omdô lipnê hā'ēdâ lammišpāṭ*
2 Sam. 15.2	*lābô' 'el hammelek lammišpāṭ*
Prov. 18.5	*lᵉhaṭṭôt ṣaddîq bammišpāṭ*

Cf. also Deut. 25.1; Isa. 3.14; 59.11; Ps. 143.2; Prov. 24.23 etc.

b. Synonymous or related terms:

rîb ûmišpāṭ	2 Sam. 15.4
dîn ûmišpāṭ	Job 36.17 (cf. also, for synonymousness, Pss. 9.5 and 35.25).

3.1.2. *mišpāṭ as Subjective Law*. This is what a just trial pursues, safeguards and affirms. In particular, when it is a matter of '*someone's rights*', it is the same as 'the case brought by someone', in the name of the law, to court, or a case that could be legally defended:

96. Cf. H.W. Hertzberg, 'Die Entwicklung des Begriffes *mšpṭ* im Alten Testament', *ZAW* 40 (1922), pp. 256-87; 41 (1923), pp. 16-76; O. Booth, 'The Semantic Development of the Term *mšpṭ* in the Old Testament', *JBL* 61 (1942), pp. 105-10; J. van der Ploeg, '*Shāpaṭ* et *mishpāṭ*', *OTS* 2 (1943), pp. 144-55; *idem*, 'Studies in Hebrew Law', *CBQ* 12 (1950), pp. 248-50; W.A.M. Beuken, 'Mišpaṭ. The First Servant Song and its Context', *VT* 22 (1972), pp. 1-30; J. Jeremias, '*Mišpāṭ* im ersten Gottesknechtslied (Jes. XLII 1-4)', *VT* 22 (1972), pp. 31-42.

97. A full treatment of the various meanings of *mišpāṭ* is to be found in Liedke, *Gestalt und Bezeichnungen*, pp. 73-100; I am putting forward a different and simpler semantic framework.

As regards the noun *mišpāṭ*, Palache makes particular reference to the semantic link between *law* and *custom* (usage, rule). 'The transition "law > custom" and vice versa is known in many languages and finds its obvious explanation in the history of civilization. Whatever is unusual is not good (cf. Gen. 29.26 etc.) and conversely, general custom tends to become the valid rule of conduct and law' (*Semantic Notes*, p. 74).

ʿśh	*mišpāṭ*	cf. the texts quoted on p. 188
šmʿ	*mišpāṭ*	1 Kgs 3.11
drš	*mišpāṭ*	Isa. 1.17; 16.5
ydʿ	*mišpāṭ*	Mic. 3.1; Qoh. 8.5
byn (*Hi*)	*mišpāṭ*	Job 32.9; Prov. 2.9 (with *ṣ*^{e}*dāqâ*); 28.5
'hb	*mišpāṭ*	Isa. 61.8
hpk	*mišpāṭ*	Amos 6.12
etc.		
mišpaṭ	*gēr yātôm w*^{e}*'almānâ*	Deut. 27.19
mišpaṭ	*gēr yātôm*	Deut. 24.17
mišpaṭ	*yātôm w*^{e}*'almānâ*	Deut. 10.18
mišpaṭ	*'ebyônîm*	Exod. 23.6; Jer. 5.28; Ps. 140.13 (// *dîn ʿānî*)
mišpaṭ	*ʿ*^{a}*niyyê ʿammî*	Isa. 10.2
mišpaṭ	*gāber*	Lam. 3.35
mišpaṭ	*'îš*	Prov. 29.26
mišpaṭ	*ʿabdô*/*ʿammô*	1 Kgs 8.59
mišpaṭ	*habb*^{e}*kōrâ*	Deut. 21.17
mišpaṭ	*yhwh*	Jer. 8.7; 2 Chron. 19.8
mišpaṭ	*hakkōh*^{a}*nîm* (*'et hāʿām*)	1 Sam. 2.13
mišpaṭ	*hammelek*	1 Sam. 8.9
mišpaṭ	*hamm*^{e}*lūkâ*	1 Sam. 10.25
mišpaṭ	+ pron. suff.	Num. 27.5; Isa. 51.4; Mic. 7.9; Ps. 17.2; Job 34.5-6
etc.		

3.1.3. *mišpāṭ as Sentence*. What is true of the verb *špṭ* holds equally good for the noun *mišpāṭ*. By metonomy, it refers to the culminating and decisive phase of a trial, the sentence. The link between the two aspects is so strong that often it is not easy to distinguish between the general meaning of 'trial' and that of 'verdict'; it seems however that the latter meaning can be recognized with certainty in these cases:

a. *Pronouncing, handing down a sentence* (cf. Prov. 16.10, where there is a link with the mouth). I believe the following syntagms should be understood in this sense: *špṭ mišpāṭ* (1 Kgs 3.28; Zech. 7.9; 8.16); *dyn mišpāṭ* (Jer. 21.12); *ḥrṣ mišpāṭ* (1 Kgs 20.40); and especially *dbr* (*Pi*) *mišpāṭ 'et* (2 Kgs 25.6; Jer. 39.5; 52.9; cf. also Jer. 1.16; 4.12); *ntn mišpāṭ* (Ezek. 23.24; Zeph. 3.5; Job 36.6; cf. also Ezek. 20.25); *yṣ'* (*Hi*) *mišpāṭ* (Isa. 42.1, 3; Ps. 37.6).[98]

98. Note should also be taken of expressions that take the 'public' (not the judge)

b. Expressions that describe *the kind of sentence*: *mišpaṭ māwet* (capital punishment): Deut. 19.6; 21.22; Jer. 26.11.16; *mišpaṭ dāmîm* (a wicked verdict): Ezek. 7.23; *mišpaṭ nō'ᵃpôt*... (sentence applied to adulteresses...): Ezek. 16.38; 23.45.

c. Perhaps the concept of a '*fair sentence*' can be made to include the use of the noun *mišpāṭ* with the prepositions *lᵉ* or *bᵉ*, of the kind: *ysr* (*Pi*) *lammišpāṭ* (Jer. 30.11; 46.28) or *bᵉmišpāṭ* (Jer. 10.24), *pdh bᵉmišpāṭ* (Isa. 1.27), etc.; these would be the opposites of the expressions *lō' bᵉmišpāṭ* (Jer. 17.11) and *bᵉlō' mišpāṭ* (Ezek. 22.29; Jer. 22.13).

3.1.4. *mišpāṭ as Law (Objective Law).* Scholars seem to be in agreement that *mišpāṭ* means *law* because, originally, it was no more than an act of jurisprudence which subsequently took on the force of law (including the apodictic) in general.[99]

1 Sam. 30.21-25 may be adduced in support (especially the last verse), but above all Deut. 17.8-11: 'If any matter arises which is too hard for you to judge, between blood and blood, between plea and plea, between blow and blow—these being matters of controversy in your towns—then you shall go up to the place the Lord your God shall choose; you shall go to the priests and to the judge appointed in those days; you shall inquire of them *wᵉhiggîdû lᵉkā 'ēt dᵉbar hammišpāṭ*. And you shall do *'al pî haddābār 'ᵃšer yaggîdû lᵉkā* in the place which the Lord your God shall choose and you shall take care to do *kᵉkōl 'ᵃšer yôrûkā. 'al pî hattôrâ 'ᵃšer yôrûkā wᵉ'al hammišpāṭ 'ᵃšer yō'mᵉrû lᵉkā* you shall do; you shall not deviate *min haddābār 'ᵃšer yaggîdû lᵉkā* either to the right or to the left.'

Two observations which seem relevant here:

a. the parallelism observable between *dābār* (*dᵉbar mišpāṭ*)–*mišpāṭ*–*tôrâ*. In particular, the link *mišpāṭ–tôrâ*[100] (cf. Isa. 42.4) suggests that both terms refer to a decision with normative value: the *tôrâ* is simply the verdict pronounced by the judging priestly body, whereas *mišpāṭ* seems to be a more general term (cf. 2 Kgs 17.27: the priest *yrh mišpāṭ*) suggesting a judicial sentence. The whole series of 'decrees' (*mišpāṭîm*,

as their subject, such as *šm' mišpāṭ* (1 Kgs 3.28) and *r'h mišpāṭ* (Ezek. 39.21).

99. Cf. H. Cazelles, 'Le sens religieux de la loi', in *Populus Dei*. I. *Israel*, p. 184: 'Le *mishpâṭ* est à l'origine le moyen juridique, la sentence par laquelle on rétablit une situation compromise par une faute ou un délit'.

100. On the concept of *tôrâ*, cf. G. Liedke and C. Petersen, '*tōrā* Weisung', *THAT*, II, pp. 1032-43 (where insistence is laid on the sapiential origin of the term).

tôrôt, etc.) later formed a code, on the basis of which the Law in Israel was drawn up.

b. the use of *'al hammišpāṭ*, which means 'in conformity with a decree', deserves attention (Num. 35.24; Ezek. 44.24b).

3.2. *dîn (mādôn, midyānîm)*

On the one hand, *dîn* seems parallel to *mišpāṭ* (Jer. 5.28);[101] on the other hand, it represents a specific kind of lawsuit—*dābār lammišpāṭ bên dām lᵉdām* ***bên dîn lᵉdîn ûbên*** *nega' lānega' dibrê rîbōt biš'āreykā* (Deut. 17.8); it may perhaps be deduced from this latter text that *dîn* refers to those lawsuits—concerning neither murder nor injury—that probably concern property or other 'civil' matters. The use of *dîn* to refer to a subjective right which has been infringed is in fact frequent:

dîn	*yātôm*	Jer. 5.28
dîn	*'ānî wᵉ'ebyôn*	Jer. 22.16
dîn	*'ānî*	Ps. 140.13
dîn	*dallîm*	Prov. 29.7
dîn	*kol bᵉnê 'ōnî*	Prov. 31.5
dîn	*kol bᵉnê ḥᵃlôp*	Prov. 31.8

The normal meaning of *mādôn* (and *midyānîm*) is that of a *dispute*, without any explicit legal reference; perhaps there is a kind of link to the judicial sphere in Prov. 6.19, given that the text deals with false witness.

3.3. *pᵉlîlâ* and *pᵉlîliyyâ*

The two terms are *hapax legomena*, and therefore do not constitute a very important element within the Hebrew juridical lexicon. However, they seem interesting enough to me to make them the object of a brief consideration, particularly because of the link they have with *pll* and *pālîl*, with which I dealt previously.

a. *pᵉlîlâ*: Isa. 16.3 (*hābî'î 'ēṣâ ᵃśû pᵉlîlâ*). The text and context are not of the clearest,[102] but the parallelism with *'ēṣâ* seems interesting.[103]

101. In Prov. 31.5 *dîn* is parallel with *mᵉḥuqqāq*; according to S.M. Paul, technical expressions are being used here: *šnh* (*Pi*) *dîn* (to alter, retract or change a verdict) and *mᵉḥuqqāq* (the text of the sentence) ('Unrecognized Biblical Legal Idioms in the Light of Comparative Accadian Expressions', *RB* 86 [1979], pp. 231-35).

102. Cf. H. Wildberger, *Jesaja* (BK, 10/2; Neukirchen, 1978), p. 593.

103. The root *y'ṣ* is closely linked by way of the sapiential world, to the sphere of government: cf. H.-P. Stähli, '*j'ṣ* raten', *THAT*, I, pp. 748-53; L. Ruppert, '*jā'aṣ*', *ThWAT*, III, pp. 718-51.

b. *p^{e}lîliyyâ*: Isa. 28.7 (*šāgû bārō'eh pāqû p^{e}lîliyyâ).* The oracle refers to priests and prophets who wander and wave under the effects of wine; if vision (*rō'eh*) belongs to the prophets, it seems that 'decision' in this case is the task of the priests.

At any rate, the nuance of 'arbitration', 'mediation', which we have noted in *pll* and perhaps *pālîl*, does not seem immediately obvious in these two nouns.

3.4. *dābār*[104]

The noun *dābār* in a legal context is particularly interesting, if only because it has always been the object of much attention. I would like to distinguish three main meanings:

a. *dispute, controversy case*

d^{e}bar š^{e}nêhem	Exod. 22.8 (refers to a *rîb*; cf. Deut. 19.17)
hyh lāhem dābār	Exod. 18.16 (refers to a *rîb*; cf. 2 Sam. 15.2)

In Deut. 22.26 and perhaps 19.4, *dābār* means a juridical 'case'.

b. *a case brought before and decided in a law court* (refers to a *mišpāṭ*)[105]

b^{e}dābār // bašša'ar	Isa. 29.21
dibrê ṣaddîqīm	Deut. 16.19
d^{e}bārîm ṭôbîm ûn^{e}kōḥîm	2 Sam. 15.3
d^{e}bar šeqer	Prov. 13.5; Exod. 23.7[106]

104. B.S. Jackson, *Theft in Early Jewish Law* (Oxford, 1972), p. 241, maintains that *dābār* means '*legal dispute*' (and quotes as texts Exod. 18.16, 22, 23, 26; Deut. 1.17; 19.15; 2 Chron. 19.6, 11; Est. 1.17-18; cf. also Exod. 24.14: *ba'al d^{e}bārîm* = 'the complainant'), or '*spoken judgment in a case*' (1 Kgs 17.24; 2 Kgs 25.6). The same author maintains that *dābār* is linked to an oracular response, but this does not seem altogether proved.

105. A typical example is that of the (involuntary) murderer who presents himself (*'md*) at the gate of a refuge town and lays his case before the elders: *dbr* (*Pi*) *b^{e}'oznê ziqnê hā'îr hahî' 'et d^{e}bārāyw* (Jos. 20.4). Along these lines mention might also be made of the noun *dibrâ* in Job 5.8: *w^{e}'el '^{e}lōhîm 'āśîm dibrātî*: the syntagm *śym dibrâ* seems to have the meaning of 'hand one's (own) case over to someone' (cf. Paul, 'Unrecognized', pp. 235-36).

106. H. Cazelles, *Etudes sur le Code de l'Alliance* (Paris, 1946), p. 89, translates: 'Tu te tiendras éloigné d'une cause mensongère', giving the noun *dābār* the nuance of an *oral* procedure, as in Exod. 22.8; with reference to this latter text, he notes: 'le mot a fréquemment le sens d' "affaire", ici d' "affaire judiciaire, contestation, procès"

dibrê rîbōt biš'āreykā		Deut. 17.8
dābār lammišpāṭ bên...l^e		Deut. 17.8 (with *rîb* in 2 Chron. 19.10)
dābār lammišpāṭ...pl' (*Ni*) *min*		Deut. 17.8
dābār... qšh min		Deut. 1.17
haddābār haggādōl...haddābār haqqāṭōn		Exod. 18.22
haddābār haqqāšeh...haddābār haqqāṭōn		Exod. 18.26
d^ebar yhwh		2 Chron. 19.11 (cf. v. 8 *mišpaṭ yhwh*)
d^ebar hā'^elōhîm		1 Chron. 26.32
d^ebar hammelek		2 Chron. 19.11; 1 Chron. 26.32
d^ebar peša'		Exod. 22.8
drš dābār		Exod. 10.16 (corr.)

c. *law court decision, sentence, verdict*

dābār...qwm (*Pi*)	= ratify an act	Ruth 4.7
dābār...qwm (*Qal*)	= institute a trial or decide a case?	Deut. 19.15
d^ebar mišpāṭ		2 Chron. 19.6
d^ebar hammišpāṭ		Deut. 17.9 (v. 11: *mišpāṭ*)

4. *The Judicial Institution*

As with almost all ancient and modern peoples, the judicial process in Israel was one of the most important institutions in civil life. As regards disputes—which have a fairly simple structure and are kept private—the jurisdictional procedure is codified into a body of State law which—more or less explicitly—lays down places, bodies and acts whereby 'justice is to be done'. Both in a controversy and in a judgment the intention is to oppose injustice by restoring a law that has been infringed; but whereas the former is entrusted to the initiative and decision of the disputants, the latter lays down strict and objective mediation by the judging authority which—in order to be recognized as a valid mediation of good—has need of a formal and universal procedure. It is precisely

comme dans la suite du Code en XXII.7 et 8 et Ex XXIV.14–E–. La procedure est orale comme dans les sociétés primitives, l'affaire est nouée par une accusation orale et dénouée après un échange de paroles (*debar šenèyhém*) parfois très long'.

this objectivity of the jurisdictional body which allows the law to impose itself even with *force*, without altering the relationship between individuals endowed with liberty; actually, the institution represents that element of constraint which makes it possible for a human community to give reasonable exercise to its vital potential.

A judge is someone who, so to speak, embodies the judicial institution: an *individual* (or a college of individuals) to whom the task and power to make decisions for everybody has been entrusted. Now people can serve an institution as individuals by giving practical expression to its good intentions, but they can also make use of it to achieve their own ends and their private interests. As the form which jurisdiction takes, a judge is the manifestation in society of objective justice; but as a historical figure, a judge is often the manifestation of structural injustice. A perverse judge, in fact, does not make a frontal assault on the law, but takes over its trappings and makes use of the force of law in order to garner an unbridled exercise of arbitrary power.

Turning the pages of Scripture in search of the juridical/lawsuit lexicon, we come across expressions and facts that demonstrate the perversion of justice more frequently than its correct functioning. This phenomenon, which may be remarked in the generic vocabulary of judging, will appear again as my work proceeds, particularly in the phase concerning trials. The cause of this is probably to be attributed to the nature and intention of the biblical texts, which are mainly the revelation of Israel in its practical historical dimension, and it is well-known that history does not often coincide with how people 'ought to be'. It is therefore important to emphasize—even if this may seem obvious—that the critical aspect (present not only in the prophetic tradition but also in the narrative and sapiential sections of the Bible) should not be confused with a depreciation of the institution as such. This holds good for all institutions and, *a fortiori*, for juridical ones; the ambiguity that marks history should not lead to the belief that human truth and justice are revealed in the abolition of what constitutes their mediation.

We have seen that the two poles at which the bad administration of justice manifests itself are, on the one hand, doing personal favours, and on the other, corruption of an economic kind.

The former pole seems to suggest that people's (social) importance risks compromising the impartiality of judgment; it may easily be imagined how the more authority an individual enjoys in society, the more respect he or she is shown in any manifestation of collective life. It follows from this that society's hierarchical organization—necessary for unity and order—can become a factor in injustice and oppression: the power that authority enjoys becomes a privileged means of defence of that power, to the detriment of the subordinate and powerless mass of people.

The second pole of injustice in judgment brings out the fact that wealth—an aspiration of the whole of society, and a legitimate condition of authority—has a logic that does not necessarily correspond to the demands of justice. Violence and the abuse of power in corrupt administration are of course condemned by the common conscience, but perhaps it is not always perceived that human communities are fatally led astray into them by the over-evaluation of economic well-being, which is activated by the profit of one at the expense of all the rest.

So we see how *politics* and *economics*, which ought to be under the control of the truth of the law, are instead ruling social forces which embrace jurisdiction in their sphere of interests and purposes. Typical in this respect is the *monarch*, who is the supreme political authority, but who is also the final court of appeal, and as a result pleasing the monarch matters more than being in the right (1 Kgs 2.6-15); and, given that royalty is accorded special prerogatives, *mišpaṭ hammelek* can become the legal organization of exploitation (e.g. 1 Sam. 8.10-18; 1 Kgs 21.4-16). If, then, the Bible is frequently critical of Israel's leaders (magistrates, leading men, the rich, and so on), it is not a question of waves of anarchy or populism, nor the anachronistic anticipation of class demands; it is rather the ethical need to recall that the better an institution is, the more subject it is to subtle perversion, as a result of which it is necessary—for real justice—that people should live in the way mapped out by these same institutions.

The institution of the law, with its bodies and procedures, has the aim of re-establishing justice. We have seen that this is the same as saying that judges, once they know who is in the right, step in to defend the innocent and punish whoever in the controversy turns out to be the guilty party. Taking the side of the innocent does not make the judge at law (the judge's cause is the cause of justice); even if the Hebrew lexicon seems to swing ambiguously between the sphere of the law court and that of the controversy, it is necessary to keep the two structures logically apart to interpret the facts and expressions found in the Bible correctly. This leads me to say, for example, that it cannot be stated—as a general axiom—that 'judging' is synonymous with 'saving', or that a judge demonstrates goodness by acquitting the guilty. A just judge saves *only the innocent* in a trial, and alternatively condemns with appropriate severity whoever is guilty. Theologically, these simple reflections have a certain importance: in the face of God's judgment, who can be declared 'just'? Well, anyone who is the *victim* of an unjust relationship, that is, all those who uphold rights while losing their own. The concept of victim (which may be expressed in different terminology) is the pole towards which the whole internal organization of the jurisdictional institution orients itself; a just judgment is one in which the victim carries off the victory, through the victory of law furthered by the just authority of a just judge. God (the judge) and the (judged) victim are two linked terms that make the drama of judgment desirable by those who love life in accordance with justice.

Now that the institution of the law court has been situated by its lexicon and its main areas of meaning, I would like to move on to an examination of its procedures: the origin and shape of the trial (Chapter 6), its centrepiece, which is the actual trial phase (Chapter 7), and its conclusion with the pronouncement and execution of sentence (Chapter 8).

Chapter 6

THE ACTS AND PROCEDURES PRECEDING THE DEBATE

The aim of this chapter is to provide the elements of law court procedure which are logically preliminary to the debate. The material of my contribution is subdivided under three main headings in the manner which I would like briefly to anticipate here:

1. the initiative of summoning a trial: a study of the role taken on by juridical individuals in putting the judicial apparatus into motion;

2. the position of the individuals in the trial: an examination, at this point, of how the principals taking part in the trial stand with respect to one another;

3. the preliminary investigation of the case—this phase is not linguistically homogeneous with the previous ones (which use verbs with a basic meaning of 'motion'); moreover, the role as analysed belongs almost exclusively to the judging magistrate (and not to the other juridical individuals); lastly, what is described may be considered co-extensive with the whole trial (so not just the preliminaries to the debate). However, I have thought it fitting to anticipate at this point everything which does not immediately look like the debate (the specific object of the next chapter), not only to create a better balance, but above all to give due emphasis to the central phase of the trial, which shows a great complexity of elements and a considerable abundance of material in the biblical texts.

1. *The Initiative to Institute a Trial*

While standing by what I said in Chapter 2 about the necessity, for any kind of juridical procedure, that a criminal deed should have occurred and be recognized as such (or at least believed so), there is necessary—for the formal institution of a trial—a specific initiative by a juridical individual who brings about the intervention of a judge's jurisdiction to settle the question and restore conditions of justice.

1.1. *The Initiative of the Disputants*

I would like to go back here to what I said about a controversy without possibility of solution by the litigants themselves: the parties at odds, and in particular the one doing the accusing, have recourse to a law court recognized as having the legitimacy and the power (force) to impose the sentence pronounced as normative.

1.1.1. *The 'Motion' towards a Court of Law*. The initiative by the parties at odds is generally expressed by *verbs of motion*: the 'grammatical subject' of the verb is whoever is submitting the case or denouncing the guilty party; the '*terminus ad quem*' is the judging person or office to whom recourse has been made. It may be noted, from the examples I shall give, that sometimes it is the one who claims to be in the right who takes the initiative in order to obtain satisfaction; but in other cases, both disputants simultaneously have recourse to the judge; in either case, however, the juridical structure set in motion always comprises three elements: the two parties and the judge. The verbs used vary, as do the prepositions with which they are construed; the act signified however appears identical.

	the one who takes the initiative	motion	court of judgment	
2 Sam. 15.2	*kol hā'îš '^{a}šer yihyeh lô rîb*	*lābô'*	*'el hammelek*	*lammišpāṭ*
2 Sam. 15.6	*kol yiśrā'ēl '^{a}šer*	*yābō'û*	*'el hammelek*	*lammišpāṭ*
Exod. 18.16	*kî yihyeh lāhem dābār*	*bā'*	*'ēlay* (Moses)	*w^{e}šāpaṭṭî…*
1 Kgs 3.16	*'āz š^{e}tayim nāšîm zōnôt*	*tābō'nâ*	*'el hammelek*	
2 Sam. 12.1	(Nathan)	*wayyābō'*	*'ēlāyw* (king David)	
2 Sam. 15.4	*kol 'îš '^{a}šer yihyeh lô rîb ûmišpāṭ*	*yābô'*	*w^{e}'ālay* (Absalom)	*w^{e}hiṣdaqtîw*
2 Chron. 19.10	*w^{e}kol rîb '^{a}šer mē'^{a}hêkem… bên…l^{e}…*	*yābô'*	*'^{a}lêkem* (priests)	*w^{e}hizhartem 'ōtām…*

	the one who takes the initiative	motion	court of judgment	
Exod. 22.8[1]			*'ad hā'elōhîm*	
		yābō'		
	debar šenêhem			*...yaršî'un...*
Job 23.3[2]	(Job)	*'ābô'*	*'ad tekûnātô*	
Job 9.32		*nābô'*		
	yaḥdāw			*bammišpāṭ*
Deut. 17.8-9	*kî yippālē' mimmekā*			
	dābār lammišpāṭ bên...le...			
	dibrê rîbōt biš'āreykā			
		weqamtā		
		we'ālîtā	*'el hammāqôm...*	
		ûbā'tā	*'el hakkōhanîm...*	
			we'el haššōpēṭ...	
				wedāraštā
				wehiggîdû
				lekā
				'ēt debar
				hammišpāṭ
Judg. 4.5		*wayya'alû*	*'ēleyhā* (Deborah)	
	benê yiśrā'ēl			*lammišpāṭ*

1. According to B.S. Jackson (*Theft in Early Jewish Law* [Oxford, 1972], p. 242), Exod. 22.8 represents a case of oracular consultation; proof would be supplied by Exod. 18.15 where we have: *bw'...lidrōš 'elōhîm.* I believe that the two Exodus texts are not a matching set: in Exod. 18.15 there is a precise description of a trial action; the fact that it is put, among other things, in the terminology of 'seeking God' means that when Moses' judgment establishes what is just or unjust in Israel, it makes reference not to previous tradition or personal wisdom, but to a privileged relationship that he enjoys with God, the ultimate principle and essential foundation of law in Israel (cf. Gamper, *Gott als Richter*, pp. 112-13). In Exod. 22.8, on the other hand, it is in effect a case of a special procedure which, although having strict juridical value, does not show the characteristics of law court procedure. It is interesting to note, however, that in both cases the terminology used (verbs of motion having as their term the 'judge') acts as description of the juridical procedure which goes on to resolve the case. On the text of Exod. 22.8, cf. also L. Koehler, 'Archäologisches Nr. 22–23', *ZAW* 46 (1928), pp. 213-20; C.H. Gordon, ''*lhym* in its Reputed Meaning of "Rulers" and "Judges"', *JBL* 54 (1935), pp. 139-44; J.R. Vannoy, 'The Use of the Word *hā'elōhîm* in Exodus 21.6 and 22.7, 8', in *The Law and the Prophets* (FS O.T. Allis; Nutley, 1974), pp. 225-41.

2. The expression used in Job 23.3 seems to call to mind the procedure of a complainant who appeals to the (royal) law court to obtain satisfaction; we might remember however that—as appears from the following verses—Job's dispute is precisely with the person sitting on the throne.

	the one who takes the initiative	motion	court of judgment	
Deut. 25.7		*w^{e}‘āl^{e}tâ*[3]		
	y^{e}bimtô		*hašša‘râ*	
			’el hazz^{e}qēnîm	
Job 34.23	(*’îš*)	*lah^{a}lōk*	*’el ’ēl*	*bammišpāṭ*
Deut. 25.1	*kî yihyeh rîb*			
	bên ’^{a}nāšîm	*w^{e}nigg^{e}šû*[4]	*’el hammišpāṭ*	
				ûš^{e}pāṭûm
				w^{e}hiṣdîqû...
				w^{e}hiršî‘û...
Exod. 24.14	*mî ba‘al d^{e}bārîm*	*yiggaš*	*’^{a}lēhem* (Aaron and Hur)	
Gen. 44.18		*wayyiggaš*	*’ēlāyw* (viceroy Joseph)	
	y^{e}hûdâ			
Gen. 18.23		*wayyiggaš*	(Judge-God cf. v. 25)	
	’abrāhām			
1 Sam. 14.38		*gōšû h^{a}lōm*		
	kōl pinnôt hā‘ām			(*yd‘* + *r’h*)
Isa. 41.1		*yigg^{e}šû...*		
	yaḥdāw			*lammišpāṭ*
		niqrābâ		
Num. 27.1[5]		*wattiqrabnâ*		
	b^{e}nôt ṣ^{e}lopḥād...			
Num. 36.1		*wayyiqr^{e}bû*		
	rā’šê hā’ābôt			
1 Sam. 14.36		*niqr^{e}bâ*		
		h^{a}lōm	*’el hā’^{e}lōhîm*	

A perusal of the texts quoted reveals that verbs of motion express going to law without any distinction between civil and criminal cases (Num. 27.1; 36.1; Deut. 25.7), between the judgment of a law court and a divine decision of an oracular kind (Exod. 22.8; 1 Sam. 14.36-38), or

3. Cf. H.A. Brongers, ‘Das Zeitwort *‘ālā* und seine Derivate’, in *Travels in the World of the Old Testament* (FS M.A. Beek; SSN, 16; Assen, 1974), p. 32, who also mentions Ruth 4.1 (*‘ālâ hašša‘ar*).

4. The special procedural value of the verbs *ngš* and *qrb* (*rḥq*) is emphasized by Z.W. Falk, ‘Hebrew Legal Terms’, *JSS* 5 (1960), pp. 253-54. Cf. also n. 35.

5. On the legal value of Num. 27.1-11, cf. J. Weingreen, ‘The Case of the Daughters of Zelophchad’, *VT* 16 (1966), pp. 518-22.

between the different jurisdictional authorities (Deut. 17.8-9). It may also be observed that, as regards my subject, the different kinds of judges (or of court of law) do not demand corresponding variations in the procedural terminology.

1.1.2. *The 'Proceedings' against the Other Party.* I would like to make it clear that the juridical formality of having recourse to a court of judgment must be kept distinct from that of *undertaking a legal action against another person.* What is expressed in the latter case is a simple controversy situation, which may or may not end up in a court of law. I make this observation because this juridical action too is expressed by *verbs of motion*, which do not, however, have the judge as their term of reference, but rather *the opposing party.*[6]

6. The distinction between the two juridical actions, that of coming for judgment in a court of law and that of coming to a controversy with someone, is not always easy to grasp, because—especially in poetic texts—the terms *rîb* and *mišpāṭ* are used in an almost synonymous way; moreover, when God is the promoter of the action, there is an instinctive feeling that he cannot be acting except as judge (which is not always true).

It should be observed, then, that the *verb of motion* only describes an initiative of a juridical kind, without specifying its nature; this may be deduced only from the relationship between the different elements in the syntagm. We have in fact at least the following figures:

a. '*coming*' *to a dispute* (proceedings against the opposing party):

Judg. 21.22	*kî **yābō'û** '^{a}bôtām 'ô '^{a}ḥêhem **lārîb** (Q) 'ēlênû . . .*
Prov. 25.8	*'al **tēṣē' lārīb** mahēr*
Isa. 66.15-16	*kî hinnēh yhwh bā'ēš **yābô'** . . . kî bā'ēš yhwh **nišpāṭ***

b. '*coming*' *to judgment* (recourse to a judge):
I would like to refer back to the texts quoted previously; in particular, a difference may be noted between Isa. 50.8 (*mî ba'al mišpāṭî yiggaš 'ēlāy* = as accuser of the other party) and Exod. 24.14 (*mî ba'al d^{e}bārîm yiggaš '^{a}lēhem* = as the party that has recourse to a judge).
c. '*coming*' *to judge* (motion by the judge towards the accused) (cf. E. Jenni, '"Kommen" im theologischen Sprachgebrauch des Alten Testaments', in *Wort–Gebot–Glaube: Beiträge zur Theologie des Alten Testaments* [ATANT, 59; Zürich, 1970], p. 258):

Ps. 96.13 (= 98.9)	*kî **bā' lišpōṭ** hā'āreṣ—yišpōṭ tēbēl b^{e}ṣedeq . . .*
Jer. 26.10	***wayya'^{a}lû*** (princes of Judah) *mibbêt hammelek bêt yhwh **wayyēš^{e}bû** b^{e}petaḥ ša'ar yhwh heḥādāš*
Jer. 1.15	***ûbā'û*** (the kings of the North) *w^{e}nāt^{e}nû 'îš **kis'ô** petaḥ ša'^{a}rê y^{e}rûšālaim*

I would like to give some examples, emphasizing on occasion the links with the terminology peculiar to the *rîb*; the resemblances to and differences from the expressions in the previous section will be easily observed.

Isa. 3.13		*niṣṣāb*	*lārîb*	
	yhwh			
		w^{e}*ʿōmēd*	*lādîn*	*ʿammîm*
Isa. 3.14	*yhwh*		*b*^{e}*mišpāṭ*	
		yābôʾ		*ʿim ziqnê ʿammô w*^{e}*śārāyw*
Ps. 143.2		*w*^{e}*ʾal tābôʾ*	*b*^{e}*mišpāṭ*	*ʾet ʿabdekā*
Job 22.4			*yōkîḥekā*	
		yābôʾ		*ʿimm*^{e}*kā*
			bammišpāṭ	
Mal. 3.5		*w*^{e}*qārabtî*		*ʾ*^{a}*lêkem*
			lammišpāṭ	
Isa. 50.8	*mî*		*yārîb*	*ʾittî…*
	mî		*baʿal mišpāṭî*	
		yiggaš		*ʾēlāy*
Isa. 1.18		*l*^{e}*kû nāʾ*	*w*^{e}*niwwāk*^{e}*ḥâ*	

1.1.3. *The 'Promotion' of a Criminal Action*. When the verbs of motion are in the *Hiphil* or *Piel* form, they seem to introduce indirectly the idea of *power* inherent in a criminal juridical action. In line with the grammatical subjects and objects, different juridical forms are seen:

a. The disputants take a juridical case to an appropriate jurisdictional body:[7]

Exod. 18.22	(lesser judges)	*w*^{e}*hāyâ kol haddābār*		
		haggādōl	*yābîʾû*	*ʾēleykā*
(Moses)				
Exod. 18.26	(lesser judges)	*ʾet haddābār haqqāšeh*	*y*^{e}*bîʾûn*	*ʾel mōšeh*
Num. 27.5			*wayyaqrēb*	
	mōšeh	*ʾet mišpāṭān*		*lipnê yhwh*
Isa. 41.21	(you)		*qār*^{e}*bû*	
		rîb^{e}*kem…*	*haggîšû*	
		ʿ^{a}*ṣumôtêkem*		

7. There is no essential difference between this form and that described in 1.1.1 of this section: it may in fact be said that by appearing in a court of law the disputants 'bring a case before' a judge. In Exod. 22.8, quoted above, the verb of motion is in the *Qal* form, and the subject is *d*^{e}*bar š*^{e}*nêhem*.

b. A disputant (accuser) brings the opposing party for judgment:[8]

Job 14.3	(God)	*w*^{e}*'ōtî*	*tābî' b*^{e}*mišpāṭ ‘immāk*
1 Sam. 20.8	(Jonathan)		*w*^{e}*‘ad 'ābîkā...*
		(= me)	*t*^{e}*bî'ēnî*

c. A judge starts a criminal action by convening the accused (or, by metonomy, what has been done) to judgment:

Qoh. 11.9					*‘al kol 'ēlleh*
		y^{e}*bî '*^{a}*kā*		(= you)	
	hā'^{e}*lōhîm*		*bammišpāṭ*		
Qoh. 12.14				*'et kol ma‘*^{a}*śeh*	
	hā'^{e}*lōhîm*	*yābī'*	*b*^{e}*mišpāṭ*		*‘al kol ne‘lām*
					'im ṭôb
					w^{e}*'im rā‘*
Num. 5.16		*w*^{e}*hiqrîb*		*'ōtāh*	
	hakkōhēn	*w*^{e}*he‘*^{e}*mīdāh*			
			lipnê yhwh		
Josh. 7.16	(*y*^{e}*hôšūa‘...*)	*wayyaqrēb*		*'et yiśrā'ēl...*	
17		*wayyaqrēb*		*'et mišpaḥat y*^{e}*hûdâ...*	
		wayyaqrēb		*'et mišpaḥat hazzarḥî...*	
18		*wayyaqrēb*		*'et bêtô...*	

1.2. *The Judge's Initiative: The Convening*

The initiative in starting a trial may be taken on by the judge in the name of the authority that belongs to him to do justice. The notice of a crime, acquired either directly or by way of prosecution witnesses, leads the jurisdictional body to issue a ‘subpoena’: once the accused is present, it will be possible to notify him or her of the accusation and proceed formally to the debate until the final verdict.

At the end of the previous section I pointed out the use of verbs of motion (in the *Hiphil*) taking as their grammatical subject the judging authority, and as their object the accused.

However, the Hebrew form most commonly used to express convening by a judge is the verb *qr' l*^{e} (sometimes *'et*, or *'el*); the person called to judgment is naturally the accused.[9]

8. This would be the equivalent of the use of the verb *y‘d* (*Hi*) (‘to convene before a court’) found in Jer. 49.19; 50.44; Job 9.19 (cf. Gemser, ‘The *rîb*- or Controversy-Pattern’, p. 123).

9. In the juridical structure of a two-sided controversy, one of the parties can summon *witnesses* in support of his case; in this case too the verb *qr'* can be used; cf. Ps. 50.1, 4: *qr' 'āreṣ...qr' 'el haššāmayim...w*^{e}*'el hā'āreṣ*; 1 Kgs 20.7: *qr' l*^{e}*ziqnê*

In order for the verb *qr' l*^{e} to have relevant reference to a judicial convening, it has to occur as a syntagmatic structure such that it more or less completely reproduces the overall trial itself. I would like to give two examples:

1 Sam. 22.9-10	(Doeg denounces the priest Ahimelek to Saul)	
	...rā'îtî...	1. 'notitia criminis'
11	*wayyišlaḥ hammelek*	2. a judge's power in the matter of a trial (*šlḥ*)
	liqrō' 'et '^{a}*ḥîmelek...* *w*^{e}*'ēt kol bêt 'ābîw...*	3. convening of the accused (*qr' 'et*)
	wayyābō'û kullām 'el hammelek	4. appearance of the accused (verbs of motion with the judge as their 'terminus ad quem')
12	*wayyō'mer šā'ûl...*	5. reading of the charge
13	*lāmmâ q*^{e}*šartem 'ālay...*	
14-15	*wayya'an '*^{a}*ḥîmelek 'et hammelek...*	6. defence speech
16	*wayyō'mer hammelek* *môt tāmût '*^{a}*ḥîmelek* *'attâ w*^{e}*kol bêt 'ābîkā*	7. sentence
17-18	*wayyō'mer hammelek lārāṣîm...* *sōbbû w*^{e}*hāmîtû kōh*^{a}*nê yhwh...*	8. order of execution
1 Kgs 2.41	*wayyugad liš*^{e}*lōmōh kî...*	1. 'notitia criminis'
42	*wayyišlaḥ hammelek*	2. the judge's power (*šlḥ*)
	wayyiqrā' l^{e}*šim'î*	3. convening of the accused (*qr' l*^{e})
	wayyō'mer 'ēlāyw...	5. reading of the charge

hā'āreṣ. The only thing which seems common to the different acts of convening is that *qr'* must take as its subject someone with a measure of authority.

43	*ûmaddûa‘ lō’šāmartā ’ēt š^{e}bū‘at yhwh w^{e}’et hammiṣwâ...*	
44-45	*wayyō’mer hammelek ’el šim‘ī...*	7. sentence
46	*wayṣaw hammelek ’et b^{e}nāyāhû...*	8. order of execution

The literary scheme outlined above (cf. also Exod. 1.17-21; Deut. 25.7-10; 2 Kgs 12.7-9) and the juridical situation whereby the accused is convened by a judge do not appear often in the Bible; this is probably because there are very few texts that describe the process of a trial;[10] on the other hand, legislative texts of a procedural kind are sparse with information on this point.

A middle position, juridically speaking, between the trial structure and that of the (two-sided) controversy occurs when the accusing party is invested with political power and authority; in this case, instead of ‘*moving*’ to charge and punish the other, the authority (who is often a sovereign) ‘*fetches*’ (convenes) the (alleged) culprit. Here too we have the use of *qr’ l^{e}*, but without the exact shape of a trial (cf. Gen. 12.18; 20.9; 26.9; Num. 16.12; Josh. 9.22 etc.).[11]

10. The Greek text of Dan. 13.1-64 (the Susannah episode) is the longest and most detailed account of a trial conducted against an individual; in it may be observed how the summons (vv. 28-30:...*aposteilate epi Sousannan*...*hoi de eutheōs ekalesan autēn. Hōs de paregenēthē*...) is located between the alleged crime and the trial proper. On the text of Daniel 13, cf. the monograph by H. Engel, *Die Susanna-Erzählung: Einleitung, Übersetzung und Kommentar zum Septuaginta-Text und zur Theodotion-Bearbeitung* (OBO, 61; Göttingen, 1985) (with abundant bibliography).

11. In this context mention might also be made of those passages in which the summoning by the authority, instead of being linked to the ‘accusation’, is designed to bring to fulfilment a (more or less clearly defined) juridical action which has been left in abeyance.

In Exod. 9.27 Pharaoh summons (*qr’ l^{e}*) Moses and Aaron in order to declare solemnly his own wrong in the controversy; this is followed by a pledge to satisfy the previous requests of those summoned (v. 28).

Even more characteristic is the situation described in 2 Samuel 21: king David becomes aware of the responsibility of the family of Saul for the massacre of the Gibeonites (v. 1); he then summons them, realizing that they fall under a law which demands reparation (vv. 2-3); sentence is pronounced by the Gibeonites themselves and ratified by the king (vv. 4-6).

The episode in 1 Samuel 29 is more complex: the princes of the Philistines, displeased that David should intervene on their side in the war, complain to king Achish, asking that David should be sent away (vv. 1-5). The king summons David (*qr’ l^{e}*). On the one hand he admits his innocence, but on the other he tells him that,

1.3. *Arrest of the Accused and Referral to Judicial Authority*
In some cases it is fairly clear that between the crime (real or alleged) and the trial the *arrest* of the accused takes place (the verbs *lqḥ* and *tpś*);[12] this seems to happen when the crime committed is such as (possibly) to deserve capital punishment. Two episodes in the biography of Jeremiah urge this meaning upon us. In ch. 26, after the Temple speech, the prophet is arrested (v. 8: *wayyitpᵉśû 'ōtô hakkōhᵃnîm wᵉhannᵉbī'îm wᵉkol hā'ām*) on a capital charge (vv. 8-9: *môt tāmût maddûa' nibbêtā*...); immediately afterwards a full trial is started and carried out, presided over by the leading men of Judah. In ch. 37, Jeremiah wants to leave the city to visit a town of Benjamin; when he reaches the gate he is 'stopped' by an officer of the guard (v. 13: *wayyitpōś 'et yirmᵉyāhû hannābî'*) on an accusation of desertion or treachery (v. 13: *'el hakkaśdîm 'attâ nōpēl*). The prophet's protestations of innocence are of no use; he is arrested and taken back to the chief

since he has been summoned as someone displeasing to the princes, he is obliged to revoke his military collaboration (vv. 6-7). To David's protest that he feels himself unjustly treated, the king restates his argument, which then becomes executive (vv. 8-11). The juridical force of this episode is that in practice David is being accused of being a traitor, and in this accusation even the king is involved. The summons allows a resolution—by way of a compromise—of a difficult situation: on the one hand, David is acquitted from the imputation of treachery, which would probably have carried a capital punishment; on the other hand, he is declared *persona non grata*, which leads to his dismissal—a decree of expulsion against a 'suspect' frees the king from any complicity whatsoever with the accused.

12. The verb *lqḥ*, although generic, can in context mean the police action mounted by a judicial authority against an alleged criminal (cf. Gen. 39.20; Deut. 19.12; 1 Kgs 22.26; Jer. 36.26 etc.). Particular note may be taken of the formula in Jer. 36.26 (*wayṣawweh hammelek...lāqaḥat*...) which is the equivalent of the 'arrest warrant'; cf. also 1 Sam. 20.31: *šᵉlaḥ wᵉqaḥ 'ōtô 'ēlay kî ben māwet hû'*.

The verb *tpś* refers to the capture (cf. in the *Ni*, with the metaphor of a net: Exod. 12.13; 17.20; 19.4, 8; Ps. 10.2), 'taking prisoners of war' (Josh. 8.23; 1 Sam. 15.8; 1 Kgs 20.18; 2 Kgs 7.12; 10.14; Jer. 34.3; Ps. 71.11 etc.). Sometimes, taking someone prisoner is linked to referral to a judging authority and execution (cf. Josh. 8.23; 1 Sam. 15.32-33; 2 Kgs 10.14; 25.6-7). Apart from the context of war, the verb *tpś* refers to the arrest of the culprit in 1 Kgs 13.14; 18.40; Jer. 26.8; 37.13-14; Ezek. 21.28-29. The act performed by parents against a rebellious child in Deut. 21.19 seems to suggest a precise juridical action: 'his father and his mother shall take hold of him and take him before the elders of the city at the gates of the place (where he lives)' (*wᵉtāpᵉśû bô...wᵉhôṣî'û 'ōtô 'el ziqnê 'îrô wᵉ'el ša'ar mᵉqōmô*).

The verb *qmṭ* seems to have the force of to arrest in Job 16.8 and 22.16.

men (v. 14: *wayyitpōś...b^eyirm^eyāhû waybī'ēhû 'el haśśārîm*).

Arrest and subsequent imprisonment seems to be a preventative[13] measure in anticipation of a formal judgment[14] which will decide acquittal or conviction. Similar cases, in which arrest and detention too look forward to a subsequent verdict, can be seen in Gen. 40.3; 42.18; Lev. 24.12; Num. 15.34; 1 Kgs 22.26-27; for referral to a judicial authority cf. Num. 5.16; 15.33; Lev. 24.11 (Deut. 21.19; Jer. 26.23).

1.4. *Public Trials*

In dealing with the act of starting a trial, due emphasis must be laid upon one of its essential aspects: anyone starting a criminal judicial action brings it out of a private dimension into a *public one*.[15] Although the structure of a law-court judgment involves basically three individuals (the prosecutor, the judge and the accused), it should be observed that

13. As de Vaux writes, 'Il y avait des prisons où l'on gardait préventivement les accusés jusqu'au jugement, Lv 24.12; Nb 15.34, et où l'on enfermait les suspects par une mesure de police parfois arbitraire, 1 R 22.27; Jr 37.15-18. La mise au carcan ou aux ceps était une rigeur supplémentaire, 2 Cron. 16,10; Jer. 20,2; 29,26' (*Institutions*, I, p. 246).

14. There appears therefore to be a formal distinction between the above and the arrest of a culprit in flight upon whom (explicitly or just implicitly) sentence has already been passed (cf. Deut. 19.12; 1 Sam. 19.19; Jer. 36.26; Amos 9.2-3 etc.).

Prison sentences seem to have existed, in the whole of the ancient Near East, only for prisoners of war (cf. A. Walther, *Das altbabylonische Gerichtswesen* [LSSt, 6; Leipzig, 1917], p. 240; E. Ebeling, 'Gefangener, Gefängnis', *Reallexicon der Assyriologie*, III [Berlin, 1957–1971], pp. 181-82; the Bible too mentions it: Judg. 1.6-7; 2 Kgs 17.4; 24.12; 25.27 etc.). For ordinary crimes, custodial sentences were not as such imposed; in fact, for crimes against property, in cases of inability to repay, the culprit was sentenced to hard labour (Ebeling, 'Gefangener, Gefängnis', p. 181) or to slavery (his own or that of his family: Exod. 22.2; Lev. 25.39-40; Deut. 15.2-3 etc.) (de Vaux, *Institutions*, I, pp. 246-47): 'l'emprisonnement par décision de justice n'apparaît qu'après l'Exil dans Esd. 7.26 et comme l'application d'une législation étrangère' (*ibid*., p. 246).

15. I would like to make reference here to a concept of criminal law, which, although drawn from modern jurists, seems to be echoed in the ancient world: 'criminal law is part of internal public law. The goods that it protects, even when they belong directly to individuals (freedom, modesty, honour, etc.) are always safeguarded from the viewpoint of public interest...It may be added that direct action for the clearing up of crimes is always public and is the concern of the State, even when its exercise depends on the manifestation of a private citizen's will' (Antolisei, *Manuale di Diritto Penale*, p. 7).

the magistrate, as such, is the (official) representative of the whole people, and that the sentence handed down concerns everybody, because it has normative value for subsequent jurisprudence.

The public nature of trials in Israel is widely accepted; my task will be only to recall the ways in which the involvement of the whole people in the juridical process is expressed in the literature of the Bible.

1.4.1. *The Assembly of the People*. Particularly in more important cases, which are the natural object of biblical accounts, the presence of the community at the trial is expressly mentioned.[16]

I would like to take as a typical example ch. 26 of Jeremiah, which together with the Greek of Daniel 13 constitutes the most detailed account of law-court procedure in the whole Bible. The point of departure is the prophet's public (cf. v. 8: *'el kol hā'ām*) prediction threatening the destruction of the Temple and the ruin of the city of Jerusalem (vv. 1-6).[17] Anyone hearing these words cannot remain

16. The importance of the citizen assembly at important juridical acts is universally accepted (Gen. 23.34; Ruth 4.11; Jer. 32.12); cf. L. Koehler, 'Archäologisches Nr. 6', *ZAW* 34 (1914), p. 148; F.S. Frick, *The City in Ancient Israel* (Missoula, MT, 1977), pp. 117-19; B. Halpern, *The Constitution of the Monarchy in Israel* (HSM, 25; Chico, CA, 1981), pp. 187-216. In particular, for a trial, cf. 1 Kgs 21.9-11; Dan. 13.28-41 (with respect to which see A. Malamat, 'Kingship and Council in Israel and Sumer: A Parallel', *JNES* 22 [1963], pp. 247-53).

According to Falk, 'the free burghers of a town formed the local *'edah*, discussed all public affairs and functioned as a court of justice' (*Hebrew Law*, p. 51); as a typical example he quotes Num. 35.12, where in fact we read: *'ad 'omdô lipnê hā'ēdâ lammišpāṭ* (cf. also Josh. 20.4-6).

As regards the problem of the 'divine' assembly, with special reference to Psalm 82, consult H.W. Robinson, 'The Council of Yahweh', *JTS* 45 (1944), pp. 151-57; F.M. Cross, 'The Council of Yahweh in Second Isaiah', *JNES* 12 (1953), pp. 274-77; W. Schmidt, *Königtum Gottes in Ugarit und Israel: Zur Herkunft der Königsprädikation Jahwes* (BZAW, 80; Berlin, 1961), pp. 32-34; H.-W. Jüngling, *Der Tod der Götter: Eine Untersuchung zu Psalm 82* (SBS, 38; Stuttgart, 1969), pp. 38-69; E.T. Mullen (Jr), *The Divine Council in Canaanite and Early Hebrew Literature* (HSM, 24; Chico, CA, 1980), pp. 226-44; M.E. Polley, 'Hebrew Prophecy within the Council of Yahweh, Examined in its Ancient Near Eastern Setting', in C.D. Evans (ed.), *Scripture in Context: Essays on the Comparative Method* (PTMS, 34; Pittsburgh, 1980), pp. 141-56.

17. The prophet's juridical role must always be kept in mind, since almost constantly in the Bible he is sent by God 'to reveal' the people's faults; he might be described as a public prosecutor (cf. Ezek. 3.26). If indeed a prophet brings out the

indifferent: either Jeremiah is right, in which case the whole people of Judah is guilty, or vice versa. At any rate, the crime is serious: destruction of the city is the punishment for the people's crime; death is the penalty for that of being a (false) prophet (vv. 6, 8-9).

'The priests, the prophets *and the whole people*' listen to those words (v. 7); their reaction shows that they consider themselves ear witnesses to a crime (*notitia criminis*); indeed, 'the priests, the prophets *and the whole people*' proceed to arrest on a capital charge (v. 8).

At this point the account says, *wayyiqqāhēl kol hā'ām 'el yirm^{e}yāhû b^{e}bêt yhwh* (v. 9). I think that this phrase does not describe the threatening press of the crowd around Jeremiah so much as the formation of a juridically competent assembly which has a decisive role within the trial. Indeed, when the 'leaders of Judah' take their seats in court to preside over the gathering (v. 10), the people then no longer side with the accusers but with the 'leaders', that is, those who, on the basis of the debate, will pass sentence. This is expressly pointed out at the important moments in the procedure: 'the priests and prophets said to the leaders *and to the whole people*' (the point when the accusation is made formal: v. 11); 'Jeremiah replied and *the whole people* said to the priests and prophets: 'This man is not worthy to die...' (verdict) (v. 16).

This account allows us to see that the public assembly acted almost like the jury in a modern assizes, making itself personally responsible for the decision taken officially by the judging magistrate (cf. 1 Sam. 14.44-45; 1 Kgs 21.13; Neh. 5.7; Dan. 13.41). This allows a better explanation of why, in the case of a death sentence by stoning, the people are called

existence of a 'crime' in the eyes of all (it is for this reason that he speaks explicitly in places where crowds gather: in the temple, in squares, at the gates), what he says cannot be restricted to a purely ethical dimension, almost as though it were a private affair left up to the individual conscience. A crime which is publicly reported necessarily requires a procedure that 'passes judgment on' the prophetic accusation, drawing the necessary juridical consequences from it. If the prophecy is a denunciation of someone (the king, the priests, false prophets, the whole people), the prophet begins a trial against others; but he himself ends up on trial (cf. Deut. 18.20), because, if he is judged 'false' in his witness, he must undergo the serious consequences of his action. Indeed, nobody can be accused lightly or falsely without incurring a punishment proportionate to the gravity of the charge (Deut. 19.16-21). But if his words are proved truthful, the public acts proportionate to the charge made are imposed on the culprits. From these observations we may conclude that prophet and trial were two extremely closely linked concepts throughout the whole history of Israel up to the time of Jesus and those who became his witnesses.

upon to execute it (cf. Lev. 24.23; Num. 15.35-36; Deut. 17.7; 21.21; 22.21).

1.4.2. *The Place of Judgment.*[18] The public element in a trial is made clear by the place in which justice is administered. It is well known that '*the gate*' (*ša'ar*) was the place in the various towns and cities of Israel where public affairs took place, trial sessions were held (cf. Deut. 16.18; 22.15; 25.7 etc.) and sentences were carried out (cf. Deut. 17.5; 22.24; Josh. 8.29; 2 Kgs 10.8).

Normally, the court of law 'at the gates' was bound up with the collegial body of the *z^eqēnîm* (Deut. 21.19; 22.15; 25.7; Josh. 20.4; Prov. 31.23; Ruth 4.11; Lam. 5.14 etc.), but this relationship should not be considered exclusive. Especially in poetic texts, the gate generally implies the court of law, without any particular indication of the kind of magistrate presiding over it (Deut. 16.18; Isa. 29.21; Amos 5.10, 12-15; Zech. 8.16; cf. also Jer. 26.10 and 38.7).

The 'gate' owes its role as a law court to the fact that it was an area given over to public events in all the (fortified) cities of Israel. The comings and goings of the population made judgment open to intervention by any passer-by, and allowed the involvement of the citizenry in the course of a juridical action.[19] From this point of view, a trial 'at the gates' is the direct opposite of a secret procedure of an inquisitorial nature, or of private vendettas or summary executions perpetrated as the opportunity presented itself.[20]

18. Qoh. 3.16 uses the descriptive expression *m^eqôm hammišpāt* and in parallel *m^eqôm haṣṣedeq* to describe a court of law; the intention is ironic, given that the author is denouncing the injustices committed in the 'seat of judgment' (to which he proposes as a cure God's just intervention: v. 17).

19. Cf. Koehler, 'Die hebräische Rechtsgemeinde', pp. 145, 147-48; E.A. Speiser, '"Coming" and "Going" at the "City" Gate', *BASOR* 144 (1952), pp. 20-23; G. Evans, '"Coming" and "Going" at the City Gate—A Discussion of Professor Speiser's Paper', *BASOR* 150 (1958), pp. 28-33.

20. It may be observed that the term *r^eḥôb* (*square*) seems to have the force of a law court in Job 29.7 (parallel to *ša'ar*) and in Isa. 59.14 (cf. also Ps. 55.12). V. Maag maintains in fact that 'unter *r^eḥôb* ist nichts anderes als der 2 Chron. 32.6 genannte *rhwb š'r h'yr* zu verstehen: der freie Platz auf der Stadtseite der Toranlage' (*Text, Wortschatz und Begriffswelt des Buches Amos* [Leiden 1951], p. 193).

As regards other places used for the administration of justice, there is debate about the term *gōren* (generally translated as *threshing-floor*). G. Münderlein (*ThWAT*, II, p. 67) observes that *grn* in Ugaritic 'dient auch als Ort der

2. *The Juridical 'Position' of Those in the Trial*

The stages of a trial are characterized by the fact that the various individuals who take part take up their 'positions' in such a way as to show what pertains to each and the role each intends to perform. In this section I shall illustrate the quite *bodily* positions taken up by the judge and those who submit to judgment, with the intention not only of visualizing the scene in a Hebrew court of law, but above all of grasping the juridical overtones of its descriptive language; on occasion, I shall also demonstrate the links with what has already been previously noted.

2.1. *The Judge's Positions*

The judge appears to have two characteristic positions in a trial: (1) that of *being seated* (both as a movement and as a state); (2) that of *rising*. The former indicates the beginning and development of the debate stage; the latter indicates the concluding stage of the sentence. Both positions can, however, by synedochy, stand for the whole activity of judging.

2.1.1. *The 'Sitting' Started by the Judge*. In a legal context, the verb *yšb* refers to a judge's action in beginning and holding a law court session.[21]

Rechtssprechung' (cf. C.H. Gordon, *Ugaritic Textbook, Glossary* [AnOr, 38; Rome, 1965], p. 622), but there does not seem to be any attestation in the Old Testament that the threshing floor was a preferred site for trials. Opinions have been voiced on this subject by S. Smith, 'The Threshing Floor at the City Gate', *PEQ* 78 (1946), pp. 5-14; *idem.*, 'On the Meaning of *goren*', *PEQ* 85 (1953), pp. 42-45; and J. Gray, 'Tell El Far'a by Nablus: A "Mother" in Ancient Israel', *PEQ* 84 (1952), p. 112; *idem*, 'The *goren* at the City Gate: Justice and the Royal Office in the Ugaritic Text *'Aqht*', *PEQ* 85 (1953), pp. 118-23. Cf. also M.M. Aranov, *The Biblical Threshing-Floor in the Light of the Ancient Near Eastern Evidence: Evolution of an Institution* (PhD Dissertation, New York University, 1977); I only have knowledge of it through *DissAbstr* 38 (1977–78), pp. 6179-80 (A). As an important text on the significance of the *gōren* (translated as *square*) in a legal context, 1 Kgs 22.10 may be cited. It may also be recalled that since the threshing floor was the place for winnowing (separating the grain from the chaff) it can become a *metaphor* for judgment (Jer. 51.33; Mic. 4.12) (cf. *ThWAT*, II, p. 68).

Finally, I would like to quote the opinion of Falk: 'Justice is administered in the name of God and quite often the court convenes in the Sanctuary or on the occasion of a religious ceremony' (*Hebrew Law*, p. 29). The texts quoted by the author as proof (Gen. 14.17ff.; Exod. 25.25; Josh. 24.25; Ps. 122.5) do not, however, seem convincing to me.

21. In Ezek. 10.16-17 we also have a precise indication of the length of a judicial session.

This is so universally accepted as not to require special comment. I would like, therefore, just to point out the texts in which there is an explicit link between the judge's *being seated* (*yšb*)[22] and the act of *judging* (root *špṭ* and synonyms), of the kind: *wayyēšeb mōšeh lišpōṭ 'et hā'ām* (Exod. 18.13); Judg. 4.4-5; Isa. 16.5; 28.6; Jer. 26.10; Joel 4.12; Ps. 9.5; Prov. 20.8.[23]

It should be noted that the judge's '*being seated*' is sometimes linked to the *movement* of those coming forward for judgment on a case (Exod. 18.13, 14, 16; Judg. 4.5; Joel 4.12; cf. also Ps. 122.4-5).

In this context we may recall that, as well as the Temple, Solomon had his own palace built; the latter was the seat of the royal law court: *w^e'ûlām hakkissē' '^ašer yišpoṭ šām 'ūlām hammišpāṭ 'āśâ* (1 Kgs 7.7).

The magistrate's 'seat' is an element linked semantically to the judicial 'session',[24] and in some texts it can symbolically stand for the judge's activity.

Nobody doubts that the 'throne' (*kissē'*) is the sign by antonomasia for the dignity, power and glory of whoever rules; but it is still important to emphasize how in the text of 1 Kgs 7.7 the 'seat' is linked to the exercise of judging as it pertains to the king (an activity which elsewhere belongs in full measure to the figure of Solomon). Whereas I emphasized the public aspect of the juridical procedure with reference to the 'gate', this term (*kissē'*) introduces the concept of power and authority. If the seat involved is *royal*, the specific nuance introduced is that of the *final* court of appeal. Indeed, recourse to it, though difficult to evaluate in practical terms, represented the possibility in Israel of equal justice for all. On the other hand, the king's throne, precisely because of its universal and supreme nature, was the institution that regulated and controlled, by directives and decrees, local jurisprudence in Israel (cf. Jer. 26.17-24).

The link between the royal throne and the administration of justice is

22. Instead of *yšb lišpōṭ*, in Ezek. 44.24 we find the syntagm *'md lišpōṭ* (according to the Ketib; the Qere is *l^emišpāṭ*), with the meaning of 'to act as a judge', 'to exercise the functions of a magistrate' (cf. n. 36).

23. Cf. also Dan. 7.9-10 (Aramaic) and 13.50 (Greek).

24. As well as the connection between 'seat' and the verb *yšb* (1 Kgs 3.6; Ps. 9.5, 9; Isa. 16.5), note should be taken of the frequent use of the verb *kwn*: the throne's foundation, on which it rests and by which it is kept firm, is indeed the exercise of justice (Isa. 9.6; 16.5; Pss. 9.8; 89.15; 97.2; Prov. 16.12; 25.5; 29.14). In Job 23.3 the seat (of God) is called *t^ekûnâ*; and in 29.7 we find a link between *kwn* and *môšāb*. The verb *s'd* in Isa. 9.6 and Prov. 20.28 has the same meaning as *kwn*.

well attested (1 Kgs 10.9; Isa. 9.6; 16.5; Ps. 94.20; Prov. 16.12; 20.8, 28; 25.5; 29.14; cf. also in Aramaic, Dan. 6.7-10). Particular mention may be made of Ps. 122.5, in which it is said of Jerusalem, *kî šāmmâ yāšᵉbû kis'ôt lᵉmišpāṭ kis'ôt lᵉbêt dāwîd*; the use of the plural ('seats') could simply indicate the eminence of the law court, but perhaps it is there to suggest the complex of appeal courts existing in the capital, courts which, under the supervision of the monarchy, guaranteed a satisfactory administration of justice to the tribes of Israel.

When God is spoken of as a king, his throne too is linked with the doing of justice (Pss. 9.5-8; 11.4; 89.15; 97.2). The universal extension of YHWH's dominion represents the guarantee of just judgment extended to the whole cosmos.[25]

2.1.2. *The Judge's 'Rising'*. In some texts, the act of judging is linked to the verbs *nṣb* (*Ni*) and *qwm*, which, and especially the latter, are the direct opposites of *yšb*. It seems reasonable to suppose[26]—even if it is not directly demonstrable from the biblical texts—that the judge was seated during the debate (when the judge's function was to give 'a hearing', that is, to listen to the parties' reasons), and rose at the time of the verdict (to give a speech pronouncing the sentence, which concluded the trial). This link between standing up and speaking seems consistent with the movements of the others taking part in the trial, as I shall show shortly.[27] The biblical texts usually quoted for the judge's rising are Pss. 76.10; 82.1, 8; Job 31.14.[28]

2.2. *'Being' on Trial*

The judge's being seated in the law court is linked—as seen above—to the movement of those who come forward for judgment; but above all it is the opposite of '*standing up*' during the course of the trial. The legal overtones of the verbs *'md, nṣb* (*Ni*) and *yṣb* (*Hitp*) do appear

25. Cf. H. Brunner, 'Gerechtigkeit als Fundament des Thrones', *VT* 8 (1958), pp. 426-28; Z.W. Falk, 'Two Symbols of Justice', *VT* 10 (1960), pp. 72-73. For the *šēbeṭ/špṭ* relationship, cf. Chapter 8 n. 90.

26. Cf. de Vaux, *Institutions*, I, p. 240; Gemser, 'The *rîb*- or Controversy-Pattern', p. 123.

27. Koehler, 'Die hebräische Rechtsgemeinde', p. 149.

28. With reference to Job 31.14, see the comment by Fra Luis de Leon (quoted by Alonso Schökel, *Job*, p. 445), which develops the symbolic value of God's 'rising' in his court of judgment.

important, both in the static sense of 'to be on trial' and in the dynamic one of 'to file an appearance', 'to appear in court'.[29]

2.2.1. *The Verb 'md*. By frequency, the verb *'md*—usually with the preposition *lipnê*[30]—is the most important of these verbs of 'appearance' for judgment; sometimes linked to verbs of motion (which emphasize the juridical initiative) it expresses the placement of the parties under the jurisdiction of the magistrate:

1 Kgs 3.16	*'āz **tābō'nâ** šᵉtayim nāšîm zōnôt 'el hammelek* ***wattaᵃmōdnâ lᵉpānāyw***
Num. 27.1	***wattiqrabnâ** bᵉnôt ṣᵉlophād...*
2	***wattaᵃmōdnâ lipnê** mōšeh*[31]

From the texts quoted it seems that two stages may be logically distinguished: that of appearance (verbs of motion) and that of submission to judgment (*'md*); indeed, the verb *'md* can stand for the totality of these acts, as can be seen from the following texts, where the verbs of motion are in synonymous parallelism with *'md* or *nṣb* (*Ni*):

a. For a juridical action undertaken *against another party*

Isa. 3.13-14	***niṣṣāb** lārîb yhwh*	
	***wᵉ'ōmēd** lādîn*	*'ammîm*
	*yhwh **bᵉmišpāṭ yābô'***	*'im ziqnê 'ammô wᵉśārāyw*
Isa. 50.8	*mî yārîb 'ittî*	***na'amdâ** yāḥad*
	mî ba'al mišpāṭî	***yiggaš** 'ēlāy*

29. As the primary meaning of *'md* Zorell proposes '*erectus stetit* (opp. iacens, sedens)' and BDB '*stand, be in a standing attitude*'; the juridical meaning of 'to stand trial' or 'to file an appearance' probably derives from the physical attitude taken up by the accused during the hearing. Standing erect seems to imply likewise winning a legal action (Pss. 76.8; 106.23, 30; 130.3 etc.).

30. In the sense which I am describing, *'md* is used absolutely in Deut. 25.8 and Nah. 1.6; with the preposition *'al* in Exod. 18.13.

31. Parallel to Num. 27.1-2 is Num. 5.16, where, however, the verbs are in the *Hiphil*:

wᵉhiqrîb 'ōtāh hakkōhēn
wᵉheᵉmîdāh lipnê yhwh.

b. For a juridical action undertaken *before a judge*

Exod. 18.13 *...wayyēšeb mōšeh lišpōṭ ’et hā‘ām*
***wayya^{a}mōd** hā‘ām **‘al** mōšeh min habbōqer ‘ad hā‘āreb*

14 *...maddûa‘ ’attâ yôšēb l^{e}baddekā*
*w^{e}kol hā‘ām **niṣṣāb ‘ālеykā** min bōqer ‘ad ‘āreb*

15-16 *...kî **yābō’ ’ēlay** hā‘ām lidrōš ’^{e}lōhîm*
*kî yihyeh lāhem dābār **bā’ ’ēlay***
w^{e}šāpaṭtî bên ’îš ûbên rē‘ēhû

The interchangeability of *‘md, nṣb* (*Ni*) and *bw’ ’el* may be noted, as well as the link to the judge’s ‘sitting’ and judging.

Deut. 19.17 ***w^{e}‘ām^{e}dû** š^{e}nê hā’^{a}nāšîm ’^{a}šer lāhem hārîb **lipnê** yhwh*
***lipnê** hakkōh^{a}nîm w^{e}haššōp^{e}ṭîm*

Cf. also Exod. 9.10; Lev. 12.4-5; Num. 35.12; Deut. 25.8; Josh. 20.4-6; Jer. 49.19; Nah. 1.6; Zech. 3.1; Pss. 76.8; 130.3; Ezek. 9.15. Perhaps there are legal overtones to Gen. 43.15 and Num. 16.18.

2.2.2. *The Verbs nṣb (Ni) and yṣb (Hitp).* We have already seen how *nṣb* (*Ni*) is synonymous with *‘md* in Exod. 18.13-14 and Isa. 3.13; later on it will be shown how both belong to the same paradigm.

The verb *yṣb* (*Hitp*) has a juridical/law court force in 1 Sam. 12.7, Job 33.5 and perhaps Ps. 5.6.

If some kind of trial background is attributed to the appearance of Moses and Aaron before Pharaoh, Exod. 5.20-21 and 7.15 may be taken into account for *nṣb* (*Ni*), and 8.16; 9.13 for *yṣb* (*Hitp*).

2.3. *The Taking up of Position by the Participants in the Trial*[32]

Heretofore I have dealt with the trial situation in which, on the one hand, is placed the *judge*, (described above all by the verb *yšb*) and, on the other hand, the *parties* standing trial (characterized mainly by the verb *‘md lipnê*). I would now like to examine further the (dynamic) part

32. It is interesting to observe how a modern penologist, in describing the workings of a trial, emphasizes the metaphorical value of individuals’ movements: ‘A trial is the expression of a *movement*, the behaviour of individuals in a trial relationship. Given that these individuals *move*, act and work together as the trial unfolds, the need arises to regulate, limit and co-ordinate their activities’ (Leone, *Manuale di Diritto processuale penale*, p. 265, my emphasis).

played by the juridical individuals, in particular clarifying the role of the *accuser* and *defender*.

In modern criminal proceedings these two juridical figures are clearly defined and distinct both from the judge and the complainant. The role of accuser is taken on by the Public Ministry which is officially in charge of criminal proceedings on behalf of the State; the defence is carried out by law professionals, to whom is given the task of assisting and representing the accused.

In Israel, as far as we can deduce from the documents at our disposal, we do not find the same sort of official apparatus; the accuser and defender are merely those who, during a public trial, *speak for or against* the accused. The situation as it appears from the texts is one that presents difficulties for interpretation, not only because any individual at all can take part in the trial, but above all because the role individuals will take in the trial itself cannot be deduced a priori; only from the context, the verbal content or sometimes from some terminological detail can the juridical significance of someone's speech be decided. The judge, moreover, sometimes personally fulfils the task of prosecuting (like a modern police magistrate) and at other times the judge appears as counsel for the accused (as noted in Chapter 5).

The conclusion of my observations is this: the dynamic expressed in the trial remains fundamentally that of the controversy: we have an accuser and an accused, and the outcome of their conflict is the chief object of interest. If someone (maybe the judge) is on the accuser's side, the sentencing of the accused follows; but if this someone (perhaps the judge) is on the accused's side, the latter gains the victory at the accuser's expense.

It comes as no surprise, then, to realize that biblical language suggesting 'taking up position' in a trial is in some respects generic, ambivalent and—by our standards—imprecise: it refers only to a *speech*, clarified by context, following a basic division: either *on behalf of* the accused (defence) or *against* (accusation).

There are two ways in which this speech is marked: (a) on the one hand, we have verbs suggesting 'being' (*'md* or its synonyms) with a particular clarification of *nearness* to the accused; (b) on the other hand, we find the verb *qwm* ('rising' in judgment) linked, as I have already noted, to speech of some kind.

2.3.1. *Closeness to or Distance from the Accused.* The fact that the verbs *'md* and its synonyms express the prosecution and defence speeches in a manner similar to the 'standing' of the parties on trial may be explained like this: someone who takes an active part in a debate, and takes a person's side, formally stands by that person—as a party—and falls under the same judgment.[33] It should be noted, however, that whereas for the parties the fundamental indication is standing '*before*' the judge (*'md lipnê*),[34] for the prosecution/defence speech the emphasis is on standing *alongside* the accused (or its opposite: standing away from the accused, that is, not speaking up).

I would like to give some examples:

Ps. 109.6	(accuser)	*w^e śāṭān ya'^amōd 'al ye mînô*[35]	(close)
Ps. 109.31	(defender)	*kî ya'^amōd lîmîn 'ebyôn*	
		l^e hôšîa' miššōp^e ṭê napšô	(nearby)

33. In modern proceedings, the position of the public prosecutor, the defence counsel and, *a fortiori*, the witnesses, cannot be defined absolutely in terms of who is on trial. From this point of view, the world of the Bible gives an altogether different implication to the different speeches at a judgment.

34. Presenting oneself before a judge is not a neutral act; it always involves some sort of charge or laying claim to a right. It may perhaps be thought that the phrase *'md lipnê*, in the sense of 'to intercede', may be regarded as a kind of speech for the defence (cf. Gen. 18.22; Jer. 15.1; 18.20).

35. Standing on someone's *right* just means '*to the side*' without specific positive (defence) or negative (prosecution) overtones: for the former aspect, cf. Pss. 16.8; 109.31; and also 142.5; for the latter, cf. Zech. 3.1; Pss. 17.7; 109.6; Job 30.12.

According to Gemser, 'be on the right hand' (in a defensive sense) is a metaphor which comes from deployment in battle: while the left side was covered by a shield, the right side was protected by a soldier (Pss. 110.5; 121.5) ('The *rîb*- or Controversy-Pattern', p. 123.) Hence—I conclude—the terrible situation of a man who finds 'on his right' his actual adversary. Z.W. Falk goes on to maintain that the vocabulary of 'being close' (*qrb* in particular) is 'a remnant of an earlier practice, settling disputes through combat. The noun *qrb* means struggle, and drawing near to the other party was primarily for the purpose of overcoming him by force. It is only in a civilised stage of society that the conflict must be referred to the judgment of an arbitrator or the divine decision by ordeal. Language, however, has preserved the memory of the old custom' ('Hebrew Legal Terms', *JSS* 5 [1960], pp. 353-54). For my part, I prefer the metaphorical interpretation of the debate to that which explains its vocabulary by way of the history of institutions. Cf. also Y. Hoffmann, 'The Root *qrb* as a Legal Term', *JNSL* 10 (1982), pp. 67-73; for the use of *qrb/rḥq* in prayer, see W.R. Mayer, '"Ich rufe dich von ferne, höre mich von nahe!". Zu einer babylonischen Gebetsformel', in *Werden und Wirken des Alten Testaments* (FS C. Westermann; Neukirchen, 1980), pp. 302-17.

Ps. 10.1	(defender)	*lāmâ yhwh ta'ᵃmōd bᵉrāḥôq*	(distant)
Ps. 38.12	(defender)	*'ōhᵃbay wᵉrē'ay minneged*	
		nig'î ya'ᵃmōdû	
		ûqᵉrôbay mērāḥōq 'āmādû	(distant)

Cf. also 2 Sam. 18.13; Zech. 3.1.

From the examples quoted above, it may be seen how 'being close' has considerable importance in referring to the speech by the accuser and, above all, the defender. The roots *qrb* and *rḥq* (even without the verb *'md* or its synonyms) can express this meaning:

a. For *qrb/qārôb*:

1. Said of the defender:

Lam. 3.57 ***qārabtā*** *bᵉyôm 'eqrā'ekkā...*
Lam. 3.58 *rabtā 'ᵃdōnāy rîbê napšî...*
Isa. 50.8 ***qārôb*** *maṣdîqî mî yārîb 'ittî*
Cf. also Isa. 51.5; Jer. 23.23; Pss. 34.19; 69.19.

2. Said of the accuser:

Ps. 27.2 ***biqrōb*** *'ālay mᵉrē'îm*
Cf. also Pss. 55.19; 119.150.

b. For *rḥq/rāḥôq*

1. Said of the defender:

Isa. 59.9 *'al kēn* ***rāḥaq*** *mišpāṭ mimmennû—wᵉlō' taśśîgēnû ṣᵉdāqâ*
Isa. 59.11 *...nᵉqawweh lammišpāṭ wā'ayin—lîšû'â* ***rāḥᵃqâ*** *mimmennû*
Isa. 59.14 *wᵉhussag 'āḥôr mišpāṭ—ûṣᵉdāqâ* ***mērāḥôq*** *ta'ᵃmōd*
Ps. 35.22 *...'al* ***tirḥaq*** *mimmennî*
Ps. 35.23 *hā'îrâ wᵉhāqîṣâ lᵉmišpāṭî—'ᵉlōhay wa'dōnāy lᵉrîbî*
Job 5.4 ***yirḥᵃqû*** *bānāyw miyyešā'—wᵉyiddakkᵉ'û bašša'ar wᵉ'ên maṣṣîl*
Cf. also Isa. 46.12-13; Pss. 10.1; 22.12, 20; 38.12, 22; 71.12; Prov. 15.29; Lam. 1.16.

2. Said of the accuser:

Exod. 23.7 *middᵉbar šeqer* ***tirḥāq***
Cf. also Isa. 54.14.

2.3.2. *Rising in Judgment.* Another important way of expressing a speech (both prosecution and defence) in a trial—often with overtones of resolution and victory—is provided by the verb *qwm*. With respect to those previously listed, this verb probably refers to a law court proceeding in which a fixed set of listeners (the assembly, the jury, the magistrates) would take part seated at a trial, while the person speaking would stand up (perhaps taking up a position next to the accused).

We may consider this verb as belonging to essentially the same syntagm as *'md* (and its synonyms), as may be seen from the following examples, in which I have juxtaposed texts which—in my opinion—have a similar meaning:

Ps. 94.16	*mî* ***yāqûm*** *lî 'im m^{e}rē'îm*	
	mî ***yityaṣṣēb*** *lî 'im pō'^{a}lê 'āwen*	(defender)
Ps. 109.6	*w^{e}śāṭān* ***ya'^{a}mōd*** *'al y^{e}mînô*	
Job 30.12	*'al yāmîn pirḥaḥ* ***yāqûmû***	(accuser)
Lev. 19.16	*lō'* ***ta'^{a}mōd*** *'al dam rē'ekā*[36]	
Deut. 19.15	*lō'* ***yāqûm*** *'ēd 'eḥād b^e'îš...*	(accuser)

36. The syntagm *'md 'al* is very frequently used with different meanings; even within the juridical sphere we come across a number of usages.

The generic meaning of 'to be over' (Exod. 3.5; 8.18; Josh. 5.15 etc.) seems sometimes to be narrowed down to that of 'to preside', 'to oversee', or more simply 'to have the task of' (Num. 7.2 for the census; Deut. 27.13 for cursing); the text of Ezek. 44.24, *w^e'al rîb hēmmâ* (the levitical priests) *ya'am^{e}dû lšpṭ* (Qeré: *l^{e}mišpāṭ*) *b^{e}mišpāṭay wīšp^{e}ṭūhû* should then be translated as: 'they will oversee judicial controversies; they will judge them according to my laws'.

In Exod. 18.13-15 we have parallelism between *'md 'al, nṣb* (*Ni*) *'al* and *bw' 'el*: the meaning seems to be clearly that of 'proceedings before' a judging authority (Moses) (cf. above).

Very often the expression *'md 'al* means 'to stand by' (Gen. 24.30; 41.1, 17; 2 Kgs 11.14 etc.); this nearness is, in certain cases, synonymous with assistance (cf. Dan. 12.1; and probably also Judg. 3.19; 1 Kgs 22.19; and elsewhere, where reference is made to the officers in the sovereign's service); but in other cases, it means *opposition* (cf. Dan. 8.25; 11.14; 1 Chron. 21.1 etc.). The meaning of *'md 'al y^{e}mîn-* (Zech. 3.1; Ps. 109.6) should probably be assigned to this sphere, that of nearness with aggressive force (cf. above). Likewise the text of Judg. 6.31, which forms part of the *rîb* between Gideon (and his father Joash) and the inhabitants of the city: *wayyō'mer yô'āš l^{e}kōl '^{a}šer 'ām^{e}dû 'ālāyw* ('Joash replied to those who were attacking him').

We may also read the passage in Lev. 19.16 along the same lines: *lō' ta'amōd 'al dam rē'ekā*. It seems preferable (with ancient and modern translations and recent commentaries) to translate the syntagm *'md 'al* (*dam*) with the meaning of *proceedings against* (life); the juridical nuance of putting on trial and starting prosecution proceedings seems a reasonable deduction from the context (cf. v. 15). Among the translators, only Vaccari, to my knowledge, shies away from this line of interpretation, giving the following meaning: 'do not stay inactive when your neighbour is in danger'. Under the heading *'md*, with reference to Lev. 19.16, Zorell upholds the following translation: '*otiosus, non iuvans, stetit* in vitae periculo proximi', quoting in support Pss. 10.1; 38.12; Isa. 59.14 (which do not, however, contain the syntagm *'md*

Like the verbs dealt with previously, *qwm* can refer to both the defence speech (cf. Pss. 12.6; 35.1, 2; 74.22; 94.16; Job 19.25 etc.) and the prosecution speech; the latter is the more frequently attested, and in some cases is qualified by the prepositions with which the verb *qwm* is construed:

qwm	Mic. 6.1; Zech. 3.8; Pss. 1.5; 35.11; Job 30.28
qwm 'et	Isa. 54.17
qwm 'al	2 Sam. 14.7; in Pss. 3.2; 54.5; 86.14; 92.12 it is difficult to distinguish between a juridical speech and a military aggression.
qwm b[e]	Deut. 19.15, 16; Mic. 7.6; Ps. 27.12; Job 16.8

3. *The Preliminary Phase*

I am taking this terminology from modern criminal proceedings, while being well aware that we do not find in the Bible such a precise distinction between 'preliminaries' and judgment. If, however, the preliminaries are 'the activity aimed at collecting proof', and more particularly that 'phase of the proceedings directed, by the collection of proof, at the *preparation for judgment* (or, more exactly, at establishing whether judgment should be passed or not)',[37] then we may correctly assume that something similar is mentioned in the biblical texts, of a kind deserving specific analysis.

The typical case in which inquiries are necessary occurs when a judging body is asked to intervene but does not have available the information necessary to accuse someone of a crime; of its own initiative, therefore, it goes in search of everything that can *establish the truth*, by inquiries, searches and so on. If, for example, information is received that

'al, but *'md + rḥq* or *minneged*; Zorell himself, on the other hand, under the heading *dām*, for the same text gives the translation: 'cooperari ad caedem alcs'. Since it is clear from Hebrew legislation that capital punishment trials are by no means prohibited (indeed, they are sometimes laid down), it is necessary to understand *dām* in the sense of 'innocent blood', 'an innocent person', or to take *'md 'al* with the nuance of unjustly aggressive proceedings; in this way Lev. 19.16 could be translated in one of the following fashions: 'you shall not take out capital punishment proceedings against the life of an *innocent* neighbour of yours', or 'you shall not mount an *unjust* trial against the life of your neighbour'.

37. Pisapia, *Compendio di procedura penale*, p. 172. In modern proceedings, one of the characteristics of the preliminary phase with respect to that of the debate is its *secrecy*; this is neither laid down nor attested in the biblical texts.

the crime of idolatry has taken place in a city, with the danger of it spreading, the judges must undertake an accurate assessment of the situation and establish whether it is a definite fact or not (Deut. 13.13-15).[38] In the same way, if a dispute arises between two individuals and they bring themselves to the court of law, the judge appealed to cannot settle for weighing the accusation of one against the other: the judge must rather go on to an inquiry that will back up the word of one of the two disputants (Deut. 19.16-21).

Structurally, this stage of the judgment is linked to the 'notice of the crime', which, as I have often mentioned, is the indispensable condition for any proceedings of a juridical nature. Investigatory activities—in Israel the task of the magistrate, but from time to time even entrusted to the prosecution, almost as though it were a question of a public ministry—had the precise aim of casting light on a particular event (crime) in such a way that—knowing what crime had been committed and knowing who was its author—it would be possible to proceed to the indictment and sentencing of the culprit in accordance with truth and justice.

3.1. *The Hebrew Lexicon Referring to Inquiries*

In this section I would like to consider the paradigm of verbs that take the judging body as their subject and express the act of acquiring enough knowledge to hand down a right judgment. The basic syntagm would be formed as follows: (1) the judge (2) *gets information* (makes inquiries) (3) in order to pronounce the sentence. This sequence of events is detectable, as we shall see, not only in strictly legal texts, but it also appears as a logical framework in narrative and poetic texts (cf., for example, Exod. 5.21; 1 Sam. 24.16, Ps. 7.9-10; Lam. 3.60-64).

3.1.1. *The First Series of Verbs Drawn from Legal Texts.* A first series of verbs referring to the inquiries is to be noted in the legislative texts of Deuteronomy (Deut. 13.15; 17.4, 9; 19.18), where emphasis is laid on the accuracy of the investigation; this seems to assume that previously

38. This is the manner in which Gen. 18.20-21 has to be interpreted: an accusation against Sodom and Gomorrah has reached the divine judge; as a result, he undertakes to clarify the facts: 'I want to go down and see if they have in fact committed all the evil of which the cry has reached me; I want *to know*' (cf. L. Alonso Schökel, *Génesis* [Los Libros Sagrados, I. 1; Madrid, 1970], p. 84).

the practice of summary judgment was not rare, to the detriment of persons unjustly accused.[39]

From Deut. 13.15 in particular we can grasp the relevance of the series of verbs *drš*, *ḥqr* and *š'l*: 'If you hear it said...that wicked men...have led astray the inhabitants of their city...you *shall make inquiries, you shall investigate, you shall ask questions* carefully'. Given that in Job 10.6 and Judg. 6.29 the verb *drš* (in a precisely investigative context) is closely linked to *bqš* (*Pi*), we may include the latter verb in our first series.[40] Here, then, is the list, with an indication of some of the important texts:

drš	Deut. 13.15; 17.4, 9; 19.18; Pss. 10.13; 142.5; Job 10.6; Ezek. 10.16 (corr.)
bqš (*Pi*)	Judg. 6.29; Job 10.6
(*Pu*)	Jer. 50.20; Est. 2.23
ḥqr[41]	Deut. 13.15; Job 13.9; 29.16; Prov. 18.17; Lam. 3.40[42]
š'l	Deut. 13.15; 2 Sam. 14.18; 2 Kgs 8.6; Jer. 18.13[43]

39. Particular note should be taken of the expression *drš hêṭēb* (Deut. 13.15; 17.4; 19.18), which is a description of an accurate investigation; to tell the truth, it could also involve an 'investigatory' attitude on the part of judges.

40. The article by C. Westermann, 'Die Begriffe für Fragen und Suchen im Alten Testament', *KD* 6 (1961) pp. 2-30, examines the verbs *bqš* (*Pi*), *š'l, drš*; the special juridical nuance of the inquiry is brought to mind by the author on p. 16.

41. The noun *ḥēqer* means inquiry in Job 34.24. B.S. Jackson observes that in *m. Sanh*. 5.1; 4.1, the law court inquiry is called *derishah weḥaqirah* (*Theft in Early Jewish Law*, p. 231 n. 3). On the root *ḥqr*, cf. P. Joüon, 'Notes de lexicographie hébraïque', *Bib* 7 (1926), pp. 72-74.

42. The text of Lam. 3.40 (*naḥp^{e}śâ d^{e}rākênû w^{e}naḥqōrâ*) gives an interesting transposition to the terminology of the inquiry: it deals with the investigation not of others but of the self, which is equivalent to an 'examination of conscience' leading to conversion (*w^{e}nāšûbâ 'ad yhwh*). The inquisitorial and accusatory character of this examination has the aim of establishing the truth (Israel has sinned) in such a way that presenting itself before God may be transformed from an act of pleading into supplication for forgiveness.

The verb *ḥpś* (*Pi*) means the act of searching for the purpose of discovering the *corpus delicti* (Gen. 31.35; 44.12), or more generally, the search to uncover the guilty (1 Sam. 23.23; 2 Kgs 10.23; Amos 9.3; Zeph. 1.12; Prov. 28.12) (L. Alonso Schökel and J. Vilchez, *Proverbios* [Madrid, 1984], pp. 487-88).

43. The investigation that the prophet invites the nation to carry out in Jer. 18.13 has the aim of highlighting by contrast the wickedness to be found in Israel (cf. also Jer. 2.10).

It is interesting to observe that these verbs are sometimes construed with a specified *object*; in this way the different forms that a judicial investigation can take are emphasized:

a. To prepare a case for trial[44]

drš	*haddābār*	Ezek. 10.16 (corr.)
bqš (*Pu*)	*haddābār*	Est. 2.23
ḥqr	*rîb-*	Job 29.16

b. To investigate a crime[45]

bqš (*Pi*)	*la'ᵃwōnî*	
drš	*lᵉḥaṭṭā'tî*	Job 10.6
bqš (*Pu*)	*'et 'ᵃwōn-*	
	'et ḥaṭṭō't-	Jer. 50.20

c. To investigate a person

ḥqr	pron. suff./*'etᵉkem*	Prov. 18.17;[46] Job. 13.9
š'l	*lā'iššâ*	2 Kgs 8.6

44. Although they appear to belong to a similar syntagm, there is a different meaning to the expressions:

drš mišpāṭ (Isa. 1.17; 16.5) = pursue right
drš dābār (1 Kgs 14.5; 22.5 etc.) and
bqš (*Pi*) *'et dᵉbar yhwh* (Amos 8.12) = consult an oracle.

45. When the object of verbs of inquiry is a 'misdeed', the meaning tends to shift from '*hold an investigation into* (a crime)' towards '*call* (a crime) *to account*' (and therefore '*to punish*') (cf., for the same phenomenon, the verb *pqd*): this is seen above all in expressions of the kind:

drš		*reša'-*		Ps. 10.15
drš			*mē'im*...	Deut. 18.19
drš	(*Ni*)	*dam-*		Gen. 42.22
drš		*dāmîm*		Ps. 9.13
drš		*dāmîm*	*miyyad*...	Gen. 9.5
drš		*dam-*	*miyyad*...	Ezek 33.6
bqš	(*Pi*)	*dam-*	*miyyad*...	2 Sam. 4.11; Ezek. 3.18, 20; 33.8
bqš	(*Pi*)		*miyyad*...	1 Sam. 20.16

Cf. H. Christ, *Blutvergiessen im Alten Testament: Der gewaltsame Tod des Menschen untersucht am hebräischen Wort* dām (Basel, 1977), pp. 119-26; S.M. Paul, 'Unrecognized Biblical Legal Idioms in the Light of Comparative Accadian Expressions', *RB* 86 (1979), pp. 237-39.

46. The meaning of Prov. 18.17 (*ṣaddîq hāri'šôn bᵉrîbô - ûbā'* [Q] *rē'ēhû waḥᵃqārô*) seems clear, even though there may be hesitation about the subject and object of the verb *ḥqr*: the *subject* could be the opposing side arriving at the judgment place (cf. Ps. 35.11 and Job 40.7, with the verb *š'l*), or an unspecified court of

3.1.2. *The Second Series of Verbs, Parallel to the First.* The verbs listed above have to be linked to a more various and more frequently used series, which has a basically identical meaning and function. Especially in poetic texts, *drš*, *bqš* (*Pi*), *ḥqr* appear in parallel with other verbs that express the investigatory side of a trial; it may reasonably be deduced from this that when these latter verbs occur on their own, they can in certain contexts suggest the investigative phase necessary for right judgment.

The phenomenon of parallelism demonstrates a basic interchangeability between all these terms, which leads me to include them in the same paradigm; in the following list, the importance of the verb *bḥn* and the pairing *r'h–yd'*[47] may be observed. I have not kept to the respective order of appearance of the verbs in the Hebrew text,[48] with the sole aim of giving greater emphasis to the ones that occur more frequently.

judgment (someone interrogates *him*); the *object* could be the one who has presented the case first (*hāri'šôn*) or the *rîb* itself (cf. Job 29.16). The term *hāri'šôn* calls to mind its reverse image in the famous text Job 19.25: *wa'ᵃnî yāda'tî gō'ᵃlî ḥāy wᵉ'aḥᵃrôn 'al 'āpār yāqûm*; here *the ultimate* juridical intervention of Job's defender seems like a guarantee of victory (cf. Alonso Schökel, *Job*, pp. 293-95).

The commentators incline towards the former of the proposed alternatives. In any case, it is obvious that what triggers an inquiry is the appearance for judgment of two parties with opposing arguments.

47. As will be shown in the next chapter, the pairing *r'h-yd'* describes the nature of the *witness*; it is clear that in certain texts these verbs refer to the role and function of the *judging* body (cf. the link with the root *špṭ* in Gen. 18.21ff.; Job 22.13-14). Rather than repeat the commonplace about the interchangeability between prosecution witness and judge in Israelite courts of law (cf. Begrich, *Deuterojesaja*, pp. 36, 37), it seems useful to observe that the *stage of (logical) certainty* (based on sensory experience or some other kind of evidence) is the only one that can guarantee correct judicial proceedings; this certainty may be gained from witnesses or acquired directly by the magistrate; but it is only when the judge is in a position of 'seeing' and 'knowing' that it becomes possible to pronounce a sentence in harmony with the law.

48. The order in which verbs of inquiry appear in the biblical texts does not seem to involve any particular nuances of meaning; for example, in Jer. 9.6 we have *ṣrp–bḥn*, and in Ps. 26.2 *bḥn–ṣrp*; in Jer. 12.3 *r'h* precedes *bḥn*, and in 20.12 it follows it; *yd'* comes before *r'h* in 1 Sam. 14.38; Job 11.11; 23.13-14, but afterwards in Gen. 18.21; and so on.

Jer. 17.9-10	*ḥqr*			*yd'*				*bḥn*				
Ps. 139.23-24	*ḥqr*			*yd'*	*r'h*			*bḥn*				
Ps. 44.22	*ḥqr*			*yd'*								
Ps. 139.1-2	*ḥqr*			*yd'*					*byn*			
2 Chron. 24.22		*drš*			*r'h*							
Ps. 10.13-14		*drš*			*r'h*		*nbṭ* (*Hi*)					
Job 10.4-7		*drš*	*bqš* (*Pi*)	*yd'*	*r'h*							
Jer. 5.1[49]			*bqš* (*Pi*)	*yd'*	*r'h*							
Job 7.18								*bḥn*		*pqd*[50]		
Ps. 17.2-3						*ḥzh*		*bḥn*		*pqd*	*ṣrp*	
Jer. 9.6, 8								*bḥn*		*pqd*	*ṣrp*	
Ps. 26.2								*bḥn*			*ṣrp*	*nsh* (*Pi*)
Jer. 6.27, 29				*yd'*				*bḥn*			*ṣrp*	
Job 23.10				*yd'*				*bḥn*				
Jer. 12.3				*yd'*	*r'h*			*bḥn*				
Jer. 20.12					*r'h*			*bḥn*				
Gen. 18.21				*yd'*	*r'h*							
1 Sam. 14.38				*yd'*	*r'h*							
Job 11.11				*yd'*	*r'h*				*byn* (*Hitp*)			
Job 22.13-14				*yd'*	*r'h*							
Ps. 11.4[51]						*ḥzh*		*bḥn*				

Whereas the first series of inquiry verbs took a different complementary object, this complementary series is used absolutely (2 Chron. 24.22) or

49. In the list of verbs of inquiry in Jer. 5.1 the verb *šwṭ* (*Pol*) also appears (cf. also 2 Chron. 16.9). In the Qal form, in Job 1.7; 2.2, it is used to describe the activity of Satan (Public Prosecutor at the divine court), who inspects the earth in search of grounds for accusation.

In Jer. 5.1 the terminology of inquiry is used in an ironic sense: the prophet is issuing an invitation to scour the city carefully, not to find (and so punish) the guilty, but to discover at least one *innocent* (so that God may forgive, according to the logic used by Abraham in Gen. 18.23-32).

50. On the force of *pqd* as an investigative (cf. also Job 31.14) and punitive act, see Fahlgren, *Ṣᵉdāḳā*, pp. 66-69. Regarding this verb, E.A. Speiser writes, 'There is probably no other Hebrew verb that has caused translators as much trouble as *pqd*. Its semantic range would seem to accommodate "to remember, investigate, muster, miss, punish, number" and the like' ('Census and Ritual Expiation in Mari and Israel', *BASOR* 149 [1958], p. 21). I would like to single out particularly J. Scharbert, 'Das Verbum PQD in der Theologie des Alten Testaments', *BZ* NS 4 (1960), pp. 209-26 (esp. pp. 217-20).

51. On Psalm 11 and its juridical/law court terminology, cf. Alonso Schökel, *Treinta Salmos*, pp. 81-87.

takes as object a human person (or, by metonomy, the person's behaviour, heart, thoughts, etc.).

The variety of combinations in which these verbs appear seems to suggest that their meaning tends to overlap: even *r'h* (and its synonyms) and *yd'* (and *byn*)—although sometimes expressing rather the *result* than the act of investigation itself—must still be placed logically in the phase prior to the handing down of the sentence.

As well as the lack of order common to the terms, a further confirmation of the synonymousness of all inquiry verbs comes from the observation of how they are used indiscriminately with a specific object such as 'the heart' and 'the kidneys' (that is, the secret depths) of a person:

bḥn	*libbî*	Ps. 17.3; Jer. 12.3[52]
bḥn	*lēbāb*	1 Chron. 29.17
bḥn	*libbôt*	Prov. 17.3
yd'	*lebābî*	Ps. 139.23
yd'	*'et lebab kol benê hā'ādām*	1 Kgs 8.39 (= 2 Chron. 6.30)
yd'	*ta'alumôt lēb*	Ps. 44.22
drš	*kol lebābôt*	1 Chron. 28.9
ḥqr	*lēb*	
bḥn	*kelāyôt*	Jer. 17.10
bḥn	*libbôt ûkelāyôt*	Ps. 7.10
bḥn	*kelāyôt wālēb*	Jer. 11.20
r'h	*kelāyôt wālēb*	Jer. 20.12
ṣrp	*kilyôtay welibbî*	Ps. 26.2.[53]

3.1.3. *Still more Synonyms. The Verb šmr.* I have given above a list of verbs that mark the investigative stage of a judgment. It would be a mistake to consider my list exhaustive because, especially in poetic texts, terms and expressions may be used which have an identical function even though they cannot be included in a specialized lexicon (cf., for

52. It seems to me that the translators are agreed on reading *libbî* as the object of *ûbāḥantā*. Keil (*ad loc.*, p. 220 English edn) in particular says that *'ittāk* is linked with *libbî*, the particle *'et* indicating the relationship that binds the heart to God (cf. 2 Sam. 16.17).

53. I would also like to single out the expressions *tkn libbôt* (= to weigh hearts) (Prov. 21.2; 24.12) and *tkn rûḥôt* (= to weigh the consciences) (Prov. 16.2), which have a similar meaning to those listed above. The concept of 'weighing' calls to mind the metaphor of the scales, in which lightness has negative overtones (*mō'zenayim*: Isa. 40.15; Ps. 62.10; Job 31.6; cf. Dan. 5.27; *peles*: Isa. 40.12; Prov. 16.11).

example, Jer. 16.17; Pss. 5.6; 66.7; 90.8; Job 31.4, 6; Prov. 20.8, 26).

In this respect, it seems to me that there may be some use in pointing to a particular force attributed to the verb *šmr*. By translating it as 'to observe', we can, even in English, retain the two semantic values contained in the meaning of the Hebrew root: (a) to see, to look, to keep an eye on; (b) to look after, to preserve, to maintain. As regards the former of these two '*semes*'—in which there is undoubtedly a link to the eye as the organ of sight—we can discern different nuances of meaning:

1. The verb *šmr* is sometimes used with the meaning of *to observe carefully, to spy on* (cf. Ps. 37.37; here the verb *šmr* is parallel to *r'h*; Jer. 20.10; Ps. 56.7; Job 24.15; 39.1; Qoh. 11.4).

2. Another frequent use is that of *to oversee*, with overtones of defence, protection (cf. Pss. 97.10; 116.6; 121.7-8; 140.5; 141.9; 145.20; 146.9; Job 10.12; 29.2; Prov. 3.26).

3. It seems that in some texts a use of *šmr* which suggests an investigative look, an *inspection*,[54] should also be acknowledged; it seems it can be included in the paradigm of perceptive seeing with a view to judgment and sanction. This is made clear when the verb takes as its (grammatical or logical) object a crime (Ps. 130.3; Job 10.14; 14.16) or human behaviour (Job 13.27; 33.11). In the latter case, it may be observed that the lexicon of the *path* (*derek* and its synonyms) is one of the frequent objects of verbs of inquiry:

šmr	*kol 'orḥōtāy*	Job 13.27; 33.11[55]
zrh (*Pi*)	*'orḥî* (*...wᵉkol dᵉrākay...*)	Ps. 139.3
yd' - bḥn	*'et darkām*	Jer. 6.27
yd' (*bḥn*)	*derek 'immādî*	Job 23.10
yd'	*nᵉtîbātî*	Ps. 142.4
r'h	*dᵉrākāyw*	Isa. 57.18
r'h	*'et darkām*	Ezek. 14.22
r'h	*dᵉrākāy*	Job 31.4
pls (*Pi*)	*kol ma'gᵉlōtāyw*	Prov. 5.21
'ênay	*'al kol darkêhem*	Jer. 16.17
'ênāyw	*'al darkê 'îš*	Job 34.21

54. In Qoh. 5.7 the term *šōmēr* refers to the authority that should oversee the course of justice.

55. Cf. also Job 10.14; 14.16.

3.2. *The Result of the Inquiry*

The aim of this section is to demonstrate how Hebrew expresses the conclusion of the investigative phase; the link between the inquiry and its result will allow us to clarify the aims of the preliminary phase and show the relevance of a lexicon that scholars of matters juridical in the Bible have not always dealt with in a consistent fashion.

3.2.1. *The Verb mṣ'*. The link between verbs suggesting 'research' (in particular *drš* and *bqš* [*Pi*]) and the verb *mṣ'* (findings) is not of course exclusive to the sphere of the law court,[56] but in this context the relationship becomes important to the extent that it shows the guilt (or otherwise) of a person, and consequently, the need (or otherwise) to proceed to sentence. Here are a few exact examples of this link:

Ps. 10.15	*tidrôš*	*riš'ô*	*bal timṣā'*
Ezra 10.16-18	*lidrôš* (corr.)	*haddābār...*	*wayyimmāṣē'...*
Jer. 50.20	*y^ebuqqaš*	*'et ^{a}wōn...*	*w^elō' timmāṣe'nâ*
Est. 2.23	*waybuqqaš*	*haddābār*	*wayyimmāṣē'*
Jer. 5.1	*ûbaqšû...*		*'im timṣ^e'û...*
Ps. 17.3	*ṣ^eraptanî*		*bal timṣā'...*

When the guilt (or innocence) of an accused is discovered or established, the result reached is that of juridical *certainty*, which allows the passing of a verdict with confidence. This may be the reason why the 'findings' after an inquiry are expressed in Hebrew by the same verb as means 'to catch red-handed', 'to catch in the act'; in fact a similar juridical ability to proceed links the two situations.[57] The use of *mṣ'* in the sense of 'to catch in the act'[58] is attested in Exod. 22.1, 3, 6-7; Num. 15.32-33;

56. Cf. G. Gerleman, '*mṣ'* finden', *THAT*, I, pp. 922-25; S. Wagner, '*māṣā'*', *ThWAT*, IV, pp. 1043-63.

57. D. Daube mentions the rabbinical interpretation, according to which *mṣ'* (*Ni*) means 'proved' (by two witnesses) ('To be Found Doing Wrong', in *Studi in onore di E. Volterra*, II [Milan, 1971], pp. 5-6). In the same article (pp. 1-3) the author emphasizes the specific nature of *mṣ'* (*Ni*) in Deut. 17.2-3; 21.1; 22.22; 24.7 (cf. also 18.10); in these texts it is supposedly not a question of 'in the act' but rather the simple singling out of a deed with disgusting overtones (= 'if there is...'). This opinion has been criticised by S. Dempster, 'The Deuteronomic Formula *kî yimmāṣē'* in the Light of Biblical and Ancient Near Eastern Law. An Evaluation of David Daube's Theory', *RB* 91 (1984), pp. 188-211, who holds rather that the aforementioned biblical passages, along with all the others, refer to different nuances of proof in cases of crime in the act.

58. Cf. Jackson, *Theft in Early Jewish Law*, p. 226; Wagner, '*māṣā'*', p. 1051.

Deut. 22.28; Jer. 2.26, 34; 48.27; Prov. 6.31.[59]

It may be useful to point out the various expressions used with the verb *mṣ'* to describe the discovery of a crime, or more exactly of a criminal:[60]

mṣ'	(*Ni*)	(something)	*b*^{e} (sack)	Gen. 44.12
mṣ'	(*Ni*)	(something)	*b*^{e}*yādô*[61]	Gen. 44.16, 17
mṣ'	(*Ni*)		*b*^{e}*yādô*	Exod. 21.16; 22.3
mṣ'		*m*^{e}*'ûmâ*	*b*^{e}*yādî*	1 Sam. 12.5
mṣ'		*'et ʿ*^{a}*wōn-*		Gen. 44.16
mṣ'		*zammōtî*		Ps. 17.3
mṣ'		*ʿāwel*	*b*^{e} (someone)	Jer. 2.5
mṣ'	(*Ni*)	*ʿawlātâ*	*b*^{e} (someone)	Ezek. 28.15
mṣ'	(*Ni*)	*ʿawlâ*	*b*^{e} (lips)	Mal. 2.6
mṣ'	(*Ni*)	*rāʿâ*	*b*^{e} (someone)	1 Sam. 25.28; 1 Kgs 1.52
mṣ'		*rāʿâ*	*b*^{e}(someone)	1 Sam. 29.6
mṣ'		*rāʿātām*	*b*^{e} (place)	Jer. 23.11
mṣ'	(*Ni*)	*pišʿê yiśrā'ēl*	*b*^{e} (place)	Mic. 1.13
mṣ'	(*Ni*)	*dam-*	*b*^{e} (clothing)	Jer. 2.34
mṣ'		*qešer*	*b*^{e} (someone)	2 Kgs 17.4
mṣ'	(*Ni*)	*qešer*	*b*^{e} (someone)	Jer. 11.9
mṣ'	(*Ni*)	*l*^{e}*šôn tarmît*	*b*^{e} (mouth)	Zeph. 3.13
mṣ'		*m*^{e}*'ûmâ*	*b*^{e} (someone)	1 Sam. 29.3
mṣ'	(*Ni*)	*d*^{e}*bārîm ṭôbîm*	*ʿim* (someone)	2 Chron. 19.3
mṣ'	(*Ni*)	*r*^{e}*šāʿîm*	*b*^{e} (people)	Jer. 5.26
mṣ'		*ṣaddîqîm*	*b*^{e} (place)	Gen. 18.26 (28, 30-32)
mṣ'		*'îš…*		Jer. 5.1

3.2.2. *The Concluding Particle hinnēh (hēn).*[62] This way of expressing

59. Num. 5.13 uses the verb *tpś*, which more usually refers to the arrest (cf. above), to express 'in the act'; perhaps there is a nuance of 'surprise', 'block' (thinking precisely of the case of adultery) at the very moment of the crime.

60. We also find two interesting expressions from a juridical point of view with the verb *mṣ'*, which are equivalent to 'to find allegations against someone': *mṣ'* (*Ni*) *šōreš dābār b*^{e} (someone) (Job 19.28); *mṣ' t*^{e}*nû'ôt 'al* (someone) (Job 33.10).

61. The expression *mṣ'* (something) *b*^{e}*yad* (of someone) gives specific emphasis to 'in the act' in cases of robbery (cf. Exod. 21.16; 22.3) or of extortion (1 Sam. 12.5). Without the verb *mṣ'*, and in the syntagm crime + *b*^{e}*yad* (of someone) we find a way of describing obvious guilt (1 Sam. 24.12; 26.18; Ezek. 23.37, 45; Ps. 26.10; cf. also Isa. 1.15).

62. Studies of the particle *hinnēh* (cf. also chapter 2, n. 60) give special space to its grammatical aspects and stylistic effects; cf. L. Alonso Schökel, 'Nota estilística sobre la partícula *hinnēh*', *Bib* 37 (1956), pp. 74-80; C.J. Labuschagne, 'The Particles

the result of an investigation is clearly marked in some texts from Deuteronomy, but is also found elsewhere:

Deut. 13.15	*w^edārašṭā*		
	w^eḥāqartā		
	w^ešā' altā hêṭēb	*w^ehinnēh*	*'^emet nākôn haddābār*
Deut. 17.4	*w^edārašṭā hêṭēb*	*w^ehinnēh*	*'^emet nākôn haddābār*
Deut. 19.18	*w^edār^ešû... hêṭēb*	*w^ehinnēh*	*'ēd šeqer hā'ēd*

hēn and *hinnēh*', *OTS* 18 (1973), pp. 1-14; D. Vetter, '*hinnē* siehe', *THAT*, I, pp. 504-507; F.I. Andersen, *The Sentence in Biblical Hebrew* (The Hague, 1974), pp. 94-96; A. Berlin, *Poetics and Interpretation of Biblical Narrative* (Bible and Literature Series, 9; Sheffield, 1983), pp. 62-63, 91-95. The article by D.J. McCarthy, 'The Uses of *w^ehinnēh* in Biblical Hebrew', *Bib* 61 (1980), pp. 330-42, concentrates on organizing the different uses of *w^ehinnēh* into traditional grammatical categories; as regards the passages from Deuteronomy considered relevant by me (cf. below), McCarthy gives the particle the force of a 'condition' (e.g. for Deut. 13.5: 'if the matter is established as true they are to put the place under the ban' [p. 336]). For a complementary view, cf. also K. Oberhuber, 'Zur Syntax des Richterbuches. Der einfache Nominalsatz und die sog. nominale Apposition', *VT* 3 (1953), pp. 2-45; J. Blau, 'Adverbia als psychologische und grammatische Subjekte/Praedikate im Bibelhebräisch', *VT* 9 (1959), pp. 130-37.

The basic identity of meaning between an inquiry concluded with the verb *mṣ'* and one with the particle *hinnēh* can be seen by comparing accounts of searches made of someone suspected of theft. A search is in fact the external and, in a manner of speaking, objective, way of carrying out an investigation of an individual's alleged guilt.

a. In Gen. 31.30-32, Laban accuses Jacob of theft (*gānabtā*); he therefore carries out a search of his tents to satisfy himself of the facts:

v. 33	*wayyābō'...*	*w^elō' māṣā'*
v. 34	*waymaššēš...*	*w^elō' māṣā'*
v. 35	*wayḥappēś*	*w^elō' māṣā'*
v. 37	*miššaštā...*	*mah māṣā'tā*

The mode of expression in Gen. 44.1ff. is identical: Joseph's brothers are accused of theft (v. 8; *nignōb*) and have to undergo a search which has a positive outcome in v. 12:

wayḥappēś... wayyimmāṣē'

b. In Josh. 7.1, the violation of the *ḥerem*, interpreted as theft (v. 11: *gān^ebû*), causes Joshua to adopt the drawing of lots to discover the guilty; the lot falls upon Achan, who confesses and reveals the hiding-place of the stolen goods. Joshua carries out a check on Achan's involvement by making a search of his tent in v. 22:

wayyārūṣû... w^ehinnēh (ṭ^emûnâ b^e'oh^olô w^ehakkesep taḥteyhā)

Exod. 32.9 (= Deut. 9.13)	*r'h*	*w^e^hinnēh*	*'am q^e^šēh 'ōrep hû'*
Lev. 10.16	*drš*	*w^e^hinnēh*	(verbal phrase)
Isa. 58.3-4	*r'h - yd'*	*hēn*	(verbal phrase)
Isa. 59.4-5	*r'h*	*hinnēh*	(verbal phrase)
Ps. 73.11-12	*yd'*	*hinnēh*	(noun phrase)
Jer. 2.10	*yd' - r'h*	*hēn*	(verbal phrase)[63]

3.2.3. *The Concluding Particle yēš (or 'ên).* The conclusion of an inquiry may be signalled in Hebrew by the particle *yēš/'ên* (followed by a noun phrase). As may be seen from the following examples, the parallelism with the verb *mṣ'* suggests that this form of expression is relevant to the sphere of the law court:

	inquiry	result		consequences
Jer. 5.1	*bqš* (*Pi*)	*'im timṣ^e^'û*	*'îš*	
		'im yēš	*'ōśeh mišpāṭ*	*slḥ*
Gen. 18.21	God carries out an inquiry in Sodom (*r'h - yd'*)			
Gen. 18.24	(Abraham says)	*'ûlay yēš*	*ḥ^a^miššîm ṣaddîqīm b^e^tôk hā'îr*	*nś'*
Gen. 18.26	(God replies)	*'im 'emṣā'*	*...ḥ^a^miššîm ṣaddîqīm b^e^tôk hā'îr*	*nś'*
Jer. 50.20	*bqš* (*Pu*) *'et '^a^wōn yiśrā'ēl w^e^'et haṭṭō't y^e^hûdâ*	*w^e^lō' timmāṣe'ynâ*	*w^e^'ênennû*	*slḥ*

The use of *yēš* (or *'ên*) at the end of an investigative activity (explicitly or implicitly) seems discernible in the following texts too:

	inquiry	result	consequences
1 Sam. 14.38-39	*yd' - r'h*[64]	*bammâ hāy^e^tâ haḥaṭṭā't hazzō't...*	
		kî 'im yešnô b^e^yônātān b^e^nî	*kî môt yāmût*
1 Sam. 20.8		*w^e^'im yeš bî '^a^wōn*	*h^a^mîtēnî 'attâ*
2 Sam. 14.32		*w^e^'im yeš bî 'āwōn*	*weh^e^mītānî*
Ps. 7.4		*'im yeš 'āwel b^e^kappāy*	(v. 5 punishment)

63. Cf. also Josh. 7.22 (*w^e^hinnēh* + noun phrase); Ps. 139.4 (*hēn* + verbal phrase); Job 4.18 (*hēn* + verbal phrase); 33.11-12 (*w^e^hinnēh* + noun phrase).

64. I would also like to mention 1 Sam. 24.12: Saul has set out to hunt David, who is accused of wanting to usurp the throne; when David can show him the edge of the royal cloak, cut off without causing the sovereign any hurt, Saul is faced with proof witnessing to the innocence of the man he has been pursuing. Here too we have the pairing *yd'* + *r'h* followed by the particle *'ên*, which expresses the side of matters establishing the absence of a crime (*'ên b^e^yādî rā'â wāpeša'*).

	inquiry	result	consequences
Job 6.30		*hᵃyēš bilšônî ʻawlâ*	
Ps. 14.2-3	*r'h*	*hᵃyēš maśkîl dōrēš 'et 'ᵉlōhîm...*	
= 53.3-4		*'ên ʻōśēh ṭôb 'ên gam 'eḥād*	(14.5 = 55.6: punishment)
Isa. 59.15	*r'h*	*kî 'ên mišpāṭ*	
	r'h	*kî 'ên 'îš*	(v. 18: punishment)

3.2.4. *Conclusions with the Verb hyh*. This manner of indicating the result of an inquiry is used in parallel with that with *yēš* in 1 Sam. 14.38-39 (cf. above), but it is found in parallel with the verb *mṣ'* in:

1 Kgs 1.52	*'im* ***yihyeh*** *lᵉben ḥayil*	*lō' yippōl miśśaʻᵃrātô 'ārṣâ*
	wᵉ'im rāʻâ ***timmāṣē'*** *bô*	*wāmēt*
Mal. 2.6	*tôrat 'ᵉmet* ***hāyᵉtâ*** *bᵉpîhû*	
	wᵉʻawlâ lō' ***nimṣā'*** *biśᵉpātāyw*	

Cf. also Deut. 21.22.

3.2.5. *The Declaration*. The methods I have pointed out so far should not be considered rigid formulae. What is relevant, formally speaking, is on the one hand the *ascertaining* or declaratory aspect, and on the other hand, that of the *evidence*. In Hebrew, these forms can be expressed in quite different ways; I have tried to give just some of the main formulae, which are equivalent to one another.

It may be observed, for example, that there is a connection between verbs of investigation and the words which reveal the result reached:

Judg. 6.29	*drš - bqš (Pi)*	*...'mr*
Deut. 17.9	*drš*	*...ngd (Hi)*

It may also be observed that in the very texts from Deuteronomy quoted at the beginning of my treatment of the judicial inquiry, in which the investigative procedure is clearly laid out, a noun phrase with *wᵉhinnēh* is clarified by a verbal phrase that reinforces the same concept:

Deut. 13.15	*wᵉhinnēh 'ᵉmet nākôn haddābār*
	neʻeśᵉtâ hattôʻēbâ hazzō't bᵉqirbekā
Deut. 17.4	*wᵉhinnēh 'ᵉmet nākôn haddābār*
	neʻeśᵉtâ hattôʻēbâ hazzō't bᵉyiśrā'ēl
Deut. 19.18	*wᵉhinnēh ʻēd šeqer hāʻēd*
	šeqer ʻānâ bᵉ'āḥîw

As regards content, the declaration of the investigating body is presented in accordance with the kind of investigation carried out; the fact that one of the basic areas of inquiry concerns accusations that are *verified* seems particularly relevant. In other words, the concept of truth and falsehood, which—as we shall see—forms an essential opposition within the prosecution, is equally bound up with the words of the judge who bends all his actions towards the pursuit of truth and certainty.

As well as the texts just quoted, I would like to single out others in which the conclusion of the investigation brings out the concept of true and false: with the term *'ᵉmet*, cf. Gen. 42.16; Deut. 22.20; Isa. 43.9; 59.14-15; Jer. 5.3 (*'ᵉmûnâ*); with the term *kēn*, cf. Gen. 42.19-20, 33-34; Num. 27.7; 36.5; Jer. 8.6; Job 5.27; with *šeqer*, cf. Deut. 19.18; Jer. 5.2; Hos. 7.1; Ps. 7.15; with *'awlâ*, cf. Mal. 2.6; Job 6.30.

3.3. *Inability to Proceed*

Up to now we have made the logical supposition that, faced with the need to acquire the proof to convict someone, a magistrate would carry out a careful investigation, and this would produce the desired result: the accused is acknowledged guilty or, alternatively, the innocence of the accused is proved.

This is abstract logic, that is, the theory of juridical proceedings; unfortunately, in reality investigative activity frequently meets with *lack of success*: the judge fails to find anything, and does not succeed in proving guilt, but neither does the investigation produce a guarantee of innocence. The juridical proceedings then find themselves in a blind alley and justice is blocked because it lacks its indispensable prerequisite of certainty.

Alternatively, and this is a different aspect of not proceeding juridically, the inquiry itself *is not carried out* or is suspended. In such a case, the reasons may be various, even the opposite of one another: the judge may connive with the evildoer to evade the duties of office; a judge may be afraid to stir up a hornets' nest and disturb the established order, or may be blocked by the intervention of a higher authority, and so on. But the inquiry may also not be carried out because an act of the sovereign authority, such as an amnesty or indult,[65] suspends the

65. Among the institutions that used to go under the name of 'sovereign clemency', and constitute cause for lifting punishment, the Italian Criminal Code lists amnesty, indult and pardon.

Pardon is not a juridical act with which I can deal at this point, in the sense that it presupposes the passing in judgment of a sentence of conviction.

Amnesty, on the other hand, is a 'general provision by which the State renounces the application of punishment for particular crimes'; in the proper sense, it

proceedings under way for the good of the nation.

I think it would be useful to point out how some of these phenomena are present and expressed in the world of the Bible; my argument will pick out the form of certain concepts, noting briefly the relevant Hebrew lexicon.

3.3.1. *The Failure of an Inquiry (Inquiry without Result).* In this section I shall suppose that an inquiry has been carried out, but it is marked by the fact that it has not brought in a useful result. The element of failure, which makes the whole proceedings undertaken useless, is what engages my attention; it seems to me that it is expressed in Hebrew in two main ways, the first being the *negation* of a useful result and the second the terminology of the *secret*.

a. *The negation of a result.* There should be no confusion between research that has a definite negative result and one that does not have a result: the former achieves certainty (of a lack of guilt), whereas the latter reaches no true conclusion.

This aspect is expressed in Hebrew above all by the negation of the verbs *r'h/yd'* (and their synonyms), the peculiarity of which is that they have several meanings—referring, that is, both to the investigative aspect (to look, to gather information, to seek to know) and the aspect of the operation's success (to see, to know, to discover) (cf. for example Isa. 29.15; Ezek. 8.12; Pss. 10.11; 94.7; Job 22.13-14).

b. *The terminology of the secret.* This is rather a wide semantic field, one which can in no way be restricted to matters juridical. What seems relevant to me is to show that an inquiry is always dealing with something which at first sight is unclear; but if the activity of the investigative body encounters something which is and remains secret, hidden, obscure, the magistrate has to declare the juridical failure of his activity.

There is almost constant distinction in the Bible between human juridical proceedings and God's. Humans frequently encounter what is unknown and secret, which blocks attempts to achieve justice; on the other hand, God can plumb the abysses of the human heart so that nothing (no crime and no guilt) can escape the just proceedings of his

is proclaimed before the jurisdictional ascertaining of the crime has been finished (cf. Antolisei, *Manuale di Diritto Penale*, pp. 605-608).

An *indult*, like an amnesty, does not presuppose an irrevocable conviction, but unlike an amnesty, it applies exclusively to the main punishment and not to secondary ones.

judgment (cf. the theme of 'testing mind and heart' mentioned above; and Jer. 16.17; Pss. 19.7; 44.22; Qoh. 12.14 etc.).

The relevant Hebrew lexicon includes the roots *str, kḥd, ksh, 'lm,* with which I shall deal in the next chapter. For now it should be enough to point out some texts in which this terminology is linked to investiga-ive activity: Josh. 7.19; 2 Sam. 14.18; 18.13; Isa. 3.9; Jer. 38.14-15; Hos. 5.3; Pss. 10.11; 69.6; 139.14-15; Job 20.12.

3.3.2. *The Suspension of an Inquiry*. The suspension of an inquiry may be considered a 'just' act to the extent to which it is justified by the circumstances: it should not just be arbitrary, but should have its reasons and tend to promote well-being and justice in society. If the suspension of inquiries (or, more radically, putting the case on file, the decree not to proceed or the like) indicates scant zeal for the re-establishment of justice, this cannot be seen as an act of clemency, but as a wicked ruling. Evil-doers, when perpetrating crimes, hope not to be found out; if they learn that the authorities (through weakness, through complicity or through inability) will not be carrying out any investigations, and therefore that crime will go unpunished, they will grow arrogant and institute a reign of systematic injustice (cf. Isa. 29.15-16; Ezek. 8.12; Pss. 10.4, 11, 13; 58.9; 64.6; 73.11; 94.7, 9; Job 22.13-14).

In the first part of my study I stated that a court of law is not a place of pardon; it is rather for the judge to establish which of the two parties is in the right and proceed against the guilty in accordance with the norms laid down in the criminal code. From this point of view, the act of a judge who does not investigate is the same as pardoning the guilty, which is alien to right-judging because it wrongs the victim unjustly hurt by the culprit.

It is nonetheless possible for a judge, who, as we have seen, was the authority in Israel, to suspend an inquiry and silence a prosecution when the evil that would result from the pursuit of justice was greater than the hoped-for good. A margin of discretion was left to a judge and even more so to the sovereign, under which a judge passed judgment on the actual mechanism of justice, in such a way that the *summum ius* did not turn into a *summa iniuria*.

In this context, mention might be made of David's decision in 2 Samuel 14, with reference to the proceedings against a fratricide (a metaphor for Absalom); in this case the king's verdict wisely takes an opposite stance to the rigid demands of the accusation, which, if they were satisfied, would only bring about a death without any good (indeed, with harm) to the injured party (vv. 7, 11, 13-17).

Thinking more generally, there are also the amnesty provisions that follow civil wars and which are intended to promote the reconciliation of minds; this was practised by David with Shimei upon his return from exile after Absalom's revolt (2 Sam. 19.22-24). In this case the judging authority interprets not the will of the prosecutor on the spot but the overall desire of the people to put an end to a situation of violence in order to begin a civilized regime of general harmony.

This juridical ruling is used metaphorically in theology. God then appears as the supreme authority who decrees the suspension of proceedings against the guilty. For the lexicon, I must refer back to what I wrote about pardon; although the two procedures do not overlap juridically, nevertheless, since they are equivalent as regards result, they are expressed in a similar vocabulary.[66]

The act of amnesty looks especially relevant when, before a 'supreme' judge, *nobody* is innocent: if the carrying out of rigorous justice involves the wiping out of the whole of humankind, this makes necessary an act of justice that cancels the past and lays the juridical basis for a different future.

66. I would like to make particular reference to the terms discussed in Chapter 4 section 2.1 of my study, which I grouped under the heading 'a series of verbs describing attention, memory, etc.' As an example, see Ps. 10.11, 13; in the phrases spoken by the *rāšā'*, in which he expresses the presumption that he will escape divine judgment, we have a parallel between verbs of inquiry (*r'h, drš*), used in the negative, and a verb that means the negation of memory (*škh)*:

v. 11	*'āmar bᵉlibbô*	*šākaḥ 'ēl*
		histîr pānāyw bal rā'â lāneṣaḥ
v. 13	*'āmar bᵉlibbô*	*lō' tidrōš.*

Chapter 7

THE DEBATE

The debate phase is the heart of law court proceedings: the two parties to the case, formally distinguished as accuser and accused, confront each other in front of a judge; each is granted the right to *speak,* outlining the facts and their juridical consequences, until the judge has what is considered to be enough certainty to hand down a verdict.

Investigations (by the magistrate) and debate (between the parties) are two separate juridical forms, even though they tend—in the world of the Bible—to overlap and become confused;[1] the inquiry may be presented as an interrogation (by the judge) to which the accused[2] or even the accuser,[3] on the other hand, must answer the arguments and proof brought in by each of the parties allow the judging body to form that 'conviction' that will inspire the sentence, which is in symmetry with the investigative activity, which seeks to discover the truth, a pre-condition for proceeding to punishment.

Despite this, it is possible to deal with the debate in itself, as a separate and essential stage of a formally constituted trial. Indeed, it is the clash between the two parties, their struggle with due regard for the law,

1. In criminal proceedings as laid down by the Italian Code, the debate goes through three quite separate phases: *the formalities of beginning*, *the examination of the proof* (also called the debate preliminaries) and the *debate* (Pisapia, *Compendio di procedura penale*, p. 353; cf. also Leone, *Manuale di diritto processuale penale*, pp. 497-508). The examination of proof, which takes in among other things the questioning of the accused and witnesses, has the purpose of making public an 'investigation' which—logically and practically prior—has the privilege, according to the Code, of being secret. Without making any claim to identify quite different juridical systems, the observations made perhaps allow a feeling for how the investigative and debate phase tend, in certain cases, to overlap in the world of the Bible.

2. Cf. 1 Sam. 22.7-15.

3. Cf. the counter-charge leveled by Daniel against the two elders accusing Susannah: Dan. 13.51-59.

which forms the core of the trial as an institution; any court that tried to frustrate this exchange of words inspired by the desire for truth would be turning the law court into a place of strength, the seat of tyranny and violence. And when strength takes the place of speech to tip the scales to one side, judgment ceases to be the affirmation of law and degenerates into a perverse and inhuman exhibition.

In the few trials recounted in the Bible, the alternation of speeches is expressed by rather generic *verba dicendi*:[4] if the specific juridical value

4. In the three trials in the Hebrew Bible described with a certain amount of completeness, the *verba dicendi* follow one another without any detectably specific juridical terminology; we could say that the terminology expresses only that *principle of contradiction* which seems essential to correct criminal proceedings (cf. Leone, *Manuale*, pp. 489-490):

1. 1 Sam. 22.7-15: A trial is begun by Saul against those who betrayed him by taking David's side:

The king accuses (*'mr*) his ministers of being disloyal (vv. 7-8).
Doeg the Idumaean intervenes (*'nh* + *'mr*) as a witness accusing Achimelech (vv. 9-10).
The king then summons Achimelech (v. 10), and accuses (*'mr*) him of treachery (vv. 12-13).
Achimelech defends himself (*'nh* + *'mr*) (vv. 14-15).
Saul decrees the death of Achimelech (*'mr*) (v. 16).

2. 1 Kgs 3.16-28: The trial of the two women before king Solomon; since the circumstances of the trial are very well known, I shall show only how the alternation of speeches between the parties involved works out, up to the judge's sentence:

v. 17 ***wattō'mer** hā'iššâ hā'aḥat...*
v. 22 ***wattō'mer** hā'iššâ hā'aḥeret...*
w^e^zō't 'ōmeret...
***watt^e^dabbērnâ** lipnê hammelek*
v. 23 ***wayyō'mer** hammelek*
*zō't **'ōmeret...***
*w^e^zō't **'ōmeret...***
v. 24 ***wayyō'mer** hammelek...*
v. 25 ***wayyō'mer** hammelek...*
v. 26 ***wattō'mer** hā'iššâ...**wattō'mer...***
*w^e^zō't **'ōmeret***
v. 27 ***wayya'an** hammelek **wayyō'mer...***

3. Jer. 26.7-16: The trial brought against the prophet Jeremiah:

Jeremiah is arrested on the capital charge (*'mr*) of having prophesied against the Jerusalem Temple (vv. 8-9).

of this terminology can be deduced only from the context, it is worth repeating the fact that a trial is a verbal confrontation in which may be distinguished, on the one hand, the *prosecution speech*, and on the other, *the defence speech*. This elementary distinction is the main framework for the current chapter; at the end, by way of conclusion, I shall add a note on the significance of *silence* in the sphere of the juridical debate.

I. THE ACCUSATION

As we saw in Chapter 2, without an accusation there cannot be criminal proceedings of any kind. The subject of a juridical action is the accuser; by exposing a criminal infraction of the norms, an accuser urges the re-establishment of justice; without this action, injustice is passed over, or not redressed.[5] So let us call an 'accusation' that juridical intervention in

Before a court of the 'leading men' of Judah, the priests and prophets read out the formal charge (*'mr*) (v. 11).
Jeremiah defends himself (*'mr*) (vv. 12-15).
The judges reject the accusation and decree (*'mr*) the acquittal of the accused (v. 16).

The account continues with the speech (*'mr*) of the 'elders of the country' (vv. 17-19), but the trial no longer proceeds in accordance with clear rules of debate.

5. The fact that prosecution witnesses are the basic *bringers* of a juridical action in the courts means that the outcome of the judgment and therefore the re-establishment of justice depends on them; it is not perhaps banal to note that the accuser is called *ba'al mišpaṭ* (+ pron. suff.) (Isa. 50.8) or *ba'al d^ebārîm* (Exod. 24.14).

This does not, however, mean that there is a confusion between the roles of *judge* and *witness* in the juridical system of Israel; on the contrary, the formal nature of both is clearly separate, even if some texts bear a doubtful interpretation and the vocabulary is sometimes common to the two functions.

I do not subscribe to the opinion of Koehler, who states, 'Wer der Rechtsgemeinde einen Rechtsfall zur Entscheidung... vorlegen will, ruft zunächst ins Gericht, und zwar zwei Gruppen: erstens die Rechtsgenossen, welche Zeuge und Richter in Einem sind oder doch sein können, und zweitens den oder die Rechtsgegner' (*Deuterojesaja*, p. 110), and again, 'Richter und Zeuge sind daher auch nicht voneinander geschieden. Derselbe Mann kann in derselben Sache und an derselben Gerichtstagung als Zeugen und als Richter angerufen werden' ('Die hebräische Rechtsgemeinde', p. 152). This thesis seems to have been accepted without question even in some later juridical literature; it is taken up, among others, by Gemser, 'The *rîb*- or Controversy-Pattern', p. 124; H.J. Boecker, 'Anklagereden und Verteidigungsreden im Alten Testament. Ein Beitrag zur Formgeschichte

a court of law which reports a crime as having occurred (in the shape of a deed carried out or attempted), demands that the guilty should be punished, and that the victim of the injustice—where possible—should be recompensed.[6] The distasteful side of an accusation arises from the fact that it is always directed *against* someone; its aggressive nature is acceptable only as an expression of the desire for justice.

In the world of the Bible, an accusation can take one of two different forms; they deserve separate treatment to the extent that each has a special juridical profile and is expressed with its own vocabulary.

The first is the *accusatory witness*. To anticipate briefly what will be developed below, we may describe it like this: one or more persons become aware that someone has committed a crime; they then appear before a judicial authority to report the culprit and demand (explicitly or implicitly) his or her punishment. This form of accusation is the one with which we are most familiar; it makes obvious its intentions *against* someone (the accused); seen as a demand made to a judge, it does call for a rigorous judgment and seems to be urging a ruthless verdict. It is notable as well that, generally speaking, the accusatory witness is not the one who has been the direct object of the wrong connected with the crime.

The second kind of accusation is an *appeal* (or suit) taken before a judicial authority.[7] Here the situation has different nuances from the one described above: first, we usually have someone who is the victim of an outrage, already carried out or hanging over the person as a threat. Moreover, the person who has suffered the wrong, rather than accusing the other (the culprit) asks the judging authority for a return of his or

alttestamentlicher Prophetenworte', *EvT* 20 (1960), pp. 407-409; Gamper, *Gott als Richter*, p. 149.

I do not see by which biblical text or by which recognized juridical institution of antiquity such a picture of the trial in ancient Israel can be sustained. I think that the reason for the aforementioned statements is, on the one hand, failure to distinguish clearly between the method or procedure of the controversy and that of the law court judgment, and on the other hand failure to recognize that terminology in common does not necessarily mean an identity of persons, roles and functions in the juridical sphere.

6. In the case of being caught in the act, there is provision for a trial *on the spot* which has the aim of setting and applying the appropriate punishment: the obvious guilt of the criminal makes the investigative preliminaries superfluous and reduces the debate stage to a minimum.

7. I would like to recall at this point the terminology that Boecker considers pre-judicial; he speaks of 'Appellation des Beschuldigers' (*Redeformen*, pp. 59-66).

her rights, that is, a judgment *in his or her favour*. Lastly, since such a person is generally a 'weakling'—the victim of someone stronger—the appellant strives to arouse feelings of compassion in the judge, calling for a verdict inspired by that compassion.[8]

Since the structure of proceedings in a law court always has three elements (judge, accuser, accused), both in the case of an accusatory witness and of an appeal the jurisdictional authority is brought to bear—with its verdict—at the same time on both the parties submitted for judgment;[9] however, the two forms may be described schematically by saying that:

a. An accusatory witness *singles out the culprit*; the judge is urged to intervene *against* the culprit (and so do justice to the innocent).
b. An appeal *singles out the innocent*: the judge is invited to intervene *on behalf of* the innocent (and hence punish the guilty).

1. *The Accusatory Witness*

In this section, after giving a definition of a witness and pointing to the relevant Hebrew lexicon, I would like to concern myself with the accusatory witness, studying its paradigmatic and syntagmatic aspects.

1.1. *The Witness: Definition*

A witness is a person who, in the knowledge of certain facts, can tell others (notify, inform them) how things happened. In the sphere of a court of law, the essential traits of a witness are specified as follows:

1. *Knowledge of the facts* is necessary: these are relevant to the extent that they concern an infraction of the law. In particular, knowledge of the 'crime' (and the criminal) is a definitive element for an accusatory witness.

8. The ultimate reason why I have made such a clear distinction in my treatment between a witness's accusation and an appeal by an injured party is the appearance of a specific vocabulary for each of these juridical forms. In its place (section I.2) I will try to justify more precisely the title *appeal* or *suit*.

9. The accuser also submits to judgment because a judge can convict him or her if it is decided that the 'testimony' is false (cf. Deut. 19.6-21; Ps. 109.7; Dan. 13.50-59).

2. It is also necessary to have words revealing the facts with a judging authority; if it is a matter of an accusation, this is the same as reporting or incriminating the culprit.

This definition in fact mirrors the text of Lev. 5.1,[10] where we read:

w^e hû' 'ēd	witness
'ô rā'â 'ô yādā'	knowledge of the facts[11]
'im lô' yaggîd	the denunciation.

10. The commentaries recognize Lev. 5.1 as an explicit reference to law court testimony (M. Noth [ATD, 6; 1962], pp. 33-34; K. Elliger [HAT, 4; 1966], pp. 73-74; G.J. Wenham [NICOT; 1979], pp. 92-93; E. Cortese [La Sacra Bibbia; 1982], pp. 44-45.

11. The verbs *r'h* and *yd'*, as can be seen from Lev. 5.1 and Is. 44.9, are used to describe the experience that is at the basis of (legal) testimony. The first term (*r'h*) suggests *eye*-witness (cf. Seeligmann, 'Zur Terminologie', pp. 265-66), which is universally recognized as certain and incontrovertible (in Isa. 11.3, however, we have indirect criticism of a judgment supposedly based on 'appearance'); the verb *r'h* on its own can refer to a witness (cf. 1 Sam. 22.9; Jer. 7.11, 17; Ezek. 8.9-10, 12; Ps. 35.21 etc.). Particularly in poetic texts, other verbs of 'sight', whether linked to the noun *'ayin* or not, can fulfil the same function (Pss. 11.4; 66.7; Job 24.15 etc.).

Because the second term (*yd'*) is semantically the polar opposite of the first (*r'h*), it ends up meaning knowledge of a deed acquired without having seen it. Gamper, *Gott als Richter*, p. 147 n. 47, quoting Judg. 11.10, recalls, for example, the existence of *ear* witnesses. In effect, this kind of witness might be thought of in the case of a pledge (promise, vow, etc.) given verbally, which may then become significant in a criminal court (cf. 1 Sam. 14.24-25). In more general terms, the experience of hearing is necessary in word-related crimes such as blasphemy, false prophecy and false accusation (Lev. 24.14; 1 Kgs 21.10; Jer. 20.10; 26.7; cf. also Mt. 26.65). In Job 29.11 the experience of witness is expressed by the parallel pairing *'ōzen šām^e'â—w^e'ayin rā'^atâ*.

For the link between *'ēd* and *yd'*, mention should also be made of Jer. 29.23: *w^e'ānōkî hwyd' wā'ēd*. The ancient translations are not in agreement: the Vulgate (*ego sum iudex et testis*) and the Syriac (*w'n' yd' 'n' wshd 'n'*) seem, with different nuances, to follow the *Qere* of the MT: *hû(') yōdēa'*; perhaps the same is true of the paraphrase in the *Targum Jonathan* (*ûq^edāmay g^elê ûmêm^erî sāhîd*). The LXX, on the other hand, has just *kai egō martys* (36.23). The hypothesis of a dittography, on the basis of the LXX (cf. *BHS*), has been raised by W. Rudolph, who translates, however, 'ich bin der Wissende und Zeuge' (HAT, 12; 3rd edn, 1968], pp. 186-87); the same line of reading is followed by Alonso Schökel, *Profetas*, I (1980), p. 546, and J.A. Thompson, *The Book of Jeremiah* (NICOT; 1980), p. 543. For his part, M. Dahood has a proposal that attempts to explain the *Ketib* by reading into it the term **hāwāh* written defectively: *w^e'ānōkî hāwā yōdēa' wā'ēd* ('for I myself know the word and the witness'); but the reasons put forward do not appear decisive to me

The same text also allows us to state that a true witness, *that is, one who authentically satisfies the above definition*, is one who brings together the two structural elements of knowledge and speech; in other words, a truthful witness is one who speaks of what he or she knows: (1) factual truth leads the person to speak; (2) the person's words correspond to the truth.

There are in fact other kinds of witness who, although they find a place—formal or real—in the sphere of law court proceedings, pervert the very meaning of witness and frustrate it.

A *false witness* is one who speaks, but whose words do not express knowledge of the real, either because of bad information—that is, because of the fact that someone claims to know but 'has seen badly'—or as a result of an ill intention which is trying to produce in the judge an erroneous evaluation of events.[12]

A *mute witness* is someone who does not speak, even though possessing knowledge of the facts (this is the case referred to in Lev. 5.1 with the expression *lô' yaggîd*). The main reasons why someone shies away from the duty to give witness seem to come down to two: fear of being involved in a trial that could rebound back upon the witness, or self-interested complicity with the evildoer.

The possibility exists that *there might be no witnesses* to a crime: if a crime has been committed in such circumstances that nobody is in a position to guarantee an exact version of events and to point with security to the guilty, then—as I will show below—there can be no proceedings under the norms laid down by criminal law, and recourse must be had, as Hebrew legislation stood, to rituals or practices more or less directly linked to religion (an appeal to God as judge).

1.2. *The Witness in Hebrew Vocabulary*

The term *'ēd* is used first of all to describe a person who acts as witness in a court of law.[13]

('Word and Witness: A Note on Jeremiah XXIX 23', *VT* 27 [1977], p. 483).

12. True knowledge makes the words of testimony true, but the mere presumption of knowledge produces deception: cf. the oppositions in Ps. 35.20-22: vv. 20-21 (enemies): *dibrê mirmôt yaḥ^{a}šōbûn...'ām^{e}rû he'āḥ he'āḥ rā'^{a}tâ 'ênênû*; v. 22 (God): *rā'îtâ yhwh 'al teḥ^{e}raš*.

13. Parallel to *'ēd* in Job 16.19 we find the Aramaicist participle *śāhēd* (cf. also, in Gen. 31.47, the Aramaic *śāh^{a}dû* with the meaning of witness) (M. Wagner, *Die lexikalischen und grammatikalischen Aramaismen im alttestamentlichen Hebräisch*

It is well known that objects are also referred to as *'ēd*: a pile of stones (Gen. 31.48), a song (Deut. 31.26), an altar (Josh. 22.27, 28, 34), and so on. These have an indisputable juridical function as the sign of a pledge or a contract between two partners,[14] but they do not enter into the area of trial witness.[15]

There also existed *notarial* witness for acts of legal importance[16] (Isa. 8.2; Jer. 32.10, 12, 25, 44; Ruth 4.9, 10, 11); this is prior to and medium and condition for possible disputes brought to trial.[17] In the latter eventuality, a witness ceases to be notarial (pre-trial) and takes part in a judgment as a qualified witness (for the prosecution or defence).

1.2.1. *'Prosecution' or 'Defence' Witnesses*. In our juridical system, the word 'witness' is generic, and has to be specified by the adjectives 'prosecution' (against) or 'defence' (for) if knowledge of their exact function is required. As regards the Hebrew vocabulary, this distinction, although relevant, is not structured by a specific lexicon: only the

[BZAW, 96; Berlin, 1966], §295). The term *'ēdâ* is used only for objects (Gen. 21.30: seven lambs; 31.52: stelae; Josh. 24.27: stone), and outside a law court context. The noun *t*^{e}*'ûdâ* (Isa. 8.16, 20; Ruth 4.7) refers to attestation by a notary.

14. I would like to observe, as a linguistic peculiarity, that the role of a *non-law court* witness is sometimes expressed by the syntagm *'ēd bên...ûbên* (Gen. 31.44, 48, 50; Josh. 22.27, 28, 34).

15. The torn remains of a beast acted as testimonial proof (*'ēd*) in questions of repayment between a hired shepherd and the owner (Exod. 22.12) (cf., however, the suggestion by F.C. Fensham, '*'d* in Exodus XXII 12', *VT* 12 [1962], pp. 337-39, who reads *'ad* in place of *'ēd*, in agreement with the LXX: *axei auton* [the owner] *epi tēn thēran*). Something similar holds good for the sheet that proves the virginity of a woman slandered by her husband (Deut. 22.17). The seal, belt and staff of Judah constitute a decisive element in discharging the proceedings under way against Tamar (Gen. 38.25), while the blood-stained tunic of Joseph seems enough to prove his accidental death (Gen. 37.31-33). Cf. other similar cases in 1 Sam. 24.12; 26.16; 2 Sam. 19.25.

Only in the case of Deut. 22.13-19, however, is an object (not called *'ēd*) entered as proof in clearly law court proceedings ('before the elders of the city'). A system of 'material proofs' as a guarantee of objectivity in judgment is not clearly documented in ancient Israel; at any rate, it seems that when an *'ēd* is referred to in a trial, it means a person.

16. Cf. G.M. Tucker, 'Witnesses and "Dates" in Israelite Contracts', *CBQ* 28 (1966), pp. 42-45.

17. Cf. Seeligmann, 'Zur Terminologie', p. 265.

context tells whether a witness is for or against someone.[18] However, we can give some guidelines of a general nature which demonstrate the predominance, for the noun *'ēd*, of prosecution witness.

a. *Defence witnesses. 'ēd* rarely means a witness 'for';[19] this meaning is linguistically discernible when the noun is construed with a *pronominal suffix*: Isa. 43.9, 10, 12; 44.8,[20] 9; Job 10.17;[21] 16.19;[22] the context of these passages seems to be judicial, and so their terminology may be deemed to be that of the law court.[23]

18. H. van Vliet, with a debatable recourse to the etymology of *'ēd* (cf. J. Barr, *The Semantics of Biblical Language* [London, 1961], pp. 107ff.) (cf. also *THAT*, II, p. 211 = 'be present'), tries to explain how the meaning of a witness *against* someone is arrived at: 'The *'d* is in the first place "one who is present" with the collateral meaning of "one who is in contact"...The fundamental idea of presence, contact, relation, originally expressed in the root *'d* must be borne in mind when we think of the witness in the OT. He is related to the wrongdoer. He was in his presence. He had contact with him' (*No Single Testimony: A Study on the Adoption of the Law of Deut. 19.15 par. into the New Testament* [STRT, 4; Utrecht, 1958], pp. 67-68).

19. C. van Leeuwen's statement seems to me inexact: 'Es ist bemerkenswert, dass *'ēd* im AT nicht als [menschlicher] Entlastungszeuge vorkommt' (*THAT*, II, p. 214). Seeligmann quotes Isa. 43.9 as the only example of a defence witness ('Zur Terminologie', p. 262).

20. H. Simian-Yofre points out the correspondence between the formula in Isa. 43.10, 12; 44.8 (*'attem 'ēday*) and that in Josh. 24.22; Ruth 4.9, 10 (*'ēdîm 'attem*) (*ThWAT*, V, pp. 1116-17). Cf. also 1 Sam. 12.5.

21. The suggestion by G.E. Watson ('The Metaphor in Job 10.17', *Bib* 63 [1982], pp. 255-57), who translates *'dyk* as 'your combatants' with the aim of guaranteeing the consistency of the warlike metaphor in the verse, does not gain my agreement. As we shall see, the Old Testament contains frequent symbolism drawn from war to describe an encounter in court (cf. in particular n. 107).

22. Cf. J.B. Curtis, 'On Job's Witness in Heaven', *JBL* 102 (1983), pp. 549-62.

23. I would also maintain that a 'notarial witness' (as in Isa. 8.2; Jer. 32.10; Ruth 4.9-10) is on the side of the summoning party within a particular juridical act; however, this side of things does not enter into my strictly judicial treatment.

An equivalent to *'ēd* + pronom. suff. might be supposed in the syntagm ***'ēd l***^{e} (as opposed to ***'ēd b***^{e}); while on the subject, the text of Isa. 19.20 seems relevant: *w*^{e}*hāyâ* (the altar and stela) *l*^{e}*'ôt ûl*^{e}*'ēd l*^{e}*yhwh...kî yiṣ'*^{a}*qû 'el yhwh* etc. This phrase, which echoes that in Gen. 21.30 (the acceptance of seven lambs *tihyeh lî l*^{e}*'ēdâ kî ḥāpartî 'et habb*^{e}*'ēr hazzō't*) supposedly means, therefore, that the altar and stela are a testimonial (not strictly legal) sign that anyone who turns to YHWH in time of oppression will be heeded (H. Wildberger [BK, 10/2; 1978], p. 740). In Isa. 55.4, in place of *'ēd l*^{e}*'ûmmîm*, *BHS* proposes reading *'ēd l*^{e}*'ammîm* (Syriac [Targum]

b. *Prosecution witnesses*. Used absolutely, in the context of clearly legal proceedings, the noun *'ēd always* means a prosecution witness.[24] Very often the syntactical structure stresses that the witness is *against* someone; for example, we frequently have the syntagm *'ēd b^e^* (or *'ēd hyh b^e^*): Num. 5.13; 1 Sam. 12.5; Mic. 1.2; Mal. 3.5; Prov. 24.28; cf. also Jer. 42.5. As we shall see later, the act of witnessing is often expressed by the verbs *qwm b^e^* and *'nh b^e^*.

1.2.2. *'Truthful' or 'False' Witnesses.* Since a witness (*'ēd*) in a trial is basically someone who is accusing, great importance is attached, in Hebrew vocabulary and juridical regulations, to the validity or otherwise of the witness's words; in fact, the whole progress of the judgment depends on them. The Hebrew lexicon referring to false witness is more various and frequently attested than that which means the opposite:

a. *truthful witness*

'ēd 'ᵉmûnîm	Prov. 14.5 (opposed to: *'ēd šāqer*)
'ēd 'ᵉmet	Prov. 14.25 (opposed to: *yāpiaḥ kᵉzābîm*)[25]

b. *false witness*[26]

'ēd šeqer	Exod. 20.16; Deut. 19.18; Ps. 27.12; Prov. 6.19; 14.5; 25.18
'ēd šᵉqārîm	Prov. 12.17; 19.5, 9
'ēd šāw'	Deut. 5.20[27]

l'mm'); if the MT is followed, the oddness of the expression should be noted (for the content of the passage, cf. J.H. Eaton, 'The King as God's Witness', *ASTI* 7 [1968–1969], pp. 25-40).

24. The case of Lev. 5.1 seems to concern the *deposition* of witness in general, perhaps with the nuance of a *denunciation* (*ngd, Hi*) brought against someone.

25. We find another three expressions meaning a 'truthful witness' in non-legal contexts: in such cases it would perhaps be better to translate as a '*trustworthy*' witness: cf. Isa. 8.2 (*'ēdîm ne'ᵉmānîm*); Jer. 42.5 (*'ēd 'ᵉmet wᵉne'ᵉmān*); Ps. 89.38 (*'ēd...ne'ᵉmān*).

26. On this subject and the relevant vocabulary, cf. M. Klopfenstein, *Die Lüge nach dem Alten Testament* (Zürich, 1964), pp. 18-31; A. Phillips, *Ancient Israel's Criminal Law: A New Approach to the Decalogue* (Oxford, 1970), pp. 141-45.

27. On the presumed semantic difference between Exod. 20.16 (*'ēd šeqer*) and Deut. 5.20 (*'ēd šāw'*), cf. Klopfenstein, *Die Lüge*, pp. 18-21; F.-L. Hossfeld, *Der Dekalog* (OBO, 45; Göttingen, 1982), pp. 75-86, on the other hand, is for a basic equality of meaning. The different nuances of meaning between expressions referring

'ēd ḥinnām	Prov. 24.28
'ēd kᵉzābîm	Prov. 21.28
'ēd bᵉliyya'al[28]	Prov. 19.28
'ēd ḥāmās[29]	Exod. 23.1; Deut. 19.16; Ps. 35.11

Alongside the terminology with *'ēd*, we may recall the parallel one expressed with *yāpîaḥ*,[30] found almost exclusively in the book of Proverbs:

to false witness are noted by H. Simian-Yofre, *ThWAT*, V, p. 1113.

28. The term *bᵉliyya'al* has been the repeated subject of articles aimed at trying to find its etymology and precise meaning: cf. W.V. Baudissin, 'The Original Meaning of "Belial"', *ExpTim* 9 (1897–1898), pp. 40-45; P. Joüon, '*bᵉliyya'al* Bélial', *Bib* 5 (1924), pp. 178-83; J.E. Hogg, '"Belial" in the Old Testament', *AJSL* 44 (1927–1928), pp. 50-58; G.R. Driver, 'Hebrew Notes', *ZAW* 52 (1934), pp. 51-56; D.W. Thomas, '*bᵉliyya'al* in the Old Testament', in *Biblical and Patristic Studies in Memory of R.P. Casey* (Freiburg, 1963), pp. 11-19; V. Maag, '*Bᵉlīja'al* im Alten Testament', *TZ* 21 (1965), pp. 287-99.

29. In *Ahiq.* 140 we have the Aramaic equivalent *śhd ḥms* (A. Cowley, *Aramaic Papyri of the Fifth Century B.C.* [Oxford, 1923], p. 217). On the specific meaning to be attributed to the expression *'ēd ḥāmās*, there is no perfect unanimity among exegetes; it seems to me that, depending on context, different aspects of interpersonal injustice caused by witness in a law court are evoked: cf. Seeligmann, 'Zur Terminologie', p. 263; H.J. Stoebe, '*ḥāmās* Gewalttat', *THAT*, I, p. 585; H. Haag, '*ḥāmās*', *ThWAT*, II, pp. 1051, 1057-58; J. Pons, *L'oppression dans l'Ancien Testament* (Paris, 1981), pp. 39-41.

30. The interpretation of *ypyḥ* is much debated, both as regards its grammatical form (verb, verbal adjective, noun), and as regards its origin (Ugaritic?), as well as regards the interpretation of the various biblical texts in which the term is or is supposed to be attested.

Among more recent contributions, which also give a history of the research on this subject, I would like to single out W. Bühlmann, *Vom rechten Reden und Schweigen: Studien zu Proverbien 10–31* (Göttingen, 1976), esp. pp. 93-96; D. Pardee, '*Ypḥ* "Witness" in Hebrew and Ugaritic', *VT* 28 (1978), pp. 204-13 (who explicitly refers back to W. McKane, *Proverbs: A New Approach* (London, 1970); P.D. Miller, '*YAPÎAḤ* in Psalm XII 6', *VT* 29 (1979), pp. 495-501; *HALAT*, pp. 866-67.

Personally, I think that in the texts quoted above, the interpretation of *ypyḥ* as a noun is more convincing than the one which considers it a verb; the meaning of the term would then in some ways be synonymous with *'ēd*. A different approach is held by E. Zurro, *Procedimientos iterativos en la poesia ugarítica y hebrea* (Biblica et Orientalia, 43; Rome, 1987), p. 68.

a. *truthful witness*

yāpîaḥ 'ᵉmûnâ	Prov. 12.17 (opposed to: *'ēd šᵉqārîm*)

b. *false witness*

yāpîaḥ kᵉzābîm	Prov. 6.19 (parallel to: *'ēd šāqer*); 14.5 (parallel to: *'ēd šāqer*; opposed to: *'ēd 'ᵉmûnîm*); 14.25 (opposed to: *'ēd 'ᵉmet*); 19.5 (parallel to: *'ēd šᵉqārîm*); 19.9 (parallel to: *'ēd šᵉqārîm*)
yᵉpēaḥ ḥāmās	Ps. 27.12 (parallel to: *'ēd šeqer*)

1.2.3. *Plurality or Singularity, Presence or Absence of Witnesses.* I would like to highlight here a peculiarity of witness that was a chief plank in the structure of Hebrew proceedings, and therefore deserves a more detailed treatment.

a. *The plurality of witnesses required by the Hebrew system.* According to Deut. 17.6; 19.15 and Num. 35.30, a (criminal) trial was correctly brought in Israel only if there was a plurality of prosecution witnesses (in agreement).[31] The most complete and explicit text is that of Deut. 19.15, which does not restrict the norm to proceedings on capital charges alone.[32]

lō' yāqûm 'ēd 'eḥād bᵉ'îš
lᵉkol 'āwōn
ûlᵉkol ḥaṭṭā't
bᵉkol ḥēṭ' 'ᵃšer yeḥᵉṭā'
'al pî šᵉnê 'ēdîm
'ô 'al pî šᵉlōšâ 'ēdîm yāqûm dābār[33]

31. The fact that the principle of excluding a single witness is repeated three times may be a sign of the importance attached to it in Old Testament legislation (cf. van Vliet, *No Single Testimony*, p. 65).

32. This is not the opinion of Jackson, *Theft in Early Jewish Law*, p. 226, who maintains that the requirement for at least two witnesses is limited to cases in which the crimes require capital punishment: Deut. 17.6 (idolatry); Num. 35.30 (murder); Deut. 19.15 (probably a reference to crimes of theft).

33. For the interpretation of the phrase 'two or three (witnesses)', cf. S.E. Loewenstamm, 'The Phrase "X (or) X plus one" in Biblical and Old Oriental Laws', *Bib* 53 (1972), p. 543; and esp. B.S. Jackson, *Essays in Jewish and Comparative Legal History* (StJudLA, 10; Leiden, 1975), pp. 153-71.

This set of norms probably did not hold for the whole history of Israel's juridical institutions,[34] and it may always be asked what its practical interpretation was in the various courts of law laid down by Hebrew legislation.

It seems to me that it has to be stated that the principle of a plurality of witnesses has first of all its internal *reasonableness*: it does in fact restrain summary judgments and reduces the possibility of judicial errors;[35] in fact, in proceedings where verbal testimony is practically the only means of proof, the agreement of the witnesses is the sole objective criterion for the judge's discretionary decision.[36] What is more, this principle is of theoretical *necessity*. Let us imagine in fact that one person accuses another of a crime; if the accused puts forward a different version of the facts or simply claims innocence, then on the hypothesis that no 'witness' can be found (after careful investigation) to confirm the word of one of the parties, the judge does not have sufficient material on which to make a decision, and must probably dismiss the case.[37] To give greater credence to the opinion of one rather

34. The fact that there is no hint of the need for a plurality of witnesses in the so-called Covenant-Code (Exod. 21–23) is especially important. In any case, it seems difficult to me to sketch in a history of this juridical norm with arguments '*e silentio*', or to draw proofs from texts such as Deut. 19.16-21 (which talks of *two* who have a controversy in a place of judgment); I therefore consider too drastic the position of Seeligmann, who downplays even the attestation of 1 Kgs 21.10, 13 when he writes that the norm regarding two witnesses 'gehört nicht den ältesten Zeiten an, doch wird sie 1 Rg. XXI im nordreich vorausgesetzt—wenn es sich nicht um eine Zufallssituation handelt' ('Zur Terminologie', p 264).

35. Cf. *THAT*, II, pp. 213-214.

36. Cf. van Vliet, *No Single Testimony*, p. 68.

37. The Bible does not offer precise rules for the circumstances, nor are cases mentioned in which proceedings for dismissal would take place. D. Daube states that 'ordinarily, in the case of one man's word against another's, any system gives preference to the *status quo*; that is to say, the party that wants a change must have some extra in his favour to win' ('The Law of Witnesses in Transferred Operation', *JANES* 5 [1973], p. 91). Philo, probably commenting on Deut. 19.15, says that a judge must not take a solitary witness into consideration (*mē prosiesthai*) because, faced with numerical equality between prosecution and defence, the best thing is to put off, that is to suspend, judgment (*epechein*) (*Spec. Leg.* 4.53-54).

From this point of view it might be of interest to observe that the denunciation of a prophet is sometimes backed up by reference to those who previously spoke similarly; in this case, as well as a denunciation of sliding back into crime, we would have a concurrence of testimony even without the physical presence of several

than the other would be to allow favouritism or partiality to sway one's judgment, the subject of repeated condemnation in Israel's legislation.

In order for a case to be 'judged', an accusation backed up in a *convincing* manner is required; thus a plurality of witnesses in agreement against someone typically constituted the evidence in the Hebrew judicial system. Two or three witnesses were enough, but an even greater number was a guarantee of greater juridical certainty: the proof became overwhelming.[38]

As far as the *Hebrew vocabulary* of witness is concerned, it is important therefore to observe the grammatical form of the *plural*, and—as I shall point out below—expressions suggesting quantity or number are also important.

b. *Absence or insufficiency of witnesses*. Going back schematically over what I stated in the previous section, we may say that a trial can be held (according to the law) only if (1) we have a prosecution witness; and (2) this is assumed to be a number of witnesses.

Now, either of these two conditions may *not* hold true:

1. Instead of the 'presence' we may have an *absence* (lack) of witnesses: if in fact nobody saw the crime and/or nobody comes to court to lay a complaint, then the trial does not possess the formal traits necessary to begin.
2. Instead of a 'plurality', we might have a *singleness* of witness: as I have said, this is the equivalent of an 'insufficiency of proof', which, as such, makes a correct judicial decision impossible.

These possibilities can arise for different reasons: for example, by chance circumstances, or by a premeditated plan of the criminal, who has a tendency to plan crimes in such a way as to ensure freedom from

witnesses (a typical case would be Jer. 26.5, 18).

38. To make reasonable progress in a courtroom it seems necessary to limit the number of these witnesses so that the evidence of the witnesses does not become superfluous and therefore uselessly burdensome to the magistrate. B.S. Jackson has dedicated a long article to a study of the expression 'two or three witnesses', coming to the conclusion that it is an editorial addition intended to clarify what was implicitly summed up in the axiom, *unus testis nullus testis*; he too thinks that plurality in the nature of testimony is the decisive semantic element in this juridical precept ('Two or Three Witnesses', in *Essays in Jewish and Comparative Legal History* [Leiden, 1975], pp. 153-71).

punishment. The disappearance of possible witnesses,[39] the phenomenon of a conspiracy of silence, the corruption of a judicial administration that looks for quibbles in order not to hear certain testimony, and so on, are other causes of the occurrence of juridical cases in which the accusation is denied convincing force.

The two situations (absence or insufficiency of witnesses) are definitely not identical: in the former case there is no possibility of formal juridical proceedings; in the latter, however, the judge can be called upon to carry out at least a preliminary investigation in the hope of finding material to back up the prosecution (or the accused).

And yet the two situations outlined, looked at in a rigorously formal way, need a treatment that unites them under one and the same juridical profile: they have as a common feature that lack (absolute or relative, i.e., absence or insufficiency) of convincing force indispensable for the prosecution's case.

This is the reason why, in Hebrew law, *when a crime has been committed*, but there are no witnesses or the testimony is insufficient (there is no certain knowledge of who the culprit might be), the normal legal path is to substitute a practice usually referred to as 'the judgment of God';[40] in other words, since it is not possible for a human tribunal to

39. The elimination of witnesses may be directly willed and carried out by a criminal in order to avoid prosecution. One way is that of killing a witness in circumstances such as to make it thought an accident; this is what David, for example, did in the case of Uriah (2 Sam. 11.14-25). Another way is to accuse the *witness* (of some crime): his or her death, in observance of the law, or at least a loss of juridical authoritativeness, will have the effect of suspending proceedings against the wrong-doer. It is in this context that the theme of a trial directed against a prophet should be placed, or, more generally, a decree pronounced summarily by authorities charged by the words of a prophet (Jeremiah 26).

40. This double system of 'just' action against a criminal still lives on today in the *popular consciousness* which, more or less explicitly, sees the intolerability of a crime that would go unpunished; it therefore attributes to divine punishment or immanent justice the possible misfortune of a wrongdoer who has escaped the mesh of human justice.

But as far as *legal provisions* go, faced with the cases to which I refer in the text, modern criminal codes simply declare 'no grounds on which to proceed' without introducing (or explicitly forbidding altogether) (restrictive) procedures referred to appeal courts of a religious nature.

In particular, it may be of interest to observe how the Italian Code of Criminal Procedure, no. 378, puts under the same heading (sentence of acquittal in preliminary judicial inquiry) both sentences not to proceed because there is a *total lack of proof*

decide with certainty whose rights to uphold and which criminal to punish, God, as the supreme guarantor of justice in the world, is asked to supply the relevant data and establish the truth; alternatively, he is given the task of intervening directly with his final verdict.[41]

As far as the *Hebrew vocabulary* is concerned, the text of Num. 5.13[42] offers us an excellent point of departure: the case is that of a woman who is accused of betraying her husband without him—although being suspicious—having proof of it (this is the reason why he is forced to have recourse to the rite of 'bitter water'):

w^{e}šākab 'îš 'ōtāh šik^{e}bat zera'	Crime
w^{e}ne'lam mē'ênê 'îšāh	Without proof
w^{e}nist^{e}râ (w^{e}hî' niṭmā'â)	
w^{e}'ēd 'ên bāh	
w^{e}hî' lō' nitpāśâ	

that there is a case to answer, or the accused did not commit it, or because there is *insufficient proof* to send the case for judgment because those who committed the crime are *unknown*. (It should be noted that in the dispositions of the acts of the C.C.P. no. 62, when proof is altogether lacking, there must be acquittal for the following reason: 'because a criminal case could not have been brought or pursued'.)

41. Cf. S.M. Paul, *Studies in the Book of the Covenant in the Light of Cuneiform and Biblical Law* (VTSup, 18; Leiden, 1970), pp. 90-91. Koehler ('Die hebräische Rechtsgemeinde', pp. 158-59) maintains that when normal juridical procedures failed, recourse was had in Israel to an oracle, which brought the 'priest' into play. It seems in accordance with the biblical texts to say that when recourse had to be had to a 'judgment of God' by an oracular reply, the priest often had a particular importance. However, it should be remembered that the priest also possessed a normal jurisdiction over matters bearing on the sacred (cf. Chapter 5 section 1.2.); moreover, it is well known that the 'judgment of God' could take place by drawing lots, oath or other ceremonies, for which the presence of a priest is not always documented (cf. de Vaux, *Institutions*, I, pp. 241-43).

42. On the text of Num. 5.11-31, which is interesting for the detailed procedure of ordeal by 'bitter water', cf. J.M. Sasson, 'Numbers 5 and the "Waters of Judgement"', *BZ* NS 16 (1972), pp. 249-51; G. Rinaldi, 'La donna che "ha deviato". Considerazioni su Num. 5.11-31', *EuntDoc* 26 (1973), pp. 535-50; M. Fishbane, 'Accusations of Adultery: A Study of Law and Scribal Practice in Numbers 5.11-31', *HUCA* 45 (1974), pp. 25-45; H.C. Brichto, 'The Case of the *śōtā* and a Reconsideration of Biblical Law', *HUCA* 46 (1975), pp. 55-70; H. McKeating, 'Sanctions against Adultery in Ancient Israelite Society with some Reflections on Methodology in the Study of Old Testament Ethics', *JSOT* 11 (1979), pp. 57-72; T. Frymer-Kensky, 'The Strange Case of the Suspected Sotah (Numbers V 11-31)', *VT* 34 (1984), pp. 11-26; J. Milgrom, 'On the Suspected Adulteress (Numbers V 11-31)', *VT* 35 (1985), pp. 368-69.

The reasons why the husband's suspicions cannot be proved in court are basically these (starting from the bottom): (1) there is *not even one witness* who saw her or caught her in the act, and (2) the crime was committed *in secret* (even the husband is not certain). The twofold form of expression allows us to organize the Hebrew lexicon of 'lack of proof'.

1. *Crimes without witnesses*. Num. 5.13 is the only text in which the noun *'ēd* is linked to the negative particle *'ên*. But if we bear it in mind that a witness is someone who 'has seen' (*r'h*) or 'knows' (*yd'*) then we find equivalent expressions that show the same syntagmatic structure: (1) negation; (2) an experience which grounds testimony. A few texts will suffice as examples:

a. with the negation *'ên*: Gen. 31.50 (***'ên 'îš 'immānû*** *r*ᵉ*'ēh* ᵉ*lōhîm 'ēd bênî ûbênekā*;[43] cf. v. 49: *yiṣep yhwh bênî ûbênekā kî* ***nissātēr*** *'îš mērē'ēhû*); Exod. 2.12 (*wayyar' kî* ***'ên 'îš***; cf. the opposite in v. 14: ***nôda'*** *haddābār*); Exod. 22.9 (***'ên rō'eh***); 1 Kgs 3.18 (***'ên zār 'ittānû*** *babbayit*); Isa. 47.10 (***'ên rō'ānî***); Ps. 14.1 = 53.2 (***'ên*** ᵉ***lōhîm***).[44]

b. with *other kinds* of negation: Deut. 21.1 (*lō' nôda'*); 21.7 (*'ênênû lō' rā'û*); with a rhetorical question: Pss. 64.6 (*mî yir'eh lāmô*); 73.11 (*'ēkâ yāda' 'ēl w*ᵉ*yēš dē'â b*ᵉ*'elyôn*).

2. *Crimes (which stay) hidden*. That a 'thing' stays hidden means, first, that nobody comes to know of it; juridical action by a prosecutor is not even imaginable, given that there is no basis or reason for proceeding.

43. N.H. Snaith proposes the correction *'ên 'îš 'ammēnû rō'eh*, and translates, 'when no man of our father's kin is watching' ('Genesis XXXI 50', *VT* 14 [1964], p. 373). The first correction (*'ammēnû* instead of *'immānû*) does not seem necessary; in Exod. 22.13-14, in fact, the presence/absence of witnesses is expressed like this: *b*ᵉ*'ālāyw 'ên 'immô/b*ᵉ*'ālāyw 'immô*. The second (*rō'eh* in place of *r*ᵉ*'ēh*) seems more acceptable, and could allow a reorganization of the phrase into parallel and opposing stichs:

'ên 'îš	*'immānû*	*rō'eh*
ᵉ*lōhîm*		*'ēd*
	bênî ûbênekā	

44. The statement, 'there is no God', should not be understood as a general declaration of atheism, but rather as a refusal to admit God's judging intervention in human history (cf. Ps. 10.4, 11, 13; Jer. 5.12; Zeph. 1.12).

From this point of view, the vocabulary of the 'secret' is an antonym of the *notitia criminis*.[45]

Secondly, it may happen that a criminal deed is known (by means of incontrovertible evidence such as, for example, the discovery of a corpse bearing signs of violence: cf. Deut. 21.1) but the author of the crime remains unknown; with the possibility of arriving—by questioning or other investigation—at a precise charge ruled out, the prosecutor cannot take action in the courts. In this case the secret (which covers the culprit) may be considered an antonym of the eyewitness's experience.[46]

As regards the Hebrew *vocabulary*, I would like to begin by picking out the terminology of 'hiding', particularly the roots *str*, *kḥd*, *'lm* (*Ni*), *ṭmn*, *ksh* (*Pi*).[47]

Consideration should also be given to the *objective* conditions that give a criminal act a specific sort of secrecy, that is, they make it structurally impossible for the magistracy to bring the case to court.

The *countryside* (*śādeh*)—as opposed to the city—is the place where people do not live, and therefore where a crime that has been

45. As has already been said, a criminal tries to wipe out the proof of guilt (cf. Prov. 30.20); the terminology of cover, hide, conceal is opposed to that of the *notitia criminis* (cf. Exod. 2.12: *wayyiṭmᵉnēhû baḥôl*; 2.14: *'ākēn nôda' haddābār*).

46. Cf. the discussion under section 3.3.1.b, Chapter 6, of the opposition between the terminology of the 'secret' and the judge's investigative activity.

47. Cf. S.E. Balentine, 'A Description of the Semantic Field of Hebrew Words for "Hide"', *VT* 30 (1980), pp. 137-53.

The root *str* has especial importance in this series and deserves a few comments which will also serve to position the verbs and texts I will be quoting later on in the note. The verb *str* (*Ni*) frequently refers to the hiding of an (alleged) criminal who is trying to avoid capture and punishment (cf. Isa. 28.15; Jer. 23.24; 36.19; Amos 9.3; Zeph. 2.3; Job 34.22); but also the conditions under which a wrongdoer works (or could work) (cf. Gen. 31.49; Num. 5.13; Jer. 16.17; see also Ps. 19.17 with the comment by Alonso Schökel, *Treinta Salmos*, p. 103). The noun *sēter* is also sometimes used to refer to a hidden crime, especially with the expression *bassēter* (Deut. 13.7; 27.15, 24; 2 Sam. 12.12; Ps. 101.5; Job 13.10; 31.27); the form *bammistār* (*îm*) in Hab. 3.14; Pss. 10.8, 9; 64.5 should be considered equivalent.

Of the texts that express the act of hiding, I would like to single out: with *kḥd*: 2 Sam. 18.13; Isa. 3.9 (*Pi*); Hos. 5.3; Ps. 69.6 (*Ni*); with *'lm*: Num. 5.13ff.; Qoh. 12.14; with *ṭmn*: Exod. 2.12; Josh. 7.21-22; 2 Kgs 7.8; Job 31.33 (in parallel with *ksh*, *Pi*); with *ṣpn*: Jer. 16.17 (*Ni*; parallel to *str*, *Ni*); Hos. 13.12 (parallel to *ṣrr*); with *ksh* (*Pi*): Ps. 32.5; Prov. 28.13; cf. also the theme of 'covering blood' (Gen. 37.26; Ezek. 24.7-8; Job 16.18).

perpetrated escapes the possibility of a prosecution witness (cf. Gen. 4.8; 37.15-20; Deut. 21.1; 22.25, 27).

Even more significant is the state of unpunishability by darkness, night, nightfall, and the like; if in fact it is *impossible to see* the wrongdoer, it becomes impossible to pursue the criminal according to the ordinary procedures laid down by the law. As a typical example, it seems of interest to call to mind Job 24.13-17:

v. 13 They are of those who rebel against the light (*'ôr*),
They do not know its ways,
Nor do they abide in its paths:
v. 14 At dawn (***lā'ôr***)[48] the murderer rises up
To kill the poor and the needy;
By night (***ûballaylâ***) he is like a thief.
v. 15 The adulterer also awaits the twilight (***nešep***),
Saying, 'No eye will see me',
And disguises (***sēter***) his face.
v. 16 In the dark (***baḥōšek***) they dig through houses,
During the day (*yômām*) they stay hidden,
They do not know the light (*'ôr*):
v. 17 For the morning (*bōqer*) is to them like the darkness (***ṣalmāwet***),
For they are friends with the terrors of the darkness (***ṣalmāwet***).

Of the numerous texts in which the element of darkness has a certain juridical significance, I would like to single out: Exod. 22.1-2; Judg. 6.25-27; 1 Sam. 28.8; 1 Kgs 3.19-20; Isa. 29.15; Jer. 49.9; Ezek. 8.12; Obad. 5; Ps. 11.2, 4; Job 22.13; 23.17; Sir. 23.18-21.

1.2.4. *Reticent or Ready Witnesses.* At the end of this chapter, when the value of 'silence in the context of legal procedures' is being dealt with, greater precision will be given to the figure of the reticent witness, defined as one who does not tell the truth he or she knows[49] in court.

We may observe that reticence can also be expressed by the negation of verbs referring to a juridical initiative (of the kind: not be present, not

48. Some exegetes prefer to read *lō' 'ôr* ('when there is no light') in order to give greater consistency to the whole, which is speaking of rebels against the light. The text translated presents not a few textual problems, for which I refer to the scientific commentaries.

49. G. Cardascia points out how the obligation to give testimony at a judgment was present in Israel (documented in Lev. 5.1) and in the ancient Near East, but is not in Roman law ('Droits cunéiformes et droit biblique', in *Proceedings of the Sixth World Congress of Jewish Studies*, I (Jerusalem, 1977), pp. 69-70.

rise, stay away, and so on); it follows that the opposite of the reticent witness is the eager witness (cf. Mal. 3.5; *'ēd m^e mahēr*).[50]

1.3. *The Syntagm of Prosecution Testimony*

What a *prosecution* testimony is, that is, what it implies and what are its constitutive elements, can be illustrated by reference to the syntagm *'ēd b^e*, separating out its essential components. The basic elements—related to one another in this syntagmatic structure in such a way that we can speak of a logic of relationships and a structure of prosecution testimony—are as follows:

1. *There is present*...This element expresses the initiative undertaken by the prosecution. It occupies a logical position in the presence–absence opposition between witnesses.
2. *a witness*...This is the element described in the previous section; its definition makes reference to some knowledge or experience which is a precondition of his juridical act. The oppositions true–false, one–many, come into play here to qualify the value of the testimony.
3. *who accuses*...The element of what is said in a trial is closely linked to the two previous elements. A reticent witness would have to be situated (as an adversary) at this point.
4. *someone*...Here we get a definition of the accused. This element may be enlarged upon by a description of the person charged, in particular giving details of the person's guilt or innocence.
5. *of a crime*...This is the element from which the prosecution draws all its juridical force and on which the punishment depends.
6. *liable to punishment*...Reference to a punitive sanction is essential for a trial, the aim of which is the re-establishment of justice by a conviction.

This syntagm was derived, in part, from a logical examination of the definition of a witness; but it was also arrived at from a comparative reading of the biblical texts, made with the intention of grasping the value of each significant element in every relevant phrase.

50. For the root *mhr* in a judicial context, cf. also Isa. 16.5: *šōpēṭ w^e dōrēš mišpāṭ ûm^e hir ṣedeq*; and, with a meaning not of eagerness but of haste, Prov. 25.8: *'al tēṣē' lārib mahēr* (cf. also 6.18). On Mal. 3.5, cf. E.D. Freudenstein, 'A Swift Witness', *Tradition* 13 (1974), pp. 114-23 (which I was unable to consult).

As a first set of examples, and with the purpose of introducing the Hebrew lexicon, I would like to take Deut. 19.15 and Num. 35.30:

	1	2	3	4	5	6
Deut. 19.15	*qwm b^e^*	*'ēd 'eḥād*		*'îš*	*l^e^kol 'āwōn...*	
Deut. 19.16	*qwm b^e^*	*'ēd ḥāmās*	*'nh b^e^...sārâ*[51]	*'îš*		(retaliation)
Num. 35.30		*'ēd 'eḥād*	*'nh b^e^*	*nepeš*		*lāmût*

The juxtaposition of these three texts reveals that, starting from the word *'ēd*, it is possible to organize the lexicon according to the main syntagmatic connections. It can also be seen that all the elements in the syntagm are necessarily represented in the actual individual texts; in fact, a few significant pointers are enough to refer to the whole relationship. Again, the lexicon offers some constants and some variants: if we make an exhaustive examination, starting with the term *'ēd*, we find that the terms most characteristic of a prosecution witness—because they occur the most frequently in clearly juridical texts—are *qwm b^e^* and *'nh b^e^*. It would, however, be a mistake to think that legal language is limited to these expressions; their appearance certainly does suggest a trial context, but a different terminology could just as well call it to mind; in fact the decisive thing is not an individual term, but the relationship of meaning in which it is engaged with the other terms in the phrase.

On the basis of these considerations, I would like to formulate my thesis: *each* of the elements in the syntagm (i.e. that of the prosecution testimony) occurs with paradigmatic variations. Even the term *'ēd* may be replaced by others that are its equivalent (by synonymousness, metonomy or metaphor) without the language ceasing to be juridically relevant. The identification of a trial structure in these cases is less certain precisely because the language is less technical; it is not however possible to set up exclusive recourse to one term or expression without incurring an extremely partial vision of the semantic field connected with matters legal.

It may be deduced from this that it is impossible to give all the paradigmatic variations on a syntagm such as the one quoted above; I think, however, that it is necessary to mention some of the most

51. For the interpretation of the syntagm *'nh b^e^...sārâ*, I am following E. Jenni, who translates '(vor Gericht) Falsches aussagen' ('Dtn. 19.16: *sarā* "Falscheit"', in *Mélanges bibliques et orientaux en l'honneur de H. Cazelles* (Neukirchen, 1981), pp. 201-11 (cf. also J. van der Ploeg, 'Notes lexicographiques', *OTS* 5 [1948], pp. 142-50).

important forms, so as to draw attention to the size of the phenomenon and its importance in the literature of the Old Testament.

1.4. *The Witness and the Paradigm*

In order to see the consistency of my argument, the syntagm of prosecution testimony must be kept clearly in mind, and it must be presupposed that the introduction of a variation into one element brings about considerable variations in all the others.

1.4.1. *Witness: An Individual.* The word *'ēd* may be replaced quite simply by the word *'person'* (*'îš*, *'ādām* or the like), which is a 'sememe' of *'ēd*. This becomes obvious when the actions proper to a prosecution witness are attributed to this 'person'.

If we take, for example, Deut. 19.16-18, we see that the relationship between the accuser and the accused is expressed first by the terms *'ēd* and *'îš*; we then have the same generic formula *šᵉnê hā'ᵃnāšîm*; and lastly *'ēd* - *'āḥîw*.

1 Kgs 21.10-13 narrates a clear episode of (false) testimony; the important fact is that the witnesses are not called *'ēdîm*, but *šᵉnayim 'ᵃnāšîm bᵉnê bᵉliyya'al* (v. 10), *šᵉnê hā'ᵃnāšîm bᵉnê bᵉliyya'al* (v. 13), *'anšê habbᵉliyya'al* (v. 13). In Prov. 25.18, the equivalence between a person and the person's witness is expressed as follows: 'club, sword and sharp arrow—*'îš 'ōneh bᵉrē'ēhû 'ēd šāqer*'; in Prov. 21.28 there is an antithetical parallelism between *'ēd kᵉzābîm* and *'îš šômēa'*.

The term *'îš* (or its synonyms) is to the point juridically not only when it is linked to the terminology of the controversy (cf. the already quoted[52] phrases *'îš rîb* + pronominal suffix and *'îš môkîaḥ*, to which may perhaps be added *'îš midyānîm* (Q) in Prov. 26.21, but also when it is construed with terms characteristic of the value of legal testimony (*šeqer*, *kāzāb*, *ḥāmās*, etc.). I would like to give some examples:

Jer. 9.4	***wᵉ'îš*** *bᵉrē'ēhû yᵉhātēllû* *we'ᵉmet lō' yᵉdabbērû* *limmᵉdû lᵉšônām dabber šeqer*
Ps. 140.2	***'ādām*** *rā'...* ***'îš*** *ḥᵃmāsîm*
5	***'îš*** *ḥᵃmāsîm*
12	***'îš*** *lāšôn...* ***'îš*** *ḥāmās*

52. Cf. pp. 37, 48.

Ps. 5.7	*dōbᵉrê kāzāb—'îš dāmîm*[53] *ûmirmâ*[54]
Ps. 31.21	*ruksê **'îš**—rîb lᵉšōnôt*
Ps. 12.3	*šāw' yᵉdabbᵉrû **'îš** 'et rē'ēhû*[55]

Cf. also Pss. 18.4 (*'îš ḥāmās*); 43.1 (*'îš mirmâ wᵉ'awlâ*); 55.24 (***'anšê** dāmîm ûmirmâ*); 62.10 (*kāzāb bᵉnê **'îš***); Ezek. 22.9 (***'anšê** rākîl*); Prov. 6.12-15 (12: ***'ādām** bᵉliyya'al **'îš** 'āwen*); 16.27-30 (27: ***'îš** bᵉliyya'al*; 28: ***'îš** tahpukôt*; 29: ***'îš** ḥāmās*); 24.1 (***'anšê** rā'â*) etc.

1.4.2. *Witness: By Mouth, Hand and Other Parts of the Body.* Another quite frequent paradigmatic substitution in Hebrew poetry is to refer to a person by way of a significant part of the body; thus, instead of saying, 'a proud person', it is possible, by metonomy, to say, 'haughty eyes'. Now since a witness's principal function is speech, the organs of that function (the mouth, tongue and lips) are seen to take the place in the paradigm of the term *'ēd*.[56]

53. Cf. N.A. van Uchelen, ''*nšy dmym* in the Psalms', *OTS* 15 (1969), pp. 205-12.

54. The link between false testimony and the noun *mirmâ* is confirmed explicitly in:

Prov. 12.17	*yāpîaḥ 'ᵉmûnâ yaggîd ṣedeq*	*wᵉ'ēd šᵉqārîm mirmâ*
Prov. 14.25	*maṣṣîl nᵉpāšôt 'ēd 'ᵉmet*	*wᵉyāpiaḥ kᵉzābîm mirmâ*

55. In many texts, the idiomatic expression *'îš 'et rē'ēhû* simply suggests a reciprocal action. I think, however, that it sometimes still retains an interpersonal connotation; in this case we would have a relationship between a person (the prosecutor, the deceiver) and a fellow-citizen.

56. In my semantic analysis of the witness (prosecutor) I have stressed the essential importance of the *speech*, with which one strives and hopes to achieve juridical victory. As my argument continues, I shall try to read many of the confrontations described in the Psalms as attacks against the one at prayer by adversaries who—making use of lies—either are or amount to false witnesses (cf. Klopfenstein, *Die Lüge*, p. 25).

It seems clear that the concept of 'enemy' cannot be reduced to a single category, nor is it plausible that every text identifies a lie with false witness in a formally constituted trial.

However, the interpretation that holds that an informal calumny or casual curse is able to plunge the Psalmist into the agony that leads to death seems insufficient; a more convincing explanation is a reference to false charges, of which the biblical texts speak as a frequent phenomenon (cf. Seeligmann, 'Zur Terminologie', p. 263; *THAT*, II, p. 213).

Also unsatisfactory is the thesis of S. Mowinckel (*Psalmenstudien*. I. *Åwän*

This kind of substitution is in a manner of speaking contained in the actual legal formulae that mention valid testimony in a trial, where we read: *l^epî ʿēdîm* (Num. 35.30), *ʿal pî š^enayim ʿēdîm...ʿal pî ʿēd ʾeḥād* (Deut. 17.6), *ʿal pî š^enê ʿēdîm* (Deut. 19.15);[57] this makes understandable the clear parallelism expressed in Prov. 19.28:

ʿēd b^eliyyaʿal	*yālîṣ mišpāṭ*
ûpî r^ešāʿîm	*y^ebalaʿ ʾāwen*

The relevant texts are especially abundant; I would therefore like to single out only some typical expressions:

Ps. 109.2	*kî* ***pî*** *rāšāʿ* ***ûpî*** *mirmâ ʿālay pātāḥû*
	dibb^erû ʾittî ***l^ešôn*** *šāqer*
Ps. 120.2	*yhwh haṣṣîlâ napšî* ***miśś^epat*** *šeqer* ***millāšôn*** *r^emiyyâ*
Ps. 31.19	*tēʾālamnâ* ***śiptê*** *šāqer haddōb^erôt ʿal ṣaddîq ʿātāq*

und die individuellen Klagepsalmen [Kristiania, 1921]), revived by N. Nicolsky (*Spuren magischer Formeln in den Psalmen* [BZAW, 46; Giessen, 1927]) and more recently by C. Hauret ('Les ennemis-sorciers dans les supplications individuelles', in *Aux grands carrefours de la révélation et de l'exégèse de l'Ancien Testament* [Recherches Bibliques, VIII; Bruges, 1967], pp. 129-137), who attributes to wizards and sorcerers (*pōʿ^alê ʾāwen*) the magic power to cause even mortal illnesses. Although it is possible to find Psalms in which the one praying represents his situation as that of someone sick (cf. K. Seybold, *Das Gebet des Kranken im Alten Testament* [BWANT, 99; Stuttgart, 1973]) in the grip of his enemies, the questions remain: (1) whether this can be extended to all the other texts, and (2) whether it is absolutely impossible to give a metaphorical interpretation to this illness (cf. C. Barth, *Die Errettung vom Tode in den individuellen Klage- und Dankliedern des Alten Testaments* [Zollikon, 1947], pp. 99-102), the symptoms of which might be being used to describe the experience of agony and the approach of death. On this subject, and in particular on the relationship between the 'lamentation' Psalms and the texts of Babylonian spells, cf. N. Lohfink, 'Projektionen. Über die Feinde des Kranken im Alten Orient und in den Psalmen', in *Unsere grossen Wörter* (Freiburg-Basel-Vienna, 1977), pp. 144-55; E.S. Gerstenberger, *Der bittende Mensch: Bittritual und Klagelied des Einzelnen im Alten Testament* (WMANT, 51; Neukirchen, 1980), pp. 64-112; L. Ruppert, 'Klagelieder in Israel und Babylonien—Verschiedene Deutungen der Gewalt', in N. Lohfink (ed.), *Gewalt und Gewaltlosigkeit im Alten Testament* (QDisp, 96; Freiburg-Basel-Vienna, 1983), pp. 111-58.

57. The expressions *l^epî* and *ʿal pî* are identical in meaning (P. Dhorme, *L'emploi métaphorique des noms de parties du corps en hébreu et en akkadien* [Paris, 1923], p. 85); although they have become idiomatic expressions, I do not think that references to the mouth as an organ of witness should be excluded.

Isa. 54.17	*wᵉkol* ***lāšôn*** *tāqûm 'ittāk lammišpāṭ taršî'î*
Job. 15.6	*yaršî'ᵃkā pîkā wᵉlō' 'ānî*
	ûśᵉpāteykā *ya'ᵃnû bāk*

Cf. also Isa. 59.3; Jer. 9.2, 7; Zeph. 3.13; Pss. 5.10; 12.3-5; 31.21; 52.4, 6; 63.12; 144.8, 11; Prov. 6.17; 10.18; 12.19, 22; 17.4; 26.28.

A different part of the body, the hand, has a certain relevance in legal testimony; to start with, this is seen from Exod. 23.1 (*'al tāšet yādᵉkā 'im rāšā' lihyōt 'ēd ḥāmās*), which seems to echo the custom of the laying of a hand on the culprit in the act of making an accusatory declaration. This would appear to be attested by Lev. 24.14 (*wᵉsāmᵉkû kol haššōmᵉ'îm 'et yᵉdêhem 'al rō'šô*)[58] and Job 9.33 (*môkîaḥ yāšēt yādô 'al šᵉnênû*).[59]

The hand also comes into play at the execution of the sentence; here too the role of the witnesses is especially emphasized: *yad hā'ēdîm tihyeh bô bārī'šōnâ lahᵃmîtô wᵉyad kol hā'ām bā'aḥᵃrōnâ* (Deut. 17.7).

From this it can be understood why the pairing *mouth–hand* is sometimes used to describe the action of an adversary in a (supposed) trial. For example:

Ps. 144.8, 11	*'ᵃšer pîhem*	*dibber šāw'*
	wîmînām	*yᵉmîn šāqer*[60]

Cf. also Isa. 59.3; for the hand alone: Ps. 26.10.

Furthermore, it may reasonably be supposed that, as well as the mouth and the hand, other parts of the body demonstrate participation in the

58. Cf. also Dan. 13.34 and the *Excursus*: 'Deutungen des Gestus und der Formel "*Die Hand/Hände aufstemmen auf das Haupt von...*" ', in H. Engel, *Die Susanna-Erzählung* (OBO, 61; Freiburg, 1985), pp. 137-41.

R. Peter, 'L'imposition des mains dans l'Ancien Testament' *VT* 27 (1977), pp. 48-55, maintains that a distinction should be made in Hebrew between the laying-on of a hand and the laying-on of *hands*: by analogy with rites of expiation, the act referred to in Lev. 24.14 (and Dan. 13.34)—where we have the plural—means that the witnesses 'ont été en quelque sorte "souillés" par la faute commise; ils se déchargent donc de cette responsabilité sur le coupable "de base" en lui imposant les mains' (p. 53). This is one of the interpretative hypotheses already suggested by D. Daube, *The New Testament and Rabbinic Judaism* (JLCR, 2 [1952]; London, 1956), p. 227.

59. Cf. H. Cazelles, *Etudes sur le Code de l'Alliance* (Paris, 1946), p. 86.

60. According to L. Kopf, in some texts *ymyn* means 'oath' ('Arabische Etymologien und Parallelen zum Bibelwörterbuch', *VT* 9 [1959], pp. 257-58), with probable reference to the gesture of raising the right hand when pronouncing an oath.

act of testimony: the *eyes*, to the extent that they are the seat of the sensory experience which is the basis for the possibility of testimony; the *heart*, as the seat of the intelligence which discerns facts and plans action; the *feet*, which permit access to the law court.

I think I am giving the correct interpretation of Prov. 6.16-19 (and by extension of 6.12-15) when I say that the '6 and 7' things held in abomination by God are nothing less than false witness, tied to the various members of the body put to wicked use:

Prov. 6.16	*šeš hēnnâ śānē' yhwh*		
	w^{e}šeba‘ tô‘^{a}bat (Q) *napšô*		
17	*‘ênayim*	*rāmôt*	(1)
	l^{e}šôn	*šāqer*	(2)
	w^{e}yādayim	*šōp^{e}kôt dām nāqî*	(3)
18	*lēb*	*ḥōrēš maḥš^{e}bôt ’āwen*	(4)
	raglayim	*m^{e}mah^{a}rôt lārûṣ lārā‘â*	(5)
19	*yāpîaḥ k^{e}zābîm ‘ēd šāqer*		(6)
	ûm^{e}šallēaḥ m^{e}dānîm bên ’aḥîm		(7)
Prov. 6.12	*’ādām b^{e}liyya‘al ’îš ’āwen*		(6)
	hôlēk ‘iqq^{e}šût	*peh*	(2)
13	*qōrēṣ*	*b^{e}‘ênāw*	(1)
	mōlēl	*b^{e}raglāw*	(5)
	môreh	*b^{e}’eṣb^{e}‘ōtāyw*	(3)
14	*tahpukôt*	*b^{e}libbô ḥōrēš rā‘*	(4)
	b^{e}kol ‘ēt midyānîm (Q) *y^{e}šallēaḥ*		(7)
15	*‘al kēn pit’ōm yābô’ ’êdô*		
	peta‘ yiššābēr w^{e}’ên marpē’		

Description of false witness by way of the parts of the body concerned in the act of testimony is sometimes reduced to three elements; for example:

Isa. 59.3	(hands–fingers). 3 (lips–tongue). 7 (feet)
Ps. 101.5	(tongue, eyes, heart)
Ps. 140.3	(heart). 4 (tongue–lips). 5 (hand)
Prov. 4.24	(mouth–lips). 25 (eyes). 26-27 (feet).

1.4.3. *Witness: By Speech.* Directly linked to the previous section, and with particular reference to a witness's verbal declaration in a trial, we have another possible paradigmatic substitution: instead of (false, violent...) 'witness' we find the (false, violent...) *speaker*, or (false, etc.) *speech*.

This substitution has already been pointed out in a number of texts in which the expression *ʻēd šeqer* is made explicit by a phrase in which the stress falls upon an act of speech, of the kind:

Deut. 19.16	*kî yāqûm ʻēd ḥāmās b*^{e}*'îš*	*la*^{ʻa}*nôt bô sārâ*
Deut. 19.18	*ʻēd šeqer hāʻēd*	*šeqer ʻānâ b*^{e}*'āḥîw*
Prov. 14.5	*ʻēd '*^{e}*mûnîm*	*lō' y*^{e}*kazzēb*
		w^{e}*yāpîaḥ k*^{e}*zābîm*
	ʻēd šāqer	

The rhetorical figure metonomy (the effect in place of the cause)[61] means that *speech* is the same as *witness*, especially when terms characteristic of false testimony are stressed. A few examples:

Ps. 101.7	*dōbēr š*^{e}*qārîm* (cf. v. 5: *m*^{e}*lošnî* (Q) *bassēter rēʻēhû*)
Ps. 63.12	*dôb*^{e}*rê šāqer*
Ps. 5.7	*dōb*^{e}*rê kāzāb* (cf. also Ps. 58.4)
Isa. 59.13	*dibrê šāqer*
Ps. 109.3	*dibrê śin'â*
Ps. 52.6	*dibrê bālaʻ* (parallel to *l*^{e}*šôn mirmâ*)
Ps. 101.3	*d*^{e}*bar b*^{e}*liyyāʻal*
Prov. 29.12	*d*^{e}*bar šāqer* (cf. Prov. 13.5)
Isa. 32.7	*'imrê šeqer*
Zech. 8.17	*š*^{e}*bûʻat šeqer*[62]

Cf. also

Isa. 59.13	*dabber ʻōšeq w*^{e}*sārâ*
Jer. 9.4	*dabber šeqer*
Isa. 58.9	*dabber 'āwen*
Isa. 59.4	*dabber šāw'*

61. H. Lausberg, *Handbuch der literarischen Rhetorik* (Munich, 1960), § 568.3.

62. As regards the relationship between an oath and the course of a trial, the interpretation of the elements is not without difficulty: cf. Klopfenstein, *Die Lüge*, pp. 32-41; Boecker, *Redeformen*, pp. 34-41; G. Giesen, 'Semantische Vorfragen zur Würzel *šbʻ "schwören"*', in *Bausteine biblischer Theologie* (FS G.J. Botterweck; BBB, 50; Bonn, 1977), pp. 127-43; *idem*, *Die Wurzel šbʻ "Schwören": Eine semasiologische Studie zum Eid im Alten Testament* (BBB, 56; Bonn, 1981), pp. 118-32; B. Lang, 'Das Verbot des Meineids in Dekalog', *TüTQ* 161 (1981), pp. 97-105.

On the oath in general, cf. also J. Pedersen, *Der Eid bei den Semiten* (SGKIO, 3; Strasbourg, 1914), especially pp. 179-89; H.S. Gehman, 'The Oath in the Old Testament: Its Vocabulary, Idiom, and Syntax; Its Semantics and Theology in the Masoretic Text and the Septuagint', in *Grace upon Grace* (FS L.J. Kuyper; Grand Rapids, 1975), pp. 51-63.

1.4.4. *Witnesses: Many...False...* We have seen the gradually growing importance attached to the nature of testimony; in fact it is the traits (generally negative) of the witness that engage the interest of the various

To start with, it seems that there was no practice of confirming witnesses' testimony; under normal circumstances, that is, when the prosecutor could count on a number of witnesses in agreement, it seems that explicit reference to the world of the sacral was not considered necessary.

An (imprecatory) oath (roots *šb‘* and *'lh*), however, had decisive value in the spheres of jurisdiction and trials when—given the need to reach a verdict—there was insufficient proof to declare one disputant or the other in the right. If my interpretation of the data is correct, an oath was a supplementary factor of the same order as the rites, ordeals, lots and so on which generally go under the heading of 'the judgment of God' (cf. de Vaux, *Institutions*, I, pp. 241-43).

A typical case is narrated in Num. 5.11-31: it is explicitly affirmed here that the suspicions of a husband with regard to an adulterous wife are not supported by proof (vv. 12-13); in this case—with the aim of resolving an intolerable conflict within the family—recourse should be had to ordeal by bitter water, which lays down as its central element an imprecatory oath by the person under suspicion (v. 21: *w^{e}hišbîa‘ hakkōhēn 'et hā'iššâ biš^{e}bū‘at hā'ālâ*) (cf. J. Morgenstern, 'Trial by Ordeal among the Semites and in Ancient Israel', in *Hebrew Union College Jubilee Volume* [Cincinnati, 1925], pp. 111-43; see also n. 42).

Another situation that seems to arise more frequently concerns disputes over property. One of the norms of the Covenant Code reads: 'If a man hands over to his neighbour an ass or an ox or a sheep or any other beast, to keep, and it dies, or is hurt, or is driven away, *without anybody seeing it*, then shall an oath of the Lord be between them both (*š^{e}bū‘at yhwh tihyeh bên š^{e}nêhem*), that he has not stretched out his hand to his neighbour's goods. The owner of it shall accept this, and the other shall not make restitution' (Exod. 22.9-10). As can be seen, the juridical problem—in a variety of cases—is basically that of the undue appropriation of what belongs to another without the possibility of clear proof (cf. also Exod. 22.7-8).

This problem is also dealt with in Lev. 5.21-24 in the wider context of loans, pledges, theft, extortion and lost objects: the Leviticus norm says that in these cases an oath is laid down, which can unfortunately be false (therefore involving a further set of reparations); my concern is to emphasize the expression in 5.22: *w^{e}kiḥeš bāh w^{e}nišba‘ ‘al šāqer*, which shows how the oath allowed borrowers to insure themselves against possible claims by owners; this still left open the possibility of 'thefts' actually underwritten by an oath.

The link between (alleged) theft and (false) oath could also be proved by Lev. 19.11-12: reading the two verses together, we would have on the one hand the theft or fraud (*lō' tignōbû w^{e}lō' t^{e}kaḥ^{a}šû w^{e}lō' t^{e}šaqq^{e}rû 'îš ba‘^{a}mîtô*) and on the other hand the false oath (*w^{e}lō' tiššāb^{e}‘û bišmî laššāqer*). A similar interpretation could be given to the vision of Zech. 5.1-4, in which the scroll of the curse is addressed to the thief

biblical authors, because it is on them that the system of justice in Israel depended. I believe that two elements in particular are frequently mentioned in such a manner as to become revelatory of (or a substitute for) prosecution witness: multiplicity and falsity.

(v. 3: *haggōnēb*; v. 4: *haggannāb*) and to the perjurer (v. 3: *hannišbā'*; v. 4: *hannišbā' bišmî laššāqer*) (J. Scharbert, ''*ālâ*', *ThWAT*, I, p. 280).

The text of Lev. 5.1 is more generic: here it is said that someone may have been witness to the facts, hears swearing (*wešāmeʿâ qôl 'ālâ*), and does not say anything ([*'im*] *lô' yaggîd*). The terminological parallel with Prov. 29.24 seems to suggest that it is a question of property matters, for that text makes explicit reference to a thief: *ḥôlēq 'im gannāb śônē' napšô—'ālâ yišma' welō' yaggîd* (cf. n. 10; also M.J. Geller, 'The Šurpu Incantations and Lev. V 1-5', *JSS* 25 [1980], pp. 181-92).

The latter texts pose a different problem: it is not clear from the expressions used who is supposed to pronounce this oath; it might be imagined that the magistrate (the person whose role it is to settle a controversy) makes appeal by an oath to those present, asking indirectly that if any are informed about the events they should come forward (cf. Mt. 26.63); or that the accused should pronounce a self-imprecatory oath, which would have an exonerating effect (cf. S.H. Blank, 'An Effective Literary Device in Job XXXI', *JJS* 2 [1950–51], pp. 105-107; Jackson, *Theft in Early Jewish Law*, pp. 218-23; Milgrom, *Cult and Conscience*, pp. 84-103).

A juridical device that in some ways brings together the two aforementioned possibilities occurs in Deut. 21.1-9, which also allows us to see that the theme of sworn testimony is not limited to adultery and theft, but also applies to murder. This is the case: a murder victim is found *in open country*, the murderer is unknown (*lō' nôda' mî hikkāhû*); the elders who act as judges carry out a measurement of the surrounding towns in order to establish which is nearest to the corpse; this operation seems to have the purpose of identifying the accused alleged to have perpetrated the crime. It is interesting to observe that the elders and priests of that city (presumably in the name of all its inhabitants) then carry out a ritual which is accompanied by a solemn declaration of freedom from guilt: 'Our hands have not shed this blood and our eyes have not seen it shed. Lord, forgive your people Israel, whom you have redeemed, and do not allow innocent blood to be spilled amidst your people Israel' (vv. 7-8). Even though we do not have the actual vocabulary or formula of the oath, it has to be admitted that the expressions used have on the one hand the purpose of exculpating the city from the charge of murder, and on the other hand act as a motivation to any possible witnesses, so that a crime may not go unpunished in Israel.

We have still more texts that mention oath (or perjury) in generic contexts where it is not possible to decide with certainty what the juridical and judicial bearing of this act is (1 Kgs 8.31; Jer. 5.2; Mal. 3.5; Pss. 15.4; 24.4; Qoh. 9.2 etc.); since oaths are frequently also used in the case of promises, vows, pledges, covenants and the like, it is not methodologically correct to include all examples of oaths and perjury in the act of juridical and law court testimony.

a. *Multiplicity*. From the point of view of the accused, the prosecution witness is often seen as a massive and overwhelming multitude, against which one has nothing to hold out in self-defence.[63] The relevant Hebrew lexicon at this point contains the term *rabbîm*,[64] (cf. Exod. 23.2), an expression that seems particularly significant to me. For example:

Ps. 3.2-3 *yhwh mâ rabbû ṣārāy*
rabbîm qāmîm ʿālāy
rabbîm ʾōmᵉrîm lᵉnapšî ʾên yᵉšûʿātâ lô bēʾlōhîm

The relationship between a crowd of adversaries and the absence of help with respect to an (unjust) victim can be seen in Pss. 7.2-3; 22.12-13; 71.10-11; 142.7; Job 19.11-19.[65] The dramatic importance granted to a surrounding (*sbb*: Pss. 22.13, 17; 109.3; Job 16.13 etc.; *ktr* [*Pi*]: Ps. 22.13; [*Hi*] Hab. 1.4) mass of enemies who hurl themselves against an innocent is one of the leitmotifs of the so-called individual lamentation: cf., for example, Jer. 20.10; Pss. 25.19; 31.14; 56.3; 119.157; 129.1; Job 30.12; 35.9. The frequently established relationship may also be observed between the crowd of adversaries and their *strength* (cf. 2 Sam. 22.18; Pss. 18.18; 38.20; 40.13; 69.5; 142.7; Job 16.7-11; 23.6 etc.).

It may be observed, however, that in two texts false witness is clearly associated with the three crimes that form part of the list condemned by the Decalogue (murder, adultery, theft): in Hos. 4.2 (*ʾālōh wᵉkaḥēš wᵉrāṣōaḥ wᵉgānōb wᵉnāʾōp*; cf. also Ps. 59.13) and in Jer. 7.9 (*hᵃgānōb rāṣōaḥ wᵉnāʾōp wᵉhiššābēaʿ laššeqer*) the element of perjury occupies the place that in the Decalogue is assigned to bearing false witness against one's neighbour. From this it might seem that falsity in court may be alleged by the accuser (*ʿēd šeqer*) or sworn to by the accused (*hannišbāʿ laššeqer*), and it can also be understood how trial testimony can end up putting the seal on other crimes such as murder, adultery and theft.

63. Cf. O. Keel, *Feinde und Gottesleugner: Studien zum Image der Widersacher in Individualpsalmen* (SBM, 7; Stuttgart, 1969), pp. 206-209.

64. Cf. *THAT*, II, p. 730.

65. The relationship of opposition between a crowd of adversaries and an absence of defenders may be a confirmation of the attribution to the term *rabbîm* of the meaning of '*all*' (cf. J. Jeremias, '*polloi*', *TWNT*, VI, pp. 536-38; G. Braulik *Psalm 40 und der Gottesknecht* [ForBib, 18; Wurzburg, 1975], pp. 116-17). This probably gives a better understanding of the repeated mention of the isolation and loneliness of the supplicant in the lamentation psalms (cf. H. Seidel, *Das Erlebnis der Einsamkeit im Alten Testament: Eine Untersuchung zum Menschenbild des Alten Testaments* [TArb, 29; Berlin, 1969], esp. pp. 21-39).

b. *Falsehood.*[66] The opposition between truthful and false witness is the one with the strongest and most decisive influence on the course of a trial; the charge of falsehood by a prosecutor is the polar concept to which many terms referring to a law-court adversary are attracted (nouns, adjectives, adverbs; even verbs). This takes two interrelated forms.

First, we have the series that refers explicitly to the deceiver,[67] the calumniator, the author of conspiracies against the innocent:[68] it is

66. As well as the other works on this subject quoted, cf. Klopfenstein, *Die Lüge*, and Bühlmann, *Vom rechten Reden und Schweigen*; see also T.W. Overholt, *The Threat of Falsehood* (SBT, 2nd Ser., 16; London, 1970), pp. 86-91.

67. Cf. Keel, *Feinde und Gottesleugner*, pp. 132-54.

68. According to Bühlmann, different nuances of meaning can be distinguished in Proverbs for what is generically referred to as *die schlechte Rede*, to wit: lies, calumny, false witness, intrigue, flattery and slander (*Vom rechten Reden und Schweigen*, pp. 16-26). This classification might be useful as a framework for the vocabulary in the other books of Scripture too. I would, however, like to be allowed to offer a few considerations with respect to this that follow on from such a methodological assumption.

It may be imagined that there was widespread in Israel, as among all peoples, a habit of slander and calumny which—as experience suggests—resulted in quarrels, social rifts and sometimes consequences of unforeseen seriousness, such as suicide and violent death. It is equally natural to believe that various forms of cheating, intrigue and calculated lying occurred, these being frequent practices in business and a large part of political life. It would be naïve, therefore, to think that 'falsehood' should always be limited to the juridical or strictly law court context; the statements made in the course of my study and the passages quoted do not claim to be a reduction of this complex social phenomenon to a single category of interpretation.

It must be observed, however, that the Hebrew expressions—not only in Proverbs, but also in the Prophets and Psalms—often have a general axiomatic value, applicable to many fields and different life situations; there cannot therefore be excluded—indeed, there is implicitly contained in the sapiential aphorism—possible reference to practices concerning the sphere of the judiciary (cf. for example the use of *nirgān* in Prov. 16.27-30; 18.6-8; 26.20-22, where we find a terminology that elsewhere refers explicitly to false witness).

Furthermore, expressions that at first sight seem limited to one sphere can be transferred to another, producing a disconcerting but effective slant of meaning. If we take, for example, the term 'swindler' and make it the subject of actions typical of the false witness, we arrive at a particularly meaningful charge with an original message (cf. for example the role of *kîlay* in Isa. 32.5-7; or the use of *'îš bᵉliyya'al* or *'îš ḥāmās* in Proverbs and the Psalms; or again expressions like *'îš lāšôn* in Ps. 140.12 and *'îš śᵉpātayim* in Job 11.2).

semantically clear that here we are faced with the person who makes lies a preferred weapon, and achieves victory by (false) words. The second form is one in which, as a result of a charge of falsehood, the accuser is described in negative terms of a different kind (proud,[69] impious, violent, etc.); these terms might, at first sight, seem semantically independent, but I believe this can be given a coherent interpretation if linked to the concept of 'false': it is in fact because the accuser is not telling the truth that his or her nature as an unjust individual is revealed, with all that means in terms of pride, abuse of power and perversion.[70]

1.4.5. *The Witness as Adversary.* The witness I am talking about is basically someone who takes up a (juridical) position *against* someone. As a result of this essential characteristic, especially when the point of view is that of the accused, the accusatory witness ends up by assuming the role and title of *adversary*.[71]

Finally, I would like to note that the background of judicial procedure is the ultimate reason that makes clear the insistence on the seriousness of lying in relations between people: the fact is that a trial shows in practical terms how false words create the premise for an infamous punishment. That one speaks without thinking (cf. Prov. 26.18-19) is in no way a mitigation of the act; the juridical comparison shows—because of its formal structure—how folly can become extremely damaging to one's neighbour and the whole of society. In this sense it could be said that all human vices reach their fulfilment and give expression to their deadly force at the judicial stage.

69. Cf. Keel, *Feinde und Gottesleugner*, pp. 159-61. For the Hebrew terminology of pride, cf. also P. Humbert, 'Démesure et chute dans l'Ancien Testament', in *Maqqél shâqédh: Hommage à W. Vischer* (Montpellier, 1960), pp. 63-68.

70. I would like to point out the special importance to be attributed to the various Hebrew expressions marked by the terms *šeqer*, *ḥāmās*, *ḥinnām*, *mirmâ*. Context alone, however, can decide—sometimes only with approximation—what the specific nature of the individual and acts mentioned is (cf. L. Ruppert, *Der leidende Gerechte* [ForBib, 5; Würzburg, 1972], pp. 30-33, who also singles out the term *rêqām* in Ps. 7.5).

71. The terminology and concept of 'adversary' are not to be identified with those of the accuser (cf. the examples given by A.F. Puukko, 'Der Feind in den alttestamentlichen Psalmen', *OTS* 8 [1950], pp. 47-65); it can however be maintained—as Puukko himself suggests (p. 47)—that conflict has a juridical root in the claim by both parties to be in the right; it may be added that this claim takes on a higher (and more dangerous) form when it can be taken to a court of appeal, aware as it then must be of the risk of denial and sentence. The most formidable adversaries are those who are so sure of their rights and success that they will go to court in order to set in

As regards the Hebrew vocabulary corresponding to this section, I would like to refer to section 1.5.1. below, under the *Accuser as Enemy*.

1.4.6. *The Guilty or Wicked Witness.*[72] Finally, the accused—who feels and claims to be innocent (*ṣaddîq*) at least relative to the accusation of which he or she is the victim—identifies the prosecution witness with the *rāšā'* (cf. Prov. 19.28). This identification may also be made by an impartial judge, who with a just sentence can condemn (*hršy'*, that is, declare *rāšā'*) the *accuser*, at the same time declaring the accused innocent (*hṣdyq*, thereby declaring the accused a *ṣaddîq*). See for example Pss. 58.4; 140.5, 9; Job 27.7.

This series of substitutions makes it difficult to mark off the semantic field of testimony strictly: in fact the readers are often in the position of not being able to decide whether they are dealing with a legal situation or not. I therefore think it necessary to make two observations of a general nature to situate what has been developed up to now in the context of an overall interpretation of biblical texts, in the quest for a coherent vision of the data being studied.

The first of my observations concerns the juridical and social system of Israel. Many of the situations involved in the Psalms and the poetic texts of the Bible in general present an innocent (sometimes a group of them) struggling with evildoers. I think that the desire is frequently to put forward a symbolic situation, a sort of model allowing the application of an interpretation to actual events with their own aspect; a precise context, a historical fact and a typical situation are as it were summed up in the language of a stereotype that repeats terms with a generic value, so that a single text can become a hermeneutic key for an almost indefinite series of events.

The interpretation of the relationship between the innocent and the evildoer therefore has an enormous range of applications, and it would seem a methodological (and historical) lessening to see a description of

motion an unstoppable procedure of which they themselves could in theory be the victim. As can be seen, the similarities with an outbreak of war or a duel are particularly obvious. On this subject, cf. H. Birkeland, *The Evildoers in the Book of Psalms* (Oslo, 1955); G.W. Anderson, 'Enemies and Evildoers in the Book of Psalms', *BJRL* 48 (1965–66), pp. 18-29; Keel, *Feinde und Gottesleugner*; N.A. van Uchelen, '*'nšy dmym* in the Psalms', *OTS* 15 (1969), pp. 205-12.

72. Cf. Keel, *Feinde und Gottesleugner*, pp. 109-31.

the trial relationship (between prosecutor and accused) in the biblical texts taken as a whole.

It has to be observed, however, that the evildoer's 'attack' on the just, the continual violence displayed against the innocent, and the constant threat that the unjust will prevail, could not have such structural importance if they were not cloaked or better backed up by a sort of legal system in which they find their 'ultimate' manifestation. The fact that there is so great an insistence on the concept of lying (linked to the terminology of violence) seems to point not to a situation of widespread banditry, but to the exercise of perversion clothed in the characteristics of the good; this leads us to the sphere of state legislation and its everyday interpretation by jurisdictional bodies. Again, there is no good reason why innocent persons, struggling with 'numberless powerful enemies', should have to direct anguished prayers to God if a normal court of law could ensure them the restitution of their rights; this becomes explicable only if it is implied that it is precisely in the trial system set up by people that the just person turns into the object of unjustified violence.[73] Susannah's prayer to God at the time of her condemnation to death (Dan. 13.42-43) may be taken as symbolic of the 'life situation' from which the lamentations of the 'just' spring.

I think, therefore, that it is by means of the legal system, including the actual trial side of it (that is, through sentences regularly handed down by a legitimate court of law) that the evildoer brings to completion the injustice committed against the innocent: not only does the evildoer steal, commit adultery, kill and so on, but, making use of complicity, lies and corruption, also gains a victory over any possible complainant: one can even heap scorn upon the adversary, being so sure of coming out of the judgment 'just'. Of course, it is not always possible to prove the relevance of this interpretation of mine in the individual texts taken singly, but it seems to me to confer greater coherence overall on the biblical texts to which I am referring.

The second consideration I mentioned turns upon a strictly literary fact. In the course of my previous argument I extracted from their context a number of expressions that, following semantic analysis and the logic of concepts, might turn out to be paradigmatic substitutions for the term 'accusatory witness' (*'ēd bᵉ*). It could be objected that this

73. Cf. H. Schmidt, *Das Gebet der Angeklagten im Alten Testament* (BZAW, 49; Giessen, 1928).

procedure of mine, although reasonable, in no way corresponds to the actual Bible texts.

Obviously, the limits of this work do not allow a demonstration of the relevance of every single text, nor the multiplication of the examples in which the relationship between the term *'ēd* and its paradigmatic substitutions appear.[74] I shall therefore limit myself to presenting a single unit of text, Psalm 35, in which the reader will easily recognize the appearance of the aforementioned terminology.

In this Psalm, the unjustly accused speaker turns in prayer to God for his defence. It has to be accepted that the 'adversaries' are the same throughout the prayer; so, putting the different expressions that describe them into paradigms, we can fix the variety and extension of the terminology used, along the exact lines of what I have tried to suggest previously:

v. 1	*y^{e}rîbay*
	lōh^{a}māy
v. 3	*rōd^{e}pāy*
v. 4	*m^{e}baqšê napšî*
	ḥōš^{e}bê rā'ātî
v. 10	(*ḥāzāq mimmennû*)
	(*gōz^{e}lô*)
v. 11	*'ēdê ḥāmās*
v. 15	*nēkîm*[75]
v. 17	*k^{e}pîrîm*
v. 19	*'ōy^{e}bay šeqer*
	śōn^{e}'ay ḥinnām
v. 26	*ś^{e}mēḥê rā'ātî*
	hammagdîlîm 'ālāy[76]

74. I refer the reader to Klopfenstein, *Die Lüge*, pp. 41-81, where the various synonymous terms in the lexicon of lying are pointed out for the Psalms.

75. As the Commentaries and the Dictionaries show, the term *nēkîm* in Ps. 35.15 (and the whole of v. 16a) has posed problems for ancient and modern translators. Many exegetes propose a correction to *nokrîm* (cf. H.-J. Kraus, *Psalmen* [BK, 15/I; 4th edn, 1972] p. 275).

76. The list given here may be integrated by the references that have been made to the *parts of the body*: eye (v. 19: *yiqr^{e}ṣû 'āyin*; v. 21: *rā'^{a}tâ 'ênênû*), mouth (v. 21: *wayyarḥîbû 'ālay pîhem*), heart (v. 25: *'al yō'm^{e}rû b^{e}libbām*). Verse 20 might also be mentioned: *lō' šālôm y^{e}dabbērû...dibrê mirmôt yaḥ^{a}šōbûn* (cf. G. Ravasi, *Il libro dei Salmi: Commento e attualizzazione*, I [Bologna, 1981], pp. 636-37).

With respect to the typical schemes that I have given before, this Psalm offers variations in an almost endless play of transformations. When we read a text in which the element of passion, a heartfelt denunciation or other emotional feelings are the creative well from which a piece of literature flows, it is normal not to expect the formal and technical language of the jurist, but the inventive personal outpouring proper to the 'poetic' genre.

In this very Psalm, moreover, we see the appearance of a new phenomenon with respect to what has been said previously: not only do we have synonymous paradigmatic substitutions (with the complementary effects of metonomy and synedochy), but the *metaphorical* variations also take on special value. In v. 1, in fact, the witnesses are called *lōḥ^{a}māy*; and in vv. 2-3 the warrior image is continued by attributing to God the role of an armed soldier. Later, in v. 17, the same witnesses are called *k^{e}pîrîm*: the image of a wild beast is preceded by mention of the 'grinding of teeth', and is probably to be taken with the 'swallowing' (*bl'*) linked to the wide-open throat (*napšēnû*) (v. 25). I would like to mention finally that in vv. 7-8 the witnesses are compared to hunters who dig a trap and spread a net to catch the speaker, this being a frequently used symbol for the deceiving side of the accusers' activity.

These latter observations allow me to introduce some thoughts on the main metaphorical transformations by which prosecution testimony (and more generally, the juridical controversy situation) is expressed.

1.5. *Metaphors for the Prosecution Witness*[77]

The aggressive side of an accusation, contained basically in the seme 'against' (*b^{e}* or *'al*), is often structured—especially in poetic texts—by

77. With reference to the 'enemies in the individual Psalms', G. Castellino writes, 'What value is to be given and what judgment passed on the language that the psalmist uses to describe evil, and what is the nature of what torments him or the adversaries who lay snares for him?...I draw the inescapable conclusion: The ease with which he passes from words to do with war (and) hunting to metaphors to do with wild and savage beasts—dogs, lions, bulls—proves that this language is altogether metaphorical and none of these expressions is to be understood literally. It is not possible to derive from them the precise identity of the enemies and the nature of their hostile activity' (*Libro dei Salmi* [Turin, 1955], p. 259). I agree about the metaphorical interpretation, but disagree that it is not possible to deduce anything about the form of the Psalmist's enemies' hostile activity: if this takes the form of *speech*, we may reasonably conclude that it takes the form of an accusation, whatever the procedure by which it is brought and followed through.

metaphorical language drawn from two precise semantic fields: that of *war* and that of *hunting*. This recourse to metaphor should not be a cause for surprise for anyone who has any familiarity with the world of literature; nobody should be amazed, therefore, that I believe it relevant to the meaning of juridical relationships and those in a trial. What matters is to understand the meaning of the various images, so as not to misunderstand the strictly juridical underlying experience.[78]

a. *The Trial as War*. A trial is not really a battle, nor is an outbreak of war a trial, yet these two events, though separate, have mutual echoes.

A trial *resembles* a battle, to the extent that it is a confrontation of two parties armed with arguments, proofs and convincing words, who run the risk of defeat, which is an embarrassing and sometimes fatal setback.[79]

78. My stance on interpretation differs from that of Gemser ('The *rîb-* or Controversy-Pattern', p. 128). Speaking of the many Psalms in which the *rîb-pattern* is found, he states, 'To interpret this class of Psalms as representing a real lawsuit and trial before a temple tribunal with decision by ordeal looks like a hermeneutic "transsubstantiation" or substantializing of metaphor into reality. Undoubtedly the phraseology is often thoroughly judicial, but with this metaphor other comparisons vary' (and in a footnote he points to the images of battle, cattle-fairs, hunting, sieges, etc.).

I do not believe in the existence of a temple tribunal before which decisions by ordeal were regularly made (except for the cases attested by Scripture, which are marked by the need to proceed without sufficient evidential proof); I would rather say that the speakers in those Psalms are directed to *God's* tribunal, which is invisible, but real by faith to the person praying. Of course, all talk about God can be no more than a 'representation', but this metaphor is coherent with the juridical reality experienced by the speaker (cf. Daniel 13); a completely different level of metaphor in fact has to be assigned to images depicting the believer struggling with fierce dogs, lions or enemy armies.

79. In this context, it may be enlightening to quote the description of a debate by an expert in criminal procedure: 'Col dibattimento il processo raggiunge la sua fase più viva e spesso più altamente drammatica. Come si evince dalla stessa espressione lessicale (la parola *dibattimento* richiama quella di *combattimento*) è in questa fase che le parti impegnano tutte le forze e sfoderano tutte le proprie armi per il trionfo delle rispettive tesi nel duello giudiziale: ed è per questo che soprattutto in questa fase si avverte l'esigenza del rispetto del principio del *contradditorio*, fondato sull'eguaglianza di posizioni (la cosiddetta *eguaglianza delle armi*) delle parti contrapposte (Pisapia, *Compendio di procedura penale*, p. 352). Cf. also Seeligmann, 'Zur Terminologie', pp. 255-56.

On the other hand—as I have already noted[80]—confrontation in battle or a duel between individuals are not events alien to a juridical consideration.[81] On the contrary, war is always motivated by reasons claimed to be just, and has as its aim the restoration of rights: the outcome of the clash decides which of the two is 'in the right' and which is 'in the wrong'. Since military victory is considered to be the triumph of right over injustice, it is normal to expect—in ancient times as in modern—that victory on the battlefield should be followed by a trial to which the defeated culprits are subjected.

b. *The Trial as a Hunt*. If hunting may be defined as the chasing of wild animals in order to catch them alive or dead,[82] and if this activity involves the exercise of strength and above all of cunning, we can understand why it is often used as the great metaphor for relationships in a trial between the prosecutor and the accused, especially in the case of a 'debate' where a treacherous, dishonest and cruel adversary is involved.[83]

80. Cf. especially Chapter 1 section 3.1.3.

81. Cf. F.C. Fensham, 'The Battle between the Men of Joab and Abner as a Possible Ordeal by Battle?', *VT* 20 (1970), pp. 356-57; *idem*, 'Ordeal by Battle in the Ancient Near East and the Old Testament', in *Studi in onore di E. Volterra*, VI (Milan, 1971), pp. 127-35; L. Alonso Schökel, 'Salvación y liberación. Apuntes de Soteriología del Antiguo Testamento', *CuadBíb* 5 (1980), pp. 112-20; *idem*, *Treinta Salmos*, pp. 426-29, 435-36. Cf. also G. Furlani, 'La sentenza di dio nella religione babilonese e assira', in *Atti della Accademia Nazionale dei Lincei* (Memorie, Classe di Scienze morali, storiche e filologiche; Serie VIII, vol. II, fasc. 5; Rome, 1950), especially pp. 263-64; *idem*, 'Le guerre quali giudizi di dio presso i Babilonesi e gli Assiri', in *Miscellanea G. Galbiati* (Fontes Ambrosianae, 27; Milan, 1951), pp. 39-47.

82. F. Palazzi, *Novissimo Dizionario della Lingua italiana* (1978), p. 223.

83. Particularly interesting is the language drawn from wild beasts when it is applied to those who have authority in Israel. The 'chief men', as is well-known, receive the title of *shepherds (rō'îm)* to the extent that they are appointed to provide for the people's needs, since they, like a flock (*ṣō'n*), have to be led to pasture and protected from the perils of predators (cf. 1 Sam. 17.34-36; 2 Sam. 24.17; Amos 3.12; Pss. 77.21; 78.70-72 etc.). Now when the chief men are called wild beasts, it means that they have lost their human face, because they treat people (especially the weak) as simple prey on which to glut themselves; instead of being 'judges', defenders of rights under threat, they become 'adversaries', accusers and condemners of the people of whom they should take care (cf. Ezek. 34.1-10). I would like to quote as an

A hunt may be carried out by one animal against another,[84] or by a human being against an animal; in the former case the 'hunter' is usually a wild beast, a fierce and bloodthirsty predator that tracks an animal, whose only possibility of escape lies in flight; in the latter case, the 'hunter' is generally a crafty man, who exploits his abilities to detect his selected victims' weak points, through which he makes them fall into a trap, surprising them with an ambush and so getting the better of them.[85]

This is a very brief and laconic description of an experience common to everybody, but especially familiar in the ancient world; these brief notes do however allow us to understand how an accusatory charge (culminating in a trial) could be translated by its victim (or by someone who shares the victim's feelings) into terms taken from the semantic field of hunting, such as being trailed, nosed out, attacked by surprise and at one's weak points and, the prey killed, the spoils being able to be divided out in an atmosphere of triumph and happiness.

example a very significant passage: 'Within it (Jerusalem) its princes are like a roaring *lion* that tears to pieces its prey; they devour the people and take possession of their treasures and wealth. They increase the number of widows among them...The chief men within it are like *wolves* that gnaw their prey; they shed blood and let the people perish for sordid gain...The lords commit violence and devote themselves to plunder; they tread down the poor and the needy, and mistreat the stranger, against every law' (Ezek. 22.25, 27, 29). Cf. also Isa. 56.9-11; Zeph. 3.3 (K. Elliger, 'Das Ende der "Abendwölfe" Zeph. 3.3 Hab. 1.8', in *Festschrift A. Bertholet* [Tübingen, 1950], pp. 158-75); Ps. 58.4.7; Prov. 28.15 etc.

In the oracle of Ezekiel directed against the chiefs of Jerusalem there could also be a double irony if it is remembered that the lion is the symbol of Judah, and the wolf of Benjamin (cf. Gen. 49.9-10, 27): the two tribes were joined in the one southern kingdom which had its capital at Jerusalem no less (on the relationship between the tribes and totemic animals, cf. *IDB*, IV, pp. 674-75).

84. A wild beast goes in pursuit of other animals, but a human may also be its victim (1 Kgs 13.24; 2 Kgs 17.25; Amos 5.19; Prov. 22.13 etc.), especially when one ventures into territory which is the domain of 'wild beasts'. The antagonism between human and animal (with a resultant destruction of life, the theme of spilled 'blood', cf. Gen. 9.4-6) becomes a metaphor for the world of violence; the eschatological kingdom of peace sees by opposition a reconciliation between humanity and the savage beasts (cf. Isa. 11.6-7; 65.25) in the wider context of a reconciliation between the weak and the strong (wolf–lamb, lion–ox, etc.).

85. C. Westermann emphasizes the aspect of a hidden, invisible threat (*Vergleiche und Gleichnisse im Alten Testament und Neuen Testament* [CalwTMon, 14; Stuttgart, 1984], p. 84).

It should also be noted that hunting is used elsewhere as a metaphor for war (Num. 23.24; Isa. 5.29; 31.4; Jer. 2.30; 4.7; 5.6; 50.17; Ezek. 19.1-9; Joel 1.6; Nah. 2.12-14; Hab. 1.6-10). If the point of view of the party that finds itself in a state of inferiority (as regards numbers, weapons, military experience) is taken into account, the enemy can only seem an irresistible animal force which, with derisory ease, smashes, tears and devours its victim.

From the observations just made, it appears that there are three interchangeable 'life situations', to which correspond three semantic fields (each with its own terminology): a trial is described as *like* a war, which in its turn may be presented as *like* a hunting expedition. Poetic language passes from one level to another, mixing and overlaying terms and images.

'Juridical' vocabulary occupies a place—with respect to the other two—on a level that we could call conceptual: it reveals the meaning underlying events by using categories that express their relationship to truth, law, good, humanity and history. But although we recognize and accept this general metaphor-making phenomenon, we must go on to recognize that a lexicon which is not technically juridical can express relationships of a highly juridical nature.

In particular, we are persuaded to enrich the paradigm of the accuser-witness with the terminology of (a) the enemy and (b) the beast of prey.

1.5.1. *The Accuser as Enemy*. The terminology used to describe a legal adversary is the same as that used for an enemy in war.[86]

In the majority of cases, *'ôyēb*[87] refers to a political or military enemy (Num. 10.19; 14.42; Deut. 1.42; 1 Sam. 4.3; 2 Sam. 3.18; 2 Kgs 17.39; Ezek. 8.22, 31 etc.), but in certain texts it clearly refers to the adversary in a controversy (Job 13.24; 27.7; 33.10 etc.) and in an actual trial (Pss. 27.6; 35.19 etc.). A similar thing is true of its synonyms such as *ṣar*, *ṣōrēr*, *šôrēr*, and the participles of the verbs *śn'*, *qwm* (*Qal* and *Hitpolel*), *rdp*, *bqš* (*Pi*) etc.[88]

86. Cf. L. Ruppert, *Der leidende Gerechte und seine Feinde: Eine Wortfelduntersuchung* (Würzburg, 1973), pp. 156-64.

87. Cf. Ruppert, *Der leidende Gerechte*, pp. 7-13; E. Jenni, '*'ōjēb* Feinde', *THAT*, I, pp. 118-22; H. Ringgren, '*'āyab*', *ThWAT*, I, pp. 228-35.

88. I would like to refer the reader to the lists of 'enemies of the individual' given by different commentators on the Psalms: H. Gunkel and J. Begrich, *Einleitung in die Psalmen* (Göttingen, 2nd edn, 1966), pp. 196-98; G. Castellino, *Libro dei Salmi*

The noun *śāṭān*,[89] as well as its use in a military context (Num. 22.22, 32; 1 Sam. 29.4; 1 Kgs 5.18; 11.14, 23, 25; 1 Chron. 21.1), is significant in the legal field (2 Sam. 19.23; Ps. 109.6; Zech. 3.1-2; Job 1.6-9, 12; 2.1-4, 6-7). The participle *śōṭēn* is only used in a juridical sense (Pss. 71.13; 109.20, 29), as are the other forms of the verb *śṭn* (Pss. 38.21; 109.4). The noun *śiṭnâ* in Ezra 4.6 (K) means a (written) accusation.[90]

As an example of the use of the terminology of a wartime and legal enemy in the same literary unit, we might take Ps. 27.2: *mᵉrē'îm—ṣāray wᵉ'ōyᵉbay*; v. 3: (*maḥᵃneh—milḥāmâ*); v. 6: *'ōyᵉbay sᵉbîbôtay*; vv. 11-12: *šôrᵉrāy—'ēdê šeqer wîpēaḥ ḥāmās*; and Ps. 120, in which we find vv. 2-3: *śᵉpat šeqer—lāšôn rᵉmiyyâ*; v. 6: *śônē' šālôm*; v. 7. *milḥāmâ*.

1.5.2. *The Accuser as 'Hunter'*.[91] Although many texts describe the activities of a legal adversary in terms of a hunter, we do not find the actual Hebrew noun, unless the participle of the verb *rdp* is considered the most relevant equivalent.

On the other hand, the presentation of a 'relentless' enemy in the guise of a fierce animal is very frequent;[92] consideration will therefore be

(Turin, 1955), pp. 260-61; H.-J. Kraus, *Psalmen* (BK, 15/I), pp. 40-43. The most detailed study of the semantic field of the 'enemy' is the one by Ruppert (*Der leidende Gerechte*), pp. 13-109.

Of particular interest are the compound expressions such as *'ōyᵉbay šeqer* (Pss. 35.19; 69.5), *śōnᵉ'ay šāqer* (Ps. 38.20), *śōnᵉ'ay ḥinnām* (Ps. 69.5; Lam. 3.52), etc.

89. Cf. G. Fohrer, *Das Buch Hiob* (KAT, 16; Gütersloh, 1963), pp. 82-83; G. Wanke, '*śāṭān* Widersacher', *THAT*, II, pp. 821-23.

90. In Israel an accusation generally took a verbal form, but in Ezra 4.6 and Job 31.35 mention is made of an accusation sent in writing. I think, however, that given a written accusation, a judge could not normally hand down sentence without inviting some sort of debate. Gemser ('The *rîb*- or Controversy-Pattern', p. 123) also quotes Isa. 65.6a; Dan. 7.10 (and, as probable, Ps. 149.9a) as proof of the existence at a court of judgment of registers [archives] ready to document important deeds and misdeeds (in this context, mention might also be made of Est. 6.1-3). Boecker (*Redeformen*, p. 14), with reference to Job 31.35, holds that this text has been influenced by the Egyptian tradition, in which the procedure for the announcement of a trial laid down the deposition of a written accusation.

91. Cf. O. Keel, *Die Welt der altorientalischen Bildsymbolik und das Alte Testament* (Zürich, 1972), pp. 75-84; Ruppert, *Der leidende Gerechte*, pp. 150-56, 166-71.

92. God too is often represented metaphorically in the guise of a fierce animal (especially a lion): cf. J. Hempel, 'Jahwegleichnisse der israelitischen Propheten',

given and examination made in context of the terminology that represents an adversary in the guise of a wild beast. Among the biblical passages which seem particularly relevant to me are: Isa. 38.13-14; Jer. 5.6; Hos. 13.7-8; Hab. 1.8; Pss. 7.3; 10.9; 17.12; 22.13, 14, 17, 21, 22; 35.17; 57.5; 58.5, 7; 59.7, 15; Job 4.10-11; 10.16-17; 29.17.

1.5.3. *The Coherence of the Images.* If the accuser is presented metaphorically as a warlike enemy, a fierce animal and a hunter, it is logical to expect that the accuser's actions should be described in a way coherent with the image chosen: each of the elements in the syntagm will therefore undergo a degree of transformation with respect to the technical term proper to legal language. It is impossible at this point to give even a summary of the endless wealth of variations that occur in the syntagmatic development of the various metaphors; I would just like to be allowed to make an outline note of some characteristic traits that the reader of the Bible will not fail to find relevant.

If a debate is imagined as a fight, then instead of (or alongside) the speech of accusation we will have the unsheathing of weapons.[93] A typical example is Prov. 25.18: *mēpîṣ wᵉḥereb wᵉḥēṣ šānûn—'îš 'ōneh bᵉrē'ēhû 'ēd šāqer* (cf. Isa. 54.17; 59.15-20; Jer. 9.2; Pss. 11.2; 37.14-15; 64.4; Job 5.15; 30.12-15; Prov. 30.14 etc.).[94]

The terminology expressing the adversary's strength (arm, hand, force, etc.) is matched by the accused's recourse to words that mean defence of a military kind (fortified city, rock, hiding-place, etc.).[95]

If the semantic field used is that of hunting, the activities of the accuser will take the form of an ambush,[96] and the vocabulary of nets,

ZAW 42 (1924), pp. 74-104; Westermann, *Vergleiche und Gleichnisse*, p. 81.

93. For everything concerning the world of warfare, see Y. Yadin, *The Art of Warfare in Biblical Lands, in the Light of Archaeological Study* (2 vols.; New York, 1963).

94. Cf. J.A. Emerton, 'The Translation of Psalm LXIV 4', *JTS* 27 (1976), pp. 391-92; B. Couroyer, 'El vocabulario del Tiro al Arco en el Antiguo Testamento', in *Servidor de la Palabra: Miscelanea Biblica en honor del P.A. Colunga* (Salamanca, 1979), pp. 111-26.

95. Cf. Westermann, *Vergleiche und Gleichnisse*, pp. 87-89. The opinion that reduces everything to the institution of the asylum city seems one-sided to me (L. Delekat, *Asylie und Schutzorakel am Zionheiligtum: Eine Untersuchung zu den privaten Feindpsalmen* [Leiden, 1967]).

96. To borrow a phrase from J. Ortega y Gasset, hunting is a 'persecución razonada', to the extent that it brings into play every trick in the book in order to achieve

traps, pits and so on will take the place of verbal testimony (Pss. 7.16; 9.16; 10.9; 35.8; 140.6 etc.). Instead of the accuser's mouth, we see the open jaws of wild beasts, their sharp teeth; instead of speech, there will be a lion's roar (Pss. 3.8; 22.14; 27.2, 12; 35.16; 37.12 etc.), and so on.

Lastly, it should be noted that the result of the action intended or pursued by the 'enemy' will take on a colouring proportionate to the metaphor being used; therefore, instead of the terms sentence, punishment and execution, which are proper to the juridical sphere, we will find the terminology of military defeat (retreat, fall, bite the dust, strike; dishonour, rout, and the like: Pss. 7.6; 10.15; 27.2; 35.4, 26; 37.15 etc.) and capture (prey, devouring, tearing, swallowing, etc.: Pss. 7.3; 9.16; 17.12; 38.8 etc.).

Although in the briefest of fashions I have opened up a perspective from which to read many biblical texts, I have digressed from an examination of the technical lexicon of the legal debate. I do not consider this a secondary parenthesis, but I think it useful now to return to a precise study of the syntagm of the prosecution witness; after concluding my study of the element 'witnesses', I would like to deal similarly—though at less length—with the elements that make up the juridical *activity* of the accuser.

1.6. *The Paradigm of an Accusatory Action*

I would like to bring together the actions typical of an accuser and the lexicon that describes them under two headings: (1) the juridical initiative undertaken by the witness; and (2) the words with which this initiative is fulfilled in a law court.

As a conclusion to this section dealing with testimony, I would like to offer some considerations on the juridical relevance of the actual 'bringing' of the accusation.

1.6.1. *The Accuser's Juridical Initiative*. This is frequently expressed by the verb *qwm*, whether we find a witness as the subject (*'ēd*) (*qwm* b^e: Deut. 19.15, 16; Ps. 27.12; Job 16.8; *qwm*: Ps. 35.11; Zeph. 3.8 [*corr.*])

success (*La caza y los toros* [Madrid, 1968], p. 101). An *ambush* is one of the favourite forms of exercise of far-sighted reasoning during a hunt; as a result it becomes a metaphor for *premeditated* murder (Exod. 21.13; Deut. 19.11 etc.); the verb *'rb* is characteristic in this context (Mic. 7.2; Ps. 10.8, 9; Prov. 1.11, 18; 12.6). On this subject, cf. B.S. Jackson, *Essays in Jewish and Comparative Legal History*, pp. 91ff.

or whether we find another equivalent term (Isa. 54.17: *kol lāšôn* + *qwm 'et*; Mic. 7.6: *bat* + *qwm bᵉ*; Ps. 1.5:[97] *rᵉšā'îm* + *qwm bammišpāṭ*; Job 30.12: *pirḥaḥ* + *qwm 'al yāmîn* etc.).

The verb *qwm* may be considered typical of a speech at a trial, as I pointed out in the previous chapter;[98] it is obvious however that it has a range of overtones and applications which go well beyond the legal semantic field. Moreover, I have already noted that other verbs of motion fulfil a similar function; I would like to note at this point that in poetic texts, when the great metaphors of war and hunting appear, the terminology of organized *aggression* acts as a natural paradigmatic substitute for the verb *qwm*. In Psalm 27, for example, the following may be considered parallel expressions: vv. 2: ***biqrōb 'ālay*** *mᵉrē'îm*; 3: *'im* ***tāḥᵃneh 'ālay*** *maḥᵃneh...'im* ***tāqûm 'ālay*** *milḥāmâ*; 6: *'ōyᵉbay sᵉbîbôtay;* 12: ***qāmû bî*** *'ēdê šeqer*.

1.6.2. *The Accusatory Speech*. The verbs that are a technical expression of the act of accusation are *'nh* and *ngd* (*Hi*).[99]

The verb *'nh* generally refers to testimony with juridical value (cf. Deut. 21.7; 25.9; Exod. 23.2: *'nh 'al rib*);[100] the syntagm *'nh bᵉ* refers more specifically to the accuser (with the subject *'ēd*: Exod. 20.16; Num. 35.30; Deut. 5.20; 19.16, 18; Job 16.8;[101] Prov. 25.18; with

97. L. Koehler, 'Archäologisches Nr. 15', *ZAW* 36 (1916), pp. 27-28; S.M. Paul, 'Unrecognized Biblical Legal Idioms in the Light of Comparative Accadian Expressions', *RB* 86 (1979), pp. 236-37.

98. Cf. Chapter 6 section 2.3.2.

99. I attribute a technical value to the verbs *'nh* and *ngd* (*Hi*) not only because they repeatedly take the term *'ēd* as their subject, but also because they appear in texts of a legal nature, where the language tends to be stricter. On these verbs, cf. also Chapter 2 section 2.2.

100. The construction *'nh 'al* is used with a personal object in 2 Sam. 19.43, where it refers to a reply against someone that has the value of an accusation.

In the text of Exod. 23.2, the expression *'nh 'al rib* clearly seems to mean 'to make deposition in a trial'; J.M. McKay, following the LXX translation, holds that in place of *rib* the vocalization should be *rōb*; this brings us to the translation, 'you shall not answer against the crowd', which, taken together with the first part of the verse, would end by defining the independence of a witness against the majority opinion ('Exodus XXIII 1-3, 6-8: A Decalogue for the Administration of Justice in the City Gate', *VT* 21 [1971], p. 315).

101. In Job 16.8 (*lᵉ'ēd hāyâ wayyāqom bî kaḥᵃšî bᵉpānay yaᵃneh*) the relationship clearly appears between the testimony (*'ēd*) and the accusation (*bᵉpānay yaᵃneh*), even if the grammatical subject of the verb *'nh* is held to be the term *kaḥᵃšî*. The latter

equivalent terms: 2 Sam. 1.16 [*pîkā*]; Job 15.6 [*śᵉpāteykā*] etc.).

The verb *ngd* (*Hi*)[102] is generally linked to the 'notitia criminis': even nowadays, the 'informer' is one of the means which a judiciary body uses during its investigations. Sometimes, *ngd* (*Hi*) refers to testimony on someone's behalf (Ps. 50.6; Job 33.23); most of the time, however, it means the complaint or charge brought against someone (with subject *'ēd*: Lev. 5.1; cf. also Prov. 12.17; with other subjects: 1 Sam. 14.33; 22.22; 27.11; Isa. 3.9, in parallel with *'nh bᵉ*; Jer. 20.10; Prov. 29.24; Est. 3.4).[103]

The verb *'wd* (*Hi*),[104] usually used with the preposition *bᵉ*, means to testify solemnly against someone. In the majority of cases this testimony precedes the crime, and so is not properly an accusation, nor, so to speak, a conditional anticipation of it (cf. Gen. 43.3; Exod. 19.21, 23; Deut. 4.26; 8.19; 30.19; 31.28; 32.46 etc.). In a few cases, however, it clearly has the meaning of 'to bear witness' in the context of juridical

is interpreted as 'my thinness/illness' (cf. Ps. 109.24) by many modern commentators (F. Delitzsch, S.R. Driver and G.B. Gray, R. Gordis, G. Fohrer, F. Horst, M.H. Pope, L. Alonso Schökel); the ancient translations on the other hand refer to the root *kḥš* = to lie, and therefore translate with 'my lie' (LXX, Syriac, Targum) or 'my calumniator' (Vulgate); this line is also followed by D. Dhorme, *Le livre de Job* (Etudes Bibliques; Paris, 1926), pp. 211-12 ('mon calomniateur', with reference to Isa. 30.9), and N.H. Tur-Sinai, *The Book of Job* (Jerusalem, 1967), p. 265 ('my lying'): this author also advances the hypothesis that a scribe has corrected the original *kaḥᵃšô* ('his false accusation') for reasons of reverence towards God (cf. also J. Vella, 'Il Redentore di Giobbe [Nota a *Giob* 16.20]', *RivB* 13 [1965], p. 165). Given the frequent semantic relationship between testimony and lying, I believe that the most acceptable translation is that of A. Vaccari, *La Sacra Bibbia*, IV, 1 (Florence, 1958), p. 47:

> Si è fatto testimone e si è levato contro di me
> il mio calunniatore, che in faccia mi accusa.

102. Cf. Seeligmann, 'Zur Terminologie', pp. 261-62: 'Das Verbum *hgyd* nimmt in sehr verschiedenen Quellen und Schichten die technische Bedeutung "beim Gericht anzeigen" an' (p. 261).

103. I ought also to point out the verb *glh*, which occupies a place in the semantic sphere of *ngd* (*Hi*): in the *Qal*, and in the form *glh 'et 'ōzen*, it can express a charge (1 Sam. 22.8, 17); in the *Piel* we have a similar meaning in Isa. 16.3; 26.21; Jer. 49.10; Job 20.27; Lam. 2.14; 4.22 (cf. also in the *Niphal*, Isa. 22.14; Ezek. 21.29; Hos. 7.1; Prov. 26.26).

104. Cf. *THAT*, II, pp. 216-17 (C. van Leeuwen); *ThWAT*, V, pp. 1107-28 (H. Simian-Yofre); Seeligmann, 'Zur Terminologie', pp. 265-66.

proceedings (on *behalf* of: Job 29.11 [with direct object]; *against*: Amos 3.13;[105] Mal. 2.14 [*bên...ûbên*]; Pss. 50.7 [*b*ᵉ],[106] 81.9). Only in 1 Kgs 21.10, 13 is the verb *'wd* (*Hi*) used (absolutely or with the preposition *'et*) to mean testimony in a clearly trial situation. Finally, I would like to note that this verb is used to mean the summoning of witnesses by one of the parties in the case: these witnesses, however, have a notarial role (Isa. 8.2; Jer. 32.10, 25, 44) or lend assistance in a two-sided controversy (Deut. 4.26; 30.19; 31.28).[107]

The verb *zkr*[108] has been conceded a certain juridical value; as regards the accusation in particular, the *Hiphil* form taking a personal pronoun as its object (Isa. 43.26) or a noun meaning a misdeed (Gen. 41.9; Num. 5.15; 1 Kgs 17.18; Ezek. 21.28-29; 29.16) is equivalent to verbs of bringing a charge, including in a court of law.

Although the verbs listed above are used to express, with different nuances, the act of accusation, it should not be forgotten that this is basically an act of speech. It follows that the various *verba dicendi*, no matter how generic, can in certain contexts take on the meaning of to accuse, especially when they are linked to terms which are characteristic of the sphere of testimony.[109] The verb *dbr* (*Pi*) itself is one of the most used: cf. Isa. 59.3-4; Pss. 12.3-5; 109.2; 144.8, 11; Prov. 30.8 etc.[110]

105. Cf. V. Maag, *Text, Wortschatz und Begriffswelt des Buches Amos* (Leiden, 1951), pp. 180-81.

106. M. Mannati ('Le Psaume 50 est-il un *rîb*?', *Sem* 23 [1973], pp. 37-40) does not accept the nuance of testimony *against*, and translates, 'je t'avertis solennellement'; despite the abundance and subtlety of his arguments, I do not accept his opinion, which seems to me inspired by a positive 'pre-understanding' of the first part of Psalm 50.

107. Cf. Isa. 43.9: *yittᵉnû 'ēdêhem* ('let them produce their witnesses'). I would also like to mention the original formula in Job 10.17: *tᵉḥaddēš 'ēdeykā negdî*; in passing, I would like to point out how this 'renew the evidence' against Job is paralleled by the metaphor of a lion hunt (v. 16: *kaššaḥal tᵉṣûdēnî*) and the image of an armed assault (*ḥªlîpôt wᵉṣābā' 'immî*) (cf. n. 21).

108. I refer the reader in particular to Boecker, *Redeformen*, pp. 105-11; cf. also W. Schottroff, '*zkr* gedenken', *THAT*, I, p. 513; and nn. 25 (Chapter 2), 62 (Chapter 4), 33.4c (Chapter 5), and Chapter 4 section 2.1.g and Chapter 6 section 3.3.2. in my own work.

109. Cf. Ruppert, *Der leidende Gerechte*, pp. 132-39.

110. Among the *verba dicendi*, I would like to single out for example *hgh* (Isa. 59.3, 13; Job 27.4) and *nb'* (*Hi*) (Pss. 59.8; 94.4; Prov. 15.28). The verb *tpl*, for which different meanings are proposed (Zorell: *excogitavit, concinnavit;* Gesenius: *anschmieren*; BDB: *smear* or *plaster* (over), *stick, glue*; *HALAT*: *anschmieren,*

The terminology discussed up to now refers generically to witness in a law court, but without saying anything directly as to its value. We have many texts in the Bible, however, which speak of *false* testimony.[111] Falsehood (or equivalent concepts) may refer to a witness (= a false witness), or may be transferred to what is said in a law court (= a false accusation). In the latter case, the terminology of calumny, *lying*, ill-saying can be used as a paradigmatic equivalent of testimony described negatively.

A series of important texts concerning false testimony will allow me to illustrate the lexicon's variation on a single theme:

Exod. 20.16	*lō' **ta'^{a}neh** b^{e}rē'^{a}kā 'ēd šāqer*
Deut. 5.20	*w^{e}lō' **ta'^{a}neh** b^{e}rē'^{a}kā 'ēd šāw'*
Lev. 19.16	*lō' **tēlēk rākîl** b^{e}'ammeykā* (cf. Jer. 9.3; Ezek. 22.9)
	lō' ta'^{a}mōd 'al dam rē'ekā
Exod. 23.1	*lō' **tiśśā' šēma' šāw'**...lihyōt 'ēd ḥāmās*[112]

zuschmieren), has a certain relationship with accusatory speech (cf. Ps. 119.69; Job 13.4; Sir. 51.5).

111. Cf. H.J. Stoebe, 'Das achte Gebot (Exod 20, Vers 16)', *WDienst* 3 (1952), pp. 108-26.

112. Following the ancient translations (LXX, Vulgate, *Targum Onkelos*), Philo (*Spec. Leg.* 4.59-61) and Rashi (cf. *L'Exode* [Paris, 1965], pp. 187, 189), H. van Vliet interprets Exod. 23.1a as a warning addressed to the *judge*, who must be on guard against accepting lying witness: 'He who tries to bear false witness must not find support, says Exod. 23.1; that can be translated by "You shall pay no heed to false report". In this way the parallelism in the sentence is preserved, which goes on to say "You shall not join hands with a wicked man, to be a malicious witness"' (*No Single Testimony*, 66).

Cazelles, on the other hand (*Etudes sur le Code de l'Alliance* [Paris, 1946], pp. 85-86), maintains that the command in Exod. 23.1 ('Tu ne feras pas de fausses déclarations') must refer to possible *witnesses*: 'Le législateur hébreu vise donc ceux qui font de fausses déclarations en justice. La procédure est orale, et ce sont les paroles qui sont les grands actes du procès. Le contexte indique qu'il s'agit plutôt de faux témoignage que de fausses dénonciations sans cependant les exclure.' This is also the line of interpretation of U. Cassuto (*A Commentary on the Book of Exodus* [Jerusalem, 1967], p. 296), M. Noth (*Das zweite Buch Mose: Exodus* [ATD, 5; Göttingen, 2nd edn, 1961], pp. 138, 152-53) and B.S. Childs (*The Book of Exodus: A Critical Theological Commentary* [Philadelphia, 1974], pp. 445, 480-81).

Regarding this latter passage, mention might also be made of:

Ps. 15.3	*lō' **rāgal** 'al l*^{e}*šōnô*[113]
	lō' 'āśâ l^{e}*rē'ēhû rā'â*
	***w*^{e}*ḥerpâ** lō' **nāśā'** 'al q*^{e}*rōbô*
Job 19.5	*'im 'omnām 'ālay **tagdîlû*** (cf. Ps. 35.26)
	w^{e}*tôkîḥû 'ālay ḥerpātî*

Along with verbs referring to the act of lying, among which the verb *kzb* (*Pi*)[114] deserves special attention (cf. Prov. 14.5; Job 6.28; 34.6); finally, I would like to mention those that emphasize the aspect of *deception*; I would like to quote, for example, *kḥš* (*Pi*),[115] this being a verb very close to the semantic field of lying (cf. Lev. 5.21-22; 19.11; Hos. 4.2), *rmh* (*Pi*) (2 Sam. 19.27; Prov. 26.19),[116] *pth* (*Pi*)[117] (1 Kgs 22.20-22; Prov. 16.29; 24.28) and so on.

1.6.3. *The Content and Motive of an Accusation*. The *content* of an accusation is not different from that which I presented in Chapter 2 of this study. To a certain extent it must be supposed, given the few explicit texts available, that the accusatory testimony brought to a court of law had to have a clearer reference to the State law regulating relations between citizens which magistrates oversaw and applied in the exercise of their function. The more explicit the 'title' of a crime is, the more explicit will the accusation's reference be to the punishment demanded from the actual juridical action.

Special consideration deserves to be given to the thesis of H.J. Boecker, who shows that, in a court of law, the prosecutor addresses the judge, and therefore speaks of the accused in the *third person*; in a controversy on the other hand (a 'pre-legal' act in this author's terminology) the

113. Cf. 2 Sam. 19.28 and Sir. 5.14 (*wblšwnk 'l trgl r'*). On Ps. 15.3, cf. J.A. Soggin, 'Il Salmo 15 (Volgata 14). Osservazioni filologiche ed esegetiche', *BeO* 12 (1970), p. 84.

114. Cf. in particular Klopfenstein, *Die Lüge*, pp. 184-87, 222-26. I would also like to mention the *Hiphil* of *kzb* with the meaning of 'to deny' in Job 24.25; and the *Niphal* ('to be denied') in Prov. 30.6.

115. On the importance of the root *kḥš*, cf. Klopfenstein, *Die Lüge*, pp. 254-310.

116. Just as the noun *šeqer* is used more and has greater juridical relevance than *šqr* (cf. Lev. 19.11; Klopfenstein, *Die Lüge*, pp. 9-11), likewise with the terms *mirmâ*, *r*^{e}*miyyâ* and *tarmît* as against the verb *rmh* (cf. *ibid.*, pp. 310-15).

117. Cf. D.J.A. Clines and D.M. Gunn, '"You tried to persuade me" and "Violence! Outrage" in Jeremiah 20.7-8', *VT* 28 (1978), pp. 20-23.

accuser appeals directly to the adversary, and so uses the second person.[118] The especially significant texts in this respect are: Deut. 21.20; 22.14; 1 Kgs 3.17, 18, 19, 21.13; Jer. 26.11; cf. also 2 Sam. 19.22; Isa. 5.3-4. Allowing for due caution, these observations are of undoubted interest, to the extent that they allow us to use a stylistic phenomenon to place certain biblical texts in their precise juridical context.

As regards the *motive of the accusation*,[119] we should be aware of using an expression not consecrated by usage: there is in fact much talk of the motive for a crime (this being a conscious element considered indispensable for a coherent interpretation of the crime that has been perpetrated), but not of an accusation. It seems obvious in fact that when giving testimony a witness is only interested in the legal pursuit of justice; like the judge, the witness should be trying to 'take evil away from Israel' by contributing to the punishment of evildoers and the protection of the innocent.

But as I have often insisted, the hypothesis must be admitted of a false accusation which makes juridical proceedings meaningless: although from the outside this looks no different from a real accusation, yet it differs from it with respect to the motive that inspires it. A false accusation is in itself 'criminal', and as such has a motive which needs to be sought out, denounced and condemned.

The reasons why a person may attack a fellow citizen in court are as numerous as those which lead one to perpetrate a crime. This seems to me an opportune moment to point out the importance—in the texts with which we are concerned—that is given to a denunciation of the accuser's *hatred* for the victim (cf. Lev. 19.17; Num. 35.20; Pss. 9.14; 18.18; 34.22; Prov. 10.18 etc.). This emphasis on the accusation as motivated and sustained by wicked feelings, born of criminal desire, whose sole aim is to wipe a person out for personal gain, is an essential description of false accusations for such accusations as malicious crime, intentional offence or premeditated murder.

When the Psalmist, for example, turns to God to denounce 'those who hate me without cause' (cf. Pss. 25.19; 35.19; 38.20; 69.5; 109.3) we see that he does not just proclaim his innocence, but opposes it to the perverse motive underlying the others' words.

118. Cf. 'Anklagereden und Verteidigungsreden im Alten Testament', *EvT* 20 (1960), pp. 398-412; *Redeformen*, pp. 75-84.

119. Cf. Chapter 4 section 1.1.3.a.

2. *The Action or Appeal*

Psalm 35 acted[120] as a typical example to illustrate the phenomenon of paradigmatic substitutions of the element 'witness', and in particular to introduce an argument on the importance of metaphorical language. When in the same Psalm the speaker turns to God to gain a just judgment which will free him from false accusations, he gives the following motive for his appeal:

v. 10	*yhwh mî kāmôkā*		
	maṣṣîl	*'ānî*	*mēḥāzāq mimmennû*
		w^e'ānî w^e'ebyôn	*miggōz^elô*

The nature of the situation expressed in the Psalm is like this: on the one hand we have some accusers who are making use of their 'strength' to make an attempt on somebody's life ('strength' should be understood as the power to get what is wanted); on the other hand we have the accused, whose rights and very life are under threat: the latter does not just represent himself as innocent (vv. 12-14: they pay me back evil for good...; v. 19: they hate me without cause), but he emphasizes his own *weakness* by referring to himself as *'ānî w^e'ebyôn*. Precisely because he belongs to that category of people habitually subjected to the whims and outrages of the powerful, the speaker claims the right to be heard, protected and saved by the One who is even stronger than the strong and the supreme guarantor of justice in the world.

The life of Israel (as elsewhere in human history) saw a constant conflict between two parties (two people or groups), in which the stronger made use of its power to overcome the weaker. This could happen on two levels.

The first is that of exploitation and/or (attempted) murder. One man beats down another, defrauds him of his basic rights, arranges his life as though it belonged to him, as Pharaoh did to Israel in Egypt (cf. Amos 8.4-6; Ezek. 22.29; Job 22.5-9 etc.). It may go as far as open murder as the (apparent) triumph of a despotic will which wields authority, and therefore makes the actual abuse of power legal (cf. Isa. 59.7; Jer. 22.17; Ezek. 22.6 etc.). The person who is oppressed, and whose life is under threat, then tries to turn to a court of justice which has a strength and authority superior to that of the oppressor; so as to be recompensed for

120. Cf. p. 291.

the wrong undergone and to be restored to rights, one brings a *suit*.

The *second level* possesses a basically similar structure, but slightly more complex and locked into legal procedures. We again have an outrage inflicted by a 'strong' party on a 'weak' party, but this outrage is carried out *in a legal manner*, following normal law court procedure. The strong party, making use of moral authority, ability in conspiracy and even knowledge of the law, drags the weak party into court and manufactures a case in order to deprive him or her of goods, honour and even life. The peculiarity of this situation is that the strength of the strong party is sublimated (enlarged and ennobled) by a shrewd use of juridical means, by which the injustice (in the heart) is legalized by the external justice. Typical in this respect is the behaviour of Jezebel towards Naboth (1 Kgs 21),[121] but many other Scripture texts mention similar perverse conduct (cf. Exod. 23.6; Deut. 24.17; 1 Sam. 12.3-4; Isa. 3.13-15; 10.1-2; Mic. 3.9-11; Prov. 22.22 etc.). It is sometimes possible to recognize this second level of oppression from an explicit mention of a trial court, but more often from the fact that the injustice is set on foot by words which, under a mask of legality or outright goodness, in fact conceal hatred, violence and a desire for death. In this case the innocent party, subjected to the strong's law court, *appeals* to a magistrate with superior jurisdiction explaining the complaint as if in a law suit; alternatively, one has recourse to the supreme tribunal of the Divine King, whose judgment is right, whose verdicts are inspired by truth and unimpeachable impartiality. In some way or other, the juridical situation in the court of law is overturned: the *accused* weakling (sometimes already sentenced) denounces the lying and violence operating against

121. The narrative in 1 Kgs 21 has been the object of numerous studies, which have tried among other things to explain the juridical problem underlying the incident that occurred between the royal house and Naboth. I would like to quote in particular K. Baltzer, 'Naboths Weinberg (1 Kön. 21). Der Konflikt zwischen israelitischem und kanaanäischem Bodenrecht', *WDienst* 8 (1965), pp. 73-88; F.I. Andersen, 'The Socio-Juridical Background of the Naboth Incident', *JBL* 85 (1966), pp. 46-57; J.M. Miller, 'The Fall of the House of Ahab', *VT* 7 (1967), pp. 307-24; P. Welten, 'Naboth Weinberg (1 Könige 21)', *EvT* 33 (1973), pp. 18-32; H. Seebass, 'Der Fall Naboth in 1 Reg. XXI', *VT* 24 (1974), pp. 474-88; D. Napier, 'The Inheritance and the Problem of Adjacency. An Essay in 1 Kings 21', *Int* 30 (1976), pp. 3-11; R. Bohlen, *Der Fall Nabot: Form, Hintergrund und Werdegang einer alttestamentlichen Erzählung (1 Kön 21)* (TThSt, 35; Trier, 1978); E. Würthwein, 'Naboth-Novelle und Elia-Wort', *ZTK* 75 (1978), pp. 375-97.

him or her, becomes the *accuser* of the accusers (and demands the condemnation of those who were plotting or had plotted the condemnation of the innocent).

The distinction between the first and second level is clear in theory, and may be discerned in some texts; often, however, the metaphorical language and generic terminology[122] do not allow a certain identification of the actual manner in which the wicked carries out their oppression.[123]

As I have several times stated, I believe that in any case steady oppression cannot be guaranteed by any perverse legislation or abuse of legitimate authority; this means that a 'rebel' (against the law or authority) will end by being sentenced. More than this: if the law is thought of as being in some way a decree by authority as to who is in the right and who in the wrong, then unjust legislation is really nothing more than an a priori condemnation of the upholders of the law and a declaration of innocence for those who are wicked.

At any rate, whether it is a matter of a complaint (a first level denunciation) or an appeal (the request for the review of a trial), the Hebrew vocabulary shows identical formulae; for this reason I think it is legitimate to deal simultaneously with the two situations without thereby denying their specific nature.

122. In Chapter 5 sections 2.2.3.–5., when dealing with partiality in judgment and perversion in the tribunal, I touched on the second level of oppression of 'the poor' and pointed out its proper lexicon. At this point in my work I find myself faced with a terminology which at first sight has no specific legal implications: it appears, in a generic way, to be the manifestation of social injustice (a serious crime), that will—possibly—give rise to judicial proceedings. The most frequently used, basically synonymous, roots are: *'šq*, *lḥṣ*, *gzl*, *ynh*, *rṣṣ*, *dk'*, *qb'*, *'nh*, *ḥms*, *ngś*. For a systematic treatment of the subject, and for appropriate bibliographical information, I refer the reader to J.L. Sicre, *Los dioses olvidados: Poder y riqueza en los profetas preexílicos* (Madrid, 1979), especially pp. 101-90, and to J. Pons, *L'oppression dans l'Ancien Testament* (Paris, 1981).

It should be noted that the terminology of oppression also appears in juridical and law court contexts: cf. 1 Sam. 12.3-4 (*'šq*, *rṣṣ*); Isa. 10.1-2 (*gzl*, *bzz*); 59.13 (*'šq*); Zech. 7.9-10 (*'šq*); Job 5.4 (*dk'*); Prov. 22.22 (*gzl*, *dk'*); Qoh. 5.7 (*'šq*, *gzl*); Lam. 3.34-36 (*dk'*) etc.

123. Cf., for example, the reflections of J. van der Ploeg, 'Le Psaume XVII et ses problèmes', *OTS* 14 (1965), pp. 273-95; J. Coppens, 'Le *ṣaddîq*—"Juste", dans le Psautier', in *De la Tôrah au Messie* (FS H. Cazelles; Paris, 1981), p. 304; G. Gerleman, 'Der "Einzelne" der Klage- und Dankpsalmen', *VT* 32 (1982), pp. 33-49, who maintains that David is the model of the just man persecuted by his enemies and heeded in his prayer.

2.1. *The Complainant/Appellant: The Hebrew Vocabulary*
As against the prosecution witness, with whom I dealt in the previous section, the complainant brings charges in his or her own name of a violation of personal rights; from this point of view, one identifies oneself as the 'injured party'. As regards the Hebrew vocabulary, we do not, however, have an equivalent of the term *'ēd*, which would allow us to mark out with certainty the semantic field, and the lexicon belonging to it, in a law suit. Despite this, on the basis of previous considerations, I can point out the chief attributes of a juridical subject who lays a complaint (or appeals to a superior court of judgment).

2.1.1. *The Injured Party*. Since the complainant is a victim and an 'injured party', expressions equivalent to 'oppressed, downtrodden, offended' and so on, take on particular emphasis. The juridical basis of the law suit is in fact to be found in the wrong undergone; as a result, whoever speaks up and becomes the bringer of the accusation is necessarily the victim of some form of violence.

Passive participles are fairly rare in Hebrew; I would like to quote *'āšûq* (Jer. 50.33; Pss. 103.6; 146.7; Qoh. 4.1) and *gāzûl* (Jer. 21.12; 22.3); the condition of the oppressed comes out above all in the description of the adversary as an oppressor (cf. Pss. 35.10; 72.4; Isa. 3.14; Jer. 22.17 etc.).

2.1.2. *The 'Deprived'*. It is also necessary to include in the same paradigmatic series terms that refer to a state of wretchedness, weakness and poverty; to these should be added the social categories of the under-privileged, such as orphans, widows, strangers and so on.[124] This

124. To refer to the concept of poverty, J. van der Ploeg selects the following terms: *'ebyôn*, *dal*, *'ānî* (*'ānāw*), *rāš*, *rêq*, *miskēn* (*m^e^sukkān*?) ('Les pauvres d'Israël et leur piété', *OTS* 7 [1950], pp. 236-70); by analysing the texts, the author shows how there existed in Israel a large number of poor people who were mortally exposed to the unjust activities of the rich (often described with the adjective *r^e^šā'îm*). It seems therefore that a juridical and not religious value is to be attributed to the coupling poor—*ṣaddîqîm* (as opposed to rich—*r^e^šā'îm*) (against the thesis of A. Kuschke, 'Arm und reich im Alten Testament mit besonderer Berücksichtigung der nachexilischen Zeit', *ZAW* 57 [1939], pp. 31-57). Cf. also J.J. Stamm, 'Ein Vierteljahrhundert Psalmenforschung', *TRu* 23 (1955), pp. 55-60; P. van den Berghe, '*'Ani* et *'Anaw* dans les Psaumes', in R. de Langhe (ed.), *Le Psautier: Ses origines. Ses problèmes littéraires. Son influence* (OrBiLov, 4; Louven, 1962), pp. 273-95; L. Delekat, 'Zum hebräischen Wörterbuch', *VT* 14 (1964), pp. 35-49; T. Donald,

terminology does not of itself directly explain the nature of the injustice experienced: impartial judgment must not in fact identify wretched with right (Exod. 23.3; Lev. 19.15). However, those who are 'poor and weak' are so often the target of outrage that in practice the implication often is that they are 'the exploited'.[125]

2.1.3. *The Innocent*. The social categories given above tend to identify the figure of the innocent with that of the just (*ṣaddîq*). Here too they are not perfect synonyms but there is an important mutual implication. Since the injustice with which I am dealing here is basically an interpersonal relationship, it is quite logical that it should be committed by someone with the strength/power to do so; a disadvantaged person, on the other hand, will be hard put to it to find the means to commit an outrage upon someone who is stronger. The 'wretched' is therefore

'The Semantic Field of Rich and Poor in the Wisdom Literature of Hebrew and Accadian', *OrAnt* 3 (1964), pp. 27-41; K. Aartun, 'Hebräisch *'ānī* und *'ānāw'*, *BO* 28 (1971), pp. 125-26.

The list given above could of course be supplemented by the characteristic list which includes *gēr*, *yātôm* and *'almānâ* (cf. F.C. Fensham, 'Widow, Orphan and Poor in Ancient Near Eastern Legal and Wisdom Literature', *JNES* 21 [1962], pp. 129-39; R.D. Patterson, 'The Widow, the Orphan and the Poor in the Old Testament and the Extra-Biblical Literature', *BS* 130 [1973], pp. 233-35; P.D. Miller (Jr), 'Studies in Hebrew Word Patterns', *HTR* 73 [1980], pp. 80-82; and also A. Tosato, 'Sul significato dei termini biblici *'Almānâ, 'Almānût* ["vedova", "vedovanza"]', *BeO* 25 [1983], pp. 193-214).

Moreover, I would like to quote *dak* (Pss. 9.10; 10.18; 74.21; Prov. 26.28) and *'ōbēd* (which I think should be translated as 'vagrant' or 'nomad' in Deut. 26.5; Job 29.13; 31.19; Prov. 31.6: different opinions on the subject are given in *ThWAT*, I, pp. 21, 24).

Finally I would like to mention that terms referring to the 'deprived' often appear in series: Ps. 146.7-10; Job 29.12-17.

125. As well as what we might call the historical or factual aspect (the observed oppression of one person by another), another motive lies behind the juridical redress of the wretched: every person has an absolute right to life, a right which under the law those who are capable must defend if they do not wish to fall into the crime of '*failure to lend assistance*'. In this case, injustice is done at the precise moment when someone who was able did not come to the aid of the disadvantaged, that is, did not hear the cry of the poor (cf. Exod. 23.20-26; Deut. 24.14-15; Ps. 72.14; Prov. 3.27-28 etc.). Cf. G. Barbiero, 'Il testo massoretico di Prov. 3.34', *Bib* 63 (1982), esp. pp. 373-74. The Bible's norms on the subject are more inclined to see it as a moral precept than as a disposition of the law (D. Patrick, 'Casuistic Law Governing Primary Rights and Duties', *JBL* 92 [1973], pp. 180-84).

ṣaddîq not only to the extent of having undergone/ been undergoing juridically unreasonable high-handed treatment (being an innocent victim),[126] but is also *ṣaddîq* at the time of the accusation and the complaint (in the sense of presenting just claims).

We can see how, if the false witness becomes identified with a *rāšā'* who attacks a *ṣaddîq* (cf. Hab. 1.4-13; Pss. 31.19; 37.12, 32), the (wretched, oppressed) appellant becomes identified with the *ṣaddîq* who levels an accusation against the *rāšā'* (cf. Pss. 34.16-17, 22; 37.25-29; 55.23-24; 59.11-12; 142.7-8 etc.).[127]

2.2. *The Act of Complaint/Appeal*

2.2.1. *The Juridical Form of the Complaint/Appeal.* The outline of the complainant sketched in the previous section is indispensable for an understanding of the particular nature of this juridical action. The complainant speaks up and appeals to the judge with formulae that so resemble a supplication as to call to mind a procedure which is not upholding the law.[128]

126. Cf. van der Ploeg, 'Les pauvres d'Israël', pp. 241, 245.

127. For the parallelism between 'poor' and 'just' (*ṣaddîq*), cf. for example, Amos 2.6 (M.A. Beek, 'The Religious Background of Amos II 6-8', *OTS* 5 [1948], pp. 132-41; J.L. Sicre, *'Con los pobres de la tierra': La justicia social en los profetas de Israel* [Madrid, 1984], p. 105); 5.12; Pss. 14.4; 34.19-20; 140.13-14; Job 36.6-7.

128. I am referring here to the fact that terms such as *t^epillâ*, *rinnâ*, *t^eḥinnâ* (or their respective verbs)—which I listed under the request for pardon (Chapter 4 section 1.1.1.)—are also used as synonyms for an appeal (cf. Pss. 6.10; 17.1; 28.2; 42.9; 80.5; 130.2; 142.2, 7 etc.).

Speaking more generally, the two kinds of request (supplication and complaint) possess a fairly similar content to the extent that persons asking for mercy sometimes find themselves—like appellants—in an objective condition of suffering; the description of the misfortune into which one is plunged (often caused by an 'enemy' in whose power one is), linked to a request to have pity in the name of justice, means that the specific character of each of these two juridical actions is less obvious.

Finally, it should be observed that a request for mercy or amnesty after an experience of harsh punishment frequently brings into play the relationship between the one undergoing punishment (the speaker) and the one inflicting it (the instrument of divine wrath); if the latter goes beyond what is just, indulging in an arbitrary kind of oppression, then the new situation created is the classic one of the tyrant and the weakling. The prayer that asks for amnesty (pardon and withholding of punishment) can be transformed into a complaint against the executor of justice (cf. Isa. 10.5-19,

And yet there is a fundamental distinction between a '*supplication*' and a '*complaint*': the former is the act of asking something that goes beyond a right, or with an altogether precise awareness of not being able to claim anything[129] (as in the case when someone asks for a loan or the forgiveness of a debt); the latter on the other hand is the procedure of someone speaking in the name of the law (cf. Isa. 32.7), addressing a judge as judge, that is, as a court of appeal with authority to decide in favour of the one who is (in the) right.

It still remains to be explained how actions with a different juridical value come to be expressed in similar vocabulary: the fundamental reason lies in the appellant's characteristic state of 'weakness'.

To start with, as we have seen, the rights of the oppressed and downtrodden are violated because they have no power; this has an echo in the law courts in the fact that their pleadings remain the words of the poor, those who do not count, who cannot make themselves felt. It may be observed, however, that a complaint is often 'individual', that is, brought by a *single* person against a crowd of adversaries: this makes the person's judicial position almost untenable according to the rules of strict procedure. The state of weakness colours the way one speaks at the trial; one tends to express oneself in laments, reproach and complaint. The consistency between the condition of being weak and the use of weak words is, however, paradoxically, what counts for the judgment, for through them shines the truth of a person's juridical testimony.

Moreover, the complainant is in a condition of structural inferiority to the judge being appealed to precisely because the judge will not brook being intimidated by anyone. One cannot 'impose oneself' on the authority, but only 'present oneself' in the humility of being and speech. One's weapons are the cry of desperation, the repeated invitation to listen and help, and the detailed description of one's own wretchedness, proving the right to pity and aid in flesh and voice.[130]

24-27; 47.6-11; Hab. 1.18-23; Zech. 1.14-16; Pss. 74.18-23; 79.3-5, 10-13 etc.). As Seeligmann writes, 'Nach dieser Interpretation wurde das Beten in Israel zu aller Zeit als eine Art Gerichtsrede vor Gott empfunden' ('Zur Terminologie', p. 278).

129. Cf. p. 156.

130. One of the characteristic traits of a complaint (which distinguishes it from a generic supplication) is the question '*why* (do you not help)?' which the speaker addresses to the judge (God). In this 'why?' lies a claim to rights which challenges the court of judgment, calling upon it to respond, justify itself or intervene (cf. Exod. 5.15; Jer. 14.9; 15.18; Pss. 22.1; 42.10; 43.2; 44.24-25 etc.). If this 'why?' is side-

If an appellant is in a position of inferiority with respect to the prosecution witness, his or her state—as it appears to a just tribunal—contrives to enjoy a certain favour; although a judge is bound to guarantee impartiality and even-handedness during a trial, he is also called upon to uphold the defenseless, to incline towards the weak, so that judgment may be fair.[131]

With the aim of placing the vocabulary of the complaint and introducing the main syntagmatic relations which express it, I would like to take the episode recounted in 2 Kgs 8.1-6. Here we have a woman, who, because of a drought, has been forced to emigrate (*gwr*: vv. 1, 2) for seven years to the land of the Philistines; it may be assumed from the account that, upon her return to the land of Israel, she could not take back possession of her house and lands because others (not identified in the account) had usurped them; it may also be deduced that the local magistrates could not or would not intervene on behalf of the woman; she then 'goes out' to address herself to the king's tribunal.

The woman's juridical action is expressed like this: *wattēṣē' liṣ'ōq 'el hammelek 'el bêtāh w^{e}'el śādāh* (v. 3); this phrase can be broken down into its component parts:

1. a verb of motion (*yṣ'*) which indicates the juridical initiative (cf. Chapter 6)
2. a verb that indicates the act of complaint (*ṣ'q 'el*)
3. the tribunal that is addressed (*hammelek*)
4. the reason for the complaint (*'el bêtāh w^{e}'el śādāh*).[132]

stepped, if the judge does not listen to the complaint, then the judge becomes an oppressor, and the speaker is the victim of a 'coalition' of oppressors (between the adversary and the judge) (Ps. 94.20) in an absurd reversal of world order.

In Chapter 2 I showed that a question (often formulated as 'why?') can be the equivalent of an accusation. The question in a complaint likewise displays a certain amount of accusation of the judging magistrate; it lacks, however, a link to any form of *punishment* of the accused; the result is that a complaint is the accusation par excellence of the weakling who cannot have recourse to anyone for defence except the very person whose justice is being called into question.

131. I am referring here to the 'principle of cross-examination', which in our legal systems is a manifestation of one of the accused's rights: it may be defined as the simultaneous and opposed participation of all the parties in the trial, who have to enjoy similar rights to speak (cf. Leone, *Manuale di diritto processuale penale*, pp. 52-53).

132. This structure is repeated with almost identical terminology in v. 5:

The 'reaction' of the judging body to the woman's juridical action comes out in the form of an inquisition: the king questions the woman with the aim of establishing the true facts (*wayyiš'al hammelek lā'iššâ*, v. 6). The complainant gives her evidence by detailing the facts (*watt^{e}sapper lô*, v. 6).

The conclusion of the affair follows the sentence of the royal tribunal: the king grants the woman's (implied) request and arranges for its execution by a decree: (1) he nominates an official (*sārîs*) to occupy the house; (2) he issues an order for restitution (*hāšêb*) both of the complainant's possessions and of the accumulated income during her absence (v. 6).

On the basis of this narrative, we may proceed to detail the Hebrew vocabulary of the complaint; in the next section I will talk about the act of complaint itself, and will therefore be concerned with the content of the request; finally, I will demonstrate the link between this juridical action and the intervention of the judging body.

2.2.2. *The Act of Complaint: The Hebrew Vocabulary*. The commonest terms referring to the complaint are the verbs (and occasionally corresponding nouns) from the roots *ṣ'q* or *z'q*, *qr'* and *šw' (Pi)*.[133] I would like to offer a few examples, showing the main elements of the complaint syntagm:

	subject	initiative	COMPLAINT *ṣ'q/z'q*	tribunal	motive
2 Kgs 8.3	(an emigrant)	*wattēṣē'*	*liṣ'ōq*	*'el hammelek*	*'el bêtāh...*[134]

1. *w^{e}hinnēh hā'iššâ* . . . : there is no verb of motion because we are already in the judge's presence; the subject of the juridical action is just made explicit.
2. *ṣō'eqet 'el*: the act of complaint.
3. *hammelek*: the tribunal being addressed.
4. *'al bêtāh w^{e} 'al śādāh*: the reason for the complaint (here expressed by the preposition *'al*, instead of *'el*).

133. The synonymous relationship between these verbs is obvious from the fact that they are often found linked to one another: cf. Jer. 20.8; Ps. 18.7; Job 19.7; 35.9; Prov. 21.13 etc. (Seeligmann, 'Zur Terminologie', pp. 257-60).

134. The motive for the complaint is more frequently expressed by the preposition *'al* (Deut. 15.9; 24.15; Job 34.28, as well as the aforementioned 2 Kgs 8.5); however, in Neh. 5.1 we have the preposition *'el*: *watt^{e}hî ṣa'^{a}qat hā'ām ûn^{e}šêhem g^{e}dôlâ 'el '^{a}ḥêhem hayy^{e}hûdîm* ('on account of their brother Jews'). On the text of Neh. 5.1-13, cf. L. Alonso Schökel, '"Somos iguales que nuestros hermanos". Para una

	subject	initiative	COMPLAINT	tribunal	motive
Exod. 5.15	*šōṭᵉrê bᵉnê yiśrā'ēl*	*wayyābō'û*[135]	*wayyiṣ'ᵃqû*	*'el par'ōh*	*lē'mōr: lāmmâ...*
Isa. 19.20	(Israel, once more in Egypt)		*kî yiṣ'ᵃqû*	*'el yhwh*	*mippᵉnê lōḥᵃṣîm*
Exod. 22.22	(vv. 20-21: *gēr; 'almānâ wᵉyātôm*)		*ṣā'ōq yiṣ'aq*	*'ēlay* (God)	oppression: *'nh* (*Pi*)
			qr'[136]		
Deut. 15.9	(*'ebyôn*)		*wᵉqārā'*	*'el yhwh*	*'āleykā*
Deut. 24.15	(*śākîr... 'ānî*)		*yiqrā'*	*'el yhwh*	*'āleykā*
			šw' (Pi)		
Ps. 72.12	*'ebyôn*		*mᵉšawwēa'*	(the king)	(v. 14: *mittôk ûmēḥāmās*)
Job 30.20	(Job)	*'āmadtî*	*'ᵃšawwa'*	*'ēleykā* (God)	

For *ṣ'q/z'q*, cf. also Gen. 4.10; 18.21; 19.13; Exod. 3.7, 9; 22.26; 1 Sam. 7.8-9; 8.18; Prov. 21.13 etc.

For *qr'*, cf. also Jer. 11.14; 20.8; Pss. 4.2, 4; 34.7 etc.

For *šw'* (*Pi*), cf. also Exod. 2.23; Hab. 1.2; Ps. 18.7; Job 19.7; 29.12; 30.28; 35.9; Lam. 3.8 etc.

The paradigmatic series of the verbs or expressions that are equivalent to the act of complaint is rather long: the vocabulary of groaning, lamentation, weeping and so on can be relevant substitutes in the aforementioned lexicon[137] (cf. Exod. 2.23, *'nḥ* (*Ni*); Exod. 2.24, *nᵉ'āqâ*; Job 24.12, *n'q*; Qoh. 4.1, *dim'â* etc.).

exégesis de Neh. 5.1-13', *Salm* 13 (1976), pp. 257-66.

135. It might be interesting to observe that the noun *ṣᵉ'āqâ* (or *šaw'â*) is sometimes construed with the verb *bw'* in the form *ṣa'ᵃqat bᵉnê yiśrā'ēl bā'â 'ēlāy* (Exod. 3.9); cf. Gen. 18.21; 1 Sam. 9.16; Pss. 18.7; 102.2; Job 34.28.

136. In certain contexts the verb *qr'* takes on the juridical nuance of a complaint (or appeal): this usage seems however to be found only in requests addressed to *God*, not in ones to human tribunals (we therefore find it frequently in the Psalms: cf. 3.5; 86.7; 120.1; 127.7 etc.).

When *qr'* refers to the opposing party, it seems to mean 'to take legal proceedings against someone', whether this in a trial situation or not (cf. Isa. 59.4; Job 9.16; 13.22).

137. Cf. R. Albertz, '*ṣ'q* schreien', *THAT*, II, pp. 569-70, where a quite long list of synonyms of the verb *ṣ'q* is given.

2.3. *The Content of a Complaint*

In a word, the content of a complaint is that the victim of an injustice cries '*violence*'.[138] Three texts link verbs of complaint directly with the noun *ḥāmās*:[139]

Hab. 1.2[140]	*'ad 'ānâ*	*yhwh šiwwa'tî*			*w^{e}lō' tišmā'*
		'ez'aq 'ēleykā	*ḥāmās*		*w^{e}lō' tôšîa'*
3	*lāmmâ*			*tar'ēnî*	
			'āwen		
			w^e'āmāl	*tabbîṭ*	
			w^{e}šōd		
			w^{e}ḥāmās	*l^{e}negdî*	
			wayhî rîb		
			ûmādôn yiššā'		
4					*'al kēn tāpûg tôrâ*
					w^{e}lō' yēṣē' lāneṣaḥ
					mišpāṭ
			kî rāšā' maktîr		
			'et haṣṣaddîq		
					'al kēn yēṣē' mišpāṭ
					m^e'uqqāl
Job 19.7	*hēn*	*'eṣ'aq*	*ḥāmās*		*w^{e}lō' 'ē'āneh*
		'^{a}šawwa'			*w^e'ên mišpāṭ*

138. Cf. Boecker, *Redeformen*, pp. 59-61.

139. It can be seen from the three texts quoted above, which have been transcribed in such a way as to bring out the different paradigms, that *ḥāmās* forms part of a cluster of terms, among which the noun *šōd* deserves special consideration (Seeligmann, 'Zur Terminologie', pp. 257-58). According to Maag, the expression *ḥāmās wāšōd* (Jer. 6.7; 20.8; Ezek. 45.9; Amos 3.10) constitutes a single concept (*Text, Wortschatz und Begriffswelt des Buches Amos*, p. 202); it should, however, be observed that the two terms are also associated in other ways (Hab. 1.3: *w^{e}šōd w^{e}ḥāmās*; Isa. 60.18 and Hab. 2.17: *ḥāmās* // *šōd*). Cf. also *kāzāb wāšōd* in Hos. 12.2 and *šōd* // *'āmāl* in Prov. 24.2.

The noun *tôk* also seems to be a close synonym of *ḥāmās*: cf. Ps. 72.14. In Pss. 10.7 and 55.12, *tôk* is associated with *mirmâ* (cf. Zeph. 1.9: *ḥāmās ûmirmâ*) but also to *'āmāl* and *'āwen*, the latter occurring in the paradigmatic series in Hab. 1.3 (cf. also Ps. 7.17).

The most detailed study of the terminology of 'violence' is to be found in J. Pons, *L'oppression dans l'Ancien Testament* (Paris, 1981), which examines in particular the roots *ḥms*, *šdd*, *'šq*, *ynh*, *rṣṣ*, *lḥṣ*, *'nh*, *ngś*.

140. On Hab. 1.2, cf. J. Jeremias, *Kultprophetie und Gerichtsverkündigung in der späten Königszeit Israels* (WMANT, 35; Neukirchen, 1970), pp. 75-81; M.D. Johnson, 'The Paralysis of Torah in Habakkuk I 4', *VT* 35 (1985), pp. 257-66.

Jer. 20.8[141] *'ez'āq*

ḥāmās

wāšōd

'eqrā'

The cry of 'violence' springs from the fact that someone is currently the victim of an injustice (Job 19.7; Jer. 20.8); the onlooker to this interprets it as the cry of an innocent overwhelmed by an evildoer (Hab. 1.4). The primary content of a complaint is therefore the denunciation of a crime being committed:[142] this may come out in the term *ḥāmās*, or in its synonyms (cf. the paradigm in Hab. 1.3-4); in a whole series of texts—I am thinking in particular of the so-called 'lamentations'—this element is developed into a detailed description of the ways in which this 'violence' is being carried out.

However, this 'cry' is not just a personal outburst or a simple instinctive reaction to suffering: it is essentially addressed to someone (*'el...*) and demands to be heard in the name of right (cf. the term *mišpāṭ* in Hab. 1.3, 4; Job 19.7). In this way a complaint reveals another aspect of what constitutes it; it is a request for help addressed to an 'authorized'[143] person, juridically bound by the actual cry. It is in accord with juridical theory and practice that a complainant should formally address a request to whoever has been appointed by the legal institution as the authoritative court of judgment; in this sense the demand for

141. Cf. S. Marrow, 'Ḥāmās ("violentia") in Jer. 20.8', *VD* 43 (1965), pp. 241-55; the author defines *ḥāmās* as 'invasionem in iura proximi, quae sponte provocat appellationem ad altiorem auctoritatem, ad arbitrum, vindicem, iudicem' (p. 253); and, with reference to Jer. 20.8 he says, 'Exclamatione "violentia!" accusator laesus invocat iustitiam, iura eius violata sunt. Extrema brevitate exhibetur et querela et appellatio' (p. 255). Cf. also Clines and Gunn, '"You Tried to Persuade Me"', pp. 24-27.

142. The term *ḥāmās* has a definite juridical meaning, since it is one of the ways in which a crime or misdeed is specified; on the other hand, there is a variety of opinions about the technical nature of its use in a law court situation (cf. H.J. Stoebe, '*ḥāmās* Gewalttat', *THAT*, I, pp. 584-86).

143. A typical case in this sense is that of a woman who is undergoing carnal violence (cf. Gen. 39.14; 15.18; 2 Sam. 13.19; and above all Deut. 22.24-27): anyone who hears her cry for help is bound to come to her defence (Boecker, *Redeformen*, p. 64). This situation, in my opinion, should be extended to similar cases of violence perpetrated against those who are not in a position to defend themselves (this would give us a case of 'analogia legis', in agreement with the maxim, *ubi eadem ratio, ibi eadem iuris dispositio*: Antolisei, *Manuale di Diritto Penale*, pp. 70-71). Cf. M. Fishbane, 'Biblical Colophons, Textual Criticism and Legal Analogies', *CBQ* 42 (1980), esp. pp. 446-49.

defence and salvation (which is indirectly equivalent to a suit against an oppressor) is at the same time a demand for judgment in accordance with justice.

This second aspect takes us on to another characteristic expression, also explicitly linked to the verbs of complaint: I am referring to the imperative: *hôšîa'*.[144]

Two episodes whose protagonist is a woman appealing to the king allow me to put my argument in context: bearing in mind the comments already made on the narrative of 2 Kgs 8.1-6 will make it easier to place these texts in the context with which we are now concerned.

2 Sam. 14.1-24 tells how Joab managed to obtain a suspension of proceedings against Absalom from David: the stratagem took the form of acting out a juridical case, ably played by a woman of Tekoa.[145] This is the structure of the case put to David:

a. The woman's juridical initiative (v. 4: [*wattābō'*][146]...*'el hammelek*) comes to a peak in the appeal addressed to the king (v. 4: *wattō'mer: hôšî'â hammelek*): this simple phrase contains the kernel of proceedings which what follows has the task of spelling out.

b. The king moves on to the questioning (v. 5: *wayyō'mer lāh hammelek: mah lāk*); in reply the woman makes her statement (vv. 5-7): she is a widow under threat (*qāmâ...'al*) from her own clan, which is demanding, under the pretext of justice, the death of the only son (guilty of murder) left to her.

c. The king gives sentence in favour of the woman (v. 8);[147] by listening favourably to the appeal addressed to him, Israel's supreme

144. On this subject, cf. the detailed treatment by Boecker, *Redeformen*, pp. 61-66. Note the association of the noun *ḥāmās* with the root *yš'* in Hab. 1.2.

145. The woman of Tekoa presents a fictitious case, but the juridical actions and vocabulary are those of normal proceedings; David is in fact only aware of the deception after having pronounced his verdict (2 Sam. 14.18-20).

146. In place of *wattābō'* in 2 Sam. 14.4, the MT has *wattō'mer*; the ancient translations all give a verb of motion, which makes the phrase run more logically. The relationship between a juridical initiative (a verb of motion) and a suit of complaint (a verb of saying) is on the other hand expressly shown in 14.3: ***ûbā't 'el hammelek*** ***wᵉdibbart*** *'ēlāyw kaddābār hazzeh*.

147. The formula *lᵉkî lᵉbêtēk wa'ᵃnî* ***'ᵃṣawweh*** *'ālāyik* surely refers to provisions favourable to the appellant. J.F.A. Sawyer also includes the verb *ṣwh* (*Pi*) in the semantic field of 'to save' (cf. Pss. 44.5; 71.3) (*Semantics in Biblical Research*, p. 38).

magistrate proves to be the saviour of a life in danger from proceedings that were certainly legal but not fair.[148]

2 Kgs 6.26-31 tells of an episode during the siege of Samaria by the Aramaeans, at the time of the prophet Elisha. The affair has some odd aspects, but we can recognize the structure of an appeal to the king:

a. While the king is 'walking along the walls'[149] (probably to inspect the city defences), a woman asks for his help (v. 26: *w*^{e}*'iššâ ṣā'*^{a}*qâ 'ēlāyw lē'mōr: hôšī'â '*^{a}*dōnî hammelek*). Here too a precise relationship is established between the complainant (*ṣ'q 'el*) and the imperative *hôšīa'*: this is so close from a juridical point of view that even though the king (guessing that it is a question of famine) declares himself powerless to resolve the case, still he carries out the usual procedural acts.

b. The king's questioning (v. 28: *wayyō'mer lāh hammelek: mah lāk*) is followed by the complainant's statement of the case; she has been cruelly tricked by another woman who failed to respect her side of a bargain, but persuaded her to kill 'without compensation' her own son.[150]

c. The king does not pronounce sentence on the matter; instead he rends his garments (v. 30), probably meaning that he has no part in this criminal event, and at the same time expressing the unease caused by such a revelation; the king is in fact aware that the city is in the grip of

148. The narrative continues with another discussion, in which the woman urges the king to guarantee with an oath (v. 11) the application of the sentence. This has the function of binding the judge to his own decision; in fact, starting from v. 12, it is David himself who is brought into question (*ûmiddabbēr hammelek haddābār hazzeh k*^{e}*'āšēm*: v. 13) and accused of injustice towards the people through his zeal against Absalom. Whether or not David's verdict is in accord with the law in force in Israel (it is a difficult conflict between the necessity to punish the guilty and safeguarding an heir [to the throne] for the good of the nation) is not the object of our consideration, which is the essential procedure in recourse to the king's supreme tribunal.

149. We have a similar situation in 1 Kgs 20.39 as well: 'When the king passed by (the prophet) appealed to the king (*ṣā'aq 'el hammelek*)'; as in 2 Sam. 14.1-24, the complainant poses a fictitious case in order to compel the sovereign to pronounce judgment on himself.

150. I would like to set down the text of the terrible barter between the two women of Samaria that made it impossible for the king to hand down a just sentence: 'This woman said to me, "Give me your son and we shall eat him today. Tomorrow we shall eat mine." We cooked and ate my child. The day after I said, "Give me your child and we shall eat him"; but she has hidden her child' (2 Kgs 6.28-29).

such mad desperation as no longer to recognize an unheard-of crime in the killing of one's own child.[151]

The observations made about these two episodes allow us to see that a complaint is in fact a request for assistance on one's own behalf (and therefore against another), which is coloured by the terminology of 'salvation' (root *yš'* [*Hi*]), on account of a death threat into which the pleader is falling. Of course, the lexicon of the complaint need not be identified just with the imperative *hôšîa'*: in the texts where the complainant enlarges on a supplication—I am thinking particularly of the Psalms—a wide range of synonyms fills the same place in the structure, giving the same meaning.

I cannot prove this statement—which I believe to be important—without offering a few model examples. I would therefore like to give a brief overview of three Psalms demonstrating the appearance of the vocabulary of the complaint and its supporting elements: Psalm 3 will act as a brief text for showing the links between the different aspects of a suit of complaint; Psalm 140 will demonstrate chiefly the development of a charge of injustice under way (series: *ḥāmās*); lastly, Psalm 11 will allow me to stress the complexity of the paradigm of the request (imperative *hôšîa'*).

Psalm 3.[152] There are basically three structural elements to this Psalm:

1. The act of complaint (*qr' 'el*) addressed to God. This element includes God's titles, which point to the 'judiciary body' to whom appeal is made; expressions that refer to the psychological condition (trust, fear, etc.) also indirectly form part of it.

2. The description of the act of violence being committed, portrayed as a massive attack (a metaphor or the reality of war?) that belittles the speaker. This is the paradigm that corresponds to the cry *ḥāmās*.

3. The request for assistance, addressed to a judge: this element is represented by the imperative *hôšîa'*, subdivided into (a) salvation of the plaintiff, and (b) counterattack against his oppressors.

151. It may be observed, however, that the king decrees the death of Elisha, considered the real culprit in the situation (2 Kgs 6.31).

152. On the general interpretation of Psalm 3, cf. in particular Alonso Schökel, *Treinta Salmos*, pp. 51-61.

	complaint	***ḥāmās***	***hôšîa‘***	
3.2	*yhwh*	*mâ rabbû ṣārāy*		
		rabbîm qāmîm ‘ālāy		
3		*rabbîm ’ōm^{e}rîm l^{e}napšî*	*’ên y^{e}šû‘ātâ lô*	
	bē’lōhîm			
4	*w^{e}’attâ yhwh*			
	māgēn ba‘^{a}dî			
	k^{e}bôdî			
	ûmērîm rō’šî			
5	***qôlî ’el yhwh ’eqrā***		*wayya‘^{a}nēnî*	
	mēhar qodšô			
6	*’^{a}nî šākabtî*			
	wā’îšānâ			
	h^{e}qîṣôtî			
	kî yhwh		*yism^{e}kēnî*	
7	*lo’ ’îrā’*	*mērib^{e}bôt ‘ām*		
		’^{a}šer sābîb šātû		
		‘ālāy		
8	*yhwh*		*qûmâ*	
			hôšî‘ēnî	
	’^{e}lōhay			*kî hikkîtā*
		kol ’ōy^{e}bay leḥî		
		šinnê r^{e}šā‘îm		*šibbartā*
9	*l^{e}yhwh*		*hayšû‘â*	
	‘al ‘amm^{e}kā		*birkātekā*	

Verses 2-3 mainly stress the element *ḥāmās*: the reference to ‘salvation’ is explicitly denied by those who are oppressing the speaker. Verses 4-7, which are central, develop the *complaint* element: in fact only in v. 5a do we find mention of what the reciter of the Psalm has done; these verses are focused on the subject and on the condition of the supplicant, which is (a) one of trust in assistance and (b) fearlessness of the violence being committed. Verses 8-9 bring to the fore the *hôšîa‘* element: here in fact we find the only imperatives in the Psalm, which have as their object (a) the salvation of the speaker and (b) the downfall of the violent.

Psalm 140. I do not believe that this Psalm (any more than the others I am putting forward as examples) has a special position among the appeals made to God; it does, however, seem to me particularly suited for emphasizing the element of *ḥāmās*. I would like to set out, therefore, just the part of the text where the terminology of oppression and trickery occurs (which calls to mind, among other things, what I have said about false witness).

140.2	*...mē'ādām rā'*	
	*mē'îš **ḥ^{a}māsîm**...*	
3		*ḥāš^{e}bû rā'ôt b^{e}lēb*
		yāgûrû milḥāmôt
4		*šān^{a}nû l^{e}šônām k^{e}mô nāḥāš*
		ḥ^{a}mat 'akšûb taḥat ś^{e}pātêmô
5	*...mîdê rāšā'*	
	*mē'îš **ḥ^{a}māsîm**...*	
		ḥāš^{e}bû lidḥôt p^{e}'āmāy
6		*ṭām^{e}nû*
	gē'îm	*paḥ lî*
		waḥ^{a}bālîm pār^{e}śû rešet
		l^{e}yad ma'gāl mōq^{e}šîm šātû lî
9	*...ma'^{a}wayyê rāšā'*	
		z^{e}māmô...
10	*rō'š m^{e}sibbāy*	
	'^{a}mal ś^{e}pātêmô...	
12	*'îš lāšôn...*	
	*'îš **ḥāmās**...*	

This Psalm takes up the traditional images of war (vv. 3, 8) and hunting (vv. 4, 6, 12) to describe metaphorically the actions of the wicked against the speaker: the insistence on the organs of speech (v. 4: tongue, lips; v. 10: lips; v. 12: tongue),[153] put at the service of an evil plot (vv. 2, 5 and above all 9: *zāmam*, which recalls Deut. 19.19), enables us to detect the activity of a false witness who—as we know—is equivalent to a 'violent witness' (*'ēd ḥāmās*). The actual term *ḥāmās* (vv. 2, 5, 12) runs through the Psalm, leading us to state that the speaker is indeed crying, 'violence' (which is taking place in the form of a judicial plot against him).

Psalm 31. This Psalm too can be read in accordance with the structure I suggested for Psalm 3; however, I intend to demonstrate here that the request addressed to the court of judgment by the appellant uses a great variety of terms which have *the same value* and therefore identical juridical relevance. Concentrating exclusively, therefore, on the paradigm of the element *hôšîa'* (and emphasizing the verbs clearly in the imperative), we arrive at:

153. Note also, in v. 3, the reference to the *heart*; and in v. 5 the mention of the *hand*. As I observed in section 1.4.2. above, this may be characteristic of the description of a false witness.

31.2	*'al 'ēbôšâ*	
	palleṭēnî	
3	***haṭṭēh** 'ēlay 'ōznekā*	
	haṣṣîlēnî	
	***heyēh** lî leṣûr mā'ôz...lehôšî'ēnî*	
4	*tanḥēnî*	
	ûtenahalēnî	
5	*tôṣî'ēnî mērešet*	
6	*pādîtâ 'ôtî*	
8	*rā'îtā 'et 'onyî*	
	yāda'tā beṣārôt napšî	
9	*welō' hisgartanî beyad 'ôyēb*	
	he'emadtā bammerḥāb raglāy	
10	***ḥonnēnî***	
16	***haṣṣîlēnî***	
17	***hā'îrâ** pāneykā 'al 'abdekā*	
18	*'al 'ēbôšâ*	
		yēbōšû rešā'îm
		yiddemû
19		*tē'ālamnâ śiptê šāqer*
21	*tastîrēm*	
	tiṣpenēm	
23	*šāma'tā qôl taḥanûnay*	
24		*mešallēm... 'ōśēh ga'awâ*

We see here the appearance of terms which I said in Chapter 5[154] were the equivalent of the verb *špṭ*: the speaker asks in fact that God 'should judge', in this way intervening on behalf of the clear upholder of right. This series of synonymous expressions provides a bridge to the following section, the object of which is indeed this link between the act of complaint and the judge's intervention.

2.4. *The Relationship between the Complaint (or Appeal) and the Judge's Action*

I stated that a complaint is a request for intervention directed to a *judge*, who does justice by giving aid to the unjustly oppressed. The terminology used to describe this intervention—as I have already noted—is quite wide-ranging; in this section I would like to demonstrate the particular relevance of the verbs *šm'* and *'nh*, which are directly linked to the complainant's request.

154. Cf. Chapter 5 section 2.3.1.-2.

2.4.1. *Appeal–Heed (ṣ‘q–šm‘)*. A complaint takes the form of an invocation and a cry, and is therefore addressed to the judge's ear. It is therefore altogether natural that there should occur a lexical relationship between the complainant's *ṣ‘q* (and synonyms) and the judge's *šm‘*.[155] From a strictly logical point of view, the act of listening is *intermediate* between the complaint and the active intervention that brings about salvation; the biblical texts, however, sometimes identify the whole of the 'saving' act with the verb of *listening* alone (which in fact means hearing the request, with all the consequences that involves), and sometimes with 'saving' alone.

We are here faced with a kind of (Deuteronomistic?)[156] literary scheme that interprets the progress of history in a juridical and judicial manner; Israel's prayer makes constant reference to it. A few examples will reveal the organization and lexicon of this scheme:

	subject	complaint	heeding	intervention
Neh. 9.27	oppressed Israel			
	(*ṣārâ*)	*ṣ‘q ’el*	*šm‘*	*yš‘ (Hi) miyyad…*
28	(*ṣārâ*)	*z‘q*	*šm‘*	*nṣl (Hi)*
Num. 20.15-16	oppressed Israel			
	(*r‘‘ [Hi]*)	*ṣ‘q ’el*	*šm‘*	(intervention: *yṣ’ [Hi]*)
Deut. 26.6-9	oppressed Israel			
	(… *‘ᵃbōdâ, ‘ᵒnî,*			
	‘āmāl, laḥaṣ)	*ṣ‘q ’el*	*šm‘*	*r’h* (intervention: *yṣ’ [Hi]*)
Exod. 3.7-8	oppressed Israel			
	(*‘ᵒnî, ngś,*			
	mak’ôb)	*ṣᵉ‘āqâ*	*šm‘*	*r’h, nṣl (Hi) miyyad…*
Exod. 2.23-25	oppressed Israel			
	(*‘ᵃbōdâ*)	*z‘q*		
		šaw‘â ’el	*šm‘*	*zkr, r’h, yd‘*

155. This is probably the reason for the relationship between *špṭ* and *šm‘* that I mentioned in Chapter 5 section 2.1.4.

156. Boecker, *Redeformen*, pp. 64-65. As regards the book of Judges in particular, I would refer the reader to W. Beyerlin, 'Gattung und Herkunft des Rahmens im Richterbuch', in *Tradition und Situation: Studien zur alttestamentlichen Prophetie* (FS A. Weiser; Göttingen, 1963), pp. 1-29; W. Richter, *Traditionsgeschichtliche Untersuchungen zum Richterbuch* (BBB, 18; Bonn, 1963); *idem*, *Die Bearbeitung des "Retterbuches" in der deuteronomischen Epoche* (BBB, 21; Bonn, 1964), especially pp. 3-13, 18-20; W. Brueggemann, 'Social Criticism and Social Vision in the Deuteronomic Formula of the Judges', in *Die Botschaft und die Boten* (FS W. Wolff; Neukirchen, 1981), pp. 101-14.

	subject	complaint	heeding	intervention
Ps. 34.7	*ʿānî*	*qr'*	*šmʿ*	*yšʿ (Hi) min (ṣārâ)*
18	(*ṣaddîqîm*)	*ṣʿq*	*šmʿ*	*nṣl (Hi) min (ṣārâ)*
Jer. 11.11	oppressed Israel			
	(*rāʿâ*)	*zʿq ʾel*	(not) *šmʿ*	
12	oppressed Israel			
	(*rāʿâ*)	*zʿq ʾel*		(not) *yšʿ* (*Hi*)
Hab. 1.2	the prophet			
	(*šōd wᵉḥāmās*)	*šwʿ* (*Pi*)	(not) *šmʿ*	
		zʿq ʾel		(not) *yšʿ* (*Hi*)
Job 27.9	the wicked			
	(*ṣārâ*)	*ṣᵉʿāqâ*	(not) *šmʿ*	
Job 34.28	the poor man			
	(*dal, ʿᵃniyyîm*)	*ṣᵉʿāqâ*	*šmʿ*	
Jer. 11.14	oppressed Israel			
	(*rāʿâ*)	*qr' ʾel*	(not) *šmʿ*	
Ps. 22.25	*ʿānî*	*šwʿ* (*Pi*) *ʾel*	*šmʿ*	
Ps. 18.7	the speaker			
	(*ṣar*)	*qr'*		
		šwʿ (*Pi*) *ʾel*	*šmʿ*	
		šawʿâ lipnê	*bwʾ bᵉʾōzen-*	
Ps. 34.16	(*ṣaddîqîm*)		*ʾōzen- ʾel*	
		šawʿâ		
Judg. 3.9	oppressed Israel			
	(*ʿbd*)	*zʿq ʾel*		*yšʿ* (*Hi*)
Judg. 10.12,	oppressed Israel			
14	(*lḥṣ*)	*ṣʿq ʾel*		*yšʿ (Hi) miyyad…*
Ps. 107.6	Israel in dire straits			
	(*ṣar*)	*ṣʿq ʾel*		*nṣl (Hi) min (mᵉṣûqâ)*
13, 19	(*ṣar*)	*zʿq ʾel*		*yšʿ (Hi) min (mᵉṣûqâ)*
28	(*ṣar*)	*ṣʿq ʾel*		*yṣ' (Hi) min (mᵉṣûqâ)*
Ps. 22.6	(forefathers:	*zʿq*		*mlṭ* (*Ni*)
	v. 5)			
Job 29.12	*ʿānî*	*šwʿ* (*Pi*)		*mlṭ* (*Pi*)
Ps. 72.12-13	*ʾebyôn*	*šwʿ* (*Pi*)		*nṣl* (*Hi*)
				ḥws
				yṣ' (*Hi*)
Ps. 18.4	the speaker			
	(*ṣar*)	*qr'*		*yšʿ (Ni) min (ʾōyēb)*
Isa. 19.20	oppressed Israel			
	(*lḥṣ*)	*ṣʿq ʾel*		*yšʿ* (*Hi*)
				ryb + pron. suff.
				nṣl (*Hi*)

2.4.2. *Appeal–Response* (*ṣ'q–'nh*). A complaint is a speech that is pronounced in a place of judgment and demands an intervention by the judge: to begin with, this intervention is a *speech* that is a response to the request made, and at the same time a decree or sentence with normative value. In fact, on the basis of this speech by the judge, *execution* subsequently occurs: this is the practical application of what the judge has laid down.[157]

Following a logical scheme, I should therefore be able to lay out 'the judge's action' vis-à-vis a complaint in the following manner:

accuser		JUDGE	
complaint	acknowledgement	response sentence	execution
ṣ'q	*šm'*	*'nh*	*yš'* (*Hi*)

157. For the purpose of illustrating the 'judge's' speech reaction to a complaint, I would like to take two episodes that resemble each other as regards the situation they describe.

1. The Hebrews in Egypt have been forced into back-breaking labour and to undergo the oppression of their foremen (Exod. 5.6-14). Israel's representatives then go to lay their complaint before Pharaoh (5.15: *ṣ'q 'el*). Faced with their request (which is an indictment of Pharaoh himself and his people), we have a royal decree (5.17: *wayyō'mer*) which rejects the claim, attributing it to culpable laziness.

2. After the death of Solomon, Jeroboam and the whole assembly of Israel appear before Rehoboam to ask him to 'lighten the harsh slavery' to which they had been subjected (1 Kgs 12.1-4); this action is expressed in generic vocabulary (v. 3: *wayyābō'û...way^{e}dabb^{e}rû 'el*), but the content of the request recalls the one in Exod. 5.15-16, where it is introduced by a technical verb, *ṣ'q 'el*. Rehoboam asks for advice from the 'elders', who urge him to put out a favourable decree (v. 7: *wa'^{a}nîtām w^{e}dibbartā '^{a}lêhem d^{e}bārîm ṭôbîm*); he then turns to the 'young men', who are of the opposite opinion. Rehoboam follows the latter suggestion, and puts out his decree: *wayya'an hammelek 'et hā'ām qāšâ...waydabbēr '^{a}lêhem...lē'mōr* (vv. 13-14). This shows how the verb *'nh* clearly expresses the reaction (in this case negative) of the judging body to the complaint; it is interesting to observe, on the other hand, how the same effect is achieved in v. 15 with the verb *šm'*: *w^{e}lō' šāma' hammelek 'el hā'ām*, which demonstrates the complementary nature of these two verbs in the syntagm I have laid out in outline form in the text.

On this latter episode, cf. D.G. Evans, 'Rehoboam's Advisors at Shechem and Political Institutions in Israel and Sumer', *JNES* 25 (1966), pp. 273-79; J.C. Trebolle Barrera, *Salomón y Jeroboán* (Bibliotheca Salmanticensis, Diss. 3; Salamanca, 1980), pp. 202-41. For the relationship between Exodus and 1 Kings 12, cf. Trebolle again, 'La liberación de Egipto narrada y creída desde la opresión de Salomón', *CuadBíb* 6 (1981), pp. 1-19.

In some biblical texts it is possible to discern all the elements listed above, but it should straightaway be recognized that each of the judge's different 'actions' is enough to bring to mind the whole judicial operation involved in a complaint. I would like to give a few examples to illustrate the variety of relationships which may occur:

	complaint	JUDGE'S ACTION		
		šmʿ	***ʿnh***	***yšʿ (Hi)***
Job 5.1	*qr'*		*ʿnh*	
Ps. 3.5	*qr'*		*ʿnh*	
Job 30.20	*šwʿ* (*Pi*)		(not) *ʿnh*	
1 Sam. 8.18	*zʿq*		(not) *ʿnh*	
1 Sam. 7.8	*zʿq 'el*			*yšʿ* (*Hi*) *miyyad*
9	*zʿq 'el*		*ʿnh*	
Ps. 120.1-2	*qr' 'el*		*ʿnh*	*nṣl* (*Hi*) *min*
Job 19.7	*ṣʿq*		(not) *ʿnh* (*Ni*)	
	šwʿ (*Pi*)			(not) *mišpāṭ*
Isa. 46.7	*ṣʿq 'el*		(not) *ʿnh*	(not) *yšʿ* (*Hi*) *min* (*ṣārâ*)
Isa. 58.9	*qr'*		*ʿnh*	
	šwʿ (*Pi*)			(*hinnēnî*)
Prov. 21.13	*z*^{e}*ʿāqâ*	*'ṭm 'ōzen*		
	qr'		(not) *ʿnh* (*Ni*)	
Job. 35.12	*ṣʿq*		(not) *ʿnh*	
13		(not) *šmʿ*		
Isa. 65.24	*qr'*		*ʿnh*	
	dbr (*Pi*)	*šmʿ*		
Isa. 30.19-20	*zʿq*	*šmʿ*	*ʿnh*	(*ntn*...)
Ps. 4.2	*qr'*		*ʿnh*	(*rḥb* [*Hi*])
	t^{e}*pillâ*	*šmʿ*		
Ps. 17.6-7	*qr'*	*nṭh* (*Hi*) *'ōzen* *šmʿ*	*ʿnh*	*yšʿ* (*Hi*)

As a conclusion to my study of the accusation, its lexicon and the ways in which it is expressed in the biblical texts, I would like to sum up in outline and mark out the respective semantic fields of the testimony, the accusation and the complaint.

1. Given a testimony, the main relationship illustrated is that of a man with his neighbour (we could call this horizontal); in a complaint, however, the emphasis falls on the relationship between the complainant and the judge (the vertical dimension). For this reason, 'witness' can be confusable with generic aggression, and a complaint with generic prayer.

2. There is frequent attestation of a witness's juridical activity with regard to human tribunals; complaints on the other hand are mostly addressed to God as the supreme judge. This looks like a denunciation, in global terms, of the imperfection of the administration of justice in Israel (cf. Ps. 58.82 etc.), which is incapable of protecting the rights of the oppressed.

3. Testimony brings in those categories that are linked together semantically under the general heading of 'force'; the complaint, by comparison, gives expression to all the nuances of 'weakness'—this is true of the subject of the juridical act, his or her acts, the so-called technical language and its metaphorical transformations.

4. When dealing with testimony the biblical texts often present us with a 'false' declaration, with all the juridical consequences that implies; the complaint of which Scripture speaks on the other hand is mainly truthful. This could be the reason why we do not have a Hebrew vocabulary for 'true' testimony comparable to that for false testimony: the two juridical forms are also, so to speak, subdivided as to what happens to their content: it is normal to expect a negative (final) response to a witness and a positive one to an appellant.

5. The person who lays a complaint is sometimes the victim of none other than the witness, but an appeal lays a charge against the witness (or even the judge). Particularly in the Psalms, it is usual to see this reversal of roles and a swing in the juridical force of the different actions described. Finally, it should be remembered that being a victim constitutes a favoured juridical condition for the obtaining of justice.

6. The semantic perspective of witness is punishment (of which the death sentence is symbolic); the complaint on the other hand takes us into the semantic field of salvation. Therefore if a judge *always* condemns and at the same time saves, these two judicial acts (condemnation–salvation) may be linked respectively with the two accusatory acts (witness–complaint). The warnings addressed to judges in Hebrew legislation take into account this essential difference, which by nature is not sociological, but highly juridical. Theologically speaking, the eschatological advent of justice will mark the definitive disappearance of the Accuser (*śāṭān*) and will hand victory to the lowly oppressed.

II. THE DEFENCE

Let us imagine that we are taking part in a typical trial, held in conformity with legal procedures, which may not guarantee, but at least make an effort to defend, truth and justice: before a judge, in the context of a public assembly, several witnesses have risen to give evidence against a man. The latter thus finds himself having to face a threat that he cannot avoid; he cannot 'let it go' (as in the case of informal calumny or slander, insults or curses) and 'go on his way' heedless of people's opinion. If a charge does not receive an adequate response, it will have precise adverse consequences in the life of the accused, to the point of bringing about his death. More than that, the accused certainly has an *interest* in defending himself, and it is his right to do so, but equally he has the *duty* to respond in the *interests* of justice: his love for truth and uprightness oblige him to fight for a fair judgement, without which justice in the world is falsified and the possibility of civilized society is undermined.

The defence speech that responds to the prosecution attack therefore has a symmetrical juridical importance, but it is surprising to see that, in the Bible, it does not receive an attention comparable to that given to testimony against someone. The legislative texts, for example, make no mention of it; even in the case of false witness, they emphasize the judge's task and duty, but do not suggest how the accused can and should conduct a defence. On the other hand, the search for a specific and technical Hebrew term meaning 'defence', which would allow an investigation of this semantic field, is an investigation that ends without any satisfactory results.

The few texts that do narrate trials are not, at first sight, particularly illuminating in this respect; yet, I believe, they put us on the track of a reasonable explanation for the absence of a specific vocabulary for the action of defence.

To this end, I would like to take two episodes that occur upon the return of David after his flight because of Absalom's revolt and the latter's defeat; the situations are not exactly those of a court of law, because the king has to judge a crime (lèse majesté, treachery) of which he himself has been the victim; nevertheless, we can still detect the format of a trial in both cases. The two accounts illustrate the two essential forms that a defence speech can take.

The first episode (2 Sam. 19.16-24) concerns Shimei, who had 'cursed' David during his flight (17.5-14). His position now has become so critical that he makes haste to meet the victorious king to show that he is no longer on the side of the rebels. His 'defence' is to recognize his wrong and ask pardon for the offence (19.20-21); despite this, Abishai takes on the role of accuser (19.22; cf. also v. 23). David grants Shimei's request, decreeing a kind of general amnesty (for the repentant) (19.23-24). In this case, as may be observed, there is no real 'defence' speech, given that the accused admits his crime; this is the kind of speech that in other circumstances would perhaps have the effect of mitigating the punishment, but would not 'defend' the accused from the judge's just penalty. As regards the vocabulary relevant to this juridical situation, I refer the reader to Chapter 3,[158] which discusses the 'admission of guilt'. To repeat, a self-confessed criminal is not 'acquitted' in court; the confession confirms the charge and therefore ensures a guilty verdict.

The second episode (2 Sam. 19.25-31) has Mephibosheth as the accused, unjustly charged by his servant Ziba with treachery against the king (16.1-4). Like Shimei, he too goes to David; the latter brings up the accusation (in the form of a question) and invites Mephibosheth to excuse himself (19.26). We then have a short speech that displays the genuine characteristics of a 'defence': in the first place, the accused gives a different version of the facts, bringing in as an element of guiltlessness his lameness (and indirectly his careless personal appearance, a sign that he had taken no pleasure in the king's exile) (19.27); next he countercharges (with falsehood) his own accuser (19.27: *rimmānî*; 19.28: *wayraggēl bᵉ'abdᵉkā 'el 'ᵃdōnî hammelek*); finally, he entrusts himself to David's wisdom, declaring that he cannot lay claim to anything (19.28-29).[159]

158. Cf. Chapter 3 section 1. In the context of a two-sided controversy, an admission of guilt may lead the accuser to pardon; in the context of a judgment, the judge may perhaps use discretion to mitigate the punishment (I have found no precise examples of this in the biblical texts except perhaps 2 Sam. 12.13-14); but in general, repentance in a court of law does not appear to have significant importance in modifying a guilty sentence (cf. for example Josh. 7.19-25).

159. The phrase *ûmah yeš lî 'ôd ṣᵉdāqâ wᵉliz'ōq 'ôd 'el hammelek* (2 Sam. 19.29) has to be taken in the context of the whole narrative. If, as I tried to show in the pages about the complaint, the expression *z'q 'el hammelek* has the force of laying claim to one's rights, Mephibosheth expressly denies that he is in that position (it could be said, in other words, that he is not the injured party in the dispute that pits him against his servant Ziba). Now this may seem strange, since the son of Jonathan has explicitly accused Ziba of calumny, and Mephibosheth therefore seems to have a legitimate expectation of a sentence favourable to him.

This second episode shows in practical terms that a true *defence* is a reversal of the *accusation*: not only are the arguments against the accused brought down, but the latter is completely exonerated (by giving, for example, a new version of the facts that shows there has been an 'error'), but this also takes the shape of a new accusation (of falsehood, wicked intent, attempted crime) against the accuser. In other words, my thesis is this: there is no such thing as a 'neutral' defence: *defence is to accuse the accuser.*[160]

My statement has a drastic and paradoxical side to it, but on the one hand, it seems to me to correspond to those texts which describe the holding of a trial,[161] and on the other hand, it supplies a reason for the

I think it is necessary to distinguish two sides to this controversy: the former concerns the accusation of treachery against David the king, with its consequent threat of death; the latter on the other hand concerns the possession of goods belonging to Mephibosheth. My opinion is that the 'claim' (*z'q 'el*) in question in the text does not so much refer to saving life as to the possessions that have been taken away from Mephibosheth (to his servant's benefit) by a previous verdict of David, as a precise consequence of a false accusation by Ziba (16.4).

Close scrutiny shows that Mephibosheth's 'defence' puts David in a difficult juridical position: if the king maintains that Ziba has told the truth, the verdict given remains just (but then he would have to take further action against Mephibosheth for attempted treachery); but if the son of Jonathan is in the right, the king has to admit to making a judicial error, and as a result would be bound to recompense the one who had been unjustly wronged.

David's new sentence looks 'Solomonic': he cuts short the appellant's speech (*lāmmâ tᵉdabbēr 'ôd dᵉbāreykā*: 19.30). As may be seen, there is no mention of an act of amnesty towards the accused (as is clearly said about Shimei in 19.24): the speech revolves exclusively around the *śādeh* and who is its owner.

So when Mephibosheth states that he has no 'right' (*ṣᵉdāqâ*) of claim, he is emphasizing that his property was not a 'family possession' at all, and as such something that would be listed in the juridical history of Israel with inalienable force; on the contrary, he had admitted that it had been freely and kindly granted to him by the king when he was on the list of those condemned to death (19.19). The force of this statement is twofold: first, Mephibosheth uses it to show that his journey to meet the king was not 'self-interested', but an act of personal fidelity to the legitimate king (after David's 'Solomonic' verdict he in fact refuses the part granted to him, thus revealing—just as in Solomon's judgment—the truth of his intentions [19.31]); secondly, it acts to free David from any charge whatever: since the property in question had been a 'royal' gift, the sovereign could dispose of it as he saw fit.

160. Cf. Chapter 3 section 2.3.

161. I cannot discuss in detail here the biblical texts that narrate trials, but I think the following observations might be useful:

observable lack of vocabulary typical of the juridical action of defence.

As regards the Hebrew lexicon of defence in particular, I can refer the reader to (1) declarations of innocence;[162] the structure of these makes

In 1 Sam. 22.6-19, the judgment given by Saul against the supporters of David (accused of rebellion) sees Ahimelech and his whole family appear before the king's court, where he is categorically accused of conspiracy (22.13). The accused defends himself: he tries to give a different interpretation to the facts surrounding him and denies any open willingness to oppose the king. As is well known, Saul decrees his death; this might look like simply a wicked and barbaric verdict, if it is not remembered that in defending himself Ahimelech has defended David (19.14) and thereby has (indirectly) accused Saul of persecuting him unjustly. If the king had acquitted the accused, he would at the same time have decreed his own guilt and would in some way have stood self-condemned (on this whole episode, cf. Whitelam, *The Just King*, pp. 83-89).

In the trial of Jeremiah (Jer. 26.1-24), the prophet's defence speech seems simply to exonerate him from the accusation; the princes in charge of the judgment do in fact pass sentence of not guilty (26.16). The narrative that follows is not a clear telling of the facts, and is therefore open to different interpretations (cf., as well as the commentaries, F.-L. Hossfeld and I. Meyer, 'Der Prophet vor dem Tribunal. Neuer Auslegungsversuch von Jer. 26', *ZAW* 86 [1974], pp. 30-50; I. Meyer, *Jeremia und die falschen Propheten* [OBO, 13; Freiburg, 1977], pp. 15-45); I think it should be stressed, however, that the acquittal of the prophet leaves 'juridically' intact the accusation brought by Jeremiah against the city (including its political and religious authorities). This means that if Jeremiah is not guilty, then his accusers are, on a twofold level: (1) because they had already been accused of capital crimes by the prophet, and (2) because they have turned into unjust accusers of a defendant. If this reading of the text is borne in mind, it is perhaps easier to understand why, after the princes' verdict, there is a further speech which follows the dynamic of criminal proceedings.

At this point I am obliged to formulate a hypothesis that I have not seen elsewhere in the commentaries or studies on this passage: *the speech by 'the elders of the land' runs from 26.17 to 26.23*; at any rate, the unity of sense does not include just the reference to the case of Micah (fairly useless, once the judges have already decreed acquittal), but also to that of Uriah. The two criminal 'precedents' have the purpose of establishing the principle of 'analogy' in jurisprudence: it is a matter of two prophets who spoke *like* Jeremiah (26.18; 26.20); therefore, by observing how *the king* judged in the past, a verdict can be formulated that is consistent with the jurisprudential history of the State of Judah. In the first case, Hezekiah judged Micah innocent (26.19a); the consequence then was that the king, finding himself in a position of guilt, encouraged an act of public penance (26.19b). On the basis of this first example, the judges (and all the inhabitants of the land) have to shoulder a grave crime, have to declare themselves seriously guilty (26.19c).

Turning instead to the second case, the verdict of the king (who is the current

use of (2) the terminology of the complaint, or, more precisely, that of the appeal;[163] the whole thing forms the essential system of a plea that is at the same time a statement of charges.

Having said this, which I believe to be the most decisive thing for an understanding of defence procedure, I would like to mention some terms or categories that bring out more clearly the aspect of the defendant's reaction and its reference to a defensive system.

1. *The Reply*

The defence speech is always *second* with respect to that for the prosecution, which has the initiative in bringing the trial and opening it with its evidence; as a result we may describe the speech for the defence as a response or reply.

Linguistically, this is not always brought out by the Hebrew lexicon,

king) is altogether different: he judged Uriah a false prophet, a liar deserving death (cf. Deut. 13.6; 18.20); as a result he pursued him fiercely to the point of extraditing him from Egypt to a shameful death (26.21-23). In accordance with this precedent—on the basis therefore of a purely juridical perspective which does not consider the prophet a priori as a true prophet (as the reader unconsciously does, contravening the need for discernment demanded by the Law)—we have a jurisprudential act opposed to the first one: which of the two then is normative? It seems logical and reasonable to go by what *the current king has decreed*, granted that prophecy is a speech that accuses particular people at the precise moment in history; if therefore Jehoiakim's sentence is followed, Jeremiah must be considered a false prophet, deserving death. It may be thought that the 'elders of the land' are implicitly reminding the 'princes' that they are judging in the name of the king; and a sentence different from that handed down by the king in person (but with the knowledge of the princes; cf. 26.21) puts them in a contradictory juridical position.

This would explain the abrupt end to the narrative (26.24). Jeremiah has by no means been acquitted; indeed, the authoritative intervention of one of the princes is necessary in order to prevent his execution (by those people who represent the judging assembly). How this intervention was carried out we are not told; perhaps unanimity was required for a capital verdict, and the opposition of Ahicham was sufficient to prevent the application of the verdict.

Out of this complicated trial affair we have confirmation that a defence of the accused coincides with a declaration the accusers' guilt. This appears quite clearly in the (Greek) text of Susannah's trial (Daniel 13): Daniel cannot defend the innocent unjustly judged without laying the blame on and condemning the false accuser (13.48-62).

162. Cf. Chapter 3 section 2.

163. Cf. Chapter 7 section 2.

which often introduces the speech for the defence with a simple *'mr* (cf. 1 Kgs 3.17, 22; Jer. 26.12 etc.). We do, however, also have the use of the verb *'nh* (2 Sam. 22.14; Job 9.3, 14-15; 13.22; 14.15; 23.5 etc.) and *šwb* (*Hi*) (Hab. 2.1; Job 13.22; 31.14; 33.5, 13, 22; 35.4; 40.4), which gives more practical expression to the aspect of rebutting the previous speech.

Along with this terminology of the oral intervention, I can also point to the force of the verb *'rk*. In prose texts, from which it seems the meaning of the root should be derived, this verb is mostly used in a military context with the meaning 'to get into position, to line up (for battle)' (1 Sam. 4.2; 2 Sam. 10.17; Jer. 6.23; 46.3; 50.14, 42), frequently in the syntagm *'rk milḥāmâ* (Gen. 14.8; Judg. 20.20, 22; 1 Sam. 17.2, 8; Joel 2.5; 1 Chron. 12.34 etc.). If, as we have seen, a trial is interpreted metaphorically as a battle, it is not strange that *'rk* should appear, in a highly legal context, to describe the taking up of position by the 'combatants' in order to gain a juridical victory.[164]

The verb *'rk* may be used absolutely (Job 33.5; 37.19 and perhaps 36.19), with a pronominal suffix (Job 6.4), with the preposition *l*^{e} (Isa. 44.7; Pss. 5.4; 50.21), in the syntagm *'rk mišpāṭ* (Job 13.18; 23.4) or *'rk millîm 'el* (Job 32.14).

Apart from Ps. 50.21, this term may be granted a certain defensive nuance, as though it meant 'to prepare to meet an attack'.[165] Since the context here is metaphorical, we could say that the verb *'rk* is the equivalent of the other images of military defence that frequently appear in poetic texts: breastplate, shield, stronghold, wall, shelter, and the like, which are the opposite of the corresponding aggressive images: spear, arrows, encampment, army and so on. Of course, this theoretical distinction is not always respected, because, as I said, a good defence is knowing how to counterattack one's adversary (Ps. 35.2: shield and buckler; 35.3: spear and battle-axe).

2. *Recourse to a 'Defender'*

If the accused is faced with a concerted attack, often by an overwhelming crowd of adverse witnesses, self-defence may be undertaken

164. As Begrich writes, ''*rk* bezeichnet im technischen Sinn das Vorlegen der Beweise vor der Gegenpartei in der Verhandlung' (*Deuterojesaja*, p. 35).

165. In Ps. 50.21 (*'ôkîḥ*^{a}*kā w*^{e}*'e'erkâ l*^{e}*'êneykā*) the verb *'rk* clearly has the meaning of an accusatory action, as may be seen from the link with the verb *ykḥ* (*Hi*) and the context. In the other texts it seems to favour a defensive nuance.

by calling upon someone to give favourable evidence; if one claims innocence, not only are there friends and close acquaintances to appeal to, but one will dare to appeal to the supreme judge, hoping that the impartial justice of an unbiased tribunal may, by rigorous inquiry and wise evaluation, find in favour of the defence. In the last of these cases (the appeal) we are dealing with the juridical situation that I described in the section dedicated to the 'accusation', and which I have likened to the complaint.

In the biblical texts in which *God* is called upon to defend the (falsely accused) innocent, I think that in the main it is a question of an appeal to the supreme judge; the vocabulary that expresses the judge's intervention and that which describes a defender's help tend to mingle because the result achieved by the two actions is basically the same: it is enough to think how Daniel, in the account of the trial of Susannah, first takes on the role of defender (Dan. 13.45-49) and then that of judge (13.50). On the other hand, in the texts where the accused appeals to *friends* and acquaintances, I think it is more a question of defence witnesses.

I would like to sum up the important elements along these lines—gathering together among other things what I have said here and there in my work—under three main headings.

2.1. *The Request for an 'Intervention' (on Behalf of)*

I have often pointed out that verbs of motion refer to a juridical initiative; now, for an accused party to ask for a defender to arise, come forward and so on, is in fact to ask for the fullness of *intervention* for the defence: the defender's movement is especially significant when it is equivalent to siding with and being close to, so as to be solid with him or her in facing the strife with enemies.

I refer the reader back to Chapter 6,[166] and repeat again that the terminology is not specific to defence but to intervention; only the context can decide the particular purpose of a juridical action.

2.2. *The Request that a Defender Should Speak*

The image frequently found (especially in the Psalms) of an innocent person at the mercy of a crowd of adversaries who are falsely accusing is matched by the insistent request that someone should speak on behalf

166. Cf. Chapter 6 section 2.3.

of the victim and break down the wall of silent complicity in order to derail the progress of the trial.

In the following section I should deal in global terms with the subject of silence in the context of juridical procedures; it will be easier to bring in this kind of request at that point under the heading of the opposition between speech and reticence.

2.3. *The Terminology most used for the Purpose of 'Defence'*

I would like here to point out the terminology that most frequently refers to the appearance of a '*defender*', that is, of someone who has the task of aiding the weak in securing their rights. I would like to make two major subdivisions that are equivalent as to meaning but are formally different as to the language used.

2.3.1. *Acting on Behalf of.* A defender is in some ways an accuser's antagonist: if the latter can be described as being *against* the accused, then the former is *for* a potential victim; if the preposition *b^e^* was the characteristic sign of the prosecution witness (cf. *'ēd b^e^*, *qwm b^e^*, *'nh b^e^*; *dibbēr b^e^*; *hyh b^e^*; *ryb b^e^* etc.),[167] then the preposition *l^e^* is often the mark of a defender. I would like to recall the force of *ryb l^e^*,[168] *'ēd l^e^*,[169] *hyh l^e^* (Gen. 31.42, Exod. 18.19; Ps. 124.1, 2), *dibbēr l^e^* (Job 13.7; cf. also 36.2) and other similar syntagms.[170]

2.3.2. *The Root 'zr*. The root *'zr* refers to the act of lending assistance in general, of joining one's forces with those of someone else for a common purpose; its field of application is as wide as that of human activity; from the world of politics (1 Kgs 1.7; Isa. 20.6; 30.5, 7; 31.3

167. Cf. Chapter 1 section 2.2, Chapter 2 section 2.2, Chapter 7 sections 1.2.1.b. and 1.6.1.

168. Cf. Chapter 1 section 2.2.

169. Cf. n. 23.

170. Cf. for example Job 36.2 and the interpretation of *yāpîaḥ lô* given by D. Miller, 'Yāpîaḥ in Psalm XII 6', *VT* 29 (1979), pp. 495-501. I could also quote the expression *'nh l^e^* in the sense of 'to testify on behalf of' in a letter from the time of Josiah, lines 10-11 (cf. J. Naveh, 'A Hebrew Letter from the Seventh Century BC', *IEJ* 10 [1960], pp. 129-139; F.M. Cross, 'Epigraphic Notes on Hebrew Documents of the Eight–Sixth Centuries BC: II. The Murabba'ât Papyrus and the Letter Found near Yabneh-yam', *BASOR* 165 [1962], pp. 34-46; S. Talmon, 'The New Hebrew Letter from the Seventh Century BC in Historical Perspective', *BASOR* 176 [1964], pp. 29-38).

etc.) to the more specifically military (Josh. 1.14; 10.4, 6, 33; 1 Sam. 7.12; 2 Sam. 8.5 etc.), from collaboration in the area of the family (Gen. 2.18-20) to the area of work (Isa. 41.6).

The sphere of the trial is also touched by this terminology: 'to assist' an accused is a common metaphor in the biblical world and in modern proceedings to describe the juridical action of defence.

In Hebrew, the root *'zr*, used in the context of trials, mainly appears alongside the terminology of 'salvation'; the overtones therefore are of a successful intervention by the defender. Just as the action of an accuser is a sort of threat that tends to become a condemnation, so the action of a defender—by bringing out the accused's innocence and the accuser's lying—tends to decide the juridical conflict favourably. I would like to give some examples of this frequent sliding between the terminology of defence and that which is often attributed to the judging authority itself. For example:

Isa. 41.4	*'zr—g'l*
Isa. 49.8	*'zr—'nh—(yš')*
Isa. 50.8-9	*'zr—ṣdq (Hi)*
Ps. 37.40	*'zr—plṭ (Pi)—yš' (Hi)*
Ps. 79.9	*'zr—nṣl (Hi)—(yš')*
Ps. 109.26	*'zr—yš' (Hi)*
Ps. 72.12	*'zr—nṣl (Hi)*
Job 29.12	*'zr—mlṭ (Pi)*

III. Silence in Juridical Proceedings

A debate may be defined as a controversy taken before a judge; as such, it consists of the alternating speeches of the two disputants: the prosecution speech is followed by the defence speech, and so on. This exchange of speeches is distinguished from polite conversation not only by the dramatic nature of its outcome, but also because each of the parties is trying to bring the conflict to the most rapid end possible; as in a brawl or duel, each tries to best the other with the minimum expenditure of energy, dealing blows in such a way as to avoid a reply.

The structure of a controversy, even when it takes the form of a trial, has an apparently contradictory shape: on the one hand, it is juridically necessary that one side should allow the other to speak, because otherwise one would not be respecting the adversary as a human being and would be denying a person's equality before the law;[171] on the other hand, the internal logic of each of the disputant's speeches is to *silence the other.* This comes out on two levels.

1. *A Speech Demands Silence*

1.1. *The 'Justificatory' Sense of a Speech*

The first level gives expression to the conditions of silence under which any speech lives: a speech is in fact given meaning if it can be *heard*, and hearing demands *silence*. As a result, a juridical speech often begins with an invitation, addressed to the other party, to listen, an invitation sometimes explicitly linked to a request to be quiet.

This may look like a rhetorical device of no great importance, but in it is hidden something decisive for an understanding of the speech relationship, especially in a juridical context. There is no real relationship between individuals, and therefore there is no justice, unless its medium, or rather its condition, is a silence that signifies an acceptance of the other, a desire for the truth and an absolute necessity to be 'questioned' as to one's own speech. In the second place, this demand for silence, if it occurs during the debate, is the same as denying value to the words the other is speaking, it is to dispute the 'justificatory' sense of the speech in progress; in general terms, it may be said that demanding silence is to deny that the other is 'right'. This is as true for a prosecution speech as a defence speech: by demanding silence, both of them dispute the truth and 'justice' of the opponent's speech; both of them say that the other is guilty.

I would like to show how my observations link up with the biblical texts, so as to prove and deepen them.

1.2. *The Request for a Hearing: The Biblical Texts*

One of the most important characteristics of the *rîb*, according to the study made by J. Harvey,[172] is that the accuser introduces his or her speech with an invitation to listen. The basic structure of this invitation has three elements: (1) an imperative demanding a hearing; (2) the

171. Cf. the aforementioned 'principle of cross-examination' (n. 131).

172. *Le plaidoyer prophétique*, pp. 54-55. The author includes the element of the appeal for attention addressed to those charged among the '*preliminaries to the trial*', along with the invocation of heaven on earth, the declaration of the judge's impartiality and the accusation of the accused party.

individual to whom it is addressed (the recipient); and (3) a reference to the speech that is about to be made.

a. The individual addressed may be the *accused*, who is not to shy away from precise and sober questioning; it is as though the charge was being personally delivered and handed over:

Ps. 50.7	*šim'â*	*'ammî*	*wa'^{a}dabbērâ*
		yiśrā'ēl	*w^{e}'ā'îdâ bāk*
Isa. 1.10	*šim'û*		*d^{e}bar yhwh*
		q^{e}ṣînê s^{e}dōm	
	ha'^{a}zînû		*tôrat '^{e}lōhênû*
		'am '^{a}mōrâ	

Cf. also 1 Sam. 22.7, 12; Isa. 41.1; Jer. 2.4; Mic. 1.2; Hos. 4.1; 5.1; Amos 3.1; 4.1; Job 15.17; 33.1 etc.

The text of Job 33.31-33 looks like a particularly important example, because it not only shows the relationship between listening and silence, but also implies that 'listening' is the same as not being able to reply:

v. 31	*haqšēb*	*'iyyôb*	
	š^{e}ma' lî		
	haḥ^{a}rēš		*w^{e}'ānōkî '^{a}dabbēr*
v. 32	if you have arguments, answer me,		
	speak, because I would like you to be right;		
v. 33	if not,		
		'attâ	
	š^{e}ma' lî		
	haḥ^{a}rēš		*wa'^{a}'allepkā ḥokmâ*

b. The recipient of the imperative may be the *witness-arbiter* (this is especially typical in prophecy). This looks new, but is consistent with what I said previously: demanding a hearing from witnesses is a device used to suggest that the accused does not want to lend an ear; in some ways it is a second charge, to the extent that not only does it declare that the person accused is guilty, but in addition the person is not even willing to hear about it.

Formally speaking, the syntagm contains four elements: (1) imperative to listen; (2) the recipient; (3) reference to speech; (4) the accused.

Isa. 1.2-3 *šîm'û* *šāmayim*
w^{e}*ha'*^{a}*zînî* *'ereṣ*
kî yhwh dibbēr
bānîm...
yiśrā'ēl...
'ammî...

Cf. also Deut. 32.1, 5; Jer. 6.18-19; Mic. 6.2-3; Job 34.2-4, 10.

Not only does the accuser demand a hearing; the *accused* also invites the accuser to be silent. This is not discernible in the prophetic texts because they represent 'the word of God' and his initiative as an accuser; other texts, however show that the defence has the same characteristics as the accusation. As with the previous point, we have:

a. an appeal for a hearing addressed to the other party: cf. Job 13.5-6, 13, 17; 21.2-3, 5.
b. an appeal addressed to the judge: the accused, unable to get a hearing from his accuser, demands a hearing from the judge as defender.[173]

2. *Juridical Silence*

The second level at which silence is significant in a juridical context lies in the intention of the speech made: the disputant wants to convince the other party, wants to prove the truth in such a way that it is not possible (for anyone) to reply. The accusation (and similarly the defence) wants to become the only speech, because it alone is truthful.

From a literary point of view, this comes out in the phrases in which a disputant tries to or succeeds in silencing the other, shutting the opponent's mouth for good: the silence to which an adversary is reduced marks the end of the juridical contest, and is equivalent to victory by one of the two litigants (Ezek. 16.63). In the context of a court of law it is the word of the judge that—externally—imposes silence on both parties (cf. Job 29.7-10, 21-22; also Hab. 2.20); in fact, however, it takes up either the prosecution speech or that for the defence, and as a result a magistrate's sentence is just a registering of the definitive victory of one argument, silencing the other for good.

The result is that the one silenced appears as guilty, and will therefore

173. Cf. esp. pp. 306-308.

be condemned;[174] silence is the symbolic foretaste of death. The trial, of course, ends in a guilty verdict: once judgment is passed, there can be no appeal against this; the culprit is handed over to death (or its symbolic equivalent), the practical application of the silence that is the end of every human being.

I will now demonstrate the relevance of these statements to an understanding of matters biblical in this case as before, by putting forward some examples.

2.1. *The Duty 'not to Keep Silent'*

'Not keeping silent' is obviously equivalent to speaking; this takes on different meanings depending on whether it is a question of the prosecution or the defence.

a. *Not Keeping Silence by the Prosecution.* Someone who does not

174. In this context I would like to be allowed, albeit briefly, to give my interpretation of Jesus' silence during his trial. All the Evangelists mention the fact, even if they do not agree on the circumstances: Matthew and Mark refer to it both in the judgment before the Sanhedrin (Mt. 26.62-63; Mk 14.61) and that before Pilate (Mt. 27.12-13; Mk 15.4); Luke on the other hand makes it specific to the trial before Herod (Lk. 23.9); John introduces it at a given point in the dialogue between Jesus and Pilate (Jn 19.9-10).

Taking Matthew's account as a basis (with the aim of setting bounds to my argument), we should observe that Jesus' silence is not absolute, but rather breaks constantly into speech: in Mt. 26.62-63 he does not respond to the accusations brought against him by the false witnesses, but does speak when the High Priest questions him; in Mt. 27.11-13 he responds to Pilate, but not to the accusations of the high priests and elders.

The response by Jesus to the judging *authorities*, I believe, means that he does not shirk giving witness about himself: he reaffirms, even in a tribunal, the truth as to his nature and messianic mission, well knowing that his words can be used against him.

But it is even more important to stress that he does not respond to the accusations: defending oneself is the same as proving that the others are lying, and therefore has the effect of condemning one's adversary. Yet Jesus gives up his legitimate right to defend himself, he allows himself to be taken for someone who cannot reply, as though silenced by the accusation, so as to show that his innocence does not condemn anyone else. He goes voluntarily to his death; he is silent before his accusers and does not shy away from condemnation so as to make it clear at his trial (the high point in the revelation of his loving intentions) that his desire was not to score a victory at the expense of others, but rather to undergo death provided that he treated nobody as an enemy.

keep silent rejects complicity with the evildoer and demonstrates desire for justice by denouncing the culprit: he or she is the antagonist of the mute witness, who indirectly is the defender of injustice. Cf. Isa. 57.11-12; 58.1; 65.6-7; Ps. 50.1, 3, 21.

b. *Not Keeping Silence by the Defence*. Since the relationship here is rather that between a victim of injustice and a defender, not keeping silence is equivalent in this case to judging and saving. This is above all a magistrate's duty, and it is a request by the innocent accused. Cf. Isa. 62.1; Pss. 35.22-24; 83.2; 109.1, 31; Prov. 31.8-9; Est. 4.14.

2.2. *The Keeping Silence that Means Defeat*

When talking about the controversy, we saw that at a certain point, when the accuser believes that words are no longer being heeded (or are being derided and distorted outright), he or she stops speaking and has recourse to more direct action. This falling silent by the accuser is an even more radical *accusation* than speaking, because one is not denouncing a misdeed but registering the impossibility of a 'reasonable' exit from an unjust situation.

The keeping silent of which I am talking, on the other hand, is the prosecution's (or defence's) inability to carry on the debate, which is equivalent to saying there are no more arguments[175] and therefore one's adversary is right.

a. For *the prosecution*, keeping silent *about a crime* may be synonymous with complicity or impotence against the evildoer. Cf. Gen. 34.5; 1 Sam. 3.13; 2 Sam. 13.20; Hab. 1.13.

In a controversy on the other hand, when the accuser is silenced we have a victory by the accused. Cf. 1 Sam. 2.9; Pss. 31.18-19; 35.15; 107.42; Job 5.16; 11.2-3; 32.1-3, 15-20.

b. For *the defence*, where a controversy situation or something like it is obviously supposed, keeping silent rather than speaking up to defend oneself is an admission of guilt.[176] Cf. Gen. 44.16; Isa. 53.7; 64.11; Mic. 7.16; Ps. 38.14-15; Job 6.24; 13.18-19; 40.4-5; Lam. 2.10; Neh. 5.8; Dan. 3.33 (Greek).

The internal dynamic of the controversy, and therefore of the judicial debate, is such that in the end someone has to fall silent, sometimes for good: this reveals the unsatisfactory inability of the judicial sphere to

175. Cf. P. Joüon, 'Notes de lexicographie hébraique', *Bib* 8 (1927), pp. 51-52, on the expression *piṯḥôn peh* (Ezek. 16.63; 29.21) as '*argument* pour se défendre'.

176. Cf. Lipiński, *La Liturgie pénitentielle*, pp. 32-35.

restore justice. If in fact justice consists of a relationship between individuals, and if an individual is someone who speaks, then the inherent aim of a trial (to silence a person for good) is revealed as contrary to justice itself. To be sure, in the face of perversion humankind can only bring to bear inadequate tools; yet the problem remains of how it is possible not to make the silence of the condemned the end or the aim of a trial but a necessary means to its end. This opens up the possibility of imagining a 'justice' that does not see its complete fulfilment in a condemnation, but which, moved by a desire for relationship, that is, love, encourages a new speech, a truthful speech from the other. If a culprit has to fall silent before the denunciation of his or her guilt, knowing of nothing more to say in self-justification, he or she can still find speech to admit that the other is so just as not to leave a person in silence and the isolation of death. Perfect justice still allows someone who has been silenced by self-perpetrated injustice to give praise.

Chapter 8

SENTENCE AND EXECUTION (THE END AND AIM OF A TRIAL)

The debate phase is the core of the trial institution because it makes it obvious that the most important and at the same time the most problematic juridical fact is the opposition between the two parties, individuals under the law, who each in their own way assert the truth of their statements, and therefore the necessity to continue with authority in accordance with the substance of their claims. As in a controversy,[1] so in a court of law, the to and fro between accuser and accused has to come to an end:[2] the whole judicial institution and its procedures is geared towards reaching a 'judgment', a concluding and *decisive* act in the original sense of the word, by which a magistrate, discerning the innocent from the guilty, can affirm and re-establish justice with the force of law. The transition from debate to 'judgment' is marked by the silence imposed on the disputants by the actual rules of judicial procedure; this silence implies that they have lost their active role, which is now taken over by the *judging magistrate*, the unquestioned protagonist of the trial's conclusion.

The judge's act that brings to an end proceedings in a court of law is the *sentence*. Sketching in its outline and illustrating its fundamental aspects are the necessary conditions for an understanding of the judgment in general; they will also act as the main links in the structure of this chapter.

A sentence is an act of *speech*, a declaration that defines the judicial truth binding on all.[3] From the outside it has some traits that look like the taking up of a position by the prosecution and/or defence; however,

1. Cf. pp. 120-21.
2. Cf. Boecker, *Redeformen*, p. 122.
3. According to Deut. 17.11-13, not agreeing with the judge's decision is a capital (*ûmēt hā'îš hahû'*) crime (*'śh bᵉzādôn, zyd*).

the judge's taking up and supporting the case of one of the disputants constitutes the legal decision; in fact, although it is the pronouncement of a single juridical individual, it is the act by which jurisdiction expresses its full force, and it therefore has normative value for all parties on trial. Although it is the fruit of the judge's free conviction and 'opinion' on the basis of the question (juridical action) brought by the prosecution, the sentence is a 'verdict', which, on the basis of the supposed etymology of the word, introduces a relationship to the concept of truth,[4] the qualities of immutability and irrevocability proper to a thing that has been *judged*.[5]

The sentence brings jurisdiction into full play, and by it the judge interprets and brings out the mind of the criminal law.[6] If this is made up of the 'praeceptum legis' and the 'sanctio legis',[7] then by the verdict the judge makes operative the punitive law laid down in the actual criminal legislation. Although there are many ways in which the sentence and its *execution* are separate, it still has to be affirmed that the sentence itself contains the order to apply punishment (to the guilty) and/or to proceed to the acquittal (of the innocent).

A judicial decision therefore represents the two sides of 'doing justice': there is the speech aspect (which demands wisdom), that declares innocence and guilt and makes it clear in truth where is the right and the wrong; and there is the practical aspect of punishment (which demands force) to be applied to the criminal, without which the judge's pronouncement would be fruitless and ineffective in human history. These two complementary aspects must always be kept in mind, even if sometimes the line of argument simplifies the data by mentioning only one side and letting the other be understood. Thus it may be said that the judge condemned (without specifying what punishment be inflicted)

4. The relationship between judicial activity and truth has already been mentioned in Chapter 6 section 3.2.5. (conclusion of the investigation/interrogation). It is worth noting that a judge, chosen according to Exod. 18.21 from among the *'anšê 'ᵉmet* (cf. also Neh. 7.2), has as his task the re-establishment of justice by making himself and his verdict agree with the truth: as a result, it seems to me, we see a link between the terminology of judging and the terms *'ᵉmet* (Isa. 16.5; 42.3; 61.8; Ezek. 18.8; Zech. 7.9; 8.16; Mal. 2.6 [in relationship with Deut. 17.11]; Prov. 29.14) and *'ᵉmûnâ* (Ps. 96.13).

5. Cf. G. Pugliese, 'Res iudicata pro veritate accipitur', in *Studi in onore di E. Volterra*, V (Milan, 1971), pp. 783-830.

6. Pisapia, *Compendio di procedura penale*, p. 381.

7. Antolisei, *Manuale di diritto penale*, pp. 31-33.

or that the judge punished (without making the premise that the accused was declared guilty).

The line of argument of this chapter will distinguish between the verdict and its execution; although the two things must be taken together, they follow one another, both logically and temporally, almost like cause and effect. At the end of the chapter I will mention the consequences intended or caused by the act of judging. Asking what is achieved, theoretically and/or practically, by a verdict—or in more general terms by the judicial institution—allows me to avoid an abstract consideration of law, dealing with it instead in the practical context of human history as a necessary means to civilized society. Punishment in particular, both from a strictly conceptual point of view and in the ways it is applied, is the perpetual subject of debate, precisely because its function (the repression of evil, social deterrent and reform of the offender) varies according to changing historical and cultural circumstances.

Since the concluding procedure of a trial and the structure of its meaning is familiar to everybody, my chapter will take a descriptive line and provide the most significant lexicographical elements.

1. *The Sentence*

In the course of my study we have often seen two phenomena appear that have notable importance for an interpretation of the biblical texts.

We might call the first one the *generic or polyvalent nature of the lexicon*: this means that one and the same *term* (or expression) is used *in different semantic fields* with different meanings (this is the case, for example, with the verbs *qr'*, *qwm*, *'śh*, etc.); the meaning is specified by 'polarization', that is, by the precise opposition set up between one word and that/those with which it is contrasted in context. It may also happen that, within one *and the same semantic field*, the same term can occupy different 'positions', depending on the context and related terms; thus, for example, the verb *špṭ* can refer to the whole of the judicial action (the relationship between crime and judgment) or just the concluding act of a trial, the pronouncing of sentence (the relationship between prosecution and judgment).

The second phenomenon may be summed up under the heading *the variety of terminology*; this means that although by nature the juridical sphere prefers a technical language, we do not find a clearly specified language in the Bible that allows the identification and separation out of terms and formulae in a strict and absolute manner. If, for example, we are looking for the formula used by a judge in a trial to pronounce sentence (of acquittal or guilt), we realize that 'fixed and repeated'[8] expressions do exist, but without the demands for formal rigour required by our legislation for an act to be juridically valid.[9]

The two phenomena I have briefly put forward form the premise for an understanding of the 'vocabulary of the sentence' which I shall now undertake to illustrate; first I shall deal with the lexicon that expresses the judge's *pronouncement* (here the 'generic' terms already seen elsewhere in my study reappear); I shall then put forward some of the main ways in which the *content* of the verdict is made explicit (there are formulae for this, but their relationships are difficult to organize); finally, I shall integrate into my argument some complementary elements which, in certain biblical texts, take on a symbolic value relative to the act of sentence.

1.1. *The Judge's Pronouncement*

Consideration has to be given at this point to the verbs (or expressions) that take the *judge* as their object, and which, more or less obviously, express the *decision-taking* act that concludes a trial.

1.1.1. *The Judicial Decision.* It is necessary to mention first of all *verbs that mean the jurisdictional function (špṭ, dyn, šm'*, etc.);[10] if, as I said in the introduction to this chapter, the sentence is jurisdiction's highest self-

8. I have adapted the definition of a formula by S. Bretón, *Vocación y misión: Formulario profético* (AnBib, 111; Rome, 1987), pp. 7-21, which goes on to note the necessity for a 'stable function within a schema'.

9. Boecker, starting from the text of Deut. 25.1 and making reference among other things to comparative studies of law in the Ancient East (*Redeformen*, pp. 122-24), maintains that the typical sentence formula (acquittal and condemnation) is to be found in the noun phrases in which the terms *ṣaddîq* and *rāšā'* appear linked to a second person pronoun (*Redeformen*, pp. 123-32, 135-37). In this context, it is worth noting that because the author does not distinguish between the structure of the controversy and that of the judgment, he says that the verdict is sometimes pronounced by one of the parties (*Redeformen*, pp. 124-25, 129), a statement with which I am not in agreement. Boecker finds the other formulae that occur at the end of trials or in Old Testament legal texts more difficult to catalogue and perhaps also less formally strict.

10. Cf. Chapter 5 section 2.1. of my study. It is to be borne in mind especially that the correct administration of justice is often represented—with a great variety of terminology—as the opposition between an action *on behalf* of the innocent (the lexicon of saving, laying claim to, etc.) and an action *against* the guilty (the lexicon of punishing, destroying, etc.).

expression, then it is obvious that these verbs can imply or refer to the handing down of a verdict by the judging authority.

In particular, I would like to refer[11] to syntagms of the kind:

špṭ	*mišpāṭ*	1 Kgs 3.28; Zech. 7.9; 8.16
dyn	*mišpāṭ*	Jer. 21.12
ḥrṣ[12]	*mišpāṭ*	1 Kgs 20.40
dbr (*Pi*)	*mišpāṭ 'et*	2 Kgs 25.6; Jer. 39.5; 52.9
		cf. Jer. 1.16; 4.12
ntn	*mišpāṭ*	Ezek. 23.24; Zeph. 3.5; Job 36.6
yṣ' (*Hi*)	*mišpāṭ*	Isa. 42.1, 3; Ps. 37.6
'mr	*mišpāṭ*	Deut. 17.11 (//*yrh* [*Hi*] *tôrâ*)
ngd (*Hi*)	*d^ebar hammišpāṭ*	Deut. 17.9
šm' (*Hi*)	*dîn*	Ps. 76.9

Verbs that express the jurisdictional function are all the more relevant at this point to the extent that they refer to the act of *separation* of the guilty from the innocent (an act that 'defines' them juridically); in other words, judging becomes more obviously the final act of a trial the more it makes explicit two opposing series of terms, the former referring to 'acquittal', the latter to 'condemnation'.[13]

Of particular importance, because of its appearance in legislative texts concerning the activity of judges, is the pairing *ṣdq* (*Hi*)–*rš'* (*Hi*);[14] the

11. Cf. Chapter 5 section 3.1.3. under *mišpāṭ* as Sentence.

12. The force of the verb *ḥrṣ* in the legal field, as well as in 1 Kgs 20.40, is attested by the expression *killāyôn ḥārûṣ* (Isa. 10.22) and by the participle (*Niphal*) *neḥ^erāṣâ* (Isa. 10.23; 28.22; Dan. 11.36), which make reference to a decision of a judicial kind. The relationship should also be mentioned between the root *špṭ* and the root *ḥrṣ* in Joel 4.12, 14: v. 12 *haggôyim 'el 'ēmeq y^ehôšāpāṭ* (*kî šām 'ēšēb lišpōṭ...*); v. 14 *h^amônîm h^amônîm b^e'ēmeq heḥārûṣ*. Note also the verb *gzr* (to decide) in Job 22.28 (obj.: *'ômer*); and, in the *Niphal*, Est. 2.1 (*'al* + pron. suff.).

13. Cf. pp. 201-202. K. Koch writes that, since a trial is begun by an overturning of community relations that has to be restored, 'sollte kein Prozess (der Theorie nach) nur mit Freispruch einer Partei ohne die Verurteilung der anderen enden. Wenn der *ṣaddīq*-Partner freigesprochen und damit wieder in sein Ansehen und seine gedeihliche Lebensmöglichkeit eingesetzt wird (*ṣdq* hi.), wird zugleich die gegnerische Partei (und sei es nur wegen ungerechtfertigter Anklage) als Frevler verurteilt (*rš'* hi.)' ('*ṣdq* gemeinschaftstreu/heilvoll sein', *THAT*, II, p. 514).

14. The verbs *ṣdq* (*Hi*) and *rš'* (*Hi*)—called 'delocutive' by D.R. Hillers ('Delocutive Verbs in Biblical Hebrew', *JBL* 86 [1967], pp. 320-24)—do not always take the *judge* as their object; they are used in a controversy situation to describe the kind of intervention that 'is equivalent' to an acquittal (*hṣdyq* = to prove right: Isa. 50.8; 53.11 (?); Job 27.5) or to a condemnation (*hršy'* = to prove wrong: Isa. 50.9;

object of these verbs shows whether the judgment is just or wicked.

	judge		acquit		condemn	
Deut. 25.1	(judges)	*špṭ*	*ṣdq (Hi)*	*'et haṣṣaddîq*	*rš‘ (Hi)*	*'et hārāšā‘*
1 Kgs 8.32	(God)	*špṭ*	*ṣdq (Hi)*	*ṣaddîq*	*rš‘ (Hi)*	*rāšā‘*
2 Chron. 6.23	(God)	*špṭ*	*ṣdq (Hi)*	*ṣaddîq*	*šwb (Hi)*	*l^{e}rāšā‘*
Prov. 17.15	(judges?)		*ṣdq (Hi)*	*rāšā‘*	*rš‘ (Hi)*	*ṣaddîq*
Isa. 5.23[15]	(judges)		*ṣdq (Hi)*	*rāšā‘*	*swr (Hi)*	*ṣidqat ṣaddîqîm mimmennû*
Exod. 23.7	(God)		not *ṣdq (Hi)*	*rāšā‘*		
Ps. 82.3	(judges)	*špṭ*	*ṣdq (Hi)*	*‘ānî wārāš*		
2 Sam. 15.4	(Absalom)	(*špṭ*)	*ṣdq (Hi)*	*kol 'îš '^{a}šer yihyeh lô rîb ûmišpāṭ*		
Exod. 22.8	(God)				*rš‘ (Hi)*	(the culprit)
Ps. 94.21	(judges, v. 20)				*rš‘ (Hi)*	*dām nāqî*
Prov. 12.2	(God)				*rš‘ (Hi)*	*'îš m^{e}zimmôt*

1.1.2. *The Assessment of a Case and Decision about it.* It seems as though the Hebrew terminology expressing the act of *assessing* a case,

54.17; Ps. 37.33; Job 9.20; 10.2; 15.6; 32.3; 34.17; 40.8). The text of 1 Sam. 14.47-48 seems strange when speaking of the king's military victories; the author seems to use a terminology that interprets these exploits in a judicial format: v. 47: *b^{e}kōl '^{a}šer yipneh yarsîa‘*...(condemnation); v. 48: *wayyaṣṣēl 'et yiśrā'ēl miyyad šōsēhû* (salvation).

15. It is possible to contrast the text of Isa. 5.23 (*maṣdîqê rāšā‘ ‘ēqeb šōḥad w^{e}ṣidqat ṣaddîqîm yāsîrû mimmennû*) with that of Job 27.5 (*ḥālîlâ lî 'im 'aṣdîq 'et^{e}kem—‘ad 'egwā‘ lō' 'asîr tummātî mimmennî*); the same vocabulary is used both in judicial proceedings and in controversies, but the difference of juridical individuals decides the particular nuance of meaning; in the former case we have a guilty verdict, in the latter a declaration of accusation (cf. also Job 27.2 and 34.5).

along with the *decision* about it, ought to be included in the general concept of judgment.[16]

The Verb ḥšb. As a verb that undoubtedly refers to the act of assessment,[17] *ḥšb* is considered a term characteristic of the priest 'sanctioning a sacrifice as in accordance with the norms by declarative formulae...or declaring it invalid', or 'declaring during the Temple entrance liturgy that anyone who enters is *ṣaddîq*, proclaiming the "attribution" to justice (for life) or vice versa'.[18]

I do not think the assessing and deciding use of the verb *ḥšb* should be limited to a liturgical context and the authority of the priest. The woman of Tekoa, while speaking to David, criticises the royal decision concerning Absalom in these terms:

> *w^elāmmâ ḥāšabtâ kāzō't 'al 'am '^elōhîm*
> *ûmiddabbēr hammelek haddābār hazzeh k^e'āšēm...* (2 Sam. 14.13).

Two of the king's 'sentences' are juxtaposed here, the former expressed by the verb *ḥšb* (the decree against Absalom and indirectly against the people), the latter by the verb *dbr* (*Pi*)[19] (the decree in favour of the woman's son).

Two texts from Zechariah give us further insight into how the verb

16. Lev. 24.10-16 and Num. 15.32-36 recount two episodes that have elements in common: they deal with two juridical cases (respectively, swearing by a foreigner and gathering wood on the Sabbath day), which lack a jurisdictional precedent; recourse is therefore had to Moses, who in his turn has recourse to God for a decision. Deciding (*prš*: Lev. 24.12; Num. 15.34) in this case is equivalent to passing sentence. It is important to note that it is not so much a question of bringing in a (new) law as of applying to an actual case a general norm already well known; it seems to me therefore that in these two episodes the importance should be recognized of the *interpretative* act in the dynamic of judgment: '*gaps* exist in the law, which it is up to the interpreter to fill. In such cases he or she has to carry forward and complete the work of the legislator, turning a general directive into a definite command. The interpreter does not establish rights, because this is the task of the law, but he or she collaborates in recuring them, integrating, as is necessary, legislative commands' (Antolisei, *Manuale di diritto penale*, p. 61).

17. W. Schottroff, '*ḥšb* denken', *THAT*, I, p. 643.

18. Schottroff, '*ḥšb* denken', pp. 644-45. According to K. Seybold, however, 'für das hebr. Verbum *ḥšb* ergeben sich zwei Konstitutive Bedeutungsmomente, das Moment des Rechnens...und das Moment des Planens' (*ḥāšaḇ*', *ThWAT*, III, p. 245).

19. Cf. Chapter 5 section 2.1.4.

ḥšb (in combination with the noun *rāʿâ*) belongs to the series of verbs concerning judgment:

mišpaṭ ʾemet šepōṭû
weḥesed weraḥamîm ʿaśû ʾîš ʾet ʾāḥîw
weʾalmānâ weyātôm gēr weʿānî ʾal taʿašōqû
werāʿat ʾîš ʾāḥîw ʾal ***taḥšebû*** *bilbabekem* (Zech. 7.9-10)

dabberû *ʾemet ʾîš ʾet rēʿēhû*
ʾemet ûmišpaṭ šālôm ***šipṭû*** *bešaʿarêkem*
weʾîš ʾet rāʿat rēʿēhû ʾal ***taḥšebû*** *bilbabekem* (Zech. 8.16-17)

The fact that the verdict in these texts is linked to an internal act (*ḥšb* 'in the heart') seems to emphasise that a judgment (*špṭ*) has its roots in a decree already made in a person's 'forum of assessment' before it is expressed in words (*dbr* [*Pi*]) in judicial proceedings.

This shows how magistrates' adjudications, like their internal thought and judgment, are far from mere opinion, to the extent that they necessarily become an expression of the truth and justice normative in social regulations, with a life (and/or death) effect of absolute relevance (cf. Mic. 2.1, 3; Lam. 2.8).

Particular relevance seems to attach to cases in which the verb *ḥšb* is construed with *le* (the accused) and with the term *ʿāwōn* (2 Sam. 19.20; Ps. 32.2; cf. also, in the *Niphal*, with *dām*: Lev. 17.4);[20] what is being expressed here is not so much the indictment as the 'holding guilty' which is proper to a sentence pronounced in judgment.

The verb yʿṣ.[21] This verb is usually translated as 'to give advice', but clearly this meaning does not fit the cases in which the opinion expressed is a deliberation by authority.[22]

20. Expressions containing *ṣedāqâ* in place of *ʿāwōn* could be considered as in contrast; some reservations are necessary, however. The text of Gen. 15.6 (*wayyaḥšebehā lô ṣedāqâ*) does not belong to the context of judgment; given the theological importance of the phrase, there have been different approaches and interpretations; cf. G. von Rad, 'Die Anrechnung des Glaubens zur Gerechtigkeit', *TLZ* 76 (1951), pp. 129-32; K. Seybold, '*ḥāšab*', *ThWAT*, III, pp. 256-57 (with bibliography). In Ps. 106.31 (*wattēḥāšeb lô liṣedāqâ*) the verb *ḥšb* (in the *Niphal*) is construed with a double *le*, which makes the expression different from all the others—the subject matter seems to me to belong to a sentence.

21. Cf. L. Ruppert, '*jāʿaṣ*', *ThWAT*, III, pp. 718-51.

22. Cf. H.-P. Stähli, '*yʿṣ* raten', *THAT*, I, p. 749: 'Aus der Bed. "raten" ergibt sich auch die daraus resultierende von "beschliessen, planen", wobei nach dem

The following seem to me to be texts that show the verb *y'ṣ* with the meaning of to decide:

y'ṣ		*'al*	Isa. 19.12; 23.8
y'ṣ	*rā'â*[23]	*'al*	Isa. 7.5
y'ṣ (pass.)	*'ēṣâ*	*'al*	Isa. 14.26
y'ṣ	*'ēṣâ*	*'al*	Isa. 19.17; Jer. 49.30[24]
y'ṣ	*'ēṣâ*[25]	*'el*	Jer. 49.20; 50.45
y'ṣ	*'ᵃṣat rā'*	(*bᵉ*)	Ezek. 11.2
y'ṣ	*zimmôt*		Isa. 32.7
y'ṣ	*nᵉdîbôt*		Isa. 32.8
y'ṣ	*bōšet*	*lᵉ*	Hab. 2.10
y'ṣ	*lᵉhašḥît*		2 Chron. 25.16
y'ṣ	*lᵉhaddîah*		Ps. 62.5

The root klh. The root *klh* expresses the idea of fulfilment; not infrequently (with the verb in the *Piel* and in the syntagm *'śh kālâ*) it takes on the negative connotation of a destructive action. It seems, however, that a special meaning should be given to the expression *kālᵉtâ hārā'â*,

Zusammenhang dieses Planen bzw. Beschliessen sowohl einen positiven (selten, vgl. Jes. 32.8) als auch einen negativen Sinn beinhaltet' (cf. also *ThWAT*, III, p. 720). The semantic shift between 'to advise' and 'to decide' (or between 'advice' and 'deliberation') is met also in the Latin 'consiliari' ('consilium'); in modern languages it is not infrequent to give the name Council to a deliberative body.

It may perhaps be maintained that in a judicial situation the verb *y'ṣ* refers to the juridical practice of the tribunal set up by a court; the opinion of the individual magistrates is summed up by the president of the jury with binding force.

23. As opposed to the syntagm *y'ṣ* + *rā'â*; (Isa. 7.5; Ezek. 11.2; cf. also other negative terms), consideration could be given to *y'ṣ* + *šālôm* (cf. Prov. 12.20 and Zech. 6.13).

24. In Jer. 49.20, 30; 50.45; Ezek. 11.2 we have a parallelism between *y'ṣ* and *ḥšb*; in Isa. 14.24 between *y'ṣ* and *dmh* (*Pi*). The latter verb does not recur in any clearly legal texts; it sometimes expresses the idea of a plan (cf. Num. 33.56; Judg. 20.5; 2 Sam. 21.5; Isa. 10.7); as with *ḥšb*, it is not easy to fix precise limits between the meanings of 'to think (about doing)' and of 'to decide (to do)'.

Cf. also the opposition between the roots *y'ṣ* and *prr* (*Hi*) in 2 Sam. 15.34; 17.14; Isa. 14.27; Ps. 33.10; Ezra 4.5; Neh. 4.9.

25. For the use of *'ēṣâ* in the sense of *decision*, cf. *THAT*, I, pp. 750-51. For a more complete discussion of the terminology and problems regarding 'advice', cf. P.A.H. de Boer, 'The Counsellor', in M. Noth and D. Winton Thomas (eds.), *Wisdom in Israel and in the Ancient Near East* (FS H.H. Rowley; VTSup, 3; Leiden, 1955), pp. 42-71.

which refers to an unfavourable decree made by authority; see in this regard:

1 Sam. 20.7	*kāl^{e}tâ hārā'â*	*mē'im...*		
20.9	*kāl^{e}tâ hārā'â*	*mē'im...*		*lābô' 'al...*
25.17	*kāl^{e}tâ hārā'â*		*'el...*	*w^{e}'al...*
Est. 7.7	*kāl^{e}tâ hārā'â*	*mē'ēt...*	*'el...*[26]	

At least in some cases, moreover, it seems that the meaning of 'what has been decided' (judged) should be given to the noun *kālâ*:

1 Sam. 20.33	*kālâ hî' mē'im...l^{e}hāmît*
Isa. 28.22	*kālâ w^{e}neḥ^{e}rāṣâ...mē'ēt...'al...*[27]

1.2. *The Formulation of the Sentence*

The sentence is the phrase pronounced by the judge at the end of a trial. Modern criminal legislation requires a wording with precise formal requirements that on the one hand guarantee its full juridical validity, and on the other hand allow the essential structure of the actual sentence to be grasped. In the biblical literature the situation is altogether more fluid, and fixing the characteristics of a judicial verdict presents not a few problems. A few examples may be enough to illustrate the problem.

In Ahimelech's trial, once the latter's defence has been concluded, king Saul addresses himself to the accused and pronounces sentence: *wayyō'mer hammelek*: *môt tāmût '^{a}ḥîmelek 'attâ w^{e}kol bêt 'abîkā* (1 Sam. 22.16). After that the king turns to his officials and gives the order for execution, adding his juridical reasoning:

wayyō'mer hammelek lārāṣîm hanniṣṣābîm 'ālāyw:
sōbbû w^{e}hāmîtû kōh^{a}nê yhwh
***kî** gam yādām 'im dāwid...* (22.17)

It seems from this text that the verdict consists of a declaration that inflicts the punishment; this declaration is then linked to a (separate and

26. For 1 Sam. 25.17 and Est. 7.7, L. Kopf proposes the translation, 'das Unheil hat ihn erreicht' ('Arabische Etymologien und Parallelen zum Bibelwörterbuch', *VT* 9 [1959], p. 284); for my part I think the context is better suited by the translation, 'the misfortune has been decided'.

27. For the pairing *kālâ w^{e}neḥ^{e}rāṣâ* ('"statutum ac decretum" metonimice "poena decreta"': Zorell, *kālâ*), cf. also Isa. 10.23 and Dan. 9.27. In Isa. 10.22 we find instead the synonymous expression *killāyôn ḥārûṣ*. I would also like to mention Exod. 11.1, where *kālâ* seems to have an adverbial force that might be translated, 'with an irrevocable decree', 'with a definitive decision', or the like.

subsequent) imperative that makes operative the actual content of the sentence. The *kî* that justifies the king's decision and order seems important.

A second case: at the end of the debate that saw the two women quarrelling over the (live) child, Solomon intervenes for the first time in these terms:

> *wayyō'mer hammelek:* *zō't 'ōmeret zeh b^{e}nî haḥay ûb^{e}nēk hammēt*
> *w^{e}zō't 'ōmeret lō' kî b^{e}nēk hammēt ûb^{e}nî heḥāy*
> (1 Kgs 3.23)

This declaration of the king has to be the equivalent of a sentence, which admittedly does not decide the case because it simply establishes that a stalemate has been reached; yet it justifies the subsequent order, which looks like one of execution:

> *wayyō'mer hammelek:* *gizrû 'et hayyeled haḥay lišnāyim*
> *ût^{e}nû 'et haḥ^{a}ṣî l^e'aḥat w^e'et haḥ^{a}ṣî l^e'eḥāt*
> (3.25)

Admittedly, Solomon is using a stratagem to cast light on the truthfulness of the two disputants' claims; but the device would not have been effective if it had not taken on the typical form of an order for execution. The real and definitive verdict comes at the end of the episode: because of the women's reaction, the king can tell with certainty which is the true mother, hence the decree:

> *wayya'an hammelek wayyō'mer:* *t^{e}nû lāh 'et hayyālûd haḥay*
> *w^{e}hāmēt lo' t^{e}mîtuhû*
> *hî' 'immô* (3.27)

In the latter expression the verdict (which points out who is right in the dispute)[28] and the reasoning behind the (favourable) order for execution

28. With reference to 1 Kgs 3.27, Boecker maintains that the biblical literature contains verdicts of a declarative nature (*Feststellungsurteil*), which supposedly do not aim to define who is guilty and/or innocent (*Redeformen*, pp. 142-43). With regard to the text quoted, it seems necessary to me to state that we are not only, as the author says, dealing with proceedings that take the form of a criminal trial (*in der Form eines Strafprozesses*), but that Solomon's judgment is effectively a decision about quite a serious crime (which, in our language, we would call changing of social status by substitution of a newborn child). It is true that the text emphasizes exclusively the king's intervention on behalf of the real mother, but the juridical recognition of her rights, like the heeding of an appeal, does not absolve the crime perpetrated by the opposing party.

are in agreement; the episode lacks any reference to the fate of the woman who unjustly laid claim both to the live child and to its 'division'.

In the trial brought against Jeremiah, after the prophet's defence the judges express their opinion:

> *wayyō'm^{e}rû haśśārîm w^{e}kol hā'ām 'el hakkōh^{a}nîm w^{e}'el hann^{e}bî'îm*
> *'ên lā'îš hazzeh mišpaṭ māwet*
> ***kî** b^{e}šēm yhwh '^{e}lōhênû dibber 'ēlênû* (Jer. 26.16)

The declarative sentence (of acquittal) is clearly motivated, but we do not find in this text an order to let the accused go free. Note how in this case the judges address the accusers, effectively rejecting their demand (cf. 26.11); it may therefore be asked whether this is just a provisional sentence, one that does not decide the dispute definitively,[29] but only denies the validity of one of the arguments put forward by the prosecution.

This brief example shows that the nature of the trials recounted by the Bible (which demonstrate all the problem elements of a judgment) and the gaps in our information that arise from the actual literary genre (which is not that of 'trial transcript') encourage us not to look for the sentence's typical formula, but rather to extract the 'formal features' that describe and express the jurisdictional moment and act.

A comparative analysis of the biblical texts shows that the most important formal features appear to be the following:

1. The verdict takes a *declarative* form: it is speech (note also, in the aforementioned passages, the importance of the verb *'mr*) that defines which of the disputants is guilty (and which innocent). A verdict may also take the form of a decree of punishment, which implicitly assumes a declaration of guilt.
2. Linked to the sentence properly so-called is the *order* that imposes the execution of what has been decreed (whether this is the application of a punitive sanction or a provision on behalf of whoever is in the right).
3. Great importance attaches to the *motivation* appended to the verdict or joined to the order of execution, which makes a judicial decision clearly in harmony with the rules of law.

On 1 Kgs 3.27, cf. also the reading proposed by E. Ruprecht, 'Eine vergessene Konjektur von A. Klostermann zu 1 Reg. 3.27', *ZAW* 88 (1976), pp. 415-18.

29. Cf. Chapter 7 n. 161.

I have already mentioned the force of the *motivation*, when I emphasized its juridical capabilities in a controversy situation.[30] From a purely lexical point of view (I am referring to the particles that introduce cause: *kî*, *ya'an*, *lākēn*, etc.), as well as the general content, there are no specific variations between the juridical situation of the *rîb* and that of the *mišpāṭ*: the discriminating element is basically *the juridical individual* (and therefore not just a person, but the role he or she takes) to whom the phrase is attributed. As we shall see, this observation also holds good for other (lexical and formal) aspects of legal proceedings; if due care is not taken, there is the risk of superimposing juridical structures and stages of a different nature.

I shall talk about the *order* that deals with the application of a sanction or commands some provision in favour of the plaintiff in the following section, which is dedicated to the execution of the sentence.

Hence therefore I would like to dwell on the main headings of the *sentence* as an act of speech, demonstrating its most common features and providing a suitable framework of reference for classifying the extremely wide variety of formulae used in the biblical literature.

1.2.1. *Guilty*. The form most strictly adhering to a sentence of the declarative kind (one that makes explicit the guilt or innocence of the accused) ought in some way to correspond to this syntagm: the judge says (to someone), 'you are guilty/innocent'. Leaving to one side the question of whether it is a just sentence or not, we can find this model of sentence in:

Job 34.18	(God)	*hā'ōmēr*[31]	*l*^{e}*melek* *'el n*^{e}*dîbîm*	*b*^{e}*liyyā'al* *rāšā'*	Condemnatory sentence
Prov. 24.24	(the judge)	*'ōmēr*	*l*^{e}*rāšā'*	*ṣaddîq 'attâ*	Acquittal

This is the formula that comes closest to making explicit the meaning of *ṣdq* (*Hi*)–*rš'* (*Hi*) attributed to a judge in the exercise of judgment; it exclusively defines the fact of guilt (or innocence) without bringing in any element—regarding the culprit in particular—that might make clear

30. Cf. p. 86.

31. Along with the majority of the commentators, I vocalize *hā'ōmēr*; the MT (*ha'*^{a}*mōr*) seems to suppose that the subject of the phrase is Job (not God). This makes the interpretation of the biblical passage as a whole difficult (cf. Alonso Schökel and Sicre, *Job*, p. 482).

the degree of and therefore the consequent sanction for the crime committed. As may be seen, there is no notable variation between expressions used here and those used to charge the adversary in a controversy situation.[32] Their purpose is to charge one's adversary or admit one's own guilt; the difference lies in the fact that, when they are pronounced by a judge, a phrase is transformed from a simple accusation into a verdict.

Legislative texts provide the equivalent of such a declarative sentence when, in a disputed case, it is established whether someone ought to be held guilty of a particular crime; however, we do not have the use of *ṣaddîq* and *rāšāʿ*, but declarations of the kind: *rōṣēaḥ hûʾ* (Num. 35.16, 17, 18, 21), *dām šāpāk* (Lev. 17.4), *ûbaʿal haššôr nāqî* (Exod. 21.28), *wᵉniqqâ hammakkeh* (Exod. 21.19), and so forth.[33]

1.2.2. *Guilty of...* A second form in which the sentence appears may be recognized in those phrases that link the punishment that legally attaches to it to a definition of guilt, thus simultaneously deciding the questions of guilt and seriousness. The syntagm of reference might be formulated like this: the judge says (of someone): 'he is guilty of...(death)'.

a. A first form uses the (Hebrew) noun *ben* as a term to define the offender's condition, a term that grammatically governs another noun referring to the sanction. We find it, for example, in the sentence pronounced by David after listening to Nathan's (fictitious) testimony:

> *wayyōʾmer ʾel nātān: ḥay yhwh*[34]
> ***kî ben māwet*** *hāʾîš hāʿōśeh zōʾt* (2 Sam. 12.5)

32. Cf. in particular Chapter 2 section 2.3. and Chapter 3 sections 1.2. and 1.3.

33. Cf. F.C. Fensham, 'Das Nicht-haftbar-sein im Bundesbuch im Lichte der altorientalischen Rechtstexte', *JNSL* 8 (1980), pp. 17-34.

34. It is important to observe that an *oath* frequently accompanies the king's judicial pronouncements (as well as 2 Sam. 12.5, cf. 1 Sam. 14.44; 19.6; 2 Sam. 4.9-11; 14.11; 19.24; 1 Kgs 1.51-52; 2.23-24 etc.). The purpose of this act, which is not mentioned in a legislative context, seems to be to guarantee the irrevocable nature of the sentence, that is, to prevent the king afterwards being moved by self-interest to go back on his word and alter his verdict.

Oaths by God (who naturally can only swear by himself) on the occasion of solemn decisions with the character of judicial decisions are probably to be understood along the same lines; among the numerous instances, see for example 1 Sam. 3.14; Isa. 14.24; 45.23; 62.8; Jer. 22.5; 44.26; 49.13; Amos 4.2; Ps. 95.11 etc.

Saul's verdict against David is just the same, even if the context is not one of a formal judgment; addressing himself to Jonathan, the king says: *w^e'attâ š^elaḥ w^eqaḥ 'ōtô 'elay kî* ***ben māwet*** *hû'* (1 Sam. 20.31). This phrase could be considered an arbitrary verdict pronounced by a despot at the end of a kangaroo court case; on the other hand, it could be interpreted as a simple accusation of a crime,[35] given that Jonathan comes to David's defence and disputes his father's statement (*lāmmâ yûmat meh 'āśâ*, 20.32). In criminal proceedings where the king is involved as one of the parties at odds, there is always the problem of establishing whether his authority enjoys the unappealable power of a judgment, or whether it lies within the perspective of a controversy, and therefore with the possibility even of a recognition of his own guilt (cf. 1 Sam. 24 and 26).

Among the texts relevant to this subsection, I would like to mention Pss. 79.11 and 102.21 (*b^enê t^emûtâ*). Deut. 25.2 on the other hand supplies the Hebrew expression referring to condemnation to flogging: *w^ehāyâ 'im bin hakkôt hārāšā'*...[36]

b. The aforementioned phrasing is not reserved exclusively for formal judicial sentences, which require as speaker a judge in the explicit context of a trial. This also holds good for another form of verdict (one including reference to the punishment) in which the term of reference is the noun *mišpāṭ*, taking as its *nomen rectum* the term referring to the punishment.

In the trial against Jeremiah, the judges hand down a sentence of acquittal in these terms: *'ên lā'îš hazzeh* ***mišpaṭ māwet*** *kî*...(Jer. 26.16). I would like to note that the accusers had introduced their lawsuit with a quite similar phrase, even though it had an opposite content: ***mišpaṭ māwet*** *lā'îš hazzeh kî*...(26.11).

35. In another episode, which definitely does not possess the characteristics of judicial proceedings, but rather those of a controversy, we encounter a similar expression, pronounced by David as an accusation against Abner and Saul's bodyguard: *ḥay yhwh kî b^enê māwet 'attem* (1 Sam. 26.16). It seems worthwhile, in this respect, to mention what I stated in Chapter 2 (pp. 87-88): an act of accusation often takes the apparent form of a verdict (note also, among other things, the oath), but is only its conditional anticipation.

36. The term *bēn* may be replaced by *'îš*: cf. 2 Sam. 19.29 (*'anšê māwet*) and 1 Kgs 2.26 (*'îš māwet 'āttâ*).

This manner of formulating a sentence seems characteristic of the legal texts in Deuteronomy:

Deut. 19.6	*w*e*lô 'ên mišpaṭ māwet kî...*
Deut. 21.22	*w*e*kî yihyeh b*e*'îš ḥēṭ' mišpaṭ māwet*
Cf. also Deut. 22.26:	*'ên lanna*ʿa*rā ḥēṭ' māwet kî...*[37]

c. A third formula expressing a verdict with an indication of (capital) punishment is to be found in phrases where the term *dām/dāmîm* is linked to the accused's responsibility (often by way of the word *rō'š*).[38]

It is used, for example, by David, to pass sentence of death on the Amalekite who admitted killing Saul: *dām*e*kā* (Q) *'al rō'šekā kî...* (2 Sam. 1.16). In this expression—which, be it noted, is pronounced by the king after the condemned man has already been executed—the description of the criminal's guilt is subordinate to a declaration that the proceedings against him (capital punishment) are in accordance with justice: the culprit is described as responsible for his own death, so that no future blood vendetta is juridically possible.[39]

Something similar was said by Solomon in connection with the order to put Joab to death: *w*e*šābû* ***d*e*mêhem b*e*rō'š*** *yô'āb ûb*e*rō'š zar'ô l*e*'ôlām* (1 Kgs 2.33);[40] and Solomon again, addressing himself to

37. Cf. K.-J. Illman, *Old Testament Formulas about Death* (Åbo, 1979), pp. 86-88.

38. The term *dām* is definitely a technical term which, linked to *b*e*rō'š...*, is used to give a practical end to responsibility in a criminal context (cf. Josh. 2.19). In a judicial context, however, alternative formulations are not ruled out, provided that they are equivalent in meaning; cf., for example, Ezek. 18.20: *riš'at hārāšā'* (Q) *'ālāyw tihyeh*; and Dan. 13.55 (Theod.): *orthōs epseusai eis tēn seautou kefalēn* (cf. also v. 59). P. Maon, 'Responsabilité', *DBSup*, X, p. 357, maintains that the simplest form in which Hebrew expresses the concept of responsibility is the preposition *'al* followed by the name of the person (responsible), or by a part of the body (for example *rō'š*) or by the person's possessions.

39. On the terminology of which I am speaking, and especially for its hermeneutic and theological implications, I would refer the reader to the debate between H. von Reventlow, 'Sein Blut komme über sein Haupt', *VT* 10 (1960), pp. 311-27, and K. Koch, 'Der Spruch "Sein Blut bleibe auf seinem Haupt" und die israelitische Auffassung vom vergossenen Blut', *VT* 12 (1962), pp. 396-416. On the 'responsibility for punishment', cf. also P. Pajardi, *Un giurista legge la Bibbia*, (Milan, 1983), pp. 253-54.

40. The expression in 1 Kgs 2.33 contains significant variations with respect to the formulae with which I have been dealing in the body of my text. First, the plural *d*e*mêhem* refers to the murders committed by Joab, not his blood (shed at the moment

Shimei, declares: ***dām^e kā*** *yihyeh* ***b^e rō'šekā*** (1 Kgs 2.37); here however we have only a conditional sentence, to be put into effect should Shimei infringe on the conditions laid down by the king.

These formulae echo ones in the legislative texts that reproduce a verdict hypothetically pronounced in a case submitted for the legislator's attention. It seems worthwhile to me, however, to call to mind a distinction:[41] although the term *dām/dāmîm* does occur with reference to the accused, in some of these legal phrases (construed with *l^e* or *'al*) it is the crime, not the punishment, that is described: cf. for example Exod. 22.1: *'ên lô dāmîm*; 22.2: *dāmîm lô*; Num. 35.27: *'ên lô dām*; Deut. 19.10: *w^e hāyâ 'āleykā dāmîm*; and so on. Closer to a sentence, on the other hand, are expressions in which the term *dām/dāmîm* is construed *b^e*-: *dāmāyw bô* (Lev. 20.9), *d^e mêhem bām* (Lev. 20.11, 12, 13 etc.). Mention might also be made of the legislative expressions in Ezekiel: *dāmāyw bô yihyeh* (Ezek. 18.13), *dāmô bô yihyeh* (Ezek. 33.5), *dāmô b^e rō'šô yihyeh* (Ezek. 33.4).[42]

1.2.3. *Sentence to (Death).* In this section I would like to deal with a fairly frequent form of expressing the sentence; in it the judge moves straight to the decree of punishment, taking the declaration of guilt altogether as read. The judge condemns and makes explicit, often by solemn formulae, what kind of punishment is to be inflicted on the criminal.

I would like to go straight to some examples. Saul concludes the trial of Ahimelech with this phrase: ***môt tāmût*** *'^a ḥîmelek 'attâ w^e kol bêt 'ābîkā*, 'you are condemned to death, Ahimelech, you and all your father's house' (1 Sam. 22.16). An absolutely identical sentence is

of execution). Moreover, the death of Joab is only one of the sentences passed on him, given that his descendants will also suffer the negative consequences of his crimes (we are not told, however, what form the punishment of his descendants will take). And again, Joab's punishment is linked to a hope for peace—which also seems to have the force of forgiveness—called down upon the throne and the king's household; this seems to emphasize the fact that failure to punish the general of David's army constituted a latent threat to the Davidic dynasty (cf. 2 Sam. 3.38-39). Lastly, note may be taken of the formal symmetry between the formula in 1 Kgs 2.33 and the ones that refer to fitting the retribution handed down by a judge to an evildoer (cf. v. 32, and section 2.1.2 below).

41. Cf. Boecker, *Redeformen*, p. 138; H. Christ, *Blutvergiessen im Alten Testament* (Basel, 1977), pp. 49, 105-15.

42. Expressions in which the term *dām/dāmîm* is construed with the preposition *b^e* also refer to cases in which there is a capital sentence for a crime other than murder.

pronounced by Saul against Jonathan after the latter is picked out as guilty by lot: ***môt tāmût*** *yônātān* (1 Sam. 14.44).[43]

Sentences that are instead the equivalent of acquittals may be read in 2 Sam. 19.24 (*lō' tāmût*: the verdict pronounced by David on Shimei) and in 2 Sam. 12.13 (*lō' tāmût*: the divine sentence that spares David, but is linked to another that strikes him in his son: *gam habbēn hayyillôd l*^{e}*kā* ***môt yāmût*** (12.14).[44]

It is clear that a verdict of capital punishment (or acquittal) is logically connected to a (sometimes implicit) declaration of the accused's guilt (or innocence); this connection is attested, in various ways, by the biblical texts:

Num. 35.31	*'*^{a}*šer hû'* ***rāšā' lāmût*** *kî môt yûmāt*
Ezek. 3.18	*b*^{e}*'omrî* ***lārāšā' môt tāmût***...
	hû' rāšā' *ba'*^{a}*wōnô* ***yāmût*** (cf. also Ezek. 33.8, 14)
Ezek. 18.4, 20	*hannepeš* ***haḥōṭē't*** *hî'* ***tāmût***
Ezek. 33.13	*b*^{e}*'omrî* ***laṣṣaddîq ḥāyōh yiḥyeh***
Ezek. 18.9	***ṣaddîq*** *hû'* ***ḥayōh yiḥyeh***
Ezek. 18.17	*hû'* ***lō' yāmût*** *ba'*^{a}*wōn 'ābîw* ***ḥayōh yiḥyeh*** (cf. also 18.21)

The formula *môt yûmat* (or simply *yûmat*)[45] is the equivalent in legislative texts of the formula *môt tāmût* used by a judge giving judgment.[46]

43. For the use of the formula (cf. also Gen. 2.17; 20.7; 1 Kgs 2.37, 42; 2 Kgs 1.4, 6, 16; Jer. 26.8; Ezek. 3.18; 33.8, 14), cf. Illman, *Old Testament Formulas about Death*, pp. 104-105 ('sentence or threat of death'). On the other hand, I would not like to make out that the judge's verdict must take the form *môt tāmût*.

44. The formula *môt yāmût* (cf. Num. 26.65; 1 Sam. 14.39; 2 Kgs 8.10) is used, according to Illmann, in cases when the person condemned is absent (*Old Testament Formulas*, pp. 105-106).

As regards 2 Samuel 12, and in particular the verdict that falls upon the son (cf. the analogy with 1 Kgs 21.27-29), I would like to single out the contribution by G. Gerleman, which does not, however, appear to me to resolve all the problems posed by the text: 'David wusste, dass der Tod des Neugeborenen eine Sühne war, durch welche Jahwe ein in Gang gekommenes Böses aufhob. Jahwe hatte die *ḥaṭṭa't* an David vorbeigehen lassen und sie auf das Kind gelegt. Davids Gebaren, als er vom Tod des Sohnes erfährt, hat den Charakter einer Gerichtsdoxologie. Nicht der Tod des Kindes, sondern die Aufhebung einer zerstörerischen Unheilwirkung wird von dem Erzähler als die allein wichtige Tatsache in den Mittelpunkt gestellt' ('Schuld und Sühne. Erwägungen zu 2 Samuel 12', in *Beiträge zur alttestamentlichen Theologie* [FS W. Zimmerli; Göttingen, 1977], p. 138). Cf. also A. Schenker, *Versöhnung und Sühne* (Freiburg, 1981), pp. 41-53.

45. Cf. Illmann, *Old Testament Formulas*, pp. 119-27.

46. Of the specific studies of the aforementioned formulae I would also like to

Naturally, other expressions can take the paradigmatic place of the sentence *môt tāmût/yûmat*, this being for reasons of a literary nature, or for a variation in the punishment in accordance with a variation in the crime.[47] For this latter case, one of the most characteristic formulae is the one regarding the repayment (of damage), which typically uses the verb *šlm* (*Pi*),[48] sometimes with a precise indication of the actual amount of the compensation:

2 Sam. 12.6	*y^ešallēm 'arba'tāyim*
Exod. 22.8	*'^ašer yaršî'un '^elōhîm y^ešallēm š^enayim l^erē'ēhû*

(cf. also Exod. 21.34, 36, 37; 22.3, 4, 5 etc.; Lev. 5.16; Ps. 37.21; Prov. 6.31 etc.).

single out: H. Gese, 'Beobachtungen zum Stil alttestamentlicher Rechtsätze', *TLZ* 88 (1960), pp. 147-50; J. Milgrom, *Studies in Levitical Terminology.* I. *The Encroacher and the Levite. The Term* 'Aboda (Berkeley, 1970), pp. 5-8; H. Schulz, *Das Todesrecht im Alten Testament: Studien zur Rechtsform der Mot-Jumat-Sätze* (BZAW, 114; Berlin, 1969); G. Liedke, *Gestalt und Bezeichnungen alttestamentlicher Rechtssätze: Eine formgeschichtlich-terminologische Studie* (WMANT, 39; Neukirchen, 1971), pp. 50-52, pp. 120-30; V. Wagner, *Rechtssätze in gebundener Sprache und Rechtssatzreihen im israelitischen Recht: Ein Beitrag zur Gattungsforschung* (BZAW, 127; Berlin, 1972), pp. 16-31.

47. Here are a few examples:

Gen. 44.17	*hā'îš '^ašer nimṣā' haggābîa' b^eyādô hû' yihyeh lî 'ābed*
1 Kgs 20.42	*...w^ehāy^etâ napš^ekā taḥat napšô w^e'amm^ekā taḥat 'ammô*
2 Sam. 12.10	*w^e'attâ lō' tāsûr ḥereb mibbêt^ekā 'ad 'ôlām*
Lev. 20.14	*zimmâ hî' bā'ēš yiśr^epû 'ōtô w^e'ethen* (cf. Gen. 38.24)
Exod. 21.22	*'ānôš yē'ānēš* (on the juridical importance of the verb *'nš*, cf. G. Liedke, *Gestalt*, pp. 43-44).
Exod. 21.20	*nāqōm yinnāqēm* (cf. Liedke, *Gestalt*, pp. 48-49).

A further important formula to be singled out is *w^enikr^etâ hannepeš hahî'* (cf. Gen. 17.14; Exod. 12.15, 19; 31.14 Lev. 7.20 etc.); on this, see the precise explanation with critical discussion by G.F. Hasel, *ThWAT*, IV, pp. 362-64; of the monographs, I would like to single out W. Zimmerli, 'Die Eigenart der prophetischen Rede des Ezechiel. Ein Beitrag zum Problem an Hand von Ez 14.1-11', *ZAW* 66 (1954), pp. 13-19 (as well as a precise examination of the formula and its variations, the author goes on to refer to similar expressions with the verb *šmd* [*Hi*] [Deut. 4.3; Ezek. 14.9] and with *'bd* [*Hi*] [Lev. 23.30]); D.J. Wold, 'The *Kareth* Penalty in P: Rationale and Cases', in P.J. Achtemeier (ed.), *SBLSP 1979,* I, (Missoula, MT, 1979), pp. 1-45.

48. Cf. W. Eisenbeis, *Die Wurzel šlm im Alten Testament* (BZAW, 113; Berlin, 1969), pp. 301-22; Liedke, *Gestalt*, pp. 42-44.

1.3. *The Accused Condemned or Acquitted*

Up to now I have looked at judgment from the judge's point of view, to the extent that a verdict is the characteristic and definitive expression of that role.

However, since I would like to provide a more complete picture of the language used to describe not only the act, but also the force, of the sentence, this is a good moment to bring in some significant elements regarding *the accused* and his or her being made the object of a judicial act.

Hebrew does not make frequent use of the passive meaning of verbs meaning 'to judge' (*špṭ*, *dyn*, etc.); and the technical terminology that we translate as 'acquit' and 'condemn', represented in Hebrew by the *Hiphil* form of *ṣdq and rš'*, has no precise parallel in the passive sense. Expressions that are familiar to us therefore, such as 'the accused is judged guilty/innocent, the accused is sentenced to.../is acquitted of...', have no direct parallels in biblical literature.

Only in three cases in fact, all of them found in the Psalms, is the verb *špṭ* used in the sense of 'to be judged'.

Ps. 9.20	*yiššāpᵉṭû gôyim 'al pāneykā*
Ps. 37.33	*yhwh...lō' yaršî'ennû bᵉhiššāpᵉṭô* (object: *ṣaddîq*, v. 32)
Ps. 109.7	*bᵉhiššāpᵉṭô yēṣē' rāšā'*

This oddity seems to be explained by the actual literary genre of the Psalms, which mostly speak from the point of view of someone who is being subjected to a trial, from which he appeals to God, the supreme judge, for his own acquittal and the condemnation of his adversary. The Psalms provide the springboard from which to deepen my research.

1.3.1. *The Juridical Relevance of the Verb yṣ': The Metaphor of Light.*[49]

Psalm 109,[50] of which I quoted v. 7 above, is a long list of charges

49. On the subject of light with reference to the matter of this section, cf. A.M. Gierlich, *Der Lichtgedanke in den Psalmen: Eine terminologisch-exegetische Studie* (FreibTSt, 56; Freiburg, 1940); S. Aalen, *Die Begriffe 'Licht' und 'Finsternis' im Alten Testament, im Spätjudentum und im Rabbinismus* (SNVAO; Oslo, 1951), esp. pp. 32-43, 71-73; consult also F. Asensio, *El Dios de la luz: Avances a través del Antiguo Testamento y contactos con el Nuevo* (Rome, 1958); P. Humbert, 'Le thème vétérotestamentaire de la lumière', *RTP* 99 (1966), pp. 1-6.

50. Whereas there is widespread agreement on classifying Psalm 109 among the 'individual lamentations', and on determining the situation as one in which a person is falsely accused and dragged into court by personal enemies (G. Castellino, *Libro*

addressed to God against enemies who are falsely accusing the speaker (vv. 1-5); among the psalmist's requests, the first (vv. 6-7) is that his adversary should be subjected to accusation by a *rāšā'*, so as to experience what it is like to be accused unjustly and 'be found' guilty (*yēṣē' rāšā'*) by a court.[51] The verb *yṣ'* suggests the conclusion of proceedings and has the purpose—via the terms linked to it—of indicating the kind of verdict passed by the judge.

It seems to me that this expression has no other parallels in the Bible. The verb *yṣ'* is however used in various forms to describe the result of a judicial action. I would like to give some examples:

a. First, when *yṣ'*[52] takes as its subject nouns such as *mišpāṭ*, *tôrâ*, *dābār*,[53] it is used to express a magistrate's judicial act:

Isa. 2.3	*kî miṣṣiyyôn tēṣē' tôrâ ûdᵉbar yhwh mîrûšālāyim*
4	*wᵉšāpaṭ bên haggôyim*
Isa. 51.4	*kî tôrâ mē'ittî tēṣē' ûmišpāṭî lᵉ'ôr 'ammîm…*
5	*qārôb ṣidqî yāṣā' yišʻî*
	ûzᵉrō'ay 'ammîm yišpōṭû
Hab. 1.7	*mimmennû mišpāṭô ûśᵉ'ētô yēṣē'*[54]

dei Salmi [Turin, 1955], p. 226), there is debate over the interpretation of the central part of the Psalm itself (vv. 6-19); some attribute it to the person at prayer, while others consider it a quotation of the adversary's words (H.J. Kraus, *Psalmen* [BK, 15/2; Neukirchen, 1972], pp. 746-47). It is not possible at this juncture to take sides in the debate; as far as my subject matter is concerned, the fact remains that the phrase *bᵉhiššāpᵉtô yēṣē' rāšā'* represents an explicit request for judicial condemnation.

51. Cf. Job 27.7: *yᵉhî kᵉrāšā' 'ōyᵉbî.*

52. In the examples quoted in my text, the verb *yṣ'* is used in the *Qal*; for the verb in the *Hiphil*, cf. Isa. 42.1-3.

53. This terminology is at least partially comparable with the series dealt with in Chapter 5 section 3.

54. The noun *śᵉ'ēt* in Hab. 1.7 has been the object of differing critical treatment. W.H. Ward (*Habakkuk* [ICC; Edinburgh, 1912], pp. 8, 9) and K. Elliger (*Das Buch der Zwölf Kleinen Propheten*, II [ATD, 25; Göttingen, 7th edn, 1975], p. 29) omit it for reasons of content and metre, thereby substantially reproducing the text of the LXX and Syr.

The majority of commentators on the other hand preserve the pairing *mišpāṭô ûśᵉ'ētô*, and—in agreement with the Dictionaries (at the word *śᵉ'ēt*)—translate: 'his law and his greatness/dignity'. As a typical example of the interpretation that follows this choice of text and semantics, I would like to quote C.F. Keil: 'von ihm nicht von Gott (vgl. Ps. 17.2) geht sein Recht aus, d.h. es bestimmt nach eigenem Ermessen Recht und Norm seines Handelns und *s'tw* seine Hoheit (Gen. 49.3; Hos. 13.1), "seine *doxa* (1 Cor. 11.7) vor allen andern Völkern" (*Hitz.*), durch seine

Hab. 1.4	*'al kēn tāpûg tôrâ w^e lō' yēṣē' lāneṣaḥ mišpāṭ...*
	'al kēn yēṣē' mišpāṭ m^e 'uqqāl
Dan. 9.23	*bitḥillat taḥ^a nûneykā yāṣā' dābār*

b. In other cases we have something more specific; the subject of *yṣ'* is not so much the 'judgment' (in the sense of verdict), but the 'subjective right' (nouns like *mišpāṭ* and *ṣedeq* with pronominal suffixes referring to the person judged), therefore the Hebrew phrase, which word for word would be translated as 'my/his rights come out', means in fact 'I am recognized as in the right, I am acquitted in a trial, I gain juridical victory'. The verb *yṣ'* can be used in the *Qal* or in the *Hiphil*; in the latter case the judge's juridical action is more clearly brought to the fore. Here are some examples:

Isa. 62.1	*...'ad yēṣē' kannōgah ṣidqāh wîšû'ātāh k^e lappîd yib'ār*[55]
Hos. 6.5	*ûmišpāṭî kā'ôr yēṣē'*[56]
Ps. 17.2	*mill^e pāneykā mišpāṭî yēṣē'*
Ps. 37.6	*w^e hôṣî' kā'ôr ṣidqekā ûmišpāṭekā kaṣṣoh^o rāyim*
Jer. 51.10	*hôṣî' yhwh 'et ṣidqōtênû*

An equivalent meaning seems to belong to the expressions in Mic. 7.9 (*...w^e 'āśâ mišpāṭî yôṣî'ēnî lā'ôr*) and Job 23.10 (*b^e ḥānanî kazzāhāb*

Waffengewalt sich zum Herrn derselben machend' (*Die zwölf Kleinen Propheten* [Leipzig, 3rd edn, 1888] p. 416).

Targum Jonathan has yet another interpretation, giving the text as *minnêh dînêh ûg^e zērātêh napqîn* (ab ipsomet ipsius judicium et decretum promanant); cf. also Zorell (at the word *ś^e 'ēt*), who for Hab. 1.7 proposes the meaning 'edictum' (with reference to the noun *maśśā'*). In L. Alonso Schökel (*Profetas*, II [Madrid, 1980], pp. 1097, 1099) we find this latter line of interpretation, with the translation: 'él con su sentencia impondrá su voluntad y su derecho'; the comment fills in the interpretative possibilities of the text: 'Tomamos *ś't* como sustantivo con valor de sentencia, decreto. Si se restringe su sentido, a "perdón" (significado conocido de *nś'*) podria componer con *mšpṭ* una polaridad, "perdón y condena". Lo importance es leerlo como respuesta al verso 4. Repitiendo y variando el sintagma, el poeta provoca la extrañeza:

lō' yēṣē'	*lāneṣaḥ*	*mišpāṭ*
mimmennû	*mišpāṭô*	*yēṣē'*.'

55. Cf. the reprise of the theme in Wis. 3.7.

56. For Hos. 6.5 I follow those commentators who follow the reading of the LXX, Syriac and Targum, dividing the Hebrew text differently from the MT (*ûmišpāṭeykā 'ôr*) (cf. H.W. Wolff [BK, 14/1; Neukirchen, 1961], pp. 134, 152).

'ēṣē'), where the subject of *yṣ'* (or the object of *yṣ'*, *Hiphil*) is the actual person upholding the law.

Of the texts quoted some deserve special consideration. Sometimes, in fact, *yṣ'* appears linked in various ways to terms that belong to the semantic field of light (*kā'ôr*: Hos. 6.5; Ps. 37.6; *kannōgah*: Isa. 62.1; *lā'ôr*: Mic. 7.9; cf. also Isa. 51.4: *lᵉ'ôr 'ammîm*). The rising of the sun,[57] which, as is well known, is expressed in Hebrew by the verb *yṣ'*,[58] seems to be one of the metaphors suggesting the advent of justice promoted by right judgment (cf. Mal. 3.20: *wᵉzārᵉḥâ lākem yir'ê šᵉmî šemeš ṣᵉdāqâ*).[59]

The analysis made so far allows the establishment of a link (of a metaphorical kind) between *being judged* (an element expressed by nouns like *mišpāṭî* and *ṣidqî* linked to the verb *yṣ'*) and *the coming of the light* (an element expressed by nouns belonging to the semantic field of light, also linked to the verb *yṣ'*).

A motive for the appearance of this symbolism may be found by recourse to general considerations that see in light a favourite image for life, truth and analogous concepts (cf. Job 17.11-14; 33.22-30). It is possible, however, to link the themes of judgment and light with greater precision by grafting them onto the institutional state of the time or *historical moment at which a trial took place in Israel.*

It is true that we do not have sufficiently certain proof of when Israel's magistrates held court and decided the cases put before them: from the data in our possession it may however be reasonably deduced that morning was the time normally given over to the course of judicial practices.

57. In certain texts the term *'ôr* is definitely an equivalent of the term *šemeš*: cf. Job 31.26; 37.31; Prov. 4.18.

58. Cf. Gen. 19.23: *haššemeš yāṣā' 'al hā'āreṣ*; also Judg. 5.31; Isa. 13.10; Ps. 19.6.

59. Cf. also Wis. 5.6: *to tēs dikaiosynēs phōs ouk epelampsen hēmin, kai ho hēlios ouk aneteilen hēmin.*

On the text of Mal. 3.20, see F. Vattioni, 'Malachia 3.20 e l'origine della giustizia in Oriente', *RivB* 6 (1958), pp. 353-60. In this context, this seems a good moment to recall the Babylonian tradition of the god *Šamaš*, the supreme judge of human actions, whose children are law (the goddess *kittu*[*m*]) and justice (the god *Mi/esaru*[*m*]) (H.-J. Kraus, *Psalmen* [BK, 15/1; Neukirchen, 1961], pp. 156-57; K. Koch, '*ṣdq* gemeinschaftstreu/heilvoll sein', *THAT*, II, p. 509; cf. also N. Sarna, 'Psalm XIX and the Near Eastern Sun-God Literature', in *Proceedings of the Fourth World Congress of Jewish Studies*, I [Jerusalem, 1967], pp. 171-75).

This seems reasonable: in fact, not only does a trial[60] require witnesses and a court of judgment, but—especially for capital charges—an assembly of citizens[61] is laid down and attested; that being so, it is easier to open court in the morning, before the citizens start leaving by the gate to get to work or set out on any sort of business. Although there are few biblical texts where it is explicitly stated that proceedings of a juridical kind began early in the day,[62] the text of 2 Sam. 15.2 clearly documents the king's custom of granting audience in the morning to anyone who had something to submit to his tribunal.

What is more, in three texts we find an attested link between judicial activity and the morning. The clearest is Jer. 21.12: here the prophet, addressing himself to the royal house, exhorts it to administer justice in a fitting manner: *dînû* ***labbōqer*** *mišpāṭ wᵉhaṣṣîlû gāzûl miyyad ʿôšēq*. In Zeph. 3.5, on the other hand, God is spoken of as a just judge who pronounces his verdict at dawn: *yhwh ṣaddîq bᵉqirbāh lō' yaʿᵃśeh ʿawlâ—* ***babbōqer babbōqer*** *mišpāṭô yittēn* ***lā'ôr*** *lō' neʿdār*. Finally, in Job 7.18 a hint may be detected to the investigative activity carried out by a judge in the morning, even though the parallelism puts more emphasis on the unceasing duration than the investigative act: *wattipqᵉdennû* ***libqārîm*** *lirgāʿîm tibḥānennû* (cf. also Pss. 73.14 and 101.8).

Another line of consideration relevant to my subject matter is supplied by recalling that the morning is the favoured time for an intervention by God,[63] an intervention that shows itself to be salvation (of the just, the

60. Civil suits also require the presence of authoritative witnesses who guarantee the regular nature of what goes on (Ruth 4.2; Jer. 32.10, 12, 25, 44). Without identifying civil and criminal proceedings (following Boecker, *Redeformen*, pp. 160-75; and M.J. Buss, 'The Distinction between Civil and Criminal Law in Ancient Israel', in *Proceedings of the Sixth World Congress of Jewish Studies*, I [Jerusalem, 1977], pp. 51-62; but cf. de Vaux, *Institutions*, I, pp. 235-36), it may be maintained that questions of a juridical nature, especially ones subject to possible dispute, took place in the same setting and had basically the same protagonists.

61. Cf. Chapter 6 section 1.4.1.

62. Cf. Gen. 20.8; Exod. 8.16; also Exod. 7.15; 9.13; Josh. 7.16; Judg. 6.28. None of these texts looks decisive for demonstrating that judicial audiences and juridical encounters usually occurred in the early hours of the day. On the other hand, it is also true that no text is to be found in the Bible that explicitly contradicts the hypothesis formulated above.

63. This is the thesis maintained by J. Ziegler, 'Die Hilfe Gottes "am Morgen"', in *Alttestamentliche Studien*, (FS F. Nötscher; BBB, 1; Bonn, 1950), pp. 281-88; cf. also Seeligmann, 'Zur Terminologie', p. 278.

appellant, the victim: cf. Isa. 33.2; Pss. 5.4; 30.6; 46.6; 57.9; 59.17; 90.14; 130.6-7; 143.8; Lam. 3.23) and also punishment (of the evildoer: cf. Gen. 19.23-25; Exod. 14.24, 27; Josh. 6.15-21). It does not seem out of place to imagine God showing himself at daybreak with a judicial verdict that re-establishes justice in the world.[64]

This shows that the fundamental opposition between light and darkness, as well as standing in general for the symbolic force of the pairs life–death, good–evil, also refers to the opposition between salvation and punishment. Since the break of day is the equivalent of the moment in which judgment in accordance with justice takes place, light becomes the symbol of the victory of the law (cf. 2 Sam. 23.3-4; Isa. 2.4-5; 5.20; 9.1-6; 58.8-10; Mic. 7.9; Pss. 97.11; 112.4; Job 11.17; 22.27-30; 38.12-15),[65] whereas darkness is the framework for images of the dominance or continuance of injustice (Isa. 50.10; 59.9-10; Pss. 30.6; 88.19; 107.10). This line of interpretation not only gives a deeper understanding of the person 'in the light' (Isa. 59.9; Jer. 13.16; Ps. 130.6-7; Job 30.26) but also of the shining appearance of God, who by the splendour of his theophany manifests and brings about right judgment in the cosmos (cf. Pss. 50.1-2; 76.5; 94.1; Hab. 3.3-4 etc.).[66]

64. C. Barth (*ThWAT*, I, pp. 751-54) takes up the opinion of L. Delekat ('Zum hebräischen Wörterbuch', *VT* 14 [1964], pp. 7-9) and criticises the various proposals of J. Ziegler (quoted above) that try to explain the literary motif of God's help occurring in the morning. In particular, he writes: 'Auch die Anknüpfung der Zeitangabe an den in Israel gebraülichen *Gerichtstermin* bereitet Schwierigkeiten. Sicher ist die Sprache des AT in mancher Hinsicht vom Rechtsleben Israels beeinflusst; aber eine bewusste oder nur faktische Analogie der Vorstellung betr. die zivile Rechtssprechung und die Offenbarung YHWHs im Tempel (Heilsorakel) erscheint zweifelhaft' (p. 753). I find no reason to doubt (Delekat says *problematisch* and *sehr unsicher*) the relationship between God's intervention and the judicial structure as regards the time of their occurrences; I therefore consider the position put forward in my text as reasonable and coherent.

65. Cf. O. Keel, *Jahwes Entgegnung an Ijob* (FRLANT, 121; Göttingen, 1978), p. 56.

66. For 'theophany', especially in relation to judgment, cf. E. Beaucamp, 'La théophanie du Psaume 50 (49). Sa signification pour l'interprétation du Psaume', *NRT* 81 (1959), pp. 897-915; F. Schnutenhaus, 'Das Kommen und Erscheinen Gottes im Alten Testament', *ZAW* 76 (1964), pp. 1-22; J. Jeremias, *Theophanie: Die Geschichte einer alttestamentlichen Gattung* (WMANT, 10; Neukirchen, 1965), esp. pp. 38-51, 62-63, 130-33; E. Lipiński, *La royauté de Yahvé dans la poésie et le culte de l'Ancien Israël* (Brussels, 1965), pp. 187-270; N.H. Ridderbos, 'Die Theophanie in Psalm 50.1-6', *OTS* 15 (1969), pp. 213-26.

So without denying the highly symbolic nature of light and darkness, I would link them with Israel's collective and institutional experience, saying that whereas the night is the customary time for an evildoer to commit a crime,[67] morning is the time when justice displays her beneficent face; whereas darkness covered the misdeed of the culprit, light allows the perceptive investigation that reveals evil (Ps. 90.8; Job 12.22; 25.3 etc.) and condemns it, thus bringing justice and salvation to innocent victims. Finally, I would like to note a last nuance with regard to my subject matter: starting judgment in the morning suggests care in the administration of justice; the first thing done in the course of the day is in fact a sign of what is most pressing and essential.[68] This makes sense of the criticism leveled by the prophets at the leaders of the people, when it is said that they rise early, but for activities that are in no way praiseworthy (Isa. 5.11 with reference to 5.20-23; Mic. 2.1-2; Zeph. 3.7; cf. also Qoh. 10.16-17).

The conclusion to my reflections is as follows: one of the ways, of a metaphorical nature, by which Hebrew describes the coming of judgment, is by the appearance of the symbol of light (or by contrast, of darkness); especially as regards the accused (or appellant) this is one of the images[69] Hebrew uses to express the desire for or result of judgment in accordance with justice.

1.3.2. *Shame (and its Opposites)*. I would like to go back to Psalm 109; the speaker's petition opens with a request for the condemnation of his

Mention might also be made of texts in which a precise relationship is established between God (as saviour) and his light: Isa. 58.10; 60.1; Pss. 4.7; 18.29; 35.10; 36.10; 43.3; 44.4; 89.16; cf. J.F.A. Sawyer, *Semantics in Biblical Research* (London, 1972), pp. 39-40.

67. Cf. p. 275.

68. Alonso Schökel, *Profetas*, I, p. 513.

69. Going back to the observations made in Chapter 7 (pp. 292-96) on debating metaphors taken from the spheres of war and hunting, I would like to repeat that their coherence extends to the result achieved, i.e. they correspond to the content of the sentence and punishment (pp. 297-99).

I would like to single out as particularly relevant the verb *'bd*, which, especially in the *Piel* and *Hiphil*, belongs to the terminology referring to military defeat (*ThWAT*, I, pp. 21-22), but which, in the Psalms and sapiential literature, is linked to the term *rāšāʿ* (*THAT*, I, p. 19; *ThWAT*, I, p. 23): the 'ruin of the wicked' is just the condemnation brought down upon the behaviour of the wicked (Seeligmann, 'Zur Terminologie', p. 269).

adversaries, and concludes with a similar demand expressed in the metaphorical language of shame (to which is opposed that of joy):

109.28 *...qāmû* ***wayyēbōšû*** *w*^e^ *'abd*^e^*kā* ***yiśmāḥ***
29 *yilb*^e^*šû* *śôṭ*^e^*nay* ***k*^e^*limmâ***
w^e^*ya'*^a^*ṭû* *kam'îl* ***bōštām***

The translation of the experience of guilt into the psychological terms of shame is so widely attested in the biblical texts that it would be worth a treatise in itself;[70] however, given that the juridical and legal force of this terminology[71] has already been singled out, it seems necessary to me at this point only to reaffirm and emphasize its relevance and special semantic force.

Although it is true that the language of 'infamy' has to be given a place in the paradigm of the judicial condemnation (or more generally, of the judicial defeat), the question remains of the reason for this. Whereas in modern proceedings the dishonourable consequences of a conviction[72] prevent the perfect reinsertion of the convicted into the

70. I would like to refer the reader to M.A. Klopfenstein, *Scham und Schande nach dem Alten Testament: Eine begriffsgeschichtliche Untersuchung zu den hebräischen Wurzeln* bôš, klm *und* ḥpr (Zürich, 1972). As the title suggest, the work is concerned with the three roots most frequently used in Hebrew to express both shame (the subjective experience) and infamy (the objective experience); an appendix (pp. 184-95) also studies the terms *qlh/qālôn/qîqālôn*, which belong to the field of objective shame (*Schande*). I would like to observe that the author has not also given consideration to the root *ḥrp*, especially the noun *ḥerpâ*, which appears frequently in the semantic field of shame.

From among the more recent contributions, I would like to single out the articles in the biblical dictionaries: for *bwš*: *THAT*, I, pp. 269-72 (F. Stolz) and *ThWAT*, I, pp. 568-80 (H. Seebass); for *ḥpr*: *ThWAT*, III, pp. 116-21 (J. Gamberoni); for *klm*: *ThWAT*, IV, pp. 196-208 (S. Wagner); for *ḥrp*: *ThWAT*, III, pp. 223-29 (E. Kutsch). For *bwš* see also L. Alonso Schökel, *Materiales para un diccionario bíblico hebreo-español* (Rome, 1985).

71. This is given varying degrees of emphasis in the aforementioned works; cf. also J.W. Olley, 'A Forensic Connotation of *bôš*', *VT* 26 (1976), pp. 230-34.

With reference to my subject matter, I deem it necessary to bring out the difference between the experience of shame that manifests itself as a feeling of (admitted) guilt in the two-sided structure of a *rîb* and the infamy represented by juridical defeat in a court of law. Whereas the former can be 'confessed' (cf. Jer. 3.25; Dan. 9.7, 8) and become a means of salvation, the latter leads only to the unacceptable situation of a definitive condemnation.

72. Whereas ancient legislation laid down directly dishonouring punishments such as branding or the pillory, modern law generally commutes these, along with its

framework of society, and as such form an active and punitive reminder of the misdeed, in the world of the Bible shame was a direct expression of juridical defeat, with a significance not very different from the actual experience of death.[73]

To say that the judge's unfavourable verdict often coincides with capital punishment does not seem sufficient explanation for this phenomenon; it is probably more correct to see the painful experience of conviction, for someone who came to court convinced of being in the right and confident of upholding it, as a radical denial of his or her image as an individual. If I assert myself as a person in relationship to the truth, then a sentence of conviction strikes me as the culprit (or allegedly such) in the spirit before it does so in the flesh; indeed, possible bodily punishment is only an expression of the silencing (without a shadow of doubt) of his false speech.

It is in fact interesting to observe that a frequent antonym of shame is not just honour (or glory) (1 Sam. 15.30; Isa. 24.23) but also 'joy'[74] (Isa. 66.5; Pss. 32.11; 35.24-27; 71.13-15), which is expressed in praise and song, an experience of life made manifest in the very act of speaking.[75]

2. *The Application of the Punishment*[76]

The judge's sentence, as well as defining the accused's juridical status of guilt, also lays down the culprit's punishment. Between the handing down of the sentence and the application of the punishment there is, however, an interval of time, during which various acts may intervene to stay execution or even lead to a complete reversal of the sentence itself.

I am referring, for example, to a possible appeal: someone convicted in a lower court may challenge the sentence and demand that a higher jurisdictional body should review the case, hoping to do away with the disadvantages arising from the previous judge's decision.[77] The convicted

chief punishments, into *accessory punishments* that involve an individual's juridical honour, that is, 'the fullness of the powers, rights, entitlements etc. which he enjoys in social life' (Antolisei, *Manuale di diritto penale*, pp. 575-83).

73. Cf. Isa. 41.11; Pss. 31.18; 37.19-20; 71.13, 83.18; 129.5-6 etc. Cf. also *THAT*, I, p. 270; and Klopfenstein, *Scham und Schande*, pp. 57, 208.

74. Cf. Barth, *Die Errettung vom Tode*, pp. 150-51.

75. Cf. Chapter 3 section 1.5.

76. Cf. E. Zingg, 'Das Strafrecht nach den Gesetzen Moses', *Judaica* 17 (1961), pp. 106-19.

77. For the juridical concept of challenging (obviously with specific reference to

person may also put forward a request for mercy, which on the one hand confirms the guilty verdict, but on the other asks for the non-application or commuting of the sentence.[78] These juridical situations, theoretically possible and frequent under modern legislation, find at least a partial echo in the biblical texts. The episode that most obviously demonstrates that a time interval between sentence and execution allows a juridical intervention capable of overturning the outcome of the trial is that of Susannah: judgment against the accused has been reached and passed, and just as she is being led off to the place of punishment Daniel lodges his appeal for a review of the trial, which ends with the death of the false accusers (Dan. 13.45ff.).

The separation between sentence and execution is also underlined by the fact that it makes protagonists out of other juridical individuals, to whom the judge authoritatively hands over the task of carrying out justice. The order given to the 'hangman' (public safety authority, executioner, etc.) to carry out the punishment shows that the judge's duties have finished, and that another body—subject to precise rules—will carry out the tribunal's decree. This is repeatedly attested in the criminal proceedings of the Old Testament, where, furthermore, for capital punishment a difference of place is also clearly laid down between the site of the trial and that of the execution of the sentence.[79]

These considerations must however take into account the fact that on occasions in the Bible, especially in poetic texts, the two stages (verdict and execution) tend to be overlaid and attributed to the same juridical individual:[80] this is not unreasonable, given that the outcome of a trial is so closely dependent on the jurisdictional decision that even subsequent actions, even ones carried out by different people, are notionally ascribed to whomever pronounced sentence. In this sense I can maintain that the 'active' juridical individual in this concluding phase is always the judge;

Italian criminal procedure), see Leone, *Manuale di diritto processuale penale*, pp. 569-655.

78. Cf. Chapter 6 n. 65; and Antolisei, *Manuale di diritto penale*, p. 608.

79. Emphasis should be given to the importance of the verb *yṣ'* in the *Hiphil* in legal texts that speak of the execution of sentence: Lev. 24.14, 23; Num. 15.36; Deut. 17.5; 22.(21), 24; Gen. 38.24. Boecker also points out how the same verb is a formula in handing over the culprit in pre-forensic proceedings (Judg. 6.30) or for trial (Deut. 21.19) (*Redeformen*, pp. 21, 75).

80. In particular, it is often said that the judge sentences and *punishes*; in both biblical and modern criminal law, more frequent emphasis is given to a decree of punishment than to one of acquittal.

and it is from this point of view that I would like to put forward the lexicon of greater importance in the biblical literature.

2.1. *Punishment*

Deut. 22.13-21 describes with a certain wealth of detail the case of a husband who accuses his wife of not having been a virgin at the time of their wedding; the elders of the city, gathered at the gate, act as the court. If the woman's parents can produce proof of their daughter's virginity,[81] the judges are to proceed against the husband; in the contrary case, it will be the wife who undergoes punishment. It may be of interest to observe the manner in which the text presents the elders' jurisdictional intervention, juxtaposing the possible outcomes:

w^{e}lāq^{e}ḥû	*ziqnê hā'îr hāhî'*	*'et hā'îš*	
w^{e}yiss^{e}rû		*'ōtô*	
w^{e}'ān^{e}šû		*'ōtô*	*mē'â kesep*...(Deut. 22.18-19)
w^{e}hôṣî'û		*'et hanna'^{a}rā 'el petaḥ bêt 'ābîhā*	
(*ûs^{e}qālûhā*	*'anšê 'îrāh*		*bā'^{a}bānîm*...) (Deut. 22.21)

What I would like to draw attention to is not so much the disparity in the punishment meted out to the two culprits,[82] but the difference in the actions attributed directly to the judges. In 22.18-19 we have the series of verbs *lqḥ*—*ysr* (*Pi*)—*'nš*: *lqḥ* seems to refer to an authoritative action against the culprit, *ysr* (*Pi*) refers to the act of punishment, while *'nš* defines as monetary[83] the kind of punishment inflicted on the slanderous

81. In Deut. 22.13-21 we have the fairly rare case in biblical texts of 'material' proof, consisting of the sheet (stained with blood) from the first night of the marriage. Given, however, the obvious scope for falsifying such proof (S.R. Driver, *Deuteronomy* [ICC, Edinburgh, 3rd edn, 1902], p. 255), it seems necessary to suppose that it was authenticated by impartial witnesses.

82. The difference in punishment laid down for a (guilty) husband as against that inflicted on a (guilty) wife goes against the norm in Deut. 19.19, which lays down that a false accuser—in accordance with the law of retribution (v. 21)—should undergo what he plotted against the accused. Since the woman risked stoning (Deut. 22.13-21), one would have expected capital punishment for a slanderous husband.

83. The amount paid by the husband is handed over by the magistrates to the woman's parents (Deut. 22.19); from this point of view it may be seen as a question of a fine paid for the injury done to the honour of the woman's house, rather than a criminal punishment. According to other codices, in fact, the fine and the damages belong to the system of criminal punishments, and consist of payment *to the State* of a certain amount of money (Antolisei, *Manuale di diritto penale*, pp. 575-79), whereas the settling of the injury is a civil matter to be taken up with the victim of the crime

husband. In this case therefore all the punitive acts are ascribed to the judge. In 22.21 on the other hand we have just the verb *yṣ'* (*Hi*), which seems used to describe the order to proceed to capital punishment, carried out by the local inhabitants. The comparison shows that it is possible to find some texts in which the act of punishment is attributed directly to the judge, and others in which punishment is meted out by people who have been officially appointed to this office.[84]

In an attempt at a more precise treatment of the lexicon concerning punishment, I would like to make a distinction between two semantic nuances that refer to the same act but illustrate a specific aspect of its meaning, one from the point of view of the punishment properly so-called, the other from the point of view of retribution.

2.1.1. *Punishment in General.* We must first consider the verbs to be assigned to the paradigm of punishment (castigation, correction, sanction); these verbs refer directly to the punishment meted out to whomever has committed (or is supposed to have committed) a crime or is in the act of a contravention.

I would like to make room here for the verbs *pqd*[85] and *ysr*, and also

(*ibid*, pp. 658-61). I doubt, however, whether this distinction was in the forefront of the mind of Israel's jurists: it seems more logical to suppose that the legislator saw payment as the main punishment, to which could be linked a secondary punishment consisting of a prohibition on the slanderous husband of bringing any future different action for repudiation against his wife (Deut. 22.19).

84. Of course, the difference in terminology between Deut. 22.18-19 and 21 arises above all from the fact that we are faced with two very different punishments; however, this does not gainsay my argument, given that I am asserting only that the punitive act can be attributed directly to the judge. In this respect, note that the verb *mwt* (*Hi*) is not reserved exclusively to the executioner (Deut. 17.7; 1 Sam. 11.12; 22.17-18; 2 Sam. 14.7; Jer. 26.24; 38.16 etc.) but is also predicated of the judge (Gen. 18.25; 1 Sam. 19.1: in relationship with v. 11; 2 Sam. 14.32; 1 Kgs 2.8, 26; Jer. 26.21 etc.).

85. The semantic complexity of the verb *pqd* has been studied by J. Scharbert, 'Das Verbum PQD in der Theologie des Alten Testaments', *BZ* NS 4 (1960), pp. 209-26. As regards the matter with which I am dealing, the author writes, 'Wenn auch *pqd* kein richterliches Strafen nach dem strengen Grundsatz der Talion oder nach bestimmten vom Strafrecht aufgestellten Normen meint, hat es doch zweifellos an vielen, ja der meisten Stellen, sofern Gott Subjekt ist, eine enge *Beziehung zum Gericht Jahwes* über die gottfeindlichen Mächte' (p. 224). Cf. also, by the same author, 'Formgeschichte und Exegese von Exod. 34.6-7, und seiner Parallelen', *Bib* 38 (1957), pp. 138-42; A. Pax, 'Studien zum Vergeltungsproblem der Psalmen', *SBF*

those, frequent in poetry, that mean to strike, to break, to knock down, to destroy, and the like.[86]

There is no doubt that these verbs are concerned with the judging authority,[87] but it is equally true that they are used for punitive action that takes place in a two-sided controversy when the accuser thinks that there is no longer the possibility of 'being heard' without handing out a lesson to the culprit. The emphasis is on an invitation to the reader of the biblical texts to try, as far as possible, to locate this terminology in the juridical framework to which it belongs, as derived from the literary context. On the other hand, however, the parallel nature of the lexicon

11 (1960–1961), pp. 72-74; see also the monographs by H. Fürst, *Die göttliche Heimsuchung: Semasiologische Untersuchung eines biblischen Begriffes* (Rome, 1965); and G. André, *Determining the Destiny: PQD in the Old Testament* (ConBOT, 16; Lund, 1980).

86. In particular, it seems that along with *mwt* (*Hi*) (cf. n. 84 in the current chapter) emphasis should be given to the verb *nkh* (*Hi*), which, linked to the terminology of 'correction' (Prov. 17.10; 23.13-14; Jer. 2.30 etc.), is also used to refer to the punitive act arising from a judicial verdict (cf. Deut. 25.2; 1 Sam. 22.19; Isa. 11.4; 14.29; Jer. 20.2; 26.23; Ps. 3.8 etc.).

The root *nqh* deserves special consideration. According to C. van Leeuwen, 'aus den Belegstellen, den Parallel- und Gegenbegriffe geht hervor, dass *nqh* im AT in der Rechtssprache beheimatet ist und das Ledig-Sein von (sozial-) ethischer Verpflichtung, Strafe oder Schuld bezeichnet' ('*nqh* ni. schuldlos sein', *THAT*, II, p. 104). The dictionaries (Zorell, BDB, *HALAT*) are also in agreement in attributing to the *Niphal* form of *nqh* the meaning of being immune from guilt, and (consequently) from punishment. For the *Piel* form, which is the one that concerns us at this point, C. van Leeuwen (*THAT*, II, p. 105) gives the generic meaning of 'ungestraft lassen', while the aforementioned dictionaries make a distinction between (a) 'declare innocent, acquit', and (b) 'leave unpunished'. From a strictly lexicographical point of view, therefore, *nqh* (*Pi*) should be included in the list of verbs that express the act of acquittal; however, it is notable that, with the exception of Ps. 19.3, it is always used with a *negative* form or meaning, with the result that the syntagm *lō'* (or *'al*) + *nqh* (*Pi*) + the guilty (or the crime) is equivalent to 'to condemn' and 'to punish' (Exod. 20.7; 34.7; Num. 14.18; Deut. 5.11; 1 Kgs 2.9; Jer. 30.11; 46.28; Nah. 1.3; Job 9.28; 10.14; for Joel 4.21, cf. the critical discussion in *THAT*, II, p. 102). The subject of *nqh* (*Pi*) is always God, except in 1 Kgs 2.9, where it is Solomon, called upon to carry out justice on Shimei.

In the paradigm of punishment, I would like also to mention the relevance of the expression *nṭh yad*, as studied by P. Humbert ('Etendre la main', *VT* 12 [1962], pp. 383-95): it is taken to refer to the gesture (attributed exclusively to God) of the hand pointed (towards the culprit) for punishment.

87. Cf. pp. 201-202.

obliges me to believe that there are shades of meaning that straddle the two juridical structures; in particular, it seems possible to assert that what a judge brings about by the execution of a sentence is just the public and authorised manifestation of the same thrust towards justice present in the *rîb*, with the specification that the character of an objective sanction is more obvious than a *mišpāṭ*. The terminology of wrath should also be considered in the same light; this was fully discussed in the first part of my work:[88] when it is attributed to a judge, it emphasizes the act of sentence passed on someone, and the punitive consequences that arise from it.[89]

Lastly, room would be made in this semantic field for the instrument used for punishment (cf. Exod. 21.20; Isa. 10.24; Prov. 10.13; 13.24; 26.3) or what stands symbolically for the authority that decrees and inflicts the punishment. I am referring in particular to the noun *šēbeṭ*;[90] linked to the lexicon of wrath (Isa. 10.5; 14.5-6; 30.30-31; Prov. 22.8; Lam. 3.1) or to that of correction (2 Sam. 7.14; Isa. 30.31-32; Prov. 10.13; 13.24; 22.15; 23.13-14; 26.3; 29.15), it means the practical act of punishment; since it is one of the symbols of sovereign authority (Isa. 9.3; 14.5-6, 29; Ps. 2.9; Job 9.34), it can be a specific reference to a properly jaundiced sanction (cf. in particular Isa. 11.4; Ps. 45.7; Job 21.9).[91]

2.1.2. *Retribution*. I would like to deal briefly in this section with the second form of expression of punishment to which I alluded above: it takes its place in the paradigm alongside the first (to which it is a literary parallel), but since it has a precise semantic force, it justifies specific treatment.

The 'retributive' nature of punishment brings out the link between

88. Cf. Chapter 1 section 3.1.4.

89. 'La ira también puede significar la sentencia condenatoria en un juicio' (Alonso Schökel, *Profetas*, II, p. 754: with reference to Ezek. 20.33, cf. also pp. 1117-18, 1148). An explicit link between wrath and the act of (condemnatory) sentence can be found in 1 Sam. 20.30-31; 2 Sam. 12.5; Isa. 65.5-7; Ezek. 7.3 etc.

90. The noun *maṭṭeh* is a synonym for *šēbeṭ* (for their use in parallel, cf. Isa. 9.3; 10.5, 24; 14.5; 30.31-32); this term, even on its own, is used as a symbolic reference to the sovereign's power, with juridical overtones (Jer. 48.17; Ezek. 7.10-11; Ps. 110.2).

91. Cf. Z.W. Falk, 'Two Symbols of Justice', *VT* 10 (1960), pp. 73-74; D.N. Freedman, 'The Broken Construct Chain', *Bib* 53 (1972), p. 534 (for Isa. 10.5); G. Wilhelmi, 'Der Hirt mit dem eisernen Szepter. Überlegungen zu Psalm II 9', *VT* 27 (1977), pp. 196-204; J.P.J. Olivier, 'The Sceptre of Justice and Ps. 45.7b', *JNSL* 7 (1979), pp. 45-54.

crime (or innocence) and punishment (or acquittal/favourable decree) in such a way that the justice of the judgment appears obvious: anyone who has done evil (in the sense of having transgressed the law and committed a crime) is made to undergo—through an action undertaken by the judicial authority—proportionate suffering;[92] those who have not done evil have their right satisfied, are repaid for any injury received, and have the exercise of their liberty guaranteed.[93]

With regard to the previous section, we can see that the concept of retribution, although it mainly expresses a punitive event, does not lack a positive meaning when it refers to the innocent. This comes out clearly in 1 Kgs 8.32, a text which, against the background of the terminology used to describe the task of judges (cf. Deut. 25.1) tells of what is expected of God's judging activity:

92. I am referring to the so-called *law of retaliation*, which, given with variant formulae in Exod. 21.23-25; Lev. 24.19-20; and Deut. 19.21 with reference to different juridical cases, seems to form a general principle of Israelite jurisprudence. On this subject, the abundant bibliography bears witness to an ongoing lively discussion over the requirements, extension and application of this norm; from among the classic studies I would like to single out J. Weismann, 'Talion und öffentliche Strafe im Mosaischen Rechte' (1913), in K. Koch (ed.), *Um das Prinzip der Vergeltung in Religion und Recht des Alten Testaments* (WegFor, 125; Darmstadt, 1972), pp. 325-406; A. Alt, 'Zur Talionsformel' (1934), in *Kleine Schriften zur Geschichte des Volkes Israel* (Munich, 1953), pp. 341-44; and, among the more recent ones, V. Wagner, *Rechtsätze in gebundener Sprache und Rechtssatzreihen im israelitischen Recht: Ein Beitrag zur Gattungsforschung* (BZAW, 127; Berlin, 1972), pp. 3-15; B.S. Jackson, 'The Problem of Exodus XXI 22-5 (Ius Talionis)', *VT* 23 (1973), pp. 273-304 (= *Essays* [1975], pp. 75-107); M. Prévost, 'A propos du talion', in *Mélanges dédiés à la mémoire de J. Teneur* (Lille, 1976), pp. 619-29; S.E. Loewenstamm, 'Exodus XXI 22-25', *VT* 27 (1977), pp. 352-60; G. Cardascia, 'La place du talion dans l'histoire du droit pénal à la lumière des droits du Proche-Orient ancien', in *Mélanges offerts à J. Dauvilliez* (Toulouse, 1979), pp. 169-83; T. Frymer-Kensky, 'Tit for Tat: The Principle of Equal Retribution in Near Eastern and Biblical Law', *BA* 43 (1980), pp. 230-34; H.-W. Jüngling, '"Auge für Auge, Zahn für Zahn". Bemerkungen zu Sinn und Geltung der alttestamentlichen Talionsformel', *TP* 59 (1984), pp. 1-38. I share the opinion of M. Gilbert, who sums up the contributions of these exegetical studies and concludes that the biblical statements about the law of retaliation 'affirment la responsabilité personnelle de chacun sur ses actes, l'égalité de tous devant la loi et, à l'encontre d'une vengeance aveugle, la juste proportion entre la peine à subir et le délit commis' ('La loi du talion', *Christus* 31 [1984], p. 81).

93. As regards punishment, the concept of *condign punishment* could be introduced here, made particularly plain in Hebrew when we find the same root referring to both crime and punishment: cf., for example, Prov. 3.34 (*lyṣ*); 22.23 (*qbʿ*).

wešāpaṭṭā 'et ᵃbādeykā	*leharšîa'*	*rāšā'*	*lātēt darkô berō'šô*
	ûlehaṣdîq	*ṣaddîq*	*lātet lô keṣidqātô*

As regards the Hebrew lectionary of retribution, I would like to point out that (as can be seen from the text quoted above) we often have a syntagm constructed out of three elements: the first consists of a verb, by which the idea of 'giving', 'handing over' and the like is expressed; the second tells of what is 'handed over' (as we shall see, we have significant variants here); the third is a reference to the subject (guilty/innocent).

The first element is expressed above all by the verbs *ntn*, *šwb* (*Hi*) and *šlm* (*Pi*),[94] taking the judicial body as their subject. Note that these verbs are also used to say what the culprit is forced (by law) to do in the event that he or she should be convicted:[95] it is in fact the guilty who has 'to give' (in the sense of to pay) (*ntn*, Exod. 21.22, 23, 30; Deut. 22.19, 29; Prov. 6.31 etc.), 'to restore' (*šwb* [*Hi*], Exod. 21.34; Lev. 5.23), 'to recompense' (*šlm* [*Pi*], Exod. 21.34, 36, 37; 22.2; 2 Sam. 12.6 etc.). We obviously have here two linguistic usages that cannot be directly superimposed, but the relationship between them puts across the idea that, through right judgment, accounts are settled in such a way that the judge's repayment agrees with the culprit's payment.

The second element is one which—as I was saying—represents a greater variety of forms. (1) The simplest is that expressed by a term (the complementary object of the verbs listed above) that means behaviour or conduct (wicked or good); translated literally, the Hebrew text would come out as: the judge repays the culprit's conduct (cf. 1 Kgs 8.32a);[96] a more fitting translation would be along the lines of: the judge gives the culprit what he or she deserves. Instead of a complementary object, we may have an expression introduced by *ke*, hence the variant: the judge repays in accordance with the conduct of the person judged (1 Kgs 8.32b). (2) A quite different form is one in which the object of the aforementioned verbs is a term that means 'recompense' or the like; in this case verb + object say basically what is already contained in the verb itself, but leaving unspecified the reason for the retribution. Form (1) and form (2) may be found in parallel, as in Ps. 28.4:

94. Cf. G. Gerleman, 'Die Wurzel *šlm*', *ZAW* 85 (1973), pp. 1-14.

95. Cf. Liedke, *Gestalt*, pp. 46-47.

96. In 1 Sam. 26.23 we have a similar expression, but formulated about a person who has acted correctly: *weyhwh yāšîb lā'îš 'et ṣidqātô we'et 'emûnātô*.

(1)	*ten*		*lāhem*
		k^e po^{ʿo} lām	
		ûk^e rōaʿ maʿal^e lêhem	
		k^e maʿ^a śēh ye dêhem	
	tēn		*lāhem*
(2)	*hašēb*	*g^e mûlām*	*lāhem*

In the third element, particular emphasis is to be laid upon the fact that different prepositions appear (*l^e*, *ʿal*, *b^e*); sometimes explicit reference is made to the imputable nature of the crime through the term *rōʾš*.[97]

Within this normal framework, I would now like to give some examples: the outline presentation allows me better to illustrate the variety of terminology within the basic identity of the syntagm.[98] The fact that in almost every example the subject who 'hands out retribution' is God seems based on the idea that he alone brings about just judgment (cf. Ps. 94.2).

1 Kgs 8.32	(God) *ntn*	*darkô*	*b^e rōʾšô*
	ntn	*k^e ṣidqātô*	*lô*
Ps. 28.4	(God) *ntn*	*k^e po^{ʿo} lām…*	*lāhem*
Jer. 32.19	(God) *ntn*	*kidrākāyw*	*l^e ʾîš*
Ezek. 7.3	(God) *ntn*	*ʾēt kol*	
		tôʿ^a bōtāyik	*ʿālayik*
4	*ntn*	*d^e rākayik*	*ʿālayik*
9	*ntn*	*kidrākayik*	*ʿālayik*
Isa. 61.8	(God) *ntn*	*p^e ʿullātām*	(*lāhem*)
Judg. 9.56	(God) *šwb* (*Hi*)	*ʾēt rāʿat ʾ^a bîmelek*	
57	*šwb* (*Hi*)	*ʾēt kol rāʿat*	
		ʾanšê š^e kem	*b^e rōʾšām*
1 Sam. 25.39	(God) *šwb* (*Hi*)	*ʾēt rāʿat nābāl*	*b^e rōʾšô*
1 Kgs 2.44	(God) *šwb* (*Hi*)	*ʾet rāʿāt^e kā*	*b^e rōʾšekā*
32	(God) *šwb* (*Hi*)	*ʾet dāmô*	*ʿal rōʾšô*
Neh. 3.36	(God) *šwb* (*Hi*)	*ḥerpātām*[99]	*ʾel rōʾšām*
2 Sam. 16.8	(God) *šwb* (*Hi*)	*kōl d^e mê bêt*	
		šāʾûl	*ʿāleykā*
Ps. 94.23	(God) *šwb* (*Hi*)	*ʾet ʾônām*[100]	*ʿ^a lêhem*

97. The noun *ḥêq* also seems to have a similar force in Isa. 65.6-7; Jer. 32.18; Ps. 79.12 (cf. *ThWAT*, II, p. 914).

98. Also for reasons of clarity, I have not followed the order of appearance of words in the Hebrew text.

99. Cf. also Dan. 11.18.

100. In Prov. 20.26 (*m^e zāreh r^e šāʿîm melek ḥākām wayyāšeb ʿ^a lêhem ʾôpān*), *BHS* suggests correcting the last word to *ʾônām* (cf. Ps. 94.23). The correction to the

Hos. 4.9	(God)	*šwb* (*Hi*)		*ma‘^{a}lālayw*	*lô*
Hos. 12.3	(God)	*šwb* (*Hi*)		*k^{e}ma‘^{a}lālāyw*	*lô*
Prov. 24.12	(God)	*šwb* (*Hi*)		*k^{e}po‘^{o}lô*	*l^{e}’ādām*
Zech. 9.12	(God)	*šwb* (*Hi*)	(*mišneh*)		*lāk*
2 Chron. 6.23	(God)	*šwb* (*Hi*)			*l^{e}rāšā‘*
Joel 4.4, 7	(God)	*šwb* (*Hi*)	*g^{e}mul^{e}kem*		*b^{e}rō’š^{e}kem*
Ps. 28.4	(God)	*šwb* (*Hi*)	*g^{e}mûlām*		*lāhem*
Ps. 94.2	(God)	*šwb* (*Hi*)	*g^{e}mûl*		*‘al gē’îm*
Prov. 12.14	(God)	*šwb* (*Hi*) (Q)	*g^{e}mûl y^{e}dê ’ādām*		*lô*
Lam. 3.64	(God)	*šwb* (*Hi*)	*g^{e}mûl*	*k^{e}ma‘^{a}śēh y^{e}dêhem*	*lāhem*
Deut. 32.41, 43	(God)	*šwb* (*Hi*)	*nāqām*[101]		*l^{e}ṣārāy*
Job 34.11	(God)	*šlm* (*Pi*)		*pō‘al ’ādām*	*lô*
Isa. 65.6-7	(God)	*šlm* (*Pi*)		*‘^{a}wōnōtêkem…*	*‘al ḥêqām*
Jer. 32.18	(God)	*šlm* (*Pi*)		*‘^{a}wōn ’ābôt*	*’el ḥêq…*
Jer. 16.18	(God)	*šlm* (*Pi*)	(*mišnēh*)[102]	*‘^{a}wōnām…*	
2 Sam. 3.39	(God)	*šlm* (*Pi*)		*k^{e}rā‘ātô*	*l^{e}‘ōśēh hārā‘â*
Ps. 62.13	(God)	*šlm* (*Pi*)		*k^{e}ma‘^{a}śēhû*	*l^{e}’îš*
Jer. 25.14	(God)	*šlm* (*Pi*)		*k^{e}po‘^{o}lām ûk^{e} ma‘^{a}śēh y^{e}dêhem*	*lāhem*
Judg. 1.7	(God)	*šlm* (*Pi*)		*ka’^{a}šer ‘āśîtî*	*lî*
Ps. 31.24	(God)	*šlm* (*Pi*)	(*‘al yeter*)		*‘ōśēh ga’^{a}wâ*.[103]

text is not convincing, even though the interpretation of the verse remains a problem: the image of a wheel (*’ôpān*) could be an allusion to the harrow (consistent with the agricultural imagery of the verse) or to some instrument of punishment unknown to us.

101. The ‘vengeance’ (*nqm*) which I spoke about in Chapter 1 section 3.2.2. is a concept that often enters into a judicial context: cf. Exod. 21.20; 1 Sam. 24.13; 2 Kgs 9.7; Jer. 51.36; Ps. 99.8.

102. According to A. Phillips, Jer. 16.18 reflects Isa. 40.2: *kî lāq^{e}ḥâ miyyad yhwh kiplayim b^{e}kol ḥaṭṭō’teyhā* (‘Double for All her Sins’, *ZAW* 94 [1982], p. 130). The article deals with the meaning to be given to the ‘double’ punishment, which would involve an innocent generation.

103. The verb *gml*, characteristic of the two-sided juridical situation (cf. Gen. 50.15, 17; 1 Sam. 24.18) is also sometimes used to express retribution of a judicial kind (2 Sam. 19.37; 22.21; Joel 4.4; Ps. 13.6); cf. further, among the texts quoted in the outline, the recurrence of the noun *g^{e}mûl*. Cf. K. Seybold, ‘Zwei Bemerkungen zu *gmwl/gml*’, *VT* 22 (1972), pp. 112-17; A. Lauha, ‘“Dominus benefecit”. Die Wortwurzel *gml* und die Psalmenfrömmigkeit’, *ASTI* 11 (1977–1978), pp. 57-62.

2.2. *The Mandatory Role of the Executor of the Sentence*

The legislative texts and stories in the Bible show that a considerable variety of punishments was laid down in Israel, depending on the crime. Some (corporal punishments), such as flogging (Deut. 25.1-3; Jer. 20.2) and mutilation (Deut. 25.11-12; cf. also Judg. 1.6) struck directly at the person; others (the financial penalties) affected a person's possessions[104] (Exod. 21.34, 37; 22.4, 5, 16 etc.); others again restricted personal liberty; rather than imprisonment,[105] I am thinking of provisions such as exile (cf. 2 Sam. 14.13) or house arrest (2 Kgs 2.36-37; Num. 35.26-28 etc.). For the most serious crimes, capital punishment was laid down, carried out by the sword (cf. 1 Sam. 22.17-19; 1 Kgs 2.31-34 etc.), by stoning (Lev. 24.14, 23; Deut. 13.10-11; 17.5-7 etc.) or by the pyre (Lev. 20.14; 21.9; cf. also Gen. 38.24).[106]

More important for my study is the fact that the execution of the sentence usually brings on—except probably in the case of a fine—the juridical figure of the executioner, an individual or collective to whom 'the order is given' to carry out the judge's decision.[107] From a lexicographical point of view, then, the formulae with which the judge *hands over* the condemned person for punishment are brought to the fore.

The following outline illustrates this terminology: the expression *ntn* b^e*yad*...is the most frequently used, but—and this is also true of paradigmatically similar expressions—not all the cases in which it is used refer to a mandate by authority to execute punishment (cf. for example Lev. 26.25; 1 Kgs 18.9; 2 Sam. 24.14 etc.). Note, moreover, that it is not always a question of capital punishment: in particular, when God is the subject the culprit is often condemned to exile or slavery (cf. Pss. 106.41; 119.18, Judg. 2.14 etc.). Finally, it should be emphasized that, since the 'executioner' is the executor of the judge's decision, to the

104. As R. de Vaux writes, 'il n'y a pas à proprement parler de peines pécuniaires, au sens d'amendes payées à l'Etat ou à la communauté...' (cf. n. 83 to this chapter). 'Par contre, le mal fait à un individu dans ses biens ou ses droits est réparé équitablement et cette compensation a un aspect pénal puisqu'elle est généralement supérieure au dommage causé' (*Institutions*, I, p. 246).

105. Cf. Chapter 6 n. 14.

106. Exposure of the corpses of the convicted, 'hanging from a gibbet' (Deut. 21.22-23; Josh. 8.29; 10.27; cf. also 2 Sam. 4.12; 21.9-11) constituted a secondary punishment, a sort of brand of infamy for the most serious crimes (de Vaux, *Institutions*, I, p. 243).

107. This happens even when the judge's sentence is favourable to the plaintiff; cf. 2 Sam. 14.8; 1 Kgs 3.27; 2 Kgs 8.6.

extent that—during the time the convict is in his charge—he commits abuses while carrying out his task, he himself runs the risk of committing a serious crime, and undergoing a punitive sanction from the same authority that gave him his power (cf. Isa. 10.5-16; 17.6-7; Deut. 32.26-30; Zech. 1.5[108]). (*See tables on the following pages.*)

3. *The Aim of Judgment*

A trial ends with a sentence, but the whole judicial proceeding reaches its fulfilment in the execution of the sentence: if the words pronounced by the judge were to remain hollow, the whole juridical process, which was intended to re-establish real justice between the citizens of a society, would be rendered vain. If a trial is the locus where the struggle for truth takes place and where the victory of the innocent over the wicked is celebrated, and if the various procedures of judgment are directed towards saving victims from violence, so that the community experiences a *mišpāṭ* as the positive route to life, then it is also true that justice is carried out by the conviction of the culprit, and his or her *inevitable punishment*.

Debate is possible, in the sphere of criminal law, as to the ultimate basis for punishment, and about the *jus puniendi* claimed by the State; history does record authors who have challenged the criminal system, maintaining that it is unjust, useless and even harmful; others have arisen in defence of the intrinsic necessity of punishment, deeming it necessary for the law to be put into effect.

It is clear at any rate that, in the Old Testament tradition, we have not just a body of legislative warnings, but also severe prescriptions that bind authorities to carrying out the dictates of the law, without leaving room for considerations or feelings that might seem to us more humanitarian; it should be enough to quote Deut. 13.9-11, which gives the norms to be followed in the case of incitement to idolatry by a relative: *lō' tō'beh lô w^{e}lō' tišma' 'ēlāyw w^{e}lō' tāḥôs 'ên^{e}kā 'ālāyw w^{e}lō' taḥmōl w^{e}lō' t^{e}kasseh 'ālāyw—kî hārōg tahargennû yād^{e}kā tihyeh bô bāri'šōnâ lah^{a}mîtô w^{e}yad kol hā'ām bā'aḥ^{a}rōnâ ûs^{e}qaltô bā'^{a}bānîm wāmēt* (cf. also Deut. 7.16; 19.13, 21; 25.12; Num. 35.32; 1 Sam. 15.9, 18-19; 1 Kgs 20.42 etc.).

108. With reference to Zech. 1.5, see Alonso Schökel: 'las naciones paganas tendrían que ser puros instrumentos para ejecutar un castigo limitado, pero se arrogan la iniciativa y se exceden en la crudeldad, por la qual incurren en la ira de Dios' (*Profetas*, II, p. 1154).

Deut. 19.12	(Elders)	*šlḥ*	*lqḥ*[109]	*ntn*	*b*^{e}*yad gō'ēl haddām*	*'ōtô*	*mwt*
2 Sam. 21.8-9	(King David)		*lqḥ*	*ntn*	*b*^{e}*yad haggib'ōnîm*	pron. suff.	*mwt* (*Ho*)
Jer. 26.24	(Prince)	(*yād*)		*ntn*	*b*^{e}*yad hā'ām*	*'ōtô*	*mwt* (*Hi*)
Jer. 38.16	(Zedekiah)			*ntn*	*b*^{e}*yad hā'*^{a}*nāšîm hā'ēlleh*	pron. suff.	*mwt* (*Hi*)
Jer. 22.25-26	(God)			*ntn*	*b*^{e}*yad m*^{e}*baqšê napšekā*[110]	pron. suff.	*mwt*
Ezek. 39.23	(God)	(*yād*) v. 21		*ntn*	*b*^{e}*yad ṣārêhem*	pron. suff.	*npl baḥereb*
Judg. 6.13	(God)			*ntn*	*b*^{e}*kap midyān*	pron. suff.	(slavery)
1 Sam. 11.12	(Samuel)			*ntn*		*hā'*^{a}*nāšîm*	*mwt* (*Hi*)
Jer. 18.21	(God)			*ntn*	*lārā'āb*	*b*^{e}*nêhem*	
				ngr (*Hi*)[111]	*'al y*^{e}*dê ḥereb*	pron. suff.	*mwt*
Jer. 25.31	(God)			*ntn*	*laḥereb*	*hār*^{e}*ša'îm*	
Isa. 43.28	(God)			*ntn*	*laḥērem l*^{e}*giddûpîm*	*ya'*^{a}*qōb yiśrā'ēl*	

109. For the relationship between *šlḥ* and *lqḥ*, cf. also 1 Sam. 20.31.

110. The executioner may even be the personal enemy of the condemned (cf. Jer. 44.30); this does not seem to have represented an obstacle in Israel to the juridical understanding of the execution of a sentence, provided that the adversary's action was authorised by the judging body.

111. For the verb *ngr* (*Hi*), cf. also Ps. 63.11 and Ezek. 35.5.

Judg. 2.14	(God)	*ntn*	*b^{e}yad šōsîm*	pron. suff.	(slavery)
		mkr	*b^{e}yad 'ôy^{e}bêhem*	pron. suff.	
Ps. 31.9	(God)	*sgr* (*Hi*)	*b^{e}yad 'ôyēb*	pron. suff.	
Josh. 20.5	(Elders)	*sgr* (*Hi*)	*b^{e}yādô* (= *gō'ēl haddām*)	*'et hārōṣēḥ*	
Zech. 11.6	(God)	*mṣ'* (*Hi*)	*b^{e}yad rē'ēhû*	*'et hā'ādām*	
Isa. 19.4	(God)	*skr* (*Pi*)	*b^{e}yad '^{a}dōnîm qāšeh*	(Egypt)	(slavery)
Neh. 9.28	(God)	*'zb*[112]	*b^{e}yad 'ōy^{e}bêhem*	pron. suff.	(slavery)
1 Kgs 2.25	(King Solomon)	*šlḥ*[113]	*b^{e}yad b^{e}nāyāhû*		*mwt*
Job 8.4	(God)	*šlḥ*	*b^{e}yad piš'ām*	pron. suff.	

112. The syntagm *'zb b^{e}yad* also occurs in 2 Chron. 12.5.

113. In the syntagm *šlḥ b^{e}yad-*, *b^{e}yad* usually means 'by means of (someone)' (cf. Exod. 4.13; 2 Sam. 10.2; 15.36; 2 Chron. 36.15 etc.); the text of 1 Kgs 2.25 should therefore correctly be translated: 'king Solomon ordered Benaiah…' Since the verb *šlḥ* lacks a complementary object, the aforementioned syntagm cannot be considered completely parallel to the ones listed previously; however, the general meaning of the verse is indeed one of authoritatively handing over a condemned person to the executioner (cf. the use of *šlḥ* in Deut. 19.12).

As regards the text of Job 8.4 (mentioned immediately below in the table), I think it should undoubtedly be translated: 'he handed them over to their crimes': it is the crime itself, by a sort of immanent justice, that acts as executioner to the culprit (cf. Isa. 64.6; Rom. 1.26).

The expressions listed above are only some of the most typical; other equivalent formulae may be seen in Jer. 15.2; 43.11; 50.35-38; Ezek. 23.46; 31.14; Ps. 118.18.

Since, therefore, punishment *has* to be applied to the culprit, the only question left is as to the purpose, that is, the effectiveness (for the re-establishment of justice) as understood by the legislator. Jurists down the centuries have often debated this problem, and to this day there is no lack of divergent opinions;[114] I shall restrict myself to highlighting what the Old Testament says, pursuing three basic ideas that seem to me the most important and frequent.

3.1. *Suppression (of Evil)*

The term 'suppression' is not one with which the reader will readily agree, given its connotation of kangaroo courts and indiscriminate massacres; the preference would probably be for talk of 'retribution', a concept connected with that of distributive justice, and which puts punishment forward as *malum passionis quod infligitur ob malum actionis* (Grotius).

The Old Testament, however, in many passages considers punishment—especially the capital kind, which because of its radical nature demands a motive in proportion—as the actual elimination of evil, and hence, in an indirect way, as the promotion of justice.

At the conclusion of norms carrying the death penalty, the legislative part of the book of Deuteronomy frequently uses the stereotyped expression: *ûbi'artā hārā' miqqirbekā*[115] (Deut. 13.6; 17.7; 19.19; 21.21; 22.21, 24; 24.7; with *miyyiśrā'ēl*: 17.12; 22.22; with *dam hannāqî* instead of *hārā'*: 19.13; cf. also 21.9).[116]

114. Cf. Antolisei, *Manuale di diritto penale*, pp. 555-56.

115. Cf. J. L'Hour, 'Une législation criminelle dans le Deutéronome', *Bib* 44 (1963), pp. 1-28; R.P. Merendino, *Das deuteronomische Gesetz* (BBB, 31; Bonn, 1969), pp. 336-45, 398-400; G. Seitz, *Redaktionsgeschichtliche Studien zum Deuteronomium* (BWANT, 93; Stuttgart, 1971), pp. 131-32; M. Weinfeld, *Deuteronomy and the Deuteronomic School* (Oxford, 1972), pp. 242-43; P.-E. Dion, 'Tu feras disparaître le mal du milieu de toi', *RB* 87 (1980), pp. 321-49.

116. In practical terms, evil is 'eradicated' by the elimination of individuals judged seriously guilty: see likewise the close relationship between the killing of assassins and the suppression of evil in Judg. 20.13: *tᵉnû 'et hā'ᵃnāšîm bᵉnê bᵉliyya'al 'ᵃšer baggib'â ûnᵉmîtēm ûnᵉba'ᵃrâ rā'â miyyiśrā'ēl.* An administrative act or a political reform that marks the onset of justice may be presented by the Bible as simply the sweeping away of delinquents and the whole of their world (cf. 2 Sam. 4.11; 1 Kgs 14.10; 21.21; 27.47; 2 Kgs 23.24); also in the passages quoted, the verb *b'r* (*Pi*) is used almost as if to underline the obvious rightness of such behaviour.

This expression in Deuteronomy is undoubtedly one of the characteristic formulae by which punitive sanctions are justified; paradigmatically, it may occur alongside others that, in different terminology, express the same concept of the suppression of evil.[117] The lexicon of retribution and the vendetta, moreover, to which I have previously referred,[118] indirectly refers the act of punishment to these same ends.

3.2. *Determent (in Society)*

The concept of the suppression of evil lays the stress on a crime that has been committed, something done in the past that demands a contrary action to mark its intrinsic wickedness; in the opinion of some jurists, this is where the so-called 'legal retaliation',[119] which achieves its aim at the very moment it is carried out, occurs.

The concept of determent, on the other hand, is from many angles different from and complementary to what has gone before when seen as the purpose of a punitive sanction, since it is directed towards the future and aims at preventing the transgression of law in society, without however automatically bringing this result about.

In the juridical tradition of Israel, the idea of punishment as *deterrent* is clearly present. Going back once more to Deuteronomy, we can see how, after the legal sanction, a comment is sometimes added to the effect: *wᵉkol yiśrāʾēl yišmᵉʿû wᵉyīrāʾûn wᵉlōʾ yôsipû laʿᵃśôt kaddābār hārāʿ hazzeh bᵉqirbekā* (Deut. 13.12; cf. also 17.13; 19.20; 21.21).

The same relationship is not infrequently recorded in Scripture: when faced with a judgment (threatened or actual), and in particular when faced with the death of the culprit, the onlookers are seized by fear; this psychological state is considered suitable for preventing the spread of evil,[120] and for encouraging people's good behaviour (cf. e.g. 1 Kgs

117. Cf. 1 Kgs 2.31 (*swr [Hi]–dᵉmê ḥinnām–min*); Ezek. 23.48 (*šbt [Hi]–zimmâ–min*); Isa. 4.4 (*dwḥ [Hi]–dᵉmê yᵉrûšālaim–min*).

These texts manifest a syntagm with three elements, *bʿr (Pi)–hārāʿ–min*. Naturally, there are other forms that can express a similar concept of the suppression of evil; cf. for example Lev. 20.14: (*bāʾēš yiśrᵉpû ʾōtô wᵉʾethen*) *wᵉlōʾ tihyeh zimmâ bᵉtôkᵉkem*; Prov. 20.8: (*melek yôšēb ʿal kissēʾ dîn*) *mᵉzāreh bᵉʿênāyw kol rāʿ*).

118. Cf. present chapter, section 2.1.2. On the subject of retribution and its consequences for theology, see especially K. Koch (ed.), *Um das Prinzip der Vergeltung in Religion und Recht des Alten Testaments* (WegFor, 125; Darmstadt, 1972).

119. Cf. Antolisei, *Manuale di diritto penale*, p. 563.

120. 'Not experiencing fear', on the other hand, can become a synonym for a

2.28; 8.40; Ps. 76.8-10; Prov. 24.21-22; and again: Exod. 14.31; Jos. 4.24; Isa. 25.2-3; 41.2-5; Zeph. 3.6-7; Pss. 52.8; 65.10; Prov. 3.7; 14.16; Neh. 15.15 etc.).

It would be possible to refer back to the concept of 'deterrence' the various biblical expressions with regard to sanctions that speak of the value of example, or, to be more precise, of an event that becomes proverbial and so represents a warning to future generations (cf. Jer. 24.9; 29.18; 42.18; 44.8, 12; Ezek. 5.14-15; Ps. 44.15 etc.).

3.3. *Correction (of the Culprit)*

The aim of punishment as expressed by the two previous concepts also holds good in the case of the death penalty; indeed, from some points of view, they are most perfectly realized in it. However, as far as the (hoped-for) rehabilitation of the criminal is concerned, a milder and temporary sanction can only be supposed: the 'correction' of the culprit not only allows the State to hold criminality in check, but also to restore fitting relations between its citizens in a civilized society. In this case, its main aim is the life of the very individual who has shown a tendency to commit crime; from this point of view, considered structurally, the punishing authority (representing the community) ends up in a two-sided relationship with the person punished, such that its aim becomes not unlike that of the accuser in a controversy, who punishes in order to rehabilitate the condemned person and make him or her capable of interpersonal justice.

Harking back to what has already been discussed in my study and to the relevant terminology,[121] I would just like to emphasize the fact that, since the concept of punitive correction is frequently applied by the biblical texts to God's intervention in history, it is not at all easy to tell whether God is acting as a judge or as a partner in a two-sided relationship. At any rate, given that in the two juridical procedures both the events that occur and the aim of their author agree at this point, the conclusion may be drawn that, where God is the subject, the in-depth aim of all criminal proceedings cannot be detached from an attempt to redeem people and restore to them their dignity as persons in communion with others.

willingness to commit crime: cf. Jer. 3.8; 44.10; Mal. 3.5; Pss. 36.2; 55.20; 64.5; Qoh. 8.11-12 etc.

121. Cf. Chapter 1 section 3.1.1; Chapter 2 section 3; Chapter 4 section 1.2.5.

CONCLUSION

At the end of this journey, which has necessarily taken an analytical route, it seems useful to pull together, by way of conclusion, the results I believe I have achieved. Since it is not easy to sum up my work in a few lines, I shall restrict myself to sketching in the aspects of overall greatest importance, starting with the more detailed and ending with the point at the core of my study.

1. As regards the study of juridical procedural *vocabulary*, I have mainly gathered together and summed up the conclusions of exegetes who have gone before me, occasionally adding to them my own careful research. But it has not been purely a matter of compilation and repetition. Precisely because of their specific nature, monograph studies of the various terms or expressions in the Hebrew lexicon do not always cleave to the juridical aspect, and it can be difficult to fit them logically into an argument; see, for example, the monographs on 'sin'[1] or the term *pqd*.[2] The theological dictionaries of the Old Testament, which necessarily call upon the contributions of various authors, do not study the terms in the (juridical) semantic field, and for the most part restrict themselves to indicating a few parallel or related terms. The brief essays by B. Gemser[3] and I.L. Seeligmann[4] supplied me with my basic material; this was filled out by the analysis of H.J. Boecker,[5] and the

1. Š. Porúbčan, *Sin in the Old Testament* (Rome, 1963); R. Knierim, *Die Hauptbegriffe für Sünde im Alten Testament* (Gütersloh, 1965).

2. J. Scharbert, 'Das Verbum PQD in der Theologie des Alten Testaments', *BZ* NS 4 (1960), pp. 209-26; H. Fürst, *Die göttliche Heimsuchung* (Rome, 1965); G. André, *Determining the Destiny* (Lund, 1980).

3. 'The *rîb*- or Controversy- Pattern in Hebrew Mentality', in M. Noth and D. Winton Thomas (eds.), *Wisdom in Israel and in the Ancient Near East* (VTSup, 3; Leiden, 1955), pp. 120-37.

4. 'Zur Terminologie für das Gerichtsverfahren im Wortschatz des biblischen Hebräisch', in J.A. Emerton *et al.* (eds.), *Congress Volume, Geneva 1965* (VTSup, 16; Leiden, 1967), pp. 251-78.

5. *Redeformen des Rechtslebens im Alten Testament* (Neukirchen, 1964).

whole was added to until it formed the most exhaustive documentation on the subject of the re-establishment of justice.

The mark of my work has been to structure the Hebrew lexicon according to the basic stages of juridical proceedings. This has allowed me to see how the function of expressing juridical concepts is not limited to one vocabulary, considered technical, but is also filled out by a 'generic' terminology, which in certain contexts and particular syntagms has a meaning quite like the former. In Chapter 7 I showed how the term *'ēd* could take the place of many other expressions and so form the complex paradigm of 'the witness'. Something similar may be seen at other points in my study, from the term *ryb* to *špṭ*; from the formulae of confession of guilt to ones used for a law court sentence.

A further important element in my research is that of always having tried to find the link between the different terms in the language of procedure. I have therefore not only considered paradigmatic relationships, but have tried to show how one element is linked to the others in a syntagmatic relation. For example, in Chapter 6 I indicated how verbs of motion reflected the nature of the juridical initiative undertaken by different individuals: the outlines supplied at this point show the verb of motion is linked to the function of judging (expressed by terms referring to the 'judge' and his or her judging); the meaning seems different, however, when the motion is directed towards the other party in the controversy. Also in Chapter 6, the verbs describing the magistrate's preliminary investigation are linked to the different ways of expressing the result of that inquiry, and so on.

On occasion, I have also drawn attention to how the various syntagmatic relations allow us to see that identical terms have a different meaning; this is true, for example, of the expressions of 'supplication' (Chapter 4: of pardon; Chapter 7: of appeal) or of similar expressions on the lips of the accuser or judge (Jer. 26.11, 16).

Lastly, the cohesive nature of my undertaking has made it possible to bring out an important fact: juridical vocabulary is to be found, though with varying frequency, in a large number of biblical texts. A concern for justice, both in human history and in the relationship between God and humanity, comes out clearly as one of the most important themes in the text of the Bible.

2. On a different level, that of the tracing of juridical/criminal *procedures*, I made no attempt to sketch a history of juridical institutions, on account of the sparseness of data, which makes the research

in question debatable. My aim has been to sketch in what seems so constantly present in the different epochs and biblical writings as to form an incontrovertible basis for interpretation. The organization of my work, which may be deduced from the chapter titles, in fact mirrors the basic forms of the controversy (Part I) and the judgment (Part II); the former (Chapter 1) was based on a structure with three fundamental elements: the accusation (Chapter 2), the response (Chapter 3) and the conclusion of the dispute (Chapter 4); the latter (Chapter 5) was also split into three stages: the start of the trial (Chapter 6), the debate (Chapter 7) and the end of the trial (Chapter 8).

Within this simple organization, I supplied broader and, so to speak, more obvious frameworks. I would like to give a list of these relationships, so as to illustrate my idea with a sort of resumé and demonstrate its practical application. In Part I, Chapter 1 gives an introduction to the individuals taking part in the juridical event that is a controversy; in Chapter 2, with the aim of defining an accusation, an outline was given of the relationship between the 'notitia criminis', the prosecution speech and the punishment; Chapter 3 laid out the structural opposition between the admission of one's guilt and a declaration of innocence; Chapter 4 was built upon the relationship between a request for pardon (both in words and in gestures) and the act that grants it. In Part II, after Chapter 5 (with its threefold structure:—judge—judging—judgment), Chapter 6 demonstrated the links between the summons to trial and the court's jurisdiction; Chapter 7 developed the concept of the debate, in which the prosecution (both under the form of witness and of appeal) and the defence take part; the link between debating speech and silence marks the passage to Chapter 8, which revolves around the sentence pronounced by the judge and the application of the punishment.

Within the basic organization, which seems solid to me precisely because it is not bound to the interpretation of an individual passage or historically uncertain institutions, the meaning of individual juridical operations was made clear. Here are a few examples: the concept of a witness has a different function and force depending on whether we are dealing with a controversy (Chapter 2) or a court of law (Chapter 7); the offer of a gift is normal and acceptable practice in a *rîb* (Chapter 4), but is synonymous with corruption in the judicial structure (Chapter 5); an accusation sometimes takes the form of a declaration of conviction, but its meaning cannot be identified with a judge's verdict (Chapter 8); and so on.

Laying a solid procedural basis for my work also seems useful to me for the clarification of some concepts relating to the juridical sphere and frequently used in biblical literature. Here too I will restrict myself to an allusion, listing chapter by chapter some of the most important concepts: wrath and vendetta (Chapter 1); an accuser who is aggressive yet eager for a communion in truth (Chapter 2); the confession of 'sins' and praise (Chapter 3); pardon, reconciliation and covenant (Chapter 4); judging and saving (Chapter 5); the closeness (or distance) of God to those who call upon him (Chapter 6); war and law; the defence of one's own rights as an accusation (of the other party) in a trial (Chapter 7); the 'justification' or punishment of the culprit (Chapter 8). I am not, of course, claiming that my study is the last word on this set of problems; I only hope that it is a useful tool for the better understanding of them.

3. The most important result I believe I have achieved, the one that in my opinion forms the core of my study, is the distinction between the procedure in a controversy and the juridical process, from the point of view both of their specific form and function, and of the necessary link between them. I believe that this can indeed form a principle for the understanding of Scripture that is capable of eliminating misunderstandings and half-truths.

In his 1962 article on the *rîb-pattern*,[6] J. Harvey posed a number of questions to which research had not yet given a satisfactory answer: why, after the introduction, did a *rîb* usually begin with a question posed by a messenger? What was the reason for the frequent reference to the uselessness of cultic practices? Why was the distinction between judge and prosecutor effectively eliminated in a *rîb*? Why was the declaration of guilt followed by threats instead of being preceded by them, or being restricted to a condemnation? Why was the law applied in a *rîb* so characteristically apodictic? Why was the pattern different from that used against foreign gods and peoples? Why do some *rîb*s have a common structure but end with a positive decree, which is not, however, a declaration of innocence?

J. Harvey believed the answer to these questions lay in locating (prophetic) *rîb*s in the same framework of international law that supplied the format for the covenant. I believe that the reader of my work can see how my treatment of the controversy, on the one hand, takes in Harvey's point of view, and on the other hand explains point by point

6. J. Harvey, 'Le "rîb-pattern", réquisitoire prophétique sur la rupture de l'alliance', *Bib* 43 (1962), pp. 179-80.

the meaning of those questions over and above reference to a literary model.[7]

Dealing with the problem posed by social justice (to which I alluded in the Introduction to my study as an interest of the whole of present-day society) is in this way enriched by the consideration of a twofold form of juridical intervention against injustice. If the purpose of judgment is more than just the regulation of relationships between citizens, and if in practical terms it is irrelevant to the relationships between States, then a different sort of effort is needed to find ways of reconciliation and peace, because this is a different manner of 'doing justice'.

Lastly, theology itself, that is, the understanding of God's revelation, is deeply affected.[8] From this point of view, it would be necessary to carry my analysis through into the New Testament, in order to pick out the elements of continuity and discontinuity with which, in the Christian perspective, the biblical tradition is interpreted through to its fulfilment. It seems of significance to me, however, to have observed already how, when the juridical metaphor is used, God's acting *in history* is described in two separate and complementary ways.

Sometimes we have the image of God as a judge; this means that *two parties* at loggerheads with each other are standing before him; in the main, one of the two disputants, making use of bullying and even legal means, is trying to do away with the weak party. God thereupon intervenes and brings justice to the latter, striking the arrogant and violent with his punishment. This manifestation of judgment demonstrates God's attention to the victims (as well as to the 'authors') of injustice in

7. Attention should be drawn to the recent contribution by M. De Roche, 'Yahweh's *rîb* against Israel: A Reassessment of the So-Called "Prophetic Lawsuit" in the Pre-exilic Prophets', *JBL* 102 (1983), pp. 563-74, which follows my work's line of interpretation.

8. In particular, the strongly-felt difficulties experienced by the modern consciousness by the image of God as judge should be taken into account; about this K. Stock writes, 'Es kann nicht zweifelhaft sein, dass eine verantwortliche Interpretation der Rechtfertigungslehre heute den Widerstand, ja den ausgesprochenen Widerwillen gegen die Prädikation Gottes als des Richters, wie er sich in repräsentativen Texten ausspricht, ernst zu nehmen hat. Ebenso ernst zu nehmen ist aber der Tatbestand, dass die biblische Überlieferung...von dem richtenden Gott redet und dass sie der Gemeinde in den vielfältigen Formen der Verkündigung, des Kirchenlieds, des Bekenntnisses und des Gebets faktisch präsent ist' ('Gott der Richter. Der Gerichtsgedanke als Horizont der Rechtfertigungslehre', *EvT* 40 [1980], p. 241).

the world, but is not to be identified with the eschatological judgment.[9]

The other image revealed in Scripture is that of God as prosecutor; in this case the other party stands before him (be it an individual, a people or the whole of humanity), and against it is brought the charge of treachery: the dynamic here is that of the controversy, with swings that are sometimes aggressive, but are always within the horizon of a possible and desired reconciliation.[10]

The person of Christ, as presented in the Gospels and St Paul, represents—in my interpretation—the synthesis of these two juridical metaphors: in his first coming (in history) he is the means and the mediator of pardon; in his second coming (at the end of time) he will appear as judge of the living and the dead. If the judgment has already been cast, the one who has been condemned is not sinful humanity but the 'prince of this world', humanity's ancient enemy.[11]

'Judgment', with its structural relationship to punishment, is a means for the correction and deterrence of evil, but it adds a dimension of fear to living; the dynamic of the controversy is a route to that understanding and love that drives out fear and opens the way to praise.

9. Cf. G. Barbiero, 'Il testo massoretico di Prov. 3.34', *Bib* 63 (1982), pp. 387-88.

10. Cf. W. Zimmerli, 'Alttestamentliche Prophetie und Apokalyptik auf dem Wege zur "Rechtfertigung des Gottlosen"', in *Rechtfertigung* (FS E. Käsemann; Tübingen, 1976), pp. 575-92.

11. Cf. S. Lyonnet, 'Justification, jugement, rédemption, principalement dans l'épître aux Romains', in *Littérature et Théologie Pauliniennes* (RechBib, V; Louven, 1960), pp. 166-84.

BIBLIOGRAPHY

The Bibliography contains only titles relating directly to the matter dealt with by me. I have not listed works of a general nature such as Grammars, Lexicons or Introductions, nor linguistic studies; the same applies to commentaries on the various books of the OT and articles in biblical Dictionaries.

Aalen, S., *Die Begriffe 'Licht' und 'Finsternis' im Alten Testament, im Spätjudentum und im Rabbinismus* (SNVAO; Oslo, 1951).

Aartun, K., 'Hebräisch 'ānī und 'ānāw', *BO* 28 (1971), pp. 125-26.

Albright, W.F., 'The Judicial Reform of Jehoshaphat', in *A. Marx Jubilee Volume* (New York, 1950), pp. 61-82.

—'Some Remarks on the Song of Moses in Deuteronomy XXXII', *VT 9* (1959), pp. 339-46.

Alonso Díaz, J., 'El Mesias y la realización de la justicia escatológica', in *Mesianismo y escatologia: Estudios en Memoria del Prof. Dr. L. Arnaldich Perot* (Bibl. Salmanticentis, XVI, Estudios 14; Salamanca, 1976), pp. 61-84.

—'Las "buenas obras" (o la "justicia") dentro de la estructura de los principales temas de teología bíblica', *EstE* 52 (1977), pp. 445-86.

—'La "justicia interhumana" idea básica de la Biblia', *CuBíb* 35 (1978), pp. 163-95.

Alonso Schökel, L., 'Nota estilística sobre la partícula *hinnēh', Bib* 37 (1956), pp. 74-80.

—'L'infaillibilité de l'oracle prophétique', in *L'infaillibilité: Son aspect philosophique et théologique* (Actes du Colloque…E. Castelli; Paris, 1970), pp. 495-503.

—'La Rédemption oeuvre de solidarité', *NRT* 93 (1971), pp. 449-72.

—'David y la mujer de Tecua: 2 Sm 14 como modelo hermenéutico', *Bib* 57 (1976), pp. 192-205.

—' "Somos iguales que nuestros hermanos", Para una exégesis de Neh 5, 1-13', *Salm* 13 (1976), pp. 257-66.

—*Treinta Salmos: Poesia y Oración* (EstAT, 2; Madrid, 1981).

Alt, A., 'Die Ursprünge des israelitischen Rechts' (1934), in *Kleine Schriften zur Geschichte des Volkes Israel*, I (Munich, 1953), pp. 278-332.

—'Zur Talionsformel' (1934), *ibid.*, pp. 341-44.

Amsler, S., 'Le thème du procès chez les prophètes d'Israël', *RTP* 24 (1974), pp. 116-31.

Andersen, F.I., 'The Socio-Juridical Background of the Naboth Incident', *JBL* 85 (1966), pp. 46-57.

—*The Sentence in Biblical Hebrew* (The Hague, 1974).

Anderson, G.W., 'Enemies and Evildoers in the Book of Psalms', *BJRL* 48 (1965–1966), pp. 18-29.

André, G., *Determining the Destiny: PQD in the Old Testament* (ConBOT, 16; Lund, 1980).

Antolisei, F., *Manuale di Diritto Penale* (Milan, 7th edn, 1975).

Ap-Thomas, D.R., 'Notes on Some Terms relating to Prayer', *VT 6* (1956), pp. 226-41.

—'Some Aspects of the Root ḤNN in the Old Testament', *JSS* 2 (1957), pp. 128-48.

Aranov, M.M., *The Biblical Threshing-Floor in the Light of the Ancient Near Eastern Evidence: Evolution of an Institution* (Diss. New York University, 1977 [*DissAbstr* 38 (1977-78) §6179-80 (A)]).

Asensio, F., *Misericordiae et veritas: El* ḥesed *y* emet *divinos. Su influjo religioso-social en la historia de Israel* (AnGr, 48; Rome, 1949).

—*El Dios de la luz: Avances a través del Antiguo Testamento y contactos con el Nuevo* (Rome, 1958).

Auld, A.G., 'Cities of Refuge in Israelite Tradition', *JSOT* 10 (1978), pp. 26-40.

Auvray, P., 'Le prophète comme guetteur', *RB* 71 (1964), pp. 191-205.

Bach, D., 'Rite et parole dans l'Ancien Testament. Nouveaux éléments apportés par l'étude de tôdâh', *VT* 28 (1978), pp. 10-19.

Bach, R., 'Gottesrecht und weltliches Recht in der Verkündigung des Propheten Amos', in *Festschrift G. Dehn* (Neukirchen, 1957), pp. 23-34.

Baker, D.W., 'Further Examples of the *waw explicativum*', *VT* 30 (1980), pp. 129-36.

Balentine, S.E., 'A Description of the Semantic Field of Hebrew Words for "Hide"', *VT* 30 (1980), pp. 137-53.

—'The Prophet as Intercessor: A Reassessment', *JBL* 103 (1984), pp. 161-73.

Baltzer, K., 'Naboths Weinberg (1 Kön. 21). Der Konflikt zwischen israelitischem und kanaanäischem Bodenrecht', *WDienst* NS 8 (1965), pp. 73-88.

Barbiero, G., 'Il testo massoretico di Prov 3,34', *Bib* 63 (1982), pp. 370-89.

Barr, J., *The Semantics of Biblical Language* (London, 1961).

—'Some Notes on *bēn* "between" in Classical Hebrew', *JSS* 23 (1978), pp. 1-22.

—'Semitic Philology and the Interpretation of the Old Testament', in G.W. Anderson (ed.), *Tradition and Interpretation* (Oxford, 1979), pp. 31-64.

Barth, C., *Die Errettung vom Tode in den individuellen Klage- und Dankliedern des Alten Testaments* (Zollikon, 1947).

Barth, M., *Rechtfertigung: Versuch einer Auslegung paulinischer Texte im Rahmen des Alten und Neuen Testamentes* (TS, 90; Zürich, 1969).

Bartlett, J.R., 'The Use of the Word *r'š* as a title in the Old Testament', *VT* 19 (1969), pp. 1-10.

Barucq, A., 'Peché et innocence dans les Psaumes bibliques et les textes religieux de l'Egypte du Nouvel-Empire', in *Etudes de critique et d'histoire religieuses* (FS L. Vaganay; Lyon, 1948), pp. 111-37.

Bassler, J.M., *Divine Impartiality: Paul and a Theological Axiom* (SBLDS, 59; Chico, CA, 1982).

Baudissin, W.V., 'The Original Meaning of "Belial"', *ExpTim* 9 (1897–98), pp. 40-45.

Baumann, E., 'Das Lied Mose's (Dt XXXII 1-43) auf seine gedankliche Geschlossenheit untersucht', *VT* 6 (1956), pp. 414-24.

Beaucamp, E., 'La théophanie du Psaume 50 (49). Sa signification pour l'interprétation du Psaume', *NRT* 81 (1959), pp. 897-915.

—'La justice de Yahvé et l'économie de l'alliance', *SBFLA* 11 (1960–61), pp. 5-55.

—'Justice divine et pardon', in *A la rencontre de Dieu* (Mém. A. Gelin; Le Puy, 1961), pp. 129-44.

—'La justice en Israël', in *Populus Dei*. I. *Israel* (Studi in onore del Card. A. Ottaviani; Rome, 1969), pp. 201-35.

—'Le péche dans l'Ancien Testament', in *Populus Dei*, pp. 299-334.

Beauchamp, P., 'Propositions sur l'alliance de l'Ancien Testament comme structure centrale', *RSR* 58 (1970), pp. 161-93.

—*L'un et l'autre Testament: Essai de lecture* (Paris, 1976).

—*Psaumes nuit et jour* (Paris, 1980).

Beek, M.A., 'The Religious Background of Amos II 6-8', *OTS* 5 (1948), pp. 132-41.

Begrich, J., *Studien zu Deuterojesaja* (BWANT, 77, Stuttgart, 1938).

—'Sofer und Mazkir. Ein Beitrag zur inneren Geschichte des davidisch-salomonischen Grossreiches und des Königreiches Juda', *ZAW* 17 (1940–1941), pp. 1-29.

Bellefontaine, E., 'Deuteronomy 21,18-21: Reviewing the Case of the Rebellious Son', *JSOT* 13 (1979), pp. 13-31.

Berghe, P. van den, '*'Ani* et *'Anaw* dans les Psaumes', in R. de Langhe (ed.), *Le Psautier. Ses origines. Ses problèmes littéraires. Son influence* (OrBiLov, 4; Louvain, 1962), pp. 273-95.

Bergmeier, R., 'Das Streben nach Gewinn—des Volkes *'āwōn*', *ZAW* 81 (1969), pp. 93-97.

Bergren, R.V., *The Prophets and the Law* (HUCA Monograph Series, 4; Cincinnati, 1974).

Berkovits, E., 'The Biblical Meaning of Justice', in *Man and God: Studies in Biblical Theology* (Detroit, 1969), pp. 224-52.

—'Ṣedeq and Ṣ'daqa', in *Man and God*, pp. 292-348.

Berlin, A., *Poetics and Interpretation of Biblical Narrative* (Bible and Literature Series, 9; Sheffield, 1983).

Bernal Giménez, J.M., 'El Siervo como promesa de "mišpāṭ". Estudio bíblico del término "mišpāṭ" en Is 42.1-4', in *Palabra y vida: Homenaje a J. Alonso Díaz* (Madrid, 1984), pp. 77-85.

Bernhardt, K.-H., *Gott und Bild: Ein Beitrag zur Begründung und Deutung des Bilderverbotes im Alten Testament* (TArb, 2; Berlin, 1956).

Bettenzoli, G., 'Gli "Anziani di Israele"', *Bib* 64 (1983), pp. 47-73.

—'Gli "Anziani" in Giuda', *Bib* 64 (1983), pp. 211-24.

Beuken, W.A.M., 'Mišpaṭ. The First Servant Song and its Context', *VT* 22 (1972), pp. 1-30.

Beyerlin, W., 'Gattung und Herkunft des Rahmens im Richterbuch', in *Tradition und Situation: Studien zur alttestamentlichen Prophetie* (FS A. Weiser; Göttingen, 1963), pp. 1-29.

—'Die *tôdā* der Heilsvergegenwärtigung in den Klageliedern des Einzelnen', *ZAW* 79 (1967), pp. 208-24.

—*Die Rettung der Bedrängten in den Feindpsalmen der Einzelnen auf institutionelle Zusammenhänge untersucht* (FRLANT, 99; Göttingen, 1970).

—'Der nervus rerum in Psalm 106', *ZAW* 86 (1974), pp. 50-64.

—*Der 52. Psalm: Studien zu seiner Einordnung* (BWANT, 111; Stuttgart, 1980).

Birkeland, H., *The Evildoers in the Book of Psalms* (Oslo, 1955).

Blank, S.H., 'The Curse, Blasphemy, the Spell, and the Oath', *HUCA* 23 (1950–51), pp. 73-95.

—'An Effective Literary Device in Job XXXI', *JJS* 2 (1950–51), pp. 105-7.

—'Irony by Way of Attribution', *Sem* 1 (1970), pp. 1-6.

Blau, J., 'Adverbia als psychologische und grammatische Subjekte/Praedikate im Bibelhebräisch', *VT* 9 (1959), pp. 130-37.

Blommerde, A.C.M., 'The Broken Construct Chain, Further Examples', *Bib* 55 (1974), pp. 549-52.

Blum, E., *Die Komposition der Vätergeschichte* (WMANT, 57; Neukirchen, 1984).

Boecker, H.J., 'Anklagereden und Verteidigungsreden im Alten Testament. Ein Beitrag zur Formgeschichte alttestamentlicher Prophetenworte', *EvT* 20 (1960), pp. 398-412.

—'Erwägungen zum Amt des Mazkir', *TZ* 17 (1961), pp. 212-16.

—*Redeformen des Rechtslebens im Alten Testament* (WMANT, 14; Neukirchen, 1964 [2nd edn, 1970]).

—*Recht und Gesetz im Alten Testament und im Alten Orient* (NStB, 10; Neukirchen, 1976).

—'Ueberlegungen zur Kultpolemik der vorexilischen Propheten', in *Die Botschaft und die Boten* (FS H.W. Wolff; Neukirchen, 1981), pp. 169-80.

Boer, P.A.H. de, 'The Counsellor', in M. Noth and D. Winton-Thomas (eds.), *Wisdom in Israel and the Ancient Near East* (VTSup, 3; Leiden, 1955), pp. 42-71.

—*Gedenken und Gedächtnis in der Welt des Alten Testaments* (Fr. Delitzsch-Vorlesungen, 1960; Stuttgart, 1962).

Boerma, C., *Rich Man, Poor Man—and the Bible* (Leiden, 1979).

Bohlen, R., *Der Fall Nabot: Form, Hintergrund und Werdegang einer alttestamentlichen Erzählung (1 Kön 21)* (TThSt, 35; Trier, 1978).

Bonnard, P.E., 'Le vocabulaire du Miserere', in *A la rencontre de Dieu* (Mém. A. Gelin; Le Puy, 1961), pp. 145-56.

Booij, T., 'Negation in Isaiah 43,22-24', *ZAW* 94 (1982), pp. 390-400.

Booth, O., 'The Semantic Development of the Term *mšpṭ* in the Old Testament', *JBL* 61 (1942), pp. 105-10.

Bornkamm, G., 'Lobpreis, Bekenntnis und Opfer', in *Apophoreta* (FS E. Haenchen; BZNW, 30; Berlin, 1964), pp. 46-63.

Botterweck, G.J., 'Die soziale Kritik des Propheten Amos', in *Die Kirche im Wandel der Zeit* (FS J. Hoeffner; Cologne, 1971), pp. 39-58.

—' "Sie verkaufen den Unschuldigen um Geld". Zur sozialen Kritik des Propheten Amos', *BibLeb* 12 (1971), pp. 215-31.

Bracker, H.-D., *Das Gesetz Israels verglichen mit den altorientalischen Gesetzen der Babylonier, der Hethiter und der Assyrer* (Hamburg, 1962).

Braulik, G., *Psalm 40 und der Gottesknecht* (ForBib, 18; Würzburg, 1975).

Bretón, S., *Vocación y misión: Formulario profético* (AnBib 111; Rome, 1987).

Brichto, H.C., 'The Case of the *śōṭā* and a Reconsideration of Biblical "Law" ', *HUCA* 46 (1975), pp. 55-70.

Brongers, H.A., 'Die Rache- und Fluchpsalmen im Alten Testament', *OTS* 13 (1963), pp. 21-42.

—'Der Eifer des Herrn Zebaoth', *VT* 13 (1963), pp. 269-84.

—'Bemerkungen zum Gebrauch des adverbialen *w^{e}'attāh* im Alten Testament (ein lexikologischer Beitrag)', *VT* 15 (1965), pp. 289-99.

—'Der Zornesbecher', *OTS* 15 (1969), pp. 177-92.

—'Das Zeitwort *'ālā* und seine Derivate', in *Travels in the World of the Old Testament: Studies presented to Prof. M.A. Beek* (SSN, 16; Assen, 1974), pp. 30-40.

—'Fasting in Israel in Biblical and Post-Biblical Times', *OTS* 20 (1977), pp. 1-21.

—'Alternative Interpretationen des sogenannten waw copulativum', *ZAW* 90 (1978), pp. 273-77.
—'Some Remarks on the Biblical Particle *h*^{a}*lō*", *OTS* 21 (1981), pp. 177-89.
Brown, J.P., 'Peace Symbolism in Ancient Military Vocabulary', *VT* 21 (1971), pp. 1-23.
Brueggemann, W.A., 'Amos' Intercessory Formula', *VT* 19 (1969), pp. 385-99.
—'Jeremiah's Use of Rhetorical Questions', *JBL* 92 (1973), pp. 358-74.
—'A Neglected Sapiential Word Pair', *ZAW* 89 (1977), pp. 234-58.
—'Social Criticism and Social Vision in the Deuteronomic Formula of the Judges', in *Die Botschaft und die Boten* (FS H.W. Wolff; Neukirchen, 1981), pp. 101-14.
Brummel, L., *et al.* (eds.), *Los pobres: Encuentro y compromiso* (Buenos Aires, 1978).
Brunner, H., 'Gerechtigkeit als Fundament des Thrones', *VT* 8 (1958), pp. 426-28.
Brunner, R., 'Das hörendes Herz', *TLZ* 79 (1954), pp. 697-700.
Bruppacher, H., *Die Beurteilung der Armut im Alten Testament* (Zürich, 1924).
Bühlmann, W., *Vom rechten Reden und Schweigen: Studien zu Proverbien 10–31* (OBO, 12; Freiburg, 1976).
Buis, P., 'Notification de jugement et confession nationale', *BZ* NS 11 (1967), pp. 193-205.
—'Les conflits entre Moïse et Israël dans l'Exode et Nombres', *VT* 28 (1978), pp. 257-70.
Buss, M.J., 'The Meaning of Cult in the Interpretation of the Old Testament', *JBR* 32 (1964), pp. 317-25.
—'The Distinction between Civil and Criminal Law in Ancient Israel', in *Proceedings of the Sixth World Congress of Jewish Studies*, I (Jerusalem, 1977), pp. 51-62.
Bussini, F., *L'homme pécheur devant Dieu: Théologie et anthropologie* (Lille, 1979).
Buttenwieser, M., 'Blood Revenge and Burial Rites in Ancient Israel', *JAOS* 39 (1919), pp. 303-21.
Callaway, P.R., 'Deut. 21.18–21. Proverbial Wisdom and Law', *JBL* 103 (1984), pp. 341-52.
Cañellas, G., 'Fundamento veterotestamentario de la reconciliación', *BibFe* 5 (1979), pp. 21-33.
Carcaterra, A., '"Ius summum saepe summast malitia"', in *Studi in onore di E. Volterra*, IV (Milan, 1971), pp. 627-66.
Cardascia, G., 'Droits cunéiformes et droit biblique', in *Proceedings of the Sixth World Congress of Jewish Studies*, I (Jerusalem, 1977), pp. 63-70.
—'La place du talion dans l'histoire du droit pénal à la lumière des droits du Proche-Orient ancien', in *Mélanges offerts a J. Dauvilliez* (Toulouse, 1979), pp. 169-83.
Carlson, R.A., *David, the Chosen King: A Traditio-Historical Approach to the Second Book of Samuel* (Stockholm, 1964).
Carmichael, C.M., *The Laws of Deuteronomy* (London, 1974).
Carrillo Alday, S., *El Cántico de Moisés (Deut 32)* (Madrid, 1970).
Castellino, G., *Le lamentazioni individuali e gli inni in Babilonia e in Israele* (Turin, 1939).
Cassuto, U., 'The Song of Moses (Deuteronomy Chapter XXXII 1-43)' (1938), in *Biblical and Oriental Studies*. I. *Bible* (Jerusalem, 1973), pp. 41-46.
Cazelles, H., *Etudes sur le Code de l'Alliance* (Paris, 1946).
—'A propos de quelques textes difficiles relatifs à la justice de Dieu dans l'Ancien Testament', *RB* 58 (1951), pp. 169-88.

—'Institutions et terminologie en Deut. I.6-17', in J.A. Emerton *et al.* (eds.), *Congress Volume, Geneva 1965* (VTSup, 15; Leiden, 1966), pp. 97-112.

—'Le sens religieux de la Loi', in *Populus Dei.* I. *Israel* (Studi in onore del Card. A Ottaviani; Rome, 1969), pp. 177-94.

—'La transgression de la loi en tant que crime et délit', in *Populus Dei*, pp. 521-528.

—'Rédactions et traditions dans l'Exode', in *Studien zum Pentateuch* (FS W. Kornfeld; Vienna, 1977), pp. 37-58.

—'Droit public dans le Deutéronome', in N. Lohfink (ed.), *Das Deuteronomium: Entstehung, Gestalt und Botschaft* (Leuven, 1985), pp. 99-106.

Charbel, A., 'Virtus sanguinis non expiatoria in sacrificio *šᵉlāmîm*', in *Sacra Pagina*, I (Gembloux, 1959), pp. 366-76.

—*Zebaḥ šᵉlāmîm: Il sacrificio pacifico; nei suoi riti e nel suo significato religioso e figurativo* (Jerusalem, 1967).

Childs, B.S., *Memory and Tradition in Israel* (SBT, 37; London, 1962).

Christ, H., *Blutvergiessen im Alten Testament: Der gewaltsame Tod des Menschen untersucht am hebräischen Wort dām* (Basel, 1977).

Clark, M., 'A Legal Background to the Yahwist's Use of "Good and Evil" in Genesis 2–3', *JBL* 88 (1969), pp. 266-78.

—'Law', in J.H. Hayes (ed.), *Old Testament Criticism* (San Antonio, 1974), pp. 99-139.

Clifford, R.J., 'The Use of *hôy* in the Prophets', *CBQ* 28 (1966), pp. 458-64.

Clines, D.J.A., and D.M. Gunn, '"You Tried to Persuade Me" and "Violence! Outrage" in Jeremiah 20.7-8', *VT* 28 (1978), pp. 20-27.

Coats, G.W., 'Self-Abasement and Insult Formulas', *JBL* 89 (1970), pp. 14-26.

—*From Canaan into Egypt: Structural and Theological Context for the Joseph Story* (CBQMS, 4; Washington, DC, 1976).

—'Strife without Reconciliation—a Narrative Theme in the Jacob Traditions', in *Werden und Wirken des Alten Testaments* (FS C. Westermann; Neukirchen, 1980), pp. 82-106.

Cody, A., 'Notes on Proverbs 22.21 and 22.23b', *Bib* 61 (1980), pp. 418-26.

Cohen, B., 'Self-Help in Jewish and Roman Law', *RIDA* 3rd ser. 2 (1955), pp. 107-33.

—*Jewish and Roman Law: A Comparative Study*, I-II (New York, 1966).

Collins, T., 'The Physiology of Tears in the Old Testament', *CBQ* 33 (1971), pp. 18-38, 185-97.

Coppens, J., 'Le roi idéal d'Is IX 5-6 et XI 1-5 est-il une figure messianique?', in *A la rencontre de Dieu* (Mém. A. Gelin; Le Puy, 1961), pp. 85-108.

—'Le *ṣaddîq*— "Juste" dans le Psautier', in *De la Torah au Messie* (Mél. H. Cazelles; Paris, 1981), pp. 299-306.

Cossmann, W., *Die Entwicklung des Gerichtsgedankens bei den alttestamentlichen Propheten* (BZAW, 29; Giessen, 1915).

Couroyer, B., 'El vocabulario del Tiro al Arco en el Antiguo Testamento', in *Servidor de la Palabra, Miscelanea Bíblica en honor del P.A. Colunga* (Salamanca, 1979), pp. 111-26.

Cowley, A., *Aramaic Papyri of the Fifth Century B.C.* (Oxford, 1923).

Cox, D., '*Ṣedaqa* and *mišpat.* The Concept of Righteousness in Later Wisdom', *SBFLA* 27 (1977), pp. 33-50.

Cramer, K., 'Der Begriff *ṣdqh* bei Tritojesaja', *ZAW* 27 (1907), pp. 79-99.

Crenshaw, J.L., '*YHWH ṣᵉba'ôt šᵉmô*: A Form-Critical Analysis', *ZAW* 81 (1969), pp. 156-75.

—'Popular Questioning of the Justice of God in Ancient Israel', *ZAW* 82 (1970), pp. 380-95.
—*Prophetic Conflict: Its Effects upon Israelite Religion* (BZAW, 124; Berlin, 1971).
—*Hymnic Affirmation of Divine Justice: The Doxologies of Amos and Related Texts in the Old Testament* (SBLDS, 24: Missoula, MT, 1975).
Croatto, J.S., 'ṬÔBĀ como "amistad (de Alianza)" en el Antiguo Testamento', *AION* 18 (1968), pp. 385-89.
Cross, F.M., 'The Council of Yahweh in Second Isaiah', *JNES* 12 (1953), pp. 274-77.
—'Epigraphic Notes on Hebrew Documents of the Eight–Sixth Centuries B.C. II. The Murabba'ât Papyrus and the Letter Found near Yabneh-yam', *BASOR* 165 (1962), pp. 34-46.
Crüsemann, F., 'Jahwes Gerechtigkeit (*ṣ*[e]*dāqā/ṣädäq*) im Alten Testament', *EvT* 36 (1976), pp. 427-50.
Curtis, J.B., 'On Job's Witness in Heaven', *JBL* 102 (1983), pp. 549-62.
Dacquino, M., 'La formula "Giustizia di Dio" nei libri dell'Antico Testamento', *RivB* 17 (1969), pp. 103-19, 365-82.
Dahood, M., 'The Phoenician Contribution to Biblical Wisdom Literature', in W.A. Ward (ed.), *The Role of the Phoenicians in the Interaction of Mediterranean Civilization* (Beirut, 1968), pp. 123-48.
—'Is the Emendation of *yādîn* to *yāzîn* Necessary in Job 36.31?', *Bib* 53 (1972), pp. 539-41.
—'Word and Witness: A Note on Jeremiah XXIX 23', *VT* 27 (1977), p. 483.
Dalglish, E.R., *Psalm Fifty-One in the Light of Ancient Near Eastern Patternism* (Leiden, 1962).
Daube, D., *Studies in Biblical Law* (Cambridge, 1947).
—'Error and Accident in the Bible', *RIDA* 2 (1949), pp. 189-213.
—'The Laying on of Hands', in *The New Testament and Rabbinic Judaism* (JLCR, 2 [1952]; London, 1956), pp. 224-46.
—'Rechtsgedanken in den Erzählungen des Pentateuchs', in *Von Ugarit nach Qumran: Beiträge zur alttestamentlichen Forschung* (FS O. Eissfeldt; BZAW, 77; Berlin, 1958), pp. 32-41.
—*The Exodus Pattern in the Bible* (All Souls Studies, 2; London, 1963).
—'To be Found Doing Wrong', in *Studi in onore di E. Volterra*, II (Milan, 1971), pp. 1-13.
—'The Law of Witnesses in Transferred Operation', *JANESCU* 5 (1973), pp. 91-93.
—*Ancient Jewish Law: Three Inaugural Lectures* (Leiden, 1981).
Daube, D., and R. Yaron, 'Jacob's Reception by Laban', *JSS* 1 (1956), pp. 60-62.
David, M., 'The Codex Hammurabi and its Relation to the Provisions of Law in Exodus', *OTS* 7 (1950), pp. 149-78.
—'Die Bestimmungen über die Asylstadte in Joshua XX: Ein Beitrag zur Geschichte des biblischen Asylrechts', *OTS* 9 (1951), pp. 30-48.
Davies, E.W., *Prophecy and Ethics: Isaiah and the Ethical Traditions of Israel* (JSOTSup, 16; Sheffield, 1981).
Deissler, A., 'Micha 6.1-8: Der Rechtsstreit Jahwes mit Israel um das rechte Bundesverhältnis', *TTZ* 68 (1959), pp. 229-34.
Delcor, M., 'Les attaches littéraires, l'origine et la signification de l'expression biblique "Prendre à témoin le ciel et la terre"', *VT* 16 (1966), pp. 8-25.
Delekat, L., 'Zum hebräischen Wörterbuch', *VT* 14 (1964), pp. 7-66.

—*Asylie und Schutzorakel am Zionheiligtum: Eine Untersuchung zu den privaten Feindpsalmen* (Leiden, 1967).

Dempster, S., 'The Deuteronomic Formula *kî yimmāṣē'* in the Light of Biblical and Ancient Near Eastern Law. An Evaluation of David Daube's Theory', *RB* 91 (1984), pp. 188-211.

Dentan, R.C., 'The Literary Affinities of Exodus XXXIV 6f', *VT* 13 (1963), pp. 34-51.

D'Ercole, G., 'The Juridicial Structure of Israel from the Time of her Origin to the Period of Hadrian', in *Populus Dei*. I. *Israel* (Studi in onore del Card. A. Ottaviani; Rome, 1969), pp. 389-461.

—'The Organic Structure of Israel in Terms of her Moral Order and Dogmatic Order of Cult', in *Populus Dei*, pp. 557-613.

Dhorme, P., *L'emploi métaphorique des noms de parties du corps en hébreu et en akkadien* (Paris, 1923).

Diamond, A.S., 'An Eye for an Eye', *Iraq* 19 (1957), pp. 151-55.

Dick, M.B., 'The Legal Metaphor in Job 31', *CBQ* 41 (1979), pp. 37-50.

Diestel, L., 'Die religiöse Delicte im israelitischen Strafrecht', *JPTh* 5 (1879), pp. 246-313.

Dietrich, W., 'Rache. Erwägungen zu einem alttestamentlichen Thema', *EvT* 36 (1976), pp. 450-72.

Dion, P-E., 'Tu feras disparaître le mal du milieu de toi', RB 87 (1980), pp. 321-49.

Donald, T., ''The Semantic Field of Rich and Poor in the Wisdom Literature of Hebrew and Accadian', *OrAnt* 3 (1964), pp. 27-41.

Donner, H., 'Die soziale Botschaft der Propheten im Lichte der Gesellschaftsordnung in Israel', *OrAnt* 2 (1963), pp. 229-45.

—*Die literarische Gestalt der alttestamentlichen Josephsgeschichte* (SHAW PH; Heidelberg, 1976).

Driver, G.R., 'Hebrew Notes', *ZAW* 52 (1934), pp. 51-56.

Ducrot, P., 'De la vendetta à la loi du talion', *RHPR* 6 (1926), pp. 350-65.

Duerr, L., 'Altorientalisches Recht bei den Propheten Amos und Hosea', *BZ* 23 (1935–36), pp. 150-57.

Durham, J.I., '*šālôm* and the Presence of God', in *Proclamation and Presence* (Fs G.H. Davies; London, 1970), pp. 272-93.

Dus, J., 'Die "Sufeten" Israels', *ArOr* 31 (1963), pp. 444-69.

Eaton, J.H., 'The King as God's Witness', *ASTI* 7 (1968–69), pp. 25-40.

Eisenbeis, W., *Die Wurzel* šlm *im Alten Testament* (BZAW, 113; Berlin, 1969).

Eissfeldt, O., *Das Lied Moses Deuteronomium 32.1-43 und das Lehrgedicht Asaphs Psalm 78 samt einer Analyse der Umgebung des Mose-Liedes* (BVSAW PH 104/5; Berlin, 1958).

Elliger, K., 'Das Ende der "Abendwölfe" Zeph. 3.3 Hab. 1.8', in *Festschrift A. Bertholet* (Tübingen, 1950), pp. 158-75.

Ellul, J., 'Réflexions sur les contradictions de la Bible au sujet de la mort', in *Filosofia e religione di fronte alla morte* (Archivio di Filosofia; Padova, 1981), pp. 315-30.

Emerton, J.A., 'The Translation of Psalm LXIV 4', *JTS* 27 (1976), pp. 391-92.

—'The Etymology of *hištaḥ^{a}wāh*', *OTS* 20 (1977), pp. 41-55

Engel, H., *Die Susanna-Erzählung: Einleitung, Übersetzung und Kommentar zum Septuaginta-Text und zur Theodotion-Bearbeitung* (OBO, 61; Freiburg, 1985).

Epsztein, L., *La justice sociale dans le Proche-Orient ancien et le peuple de la Bible* (Paris, 1983).

Erlandsson, L., 'The Wrath of Yhwh', *TynBul* 23 (1972), pp. 111-16.
Evans, G., '"Coming" and "Going" at the City Gate—A discussion of Professor Speiser's Paper', *BASOR* 150 (1958), pp. 28-33.
—'Rehoboam's Advisors at Shechem and Political Institutions in Israel and Sumer', *JNES* 25 (1966), pp. 273-79.
Eybers, I.H., 'The Stem š-p-ṭ in the Psalms', in *Studies on the Psalms* (OTWerkSuidA, 6; Potchefstroom, 1963), pp. 58-63.
Fahlgren, K.H.J., *Ṣ^{e}dāḳā, nahestehende und entgegengesetzte Begriffe im Alten Testament* (Uppsala, 1932).
Falk, Z.W., 'Gesture Expressing Affirmation', *JSS* 4 (1959), pp. 268-69.
—'Hebrew Legal Terms', *JSS* 5 (1960), pp. 350-54.
—'Two Symbols of Justice', *VT* 10 (1960), pp. 72-74.
—*Hebrew Law in Biblical Times: An Introduction* (Jerusalem, 1964).
—'"Words of God" and "Judgments"', in *Studi in onore di E. Volterra*, VI (Milan, 1971), pp. 155-59.
—*Introduction to Jewish Law of the Second Commonwealth* (2 vols.; Leiden, 1972, 1978).
Fendler, M., 'Zur Sozialkritik des Amos. Versuch einer wirtschafts- und sozialgeschichtlichen Interpretation alttestamentlicher Texte', *EvT* 33 (1973), pp. 32-53.
Fensham, F.C., 'The Judges and Ancient Israelite Jurisprudence', in *OTWerkSuidA* 2 (Potchefstroom, 1959), pp. 15-22.
—'Widow, Orphan and the Poor in Ancient Near Eastern Legal and Wisdom Literature', *JNES* 21 (1962), pp. 129-39.
—'*'d* in Exodus XXII 12', *VT* 12 (1962), pp. 337-39.
—'Legal Aspects of the Dream of Solomon', in *Proceedings of the Fourth World Congress of Jewish Studies*, I (Jerusalem, 1967), pp. 67-70.
—'The Battle between the Men of Joab and Abner as a Possible Ordeal by Battle?', *VT* 20 (1970), pp. 356-57.
—'Ordeal by Battle in the Ancient Near East and the Old Testament', in *Studi in onore di E. Volterra*, VI (Milan, 1971), pp. 127-35.
—'Father and Son as Terminology for Treaty and Covenant', in *Near Eastern Studies* (FS W.F. Albright; Baltimore, 1971), pp. 121-35.
—'Transgression and Penalty in the Book of the Covenant', *JNSL* 5 (1977), pp. 23-41.
—'Das Nicht-haftbar-sein im Bundesbuch im Lichte der altorientalischen Rechtstexte', *JNSL* 8 (1980), pp. 17-34.
Ferguson, H., 'The Verb *špṭ*', *JBL* 8 (1888), pp. 130-36.
Fichtner, J., 'Die "Umkehrung" in der prophetischen Botschaft. Eine Studie zu dem Verhältnis von Schuld und Gericht in der Verkündigung Jesajas', *TLZ* 78 (1953), pp. 459-66.
Finkelstein, J., 'The Middle Assyrian *Šulmānu-* Texts', *JAOS* 72 (1952), pp. 77-80.
Fishbane, M., 'Accusations of Adultery: A Study of Law and Scribal Practice in Numbers 5.11-31', *HUCA* 45 (1974), pp. 25-45.
—'Biblical Colophons, Textual Criticism and Legal Analogies', *CBQ* 42 (1980), pp. 438-49.
Fohrer, G., 'Umkehr und Erlösung beim Propheten Hosea', *TZ* 11 (1955), pp. 161-85.
—'Jesaja 1 als Zusammenfassung der Verkündigung Jesajas', *ZAW* 74 (1962), pp. 251-68.

—'Kritik an Tempel, Kultus und Kultusausübung in nachexilischer Zeit', in *Archäologie und Altes Testament* (FS K. Galling; Tübingen, 1970), pp. 101-16.

Fokkelman, J.P., *Narrative Art in Genesis: Specimens of Stylistic and Structural Analysis* (SSN, 17; Assen, 1975).

—*Narrative Art and Poetry in the Book of Samuel: A Full Interpretation Based on Stylistic and Structural Analyses*. I. *King David* (*II Samuel 9–20 & I Kings 1–2*) (SSN, 20; Assen, 1981).

Fox, M., 'Ṭôḇ as Covenant Terminology', BASOR 209 (1973), pp. 41-42.

Frankena, R., 'Einige Bemerkungen zum Gebrauch des Adverbs *'al kēn* im Hebräischen', in *Studia Biblica et Semitica* (FS T.C. Vriezen; Wageningen, 1966), pp. 94-99.

—'Some Remarks on the Semitic Background of Chapters XXIX–XXXI of the Book of Genesis', *OTS* 17 (1972), pp. 53-64.

Freedman, D.N., 'The Broken Construct Chain', *Bib* 53 (1972), pp. 534-36.

Freudenstein, E.D., 'A Swift Witness', *Tradition* 13 (1974), pp. 114-23.

Frick, F.S., *The City in Ancient Israel* (Missoula, MT, 1977).

Frost, S.B., 'Asseveration by Thanksgiving', *VT* 8 (1958), pp. 380-90.

Frymer-Kensky, T., 'Tit for Tat: the Principle of Equal Retribution in Near Eastern and Biblical Law', *BA* 43 (1980), pp. 230-34.

—'The Strange Case of the Suspected Sotah (Num. 5.11-31)', *VT* 34 (1984), pp. 11-26.

Fuhrmann, M., 'Philologische Bemerkungen zur Sentenz "Summum ius summa iniuria" ', in *Studi in onore di E. Volterra*, II (Milan, 1971), pp. 53-81.

Furlani, G., 'La sentenza di dio nella religione babilonese e assira', in *Atti della Accademia Nazionale dei Lincei, 1949* (Memorie, Classe di Scienze morali, storiche e filologiche, Serie VIII, vol. 2, fasc. 5; Rome, 1950), pp. 219-79.

—'Le guerre quali giudizi di dio presso i Babilonesi e gli Assiri', in *Miscellanea G. Galbiati* (Fontes Ambrosianae, 27; Milan, 1951), pp. 39-47.

Fürst, H., *Die göttliche Heimsuchung: Semasiologische Untersuchung eines biblischen Begriffes* (Rome, 1965).

Galling, K., 'Der Beichtspiegel. Eine gattungsgeschichtliche Studie', *ZAW* 47 (1929), pp. 125-30.

—'Tafel, Buch und Blatt', in *Near Eastern Studies* (FS W.F. Albright; Baltimore, 1971), pp. 207-23.

Gamper, A., *Gott als Richter in Mesopotamien und im Alten Testament: Zum Verständnis einer Gebetsbitte* (Innsbruck, 1966).

Garcia de la Fuente, O., 'Sobre la idea de contrición en el antiguo Testamento', in *Sacra Pagina* (BETL, XII-XIII, vol. 1; Gembloux, 1959), pp. 559-79.

Gehman, H.S., 'The Oath in the Old Testament: Its Vocabulary, Idiom, and Syntax; its Semantics and Theology in the Masoretic Text and the Septuagint', in *Grace upon Grace* (FS L.J. Kuyper; Grand Rapids, 1975), pp. 51-63.

Gelin, A., 'La péché dans l'Ancien Testament', in *Théologie du péché* (Bibl. de Théologie, Sér. II, Théol. morale, vol. 7; Tournai, 1960), pp. 23-47.

—*Les pauvres que Dieu aime* (Paris, 1967).

Geller, M.J., 'The *šurpu* Incantations and Lev. V 1-5', *JSS* 25 (1980), pp. 181-92.

Gemser, B., 'The *rîb*- or Controversy-Pattern in Hebrew Mentality', in M. Noth and D. Winton Thomas (eds.), *Wisdom in Israel and the Ancient Near East* (FS H.H. Rowley; VTSup, 3; Leiden, 1955), pp. 120-37.

Gennaro, G. de (ed.), *Amore–Giustizia; analisi semantica dei due termini e delle loro correlazioni nei testi biblici veterotestamentari e neotestamentari* (L'Aquila, 1980).
Gerleman, G., 'Die Wurzel *šlm*', *ZAW* 85 (1973), pp. 1-14.
—'Schuld und Sühne. Erwägungen zu 2 Samuel 12', in *Beiträge zur alttestamentlichen Theologie* (FS W. Zimmerli; Göttingen, 1977), pp. 132-39.
—'Das übervolle Mass. Ein Versuch mit *ḥaesed*', *VT* 28 (1978), pp. 151-64.
—'Der "Einzelne" der Klage- und Dankpsalmen', *VT* 32 (1982), pp. 33-49.
Gerlitz, P., 'Religionsgeschichtliche und ethische Aspekte des Fastens', in *Ex orbe religionum*, II (FS G. Widengren; Leiden, 1972), pp. 255-65.
Gerstenberger, E., 'The Woe-Oracles of the Prophets', *JBL* 81 (1962), pp. 249-63.
—*Wesen und Herkunft des apodiktischen Rechts* (WMANT, 20; Neukirchen, 1965).
—*Der bittende Mensch: Bittritual und Klagelied des Einzelnen im Alten Testament* (WMANT, 51; Neukirchen, 1980).
Gese, H., 'Beobachtungen zum Stil alttestamentlicher Rechtssätze', *TLZ* 88 (1960), pp. 147-50.
—'Psalm 50 und das alttestamentliche Gesetzesverständnis', in *Rechtfertigung* (FS E. Käsemann; Tübingen, 1976), pp. 57-77.
Geus, C.H.J. de, *The Tribes of Israel: An Investigation into Some of the Presuppositions of Martin Noth's Anphictyony Hypothesis* (SSN, 18; Assen, 1976).
—'Die Gesellschaftskritik der Propheten und die Archäologie', *ZDPV* 98 (1982), pp. 50-57.
Gierlich, A.M., *Der Lichtgedanke in den Psalmen: Eine terminologisch-exegetische Studie* (FreibTSt, 56; Freiburg, 1940).
Giesen, G., 'Semantische Vorfragen zur Wurzel *šb'* "schwören"', in *Bausteine biblischer Theologie* (FS G.J. Botterweck; BBB, 50; Bonn, 1977), pp. 127-43.
—*Die Wurzel šb' 'Schwören': Eine semasiologische Studie zum Eid im Alten Testament* (BBB, 56; Bonn, 1981).
Gilbert, M., 'La prière de Daniel, Dan. 9.4-19', *RTL* 3 (1972), pp. 284-310.
—'La prière d'Azarias (Dan. 3.26-45. Théodotion)', *NRT* 96 (1974), pp. 561-82.
—'La place de la loi dans la prière de Néhémie 9', in *De la Tôrah au Messie* (FS H. Cazelles; Paris, 1981), pp. 307-16.
—'La loi du talion', *Christus* 31 (1984), pp. 73-82.
Giraudo, C., *La struttura letteraria della preghiera eucaristica: Saggio sulla genesi letteraria di una forma. Toda veterotestamentaria, Beraka giudaica, Anafora cristiana* (AnBib, 92; Rome, 1981).
Gitay, Y., *Prophecy and Persuasion: A Study of Isaiah 40–48* (ForTLing, 14; Bonn, 1981).
Glueck, N., *Das Wort ḥesed im alttestamentlichen Sprachgebrauche als menschliche und göttliche gemeinschaftsgemässe Verhaltungsweise* (BZAW, 47; Berlin, 2nd edn, 1961).
Goldin, H.E., *Hebrew Criminal Law and Procedure* (New York, 1952).
Goldman, M.D., 'The Root *pll* and its Connotation with Prayer (Attempted Explanation of Deuteronomy 32.31)', *AusBR* 3 (1953), pp. 1-6.
Good, E.M., *Irony in the Old Testament* (Bible and Literature Series, 3; Sheffield, 2nd edn, 1981).
Goodman, A.E., '*ḥsd* and *twdh* in the Linguistic Tradition of the Psalter', in *Words and Meanings* (FS D.W. Thomas; Cambridge, 1968), pp. 105-15.

Gordis, R., 'A Rhetorical Use of Interrogative Sentences in Biblical Hebrew', *AJSL* 49 (1932–33), pp. 212-17.

Gordon, C.H., '*'lhym* in its Reputed Meaning of "Rulers" and "Judges"', *JBL* 54 (1935), pp. 139-44.

—'The Story of Jacob and Laban in the Light of the Nuzi Tablets', *BASOR* 66 (1937), pp. 25-27.

Gordon, R.P., 'David's Rise and Saul's Demise: Narrative Analogy in 1 Samuel 24–26', *TynBul* 31 (1980), pp. 37-64.

Gowan, D.E., 'The Use of *ya'an* in Biblical Hebrew', *VT* 21 (1971), pp. 168-85.

Graffy, A., 'The Literary Genre of Isa. 5.1-7', *Bib* 60 (1979), pp. 400-409.

—*A Prophet Confronts his People: The Disputation Speech in the Prophets* (AnBib, 104; Rome, 1984).

Gray, J., 'Tell El Far'a by Nablus: A "Mother" in Ancient Israel', *PEQ* 84 (1952), pp. 110-13.

—'The *goren* at the City Gate: Justice and the Royal Office in the Ugarit Text 'Aqht', *PEQ* 85 (1953), pp. 118-23.

Greenberg, M., 'On Ezekiel's Dumbness', *JBL* 77 (1958), pp. 101-105.

—'The Biblical Concept of Asylum', *JBL* 78 (1959), pp. 125-32.

—'Some Postulates of Biblical Criminal Law', in *Studies in Bible and Jewish Religion* (Y. Kaufmann Jubilee Volume; Jerusalem, 1960), pp. 5-28.

—'Another Look at Rachel's Theft of the Teraphim', *JBL* 81 (1962), pp. 239-48.

Gressmann, H., *Die älteste Geschichtsschreibung und Prophetie Israels (von Samuel bis Amos und Hosea)* (Göttingen, 1910).

—'Die literarische Analyse Deuterojesajas', *ZAW* 34 (1914), pp. 254-97.

Grether, O., 'Die Bezeichnung "Richter" für die charismatischen Helden der vorstaatlichen Zeit', *ZAW* 57 (1939), pp. 110-21.

Grimme, H., 'Der Begriff von hebräischem *hwdh* und *twdh*', *ZAW* 58 (1940–41), pp. 234-40.

Gross, H., *Die Idee des ewigen und allgemeinen Weltfriedens im Alten Orient und im Alten Testament* (TThSt, 7; Trier, 1956).

—'Theologische Eigenart der Psalmen und ihre Bedeutung für die Offenbarung des Alten Testaments. Dargestellt an Psalm 51', *BibLeb* 8 (1967), pp. 248-56.

—'"Rechtfertigung" nach dem Alten Testament', in *Kontinuität und Einheit* (FS F. Mussner; Freiburg, 1981), pp. 17-29.

—'"Anfang und Ende". Beobachtungen zum prophetischen Reden von Schöpfung, Gericht und Heil', in *Künder des Wortes: Beiträge zur Theologie der Propheten* (FS J. Schreiner; Würzburg, 1982), pp. 287-99.

Gruber, M.I., *Aspects of Nonverbal Communication in the Ancient Near East*, I-II (Studia Pohl, 12; Rome, 1980).

Gunkel, H., 'Die Propheten als Schriftsteller und Dichter', in H. Schmidt, *Die grossen Propheten* (Die Schrift des AT, 2.2; Göttingen, 1915), pp. XXXVI-LXXII.

—*Einleitung in die Psalmen: Die Gattungen der religiösen Lyrik Israels* (Göttingen, 2nd edn, 1966 [1933]).

Gunn, D.M., *The Story of King David: Genre and Interpretation* (JSOTSup, 6; Sheffield, 1978).

—*The Fate of King Saul: An Interpretation of a Biblical Story* (JSOTSup, 14; Sheffield, 1980).

Haag, H., '"Gegen dich allein habe ich gesündigt". Eine Exegese von Ps. 51.6', *TüTQ* 155 (1975), pp. 49-50.

Haase, R., 'Körperliche Strafen in den altorientalischen Rechtssammlungen. Ein Beitrag zum altorientalischen Strafrecht', *RIDA*, 3 Sér. 10 (1963), pp. 55-75.

Halpern, B., 'Yahweh's Summary Justice in Job 14.20', *VT* 28 (1978), pp. 472-74.

—*The Constitution of the Monarchy in Israel* (HSM, 25; Chico, CA, 1981).

Hardmeier, C., *Texttheorie und biblische Exegese: Zur rethorischen Funktion der Trauermetaphorik in der Prophetie* (BEvT, 79; Munich, 1978).

Harrelson, W., 'A Meditation on the Wrath of God: Psalm 90', in *Scripture in History and Theology* (FS J.C. Rylaarsdam; Pittsburgh, 1977), pp. 181-91.

Harvey, J., '"Le Rîb-Pattern", réquisitoire prophétique sur la rupture de l'alliance', *Bib* 43 (1962), pp. 172-96.

—*Le plaidoyer prophétique contre Israël après la rupture de l'alliance: Etude d'une formule littéraire de l'Ancien Testament* (Studia, 22; Bruges, 1967).

Haulotte, E., *Symbolique du vêtement selon la Bible* (Théologie, 65; Paris, 1966).

Hauret, C., 'Les ennemis-sorciers dans les supplications individuelles', in *Aux grands carrefours de la révélation et de l'exégèse de l'Ancien Testament* (Rech. bibliques, 8; Bruges, 1967), pp. 129-37.

Hauser, J., 'The "Minor Judges"—A Re-Evaluation', *JBL* 94 (1975), pp. 190-200.

Heinisch, P., *Die Trauergebräuche bei den Israeliten* (BZfr 13 F., 7/8; Münster, 1931).

—*Die Totenklage im Alten Testament* (BZfr 13 F., 9/10; Münster, 1931).

Hempel, J., 'Jahwegleichnisse der israelitischen Propheten', *ZAW* 42 (1924), pp. 74-104.

—*Die althebräische Literatur und ihr hellenistisch-jüdisches Nachleben* (Handbuch Lit.-Wiss, Ergänzungsheft; Wildpark-Postdam, 1930).

—*Heilung als Symbol und Wirklichkeit im biblischen Schrifttum* (NAWG PH; Göttingen, 1958), no. 3, pp. 237-314.

Hentschel, G., *Die Elijaerzählungen: Zum Verhältnis von historischem Geschehen und geschichtlicher Erfahrung* (ErfTSt, 33; Leipzig, 1977).

Hentschke, R., *Die Stellung der vorexilischen Schriftpropheten zum Kultus* (BZAW, 75; Berlin, 1957).

—*Satzung und Setzender: Ein Beitrag zur israelitischen Rechtsterminologie* (BWANT, 5/3; Stuttgart, 1963).

Hermisson, H.J., *Sprache und Ritus im altisraelitischen Kult: Zur 'Spiritualisierung' der Kultbegriffe im Alten Testament* (WMANT, 19; Neukirchen, 1965).

Hernando, E., 'Los profetas y el derecho de gentes', *LuVitor* 28 (1979), pp. 129-52.

Herrmann, J., *Die Idee der Sühne im Alten Testament: Eine Untersuchung über Gebrauch und Bedeutung des Wortes kipper* (Leipzig, 1905).

Hertzberg, H.W., 'Die Entwicklung des Begriffes *mšpṭ* im Alten Testament', *ZAW* 40 (1922), pp. 256-87; *ZAW* 41 (1923), pp. 16-76.

—'Die prophetische Kritik am Kult', *TLZ* 75 (1950), pp. 219-26.

—'Die "Abtrünnigen" und die "Vielen". Ein Beitrag zu Jesaja 53', in *Verbannung und Heimkehr* (FS W. Rudolph; Tübingen, 1961), pp. 97-108.

—'Sind die Propheten Fürbitter?', in *Tradition und Situation: Studien zur alttestamentlichen Prophetie* (FS A. Weiser; Göttingen, 1963), pp. 63-74.

Hesse, F., 'Wurzelt die prophetische Gerichtsrede im israelitischen Kult?', *ZAW* 65 (1953), pp. 45-53.

Hillers, D.R., 'Amos 7.4 and Ancient Parallels', *CBQ* 26 (1964), pp. 221-25.

—'A Note on Some Treaty Terminology in the Old Testament', *BASOR* 176 (1964), pp. 46-47.

—'Delocutive Verbs in Biblical Hebrew', *JBL* 86 (1967), pp. 320-24.

—'*Hôy* and *Hôy*-Oracles: A Neglected Syntactic Aspect', in *The Word of the Lord Shall Go Forth* (FS D.N. Freedman; Winona Lake, IN, 1983), pp. 185-88.

Hoffman, Y., 'The Root *qrb* as a Legal Term', *JNSL* 10 (1982), pp. 67-73.

Hoffmann, H.W., 'Form—Funktion—Intention', *ZAW* 82 (1970), pp. 341-46.

—*Die Intention der Verkündigung Jesajas* (BZAW, 136; Berlin, 1974).

Hoftijzer, J., 'David and the Tekoite Woman', *VT* 20 (1970), pp. 419-44.

Hogg, J.E., '"Belial" in the Old Testament', *AJSL* 44 (1927–1928), pp. 56-58.

Holladay, W.L., *The Root šûbh in the Old Testament with Particular Reference to its Usages in Covenantal Contexts* (Leiden, 1958).

Holm-Nielsen, S., 'Die Sozialkritik der Propheten', in *Denkender Glaube* (FS C.H. Ratschow; Berlin, 1976), pp. 7-23.

Hornig, B., 'Das Prosagebet der nachexilischen Literatur', *TLZ* 83 (1958), pp. 644-46.

Horst, F., 'Die Doxologien im Amosbuch', *ZAW* 47 (1929), pp. 45-54.

—'Der Eid im Alten Testament', *EvT* 17 (1957), pp. 366-84.

—'Recht und Religion im Bereich des Alten Testament', *EvT* 16 (1956), pp. 49-75.

Hossfeld, F-L., *Der Dekalog: Seine späten Fassungen, die originale Komposition und seine Vorstufen* (OBO, 45; Göttingen, 1982).

Hossfeld, F.-L., and I. Meyer, *Prophet gegen Prophet: Eine Analyse der alttestamentlichen Texte zum Thema: wahre und falsche Propheten* (BiB, 9; Fribourg, 1973).

—'Der Prophet vor dem Tribunal. Neuer Auslegungsversuch von Jeremiah 26', *ZAW* 86 (1974), pp. 30-50.

Hruby, K., 'Le Yom ha-kippurim ou Jour de l'Expiation', *OrSyr* 10 (1965), pp. 43-74, 161-92, 413-42.

Hubbard, R.L., 'Dynamistic and Legal Processes in Psalm 7', *ZAW* 94 (1982), pp. 267-79.

Huffmon, H.B., 'The Covenant Lawsuit in the Prophets', *JBL* 78 (1959), pp. 285-95.

—'The Social Role of Amos' Message', in *The Quest for the Kingdom of God* (FS G.E. Mendenhall; Winona Lake, IN, 1983), pp. 109-16.

Humbert, P., 'Die Herausforderungsformel "hinnenî êlékâ"', *ZAW* 51 (1933), pp. 101-108.

—'La formule hébraïque en hineni suivi d'un participe', *REJ* 97 (1934), pp. 58-64.

—'L'emploi du verbe *pā'al* et de ses dérivés substantifs en hébreu biblique', *ZAW* 65 (1953), pp. 35-44.

—'Le substantif *to'ēbā* et le verbe *t'b* dans l'Ancien Testament', *ZAW* 72 (1960), pp. 217-37.

—'Démesure et chute dans l'Ancien Testament', in *Maqqél shâqédh: Hommage à W. Vischer* (Montpellier, 1960), pp. 63-82.

—'L'étymologie du substantif *to'ēbā*'', in *Verbannung und Heimkehr* (FS W. Rudolph; Tübingen, 1961), pp. 157-60.

—'Etendre la main', *VT* 12 (1962), pp. 383-95.

—'Le thème vétérotestamentaire de la lumière', *RTP* 99 (1966), pp. 1-6.

Hurvitz, A., 'The Chronological Significance of "Aramaisms" in Biblical Hebrew', *IEJ* 18 (1968), pp. 234-40.

—*Bein Lashon Lelashon (Biblical Hebrew in Transition. A Study in Post-Exilic Hebrew and its Implications for the Dating of the Psalms)* (Jerusalem, 1972 [Hebrew]).
—'The Evidence of Language in Dating the Priestly Code. A Linguistic Study in Technical Idioms and Terminology', *RB* 81 (1974), pp. 24-56.
—'The Date of the Prose-Tale of Job Linguistically Reconsidered', *HTR* 67 (1974), pp. 17-34.
—*A Linguistic Study of the Relationship between the Priestly Source and the Book of Ezekiel: A New Approach to an Old Problem* (Cahiers de la Revue Biblique, 20; Paris, 1982).
Hvidberg, F.F., *Weeping and Laughter in the Old Testament: A Study of Canaanite-Israelite Religion* (Leiden, 1962).
Ibañez Arana, A., 'Una etiologia etimológica atípica', *CuadBíb* 9 (1983), pp. 1-20.
Illman, K.-J., *Old Testament Formulas about Death* (Åbo, 1979).
Irsigler, H., *Gottesgericht und Jahwetag: Die Komposition Zef 1.1–2.3, untersucht auf der Grundlage der Literarkritik des Zefanjabuches* (Münchener Univ., Fachbereich Kath. Theol. Arbeiten zu Text und Sprache im AT, 3; St Ottilien, 1973).
Ishida, T., 'The Leaders of the Tribal Leagues "Israel" in the Pre-monarchic Period', *RB* 80 (1973), pp. 514-30.
Iwry, S., '*whnmṣ*—A Striking Variant Reading in 1QIs[a]', *Textus* 5 (1966), pp. 34-43.
Jackson, B.S., 'Liability for Mere Intention in Early Jewish Law', *HUCA* 42 (1971), pp. 197-225.
—*Theft in Early Jewish Law* (Oxford, 1972).
—'The Problem of Exodus 21.22-5 (ius talionis)', *VT* 23 (1973), pp. 273-304.
—*Essays in Jewish and Comparative Legal History* (SJLA, 10; Leiden, 1975).
Jacob, B., 'Erklärung einiger Hiob-Stellen', *ZAW* 32 (1912), pp. 278-87.
Jacob, E., 'Prophètes et Intercesseurs', in *De la Tôrah au Messie* (FS H. Cazelles; Paris, 1981), pp. 205-17.
Jaeger, N., *Il diritto nella Bibba: Giustizia individuale e sociale nell'Antico e Nuovo Testamento* (Assisi, 1960).
Jahnow, H., *Das hebräische Leichenlied im Rahmen der Völkerdichtung* (BZAW, 36; Giessen, 1923).
Janowski, B., *Sühne als Heilsgeschehen: Studien zur Sühnetheologie der Priesterschrift und zur Wurzel* KPR *im Alten Orient und im Alten Testament* (Neukirchen, 1982).
Janzen, W., '"*'Ašrê*" and "*hôy*" in the Old Testament', *HTR* 62 (1970), pp. 432-33.
—*Mourning Cry and Woe Oracle* (BZAW, 125; Berlin, 1972).
Jastrow, M. (Jr), 'Dust, Earth and Ashes as Symbols of Mourning among the Ancient Hebrews', *JAOS* 20 (1900), pp. 133-50.
Jenni, E., *Das hebräische Pi'el* (Zürich, 1968).
—'"Kommen" im theologischen Sprachgebrauch des Alten Testaments', in *Wort—Gebot—Glaube: Beiträge zur Theologie des Alten Testaments* (FS W. Eichrodt; ATANT, 59; Zürich, 1970), pp. 251-61.
—'Zur Verwendung von *'attā* "jetzt" im Alten Testament', *TZ* 28 (1972), pp. 5-12.
—'Deut. 19.16: *sarā* "Falschheit"', in *Mélanges bibliques et orientaux en l'honneur de H. Cazelles* (Neukirchen, 1981), pp. 201-11.
Jepsen, A., 'Gnade und Barmherzigkeit im Alten Testament', *KD* 7 (1961), pp. 261-71.
—'*ṣdq* und *ṣdqh* im Alten Testament', in *Gottes Wort und Gottes Land* (FS H.-W. Hertzberg; Göttingen, 1965), pp. 78-89.

—'Warum? Eine lexikalische und theologische Studie', in *Das ferne und nahe Wort* (FS L. Rost; BZAW, 105; Berlin, 1967), pp. 106-13.
—'Ahabs Busse. Ein kleiner Beitrag zur Methode literarhistorischer Einordnung', in *Archäologie und Altes Testament* (FS K. Galling; Tübingen, 1970), pp. 145-55.
Jeremias, J., *Theophanie: Die Geschichte einer alttestamentlichen Gattung* (WMANT, 10; Neukirchen, 1965).
—*Kultprophetie und Gerichtsverkündigung in der späten Königszeit Israels* (WMANT, 35; Neukirchen, 1970).
—'*mišpāṭ* im ersten Gottesknechtslied (Jes. 42.1-4)', *VT* 22 (1972), pp. 31-42.
—*Die Reue Gottes: Aspekte alttestamentlicher Gottesvorstellung* (BiblSt, 65; Neukirchen, 1975).
Jirku, A., *Das weltliche Recht im Alten Testament: Stilgeschichtliche und rechtsvergleichende Studien zu den juristischen Gesetzen des Pentateuchs* (Gütersloh, 1927).
Johag, I., '*Ṭôb*—Terminus technicus in Vertrags- und Bündnisformularen des Alten Orients und des Alten Testaments', in *Bausteine biblischer Theologie* (FS G.J. Botterweck; BBB, 50; Cologne-Bonn 1977), pp. 3-23.
Johansson, N., *Parakletoi. Vorstellungen von Fürsprechern für die Menschen vor Gott in der alttestamentlichen Religion, im Spätjudentum und Urchristentum* (Lund, 1940).
Johnson, A.R., 'The Primary Meaning of √*g'l*', in J.A. Emerton *et al.* (eds.), *Congress Volume, Copenhagen 1953* (VTSup, 1; Leiden, 1953), pp. 67-77.
—'ḤESED and ḤĀSÎḎ', in *Interpretationes ad Vetus Testamentum pertinentes* (FS S. Mowinckel; Oslo, 1955), pp. 100-12.
Johnson, B., 'Der Bedeutungsunterschied zwischen *ṣädäq* und *ṣedaqa*', *ASTI* 11 (1977–78), pp. 31-39.
Johnson, M.D., 'The Paralysis of Torah in Habakkuk 1.4', *VT* 35 (1985), pp. 257-66.
Jones, B.W., 'The Prayer in Daniel 9', *VT* 18 (1968), pp. 488-93.
Jones, G.H., 'The Decree of Yahweh (Ps. 2.7)', *VT* 15 (1965), pp. 336-44.
Jongeling, B., '*Lākēn* dans l'Ancien Testament', *OTS* 21 (1981), pp. 190-200.
Joüon, P., 'Etudes de sémantique hébraïque', *Bib* 2 (1921), pp. 336-42.
—'Reconnaissance et remercîment en hébreu biblique', *Bib* 4 (1923), pp. 381-85.
—'*b^{e}liyya'al* Bélial', *Bib* 5 (1924), pp. 178-83.
—'Notes de lexicographie hébraïque', *Bib* 6 (1925), pp. 311-21; *Bib* 7 (1926), pp. 72-74; *Bib* 8 (1927), pp. 51-64; *Bib* 17 (1936), pp. 229-33; *Bib* 18 (1937), pp. 205-206; *Bib* 19 (1938), pp. 454-59.
Jüngling, H.-W., *Der Tod der Götter: Eine Untersuchung zu Psalm 82* (SBS, 38; Stuttgart, 1969).
—'"Auge für Auge, Zahn für Zahn". Bemerkungen zu Sinn und Geltung der alttestamentlichen Talionsformel', *TP* 59 (1984), pp. 1-38.
Justesen, J.P., 'On the Meaning of ṣāḏaq', *AUSS* 2 (1964), pp. 53-61.
Kaddari, M.Z., 'Syntactic Presentation of a Biblical Hebrew Verb (*mṣ'*)', in *Studies in Hebrew and Semitic Languages* (FS E.Y. Kutscher; Ramat-Gan, 1980), pp. 18-25 (also p. LXI).
Kalugila, L., *The Wise King: Studies in Royal Wisdom as Divine Revelation in the Old Testament and its Environment* (ConBOT, 15; Lund, 1980).
Kautzsch, E., *Über die Derivate des Stammes* ṣdq *im alttestamentlichen Sprachgebrauch* (Tübingen, 1881).

Keel, O., *Feinde und Gottesleugner: Studien zum Image der Widersacher in den Individualpsalmen* (SBM, 7; Stuttgart, 1969).

—*Die Welt der altorientalischen Bildsymbolik und das Alte Testament* (Zürich, 1972).

—*Jahwes Entgegnung an Ijob: Eine Deutung von Ijob 38–41 vor dem Hintergrund der zeitgenössischen Bildkunst* (FRLANT, 121; Göttingen, 1978).

Kellenberger, E., *häsäd wä'ᵃmät als Ausdruck einer Glaubenserfahrung: Gottes Offen-Werden und Bleiben als Voraussetzung des Lebens* (Zürich, 1982).

Kendall, D., 'The Use of Mišpaṭ in Isaiah 59', *ZAW* 96 (1984), pp. 391-405.

Kenik, H.A., *Design for Kingship: The Deuteronomistic Narrative Technique in 1 Kings 3.4-15* (SBLDS, 69; Chico, CA, 1983).

Kent, C.F., *Israel's Laws and Legal Precedents* (London, 1907).

Kidner, D., 'Sacrifice—Metaphors and Meanings', *TynBul* 33 (1982), pp. 119-36.

Kimbrough, S.T., *Israelite Religion in Sociological Perspective: The Work of Antonin Causse* (Wiesbaden, 1978).

Kleinert, P., *Die Propheten Israels in sozialer Beziehung* (Leipzig, 1905).

Kline, M.G., *By Oath Consigned: A Reinterpretation of the Covenant Signs of Circumcision and Baptism* (Grand Rapids, 1968).

Klopfenstein, M.A., *Die Lüge nach dem Alten Testament: Ihr Begriff, ihre Bedeutung und ihre Beurteilung* (Zürich, 1964).

—*Scham und Schande nach dem Alten Testament: Eine begriffsgeschichtliche Untersuchung zu den hebräischen Wurzeln* bôš, klm *und* ḥpr (ATANT, 62; Zürich, 1972).

Knierim, R., 'Exodus 18 und die Neuordnung der mosaischen Gerichtsbarkeit', *ZAW* 73 (1961), pp. 146-71.

—*Die Hauptbegriffe für Sünde im Alten Testament* (Gütersloh, 1965).

Koch, K., 'Gibt es ein Vergeltungsdogma im Alten Testament?', *ZTK* 52 (1955), pp. 1-42.

—'Der Spruch "Sein Blut bleibe auf seinem Haupt" und die israelitische Auffassung vom vergossenen Blut', *VT* 12 (1962), pp. 396-416.

—'Sühne und Sündenvergebung um die Wende von der exilischen zur nachexilischen Zeit', *EvT* 26 (1966), pp. 217-39.

—'Die Entstehung der sozialen Kritik bei den Propheten', in *Probleme biblischer Theologie* (FS G. von Rad; Munich, 1971), pp. 236-57.

—(ed.), *Um das Prinzip der Vergeltung in Religion und Recht des Alten Testaments* (WegFor, 125; Darmstadt, 1972).

Köhler, L., 'Archäologisches Nr. 6', *ZAW* 34 (1914), p. 148.

—'Archäologisches Nr. 15', *ZAW* 36 (1916), pp. 27-28.

—*Deuterojesaja stilkritisch untersucht* (BZAW, 37; Giessen, 1923).

—'Archäologisches Nr. 22-23. Zu Ex 22.8. Ein Beitrag zur Kenntnis des hebräischen Rechts', *ZAW* 46 (1928), pp. 213-20.

—'Die hebräische Rechtsgemeinde' (1931), in *Der hebräische Mensch* (Tübingen, 1953), pp. 143-71.

—'Problems in the Study of the Language of the Old Testament', *JSS* 1 (1956), pp. 3-24.

Kopf, L., 'Arabische Etymologien und Parallelen zum Bibelwörterbuch', *VT* 9 (1959), pp. 247-87.

Kraus, H.-J., 'Die prophetische Botschaft gegen das soziale Unrecht Israels', *EvT* 15 (1955), pp. 295-307.

—*Die prophetische Verkündigung des Rechts in Israel* (TS, 51; Zollikon, 1957).
—*Prophetie in der Krisis: Studien zu Texten aus dem Buch Jeremia* (BiblSt, 43; Neukirchen, 1964).
—'Die Anfänge der religionssoziologischen Forschungen in der alttestamentlichen Wissenschaft. Eine forschungsgeschichtliche Orientierung', in *Biblisch-theologische Aufsätze* (Neukirchen, 1972), pp. 296-310.
Krause, H.-J., '*hôj* als prophetische Leichenklage über das eigene Volk im 8. Jahrhundert', *ZAW* 85 (1973), pp. 15-46.
Kreuzer, S., 'Zur Bedeutung und Etymologie von *hištaḥ^{a}wāh/yšt̲ḥwy*', *VT* 35 (1985), pp. 39-60.
Kselman, J.S., 'A Note on Ps. 51.6', *CBQ* 39 (1977), pp. 251-53.
Küchler, F., 'Der Gedanke des Eifers Jahwes im Alten Testament', *ZAW* 28 (1908), pp. 42-52.
Kuschke, A., 'Arm und reich im Alten Testament mit besonderer Berücksichtigung der nachexilischen Zeit', *ZAW* 57 (1939), pp. 31-57.
Kutsch, E., '"Trauerbräuche" und "Selbstminderungsriten" im Alten Testament', in K. Lüthi, E. Kutsch and W. Dantine, *Drei Wiener Antrittsreden* (TS, 78; Zürich, 1965), pp. 23-42.
—'"Wir wollen miteinander rechten". Zu Form und Aussage von Jes 1.18-20', in *Künder des Wortes: Beiträge zur Theologie der Propheten* (FS J. Schreiner; Würzburg, 1982), pp. 23-33.
Kuyper, L.J., 'The Repentance of Job', *VT* 9 (1959), pp. 91-94.
—'Righteousness and Salvation', *SJT* 30 (1977), pp. 233-52.
Labuschagne, C.J., 'The Emphasizing Particle *gam* and its Connotations', in *Studia Biblica et Semitica* (FS T.C. Vriezen; Wageningen, 1966), pp. 193-203.
—'The particles *hēn* and *hinnēh*', *OTS* 18 (1973), pp. 1-14.
Lacocque, M.-J., 'The Liturgical Prayer in Daniel 9', *HUCA* 47 (1976), pp. 119-42.
—'L'homicide d'après le Code de Hammourabi et d'après la Bible', *RB* 13 (1916), pp. 440-71.
Lákatos, E., *La religión verdadera: Estudio exegético del Salmo 51* (Madrid, 1972).
Lamadrid, A.G., 'Pax et bonum. "Shalôm" y "ṭôb" en relación con "berit"', *EstBíb* 28 (1969), pp. 61-77.
Landes, G.M., 'Linguistic Criteria and the Date of the Book of Jonah', *Eretz-Israel* 16 (1982), pp. 147*-70*.
Lang, B., 'Das Verbot des Meineids in Dekalog', *TüTQ* 161 (1981), pp. 97-105.
—'Sklaven und Unfreie im Buch Amos (2.6, 8.6)', *VT* 31 (1981), pp. 482-88.
—'The Social Organisation of Peasant Poverty in Biblical Times', *JSOT* 24 (1982), pp. 47-63.
Lapointe, R., 'Foi et vérifiabilité dans le langage sapiential de rétribution', *Bib* 51 (1970), pp. 349-68.
Lauha, A., '"Dominus benefecit". Die Wortwurzel *gml* und die Psalmenfrömmigkeit', *ASTI* 11 (1977–78), pp. 57-62.
Laurentin, A., '*w^e'attah—kai nun*. Formule caractéristique des textes juridiques et liturgiques (à propos de Jean 17.5)', *Bib* 45 (1964), pp. 168-97 (413-32).
Leeuwen, C. van, *Le développement du sens social en Israël avant l'ère chrétienne* (SSN, 1; Assen, 1955).
—'Die Partikel *'im*', *OTS* 18 (1973), pp. 15-48.
Lehmann, M.R., 'Biblical Oaths', *ZAW* 81 (1969), pp. 74-92.

Leone, G., *Manuale di Diritto Processuale Penale* (Naples, 9th edn, 1975).

Lescow, T., 'Die dreistufige Tora. Beobachtungen zu einer Form', *ZAW* 82 (1970), pp. 362-79.

Levenson, J.D., '1 Samuel 25 as Literature and as History', *CBQ* 40 (1978), pp. 11-28.

Lévêque, J., 'Anamnèse et disculpation: La conscience du juste en Job 29–31', in M. Gilbert (ed.), *La Sagesse de l'Ancien Testament* (BETL, 51; Gembloux, 1979), pp. 231-48.

L'Hour, J., 'Une législation criminelle dans le Deutéronome', *Bib* 44 (1963), pp. 1-28.

Liaño, J.M., 'Los pobres en el Antiguo Testamento', *EstBíb* 25 (1966), pp. 117-67.

Liebreich, L.J., 'The Impact of Nehemia 9.5-37 on the Liturgy of the Synagogue', *HUCA* 32 (1961), pp. 227-37.

Liedke, G., *Gestalt und Bezeichnungen alttestamentlicher Rechtssätze: Eine formgeschichtlich-terminologische Studie* (WMANT, 39; Neukirchen, 1971).

Limburg, J., 'The Root *ryb* and the Prophetic Lawsuit Speeches', *JBL* 88 (1969), pp. 291-304.

Lind, M.C., *Yahweh is a Warrior: The Theology of Warfare in Ancient Israel* (Scottdale, 1980).

Lindblom, J., *Die literarische Gattung der prophetischen Literatur: Eine literaturgeschichtliche Untersuchung zum Alten Testament* (Uppsala, 1924).

Lipiński, E., *La royauté de Yahvé dans la poésie et le culte de l'Ancien Testament* (Brussels, 1965).

—*La liturgie penitentielle dans la Bible* (LD, 52; Paris, 1969).

Lods, A., *La croyance à la vie future et le culte des morts dans l'antiquité israélite* (Paris, 1906).

Loewenclau, I. von, 'Zur Auslegung von Jesaja, 1.2-3', *EvT* 26 (1966), pp. 294-308.

Loewenstamm, S.E., 'The Phrase "X (or) X plus one" in Biblical and Old Oriental Laws', *Bib* 53 (1972), p. 543.

—'Exodus 21.22-25', *VT* 27 (1977), pp. 352-60.

Lofthouse, W.F., 'Ḥen and Ḥesed in the Old Testament', *ZAW* 51 (1933), pp. 29-35.

—'The Righteousness of Yahweh', *ExpTim* 50 (1938–39), pp. 341-45.

—'The Righteousness of God', *ExpTim* 50 (1938–39), pp. 441-45.

Lohfink, N., 'Enthielten die im Alten Testament bezeugten Klageriten eine Phase des Schweigens?', *VT* 12 (1962), pp. 260-77.

—'Gewaltenteilung. Die Ämtergesetze des Deuteronomiums als gewaltenteiliger Verfassungsentwurf und das katholische Kirchenrecht', in *Unsere grossen Wörter: Das Alte Testament zu Themen dieser Jahre* (Freiburg, 1977), pp. 57-75, 252.

—'Projektionen. Über die Feinde des Kranken im alten Orient und in den Psalmen', in *Unsere grossen Wörter*, pp. 145-55.

—(ed.), *Gewalt und Gewaltlosigkeit im Alten Testament* (QDisp, 96; Freiburg, 1983).

Long, B.O., 'Two Question-and-Answer Schemata in the Prophets', *JBL* 90 (1971), pp. 129-39.

Luck, U., 'Gerechtigkeit in der Welt—Gerechtigkeit Gottes', *WDienst* 12 (1973), pp. 71-89.

Luke, K., '"Eye for Eye, Tooth for Tooth..." ', *IndTSt* 16 (1979), pp. 326-43.

Lust, J., 'The Immanuel Figure: A Charismatic Judge-Leader', *ETL 47* (1971), pp. 464-70.

Lyonnet, S., 'De "Iustitia Dei" in Epistola ad Romanos (1.17 et 3.21-22; 10.3 et 3.5; 3.25-26)', *VD* 25 (1947), pp. 23-34; 118-21; 129-44; 193-203; 255-63.

—*De peccato et redemptione*. I. *De notione peccati*. II. *De vocabulario redemptionis* (Rome, 2nd edn, 1972 [1957]).
—'De notione expiationis', *VD* 37 (1959), pp. 336-52.
—'La notion de Justice de Dieu en Rom 3.5 et l'exégèse paulinienne du "Miserere"', in *Sacra pagina* (BETL, 13; Paris, 1959), pp. 342-56.
—'Expiation et intercession. A propos d'une traduction de saint Jérôme', *Bib* 40 (1959), pp. 885-901.
Lyonnet, S., and L. Sabourin, *Sin, Redemption and Sacrifice: A Biblical and Patristic Study* (AnBib, 48; Rome, 1970).
Maag, V., *Text, Wortschatz und Begriffswelt des Buches Amos* (Leiden, 1951).
—'B^{e}līja'al im Alten Testament', *TZ* 21 (1965), pp. 287-99.
—'Unsühnbare Schuld', *Kairos* 2 (1966), pp. 90-106.
Maarsingh, B., 'Das Verbum *nāḥam, ni.*', in *Übersetzung und Deutung* (FS A.R. Hulst; Nijkerk, 1977), pp. 113-25.
Mabee, C., 'Jacob and Laban. The Structure of Judicial Proceedings (Genesis 31.25-42)', *VT* 30 (1980), pp. 192-207.
Macholz, G.C., 'Die Stellung des Königs in der israelitischen Gerichtsverfassung', *ZAW* 84 (1972), pp. 157-82.
—'Zur Geschichte der Justizorganisation in Juda', *ZAW* 84 (1972), pp. 314-40.
—'Gerichtsdoxologie und israelitisches Rechtsverfahren', *DielhBlAT* 9 (1975), pp. 52-79.
Malamat, A., 'Kingship and Council in Israel and Sumer: A Parallel', *JNES* 22 (1963), pp. 247-53.
—'Organs of Statecraft in the Israelite Monarchy', *BA* 28 (1965), pp. 34-65.
—'Charismatic Leadership in the Book of Judges', in *Magnalia Dei: The Mighty Acts of God. Essays on the Bible and Archaeology in Memory of G.E. Wright* (Garden City, NY, 1976), pp. 152-68.
Malchow, B.V., 'Social Justice in the Wisdom Literature', *BibTB* 12 (1982), pp. 120-24.
Mand, F., 'Die Eigenständigkeit der Danklieder des Psalters als Bekenntnislieder', *ZAW* 70 (1958), pp. 185-99.
Mannati, M., 'Le Psaulme 50 est-il un *rîb*?', *Sem* 23 (1973), pp. 27-50.
—'Les accusations de Psaume 50.18-20', *VT* 25 (1975), pp. 659-69.
Markert, L., *Struktur und Bezeichnung des Scheltworts: Eine gattungskritische Studie anhand des Amosbuches* (BZAW, 140; Berlin, 1977).
Marrow, S., '*Ḥāmās* ("violentia") in Jer. 20.8', *VD* 43 (1965), pp. 241-55.
Martin-Achard, R., 'Yahwé et les *^{a}nāwīm*', *TZ* 21 (1965), pp. 349-57.
Martino, E. de, *Morte e pianto rituale nel mondo antico: Dal lamento pagano al pianto di Maria* (Turin, 1958).
Masing, U., 'Der Begriff *ḥesed* im alttestamentlichen Sprachgebrauch', in *Charisteria*, I (Köpp...oblata; Holmiae, 1954), pp. 26-63.
Mastin, B.A., '*Wāw explicativum* in 2 Kings 8.9', *VT* 34 (1984), pp. 353-55.
Mayer, R., 'Sünde und Gericht in der Bildersprache der vorexilischen Prophetie', *BZ* 8 (1964), pp. 22-44.
Mayer, W.R., '"Ich rufe dich von ferne, höre mich von nahe!". Zu einer babylonischen Gebetsformel', in *Werden und Wirken des Alten Testaments* (FS C. Westermann; Neukirchen, 1980), pp. 302-17.
Mayes, A.D.H., *Israel in the Period of the Judges* (SBT 2nd Ser., 29; London, 1974).

McCarthy, D.J., 'Hosea 12.2: Covenant by Oil', *VT* 14 (1964), pp. 215-21.
—'Notes on the Love of God in Deuteronomy and the Father–Son Relationship between Yahweh and Israel', *CBQ* 72 (1965), pp. 144-47.
—'Moses' Dealings with Pharaoh: Exod. 7.8–10.27', *CBQ* 27 (1965), pp. 336-47.
—'The Wrath of Yahweh and the Structural Unity of the Deuteronomistic History', in *Essays in Old Testament Ethics* (FS J.P. Hyatt; New York, 1974), pp. 97-110.
—*Treaty and Covenant: A Study in Form in the Ancient Oriental Documents and in the Old Testament* (AnBib, 21A; Rome, 2nd edn, 1978).
—'The Uses of *wᵉhinnēh* in Biblical Hebrew', *Bib* 61 (1980), pp. 330-42.
—'Les droits de l'homme et l'Ancien Testament', in *Droits de l'homme: Approche chrétienne* (Fédération Internationale des Universités Catholiques. Centre de coordination de la recherche; Rome, 1984), pp. 11-25.
McCree, W.T., 'The Covenant Meal in the Old Testament', *JBL* 45 (1926), pp. 120-28.
McKane, W., 'The *Gibbôr Ḥayil* in the Israelite Community', *GUOST* 17 (1957–58), pp. 28-37.
McKay, J.W., 'Exodus 23.1-3, 6-8: A Decalogue for the Administration of Justice in the City Gate', *VT* 21 (1971), pp. 311-25.
McKeating, H., 'Vengeance is Mine. A Study of the Pursuit of Vengeance in the Old Testament', *ExpTim* 74 (1962–63), pp. 239-45.
—'The Development of the Law of Homicide in Ancient Israel', *VT* 25 (1975), pp. 46-68.
—'Sanctions against Adultery in Ancient Israelite Society with some Reflections on Methodology in the Study of Old Testament Ethics', *JSOT* 11 (1979), pp. 57-72.
McKenzie, D.A., 'Judicial Procedure at the Town Gate', *VT* 14 (1964), pp. 100-104.
—'The Judge of Israel', *VT* 17 (1967), pp. 118-21.
McKenzie, J.L., 'The Elders in the Old Testament', *Bib* 40 (1959), pp. 522-40.
—'Vengeance is Mine', *Script* 12 (1960), pp. 33-39.
Mendelsohn, I., 'Authority and Law in Canaan-Israel', in *Authority and Law in the Ancient Orient* (JAOS Supplement, 17; Baltimore, 1954), pp. 25-33.
Mendenhall, E., 'Ancient Oriental and Biblical Law', *BA* 17 (1954), pp. 26-46.
—'The Vengeance of Yahweh', in *The Tenth Generation: The Origins of the Biblical Tradition* (Baltimore, 1973), pp. 69-104.
Merendino, R.P., *Das deuteronomistische Gesetz: Eine literarkritische, gattungs- und überlieferungsgeschichtliche Untersuchung zu Deuteronomy 12–26* (BBB, 31; Bonn, 1969).
Merz, E., *Die Blutrache bei den Israeliten* (BWAT, 20; Leipzig, 1916).
Mettinger, T.N.D., *Solomonic State Officials: A Study of the Civil Government Officials of the Israelite Monarchy* (ConBOT, 5; Lund, 1971).
—*Kings and Messiah: The Civil and Sacral Legitimation of the Israelite Kings* (ConBOT, 8; Lund, 1976).
Meyer, I., *Jeremia und die falschen Propheten* (OBO, 13; Freiburg, 1977).
Miguélez, S., 'La justicia de Dios ante el pecado del hombre', *BibFe* 1 (1975), pp. 191-200.
Milgrom, J., 'The Cultic *šᵉgāgā* and its Influence in Psalms and Job', *JQR* 58 (1967), pp. 115-25.
—*Studies in Levitical Terminology*. I. *The Encroacher and the Levite. The Term 'Aboda* (Berkeley, 1970).
—'The Priestly Doctrine of Repentance', *RB* 82 (1975), pp. 186-205.

—*Cult and Conscience: The* Asham *and the Priestly Doctrine of Repentance* (SJLA, 18; Leiden, 1976).

—'The Concept of *ma'al* in the Bible and the Ancient Near East', *JAOS* 96 (1976), pp. 236-47.

—'Two Kinds of *ḥaṭṭā't*', *VT* 26 (1976), pp. 333-37.

—'The Cultic *'šm*: A Philological Analysis', in *Proceedings of the Sixth World Congress of Jewish Studies*, I (Jerusalem, 1977), pp. 299-308.

—'Concerning Jeremiah's Repudiation of Sacrifice', *ZAW* 89 (1977), pp. 273-75.

—'Sancta Contagion or Altar/City Asylum', in J.A. Emerton (ed.), *Congress Volume, Vienna 1980* (VTSup, 32; Leiden, 1981), pp. 278-310.

—'On the Suspected Adulteress (Numbers 5.11-31)', *VT* 35 (1985), pp. 368-69.

Miller, J.M., 'The Fall of the House of Ahab', *VT* 17 (1967), pp. 307-24.

Miller, P.D., 'YĀPÎAḤ in Psalm 12.6)', *VT* 29 (1979), pp. 495-501.

—'Studies in Hebrew Word Patterns', *HTR* 73 (1980), pp. 79-89.

—*Sin and Judgment in the Prophets: A Stylistic and Theological Analysis* (SBLMS, 27; Chico, CA, 1982).

Mogensen, B., '*ṣᵉdāqā* in the Scandinavian and German Research Traditions', in K. Jeppesen and B. Otzen (eds.), *The Productions of Time: Tradition History in the Old Testament Scholarship* (Sheffield, 1984), pp. 67-80.

Monty, V., 'La nature du péché d'après le vocabulaire hébreu', *ScEccl* 1 (1948), pp. 95-109.

—'Péchés graves et légers d'après le vocabulaire hébreu', *ScEccl* 2 (1949), pp. 129-68.

Moraldi, L., *Espiazione sacrificale e riti espiatori nell'ambiente biblico e nell'Antico Testamento* (AnBib, 5; Rome, 1956).

—'Espiazione nell'Antico e nel Nuovo Testamento', *RivB* 9 (1961), pp. 289-304; *RivB* 10 (1962), pp. 3-17.

Moran, W.L., 'Some Remarks on the Song of Moses', *Bib* 43 (1962), pp. 317-27.

Morgenstern, J., 'Trial by Ordeal among the Semites and in Ancient Israel', in *Hebrew Union College Jubilee Volume* (Cincinnati, 1925), pp. 111-43.

Morris, L., ''Asham', *EvQ* 30 (1958), pp. 196-210.

—'The Punishment of Sin in the Old Testament', *AusBR* 6 (1958), pp. 61-86.

Morrison, M.A., 'The Jacob and Laban Narrative in the Light of Near Eastern Sources', *BA* 46 (1983), pp. 155-64.

Moule, C.F.D., '"...As we forgive...". A Note on the Distinction between Deserts and Capacity in the Understanding of Forgiveness', in *Donum Gentilicium: New Testament Studies in Honor of D. Daube* (Oxford, 1978), pp. 68-77.

Mowinckel, S., *Psalmenstudien*. I. *Åwän und die individuellen Klagepsalmen* (Kristiania, 1921).

Muilenberg, J., 'The Linguistic and Rhetorical Usages of the Particle *ky* in the Old Testament', *HUCA* 32 (1961), pp. 135-60.

Mulder, M.J., 'Die Partikel *ya'an* ', *OTS* 18 (1973), pp. 49-83.

Mullen, E.T. (Jr), *The Divine Council in Canaanite and Early Hebrew Literature* (HSM, 24; Chico, CA, 1980).

Napier, D., 'The Inheritance and the Problem of Adjacency. An Essay on I Kings 21', *Int* 30 (1976), pp. 3-11.

Naveh, J., 'A Hebrew Letter from the Seventh Century B.C.', *IEJ* 10 (1960), pp. 129-39.

Nel, P., 'The Concept "Father" in the Wisdom Literature of the Ancient Near East', *JNSL* 5 (1977), pp. 53-66.
Neubauer, K.W., *Der Stamm CH N N im Sprachgebrauch des Alten Testaments* (Berlin, 1964).
Neufeld, E., 'Self-Help in Ancient Hebrew Law', *RIDA* (3rd Ser.) 5 (1958), pp. 291-98.
—'The Emergence of a Royal–Urban Society in Ancient Israel', *HUCA* 31 (1960), pp. 31-53.
Nicolsky, N., *Spuren magischer Formeln in den Psalmen* (BZAW, 46; Giessen, 1927).
—'Das Asylrecht in Israel', *ZAW* 48 (1930), pp. 146-75.
Nielsen, K., *Yahweh as Prosecutor and Judge: An Investigation of the Prophetic Lawsuit (Rib-Pattern)* (JSOTSup, 9; Sheffield, 1978).
—'Das Bild des Gerichts (*Rib*-Pattern) in Jes. I–XII. Eine Analyse der Beziehungen zwischen Bildsprache und dem Anliegen der Verkündigung', *VT* 29 (1979), pp. 309-24.
North, R., 'Angel-Prophet or Satan-Prophet?', *ZAW* 82 (1970), pp. 31-67.
—'Civil Authority in Ezra', in *Studi in onore di E. Volterra*, VI (Milan, 1971), pp. 377-404.
Noth, M., 'Das Amt des "Richters Israels"', in *Festschrift A. Bertholet* (Tübingen, 1950), pp. 404-17.
—'Die Bewährung von Salomos "Göttlicher Weisheit"', in M. Noth and D. Winton Thomas (eds.), *Wisdom in Israel and in the Ancient Near East* (FS H.H. Rowley; VTSup, 3; Leiden, 1955), pp. 225-37.
Nötscher, F., *Die Gerechtigkeit Gottes bei den vorexilischen Propheten: Ein Beitrag zur alttestamentlichen Theologie* (ATA VI/1; Münster, 1915).
Oberhuber, K., 'Zur Syntax des Richterbuches. Der einfache Nominalsatz und die sog. nominale Apposition', *VT* 3 (1953), pp. 2-45.
Ogushi, M., *Der Tadel im Alten Testament: Eine formgeschichtliche Untersuchung* (EurHS XXIII/115; Frankfurt, 1978).
Olivier, J.P.J., 'The Sceptre of Justice and Ps. 45.7b', *JNSL* 7 (1979), pp. 45-54.
Olley, J.W., 'A Forensic Connotation of *bôš*', *VT* 26 (1976), pp. 230-34.
Olmo Lete, G. Del, 'Estructura literaria de Ez 33, 1-20', *EstBíb* 22 (1963), pp. 5-31.
O'Rourke Boyle, M., 'The Covenant Lawsuit of the Prophet Amos: III.1 IV.13', *VT* 21 (1971), pp. 338-62.
Osborn, G., *Tōrāh in the Old Testament: A Semantic Study* (Lund, 1945).
Otto, E., 'Die Stellung der Wehe-Worte in der Verkündigung des Propheten Habakuk', *ZAW* 89 (1977), pp. 73-107.
Overholt, T.W., *The Threat of Falsehood: A Study in the Theology of the Book of Jeremiah* (SBT 2nd Ser., 16; London, 1970).
Oyen, H. van, 'Schalom. Gesetz und Evangelium unter dem Aspekt des Friedens', in *Wort—Gebot—Glaube: Beiträge zur Theologie des Alten Testaments* (FS W. Eichrodt; ATANT, 59; Zürich, 1970), pp. 157-70.
Pajardi, P., *Un giurista legge la Bibbia: Ricerche e meditazioni di un giurista cattolico sui valori giuridici del messaggio biblico ed evangelico* (Milan, 1983).
Palache, J.L., 'Ueber das Weinen in der jüdischen Religion', *ZDMG* 70 (1916), pp. 251-56.
—*Semantic Notes on the Hebrew Lexicon* (Leiden, 1959).
Pardee, D., '*Ypḥ* "Witness" in Hebrew and Ugaritic', *VT* 28 (1978), pp. 204-13.

Parunak, H. van Dyke, 'A Semantic Survey of NḤM', *Bib* 56 (1975), pp. 512-32.

Paschen, W., *Rein und Unrein: Untersuchung zur biblischen Wortgeschichte* (SANT, 24; Munich, 1970).

Patrick, D., 'Casuistic Law Governing Primary Rights and Duties', *JBL* 92 (1973), pp. 180-84.

—'The Translation of Job XLII.6', *VT* 26 (1976), pp. 369-71.

Patterson, R.D., 'The Widow, the Orphan and the Poor in the Old Testament and the Extra-Biblical Literature', *BS* 130 (1973), pp. 223-35.

Paul, S.M., *Studies in the Book of the Covenant in the Light of Cuneiform and Biblical Law* (VTSup, 18; Leiden, 1970).

—'Unrecognized Biblical Legal Idioms in the Light of Comparative Accadian Expressions', *RB* 86 (1979), pp. 231-39.

Pautrel, R., '"Immola Deo sacrificium laudis". Ps. 50.15', in *Mélanges bibliques...en l'honneur de A. Robert* (Paris, 1957), pp. 234-40.

Pax, E., 'Studien zum Vergeltungsproblem der Psalmen', *SBFLA* 11 (1960–1961), pp. 56-112.

Pedersen, J., *Der Eid bei den Semiten in seinem Verhältnis zu verwandten Erscheinungen sowie die Stellung des Eides im Islam* (SGKIO, 3; Strasbourg, 1914).

—*Israel: Its Life and Culture*, I-II (Copenhagen, 1926).

Penna, A., 'I diritti umani nel Vecchio Testamento', in *I diritti umani: Dottrina e prassi, Opera collettiva diretta da G. Concetti* (Rome, 1982), pp. 61-95.

Péter, R., 'L'imposition des mains dans l'Ancien Testament', *VT* 27 (1977), pp. 48-55.

Pettazzoni, R., *La confessione dei peccati* (Parte seconda, volume secondo: Egitto—Babilonia—Israele—Arabia meridionale; Bologna, 1935).

Pfeiffer, E., 'Die Disputationsworte im Buche Maleachi (Ein Beitrag zur formgeschichtlichen Struktur)', *EvT* 12 (1959), pp. 546-68.

Phillips, A., 'The Interpretation of II Sam. 12.5-6', *VT* 16 (1966), pp. 242-44.

—'The Ecstatics' Father', in *Words and Meanings* (FS D.W. Thomas; Cambridge, 1968), pp. 183-94.

—*Ancient Israel's Criminal Law: A New Approach to the Decalogue* (Oxford, 1970).

—'Some Aspects of Family Law in Pre-Exilic Israel', *VT* 23 (1973), pp. 349-61.

—'Nebalah—A Term for Serious Disorderly and Unruly Conduct', *VT* 25 (1975), pp. 237-41.

—'Another Look at Murder', *JJS* 28 (1977), pp. 105-26.

—'Prophecy and Law', in *Israel's Prophetic Tradition* (FS P.R. Ackroyd; Cambridge, 1982), pp. 217-32.

—'"Double for all her Sins"', *ZAW* 94 (1982), pp. 130-32.

Pidoux, G., 'Quelques allusions au droit d'asile dans les Psaumes', in *Maqqél Shâqédh* (FS W. Vischer; Montpellier, 1960), pp. 191-97.

Pirenne, J., 'Les Institutions du peuple hébreu', *Archives du Droit Oriental* 4 (1949), pp. 51-75; *Archives du Droit Oriental* 5 (1950–1951), pp. 99-131; *Archives d'Histoire du Droit Oriental et RIDA* 1 (1952), pp. 33-86, *Archives d'Histoire du Droit Oriental et RIDA* 2 (1953), pp. 109-49; *RIDA* (3rd Ser.) 1 (1954), pp. 195-235.

Pisapia, G.D., *Compendio di procedura penale* (Padova, 2nd edn, 1979).

Ploeg, J. van der, 'Le sens de *gibbôr ḥail*', *RB* 50 (1941) = *Vivre et penser*, I, pp. 120-25.

—'*Shāpaṭ* et *mishpāṭ*', *OTS* 2 (1943), pp. 144-55.
—'Notes lexicographiques', *OTS* 5 (1948), pp. 142-50.
—'Studies in Hebrew Law', *CBQ* 12 (1950), pp. 248-59, 416-27; *CBQ* 13 (1951), pp. 28-43, 164-71, 296-307.
—'Les chefs du peuple d'Israël et leur titres', *RB* 57 (1950), pp. 40-61.
—'Les pauvres d'Israël et leur piété', *OTS* 7 (1950), pp. 236-70.
—'Les "nobles" israélites', *OTS* 9 (1951), pp. 49-64.
—'Les *šoṭᵉrim* d'Israël', *OTS* 10 (1954), pp. 185-96.
—'Les anciens dans l'Ancien Testament', in *Lex tua Veritas* (FS H. Junker; Trier, 1961), pp. 175-91.
—'Le Psaume XVII et ses problèmes', *OTS* 14 (1965), pp. 273-95.
—'Les juges en Israël', in *Populus Dei*. I. *Israel* (Studi in onore del Card. A. Ottaviani; Rome, 1969), pp. 463-507.
—'Le pouvoir exécutif en Israël', in *Populus Dei*, pp. 509-19.
Polley, M.E., 'Hebrew Prophecy within the Council of Yahweh, Examined in its Ancient Near Eastern Setting', in C.D. Evans *et al.* (eds.), *Scripture in Context: Essays on the Comparative Method* (PTMS, 34; Pittsburgh, 1980), pp. 141-56.
Polzin, R., *Late Biblical Hebrew: Toward an Historical Typology of Biblical Hebrew Prose* (HSM, 12; Missoula, MT, 1976).
Pons, J., *L'oppression dans l'Ancien Testament* (Paris, 1981).
Porteous, N.W., 'Semantics and Old Testament Theology', *OTS* 8 (1950), pp. 1-14.
—'Royal Wisdom', in M. Noth and D. Winton Thomas (eds.), *Wisdom in Israel and in the Ancient Near East* (FS H.H. Rowley; VTSup, 3; Leiden, 1955), pp. 247-61.
—'Actualization and the Prophetic Criticism of the Cult', in *Tradition und Situation: Studien zur alttestamentlichen Prophetie* (FS A. Weiser; Göttingen, 1963), pp. 93-105.
Porter, J.R., 'The Legal Aspects of the Concept of "Corporate Personality" in the Old Testament', *VT* 15 (1965), pp. 361-80.
Porúbčan, Š., *Sin in the Old Testament: A Soteriological Study* (Rome, 1963).
Preiser, W., 'Vergeltung und Sühne im altisraelitischen Strafrecht', in *Festschrift E. Schmidt* (Göttingen, 1961), pp. 7-38.
Press, R., 'Die Gerichtspredigt der vorexilischen Propheten und der Versuch einer Steigerung der kultischen Leistung', *ZAW* 70 (1958), pp. 181-84.
Prevost, M.H., 'A propos du talion', in *Mélanges dédiés à la mémoire de J. Teneur* (Lille, 1976), pp. 619-29.
—'L'oppression dans la Bible', in *Mélanges à la mémoire de M.-H. Prevost* (Paris, 1982), pp. 3-16.
Price, I.M., 'The Oath in Court Procedure in Early Babylonia and the Old Testament', *JAOS* 49 (1929), pp. 22-39.
Priest, J.E., *Governmental and Judicial Ethics in the Bible and Rabbinic Literature* (New York, 1980).
Pugliese, G., '"Res iudicata pro veritate accipitur"', in *Studi in onore di E. Volterra*, V (Milan, 1971), pp. 783-830.
Puukko, A.F., 'Der Feind in den alttestamentlichen Psalmen', *OTS* 8 (1950), pp. 47-65.
Rabello, A.M., 'Les effets personnels de la puissance paternelle en droit hébraïque, à travers la Bible et le Talmud', in *Mélanges à la mémoire de M.-H. Prevost* (Paris, 1982), pp. 84-101.

Rad, G. von, '"Gerechtigkeit" und "Leben" in den Psalmen', in *Festschrift A. Bertholet* (Tübingen, 1950), pp. 418-37.
—'Die Anrechnung des Glaubens zur Gerechtigkeit', *TLZ* 76 (1951), pp. 129-32.
—*Theologie des Alten Testaments*, I-II (Munich, 1957, 1960).
—*Die Josephgeschichte* (BiblSt, 5; Neukirchen, 4th edn, 1964).
—'Gerichtsdoxologie', in *Schalom: Studien zu Glaube und Geschichte Israels* (FS A. Jepsen; Stuttgart, 1971), pp. 28-37.
—'Zwei Überlieferungen von König Saul' (1968), in *Gesammelte Studien zum Alten Testament*, II (TBü, 48; Munich, 1973), pp. 199-211.
Raitt, T.M., 'The Prophetic Summons to Repentance', *ZAW* 83 (1971), pp. 30-49.
Ramsey, G.W., 'Speech-Forms in Hebrew Law and Prophetic Oracles', *JBL* 96 (1977), pp. 45-58.
Redford, D.B., *A Study of the Biblical Story of Joseph (Genesis 37–50)* (VTSup, 20; Leiden, 1970).
Reed, W.L., 'Some Implications of Ḥēn for Old Testament Religion', *JBL* 73 (1954), pp. 36-41.
Rehm, M., 'Nehemias 9', *BZ* NS 1 (1957), pp. 59-63.
Reindl, J., *Das Angesicht Gottes im Sprachgebrauch des Alten Testaments* (ErfTSt, 25; Leipzig, 1970).
Reiterer, F.V., *Gerechtigkeit als Heil: ṣdq bei Deuterojesaja. Aussage und Vergleich mit der alttestamentlichen Tradition* (Graz, 1976).
Rémy, P., 'Peine de mort et vengeance dans la Bible', *ScEccl* 19 (1967), pp. 323-50.
Renaud, B., *Je suis un Dieu jaloux: Evolution sémantique et signification théologique de qin^{e}'ah* (LD, 36; Paris, 1963).
Rendtorff, R., 'Priesterliche Kulttheologie und prophetische Kultpolemik', *TLZ* 81 (1956), pp. 341-44.
—*Studien zur Geschichte des Opfers im Alten Israel* (WMANT, 24; Neukirchen, 1967).
Renker, A., *Die Tora bei Maleachi: Ein Beitrag zur Bedeutungsgeschichte von* tôrā *im Alten Testament* (FreibTSt, 112; Freiburg, 1979).
Reventlow, H. von, 'Das Amt des Mazkir. Zur Rechtsstruktur des öffentlichen Lebens in Israel', *TZ* 15 (1959), pp. 161-75.
—'Die Völker als Jahves Zeugen bei Ezechiel', *ZAW* 71 (1959), pp. 33-43.
—'"Sein Blut komme über sein Haupt"', *VT* 10 (1960), pp. 311-27.
—*Wächter über Israel: Ezechiel und seine Tradition* (BZAW, 82; Berlin, 1962).
—*Liturgie und prophetisches Ich bei Jeremia* (Gütersloh, 1963).
—*Rechtfertigung im Horizont des Alten Testaments* (BEvT, 58; Munich, 1971).
Reviv, H., 'Elders and "Saviors"', *OrAnt* 16 (1977), pp. 201-204.
—'The Traditions concerning the Inception of the Legal System in Israel. Significance and Dating', *ZAW* 94 (1982), pp. 566-75.
—*The Elders in Ancient Israel: A Study of a Biblical Institution* (Jerusalem, 1983 [Hebrew]).
Reymond, P., 'Le rêve de Salomon (1 Rois 3,4-15)', in *Maqqél Shâqédh* (FS W. Vischer; Montpellier, 1960), pp. 210-15.
—'Sacrifice et "spiritualité", ou sacrifice et alliance? Jér 7.22-24', *TZ* 21 (1965), pp. 314-17.
Rhodes, A.B., 'Israel's Prophets as Intercessors', in *Scripture in History and Theology* (FS J.C. Rylaarsdam; Pittsburgh, 1977), pp. 107-28.

Richter, H., *Studien zu Hiob: Der Aufbau des Hiobbuches, dargestellt an den Gattungen des Rechtsleben* (TArb, 11; Berlin, 1959).
Richter, W., *Traditionsgeschichtliche Untersuchungen zum Richterbuch* (BBB, 18; Bonn, 1963).
—*Die Bearbeitung des 'Retterbuches' in der deuteronomischen Epoche* (BBB, 21; Bonn, 1964).
—'Zu den "Richtern Israels"', *ZAW* 77 (1965), pp. 40-72.
—'Die *nāgīd*-Formel. Ein Beitrag zur Erhellung des *nāgīd*-Problems', *BZ* NS 9 (1965), pp. 71-84.
Ricoeur, P., *Finitude et culpabilité* (Paris, 1960).
Ridderbos, N.H., '*'apar* als Staub des Totenortes', *OTS* 5 (1948), pp. 174-78.
—'Psalm 51.5-6', in *Studia biblica et semitica* (FS T.C. Vriezen; Wageningen, 1966), pp. 299-312.
—'Die Theophanie in Psalm 50.1-6', *OTS* 15 (1969), pp. 213-26.
Riesener, I., *Der Stamm* 'bd *im Alten Testament: Eine Wortuntersuchung unter Berücksichtigung neuerer sprachwissenschaftlicher Methode* (BZAW, 149; Berlin, 1979).
Rinaldi, G., 'La donna che "ha deviato". Considerazioni su Num. 5.11-31', *EuntDoc* 26 (1973), pp. 535-50.
Ring, E., *Israels Rechtsleben im Lichte der neuentdeckten assyrischen und hethitischen Gesetzesurkunden* (Stockholm, 1926).
Ringgren, H., 'Einige Schilderungen des göttlichen Zorns', in *Tradition und Situation: Studien zur alttestamentlichen Prophetie* (FS A. Weiser; Göttingen, 1963), pp. 107-13.
Roberts, J.J.M., 'The Divine King and the Human Community in Isaiah's Vision of the Future', in *The Quest for the Kingdom of God* (FS G.E. Mendenhall; Winona Lake, IN, 1983), pp. 127-36.
Robertson, D.A., *Linguistic Evidence in Dating Early Hebrew Poetry* (SBLDS, 3; Missoula, MT, 1972).
Robinson, H.W., 'The Council of Yahweh', *JTS* 45 (1944), pp. 151-57.
Roche, M. de, 'Yahweh's *rîb* against Israel: A Reassessment of the So-Called "Prophetic Lawsuit" in the Preexilic Prophets', *JBL* 102 (1983), pp. 563-74.
Rösel, H.N., 'Jephtah und das Problem der Richter', *Bib* 61 (1980), pp. 251-55.
Rosenthal, F., 'Ṣedaqa, charity', *HUCA* 23 (1950–1951), pp. 411-30.
Rost, L., 'Die Gerichtshoheit am Heiligtum', in *Archäologie und Altes Testament* (FS K. Galling; Tübingen, 1970), pp. 225-31.
—'Erwägungen zum Begriff *šālôm*', in *Schalom: Studien zu Glaube und Geschichte Israels* (FS A. Jepsen; Stuttgart, 1971), pp. 41-44.
Roubos, K., *Profetie en Cultus in Israël (Prophecy and Cult in Israel)* (Wageningen, 1956).
Rouillard, H., 'Les feintes questions divines dans la Bible', *VT* 34 (1984), pp. 237-42.
Rozenberg, M.S., 'The *šōfᵉṭīm* in the Bible', *Eretz-Israel* 12 (1972), pp. 77*-86*.
Ruppert, L., *Die Josepherzählung der Genesis: Ein Beitrag zur Theologie der Pentateuchquellen* (SANT, 11; Munich, 1965).
—*Der leidende Gerechte: Eine motivgeschichtliche Untersuchung zum Alten Testament und zwischentestamentliche Judentum* (ForBib, 5; Würzburg, 1972).
—*Der leidende Gerechte und seine Feinde: Eine Wortfelduntersuchung* (Würzburg, 1973).

—'Klagelieder in Israel und Babylonien—Verschiedene Deutungen der Gewalt', in *Gewalt und Gewaltlosigkeit im Alten Testament* (QDisp, 96; Freiburg, 1983), pp. 111-58.

Ruprecht, E., 'Eine vergessene Konjektur von A. Klostermann zu 1. Reg. 3.27', *ZAW* 88 (1976), pp. 415-18.

Rüterswörden, U., *Die Beamten der israelitischen Königszeit: Eine Studie zu* śr *und vergleichbaren Begriffen* (BWANT, 117; Stuttgart, 1985).

Ruwet, J., 'Misericordia et Iustitia Dei in Vetere Testamento', *VD* 25 (1947), pp. 35-42, 89-98.

Sakenfeld, K.D., *The Meaning of Ḥesed in the Hebrew Bible: A New Inquiry* (HSM, 17; Missoula, MT, 1978).

Santos Olivera, B., '"Vindex" seu "Redemptor" apud hebreos', *VD* 11 (1931), pp. 89-94.

Sarna, N., 'Psalm XIX and the Near Eastern Sun-God Literature', in *Proceedings of the Fourth World Congress of Jewish Studies*, I (Jerusalem, 1967), pp. 171-75.

Sasson, J.M., 'Numbers 5 and the "Waters of Judgment"', *BZ* NS16 (1972), pp. 249-51.

Sauer, G., 'Die Umkehrforderung in der Verkündigung Jesajas', in *Wort—Gebot—Glaube: Beiträge zur Theologie des Alten Testaments* (FS W. Eichrodt; ATANT, 59; Zürich, 1970), pp. 277-97.

Savage, M., 'Literary Criticism and Biblical Studies: A Rhetorical Analysis of the Joseph Narrative', in C.D. Evans *et al.* (eds.), *Scripture in Context: Essays on the Comparative Method* (PTMS, 34; Pittsburgh, 1980), pp. 79-100.

Sawyer, J.F.A., 'What was a Mošia'?', *VT* 15 (1965), pp. 475-86.

—*Semantics in Biblical Research: New Methods of Defining Hebrew Words for Salvation* (SBT 2nd Ser., 24; London, 1972).

—'Types of Prayer in the Old Testament. Some Semantic Observations on *Hitpallel, Hitḥannen*, etc.', *Semitics* 7 (1980), pp. 131-43.

Schäfer-Lichtenberger, C., *Stadt und Eidgenossenschaft im Alten Testament: Eine Auseinandersetzung mit Max Webers Studie 'Das antike Judentum'* (BZAW, 156; Berlin, 1983).

Scharbert, J., *Der Schmerz im Alten Testament* (BBB, 8; Bonn, 1955).

—'Formgeschichte und Exegese von Ex 34,6f und seiner Parallelen', *Bib* 38 (1957), pp. 130-50.

—'Das Verbum PQD in der Theologie des Alten Testaments', *BZ* NS 4 (1960), pp. 209-26.

—'*šlm* im Alten Testament', in *Lex tua veritas* (FS H. Junker; Trier, 1961), pp. 209-29.

—*Heilsmittler im Alten Testament und im Alten Orient* (QDisp, 23/24; Freiburg, 1964).

Schenker, A., *Versöhnung und Sühne: Wege gewaltfreier Konfliktlösung im AT mit einem Ausblick auf das NT* (BibB, 15; Freiburg, 1981).

—*Der Mächtige im Schmelzofen des Mitleids: Eine Interpretation von 2 Sam. 24* (OBO, 42; Freiburg, 1982).

Schilling, O., 'Die alttestamentliche Auffassung von Gerechtigkeit und Liebe', in *Vom Wort des Lebens* (FS M. Meinertz; Münster, 1951), pp. 9-27.

Schmid, H.H., *Gerechtigkeit als Weltordnung: Hintergrund und Geschichte des alttestamentlichen Gerechtigkeitsbegriffes* (BHT, 40; Tübingen, 1968).

—*Šalôm 'Frieden' im Alten Orient und im Alten Testament* (SBS, 51; Stuttgart, 1971).

—'Gerechtigkeit und Barmherzigkeit im Alten Testament', *WDienst* 12 (1973), pp. 31-41.
—'Rechtfertigung als Schöpfungsgeschehen. Notizen zur alttestamentlichen Vorgeschichte eines neutestamentlichen Themas', in *Rechtfertigung* (FS E. Käsemann; Tübingen, 1976), pp. 403-14.
Schmid, R., *Das Bundesopfer in Israel: Wesen, Ursprung und Bedeutung der alttestamentlichen Schelamim* (SANT, 9; Munich, 1964).
Schmidt, H., *Das Gebet der Angeklagten im Alten Testament* (BZAW, 49; Giessen, 1928).
Schmidt, L., *'De Deo': Studien zur Literarkritik und Theologie des Buches Jona, des Gesprächs zwischen Abraham und Jahwe in Gen. 18.22ff. und von Hi 1* (BZAW, 143; Berlin, 1976).
Schmidt, W.H., *Königtum Gottes in Ugarit und Israel: Zur Herkunft der Königsprädikation Jahwes* (BZAW, 80; Berlin, 1961).
—*Zukunftsgewissheit und Gegenwartskritik: Grundzüge prophetischer Verkündigung* (BiblSt, 64; Neukirchen, 1973).
—' "Rechtfertigung des Gottlosen" in der Botschaft der Propheten', in *Die Botschaft und die Boten* (FS H.W. Wolff; Neukirchen, 1981), pp. 157-68.
Schmitt, H.-C., *Die nichtpriesterliche Josephgeschichte: Ein Beitrag zur neuesten Pentateuchkritik* (BZAW, 154; Berlin, 1980).
Schmökel, H., *Das angewandte Recht im Alten Testament: Eine Untersuchung seiner Beziehungen zum kodifizierten Recht Israels und des alten Orients* (Leipzig, 1930).
Schmuttermayr, G., 'RḤM—Eine lexikalische Studie', *Bib* 51 (1970), pp. 499-532.
Schnutenhaus, F., 'Das Kommen und Erscheinen Gottes im Alten Testament', *ZAW* 76 (1964), pp. 1-22.
Scholnick, S.H., 'The Meaning of *mišpaṭ* in the Book of Job', *JBL* 101 (1982), pp. 521-29.
Schoors, A., *I Am God Your Saviour. A Form-critical Study of the Main Genres in Is XL-LX* (VTSup, 24; 1973).
—'The Particle *ky*', *OTS* 21 (1981), pp. 240-76.
Schottroff, W., *'Gedenken' im Alten Orient und im Alten Testament: Die Wurzel* zākar *im semitischen Sprachkreis* (WMANT, 15; Neukirchen, 1964).
—'Das Weinberglied Jesajas (Jes 5.1-7). Ein Beitrag zur Geschichte der Parabel', *ZAW* 82 (1970), pp. 68-91.
—'Zum alttestamentlichen Recht', *VF* 22 (1977), pp. 3-29.
Schottroff, W., and W. Stegeman (eds.), *Traditionen der Befreiung: Sozialgeschichtliche Bibelauslegung*. I. Methodische Zugänge (Munich, 1980).
Schötz, D., *Schuld- und Sündopfer im Alten Testament* (BSHT, 18; Breslau, 1930).
Schulz, H., *Das Todesrecht im Alten Testament: Studien zur Rechtsform der Mot—Jumat—Sätze* (BZAW, 114; Berlin, 1969).
Schunck, K.-D., 'Die Richter Israels und ihr Amt', in J.A. Emerton *et al.* (eds.), *Congress Volume, Geneva 1965* (VTSup, 15; Leiden, 1966), pp. 252-62.
Schüngel-Straumann, H., *Gottesbild und Kultkritik vorexilischer Propheten* (SBS, 60; Stuttgart, 1972).
Schwantes, M., *Das Recht der Armen* (BeiBibExT, 4; Frankfurt, 1977).
Scullion, J.J., 'Ṣedeq - ṣedaqah in Isaiah cc. 40–66 with Special Reference to the Continuity in Meaning between Second and Third Isaiah', *UF* 3 (1971), pp. 335-48.

Seebass, H., 'Nathan und David in II Sam 12', *ZAW* 86 (1974), pp. 203-11.
—'Der Fall Naboth in 1 Reg XXI', *VT* 24 (1974), pp. 474-88.
—*Geschichtliche Zeit und theonome Tradition in der Joseph-Erzählung* (Gütersloh, 1978).
—'Die Stämmesprüche Gen. 49.3-27', *ZAW* 96 (1984), pp. 333-50.
Seeligmann, I.L., 'Menschliches Heldentum und göttliche Hilfe. Die doppelte Kausalität im alttestamentlichen Geschichtsdenken', *TZ* 19 (1963), pp. 385-411.
—'Zur Terminologie für das Gerichtsverfahren im Wortschatz des biblischen Hebräisch', in *Hebräische Wortforschung* (VTSup, 16; FS W. Baumgartner; Leiden, 1967), pp. 251-78.
Segert, S., 'Form and Function of Ancient Israelite, Greek and Roman Legal Sentences', in *Orient and Occident: Essays presented to C.H. Gordon* (AOAT, 22; Neukirchen, 1973), pp. 162-65.
Seidel, H., *Das Erlebnis der Einsamkeit im Alten Testament: Eine Untersuchung zum Menschenbild des Alten Testament* (TArb, 29; Berlin, 1969).
Seitz, G., *Redaktionsgeschichtliche Studien zum Deuteronomium* (BWANT, 93; Stuttgart, 1971).
Sekine, M., 'Das Problem der Kultpolemik bei den Propheten', *EvT* 28 (1968), pp. 605-609.
Seybold, K., 'Zwei Bemerkungen zu *gmwl/gml*', *VT* 22 (1972), pp. 112-17.
—*Das Gebet des Kranken im Alten Testament* (BWANT, 99; Stuttgart, 1973).
Shaviv, S., '*Nābî* and *nāgîd* in 1 Sam. IX 1–X16', *VT* 34 (1984), pp. 108-13.
Sicre, J.L., *Los dioses olvidados: Poder y riqueza en los profetas preexílicos* (Madrid, 1979).
—'La monarquía y la justicia. La práctica de la justicia como elemento aglutinante en la redacción de Jr. 21.11–23.8', in *El misterio de la Palabra: Homenaje… L. Alonso Schökel* (Madrid, 1983), pp. 193-206.
—*'Con los pobres de la tierra': La justicia social en los profetas de Israel* (Madrid, 1984).
Simon, V., 'The Poor Man's Ewe-Lamb. An Example of a Juridical Parable', *Bib* 48 (1967), pp. 207-42.
Ska, J.L., 'La sortie d'Egypte (Ex. 7–14) dans le récit sacerdotal (P^g) et la tradition prophétique', *Bib* 60 (1979), pp. 191-215.
Skehan, P.W., 'The Structure of the Song of Moses in Deuteronomy (Deut. 32:1-43)', *CBQ* 13 (1951), pp. 153-63.
Smith, C.R., *The Bible Doctrine of Sin* (London, 1953).
Smith, S., 'The Threshing Floor and the City Gate', *PEQ* 78 (1946), pp. 5-14.
—'On the Meaning of *goren*', *PEQ* 85 (1953), pp. 42-45.
Smitten, W.T. in der, *Esra: Quellen, Überlieferung und Geschichte* (SSN, 15; Assen, 1973).
Snaith, N.H., *The Distinctive Ideas of the Old Testament* (London, 1944).
—'The Hebrew Root *g'l* (I)', *ALUOS* 3 (1961–62), pp. 60-67.
—'Genesis XXXI 50', *VT* 14 (1964), p. 373.
—'The Sin-Offering and the Guilt-Offering', *VT* 15 (1965), pp. 73-80.
Snijders, L.A., 'Psaume XXVI et l'innocence', *OTS* 13 (1963), pp. 112-30.
Soggin, J.A., 'Der prophetische Gedanke über den heiligen Krieg, als Gericht gegen Israel', *VT* 10 (1960), pp. 79-83.

—'Il Salmo 15 (Volgata 14). Osservazioni filologiche ed esegetiche', *BO* 12 (1970), pp. 83-90.
—'Das Amt der "kleinen Richter" in Israel', *VT* 30 (1980), pp. 245-48.
Speiser, E.A., '"Coming" and "Going" at the "City" Gate', *BASOR* 144 (1952), pp. 20-23.
—'Census and Ritual Expiation in Mari and Israel', *BASOR* 149 (1958), pp. 17-25.
—'Background and Function of the Biblical Nāśī'', *CBQ* 25 (1963), pp. 111-17.
—'The Stem PLL in Hebrew', *JBL* 82 (1963), pp. 301-306.
Stamm, J.J., *Erlösen und Vergeben im Alten Testament: Eine begriffsgeschichtliche Untersuchung* (Bern, 1940).
—'Ein Vierteljahrhundert Psalmenforschung', *TRu* 23 (1955), pp. 1-68.
—'Der Weltfriede im Alten Testament', in J.J. Stamm and H. Bietenhard, *Der Weltfriede im Alten und Neuen Testament* (Zürich, 1959), pp. 7-63.
Steck, O.H., *Überlieferung und Zeitgeschichte in den Elia-Erzählungen* (WMANT, 26; (Neukirchen, 1968).
Stek, J.H., 'Salvation, Justice and Liberation in the Old Testament', *CTJ* 13 (1978), pp. 133-65.
Stock, K., 'Gott der Richter. Der Gerichtsgedanke als Horizont der Rechtfertigungslehre', *EvT* 40 (1980), pp. 240-56.
Stoebe, H.J., 'Das achte Gebot (Exod 20. Vers 16)', *WDienst* 3 (1952), pp. 108-26.
—'Die Bedeutung des Wortes *ḥäsäd* im Alten Testament', *VT* 2 (1952), pp. 244-54.
Stroete, G. te, 'Sünde im Alten Testament. Die Wiedergabe einiger hebräischer Ausdrücke für "Sünde" in fünf gangbaren west-europäischen Bibelübersetzungen', in *Übersetzung und Deutung* (FS A.R. Hulst; Nijkerk, 1977), pp. 164-75.
Subilia, V., *La giustificazione per fede* (Brescia, 1976).
Swartzback, R.H., 'A Biblical Study of the Word "Vengeance"', *Int* 6 (1952), pp. 451-57.
Talmon, S., 'The New Hebrew Letter from the Seventh Century B.C. in Historical Perspective', *BASOR* 176 (1964), pp. 29-38.
—'*Amen* as an Introductory Oath Formula', *Textus* 7 (1969), pp. 124-29.
Tasker, R.V., *The Biblical Doctrine of the Wrath of God* (London, 1951).
Thomas, D.W., '*b^{e}liyya'al* in the Old Testament' in *Biblical and Patristic Studies in Memory of R.P. Casey* (Freiburg, 1963), pp. 11-19.
Thompson, J.A., 'Expansion of the *'d* Root', *JSS* 10 (1965), pp. 222-40.
Thompson, R.J., *Penitence and Sacrifice in Early Israel outside the Levitical Law* (Leiden, 1963).
Thomson, H.C., 'The Significance of the Term 'Asham in the Old Testament', *GUOST* 14 (1953), pp. 20-26.
—'*Shopeṭ* and *Mishpaṭ* in the Book of Judges', *GUOST* 19 (1961–62), pp. 74-85.
Thyen, H., *Studien zur Sündenvergebung im Neuen Testament und seinen alttestamentlichen und jüdischen Voraussetzungen* (FRLANT, 96; Göttingen, 1970).
Tigay, J.H., 'Psalm 7.5 and Ancient Near Eastern Treaties', *JBL* 89 (1970), pp. 178-86.
Toaff, E., 'Evoluzione del concetto ebraico di zedāqa', *AnStEbr* (1968–69), pp. 111-22.
Toombs, L.E., 'Love and Justice in Deuteronomy', *Int* 19 (1965), pp. 399-411.
Tosato, A., 'Sul significato dei termini biblici *'Almānâ*, *'Almānût* ("vedova", "vedovanza")', *BeO* 25 (1983), pp. 193-214.
Trebolle Barrera, J.C., *Salomón y Jeroboán: Historia de la recensión y redacción de I. Reyes 2-12.14* (Bibliotheca Salmanticensis Diss., 3; Salamanca, 1980).

—'La liberación de Egipto narrada y creída desde la opresión de Salomón', *CuadBíb* 6 (1981), pp. 1-19.
Tromp, N.J., 'Tibi soli peccavi—Ps. 51.6', *OnsGeestLev* 54 (1977), pp. 226-34.
—'The Hebrew Particle *bal*', *OTS* 21 (1981), pp. 277-87.
Tsevat, M., "God and the Gods in Assembly. An Interpretation of Psalm 82', *HUCA* 40-41, (1969–70), pp. 123-37.
Tucker, G.M., 'Witness and "Dates" in Israelite Contracts', *CBQ* 28 (1966), pp. 42-45.
Uchelen, N.A. van, '*'nšy dmym* in the Psalms', *OTS* 15 (1969), pp. 205-12.
Valgiglio, E., *Confessio nella Bibbia e nella letteratura cristiana antica* (Turin, 1980).
Vannoy, J.R., 'The Use of the Word *hā'ᵉlōhîm* in Exodus 21.6 and 22.7-8', in *The Law and the Prophets* (FS O.T. Allis; Nutley, 1974), pp. 225-41.
Vattioni, F., 'I precedenti letterari di Is. 32.17. Et erit opus iustitiae pax', *RivB* 6 (1958), pp. 23-32.
—'Malachia 3.20 e l'origine della giustizia in Oriente', *RivB* 6 (1958), pp. 353-60.
Vaux, R. de, 'Titres et fonctionnaires égyptiens à la cour de David et de Salomon', *RB* 48 (1939), pp. 395-97.
—*Les Institutions de l'Ancien Testament*, I-II (Paris, 1958, 1960).
—*Les sacrifices de l'Ancien Testament* (Cahiers de la Revue Biblique, 1; Paris, 1964).
Vella, J., *La giustizia forense di Dio* (Supplementi alla Rivista Biblica; Brescia, 1964).
—'Il Redentore di Giobbe (Nota a *Giob* 16.20)', *RivB* 13 (1965), pp. 161-68.
—'Una trama letteraria di liti di Dio con il suo popolo: schema di teologia biblica', in *Jalones de la Historia de la salvación en el Antiguo y Nuevo Testamento*, (XXVI SemBEsp [1965]; Madrid, 1969), pp. 113-31.
Vesco, J.-L., 'Amos de Teqoa, défenseur de l'homme', *RB* 87 (1980), pp. 481-513.
Vetter, D., 'Satzformen prophetischer Rede', in *Werden und Wirken des Alten Testaments* (FS C. Westermann; Neukirchen, 1980), pp. 174-93.
Victor, P., 'A Note on *ḥōq* in the Old Testament', *VT* 16 (1966), pp. 358-61.
Vílchez, J., 'El binomio justicia–injusticia en el libro de la Sabiduría', *CuadBíb* 7 (1981), pp. 1-16.
Vliet, H. van, *No Single Testimony: A Study on the Adoption of the Law of Deut. 19.15 par. into the New Testament* (STRT, 4; Utrecht, 1958).
Vogt, E., 'Die Lähmung und Stummheit des Propheten Ezechiel', in *Wort—Gebot—Glaube: Beiträge zur Theologie des Alten Testaments* (FS W. Eichrodt; ATANT, 59; Zürich, 1970), pp. 87-100.
Volz, P., *Die biblische Altertümer* (Stuttgart, 1914).
—'Die radikale Ablehnung der Kultreligion durch die alttestamentlichen Propheten', *ZST* 14 (1937), pp. 63-85.
Vries, S.P. de, *Jüdische Riten und Symbole* (Wiesbaden, 1981).
Wagner, V., 'Umfang und Inhalt der *mōt-jūmaṯ*-Reihe', *OLZ* 63 (1968), pp. 325-28.
—*Rechtssätze in gebundener Sprache und Rechtssatzreihen im israelitischen Recht: Ein Beitrag zur Gattungsforschung* (BZAW, 127; Berlin, 1972).
Waldow, E. von, *Der traditionsgeschichtliche Hintergrund der prophetischen Gerichtsreden* (BZAW, 85; Berlin, 1963).
—'Social Responsibility and Social Structure in Early Israel', *CBQ* 32 (1970), pp. 182-204.
Walther, A., *Das altbabylonische Gerichtswesen* (LSSt, 6; Leipzig, 1917).
Wambacq, B.N., 'La prière de Baruch (1.15–2.19) et de Daniel (9.5-19)', *Bib* 40 (1959), pp. 463-75.

Wanke, G., *''oy* und *hôy*', *ZAW* 78 (1966), pp. 215-18.
—'Zu Grundlagen und Absicht prophetischer Sozialkritik', *KD* 18 (1972), pp. 2-17.
Ward, E.F. de, 'Mourning Customs in 1.2 Samuel', *JJS* 23 (1972), pp. 1-27, 145-66.
Warmuth, G., *Das Mahnwort: Seine Bedeutung für die Verkündigung der vorexilischen Propheten Amos, Hosea, Micha, Jesaja und Jeremia* (BeiBibExT, 1; Frankfurt, 1976).
Warner, S.M., 'The Period of the Judges within the Structure of Early Israel', *HUCA* 47 (1976), pp. 57-79.
Watson, W.G.E., 'Reclustering Hebrew *l'lyd*', *Bib* 58 (1977), pp. 213-15.
—'The Metaphor in Job 10.17', *Bib* 63 (1982), pp. 255-57.
Weijden, A.H. van der, *Die 'Gerechtigkeit' in den Psalmen* (Nimwegen, 1952).
Weil, H.-M., 'Exégèse d'Isaïe 3.1-15', *RB* 49 (1940), pp. 76-85.
Weinfeld, M., *Deuteronomy and the Deuteronomic School* (Oxford, 1972).
—'The Origins of the Apodictic Law. An Overlooked Source', *VT* 23 (1973), pp. 63-75.
—'Judge and Officer in Ancient Israel and in the Ancient Near East', *IsrOrSt* 7 (1977), pp. 65-88.
Weingreen, J., 'The Case of the Daughters of Zelophchad', *VT* 16 (1966), pp. 518-22.
Weisman, Z., 'Charismatic Leadership in the Era of the Judges', *ZAW* 89 (1977), pp. 399-412.
Weismann, J., 'Talion und öffentliche Strafe im Mosaischen Rechte' (1913), in K. Koch (ed.), *Um das Prinzip der Vergeltung in Religion und Recht des Alten Testaments* (WegFor, 125; Darmstadt, 1972), pp. 325-406.
Welch, A.C., 'The Source of Nehemiah IX', *ZAW* 47 (1929), pp. 130-37.
Welten, P. 'Naboth Weinberg (1 Könige 21)', *EvT* 33 (1973), pp. 18-32.
Wenham, G.J., 'Legal Forms in the Book of the Covenant', *TynBul* 22 (1971), pp. 95-102.
Westermann, C., 'Struktur und Geschichte der Klage im Alten Testament', *ZAW* 66 (1954), pp. 44-80.
—*Das Loben Gottes in den Psalmen* (Göttingen, 1954).
—'Die Begriffe für Fragen und Suchen im Alten Testament', *KD* 6 (1960), pp. 2-30.
—*Grundformen prophetischer Rede* (BEvT, 31; Munich, 1960).
—'Boten des Zorns. Der Begriff des Zornes Gottes in der Prophetie', in *Die Botschaft und die Boten* (FS H.W. Wolff; Neukirchen, 1981), pp. 147-56.
—*Vergleiche und Gleichnisse im Alten Testament und Neuen Testament* (CalwTMon, 14; Stuttgart, 1984).
Whitelam, K.W., *The Just King: Monarchical Judicial Authority in Ancient Israel* (JSOTSup, 12; Sheffield, 1979).
Whitley, C.F., 'Deutero-Isaiah's Interpretation of *ṣedeq*', *VT* 22 (1972), pp. 469-75.
—'The Semantic Range of *Ḥesed*', *Bib* 62 (1981), pp. 519-26.
Wildberger, H., 'Die Thronnamen des Messias, Jes. 9.5b', *TZ* 16 (1960), pp. 314-32.
Wildeboer, G., 'Die älteste Bedeutung des Stamme *tsdq* [= *ṣdq]*', *ZAW* 22 (1902), pp. 167-69.
Wilhelmi, G., 'Der Hirt mit dem eisernen Szepter. Überlegungen zu Psalm II.9', *VT* 27 (1977), pp. 196-204.
Williams, J.G., 'The Alas-Oracles of the Eighth Century Prophets', *HUCA* 38 (1967), pp. 75-91.
Willis, J.T., 'The Genre of Isaiah 5.1-7', *JBL* 96 (1977), pp. 337-62.

Wilson, R.R., 'An Interpretation of Ezekiel's Dumbness', *VT* 22 (1972), pp. 91-104.
—'Enforcing the Covenant: The Mechanisms of Judicial Authority in Early Israel', in *The Quest for the Kingdom of God* (FS G.E. Mendenhall; Winona Lake, IN, 1983), pp. 59-75.
Wiseman, D.J., '"Is it Peace?"—Covenant and Diplomacy', *VT* 32 (1982), pp. 311-26.
Wold, D.J., 'The *kareth* Penalty in P: Rationale and Cases', in P.J. Achtmeier (ed.), *SBLSP 1979*, I (Missoula, MT, 1979), pp. 1-45.
Wolff, H.W., 'Die Begründungen der prophetischen Heils- und Unheilssprüche', *ZAW* 52 (1934), pp. 1-22.
—'Das Thema "Umkehr" in der alttestamentlichen Prophetie', *ZTK* 48 (1951), pp. 129-48.
—'Der Aufruf zur Volksklage', *ZAW* 76 (1964), pp. 48-56.
—'"Wissen um Gott" bei Hosea als Urform von Theologie', in *Gesammelte Studien zum Alten Testament* (Munich, 2nd edn, 1973), pp. 182-205.
Wolverton, W.I., 'The King's "Justice" in Pre-Exilic Israel', *ATR* 41 (1959), pp. 276-86.
Wright, G.E., 'The Lawsuit of God: A Form-Critical Study of Deuteronomy 32', in *Israel's Prophetic Heritage* (FS J. Muilenburg; New York, 1962), pp. 26-67.
Würthwein, E., 'Der Ursprung der prophetischen Gerichtsrede', *ZTK* 49 (1952), pp. 1-16.
—'Kultpolemik oder Kultbescheid? Beobachtungen zu dem Thema "Prophetie und Kult"', in *Tradition und Situation: Studien zur alttestamentlichen Prophetie* (FS A. Wieser; Göttingen, 1963), pp. 115-31.
—'Naboth-Novelle und Elia-Wort', *ZTK* 75 (1978), pp. 375-97.
Yadin, Y., *The Art of Warfare in Biblical Lands in the Light of Archaeological Study* (2 vols.; New York, 1963).
Yaron, R., 'Jewish Law and Other Legal Systems of Antiquity', *JSS* 4 (1959), pp. 308-31.
Yee, G.W., 'A Form-Critical Study of Isaiah 5.1-7 as a Song and a Juridical Parable', *CBQ* 43 (1981), pp. 30-40.
Zeitlin, I.M., *Ancient Judaism: Biblical Criticism from Max Weber to the Present* (Cambridge, 1984).
Ziegler, J., 'Die Hilfe Gottes "am Morgen"', in *Alttestamentliche Studien* (FS F. Noetscher; BBB, 1; Bonn, 1950), pp. 281-88.
Zimmerli, W., 'Die Eigenart der prophetischen Rede des Ezechiel. Ein Beitrag zum Problem an Hand von Ez. 14.1-11', *ZAW* 66 (1954), pp. 1-26.
—'Alttestamentliche Prophetie und Apokalyptik auf dem Wege zur "Rechtfertigung des Gottlosen"', in *Rechtfertigung* (FS E. Käsemann; Tübingen, 1976), pp. 575-92.
—'Das Gottesrecht bei den Propheten Amos, Hosea und Jesaja', in *Werden und Wirken des Alten Testaments* (FS C. Westermann; Neukirchen, 1980), pp. 216-35.
Zingg, E., 'Das Strafrecht nach den Gesetzen Moses', *Judaica* 17 (1961), pp. 106-19.
Zink, J.K., 'Uncleanness and Sin. A Study of Job XIV 4 and Psalm LI 7', *VT* 17 (1967), pp. 354-61.
Zurro Rodriguez, E., *Procedimientos iterativos en la poesia ugarítica y hebrea* (Biblica et Orientalia, 43; Rome, 1987).

Indexes

Index of References

Bible

Index of Authors

Jenni, E. 21, 86, 174, 221, 277
Jepsen, A. 18, 76, 142, 155
Jeremias, J. 18, 153, 208, 286, 316, 368
Johag, I. 162
Johansson, N. 59, 132
Johnow, H. 90
Johnson, A.R. 155
Johnson, B. 18
Johnson, E. 50
Johnson, M.D. 316
Jones, G.H. 59, 188
Jongeling, B. 59, 86
Joüon, P. 59, 68, 89, 96, 157, 194, 207, 242, 267, 342
Jüngling, H.-W. 173, 228

Kamlah, E. 155
Kautzsch, E. 18
Keel, O. 286-89, 297, 368
Keil, C.F. 364
Kellenberger, E. 155
Kellermann, D. 197
Kenik, H.A. 179, 187
Kidner, D. 138
Kline, M.G. 165
Klopfenstein, M.A. 266, 279, 283, 287, 291, 304, 370, 371
Knierim, R. 26, 64, 65, 68, 101, 179
Koch, K. 16, 158, 348, 359, 366, 386
Koehler, L. 21, 23, 24, 65, 176, 187, 206, 219, 228, 230, 233, 259, 272, 300
Kopf, L. 283, 353
Kraus, H.-J. 16, 69, 107, 291, 297, 364, 366
Krause, H.-J. 90
Kreuzer, S. 135
Kuschke, A. 309
Kutsch, E. 44, 136, 159, 370
Kuyper, L.J. 17
Küchler, F. 52

L'Hour, J. 385
Labuschagne, C.J. 85, 249
Lacocque, M.-J. 97
Lagrange, M.-J. 57
Lamadrid, A.G. 162
Landes, G.M. 21
Lang, B. 16, 145, 283
Lauha, A. 380
Laurentin, A. 86
Lausberg, H. 78, 283
Leeuwen, C. van89, 265, 375
Leidke, G. 44, 186, 188, 195, 208, 210
Leone, G. 84, 185, 235, 257, 313, 372
Lesêtre, H. 137
Levenson, J.D. 124
Liedke, G. 36, 175, 185, 362, 378
Limburg, J. 25, 34, 37, 39
Lindblom, J. 24
Lipínski, E. 97, 135, 136, 342, 368
Lods, A. 136
Loewenclau, I. von 268
Loewenstamm, S.E. 377
Lofthouse, W.F. 154
Lohfink, N. 177, 178, 280
Long, B.O. 102
Luck, U. 17
Lust, J. 184
Lyonnet, S. 52, 53, 64, 104, 125, 145, 393
Lyons, J. 20
Lévêque, J. 113

Maag, V. 44, 192, 230, 267, 302, 316
Maarsingh, B. 153
Maas, F. 145, 197
Mabee, C. 59, 73, 114
Macholz, G.C. 22, 177, 180
Malamat, A. 177, 183, 228
Mand, F. 96
Mannati, M. 79, 200, 206, 302
Maon, P. 63, 68, 359
Markert, L. 69, 90
Marrow, S. 317
Martino, E. de136
Masing, U. 155
Mastin, B.A. 183
Mayer, G. 97
Mayer, R. 237
Mayes, A.D.H. 182
Mays, J.L. 40, 164
McCarthy, D.J. 16, 52, 138, 165, 166, 174, 250
McCree, W.T. 165

INDEX OF HEBREW WORDS

INDEX OF SUBJECTS